Frommer's

KU-602-853

South Florida
with the best of Miami & the Keys

6th Edition

by Lesley Abravanel

Here's what the critics say about Frommer's:

"Amazingly easy to use. Very portable, very complete."
—*Booklist*

"Detailed, accurate, and easy-to-read information for all price ranges."
—*Glamour Magazine*

"Hotel information is close to encyclopedic."
—*Des Moines Sunday Register*

"Frommer's Guides have a way of giving you a real feel for a place."
—*Knight Ridder Newspapers*

WILEY

Wiley Publishing, Inc.

About the Author

Lesley Abravanel is a freelance journalist and a graduate of the University of Miami School of Communication. When she isn't combing South Florida for the latest hotels, restaurants, and attractions, she is on the lookout for vacationing celebrities and covers them in her weekly nightlife and gossip column, "Velvet Underground," in the *Miami Herald.* She is a contributor to *Business Traveler, Time Out,* all three illustrious supermarket tabloids, and is the author of *Florida For Dummies, Frommer's Florida,* and *Frommer's Portable Miami.*

Published by:

Wiley Publishing, Inc.

111 River St.
Hoboken, NJ 07030-5774

ISBN 978-0-470-28973-0

Editor: Stephen Bassman
Production Editor: Suzanna R. Thompson
Cartographer: Andrew Dolan
Photo Editor: Richard Fox
Production by Wiley Indianapolis Composition Services

Front cover photo: Miami, South Beach: Art Deco–style lifeguard hut
Back cover photo: Key West: Sloppy Joe's Bar at night

For information on our other products and services or to obtain technical support, please contact our Customer Care Department within the U.S. at 800/762-2974, outside the U.S. at 317/572-3993 or fax 317/572-4002.

Wiley also publishes its books in a variety of electronic formats. Some content that appears in print may not be available in electronic formats.

Manufactured in the United States of America

5 4 3 2 1

Contents

List of Maps   vii

What's New in South Florida   1

1   The Best of South Florida   5

1 Frommer's Favorite South Florida
Experiences .8

2 The Best Beaches 10

3 Best Hotel Bets 11

4 Best Dining Bets 13

5 The Rest of the Best 16

2   South Florida in Depth   18

1 The Land & Its People 18

2 A Look at the Past 19

3 Recommended Books, Movies
& Music 25

3   Planning Your Trip to South Florida   27

1 Visitor Information 27

2 Entry Requirements & Customs 28

3 Money 29

4 When to Go 30

    South Florida Calendar of Events . . .31

5 Getting There & Getting Around 37

6 Travel Insurance 40

7 Health & Safety 41

8 Specialized Travel Resources 43

    Online Traveler's Toolbox 44

9 Planning Your Trip Online 45

    *Frommers.com: The Complete
Travel Resource* 45

10 The Top Websites for Miami
& South Florida 46

11 The 21st-Century Traveler 47

12 Packages for the Independent
Traveler 48

13 Escorted General-Interest Tours 49

4   Suggested South Florida Itineraries   50

1 Beachy Keen South Florida in
1 Week 50

2 South Florida in 2 Weeks 52

3 South Florida, Family Style, in
1 Week 55

    *Hollywood South—Celebrities'
South Beach (& Beyond)* 56

4 Cultural South Florida 58

    South Florida Literary Tour 59

5   Getting to Know Miami   60

1 Orientation .60

    The Neighborhoods in Brief 62

2 Getting Around 66

    Fast Facts: Miami 68

6 Where to Stay in Miami   74

1 South Beach 76
  The Best Hotel Spas 88
2 Miami Beach: Surfside, Bal
  Harbour & Sunny Isles 96
3 Key Biscayne 100
4 Downtown 101

5 Coral Gables 104
6 Coconut Grove 106
7 West Miami/Airport Area 108
8 North Dade County 110

7 Where to Dine in Miami   113

1 South Beach 114
2 Miami Beach, North Beach,
  Surfside, Bal Harbour, Sunny Isles
  & North Miami 132
3 North Miami Beach 134
4 Downtown Miami 137
5 Little Havana 145

  Cuban Coffee 146
  *From Ceviche to Picadillo: Latin
  Cuisine at a Glance* 147
6 Key Biscayne 148
7 Coconut Grove 150
8 Coral Gables 152
9 South Miami & West Miami 156

8 What to See & Do in Miami   160

1 Miami's Beaches 160
2 The Art Deco District
  (South Beach) 163
3 Miami's Museum & Art Scene 166
  Roadside Attractions 167
  Miami Art Galleries 170
4 Historic Homes & Sites 174
  Freedom Tower 175
  Digging Miami 176
5 Nature Preserves, Parks
  & Gardens 177
6 Sightseeing Cruises &
  Organized Tours 179

  Vintage Miami 181
7 Watersports 183
8 More Ways to Play, Indoors
  & Out 185
  A Berry Good Time 186
  On Location in Miami 191
9 Spectator Sports 191
  Jai Alai Explained 193
10 Animal Parks 193
11 Video Arcades & Entertainment
  Centers .196

9 Miami Shopping   197

1 The Shopping Scene 197

2 Shopping A to Z 199

10 Miami After Dark   210

1 Bars & Lounges 211

Swank Hotel Bars 216

2 Dance Clubs, Live Music, the Gay & Lesbian Scene & Latin Clubs 217

Ground Rules: Stepping Out in Miami 218

Winter Music Conference 220

The Rhythm Is Gonna Get You 224

3 The Performing Arts 224

4 Cinemas, the Literary Scene, Spectator Sports & a Video Arcade 228

5 Late-Night Bites 229

11 The Everglades & Biscayne National Park   230

1 A Glimpse of Everglades National Park 230

2 Biscayne National Park 244

12 The Keys & the Dry Tortugas   248

1 The Upper & Middle Keys: Key Largo to Marathon 251

The 10 "Keymandments" 258

2 The Lower Keys: Big Pine Key to Coppitt Key 270

3 Key West .275

Going, Going, Gone: Where to Catch the Famous Key West Sunset 282

Literary Key West 284

4 The Dry Tortugas 303

13 The Gold Coast: Hallandale to the Palm Beaches   306

1 Broward County: Hallandale & Hollywood to Fort Lauderdale 308

One If by Land, Taxi If by Sea 314

2 Boca Raton & Delray Beach 329

3 Palm Beach & West Palm Beach . . .339

The Sport of Kings 342

Unreal Estate 344

4 Jupiter & Northern Palm Beach County 354

Discovering a Remarkable Natural World 356

14 The Treasure Coast: Stuart to Sebastian   361

1 Hobe Sound, Stuart (North Hutchinson Island) & Jensen Beach 363

Wildlife Exploration: From Gators to Manatees to Turtles 365

2 Port St. Lucie & Fort Pierce 370

3 Vero Beach & Sebastian 373

4 A Side Trip Inland: Fishing at Lake Okeechobee 379

Going After the Big One 381

Appendix: Fast Facts, Toll-Free Numbers & Websites   382

1 Fast Facts: South Florida 382   **2** Toll-Free Numbers & Websites 388

Index   394

List of Maps

Florida 6

Suggested South Florida Itineraries 51

More Suggested South Florida
Itineraries 53

Greater Miami Accommodations 77

South Beach Accommodations 79

Miami Beach 98

Downtown Miami 103

South Beach Dining 115

North Dade 135

Miami's Design District, Little Haiti
& Upper East Side 139

Key Biscayne, Virginia Key &
Fisher Island 149

Coconut Grove 151

Coral Gables 153

Greater Miami Dining 157

Miami's Best Beaches 161

South Beach Attractions 165

Miami Area Attractions 169

South Beach After Dark 213

The Everglades 232

The Florida Keys 250

Key West 276

The Gold Coast 307

Fort Lauderdale 309

Boca Raton 331

Palm Beach & West Palm Beach 341

The Treasure Coast 363

Acknowledgments

Thanks to all the intrepid publicists out there, for whom no question is an inane one. Hair dryers in rooms? Wi-Fi vs. high speed Internet? I needed it now, and you gave it to me when I asked for it. Well, most of you did. Thanks to my husband, the Swede, for trekking through the long state of Florida and for insight and entertainment. Most of all, thanks to my parents for convincing me that Florida really would be a good experience. Fifteen years later, I admit it: They were right.

—Lesley Abravanel

An Invitation to the Reader

In researching this book, we discovered many wonderful places—hotels, restaurants, shops, and more. We're sure you'll find others. Please tell us about them, so we can share the information with your fellow travelers in upcoming editions. If you were disappointed with a recommendation, we'd love to know that, too. Please write to:

Frommer's South Florida, 6th Edition
Wiley Publishing, Inc. • 111 River St. • Hoboken, NJ 07030-5774

An Additional Note

Please be advised that travel information is subject to change at any time—and this is especially true of prices. We therefore suggest that you write or call ahead for confirmation when making your travel plans. The authors, editors, and publisher cannot be held responsible for the experiences of readers while traveling. Your safety is important to us, however, so we encourage you to stay alert and be aware of your surroundings. Keep a close eye on cameras, purses, and wallets, all favorite targets of thieves and pickpockets.

Other Great Guides for Your Trip:

Frommer's Florida

Frommer's Cruises & Ports of Call

Frommer's Portable Miami

Frommer's Walt Disney World® & Orlando

The Unofficial Guide to Florida with Kids

The Unofficial Guide to Walt Disney World®

The Unofficial Guide to Walt Disney World® with Kids

The Unofficial Guide to Walt Disney World® for Grown-Ups

Frommer's Star Ratings, Icons & Abbreviations

Every hotel, restaurant, and attraction listing in this guide has been ranked for quality, value, service, amenities, and special features using a **star-rating system.** In country, state, and regional guides, we also rate towns and regions to help you narrow down your choices and budget your time accordingly. Hotels and restaurants are rated on a scale of zero (recommended) to three stars (exceptional). Attractions, shopping, nightlife, towns, and regions are rated according to the following scale: zero stars (recommended), one star (highly recommended), two stars (very highly recommended), and three stars (must-see).

In addition to the star-rating system, we also use **seven feature icons** that point you to the great deals, in-the-know advice, and unique experiences that separate travelers from tourists. Throughout the book, look for:

Finds	Special finds—those places only insiders know about
Fun Fact	Fun facts—details that make travelers more informed and their trips more fun
Kids	Best bets for kids and advice for the whole family
Moments	Special moments—those experiences that memories are made of
Overrated	Places or experiences not worth your time or money
Tips	Insider tips—great ways to save time and money
Value	Great values—where to get the best deals

The following **abbreviations** are used for credit cards:

AE	American Express	DISC	Discover	V	Visa
DC	Diners Club	MC	MasterCard		

Frommers.com

Now that you have this guidebook to help you plan a great trip, visit our website at **www. frommers.com** for additional travel information on more than 4,000 destinations. We update features regularly to give you instant access to the most current trip-planning information available. At Frommers.com, you'll find scoops on the best airfares, lodging rates, and car rental bargains. You can even book your travel online through our reliable travel booking partners. Other popular features include:

- Online updates of our most popular guidebooks
- Vacation sweepstakes and contest giveaways
- Newsletters highlighting the hottest travel trends
- Podcasts, interactive maps, and up-to-the-minute events listings
- Opinionated blog entries by Arthur Frommer himself
- Online travel message boards with featured travel discussions

What's New in South Florida

At last, South Florida has broken free from its tired stereotypes. No longer equated with sleepy retirement communities and rowdy Spring Break beaches, South Florida's varied regions, from the Palm Beaches down to the Keys, offer something for everyone. Here's a rundown of what's new and what's closed.

MIAMI

Miami is a city on the verge—of everything. Whereas supermodels were once the city's cottage industry, today condo models are all the rage. Look at the skyline and you'll see what we mean. Despite the shaky real estate market and predicted bust, the city remains as photogenic as ever. Still beautiful, especially at night and during sunset, the photogenic Miami skyline is peppered with cranes working hard to raise swank, zillion-dollar condos and hotels—or, for the really trendy, condo-hotels for which buyers plunk down millions to live like Eloise in a bona fide hotel. A cash crop of hyperluxe hotels and restaurants has proven that, yes, people will spend thousands of dollars per night on a hotel room and $30 for a drink. Today there's more culture than what is dubiously found inside the city's nightclubs. The nearly $500-million Carnival Center for the Performing Arts is finally done and ready for its own close-up—despite the fact that, in typical Miami fashion, they forgot to build a parking lot. But that's another story.

On the downside, while some are hesitant to use the "r" word (recession), 2008 saw the closing of a slew of Miami businesses, even a Burger King. That said, the beach still goes on and optimists continue to see South Florida as a land of booming business opportunities, as they should.

WHERE TO STAY Not too much progress has been made on hotels under construction due to permit issues, financial issues, and, well, unreliable contractors. That said, a few are expected to be done by the time this book is in your hands. While we wait for the rest, other mainstays have undergone or are in the throes of some nips and tucks.

Miami Beach's famed **Eden Roc Renaissance Resort & Spa** (© 305/531-0000) closed in April 2007 for $110 million worth of renovations. In the multimillion-dollar makeover, the hotel plans to add a second tower with 283 rooms. The existing tower's 349 rooms will be gutted and restored, complete with plasma televisions in each room and upgraded bathrooms. When complete in the fall of 2008, the renovations will include five pools, two signature restaurants, and 17 "bungalow" suites.

Fontainebleau Resorts (© 800/548-8886 or 305/538-2000) is still in the throes of a 2-year, $500-million reconstruction/expansion of the original resort. Gone are all the Art Deco details and new will be 11 restaurants, nightclubs, spa, 825 ultramodern rooms—and a 70% increase on room rates. During the construction period, the new, 37-story, stand-alone Fontainebleau Suites hotel is fully operational.

The Tides South Beach (✆ 800/439-4095) unveiled a distinctive new look by trendsetting designer Kelly Wearstler in July 2007. The 45 guest rooms received a makeover with new colors and lush fabrics. An exclusive new entryway greets guests, and signature poolside cabanas will enhance the pool.

The Blue (✆ 305/597-8500), a new luxury resort hotel condominium, is slated for 2008 completion as the only property ever to be built along the legendary fairways of the Blue Monster golf course at the Doral Resort & Spa in Miami. Prices range from the $400,000s to $1.4 million.

Regent Bal Harbour (✆ 800/545-4000), set for a late-2008 opening, has 17 stories, panoramic views of the Atlantic, and 1,650-square-foot guest rooms.

NYC's hot meatpacking district **Gansevoort South** (✆ 305/604-1000) has taken over the old Roney Palace Hotel at 23rd Street and Collins Avenue on South Beach. It opened in late 2007 as a 332-room boutique hotel with a rooftop pool, upgraded oceanfront pool deck, spa, beach club, and a block of upscale shops and restaurants including the legendary **Mr. Chow.**

Nearby, at 2201 Collins Ave., the **W** hotel chain plans to take over an old Holiday Inn and turn it into a 25-story hotel/condo with 511 units, trademark Bliss spa, two pools, and a Rande Gerber–owned hip hotel bar. Completion is slated for mid-2009.

The Kimpton Hotels and Restaurants Group has announced the construction of **Solé on the Ocean** (✆ 800/KIMPTON), a 250-room high-rise boutique resort on the ocean in Sunny Isles. The resort will have suites with floor-to-ceiling windows and Alba, a Mediterranean restaurant. Completion is slated for 2008.

Designer Todd Oldham, responsible for the whimsical decor of South Beach's The Hotel, has been tapped to redesign **The Fairfax,** 1776 Collins Ave. (✆ 305/398-7888), a 53-suite condo/hotel that will feature Enoteca Spiaggia, a spin-off of Chicago's acclaimed Spiaggia. Completion is expected for late 2008.

A **Shangri-La Hotel** is slated to open in Miami in late 2008. The 147-room hotel will be set on Watson Island, near Jungle Island, and will be the first hotel ever on that site. Chi, a spa using Chinese and Himalayan healing therapies, will be on-site.

Giuseppe Cipriani of the famous Italian hotel and Harry's Bar plans to transform the deco Saxony Hotel into a 170-room luxury condo/hotel. **The Cipriani Resort and Residences South Beach** is expected to open in 2009.

WHERE TO DINE Some major upsets occurred in 2007 when Norman Van Aken closed his Coral Gables eatery in favor of a move to Key West, Jonathan Eismann was forced to close his Lincoln Road mainstay, Pacific Time, because the rent was too high, and Johnny V South Beach closed after disappointing reviews. More casualties of the economy: Cafe Tu Tu Tango in Coconut Grove, Mark's South Beach, Wolfie Cohen's Rascal House, Bouley, Vivi, and Karu & Y.

New to Miami dining is Danny DeVito's latest production, **DeVito South Beach,** 150 Ocean Dr. (✆ 305/531-0911), a pricey Italian chophouse where steaks—and checks—are bigger than the diminutive actor himself. Former Nemo chef Michael Schwartz introduced **Michael's Genuine Food & Drink,** 130 NE 40th St. (✆ 305/573-5550), which debuted to raves in the ever-emerging Miami Design District in early 2007. The unpretentious yet hip eatery showcases the former Nemo chef's trademark new American cuisine at prices designed to encourage frequent dining. A newcomer to downtown Miami is **The Oceanaire Seafood Room,** 900 S. Miami Ave.

(© 305/372-8862), a 290-seat restaurant, which is the 12th restaurant of Minneapolis-based The Oceanaire, Inc., and the first to open in Florida. Right next door is **Rosa Mexicano,** 900 S. Miami Ave. (© 786/425-1001), where guacamole is prepared tableside and tortillas are tossed smack in the middle of the restaurant.

At the Fairmont Turnberry Isle Resort & Club, 1999 West Country Club Dr. (© 800/327-7028 or 305/936-2929), early 2008 saw the opening of **Bourbon Steak, A Michael Mina Restaurant,** featuring a cutting-edge design and major cuts of meat.

AFTER DARK Over the causeway, a burgeoning nocturnal buzz is still emanating from the once-desolate area of downtown Miami off Biscayne Boulevard.

The masterminds behind Opium, Prive, and Mansion debuted **SET,** 320 Lincoln Rd. (© 305/531-2800), yet another den of hipster iniquity where the likes of Britney Spears, Simon Cowell, and Ryan Seacrest have been known to lounge. **PURE,** the nightclub that revolutionized nightlife on the Las Vegas Strip, is en route to Miami Beach. PURE will open a new location at the freshly renovated and expanded Fontainebleau Miami Beach in 2008.

One unfortunate closing: Studio A, a favorite among indie music fans, will now join New York's CBGB in indie heaven.

THE KEYS

The newest luxury resort to hit Key West, **Beachside Resort & Conference Center,** 3841 N. Roosevelt Blvd. (© 800/546-0885 or 305/296-8100), features hyperluxe one-, two-, and three-bedroom suites as well as king bedrooms, all adorned with oversize balconies with waterfront views, open gourmet kitchens, marble Jacuzzi tubs, and, on the third floor, private sundecks. For gourmands, star chef Norman Van Aken opened two

restaurants here, **Tavern n Town,** two separate eateries within a bilevel space—Van Aken calls it a hyphenated restaurant, with Tavern featuring tapas and small plates and Town a more world-class dining experience, but both equally good—and pricey.

THE GOLD COAST

While the Gold Coast's beaches remain less congested than those in Miami, the area isn't impervious to development—especially when it comes to resorts, restaurants, and nightlife.

WHERE TO STAY Newly opened is Florida's first **St. Regis Resort** (© 954/568-4623), a $135-million, 23-story luxe property in Fort Lauderdale with nearly 200 rooms, a gourmet restaurant, an air-conditioned walkway to the beach, a massive spa, and more.

In early 2008, the **W Fort Lauderdale Hotel & Residences** (© 954/525-8133) will open on Fort Lauderdale Beach. The $220-million boutique-hotel-condominium features the usual W hotel bells and whistles, including the signature bar and restaurant.

Donald Trump is converting a private condo on Fort Lauderdale Beach into the **Trump International Beach Club.** True to Trump's character, some of the 14-story building's suites will be available for purchase. Opening is slated for mid-2009. Construction has also begun on the **Trump International Hotel & Tower Fort Lauderdale,** a 24-story building designed by world-renowned Michael Graves & Associates. The property will be composed of residences as well as hotel rooms, and its location will afford views of both the Atlantic Ocean and Greater Fort Lauderdale's Intracoastal Waterway. Completion is scheduled for the fall of 2008. Also planned is **Trump Las Olas,** a 95-unit resort on Fort Lauderdale beach scheduled for completion by fall 2008.

The **Lago Mar Resort & Spa,** 1700 S. Ocean Lane (© **954/523-6511;** www. lagomar.com), received a $15 million addition that consists of a six-story wing of one- and two-bedroom oceanfront suites with individual balconies and larger luxurious bathrooms, as well as 24-hour concierge service. The 76-room project also includes a deck of native tropical landscaping and a 5,000-square-foot saltwater lagoon.

Fort Lauderdale's **Holiday Inn,** at Sunrise Boulevard and A1A, is getting a chic makeover into the country's first Stay Social, a name with links to the Social restaurants in Miami Beach and Los Angeles, run by China Grill Management. LXR Luxury Resorts is investing $20 million into a conversion project that would transform the 38-year-old structure into a boutique hotel aimed at celebrities, fashion figures, and jet-setters. Date of completion to be announced. For more information visit www.luxury resorts.com.

Refurbishments have been made to the Tower and deluxe lanai guestrooms of the **Regency Pier Sixty-Six Resort & Spa** (© **954/525-6666;** www.luxuryresorts. com), including luxurious retro-modern appointments. Lush landscaping has been added to the resort's lanai courtyard, and a spectacular three-pool waterfall oasis with an additional eight deluxe cabanas tops off this enchanting space.

In the midst of the most ambitious coastal redevelopment initiative in the State of Florida, with more than $120 million in public improvements and several private development projects in the works, Hollywood Beach has become a sought-after location for investors and visitors. With the first phase now completed, the Hollywood Broadwalk features Old Florida charm, dining, shopping, and a variety of accommodations, including several Superior Small Lodging properties.

Swedish meatballs, anyone? Florida's first-ever **IKEA,** 151 NW 136th Ave. (© **954/838-9292**), opened in Sunrise near Sawgrass Mills in late 2007. People actually quit their jobs and slept outside to make the opening. We're not kidding.

The **Boca Resort & Club,** 501 E. Camino Real (© **561/395-3000;** www. bocaresort.com), continues its remarkable $100-million renovation, becoming a culinary destination with South Florida's first-ever Gordon Ramsay eatery, **Cielo.**

1

The Best of South Florida

A week in Miami is not unlike watching an episode of, say, *Access Hollywood*—with a little CNN thrown in for good measure. Miami: the city to which Britney Spears flees when things aren't going her way, where Tom Cruise took Katie Holmes to celebrate her never-ending 27th birthday, where the paparazzi camps out for days hoping to catch a glimpse of something or someone fabulous, where former President Bill Clinton kibitzes with modeling agency executives at St. Tropez-ish beach clubs, and where Janet Reno throws a politically driven dance party at a South Beach nightclub. And that's just a small sampling of the surreal, Fellini-esque world that exists way down here at the bottom of the map. Nothing in Miami is ever what it seems.

What used to be a relatively sleepy beach vacation destination has awakened from its humid slumber, upped its tempo, and finally earned its place in the Blackberries and iPhones of cutting-edge jet-setters worldwide—but don't be fooled by the hipper-than-thou, celebrity-drenched playground that is South Beach. While the chic elite do indeed flock here, it is surprisingly accessible to the average Joe, Jane, or José. For every Phillippe Starck–designed, bank-account-busting boutique hotel on South Beach, there's a kitschy, candy-coated Art Deco one that's much less taxing on the pockets. For each Pan-Mediterranean-Asian haute cuisinerie, there's always the down-home, no-nonsense Cuban bodega offering hearty food at ridiculously cheap prices.

Beyond the glitzy, *Us Weekly*–meets–beach blanket bacchanalia, Miami has an endless number of sporting, cultural, and recreational activities to keep you entertained. Our sparkling beaches are beyond compare. Plus, there's excellent shopping; nightlife activities including ballet, theater, and opera; as well as the celebrity-saturated hotels, restaurants, bars, and clubs that helped make Miami so famous.

Leave Miami—maybe for the Keys, the Gold Coast, or the Treasure Coast—and you'll expose yourself not only to more UV rays, but to a world of cultural, historical, and sybaritic surprises where you can take in a spring baseball game, walk in the footsteps of Hemingway, get up close and personal with the area's sea life, soak up the serenity of unspoiled landscapes, catch the filming of *CSI: Miami* (or a big-budget Hollywood flick), and much more.

Forget that idea that South Florida is "Heaven's Waiting Room." That slogan is as passé as the concept of early-bird dinners (which you can still get—they just no longer define the region). In fact, according to some people, South Florida *is* heaven. So what are *you* waiting for?

Florida

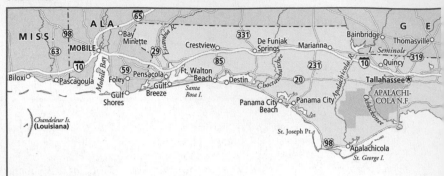

1 Frommer's Favorite South Florida Experiences

- **Driving Along Florida A1A:** This oceanfront route, which runs north up Miami Beach, through Sunny Isles and Hollywood, and into Fort Lauderdale (starting at Ocean Dr. and First St. in Miami and merging onto Collins Ave. before running north), embodies the essence that is South Florida. From time-warped hotels steeped in Art Deco kitsch to multimillion-dollar modern high-rises, A1A is one of the most scenic, albeit heavily trafficked, roads in all of Florida.

- **South Beach Nightlife:** If you can handle it, you can boogie down until the sun comes up in cavernous, pulsating dance clubs, which are considered among the best in the world. Lounges aren't too shabby either. There's **SET** and **Mokai**, where the likes of Justin Timberlake, Scarlett Johansson, Tom Cruise, Katie Holmes, Paris Hilton, and Sting mix with a colorful crowd of local and international hipsters and then there's **Skybar, Cameo, Prive, Mansion, Opium, the Setai, The Forge,** and, well, the list goes on. Where else can us ordinary folk brush elbows with— or spill Cosmopolitans on—Hollywood starlets, entertainment moguls, and living legends but in South Beach's hot clubs, bars, and restaurants, many of which don't get going until the crack of dawn? See chapter 10 for more on Miami's nightlife.

- **Airboat Ride Through the Outskirts of the Everglades:** Unfettered by jet skis, cruise ships, and neon bikinis, the Everglades are Florida's outback, resplendent in their swampy nature. The Everglades are best explored either by slow-moving canoes that really get you acquainted with your surroundings or via an airboat that can quickly navigate its way through the most stubborn of saw grass while providing you with an up-close and personal (as well as fun) view of the land's inhabitants, from alligators and manatees to raccoons and Florida panthers. See p. 239.

- **Dining at Big Fish Restaurant on the Miami River:** Some consider dining on the Miami River to be industrial chic; others consider it seedy in a *Miami Vice* sort of way. However you choose to look at it, by all means *do* look at it; the sleepy Miami River is nestled below the sweeping downtown Miami skyline, reminding you that even though you're in a major metropolis, things in this often-frenetic city are capable of slowing down to a more soothing pace. See p. 138.

- **Vizcaya Museum and Gardens:** Built in 1916, this Italian Renaissance–style manse on Biscayne Bay in Miami features 34 rooms of antiques, art, and tapestries; 10 acres of Italian gardens, statues, and fountains; a new orchid display; and a picture-perfect view of the skyline and Key Biscayne. See p. 176.

- **Joe's Stone Crab Restaurant:** You *will* wait in line at Miami Beach's landmark spot for crab, but it's never dull, and the cacophony of mostly Northeastern U.S. accents and the occasional celebrity will keep you entertained until you are seated for your feast of crustacean. Dip medium, large, or jumbo crab into a tasty mustard-mayo sauce or just mustard, and save room for Key lime pie. Open October through May only. See p. 117.

- **Moonlight Concerts at the Barnacle State Historic Site:** Once a month, on or near the full moon (except in July–Aug), the Barnacle State Historic Site hosts a concert in the backyard of its charming 1908 Coconut Grove bungalow built on 5 acres of waterfront property. Listeners are welcome to picnic and bask in this sublime setting for a mere $5. See p. 174.

- **Midnight Snacking at Versailles:** This iconoclastic, gaudy Cuban diner in the heart of Miami's Little Havana is humming with the buzz of old-timers reminiscing about pre-Castro Cuba, local politicos trying to appease them, and a slew of detached people there only for the fantastically cheap and authentic Cuban fare. Much like its French namesake in whose image it's been literally mirrored, Miami's Versailles provides a palatial view of Miami's ever-changing Cuban landscape. See p. 148.

- **Watching the Cruise Ships Set Sail from South Pointe Park:** Unless you're already on a boat, you can't get a better view of the monstrous cruise ships leaving the Port of Miami than from South Pointe Park, located at the southern tip of South Beach. If you stare long enough, you *will* feel like you're moving, which is almost as much fun as being on board. See p. 187.

- **Lunch at News Cafe on Ocean Drive:** The quintessential South Beach experience, lunching at News Café is more of a spectator sport than a dining experience. What the Big Mac is to McDonald's, people-watching is to News Café, whose Ocean Drive location is one of the best sidewalk spots from which to observe the wacky, colorful mix of pedestrians on parade. See p. 130.

- **Sunset Cocktails at the Setai:** The most luxe, most expensive hotel on South Beach may not be in everyone's budget, but the Friday night cocktail parties there are, and should not be missed. See p. 83.

- **Partying at the Pawn Shop Lounge:** Forget about Miami being stuffy and swank. This downtown Miami club is one of the coolest places on the planet—housed in a former pawn shop and complete with a full-blown, big yellow school bus cum cocktail lounge, Airstream trailer cum VIP lounge, and jetliner fuselage in which you can enjoy more than a sample size of your favorite beverage. See p. 220.

- **Relishing the View from Bill Baggs Cape Florida State Recreation Area:** You haven't truly seen South Florida until you've checked out the view from the southern point of Key Biscayne. Whether it's the turquoise water or the sight of Stiltsville—seven still-inhabited aquatic cabins dating back to the 1930s, perched smack in the middle of the Biscayne Channel—it may take a little coercing to get you to leave. See p. 177.

- **Scuba Diving off Jupiter Beach:** In 1988, Jupiter Beach lifeguard Peter Leo spotted an anchor and a cannon while on his routine morning swim. Turns out, they belonged to what is believed to be the shipwreck of a Spanish galleon dating back to the 16th or 17th century. Giving literal meaning to South Florida's Treasure and Gold coasts, this wreck is worth holding your breath for. See p. 357.

- **Happy Hour at Mai Kai:** Polynesia meets Fort Lauderdale at Mai Kai, the trippiest Tiki hut this side of Tahiti, with its sarong-clad bartenders, a fiery hula show, and an exhaustive menu of frozen concoctions. See p. 328.

- **Discovering Your Inner Flipper at the Dolphin Research Center:** Learn to communicate with and touch, swim, or play with the mammals at the nonprofit Dolphin Research Center in Marathon Key,

Impressions
What could be better than to sit on the beach playing cards in my shirt-sleeves in January?

—Anonymous Miami Beach resident

home to a school of approximately 15 dolphins. See p. 255.

- **Eyeing the Estates on Palm Beach:** The winter playground for the *Lifestyles of the Rich and Famous* set, Palm Beach is lined with jaw-dropping palatial estates. Though many of them are hidden behind towering shrubbery, head south on South County Road, from Brazilian Avenue, where you will see some of the most opulent homes ever built. Make sure someone holds the steering wheel if you're driving, because you *will* do a double take. See p. 339.

- **Boating Through the Intracoastal Waterway:** The waterway that connects the natural bays, lagoons, and rivers along Florida's East Coast snakes around from the Florida-Georgia border all the way to the port of Miami. A ride through the Fort Lauderdale Intracoastal provides a sublime view of million-dollar waterfront houses. See p. 312.

- **Salsa Lessons at Bongo's Cuban Café:** If the only salsa you're familiar with is the kind you put on your tacos, get over to Bongo's, the hottest salsa club north of Havana, where Miami's most talented salsa dancers will teach you how to move your two left feet in the right direction. See p. 218.

- **Exploring the Design District After Dark:** After waiting patiently for this arty, funky area to hit its comeuppance, Miami's hipsters have finally been rewarded with cool bars, lounges, and restaurants that exude that New York City SoHo–meets–Meatpacking District vibe.

- **Sundays at Alabama Jack's:** There is nothing like hanging out, chugging a cheap beer, chowing down on amazing conch fritters, and watching a bunch of sauced octogenarians dressed like extras from Hee Haw line dancing to incredible live country music, all in a Sunday's afternoon. Even better is the spectacular waterfront setting that makes you truly appreciate why you're in Florida in the first place. See p. 250.

2 The Best Beaches

- **For Tranquillity: Matheson Hammock Park Beach** (© **305/665-5475**) in South Miami features an enclosed man-made lagoon that is flushed naturally by the tidal action of the adjacent Biscayne Bay. The serene beach is surrounded by the bay's warm, calm waters and a backdrop of tropical hardwood forest. See p. 163.

  The beach at **Bahia Honda State Park** (© **305/872-2353**) in Bahia Honda Key is one of the nicest and most peaceful in Florida, located amid 635 acres of nature trails and even a portion of Henry Flagler's railroad. See p. 270.

- **For Watersports: Hobie Beach** (© **305/361-2833**), located on the south side of Key Biscayne's Rickenbacker Causeway, is one of the most popular beaches for watersport enthusiasts, featuring jet ski, sailboat, windsurfing, and sailboard rentals;

shade, if necessary, from the Australian pine; and a sublime view of the picturesque downtown Miami skyline. See p. 163.

- **For People-Watching: Lummus Park Beach** (© 305/673-7714) is world renowned, not necessarily for its pristine sands, but for its more common name of **South Beach.** Here, seeing, being seen, and, at times, the obscene, go hand in hand with the sunscreen and beach towels. See p. 162.

Not nearly as scenic, but still heavily populated, **Fort Lauderdale Beach** (© 954/468-1597) is the site of many a bacchanalian Spring Break, Frankie and Annette, and now, an eclectic—albeit calmer—mix of young, buff beach bums. See p. 311.

- **For Nature Lovers: MacArthur Beach** (© 561/624-6950), in West Palm Beach, is considered by many nature enthusiasts to be the most beautiful nature park in South Florida, with a nice stretch of beach set against a lush and diverse background of foliage, plus a state-of-the-art nature center and renowned sea turtle awareness program. See p. 355.

- **For Nude Sunbathing:** For that all-over tan, the place to be is the north end of **Haulover Beach** (© 305/944-3040), nestled between the Intracoastal Waterway and the ocean. A gay, nude beach is also there, as is an area for nude volleyball. See p. 163.

- **For Seclusion:** The producers of *Survivor* could feasibly shoot their show on the ultra-secluded, picturesque, and deserted **Virginia Key** (© 305/361-2749), on Key Biscayne, where people go purposely not to be found. See p. 163.

John U. Lloyd Beach State Park (© 954/923-6711) in Dania Beach is unfettered by high-rise condos, T-shirt shops, and hotels, and remains intact with an untouched shoreline surrounded by a canopy of Australian pine to ensure that your seclusion is, indeed, highly guarded. See p. 311.

- **For Gay Beachgoers:** South Beach's **12th Street Beach** (© 305/673-7714) is the beach of choice for gay residents and travelers who come to show off just how much time they've spent in the gym, and, of course, catch up on the latest gossip and upcoming must-attend parties and events. Oftentimes, this beach is the venue for some of the liveliest parties South Beach has ever seen. See p. 163.

- **For Kids:** Miami's **Crandon Park Beach** (© 305/361-5421) is extremely popular for families with kids because of the shallow water created by a neighboring sandbar. Convenient parking, picnic areas, a winding boardwalk, eco adventure tours, and a multiethnic mix of families grilling, dancing, and relaxing are the benchmarks of this beach. See p. 162.

3 Best Hotel Bets

- **Best Historic Hotel:** With a guest registry that reads like a who's who of history crossed with an engrossing whodunit, Miami's monumental, Mediterranean revivalist–style **Biltmore Hotel** (© 800/727-1926 or 305/445-1926) opened its doors in 1926. Guests ranging from Al Capone to the duke and duchess of Windsor loved the stately hotel so much that they never left, so say those who claim the hotel is haunted. Ghosts aside, this national landmark boasts the largest hotel pool in the continental United States as well as a 300-foot bell tower modeled after the Cathedral of Seville. See p. 105.

- **Most Expensive Luxury Hotel:** With room rates *starting* at $1,000 a night, a guest list that reads straight off of a Hollywood premiere, **the Setai** (© 305/520-6100) and its doting, professional Asian staff, awe-inspiring decor, and outstanding cuisine, is decadence and extravagance at its fullest. See p. 83.

- **Best Cheap-Chic Hotel:** West Palm Beach's **Hotel Biba** (© 561/832-0094) is a funky, single-story, converted 1940s motor-lodge-turned-boutique hotel featuring an oversized swimming pool, Asian gardens with sitting areas, a reflection pond, and the ultrahip Biba Bar. Rooms start at $100. See p. 349.

- **Best Celebrity-Saturated Hotel:** The Shore Club (© 877/640-9500 or 305/695-3100) still reigns as Miami's number one celebrity magnet, attracting stars and starlets whom you'd find at A-list Hollywood parties. While the terminally trendy Skybar isn't necessarily the hottest spot in town, swank sushi joint Nobu always brings 'em in. See p. 83.

- **Best Role-Playing Hotel:** With rooms such as "Me Tarzan, You Vain," or "Best Whorehouse," South Beach's **Pelican Hotel** (© 800/7-PELICAN or 305/673-3373) takes the concept of escapism to an entirely new level. See p. 93.

- **Best Out-of-Place Bed-and-Breakfast:** Located on the outskirts of gritty, bustling downtown Miami is the historic **Miami River Inn** (© 800/468-3589 or 305/325-0045), housed in five restored clapboard buildings dating back to 1906. By the looks of this place, you could swear you were somewhere in New England—until you step out for a breath of the balmy air. See p. 104.

- **Best Hotel in a League of Its Own:** Jules' Undersea Lodge (© 305/451-2353) in Key Largo really gives you the low-down on the full Keys experience by requiring all guests to scuba 30 feet underwater to get to their rooms, which are literally located under the sea, in the mangrove habitat of Emerald Lagoon. See p. 262.

- **Best Art Deco Hotel:** The **Raleigh Hotel** (© 800/848-1775 or 305/534-6300) in Miami is the reigning diva of Deco, dating back to 1940. It features one of the most photographed palm-lined swimming pools, reminiscent of the days of Esther Williams. See p. 87.

- **Best Gatsby-esque Hotel:** As you drive up to the **Breakers** (© 800/833-3141) in posh Palm Beach, you can't help but feel the spirit of Jay Gatsby beckoning you into this mammoth Italian Renaissance–style hotel. See p. 347.

- **Best Beach Hotel:** Miami's **Ritz Carlton South Beach** (© 800/241-3333 or 786/276-4000) is a lot more than just a drop in the sand thanks to its DiLido Beach Club, providing stellar food, drink, entertainment, and beach toys whenever and wherever you feel like it. See p. 81.

- **Best Inexpensive Hotel:** It's hard to find a hotel on South Beach with both good value and excellent service, but the **Crest Hotel Suites** (© 800/531-3880 or 305/531-0321) delivers as one of Miami's best bargains as well as coolest hotels. See p. 91.

  In Key West, the **Grand** (© 888/947-2630 or 305/294-0590), despite its name, will not leave you with a huge tab at the end of your stay. The rooms in this hotel are bright and airy and the proprietor works hard to keep you happy. See p. 296.

- **Best for Families:** On South Beach, the **Loews** (© 800/23-LOEWS or 305/604-1601) is known for its

Loews Loves Kids program including activities for kids and kids at heart including Dive-in Movies at the pool, salsa lessons, and bingo. See p. 81.

In Fort Lauderdale, **Marriott's Harbor Beach** (© **800/222-6543** or 954/525-4000) has a Beachside Buddies program for children ages 5 to 12, offering half-day and all-day children's activities that range from seashell collecting to hula-hoop contests. The 8,000-square-foot, freeform swimming pool, expansive sand beach, and instant access to water toys also keep kids entertained. See p. 318.

The **Boca Raton Resort & Club** (© **800/327-0101** or 561/395-3000) has activity programs designed for distinct age groups. Upon registering children in the program, each parent is given a beeper with a 60-mile radius so that each may be contacted by the children at any time. See p. 334.

• **Best for Romance:** In Miami, the **Hotel St. Michel** (© **800/848-HOTEL** or 305/444-1666) is a cozy European-style hotel whose wood-floored dark-paneled rooms are adorned in antiques, transporting you from sunny Florida to gay Paris. See p. 106.

Imagine an intimate haven on your own private island and you've got **Little Palm Island** (© **800/343-8567** or 305/872-2524), located just 3 miles offshore in the Florida Keys, accessible only by boat or seaplane, and quite possibly the closest thing to paradise, with only one telephone on the entire island. See p. 272.

Although it's 2 blocks from Duval Street—Bourbon Street South—**The Gardens Hotel** (© **800/526-2664** or 305/294-2661) is Key West's most romantic, Eden-istic hideaway that's worlds away from the madness. See p. 290.

In Palm Beach, modeled after a quaint English inn, the **Chesterfield Hotel** (© **800/243-7871** or 561/659-5800) is absolutely seductive, thanks in part to its sexy, sultry Leopard Lounge, its cozy fireside library, and Churchill's Cigar Room. See p. 90.

• **Best Guesthouses/B&Bs:** The **Villa Paradiso** (© 305/532-0616) may be smack in the heart of frenetic South Beach, but once you're inside you're worlds away, with rooms facing a sun-drenched courtyard and a host who is genuinely glad to see you, unlike some of the more attitudinal staff found in other nearby hotels. See p. 95.

4 Best Dining Bets

• **Best for Celebrating a Big Deal:** **Prime One Twelve** on Miami Beach (© **305/532-8112**) is where everyone from Gorbachev and Clinton to Madonna and Beyoncé come to satisfy their carnivorous sides with fare such as $20 Kobe beef hot dogs, dried sticks of bacon at the bar in lieu of peanuts, and, if you must cheat, the best truffle-infused macaroni and cheese you'll ever eat. See p. 119.

• **Best Romantic Restaurant:** Casa Tua, in South Beach (© **305/673-1010**), offers exquisite Italian cuisine

in a Mediterranean villa that's hidden from the street with lush landscaping and an iron gate, resplendent outdoor garden, cozy Hamptons-esque dining room, communal kitchen, and intimate upstairs lounge and patio. See p. 116.

• **Best Restaurant for Zone Dieters Not on a Budget:** The **Forge,** in Miami Beach (© **305/538-8533**), serves the best aged beef this side of Chicago, not to mention a massive slab of meat known officially and appropriately as The Super Steak. See p. 132.

• **Best Waterfront Dining:** It's a tossup between Biscayne Bay and the Atlantic Ocean, but whichever you prefer, there are two restaurants that provide front-row seats to both. The Mandarin Oriental Hotel's global fusion restaurant, **Azul** (© **305/913-8258**), faces the Miami skyline and beautiful, tranquil Biscayne Bay, while **Joe's Seafood** (© **305/381-9329**) faces the scenic Miami River. Tough decisions, but both are winners. See p. 137 and p. 142.

Louie's Backyard in Key West (© **305/294-1061**) offers Caribbean cuisine and one of the best views of the gulf you'll ever have. See p. 297.

• **Best Restaurant Not Worth the Wait for a Table:** The legendary South Florida institution known as **Joe's Stone Crab Restaurant,** in Miami Beach (© **305/673-0365**), refuses to take reservations, but that doesn't stop people from clawing their way into the restaurant for a table—despite a wait that's often in excess of 3 hours. Thing is, if only they knew about **Joe's Take Away,** directly next door, the only thing they'd be waiting for is seconds. See p. 117.

• **Best Cuban Restaurant:** There's always a debate on who has the best, most authentic Cuban cuisine, but for those of you who have never been to Havana, Miami's **Versailles,** in Little Havana (© **305/444-0240**), is *the* quintessential Cuban diner, featuring enormous portions at paltry prices. See p. 148.

• **Best Old School Steakhouse:** Miami's **Capital Grille** (© **305/374-4500**) may be part of a chain, but its dry-aged steaks are still a cut above the rest. See p. 138.

In addition to the **Forge Restaurant** (see above), **Christy's,** in Coral Gables (© **305/446-1400**), is another top carnivorous choice, with superb steaks and famous Caesar salads. See p. 152.

• **Best New World Cuisine:** This one's been a tossup for years, but now that Mark's South Beach bit the dust, the contest easily goes to **Chef Allen's,** in Aventura (© **305/935-2900**), owned by chef Allen Susser. He does wonders with mangos, mostly in the service of fresh fish. The locale isn't ideal (it's in the rear of a strip mall), but Susser is royalty around here and commands the crowds. See p. 134.

• **Sexiest Restaurant: The Restaurant at the Setai,** on South Beach (© **305/573-3355**), brings an exotic, authentic Asian vibe to a place where even Italian restaurants serve sushi. The Indo-Asian decor, dim lighting, and reflecting pools give way to a very exotic, erotic Kama Sutra vibe. See p. 83.

• **Best Scene: Nobu,** in Miami Beach (© **305/695-3232**), is the unrivaled sushi den in which everyone from Justin Timberlake to Madonna have been spotted swooning over their sashimi. See p. 118.

Taverna Opa, also in Miami Beach, Hollywood, and Ft. Lauderdale (© **305/673-6730,** 954/929-4010, and 954/567-1630, respectively), makes the film *My Big Fat Greek Wedding* look like a big fat bore with its own plate breaking, table dancing, ouzo pouring version of a Greek bacchanalia. See p. 216.

• **Best Sunday Brunch: The Blue Door** on Miami Beach (© **305/674-6400**) turns the sleek and chic Delano lobby into a help-yourself-to-anything, calorie-busting Sunday brunch of gourmet fare and insanely good desserts. See p. 114.

At the stately Biltmore Hotel in Coral Gables, **Palme d'Or** (© 305/445-1926) rolls out a regal buffet that's good enough to feed royalty. Delray Beach's **Sundy House Restaurant** (© 561/272-5678) features a gourmet all-you-can-eat $40 brunch *including* alcoholic beverages—an unheard-of value that comes complete with a stunning outdoor garden setting. See p. 153 and 336.

- **Best View: Big Fish,** in Miami (© 305/373-1770), is all about gritty-chic, located on the Miami River, where tugboats and cargo ships slink by as you indulge in fresh fish and sip good Italian wine under the glow of the brilliant downtown skyline hovering above. See p. 138. On South Beach, **Smith & Wollensky** (© 305/673-2800) has views of Fisher Island, Government Cut, and the occasionally passing cruise ship. See p. 120. **Red Fish Grill** (© 305/668-8788) is ensconced in Coral Gables' Matheson Hammock Park and located on the edge of a saltwater lagoon, a setting so blissfully distracting, you may forget to pay attention to what's on your plate. See p. 155. **Le Tub** (© 954/921-9425) may not be considered fine dining, but when you sink your teeth into one of their incredible burgers while overlooking the Intracoastal, nothing could be finer. See p. 327.

- **Best Haute Cuisine: Mark's Las Olas,** in Fort Lauderdale (© 954/463-1000), and Miami's **Table 8** (© 305/695-4114) are both run by celebrity chefs Mark Militello (whose New American cuisine restores the faith of gourmands whose palates once belonged to the Pan-Asian Fusion movement) and Govind Armstrong, a charismatic chef who launched his career at the tender age

of 13 with Wolfgang Puck at L.A.'s legendary Spago. See p. 322 and 120.

- **Best People-Watching:** The **News Cafe,** in South Beach (© 305/538-6397), practically invented the sport of people-watching, encouraging its customers to sit at an outdoor table all day if they want, lingering over the passing parades of people while sipping a cappuccino. Lincoln Road's Euro-fabulous **Segafredo Espresso** cafe (© 305/673-0047), provides a front-row seat to the hordes of people who parade along the pedestrian mall. See p. 130 and 215.

- **Best Comfort Food: Big Pink,** in Miami Beach (© 305/532-4700), serves kitsch in large doses, featuring TV dinners served in compartmentalized trays. It's fun and funky, and the food's pretty good, too. See p. 125.

- **Best Italian Food:** Miami Beach's **Macaluso's** (© 305/604-1811) would make Tony Soprano very proud of his Italian heritage, thanks to Chef Michael's expertly prepared Staten Island–meets–SoHo cuisine. See p. 127. **Café Martorano,** in Ft. Lauderdale (© 954/561-2554), is where the cast of the former hit show The Sopranos eats when they're in town. Fugheddaboutit. See p. 322.

- **Best Kids' Restaurant:** South Miami's **GameWorks** (© 305/667-4263) is the brainchild of co-owner Steven Spielberg, whose virtual reality and video games contribute to the actual reality of kids cleaning their plates so that they can play. The video games also appeal to adults, as do the restaurant and full bar, which make nights at GameWorks a 21-and-over hangout. See p. 196.

- **Best Mexican:** The fresh, authentic Mexican fare at **Baja Cafe,** in Boca Raton (© 561/394-5449), will have you swearing off Taco Bell forever.

See p. 337. And the gourmet Mexican fare in Fort Lauderdale's lauded **Eduardo de San Angel** (© 954/772-4731) is *Like Water for Chocolate* and from the Gods. See p. 323.

- **Best Star-Studded Sushi Restaurant: Nobu,** at The Shore Club hotel in Miami Beach (© 305/695-3100), is known for its star sushi chef and owner, the legendary Nobu Matsuhisa, but the raw facts about this restaurant are as simple as its stellar clientele (which includes Madonna, among others): It's unquestionably the best sushi in town. For fabulous sushi minus the Hollywood vibe, Miami Beach's **Shoji Sushi** (© 305/532-4245) is at the top of the A-list. See p. 118 and 123.
- **Best Seafood: Sunfish Grill,** in Pompano Beach (© 954/788-2434), is simple, unpretentious, and consistently serves the freshest fish in town—any which way you desire. See p. 324.
- **Best Late-Night Dining:** In addition to the 24-hour **News Cafe** (see above and p. 130) and **Big Pink** (see above

and p. 125), **Jerry's Famous Deli** (© 305/534-3244) on South Beach serves a deluge of deli food 24/7. See p. 126. Ft. Lauderdale's **Lester's Diner** (© 954/525-5641) is a 24-hour institution, serving classic greasy-spoon fare at ridiculously cheap prices. See p. 326. The **Floridian Restaurant,** also in Fort Lauderdale (© 954/463-4041), serves everything from eggs to steaks, 24 hours a day, but the vantage point for people-watching rates higher than the food. See p. 326.

- **Kitschiest Dining: Anthony's Runway 84** (© 954/467-8484) in Fort Lauderdale is pure *Goodfellas* kitsch, complete with mirrored walls, servers and waiters who all seem to be named Tony, and a cheesy '70s airliner theme—the bar is even crafted out of plane fuselage. This is a good place to dine family style. See p. 323. **Dogma Grill** (© 305/759-8434) is a cool little hotdog stand whose motto is "A Frank Philosophy." See p. 144.

5 The Rest of the Best

- **Best Museum:** A collector's dream come true, Miami's **Wolfsonian** is a treasure trove of miscellany (a matchbook that once belonged to the King of Egypt) and artifacts hailing from the propaganda age of World War II. See p. 173.
- **Best Spa: The Spa at The Standard Hotel** (South Beach; © 305/673-1717). What used to be an old school, Borscht Belt-style Miami Beach health spa is now one of the hottest, trendiest places to take a Turkish bath in a bona fide Hamam, let out steam in a cedar sauna, or get spritzed in the hotel's sublime Wall of Sound Shower.

- **Best Cultural Experience:** A walk through **Little Havana** is a fascinating study in the juxtaposition and fusion of two very vibrant cultures in which pre-Castro Cuba is as alive and well as the McDonald's right next door. See p. 65.
- **Best Cheap Thrill:** Riding the **Metrorail** in Miami. Originally created to relieve traffic congestion, the city's billion-dollar transportation network is hardly used by commuters and is little more than Miami's own version of Disney's Monorail. Nonetheless, for little more than a dollar, you can tour many of Miami's neighborhoods and see much of its skyline

without having to stop, look at a map, or ask for directions. See p. 66.

• **Best Snorkeling Spot: Looe Key National Marine Sanctuary,** Bahia Honda State Park. With 5.3 square miles of gorgeous coral reef, rock ledges up to 35 feet tall, and a colorful and motley marine community, you may never want to come up for air. See p. 272.

• **Best Public Golf Course:** Miami's **Biltmore Golf Course,** Biltmore Hotel. If it's good enough for former President Clinton, it's good enough for those of you who don't travel with a bevy of Secret Service agents. But the real question is: Are *you* good enough for the course? The 6th hole is notoriously difficult, with distracting water hazards among other difficulties. Nonetheless, it's an excellent course with picture-postcard setting. See p. 189.

• **Best Dive Bar: Jose Cuervo Underwater Bar.** In May 2000, the legendary tequila company celebrated Cinco de Mayo by submerging an actual, $45,000 full-size bar and six stools about 600 feet off South Beach's First Street beach. For expert divers, this bar is more than your average watering hole. Check out www.sinkodemayo.com See p. 185.

• **Best Place to Satisfy Your Morbid Curiosity: The Mystery, Mayhem and Vice Crime Bus Tour.** Not that we're implying anything here, but Miami is a haven for people like O. J. Simpson and, at one time, Al Capone. It's a place where shady characters come to reinvent themselves. However, at times, they also tend to reincriminate themselves. See the spots where some of these criminals fell off the wagon—it's morbidly delicious. See p. 183.

• **Best Latin Club:** Although the predominant language spoken at Miami's **La Covacha** is Spanish, the only word you really need to know here is *agua,* because you will certainly need it after working up a sweat on the dance floor. Music—the best Latin music in town—is, in fact, the common language at this rustic, open-aired Latin dance club that features salsa, merengue, and Latin rock. See p. 223.

• **Best Dance Club:** You know you're in a serious dance club when patrons are fawning all over the star DJ who flew in from Germany rather than Christina Aguilera, who has been seen grinding against the stripper pole in Vice, the club's upstairs VIP area. The aforementioned happens all the time at **Cameo,** South Beach's proven dance club champion. See p. 218.

• **Best Offbeat Experience:** Although it's little more than a tropical shantytown, **Jimbo's,** located at the tip of Virginia Key, is consistently fantastic, with no-frills smoked fish, beer out of the bucket, and colorful locals, all of which make it the best offbeat and off-the-beaten-track experience in South Florida. See p. 149.

2

South Florida in Depth

Since the roaring '20s, South Florida has been a playground for the rich, famous, and freezing. But the area has been inhabited for at least 10 centuries, making the stereotypical blue hairs of the area seem downright young. Par for the course, South Florida's history is an illustrious and rich one.

1 The Land & Its People

Because the population of South Florida is largely confined to a strip of land between the Atlantic Ocean and the Everglades, the Miami Urbanized Area (that is, the area of contiguous urban development) is about 110 miles long (north to south), but never more than 20 miles wide, and in some areas only 5 miles wide (east to west). South Florida is longer than any other urbanized area in the United States except for the New York metropolitan area. It was the eighth most densely populated urbanized area in the United States in the 2000 census. As of the 2000 census, the urbanized area had a land area of 1,116 square miles, with a population of 4,919,036, for a population density of 4,407.4 per square mile. Miami and Hialeah (the second largest city in the metropolitan area) had population densities of more than 10,000 per square mile. The Miami Urbanized Area was the fifth largest Urbanized Area in the United States in the 2000 census, ahead of the Dallas–Fort Worth–Arlington, Texas Urbanized Area.

In 2006, the area, including Fort Lauderdale and Palm Beach, had an estimated 5,463,857 persons, of which 1,671,398 live in unincorporated areas. Considering that the area has an urban population of 4,919,036, only 544,821 residents live outside of the urban area, meaning that *at least* 1,126,577 persons live in urban unincorporated areas, but the number is actually higher. Palm Beach County was added to the Miami–Fort Lauderdale metropolitan area for the first time in 2000, giving it a considerable boost in population and in ranking among U.S. metropolitan areas.

There are bigger issues than population growth, however. Scientists have observed changes in Florida consistent with the early effects of global warming: retreating and eroding shorelines, dying coral reefs, saltwater intrusion into inland freshwater aquifers, an upswing in forest fires, and warmer air and sea-surface temperatures. As glaciers melt and warming waters expand, sea levels will rise anywhere from 8 inches to 2½ feet over the next century. In Florida, seawater will advance inland as much as 400 feet in low-lying areas, flooding shoreline homes and hotels, limiting future development, and eroding the state's beloved beaches. People aren't kidding when they say that one day, Florida will be underwater.

On a more positive note, some say this perceived global warming threat has been greatly exaggerated. Though preliminary research raised concerns that warmer ocean temperatures would lead to more frequent hurricanes, scientists now discount this theory. Nevertheless, global warming may increase hurricanes' maximum intensity, which will serve to exacerbate a natural cyclical trend toward more severe storms—a trend likely to persist for the next 25 to 40 years.

2 A Look at the Past

PREHISTORIC SOUTH FLORIDA

Fourteen thousand years ago, Florida would have made an ideal location for the show Land of the Lost—that is, if there were actually dinosaurs down here. Not so much. During the age of dinosaurs, the Florida peninsula was underwater and did not exist as a land mass. Therefore, no dinosaur remains were ever deposited in Florida.

However, in 1998, archaeologists discovered a slew of artifacts in downtown Miami in an area now known as The Miami Circle. With origins dating back to at least 2,000 years, it was discovered that the artifacts belonged to the Calusa or Tequesta tribes.

Paleo-Indians got here by crossing over to North America from Asia. Most of their activity was around the watering holes, sinkholes and basins in the beds of modern rivers.

Paleo-Indian culture was eventually replaced by, or evolved into, the Early Archaic culture. There were now more people in Florida, and as they were no longer tied to a few water holes in an arid land, they left their artifacts in many more locations.

The Early Archaic period evolved into the Middle Archaic period around 5000 B.C. People started living in villages near wetlands, and favored sites may have been occupied for multiple generations. The Late Archaic period started around 3000 B.C., when Florida's climate had reached current conditions and the sea had risen close to its present level. People now lived everywhere there were fresh or saltwater wetlands. Many people lived in large villages with purpose-built mounds. Fired pottery appeared in Florida by 2000 B.C. By about 500 B.C., the Archaic culture that had been fairly uniform across Florida began to fragment into regional cultures.

The post-Archaic cultures of eastern and southern Florida developed in relative isolation, and it is likely that the peoples living in those areas at the time of first European contact were direct descendants of the inhabitants of the areas in late Archaic times. The cultures of the Florida panhandle and the north and central gulf coast of the Florida peninsula were strongly influenced by the Mississippian culture, although there is continuity in cultural history, suggesting that the peoples of those cultures were also descended from the inhabitants of the Archaic period. Cultivation of maize was adopted in the panhandle and the northern part of the peninsula, but was absent or very restricted in the tribes that lived south of the Timucuan-speaking people (that is, south of a line approximately from present-day Daytona Beach to a point on or north of Tampa Bay).

NATIVE AMERICANS Spanish explorers of the early 16th century were likely the first Europeans to interact with the native population of Florida. The first documented encounter of Europeans with Native Americans of the United States came with the first expedition of Juan Ponce de Leon to Florida in 1513, although he encountered at least one native that spoke Spanish. In 1521, he encountered the Calusa Indians, who established 30 villages in the Everglades, during a failed colonization attempt in which they drove off the Europeans.

The Spanish recorded nearly 100 names of groups they encountered, ranging from organized political entities such as the Apalachee, with a population of around 50,000, to villages with no known political affiliation. There were an estimated 150,000 speakers of dialects of the Timucua language, but the Timucua were organized only as groups of villages, and did not share a common culture. Other tribes in Florida at the time of first contact included the Ais, Calusa, Jaega, Mayaimi, Tequesta, who lived on the southeast coast of the Everglades, and Tocobaga. All of these tribes diminished in numbers during the period of Spanish control of Florida.

At the beginning of the 18th century, tribes from areas to the north of Florida—supplied, encouraged, and occasionally accompanied by white colonists from the Province of Carolina—raided throughout Florida, burning villages, killing many of the inhabitants, and carrying captives back to Charles Towne to be sold as slaves. Most of the villages in Florida were abandoned and the survivors sought refuge at St. Augustine, or in isolated spots around the state. Some of the Apalachee eventually reached Louisiana, where they survived as a distinct group for at least another century.

The few surviving members of these tribes were evacuated to Cuba when Spain transferred Florida to the British Empire in 1763. The Seminole, originally an offshoot of the Creek people who absorbed other groups, developed as a distinct tribe in Florida during the 18th century, and are now represented in the Seminole Nation of Oklahoma, the Seminole Tribe of Florida, and the Miccosukee Tribe of Indians of Florida.

SPANISH RULE   Once Ponce de Leon laid his eyes on Florida in 1513, a slew of competitive Conquistadors made futile efforts to find gold there and colonize the region. The first to establish a fort in Florida were the French, actually, but it was ultimately destroyed by the Spanish, who introduced Christianity, horses, and cattle to the region. Unfortunately they also introduced diseases and conquistador brutality, which ultimately decimated Indian populations. Eager to expand its own American colony collection, Britain led several raids into Florida in the 1700s to overthrow Spanish rule. Among the most notable Spaniards in Florida included the aforementioned de Leon; Hernando de Soto, the most ruthless of the explorers whose thirst for gold led to the massacre of many Indians; Panfilo de Narvaez, whose quest for El Dorado—the land of gold—landed him in Tampa Bay; and Pedro Menendez de Aviles, who founded St. Augustine after defeating the French.

BRITISH RULE   The Brits weren't interested in gold—they were all about Florida's bounty of hides and furs and they'd stop at nothing to get them. After taking control in 1763, the Brits divided Florida into two. Because Florida was subsidized by the English, Floridians remained loyal to Mother England during the American Revolution—that is, until the Spanish returned and regained West Florida in 1781 and, 2 years later, East Florida. During the Spanish re-conquest, American slaves fled to Florida, causing major turmoil between Spain and the U.S. Combined with Indian raids in the north and an Indian alliance with runaway slaves, Florida was, well, a mess, until General Andrew Jackson invaded Spanish Florida, captured Pensacola and occupied West Florida. Then Florida was a disaster. Jackson's invasion kicked off the First Seminole War in 1817. Finally, to settle Spain's $5 million debt to the U.S., all Spanish land east of the Mississippi, including Florida, was ceded to the U.S. in 1819.

AMERICAN RULE Florida became an organized territory of the United States on March 30, 1822. The Americans merged East Florida and West Florida (although the majority of West Florida was annexed to Orleans Territory and Mississippi Territory), and established a new capital in Tallahassee, conveniently located halfway between the East Florida capital of St. Augustine and the West Florida capital of Pensacola. The boundaries of Florida's first two counties, Escambia and St. Johns, approximately coincided with the boundaries of West and East Florida, respectively.

At this time, the plantation system was adopted by north Florida and because the settlers wanted the best possible land, the Federal government tried moving all Indians west of the Mississippi, resulting in the Second and Third Seminole Wars. When Abraham Lincoln was elected president in 1860, Florida became the third state to secede from the Union. Florida saw little action during the Civil war—its main role was to supply beef and salt to the Confederates. The state got off easy for a change.

After meeting the requirements of Reconstruction, including amendments to the U.S. Constitution, Florida was readmitted to the United States on July 25, 1868.

MIAMI It wasn't long after Florida became the 27th state in the union that Miami began to emerge as a city—or somewhat one. During the war, the U.S. created Fort Dallas on the north bank of a river that flowed through southern Florida. When the soldiers left, the fort became the base for a small village established by William H. English, who dubbed it Miami, from the Indian word Mayami, meaning big water.

In 1822, the Homestead Act offered 160 acres of free land to anyone who would stay on it for at least 5 years. Edmund Beasley bit and in 1868 moved into what is now Coconut Grove. Two years later, William Brickell bought land on the south bank of the Miami River and Ephraim Sturtevant took over the area called Biscayne. In 1875, his daughter Julia Tuttle visited him and fell in love with the area, although not returning for another 16 years, when she would further transform the city.

In the meantime, Henry Flagler, who made a $50 million fortune working with John Rockefeller in the Standard Oil company, came to Florida in the late 1800s because he thought the warm weather would help his wife's frail health. After moving to the area, he built a railroad all the way down the east coast of Florida, stopping in each major town to build a hotel. Another railway honcho, Henry Plant, laid his tracks on the opposite coast, from Jacksonville to Tampa.

When her husband died in 1886, Julia Tuttle decided to leave Cleveland for Florida and asked Plant to extend his railroad to Miami. Plant declined so Tuttle went to Flagler, whose own railroad stopped 66 miles away in what is now known as Palm Beach. Flagler laughed at Tuttle's request, saying he didn't see what Miami had to offer in terms of tourism.

After a devastating winter that killed all crops north of the state, Tuttle sent Flagler a bounty of orange blossoms to prove that Miami did, indeed, have something to offer. After Tuttle agreed to give Flagler some of her land along with William Brickell's, Flagler agreed to extend the railway. When the first train arrived in Miami on April 15, 1896, all 300 (!) of the city's residents showed up to see it. Miami had arrived and newspapers and magazines began touting the city as "the sun porch of America, where winter is turned to summer."

FLORIDA KEYS No one knows exactly when the first European set foot on one of the Florida Keys, but as exploration and shipping increased, the islands became prominent on nautical maps. The nearby treacherous coral reefs claimed many lives. The chain was eventually called "keys," also attributed to the Spanish, from *cayos*, meaning "small islands." In 1763, when the Spanish ceded Florida to the British in a trade for the port of Havana, an agent of the King of Spain claimed that the islands, rich in fish, turtles, and mahogany for shipbuilding, were part of Cuba, fearing that the English might build fortresses and dominate the shipping lanes.

The British realized the treaty was ambiguous, but declared that the Keys should be occupied and defended as part of Florida. The British claim was never officially contested. Ironically, the British gave the islands back to Spain in 1783, to keep them out of the hands of the United States, but in 1821 all of Florida, including the necklace of islands, officially became American territory.

Many of the residents of Key West were immigrants from the Bahamas, known as Conchs (pronounced "Conks") who arrived in increasing numbers after 1830. Many were sons and daughters of Loyalists who fled to the nearest crown soil during the American Revolution.

In the 20th century many residents of Key West started referring to themselves as "Conchs," and the term is now generally applied to all residents of Key West. In 1982, Key West, and the rest of the Florida Keys, briefly declared its "independence" as the Conch Republic in a protest over a United States Border Patrol blockade. This blockade was set up on U.S. 1 where the Northern end of the Overseas Highway meets the mainland at Florida City. This blockade was in response to the Mariel Boatlift. A 17-mile (27km) traffic jam ensued while the Border Patrol stopped every car leaving the Keys supposedly searching for illegal aliens attempting to enter the mainland United States. This paralyzed the Florida Keys. The Conch Republic Independence Celebration—including parades and parties—is celebrated every April 23.

THE EVERGLADES   Thanks to the work of the Everglades' foremost supporter, Ernest F. Coe, Congress passed a park bill in 1934. Dubbed by opponents as the "alligator and snake swamp bill," the legislation stalled during the Great Depression and World War II. Finally, on December 6, 1947, President Harry Truman dedicated the Everglades National Park. In that same year, Marjory Stoneman Douglas first published *The Everglades: River of Grass*. She understood its importance as the major watershed for South Florida and as a unique ecosystem.

FORT LAUDERDALE   Fort Lauderdale is named after a series of forts built by the United States during the Second Seminole War. However, development of the city did not begin until 50 years after the forts were abandoned at the end of the conflict. Three forts named "Fort Lauderdale" were constructed; the first was at the fork of the New River, the second at Tarpon Bend, and the third near the site of the Bahia Mar Marina. The forts took their name from Major William Lauderdale, who was the commander of the detachment of soldiers who built the first fort.

The area in which the city of Fort Lauderdale would later be founded was inhabited for more than 1,000 years by the Tequesta Indians. Contact with Spanish explorers in the 16th century proved disastrous for the Tequesta, as the Europeans unwittingly brought with them diseases to which the native populations possessed no resistance, such as smallpox. For the Tequesta, disease, coupled with continuing conflict with their Calusa neighbors, contributed greatly to their decline over the next 2 centuries. By 1763, there were only a few Tequesta left in Florida, and most of them were evacuated to Cuba when the

Spanish ceded Florida to the British in 1763, under the terms of the Treaty of Paris (1763), which ended the Seven Years' War. Although control of the area changed between Spain, England, the United States, and the Confederate States of America, it remained largely undeveloped until the 20th century.

It was not until Frank Stranahan arrived in the area in 1893 to operate a ferry across the New River, and the Florida East Coast Railroad's completion of a route through the area in 1896, that any organized development began. The city was incorporated in 1911, and in 1915 was designated the county seat of newly formed Broward County.

Fort Lauderdale's first major development began in the 1920s, during the Florida land boom of the 1920s. The 1926 Miami Hurricane and the Great Depression of the 1930s caused a great deal of economic dislocation. When World War II began, Fort Lauderdale became a major US Navy base, with a Naval Air Station to train pilots, radar and fire control operator training schools, and a Coast Guard base at Port Everglades.

After the war ended, service members returned to the area, spurring an enormous population explosion, which dwarfed the 1920s boom. Today, Fort Lauderdale is a major yachting center, one of the nation's largest tourist destinations, and the center of a metropolitan division with 1.8 million people.

PALM BEACH Palm Beach County was created in 1909. It was named for its first settled community, Palm Beach, in turn named for the palm trees and beaches in the area. The County was carved out of what was then the northern half of Dade County. The southern half of Palm Beach County was subsequently carved out to create the northern portion of Broward County in 1915. Henry Flagler was instrumental in the county's development in the early 1900s with the extension of the Florida East Coast Railway through the county from Jacksonville to Key West. After Flagler, came Addison Mizner, an architect with a flair for Mediterranean styles. You can blame or thank Mizner for all those pink houses. As Palm Beach became a haven for the über-rich, it also became a political focal point as was one of the counties at the center of the 2000 U.S. Presidential election recount controversy, and ended up turning the state in favor of George W. Bush by 537 votes.

TREASURE COAST The name "Treasure Coast" is derived from a number of ships of Spanish galleons (especially those of the 1715 Spanish treasure fleet) that wrecked off the coast during the 17th and 18th centuries. Artifacts from these ships are still being recovered today, by both amateur and professional treasure-hunters.

For 2 centuries, Spain sent fleets twice a year to collect treasure from her New World colonies. In 1715, eleven Spanish ships crashed into the treacherous reefs off the Florida coast. The survivors swam to the beaches but the violent winds sucked many back into the water. Daybreak found more than 700 men missing, with wreckage and bodies scattered across 30 miles.

The senior surviving officer ordered a damaged lifeboat repaired, and then sent the Chaplain and a young pilot for help. Three days later they landed 120 miles to the north.

The Spanish attempted to salvage the treasure for the next 4 years; however, the hazards of sharks, barracudas, buccaneers, and Indians led them to abandon the operation. Records indicate that only 30 percent of the treasure was recovered; the rest lay buried in the sands of the Treasure Coast.

MODERN SOUTH FLORIDA

South Florida today is a fascinating study in, well everything. It seems as if the state is always in the news for *something*, and with this timeline, you'll understand why.

1980: Race riots tear apart city. The Mariel boatlift brings 140,000 Cubans to Florida. The Miami Seaquarium celebrates its 25th anniversary.

1983: Thirty-eight overseas highway bridges from Key Largo to Key West are completed under the Florida Keys Bridge Replacement Program.

1984: The Miami Metro Rail, the only inner city, elevated rail system in Florida, begins service in May.

1986: Treasure hunter Mel Fisher continues to salvage vast amounts of gold and silver from his discovery of the Spanish galleon *Nuestra Senora de Atocha,* which sank in 1622 during a hurricane off Key West. The television series *Miami Vice* continues to capture the nation's imagination, revitalizing interest and tourism for South Florida.

1987: U.S. Census Bureau estimates indicate that Florida has surpassed Pennsylvania to become the fourth most populous state in the nation. The ranking will not become official until the Bureau publishes its report in early 1988. It is predicted that Florida will be the third most populous state by the year 2000.

1990: Panama's governor Manuel Noriega is brought to Miami in January for trial on drug charges. Joe Robbie, Miami Dolphins founder, dies in January.

1991: Queen Elizabeth II visits Miami. Five Navy bombers found by treasure salvers are determined not to be the "Lost Squadron" of Bermuda Triangle fame that went down in 1945 off the coast of Florida. Miami and Denver are awarded new national major league baseball franchises. The 1990 Federal Census puts Florida's population at 12,937,926, a 34% increase from 1980.

1992: Homestead and adjacent South Florida are devastated on August 24 by the (then) costliest natural disaster in American history, Hurricane Andrew, demanding billions in aid. There were 58 deaths directly or indirectly related to Andrew. The hurricane destroyed 25,000 homes and damaged 10,000 others. Twenty-two thousand Federal troops were deployed. Shelters housed 80,000 persons.

Among African Americans elected to Congress was Carrie Meek of Miami. Sixty-six in 1993, her political career saw her elected first to the Florida House of Representatives, next the Florida Senate, and then the U.S. House of Representatives.

1993: Janet Reno, State Attorney for Dade County (Miami) for 15 years is named Attorney General of the U.S. by President Bill Clinton; Reno is the first woman to so serve in U.S. history. Although a pro-choice Democrat, she managed to win reelection four times in a conservative stronghold, the last time without opposition.

1996: Miami turns 100.

2000: Florida became the battleground of the controversial 2000 US presidential election, when a count of the popular votes held on Election Day was extremely close and mired in accusations of fraud and manipulation. Subsequent recount efforts degenerated into arguments over mispunched ballots, "hanging chads," and controversial decisions by the Florida Secretary of State Katherine Harris and the Florida Supreme Court. Ultimately, the United States Supreme Court ended all recounts and let stand the official count by Harris, which was accepted by Congress.

2003: The Florida Marlins win the World Series.

2004: George W. Bush wins the presidential election again. His brother Jeb celebrates in Florida's State Capitol.

2006: The Miami Heat win the NBA championships.

2007: Jeb Bush vacates the governor's office, which is taken over by Charlie Crist.

2008: Florida continues to be one of the fastest growing states in the country. The economy still depends greatly on tourism, but expanding industries in business and manufacturing are strengthening its growth potential. State leaders are working on problems created due to huge population increases and environmental concerns.

3 Recommended Books, Movies & Music

South Florida—and Florida in general—is an author's dream come true. In this state of much diversity (read: bizarre characters, to say the least), inspiration is practically hanging from the palm trees.

FICTION

- *The Perez Family* (W. W. Norton & Co. Inc.) by Christine Bell—Cuban immigrants from the Mariel Boatlift exchange their talents for an immigration deal in Miami (also a 1995 movie by Mira Nair).
- *Miami, It's Murder* (Avon) by Edna Buchanan—Miami's Agatha Christie keeps you in suspense with her reporter protagonist and her life as an investigative crime solver in Miami.
- *To Have and Have Not* (Scribner) by Ernest Hemingway—One of the many must-reads by Key West's most famous resident.
- *Naked Came the Manatee* (Ballantine Books) by Carl Hiassen—Thirteen *Miami Herald* writers contributed to this hilarious story about the discovery of Castro's head.
- *Killing Mister Watson* (Vintage Books USA) by Peter Matthiessen—A fascinating story about the settlement of the Everglades and the problems that ensued.
- *The Yearling* (Collier MacMillan Publishers) by Marjorie Kinnan Rawlings—A classic about life in the Florida backwoods.
- *Seraph on the Suwanee* (Harper Perennial) by Zora Neale Hurston—A novel about turn of the century Florida "white crackers."
- *Nine Florida Stories* (University Press of Florida) by Marjory Stoneman Douglas—The beloved Florida naturalist's fictional take on Florida, set in a scattering of settings—Miami, Ft. Lauderdale, the Tamiami Trail, the Keys, the Everglades—and revealing the drama of hurricanes and plane crashes, of kidnappers, escaped convicts, and smugglers.
- *Swim to Me* (Algonquin Books) by Betsy Carter—A wacky novel set in Weeki Wachee about a shy teenager who finds her purpose at the mermaid-happy theme park.

NONFICTION

- *Miami* (Vintage) by Joan Didion—An intriguing compilation of impressions of the Magic City.
- *Miami, the Magic City* (Centennial Press) by Arva Moore Parks—An authoritative history of the city.
- *The Everglades: River of Grass* (Pineapple Press) by Marjory Stoneman Douglas—Eco-maniacs will love this personal account of the treasures of Florida's most famous natural resource.
- *Celebration USA: Living in Disney's Brave New Town* (Holt Paperbacks) by Douglas Frantz and Catherine Collins—An eye-opening true story about living in Disney's "model town."

MOVIES FILMED IN FLORIDA

- Clarence Brown's *The Yearling* (1946) based on novel by M.K. Rawlings
- John Huston's *Key Largo* (1948) based on novel by Hemingway (gangsters, hurricanes, and Bogey and Bacall)
- Harry Levin's *Where the Boys Are* (1960) (spring break in Ft. Lauderdale)
- John Schlesinger's *Midnight Cowboy* (1969) based on novel by James Leo Herlihy
- Ernest Lehman's *Portnoy's Complaint* (1972) based on novel by Philip Roth (Jewish culture)
- Lawrence Kasdan's *Body Heat* (1981) (crime)
- Ron Howard's *Cocoon* (1985) based on novel by David Saperstein (retirees)
- Tim Burton's *Edward Scissorhands* (1990) (modern fairy tale filmed in Dade City and Lakeland)
- Mike Nichols' *Birdcage* (1996) (South Beach comedy)
- Andrew Bergman's *Striptease* (1996) based on novel by Carl Hiassen
- John Singleton's *Rosewood* (1997) based on historic Rosewood massacre (African-American culture)
- Victor Nunez's *Ulee's Gold* (1997) (Panhandle family drama)
- Peter Weir's *The Truman Show* (1998) (sci-fi in Seaside)
- Spike Jonze's *Adaptation* (2002) loosely based on Susan Orleans' *The Orchid Thief*
- Patty Jenkins' *Monster* (2003) biopic of serial killer Aileen Wournos
- Taylor Hackford's *Ray* (2004) biopic of musician Ray Charles, born in Florida

MUSIC OF SOUTH FLORIDA

The Miami recording industry did not begin with Gloria Estefan's Miami Sound Machine, contrary to popular belief. In fact, some major rock albums were recorded in Miami's Criteria Studios. Among them: *Rumours* by Fleetwood Mac and *Hotel California* by The Eagles. Long-time local music entrepreneur Henry Stone and his label, TK Records, created the local indie scene in the 1970s. TK Records produced the R&B group KC and the Sunshine Band along with soul singers Betty Wright, George McCrae, and Jimmy "Bo" Horne, as well as a number of minor soul and disco hits, many influenced by Caribbean music. In the 2000s, Miami has seen an enormous rap boom in the form of Daddy Yankee, Pitbull, Rick Ross, and more.

3

Planning Your Trip to South Florida

Peak season in South Florida runs from October to March. And while peak season is the most popular time to visit, pre- and postseason offer you a less congested, less expensive travel experience. Regardless of when you choose to travel, a little advanced planning will help you make the most of your trip.

1 Visitor Information

The **Greater Miami Convention and Visitor's Bureau,** 701 Brickell Ave., Miami, FL 33131 (© **800/933-8448;** www.miamiandbeaches.com), is the best source for specialized information about the city and its beaches. Even if you don't have a specific question, you should request a free copy of *Tropicool,* the bureau's vacation planner for greater Miami and the beaches. And remember that just because information on a particular establishment you're inquiring about is not available, that doesn't mean the place doesn't exist: The GMCVB only endorses member businesses.

The **Greater Miami and Beaches Hotel Association,** 407 Lincoln Rd., Miami Beach, FL 33139 (© **800/531-3553;** www.gmbha.org), provides information on accommodations and tours.

Because Miami is such a vast city, some of the more popular neighborhoods have their own chambers of commerce that will provide you with specific information on events, accommodations, and attractions in their areas. Here's a partial list:

- **Miami Beach Chamber of Commerce,** 420 Lincoln Rd., Miami Beach, FL 33139 (© **305/672-1270;** www.miamibeachchamber.com)
- **Coral Gables Chamber of Commerce,** 2333 Ponce de León Blvd., Suite 650, Coral Gables, FL 33134 (© **305/446-1657;** www.gableschamber.org)
- **Coconut Grove Chamber of Commerce,** 2820 McFarlane Rd., Coconut Grove, FL 33133 (© **305/444-7270;** www.coconutgrove.com)

For information on visiting the Fort Lauderdale area, the **Greater Fort Lauderdale Convention & Visitor's Bureau,** 1850 Eller Dr., Suite 303, Fort Lauderdale, FL 33316 (© **954/765-4466;** www.sunny.org), offers a 71-page vacation planner, as well as maps and other helpful information on the area and its beaches.

The **Palm Beach County Convention and Visitors Bureau,** 1555 Palm Beach Lakes Blvd., Suite 204, West Palm Beach, FL 33401 (© **561/471-3995;** www.palmbeachfl.com), offers maps, brochures, and, if you request it, a coupon book of over $500 in savings in the Palm Beach area. Ask for it!

Because there are so many islands in the Florida Keys, the best place for information is at www.florida-keys.fl.us/chamber.htm, where you can send e-mail requests to each individual Florida Keys chamber of commerce. To call, contact the chambers of commerce at the following numbers: **Key Largo** (© 800/822-1088 or 305/451-1414); **Islamorada** (© 800/332-5397 or 305/664-4503); **Marathon** (© 800/262-7284 or 305/743-5417); **Lower Keys** (© 800/872-3722 or 305/872-2411); and **Key West** (© 800/527-8539 or 305/294-2587).

For the Everglades, the **Tropical Everglades Visitor's Center,** 160 U.S. 1, Florida City, FL 33034 (© **305/245-9180**), will provide you with information on tours, sites, and parks in the area.

For information on traveling throughout Florida, including a calendar of events, a guide to accommodations, and a list of useful websites, contact **Visit Florida,** P.O. Box 1100, 66 E. Jefferson St., Tallahassee, FL 32302 (© **888/7-FLA-USA;** www.flausa.com).

For Florida State Parks, see www.florida stateparks.org.

2 Entry Requirements & Customs

ENTRY REQUIREMENTS
PASSPORTS

For information on how to get a passport, see the "Passports" section in the appendix—the websites listed provide downloadable passport applications as well as the current fees for processing passport applications. For an up-to-date, country-by-country listing of passport requirements around the world, go to the "Foreign Entry Requirement" Web page of the U.S. State Department at **http://travel.state.gov.** International visitors can obtain a visa application at the same website.

VISAS

For information on how to get a Visa, see the "Visas" section in the appendix.

The U.S. State Department has a **Visa Waiver Program** allowing citizens of the following countries (at press time) to enter the United States without a visa for stays of up to 90 days: Andorra, Australia, Austria, Belgium, Brunei, Denmark, Finland, France, Germany, Iceland, Ireland, Italy, Japan, Liechtenstein, Luxembourg, Monaco, the Netherlands, New Zealand, Norway, Portugal, San Marino, Singapore, Slovenia, Spain, Sweden, Switzerland, and the United Kingdom. Citizens of these nations need only a valid passport

and a round-trip air or cruise ticket upon arrival. If they first enter the United States, they may also visit Mexico, Canada, Bermuda, and/or the Caribbean islands and return to the United States without a visa. Further information is available from any U.S. embassy or consulate. Canadian citizens may enter the United States without visas; they need only proof of residence.

Citizens of all other countries must have (1) a valid passport that expires at least 6 months later than the scheduled end of their visit to the United States, and (2) a tourist visa, which may be obtained without charge from any U.S. consulate.

MEDICAL REQUIREMENTS

Unless you're arriving from an area known to be suffering from an epidemic (particularly cholera or yellow fever), inoculations or vaccinations are not required for entry into the United States. If you have a medical condition that requires **syringe-administered medications,** carry a valid signed prescription from your physician—the Federal Aviation Administration (FAA) no longer allows airline passengers to pack syringes in their carry-on baggage without documented proof of medical need. If you have a disease that requires treatment with **narcotics,** you should also carry documented proof with you—smuggling narcotics aboard a plane is a serious offense that carries severe penalties in the U.S.

For **HIV-positive visitors,** requirements for entering the United States are somewhat vague and change frequently. For up-to-the-minute information, contact **AIDSinfo** (© 800/448-0440 or 301/519-6616 outside the U.S.; www. aidsinfo.nih.gov) or the **Gay Men's Health Crisis** (© 212/367-1000; www. gmhc.org).

CUSTOMS
WHAT YOU CAN BRING INTO SOUTH FLORIDA

Every visitor more than 21 years of age may bring in, free of duty, the following: (1) 1 liter of wine or hard liquor; (2) 200 cigarettes, 100 cigars (but not from Cuba), or 3 pounds of smoking tobacco; and (3) $100 worth of gifts. These exemptions are offered to travelers who spend at least 72 hours in the United States and who have not claimed them within the preceding 6 months. It is altogether forbidden to bring into the country foodstuffs (particularly fruit, cooked meats, and canned goods) and plants (vegetables, seeds, tropical plants, and the like). Foreign tourists may carry in or out up to $10,000 in U.S. or foreign currency with no formalities; larger sums must be declared to U.S. Customs on entering or leaving, which includes filing form CM 4790. For details regarding U.S. Customs

and Border Protection, consult your nearest U.S. embassy or consulate, or **U.S. Customs** (© 202/927-1770; www. customs.ustreas.gov).

WHAT YOU CAN TAKE HOME FROM SOUTH FLORIDA
Canadian Citizens

For a clear summary of Canadian rules, write for the booklet *I Declare,* issued by the **Canada Border Services Agency** (© 800/461-9999 in Canada, or 204/ 983-3500; www.cbsa-asfc.gc.ca).

U.K. Citizens

For information, contact **HM Customs & Excise** at © 0845/010-9000 (from outside the U.K., 020/8929-0152), or consult their website at www.hmce. gov.uk.

Australian Citizens

A helpful brochure available from Australian consulates or Customs offices is *Know Before You Go.* For more information, call the **Australian Customs Service** at © 1300/363-263, or log on to www.customs.gov.au.

New Zealand Citizens

Most questions are answered in a free pamphlet available at New Zealand consulates and Customs offices: *New Zealand Customs Guide for Travellers, Notice no. 4.* For more information, contact **New Zealand Customs,** The Customhouse, 17–21 Whitmore St., Box 2218, Wellington (© 04/473-6099 or 0800/428-786; www.customs.govt.nz).

3 Money

CREDIT CARDS & ATMs

For as many palm trees as there are in South Florida, there are just as many, if not more, ATMs linked to a major national network that will likely include your bank at home. The easiest way to pay for almost everything in Florida is

with a credit card. MasterCard and Visa credit and debit cards are accepted almost everywhere. American Express, Diner's Club, and Discover cards also are accepted, although not as widely as MasterCard and Visa.

The best way to get cash while you're traveling in Florida is to use your debit or credit cards at **ATMs.** Of the big national banks, **First Union Bank** and **Bank of America** have offices with ATMs throughout Florida.

Nearly all ATMs are linked to a national network that most likely includes your bank at home. **Cirrus** (© **800/424-7787;** www.mastercard.com/atmlocator) and **PLUS** (© **800/843-7587;** www.visa.com/atms) are the two most popular networks; check the back of your ATM card to see which network your bank belongs to. Use the toll-free numbers or check online to locate ATMs in your destination. Be sure to check your bank's daily withdrawal limit and your credit limits before leaving home.

Also be sure to have your personal identification number (PIN), which you will need to activate the cash withdrawal functions at all ATMs. *Note:* Remember that many banks impose a fee every time you use a card at another bank's ATM, and that fee can be higher for international transactions (up to $5 or more) than for domestic ones (where they're rarely more than $2). In addition, the bank from which you withdraw cash may charge its own fee. To compare banks' ATM fees within the U.S., use **www.bankrate.com**. For international withdrawal fees, ask your bank.

TRAVELER'S CHECKS

Traveler's checks are widely accepted in the U.S., but foreign visitors should make sure that they're denominated in U.S. dollars; foreign-currency checks are often difficult to exchange.

You can buy traveler's checks at most banks. Most are offered in denominations of $20, $50, $100, $500, and sometimes $1,000. Generally, you'll pay a service charge ranging from 1% to 4%.

The most popular traveler's checks are offered by **American Express** (© **800/807-6233;** 800/221-7282 for cardholders—this number accepts collect calls, offers service in several foreign languages, and exempts Amex gold and platinum cardholders from the 1% fee.); **Visa** (© **800/732-1322**)—AAA members can obtain Visa checks for a $9.95 fee (for checks up to $1,500) at most AAA offices or by calling © **866/339-3378;** and **MasterCard** (© **800/223-9920**).

If you do choose to carry traveler's checks, keep a record of their serial numbers separate from your checks in the event that they are stolen or lost. You'll get a refund faster if you know the numbers.

4 When to Go

Contrary to popular belief, the notion of sunny Florida isn't always 100% correct. While the term is hardly an oxymoron, when it comes to weather, sunny Florida undergoes major mood swings. While it may be pouring rain on the ocean side of Miami Beach, on the bay side, the only thing pouring down may be UV rays.

Rain showers aside, the most pressing concern for every South Florida visitor is the dreaded "H" word—the un-predictable, unstoppable hurricane. Official hurricane season is from June to November, and while the hurricane's actual pattern is unpredictable, for the most part, the meteorologists at the National Hurricane Center in Coral Gables are able to give fair enough warning so that people can take proper precautions. One of the safest places during a hurricane happens to be in a hotel, because most hotels are sturdy enough to withstand high winds and have generators in case of power failures.

For many people, the worst time to come to South Florida is during the summer, when temperatures are usually scorching, humidity is oppressive, and rain at 4pm is a daily occurrence. Wintertime in South Florida is spectacular—not too hot, not too cool. Temperatures can, however, dip down into the low 50s (teens Celsius) during a cold front.

Weather aside, peak season in South Florida means more tourists, snowbirds, and models—and the influx of celebrities, who also call South Florida their winter home.

In the summer, South Florida practically comes to a standstill as far as special events, cultural activities, and overall pace is concerned. Locals love it; it is their time to reclaim their cities. Tourists may want to take advantage of the summers down here as long as they can stand the heat. If you can brave the temperature, you will not have to face the long lines in restaurants and at attractions that you will encounter during peak season. For some people, however, the lines and the waiting are all part of the allure of South Florida, as they provide an opportunity to see and be seen.

Miami's Average Monthly High/Low Temperatures & Rainfall

	Jan	Feb	Mar	Apr	May	June	July	Aug	Sept	Oct	Nov	Dec
High (°F)	76	77	80	83	86	88	89	90	88	85	80	77
High (°C)	24	25	27	28	30	31	32	32	31	29	27	25
Low (°F)	60	61	64	68	72	75	76	76	76	72	66	61
Low (°C)	15.6	16	18	20	22	24	24	24	24	22	19	16
Rain (in.)	2.0	2.1	2.4	3.0	5.9	8.8	6.0	7.8	8.5	7.0	3.1	1.8

SOUTH FLORIDA CALENDAR OF EVENTS

January

FedEx Orange Bowl Classic, Miami. Football fanatics flock down to the big Orange Bowl game (oddly taking place not at the Orange Bowl in seedy downtown, but at the much more savory Pro Player Stadium) on New Year's Day, featuring two of the year's best college football teams. Tickets are available from March 1 of the previous year through the Orange Bowl Committee (© 305/371-4600; www.orangebowl. org), but call early as they sell out quickly. January 1.

Polo Season, Palm Beach. Join the crisp and clean Ralph Lauren–clad polo fanatics (including stars and socialites) at the Palm Beach Polo and Country Club for polo season. Call © 561/793-1440 for details. Begins in early January.

Three Kings Parade, Miami. Miami's Cuban community makes up for the fact that Castro banned this religious celebration over 25 years ago by throwing a no-holds-barred parade throughout the streets of Little Havana's Calle Ocho neighborhood. Call © 305/447-1140. Usually the first Sunday of January.

Art Deco Weekend, South Beach. Gain a newfound appreciation for the Necco-wafered Art Deco buildings, Deco furniture, history, and fashion at this weekend-long festival of street fairs, films, lectures, and other events. Call © 305/672-2014. Mid- to late January.

Martin Luther King, Jr., Day Parade, Miami. The culmination of the week's celebration of Dr. King's birthday, this parade occurs in the not-so-great neighborhood of Liberty City, along NW 54th Street, between NW

12th and 32nd avenues. For information, call © **305/636-1924.** Mid-January.

Palm Beach International Art and Antiques Fair, West Palm Beach. With antiques and art older than some of Palm Beach's very own residents, this fair has become a premier stomping ground for domestic artifacts. Call © **561/220-2690.** Late January or early February.

Key West Literary Seminar, Key West. Literary types get a good reason to put down the books and head to Key West. This annual 3-day event features a different theme every year, such as "the Memoir" or "Science Fiction," and a roster of incredible authors, writers, and other literary types such as Joyce Carol Oates, Barbara Ehrenreich, and Jamaica Kincaid. The event is so popular it sells out well in advance, so call early for tickets (available for individual lectures or events, or the entire conference). For information, call © **888/293-9291** or visit www.key westliteraryseminar.org. Mid-January.

February

Miami Film Festival. Though not exactly Cannes, the Miami Film Festival, sponsored by the Film Society of America, is an impressive 10-day celluloid celebration, featuring world premiers of Latin American, domestic, and other foreign and independent films. Actors, producers, and directors show up to plug their films and participate in Q&A sessions with the audiences. Call © **305/377-FILM.** Early to mid-February.

Everglades Seafood Festival, Florida City. What seems like schools of fish-loving people flock down to Florida City for a 2-day feeding frenzy, in which Florida delicacies from stone crab to gator tails are served from shacks and booths on the outskirts of this quaint old Florida town. Free admission, but you pay for the food you eat, booth by booth. Call © **941/ 695-4100.** First full weekend in February.

Homestead Rodeo, Homestead. One of South Florida's only rodeo shows, this one features clowns, competitions, and bucking broncos. Call © **305/ 247-3515.** Early February.

Coconut Grove Arts Festival, Coconut Grove. Florida's largest art festival features over 300 artists who are selected from thousands of entries. Possibly one of the most crowded street fairs in South Florida, the festival attracts art lovers, artists, and lots of college students who seem to think this event is the Mardi Gras of art fairs. Call © **305/447-0401** for information. Presidents' Day weekend.

Miami International Boat Show, Miami Beach. Agoraphobics beware, as this show draws a quarter of a million boat enthusiasts to the Miami Beach Convention Center. Some of the world's priciest megayachts, speedboats, sailboats, and schooners are displayed for purchase or for gawking. Call © **305/531-8410.** Mid-February.

Winter Equestrian Festival, West Palm Beach. With over 1,000 horses and three grand-prix equestrian events, the Palm Beach Polo Club's winter festival is an equestrian's dream. For information, call © **561/798-7000.** Late February.

Doral Ryder Golf Open, West Miami. This prestigious annual golf tournament swings into Miami at the legendary courses at the Doral Resort and Club. Call © **305/477-GOLF.** Late February.

Hatsume Fair, Delray Beach. A 2-day fair celebrating the first buds of spring in a state that barely has seasons may seem like an odd notion, but the Hatsume Fair takes place at the Morikami Japanese Museum and Gardens—a place where visitors can appreciate truly exotic flora and fauna. Call ℂ **561/495-0233.** Last weekend in February.

South Beach Wine & Food Festival, South Beach. A 3-day celebration featuring some of the Food Network's and the world's best chefs who do their thing in the kitchens of various restaurants and events around town. In addition, there are tastings, lectures, seminars, and parties that are all open to the public—for a price, of course. Call ℂ **877/762-3933** or go online to www.sobewineandfoodfest.com. Last weekend in February.

March

Winter Party, Miami Beach. Gays and lesbians from around the world book trips to Miami as far as a year in advance to attend this weekend-long series of parties and events benefiting the Dade Human Rights Foundation. Travel arrangements can be made through Different Roads Travel, the event's official travel company, by calling ℂ **888/ROADS-55,** ext. 510. For information on the specific events and prices, call ℂ **305/538-5908** or visit www.winterparty.com. Early March.

Winter Music Conference, South Beach/Miami. In one word: DJpalooza. Basically, the WMC is the Westminster Dog Show of DJs and electronic music artists, in which people from all over the world descend on the Magic City for 5 consecutive, exhausting days and nights of shows, kibitzing, and networking. Late March.

Italian Renaissance Festival, Miami. Villa Vizcaya gets in touch with its Renaissance roots at this festival, which features strolling musicians, stage plays, and a cast of period-costumed characters who do their best to convince you that you're in a time warp. Call ℂ **305/250-9133.** Mid-March.

Miami Gay & Lesbian Film Festival, Miami Beach. This 10-day event is the Sundance of festivals for gay and lesbian films and filmmakers. It features an impressive roster of independent and commercial films, plus appearances by some of the films' directors, actors, and writers. Call ℂ **305/532-7256.** Mid-March.

Calle Ocho Festival, Little Havana. What Carnavale is to Rio, the Calle Ocho Festival is to Miami. This 10-day extravaganza, also called Carnival Miami, features a lengthy block party spanning 23 blocks, live salsa music, parades, and, of course, tons of savory Cuban delicacies. Those afraid of mob scenes should avoid this party at all costs. Call ℂ **305/644-8888.** Mid-March.

Grand Prix of Miami, Homestead. A little bit of Daytona in Miami, the Grand Prix is a premier racing event, attracting celebrities, Indy car drivers, and curious spectators who get a buzz off the smell of gasoline. Get tickets early, as this event sells out quickly. Call ℂ **305/250-5200.** Late March.

NASDAQ 100 Open, Key Biscayne. Agassi, Kournikova, and the Williams sisters are only a few of the Grand Slammers who appear at this, one of the world's foremost tennis tournaments. Tickets for the semifinals and finals are hard to come by, so order early. Call ℂ **305/446-2200.** End of March.

April

World Cup Polo Tournament, Palm Beach. The last tournament of the polo season, this event draws the diamond-studded mallet set who gather one more time in the name of scene and sport. Call ☏ **561/793-1440**. Mid-April.

PGA Seniors Golf Championship, Palm Beach Gardens. This is the oldest and most prestigious of the senior golf tournaments in which aging swingers prove they've still got spunk in their swing. Call ☏ **561/624-8400**. Mid-April.

Little Acorns International Kite Festival, South Beach. A great event for the kids and kids at heart, this free kite festival is a true spectacular in the sky, attracting thousands of expert flyers and their flying works of art from 5th to 15th streets. Kids can build their own kites and scrounge for candy, which is dropped piñata style along the beach. Call ☏ **888/298-9815**. Third weekend in April.

Sunfest, West Palm Beach. Sleepy downtown West Palm comes alive at the end of April for this street fair and concert, featuring big-name entertainment, food stands, a youth fair, and hordes of people. Admission charges are reasonable, but, unless there's someone performing whom you must see, not always worth the price. Stick to the free nontented area on Clematis Street for excellent people-watching. For information, call ☏ **561/659-5992**. Late April.

Texaco Key West Classic, Key West. This catch-and-release fishing competition offers $50,000 in prizes to be divided among the top anglers in three divisions: sailfish, marlin, and light tackle. You won't believe the size of some of these catches. Call ☏ **305/294-4042**. Late April.

May

McDonald's Air & Sea Show, Fort Lauderdale. It's a tough call as far as what's more crowded—the air, the sea, or the ground, which attracts over 2 million onlookers craning their necks for a view of big-name airwolves such as the Blue Angels and the Thunderbirds. In addition to the various planes doing tricks in the sky, you'll also see battleships pull into port. *Remember:* It's an *air* and *sea* show, not a car show, so consider leaving yours at the hotel. Call ☏ **954/467-3555**. Early May.

Cajun Zydeco Crawfish Festival, Fort Lauderdale. A little bit of Nawlins in South Florida. Enjoy the crawfish delicacies at this 3-day festival paying homage to all things hot, spicy, and, er, crunchy. Call ☏ **954/761-5934**. Early May.

Arabian Nights Festival, Hialeah. A colorful celebration of Hialeah's Moorish architecture, this festival features a mix of entertainment, food, and fantasy inspired by Arabian culture. Call ☏ **305/758-4166**. Mid-May.

June

Coconut Grove Goombay Festival, Coconut Grove. They may say it's better in the Bahamas, but that's questionable after you've attended Miami's own Bahamian bash, featuring lots of dancing in the streets, marching bands, scorching Caribbean temperatures, and the ever buzz-worthy and refreshing Goombay punch. For information, call ☏ **305/372-9966**. Early June.

July

Independence Day, Miami. Watch as one of the nation's most spectacular skylines is further illuminated with the masterful display of professional fireworks throughout the entire city. Best views are from Key Biscayne and Bayfront Park. For specific information on events, check the local newspapers or contact the Miami Chamber of Commerce (see above). July 4th.

Lower Keys Underwater Music Fest, Looe Key. When you hear the phrase "the music and the madness," you may want to think of this amusing aural aquatic event in which boaters head out to the underwater reef at the Looe Key Marine Sanctuary, drop speakers into the water, and pipe in all sorts of music, creating a disco-diving spectacular. Considering the heat at this time of year, underwater is probably the coolest place for a concert. Call © 800/872-3722. Early July.

Miccosukee Everglades Festival, West Miami (close to the Everglades). South Florida's Native American community celebrates its own unique heritage with music, food, and fanfare including shriek-inducing alligator wrestling. Call © 305/223-8380 for prices and information. Late July.

Hemingway Days Festival, Key West. The legendary author is alive and well—many times over—at this celebration of the literary world's most famous papa, to which eerily accurate Hemingway clones flock in the hopes of winning the big look-alike contest. Call © 305/294-4440. Mid- to late July.

Wine and All That Jazz, Boca Raton. Though the experts may recommend water as the ideal summer thirst quencher, the organizers of this event prefer the fruits of the vine. Sip over 100 vintages to the tune of jazz at this swank wine-tasting party. Call © 561/278-0424. Late July.

Beethoven by the Beach, Fort Lauderdale. The Florida Philharmonic takes Beethoven to the beach with its summer music festival, featuring symphonies, chamber pieces, and piano concertos. Call © 954/561-2997. Mid- to late July.

August

This month is possibly the most scorching, which is why event planners try to avoid it altogether. Your best bet? Try the beach, pool, or anywhere with air-conditioning.

September

Festival Miami, Miami. The University of Miami School of Music presents a 4-week program of performing arts, classical, jazz, and world music. For a schedule of performances, call © 305/284-4940. Mid-September.

October

Caribbean Carnival, Miami. If you've never been to the Caribbean, then this can be your introduction to the colorful, multicultural island nations of Trinidad, Jamaica, Haiti, St. Vincent, Barbados, and St. Croix, as natives from the islands participate in a masquerade parade in their traditional costumes. Call © 305/653-1877. Early October.

Columbus Day Regatta, Miami. On the day that Columbus discovered America, the party-hearty of today's Florida discover their fellow Americans' birthday suits—this bacchanalia in the middle of Biscayne Bay encourages participants in this so-called regatta (there is a boat race at some point during the day, but most people are too preoccupied to notice) to strip down to their bare necessities and party at the sandbar in the middle of the bay. You may not need a bathing suit, but you will need a boat to get out to where all the action is. Consider renting one on Key Biscayne, which is the closest to the sandbar. Columbus Day (a Mon in early Oct).

Fort Lauderdale International Boat Show, Fort Lauderdale. The world's largest boat show, this one's got boats of every size, shape, and status symbol displayed at the scenic Bahia Mar marina and four other locations in the area. Traffic-phobes beware. Call © 954/764-7642. Mid-October.

Fantasy Fest, Key West. Mardi Gras takes a Floridian holiday as the streets of Key West are overtaken by wildly costumed revelers who have no shame and no parental guidance. This week-long, hedonistic, X-rated Halloween party is not for children 17 and under. Make reservations in Key West early, as hotels tend to book up quickly during this event. Call ✆ **305/296-1817.** Last week of October.

November

Blues Festival at Riverwalk, Fort Lauderdale. The scenic landscape of downtown Fort Lauderdale's River-walk will make your own personal blues go away, but you'll want to immerse yourself in the music of big-name performers who sing and play the blues here at various venues. Call ✆ **954/761-5934.** Early November.

South Florida International Auto Show, Miami Beach. Cars are every-where—literally—at this massive auto show, displaying the latest and most futuristic modes of transportation on the market. Try to take public trans-portation or call a cab to get to this gridlocked event. Call ✆ **305/947-5950.** Early November.

Jiffy Lube Miami 300 Weekend of NASCAR, Homestead. World-class racing takes place on Miami's world-class 344-acre motor sports complex. Rev your engines early for tickets to this event. Call ✆ **305/230-5200.** Mid-November.

Miami Book Fair International, downtown Miami. Bibliophiles, literati, and some of the world's most presti-gious and prolific authors descend upon downtown Miami for a weeklong hom-age to the written word, which also hap-pens to be the largest book fair in the United States. The weekend street fair is the most well attended of the entire event, in which regular folk mix with wordsmiths such as Tom Wolfe and Jane Smiley while indulging in snacks, antiquarian books, and literary gossip.

All lectures are free, but they fill up quickly, so get there early. Call ✆ **305/ 237-3258** for lecture schedules. Mid-November.

White Party Week, Miami and Fort Lauderdale. This week-long series of parties to benefit AIDS research is built around the main event, the White Party, which takes place at Villa Vizcaya and sells out as early as a year in advance. Philanthropists and celebrities such as Calvin Klein and David Geffen join thousands of white-clad, mostly gay men (and some women) in what has become one of the world's hottest and hardest-to-score party tickets. Call ✆ **305/667-9296** or visit www.whitepartyweek.com for a schedule of parties and events. Thanks-giving week.

Santa's Enchanted Forest, Miami. Billing itself as the world's largest Christmas theme park, Santa's Enchanted Forest is an assault on the eyes, with thousands of lights lining Tropical Park plus rides, games, and lots of food. This is a great place to bring younger kids. Call ✆ **305/893-0090.** Early November to mid-January.

December

Art Basel Miami Beach, Miami Beach/Design District. Switzerland's most exclusive art fair and the world's most prominent collectors fly south for the winter and set up shop on South Beach and in the Design District with thousands of exhibitions, not to men-tion cocktail parties, concerts, and con-tainers—as in shipping—that are set up on the beach and transformed into makeshift galleries. Early December.

Seminole Hard Rock Winterfest Boat Parade, Fort Lauderdale. People who complain that the holiday season just isn't as festive in South Florida as it is in colder parts of the world haven't been to this spectacular boat parade along the Intracoastal Waterways. Forget decking the halls. At this parade, the decks are decked out in magnificent holiday regalia as they gracefully—and boastfully—glide up and down the water. If you're not on a boat, the best views are from waterfront restaurants or anywhere you can squeeze in along the water. Call © **954/767-0686.** Mid-December.

Taste of the Grove Food and Music Festival, Coconut Grove. Brave massive crowds of hungry folk at this festival featuring booths from various neighborhood eateries hawking their goods for the price of a few prepurchased tickets. Call © **305/444-7270.** Usually held the week after Christmas.

5 Getting There & Getting Around

For contact information of any airline or car rental service listed below, see the appendix.

GETTING THERE
BY PLANE

Miami is one of **American Airlines'** biggest hubs, and most major domestic airlines fly to and from many Florida cities, including **Continental, Delta, Northwest/KLM, TWA, United,** and **US Airways.**

Several budget airlines also fly to South Florida, including **Southwest Airlines, Delta Song, Air Tran, Spirit,** and **Jet Blue.**

IMMIGRATION & CUSTOMS CLEARANCE Foreign visitors arriving by air, no matter what the port of entry, should cultivate patience and resignation before setting foot on U.S. soil. Clearing immigration control can take as long as 2 hours. This is especially true in the aftermath of the September 11, 2001, terrorist attacks, when U.S. airports considerably beefed up security clearances. People traveling by air from Canada, Bermuda, and certain Caribbean countries can sometimes clear Customs and Immigration at the point of departure, which is much faster.

BY CAR

Although four major roads run to and through Miami—I-95, S.R. 826, S.R. 836, and U.S. 1—chances are you'll reach Miami and the rest of South Florida by way of I-95. This north-south interstate is South Florida's lifeline and an integral part of the region. The highway connects all of Miami's different neighborhoods, the airport, the beaches, and all of South Florida to the rest of the country. Miami's road signs are notoriously confusing and notably absent when you most need them. Think twice before you exit from the highway if you aren't sure where you're going: Some exits lead to unsavory neighborhoods.

Other highways that will get you to Florida include I-10, which originates in Los Angeles and terminates at the tip of Florida in Jacksonville, and I-75, which begins in North Michigan and runs through the center of the state to Florida's west coast.

Florida law allows drivers to make a right turn on a red light after a complete

---

Tips **Fly for Less**

When booking airfare to Miami, consider flying into the Fort Lauderdale Hollywood International Airport for considerably cheaper fares. The airport is only a half-hour from downtown Miami.

Tips Prepare to Be Fingerprinted

As of January 2004, many international visitors traveling on visas to the United States will be photographed and fingerprinted at Customs in a new program created by the Department of Homeland Security called **US-VISIT**. Non-U.S. citizens arriving at airports and on cruise ships must undergo an instant background check as part of the government's efforts to deter terrorism by verifying the identity of incoming and outgoing visitors. Exempt from the extra scrutiny are visitors entering by land or those (mostly in Europe; see p. 28) who don't require a visa for short-term visits. For more information, go to the Homeland Security website at **www.dhs.gov/dhspublic**.

stop, unless otherwise indicated. In addition, all passengers are required to wear seat belts, and children younger than 3 must be securely fastened in government-approved car seats.

If you plan to be in your car quite a bit during your visit, you may want to join the **American Automobile Association (AAA),** which has hundreds of offices nationwide. Members receive excellent maps, emergency road service, and, upon request, planned, detailed itineraries.

For information on car-rental companies with offices in South Florida, see p. 67.

Saving Money on a Rental Car   Car-rental rates vary even more than airline fares. The price you pay will depend on the size of the car, where and when you pick it up and drop it off, the length of the rental period, where and how far you drive it, whether you purchase insurance, and a host of other factors. A few key questions could save you hundreds of dollars:

- Are weekend rates lower than weekday rates? Ask if the rate is the same for pickup Friday morning, for instance, as it is for Thursday night.
- Is a weekly rate cheaper than the daily rate? Even if you only need the car for 4 days, it may be cheaper to keep it for 5.
- Does the agency assess a drop-off charge if you don't return the car to

the same location where you picked it up? Is it cheaper to pick up the car at the airport compared to a downtown location?

- Are special promotional rates available? If you see an advertised price in your local newspaper, be sure to ask for that specific rate; otherwise you may be charged the standard cost.
- Are discounts available for members of AARP, AAA, frequent-flier programs, or trade unions?
- How much tax will be added to the rental bill? Local tax? State tax?
- What is the cost of adding an additional driver's name to the contract?
- How many free miles are included in the price? Free mileage is often negotiable, depending on the length of your rental.
- How much does the rental company charge to refill your gas tank if you return with the tank less than full? Fuel is almost always cheaper in town; try to allow enough time to refuel the car yourself before returning it.

Many packages are available that include airfare, accommodations, and a rental car with unlimited mileage. Compare these prices with the cost of booking airline tickets and renting a car separately to see whether these offers are good deals.

Arranging Car Rentals on the Web   Internet resources can make comparison shopping easier. **Expedia.com** (www. expedia.com) and **Travelocity** (www. travelocity.com) help you compare prices and locate car-rental bargains from various companies nationwide. They will even make your reservation for you once you've found the best deal.

BY TRAIN

Amtrak (© 800/USA-RAIL; www. amtrak.com) offers train service to Florida from both the East and West coasts. It takes some 26 hours from New York to Miami and 68 hours from Los Angeles to Miami; Amtrak's fares aren't much less—if not more—than many of the airlines' lowest fares.

Amtrak's *Silver Meteor* and *Silver Star* both run twice daily between New York and either Miami or Tampa, with intermediate stops along the East Coast and in Florida. Amtrak's Thruway Bus Connections are available from the Fort Lauderdale Amtrak station and Miami International Airport to Key West; from Tampa to St. Petersburg, Treasure Island, Clearwater, Sarasota, Bradenton, and Fort Myers; and from Deland to Daytona Beach. From the West Coast, the *Sunset Limited* runs three times weekly between Los Angeles and Orlando. It stops in Pensacola, Crestview (north of Fort Walton Beach and Destin), Chipley (north of Panama City Beach), and Tallahassee. Sleeping accommodations are available for an extra charge.

Amtrak's **Auto Train** runs daily from Lorton, Virginia (12 miles south of Washington, D.C.), to Sanford, Florida (just northeast of Orlando). You ride in a coach while your car is secured in an enclosed vehicle carrier.

If you intend to stop along the way, you can save money with Amtrak's **Explore America** (or All Aboard America) fares, which are based on three regions of the country.

International visitors can buy Amtrak's **USA Rail Pass,** good for 5, 15, or 30 days of unlimited travel. The pass is available online or through many overseas travel agents. See Amtrak.com for the cost of travel within the western, eastern, or northwestern United States. Reservations are generally required and should be made as early as possible.

GETTING AROUND

For details on getting around Miami, see p. 66. For details on exploring the Keys by car, see p. 250.

Having a car is the best and easiest way to see South Florida's sights or to get to and from the beach. Public transportation is available only in the cities and larger towns, and even there, it may provide infrequent or inadequate service.

If you're heading upstate, a flight may be best. Jacksonville is about 350 miles north of Miami and 500 miles north of Key West, so don't underestimate how long it will take you to drive around the state.

BY CAR

If you're visiting from abroad and plan to rent a car in South Florida, keep in mind that foreign driver's licenses are usually recognized in the U.S., but you should get an international one if your home license is not in English.

The speed limit is either 65 mph or 70 mph on the rural interstate highways, so you can make good time between cities. Not so on U.S. 1, U.S. 17, U.S. 19, U.S. 41, and U.S. 301; although most have four lanes, these older highways tend to be heavily congested, especially in built-up areas.

Every major car rental company is represented here, including **Alamo, Avis, Budget, Dollar, Enterprise, Hertz, National,** and **Thrifty.**

State and local **taxes** will add as much as 20% to your final bill. You'll pay an additional $2.05 per day in statewide use tax, and local sales taxes will tack on at least 6% to the total, including the statewide use tax. Some airports add another 35¢ per day and as much as 10% in "recovery" fees. You can avoid the recovery fee by picking up your car in town rather than at the airport. Budget and Enterprise both have numerous rental locations away from the airports. But be sure to weigh the cost of transportation to and from your hotel against the amount of the fee.

Competition is so fierce among Florida rental firms that most have now stopped charging **drop-off fees** if you pick up a car at one place and leave it at another within the state. Be sure to ask in advance if there's a drop-off fee.

To rent a car, you must have a valid **credit card** (not a debit or check card) in your name, and most companies require you to be at least 25 years old. Some also set maximum ages and may deny cars to anyone with a bad driving record. Ask about requirements and restrictions when you book, in order to avoid problems once you arrive.

BY PLANE

The commuter arms of **Continental, Delta,** and **US Airways** provide extensive service between Florida's major cities and towns. Fares for these short hops tend to be reasonable.

Cape Air flies between Key West and Naples, which means you can avoid backtracking to Miami from Key West if you're touring the state. You can also take a 3-hr. boat ride between Key West and Fort Myers Beach or Marco Island during the winter months; try **Key West Express** (© 888/539-2628; www.seakeywestexpress.com). **Collins Aviation** connects Fort Lauderdale with Marathon.

Overseas visitors can take advantage of the APEX (Advance Purchase Excursion) reductions offered by all major U.S. and European carriers. In addition, some large airlines offer transatlantic or transpacific passengers special discount tickets under the name **Visit USA,** which allows mostly one-way travel from one U.S. destination to another at very low prices. Unavailable in the U.S., these discount tickets must be purchased abroad in conjunction with your international fare. This system is the easiest, fastest, and cheapest way to see the country.

BY TRAIN

You'll find that train travel isn't terribly feasible within Florida, and it's not significantly less expensive than flying, if at all. See "Getting There," above, for Florida towns served by **Amtrak.**

6 Travel Insurance

The cost of travel insurance varies widely, depending on the cost and length of your trip, your age and health, and the type of trip you're taking, but expect to pay between 5% and 8% of the vacation itself. You can get estimates from various providers through **InsureMyTrip.com.** Enter your trip cost and dates, your age, and other information, for prices from more than a dozen companies.

TRIP-CANCELLATION INSURANCE

Trip-cancellation insurance will help retrieve your money if you have to back out of a trip or depart early, or if your travel supplier goes bankrupt. Permissible reasons for trip cancellation can range from sickness to natural disasters to the State Department declaring a destination unsafe for travel.

For more information, contact one of the following recommended insurers: **Access America** (© 866/807-3982; www.accessamerica.com); **Travel Guard International** (© 800/826-4919; www.travelguard.com); **Travel Insured International** (© 800/243-3174; www.travelinsured.com); and **Travelex Insurance**

Services (℡ 888/457-4602; www.travelex-insurance.com).

MEDICAL INSURANCE

Although it's not required of travelers, health insurance is highly recommended. Most health insurance policies cover you if you get sick away from home—but verify that you're covered before you depart, particularly if you're insured by an HMO.

International visitors should note that unlike many European countries, the United States does not usually offer free or low-cost medical care to its citizens or visitors. Doctors and hospitals are expensive, and in most cases will require advance payment or proof of coverage before they render their services. Good policies will cover the costs of an accident, repatriation, or death. Packages such as **Europ Assistance's "Worldwide Healthcare Plan"** are sold by European automobile clubs and travel agencies at attractive rates. **Worldwide Assistance Services, Inc.** (℡ 800/777-8710; www.worldwideassistance.com) is the agent for Europ Assistance in the United States.

Though lack of health insurance may prevent you from being admitted to a hospital in nonemergencies, don't worry about being left on a street corner to die: The American way is to fix you now and bill the living daylights out of you later.

INSURANCE FOR BRITISH TRAVELERS Most big travel agents offer their own insurance and will probably try to sell you their package when you book a holiday. Think before you sign. **Britain's Consumers' Association** recommends that you insist on seeing the policy and reading the fine print before buying travel insurance. **The Association of British Insurers** (℡ 020/7600-3333; www.abi.org.uk) gives advice by phone and publishes *Holiday Insurance,* a free guide to policy provisions and prices. You might also shop around for better deals: Try **Columbus Direct** (℡ 0870/033-9988; www.columbusdirect.net).

INSURANCE FOR CANADIAN TRAVELERS Canadians should check with their provincial health plan offices or call **Health Canada** (℡ 866/225-0709; www.hc-sc.gc.ca) to find out the extent of their coverage and what documentation and receipts they must take home in case they are treated in the United States.

LOST-LUGGAGE INSURANCE

On flights within the U.S., checked baggage is covered up to $2,500 per ticketed passenger. On flights outside the U.S. (and on U.S. portions of international trips), baggage coverage is limited to approximately $9.07 per pound, up to approximately $635 per checked bag. If you plan to check items more valuable than what's covered by the standard liability, see whether your homeowner's policy covers your valuables, get baggage insurance as part of your comprehensive travel-insurance package, or buy Travel Guard's "BagTrak" product.

If your luggage is lost, immediately file a lost-luggage claim at the airport, detailing the luggage contents. Most airlines require that you report delayed, damaged, or lost baggage within 4 hours of arrival. The airlines are required to deliver luggage, once found, directly to your house or destination free of charge.

7 Health & Safety

STAYING HEALTHY

GENERAL AVAILABILITY OF HEALTH CARE

Contact the **International Association for Medical Assistance to Travelers** **(IAMAT)** (℡ 716/754-4883 or, in Canada, 416/652-0137; **www.iamat.org**) for tips on travel and health concerns in the countries you're visiting, and for lists of local, English-speaking doctors. The United States **Centers for Disease Control and Prevention** (© 800/ 311-3435; www.cdc.gov) provides up-to-date information on health hazards by region or country and offers tips on food safety. The website **www.tripprep.com**, sponsored by a consortium of travel medicine practitioners, may also offer helpful advice on traveling abroad. You can find listings of reliable clinics overseas at the **International Society of Travel Medicine** (www.istm.org).

WHAT TO DO IF YOU GET SICK AWAY FROM HOME

In most cases, your existing health plan will provide the coverage you need. But double-check; you may want to buy **travel medical insurance** instead. Always bring your insurance ID card with you when you travel.

Pack **prescription medications** in your carry-on luggage, and carry prescription medications in their original containers, with pharmacy labels—otherwise they won't make it through airport security. Also bring along copies of your prescriptions in case you lose your pills or run out. And don't forget sunglasses and an extra pair of contact lenses or prescription glasses.

If you get sick, consider asking your hotel concierge to recommend a local doctor—even his or her own. You can also try the emergency room at a local hospital; many have walk-in clinics for emergency cases that are not life threatening. You may not get immediate attention, but you won't pay the high price of an emergency room visit.

SUN Paramount to staying well in South Florida (and maintaining a sunny disposition) is sunscreen. Even on the cloudiest of days, you *will* feel the effects of the powerful UV rays, so it's best to take precautions at all times. Limit your exposure to the sun, especially during the first few days of your trip and thereafter from 11am to 2pm. Use a sunscreen with a high sun protection factor (SPF) and apply it liberally. Remember that children need more protection than do adults. Mosquito repellent, especially if you travel to the Everglades or other swampy areas and parks, is a good idea.

STAYING SAFE

Although tourist areas in Florida are generally safe, you should always stay alert. This is particularly true in the large cities such as Miami, Orlando, Tampa, and St. Petersburg. It is wise to ask your hotel's front-desk staff or the city's or area's tourist office if you're in doubt about which neighborhoods are safe.

Remember also that hotels are open to the public, and in a large hotel, security may not be able to screen everyone entering. Always lock your room door. Don't assume that once inside your hotel you are automatically safe and no longer need to be aware of your surroundings.

ECOTOURISM

You can find eco-friendly travel tips, statistics, and touring companies and associations—listed by destination under "Travel Choice"—at the TIES website, www.ecotourism.org. **Ecotravel.com** is part online magazine and part ecodirectory that lets you search for touring companies in several categories (water-based, land-based, spiritually oriented, and so on). Also check out **Conservation International** (www.conservation.org)— which, with *National Geographic Traveler,* annually presents **World Legacy Awards** (www.wlaward.org) to those travel tour operators, businesses, organizations, and places that have made a significant contribution to sustainable tourism.

For information about the ethics of swimming with dolphins and other outdoor activities, visit the **Whale and Dolphin Conservation Society** (www.wdcs. org) and **Tread Lightly** (www.tread lightly.org).

8 Specialized Travel Resources

TRAVELERS WITH DISABILITIES

Most disabilities shouldn't stop anyone from traveling in the U.S. There are more options and resources out there than ever before.

The **Golden Access Passport** gives visually impaired or permanently disabled persons (regardless of age) free lifetime entrance to all properties administered by the National Park Service, the U.S. Fish and Wildlife Service, the U.S. Forest Service, the U.S. Army Corps of Engineers, the Bureau of Land Management, and the Tennessee Valley Authority. This may include national parks, monuments, historic sites, recreation areas, and national wildlife refuges.

GAY & LESBIAN TRAVELERS

South Florida, particularly Key West, South Beach, and Fort Lauderdale, has a thriving gay community, supported by a wide range of services and establishments. There are several local gay-oriented publications full of information on gay and gay-friendly events, businesses, and services. *TWN, Wire, Hot Spots,* and *Miamigo* are among the free publications available in boxes on street corners, in stores, and on newsstands.

For a map and directory of gay businesses or a copy of the gay and lesbian community calendar sponsored by the **Dade Human Rights Foundation,** call ⓒ **305/572-1841.** For a copy of the calendar and other information, you can also visit www.dhrf.com. Two organizations that are extremely helpful for gay and lesbian travelers are the **Miami Dade and South Beach Business Guild** (better known as the Gay Chamber of Commerce; ⓒ **305/751-8855**), and the **Gay and Lesbian Community Center of Fort Lauderdale** (ⓒ **954/563-9500**).

You can also contact the **Gay, Lesbian & Bisexual Community Services of Central Florida,** 946 N. Mills Ave.,

Orlando, FL 32803 (ⓒ **407/228-8272;** www.glbcc.org), whose welcome packets usually include the latest issue of the *Triangle,* a quarterly newsletter dedicated to gay and lesbian issues, and a calendar of events pertaining to the gay and lesbian community. Although not a tourist-specific packet, it includes information and ads for the area's gay and lesbian clubs.

SENIOR TRAVEL

With one of the largest retired populations of any state, Florida offers a wide array of activities and benefits for seniors. Don't be shy about asking for discounts, but always carry some kind of identification, such as a driver's license, that shows your age/date of birth. Mention the fact that you're a senior when you make your travel reservations. In most cities, people over the age of 60 qualify for reduced admission to theaters, museums, and other attractions, as well as discounted fares on public transportation.

Members of **AARP** (formerly known as the American Association of Retired Persons), 601 E St. NW, Washington, DC 20049 (ⓒ **888/687-2277** or 202/434-2277; www.aarp.org), get discounts on hotels, airfares, and car rentals. AARP offers members a wide range of benefits, including *AARP: The Magazine* and a monthly newsletter. Anyone over 50 can join.

FAMILY TRAVEL

South Florida is chock-full of kid-friendly hotels, attractions, and restaurants. When visiting the Keys, be sure to check that the hotel or inn allows children, as many do not. Look for the "Kids" icon throughout this book.

You may also want to consult *The Unofficial Guide to Florida with Kids* as well as *How to Take Great Trips with Your Kids* (The Harvard Common Press), which is full of good general advice that can apply to travel anywhere.

Online Traveler's Toolbox

Veteran travelers usually carry some essential items to make their trips easier. Following is a selection of handy online tools to bookmark and use.

- **Airplane Food** (www.airlinemeals.net)
- **Airplane Seating** (www.seatguru.com or www.airlinequality.com)
- **Foreign Languages for Travelers** (www.travlang.com)
- **Maps** (www.mapquest.com)
- **Subway Navigator** (www.subwaynavigator.com)
- **Time and Date** (www.timeanddate.com)
- **Travel Warnings** (http://travel.state.gov, www.fco.gov.uk/travel, www.voyage.gc.ca, or www.dfat.gov.au/consular/advice)
- **Universal Currency Converter** (www.xe.com/ucc)
- **Visa ATM Locator** (www.visa.com), **MasterCard ATM Locator** (www.mastercard.com)
- **Weather** (www.intellicast.com or www.weather.com).

To locate accommodations, restaurants, and attractions that are particularly kid-friendly, refer to the "Kids" icon throughout this guide.

Familyhostel (✆ 800/733-9753; www.learn.unh.edu/familyhostel) takes the whole family, including kids ages 8 to 15, on moderately priced U.S. and international learning vacations. Lectures, field trips, and sightseeing are guided by a team of academics.

Recommended family travel websites include **Family Travel Forum** (www.familytravelforum.com), a comprehensive site that offers customized trip planning; **Family Travel Network** (www.familytravelnetwork.com), an award-winning site that offers travel features, deals, and tips; **Traveling Internationally with Your Kids** (www.travelwithyourkids.com), a comprehensive site offering sound advice for long-distance and international travel with children; and **Family Travel Files** (www.thefamilytravelfiles.com), which offers an online magazine and a directory of off-the-beaten-path tours and tour operators for families.

WOMEN TRAVELERS

Check out the award-winning website **Journeywoman** (www.journeywoman.com), a "real life" women's travel-information network where you can sign up for a free e-mail newsletter and get advice on everything from etiquette and dress to safety; or the travel guide *Safety and Security for Women Who Travel* by Sheila Swan and Peter Laufer (Travelers' Tales, Inc.), offering common-sense tips on safe travel.

AFRICAN-AMERICAN TRAVELERS

Black Travel Online (www.blacktravelonline.com) posts news on upcoming events and includes links to articles and travel-booking sites. **Soul of America** (www.soulofamerica.com) is a comprehensive website, with travel tips, event and family-reunion postings, and sections on historically black beach resorts and active vacations.

Agencies and organizations that provide resources for black travelers include **Rodgers Travel** (✆ 800/825-1775;

www.rodgerstravel.com); the **African American Association of Innkeepers International** (© 877/422-5777; www. africanamericaninns.com); and **Henderson Travel & Tours** (© 800/327-2309 or 301/650-5700; www.hendersontravel. com), which has specialized in trips to Africa since 1957. For more information, check out the following collections and guides: *Go Girl: The Black Woman's Guide to Travel & Adventure* (Eighth Mountain Press), a compilation of travel essays by writers including Jill

Nelson and Audre Lorde; *The African American Travel Guide* by Wayne Robinson (Hunter Publishing; www. hunterpublishing.com); *Steppin' Out* by Carla Labat (Avalon); *Travel and Enjoy Magazine* (© 866/266-6211; www.travel andenjoy.com); and *Pathfinders Magazine* (© 877/977-PATH; www.path finderstravel.com), which includes articles on everything from Rio de Janeiro to Ghana as well as information on upcoming ski, diving, golf, and tennis trips.

9 Planning Your Trip Online

SURFING FOR AIRFARE

The most popular online travel agencies are **Travelocity** (www.travelocity.com, or www.travelocity.co.uk); **Expedia** (www. expedia.com, www.expedia.co.uk, or www. expedia.ca); and **Orbitz** (www.orbitz.com).

In addition, most airlines now offer online-only fares that even their phone agents know nothing about. For the websites of airlines that fly to and from your destination, see "Getting There", p. 37.

Other helpful websites for booking airline tickets online include:

- www.biddingfortravel.com
- www.cheapflights.com
- www.hotwire.com
- www.kayak.com
- www.lastminutetravel.com
- www.opodo.co.uk
- www.priceline.com
- www.sidestep.com
- www.site59.com
- www.smartertravel.com

Frommers.com: The Complete Travel Resource

For an excellent travel-planning resource, we highly recommend **Frommers.com** (www.frommers.com), voted Best Travel Site by *PC Magazine*. We're a little biased, of course, but we guarantee that you'll find the travel tips, reviews, monthly vacation giveaways, bookstore, and online-booking capabilities thoroughly indispensable. Among the special features are our popular **Destinations** section, where you'll get expert travel tips, hotel and dining recommendations, and advice on the sights to see for more than 3,500 destinations around the globe; the **Frommers.com Newsletter,** with the latest deals, travel trends, and money-saving secrets; our **Community** area featuring **Message Boards,** where Frommer's readers post queries and share advice (sometimes even our authors show up to answer questions); and our **Photo Center,** where you can post and share vacation tips. When your research is finished, the **Online Reservations System** (www.frommers. com/book_a_trip) takes you to Frommer's preferred online partners for booking your vacation at affordable prices.

SURFING FOR HOTELS

In addition to **Travelocity, Expedia, Orbitz, Priceline,** and **Hotwire** (see above), the following websites will help you with booking hotel rooms online:

- www.hotels.com
- www.quickbook.com
- www.travelaxe.net
- www.travelweb.com
- www.tripadvisor.com

It's a good idea to **get a confirmation number** and **make a printout** of any online booking transaction.

SURFING FOR RENTAL CARS

For booking rental cars online, the best deals are usually found at rental-car company websites, although all the major online travel agencies also offer rental-car reservations services. Priceline and Hotwire work well for rental cars, too; the only "mystery" is which major rental company you get, and for most travelers the difference between Hertz, Avis, and Budget is negligible.

TRAVEL BLOGS & TRAVELOGUES

- www.gridskipper.com
- www.salon.com/wanderlust
- www.travelblog.com
- www.travelblog.org
- www.worldhum.com
- www.writtenroad.com

10 The Top Websites for Miami & South Florida

GENERAL SOUTH FLORIDA SITES

- For entertainment, dining, sports, and festival information produced in cooperation with the *Sun-Sentinel:* **southflorida.digitalcity.com**.
- The site of Florida's official tourism bureau, this extensive website includes information on attractions, beaches, golfing, and watersports, as well as airport information, weather, and maps: **www.flausa.com**.
- This site links to more than a dozen convention bureaus throughout the state. Most of the sites include information on attractions, dining, lodging, and shopping: **www.facvb.org**.
- Detailed information on state parks, right down to what kind of wildlife hangs out where, and the lowdown on fees, attractions, and facilities: **www.dep.state.fl.us/parks**.
- A nicely organized guide to theme parks, marine attractions, museums, boating, fishing, and much more, as well as advice for first-time visitors to the Sunshine State: **www.see-florida.com**.

CITY GUIDES, DINING & ENTERTAINMENT SITES

- A collection of websites regarding Miami, all with links to other relevant websites: **www.gomiami.about.com**.
- For listings and reviews for Miami arts and entertainment events, restaurants, shopping, and attractions: **www.miami.citysearch.com**.
- A well-rounded guide to Key West, including an events calendar and extensive listings for attractions, sightseeing and ecotours, theater, art galleries, dining, lodging, fishing, and shopping: **www.key-west.com**.
- A guide to gay-friendly Key West: **www.gaykeywestfl.com**.
- Featuring local news and up-to-date information on events and entertainment options from the *Miami Herald:* **www.miami.com**.
- This site offers reviews and listings for attractions, entertainment, restaurants, hotels, and shopping, and includes categories for kids, and gays and lesbians. Unlike some other city guides, *Time Out: Miami* makes a

concerted effort to cater to tourists as well as locals: **www.timeout.com/miami**.

- Miami's leading alternative weekly includes features and listings for music, theater, film, and more: **www.miaminewtimes.com**.
- Here's a nice roundup of music, theater, sports, and dining choices in South Florida: **www.sun-sentinel.com/showtime**.
- Listings and reviews for Miami: Each restaurant has a capsule review and ratings based on surveys received from site users. For many restaurants, only two or three people have bothered to submit ratings, so they may not be statistically significant. However, comments can be instructive, as CuisineNet's readers discuss service, parking, free birthday desserts, and a host of other insightful topics: **www.cuisinenet.com**.
- Reviewing top restaurants, Zagat has made a name for itself as the people's choice, as its listings are based on extensive surveys: **www.zagat.com**.

11 The 21st-Century Traveler

INTERNET ACCESS AWAY FROM HOME
WITHOUT YOUR OWN COMPUTER

To find cybercafes in your destination check **www.cybercaptive.com** and **www.cybercafe.com**.

Aside from formal cybercafes, most **youth hostels** and **public libraries** offer Internet access. Avoid **hotel business centers** unless you're willing to pay exorbitant rates.

Most major airports now have **Internet kiosks** scattered throughout their gates. These give you basic Web access for a per-minute fee that's usually higher than cybercafe prices.

WITH YOUR OWN COMPUTER

More and more hotels, cafes, and retailers are signing on as Wi-Fi (wireless fidelity) "hotspots." Mac owners have their own networking technology, Apple AirPort. **T-Mobile Hotspot** (www.t-mobile.com/hotspot) serves up wireless connections at more than 1,000 Starbucks coffee shops nationwide. **Boingo** (www.boingo.com) and **Wayport** (www.wayport.com) have set up networks in airports and high-class hotel lobbies. IPass providers (see below) also give you access to a few hundred wireless hotel lobby setups. To locate other hotspots that provide **free wireless networks** in cities around the world, go to **www.personaltelco.net/index.cgi/WirelessCommunities**.

For dial-up access, most business-class hotels in the U.S. offer dataports for laptop modems, and a few thousand hotels in the U.S. and Europe now offer free high-speed Internet access. In addition, major Internet Service Providers (ISPs) have **local access numbers** around the world, allowing you to go online by placing a local call. The **iPass** network also has dial-up numbers around the world. You'll have to sign up with an iPass provider, who will then tell you how to set up your computer for your destination(s). For a list of iPass providers, go to www.ipass.com and click on "Individuals Buy Now." One solid provider is **i2roam** (© **866/811-6209** or 920/235-0475; www.i2roam.com).

Wherever you go, bring a **connection kit** of the right power and phone adapters, a spare phone cord, and a spare Ethernet network cable—or find out whether your hotel supplies them to guests.

For information on electrical currency conversions, see the "Electricity" section in the appendix.

CELLPHONE USE IN THE U.S.

Just because your cellphone works at home doesn't mean it'll work everywhere in the U.S. (thanks to our nation's fragmented cellphone system). It's a good bet that your phone will work in major cities, but take a look at your wireless company's coverage map on its website before heading out; T-Mobile, Sprint, and Nextel are particularly weak in rural areas. If you need to stay in touch at a destination where you know your phone won't work, **rent** a phone that does from **InTouch USA** (© **800/872-7626;** www.intouch global.com) or a rental car location, but beware that you'll pay $1 a minute or more for airtime.

If you're venturing deep into national parks, you may want to consider renting a **satellite phone (satphones).** It's different from a cellphone in that it connects to satellites rather than ground-based towers. Unfortunately, you'll pay at least $2 per minute to use the phone, and it only works where you can see the horizon (usually not indoors). In North America, you can rent Iridium satellite phones from **RoadPost** (© **888/290-1606** or 905/272-5665; www.roadpost. com). InTouch USA (see above) offers a wider range of satphones but at higher rates.

If you're not from the U.S., you'll be appalled at the poor reach of our **GSM** (Global System for Mobiles) **wireless network,** which is used by much of the rest of the world. Your phone will probably work in most major U.S. cities; it definitely won't work in many rural areas. (To see where GSM phones work in the U.S., check out www.t-mobile.com/coverage/national_popup.asp.) And you may or may not be able to send SMS (text messaging) home.

12 Packages for the Independent Traveler

Before you start your search for the lowest airfare, you may want to consider booking your flight as part of a travel package. Package tours are not the same thing as escorted tours. Package tours are simply a way to buy the airfare, accommodations, and other elements of your trip (such as car rentals, airport transfers, and sometimes even activities) at the same time and often at discounted prices—kind of like one-stop shopping. Packages are sold in bulk to tour operators—who resell them to the public at a cost that usually undercuts standard rates.

One good source of package deals is the airlines themselves. Most major airlines offer air/land packages, including **American Airlines Vacations** (© 800/321-2121; www.aavacations.com), **Delta Vacations** (© 800/221-6666; www.delta vacations.com), **Continental Airlines Vacations** (© 800/301-3800; www.co vacations.com), and **United Vacations** (© 888/854-3899; www.unitedvacations.

com). Several big **online travel agencies**—Expedia, Travelocity, Orbitz, Site59, and Lastminute.com—also do a brisk business in packages.

For information on package tours to South Florida, consult the following companies: **CWS Tours & Transportation** (© **407/448-3969;** www.cwstours. com/sfltour.htm), **Eyre Tour and Travel** (© **800/321-EYRE;** www.eyre.com), and **Miami City Web** (© **888/MIAMI-MALL** or 305/715-9080; www.miami city.net).

Package tours can vary by leaps and bounds. Some offer a better class of hotels than others. Some offer the same hotels for lower prices. Some offer flights on scheduled airlines, while others book charters. Some limit your choice of accommodations and travel days. You are often required to make a large payment up front. On the plus side, packages can save you money, offering group prices but allowing for independent travel. Some even let you add on a few guided excursions or escorted day trips (also at prices lower than if you booked them yourself) without booking an entirely escorted tour.

Before you invest in a package tour, get some answers. Ask about the **accommodations choices** and prices for each. Then look up the hotels' reviews in a Frommer's guide and check their rates online for your specific dates of travel.

You'll also want to find out what **type of room** you get. If you need a certain type of room, ask for it; don't take whatever is thrown your way. Request a nonsmoking room, a quiet room, a room with a view, or whatever you fancy.

Finally, look for **hidden expenses.** Ask whether airport departure fees and taxes, for example, are included in the total cost.

13 Escorted General-Interest Tours

Escorted tours are structured group tours, with a group leader. The price usually includes everything from airfare to hotels, meals, tours, admission costs, and local transportation.

Despite the fact that escorted tours require big deposits and predetermine hotels, restaurants, and itineraries, many people derive security and peace of mind from the structure they offer. Escorted tours—whether they're navigated by bus, motor coach, train, or boat—let travelers sit back and enjoy the trip without having to drive or worry about details. They take

you to the maximum number of sights in the minimum amount of time with the least amount of hassle. They're particularly convenient for people with limited mobility and they can be a great way to make new friends.

On the downside, you'll have little opportunity for serendipitous interactions with locals. The tours can be jam-packed with activities, leaving little room for individual sightseeing, whim, or adventure—plus they often focus on the heavily touristed sites, so you miss out on many a lesser-known gem.

4

Suggested South Florida Itineraries

Contrary to popular belief, South Florida isn't just Miami. There's the Keys, the Everglades, the Gold Coast, the Treasure Coast and, well, you get the picture. Set your sights on what you want to do and see the most, and simply unwind.

The range of possible itineraries is endless; what we've suggested below is a very full program covering Florida over a **2-week period.** If possible, you should extend your time—2 weeks is not really enough time if you plan to actually explore the Sunshine State, but if you plan to veg out on a beach, then it's plenty of time—or cut out some of the destinations suggested. You can always tack on one itinerary to the next. We've done our best to keep it geographically viable and logical. Whatever you finally decide to do, we highly recommend that you at least include a stop at one of Florida's natural wonders, be it the beaches, the Everglades or the Keys.

Important: Should limited time force you to include only the most obvious stops in your itinerary, you will invariably make contact with only those who depend on you to make a living, which regrettably could leave you with a frustrated sense that Florida is one big, long tourist trap. This is why it is so important to *get off the beaten tourist track*—to experience the wacky, the kitschy, the stunning, the baffling, and the fascinating people, places, and things that make Florida an incredible destination.

1 Beachy Keen South Florida in 1 Week

South Florida's beaches have been more photographed—we think—than Paris Hilton. In addition to the sand and sparkling waters of the Atlantic, the beaches have various personalities, from laid back and remote to year-round MTV Spring Break. It may be fun to get a taste of all of these, if not for an hour or two at a time.

Day ❶: Arrive in Islamorada 𝓰𝓰𝓰
Check into the Cheeca Lodge and Spa and take in the panoramic ocean views. Park yourself on a chair and enjoy one of the Florida Keys best—and only—private beaches. Waste no time making a dinner reservation for an outside table on the upstairs verandah at Pierre's where you must, *must,* try the potato-crusted black grouper with seasonal greens and a roasted tomato sauce. After dinner, park yourself on the beach at the Morada Bay Café and listen to some live music while sipping a piña colada.

Day ❷: Bahia Honda State Park 𝓰𝓰𝓰
Just an hour south of Islamorada is one of South Florida's most resplendent beaches. Spend the day on the 524-acre park and lose yourself in the mangroves, beach dunes, and tropical hammocks. Head

Suggested South Florida Itineraries

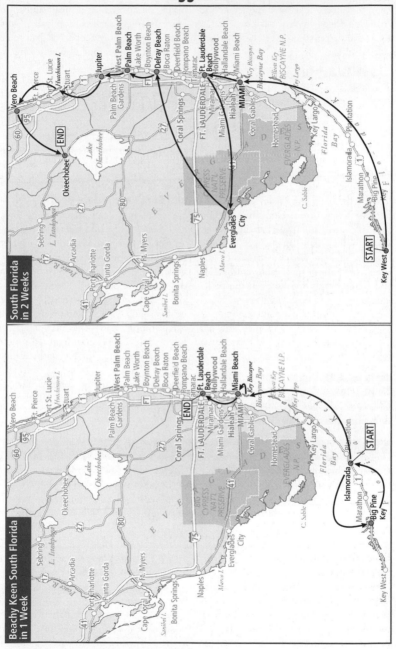

South Florida in 2 Weeks

Beachy Keen South Florida in 1 Week

back to Cheeca and have dinner at the Atlantic's Edge, which also happens to be, figuratively speaking, over the top. See p. 270.

Day ❸: To Key Biscayne 𝒶𝒶

Take the scenic, sleepy, and often slow-moving Overseas Highway north to Key Biscayne and check into the Ritz Carlton Key Biscayne. On this, Miami's only bona fide Florida Key, you will be able to beach hop until the sun goes down. For the party people, Crandon Park Beach is the place to be, with 2 miles of beach and lots of salsa emanating from various sun-bathers' boom boxes. Grab some much-needed peace and quiet at Bill Baggs Cape Florida State Park where you will forget you're in Miami, thanks to the miles of nature trails and completely unfettered beach. Do lunch at the park's charming Lighthouse Café before heading over to Virginia Key and Jimbo's, the place where Flipper was filmed and old Florida cracker-style houses serve as a backdrop to a beachfront bacchanal.

Days ❹ & ❺: South Beach/ Miami Beach 𝒶𝒶𝒶

Going to "the beach" takes on a totally different meaning when you're on South Beach. Not only does it mean sunbathing on Lummus Park Beach, aka South Beach, for a cornucopia of half-naked beautiful people, but also enjoying the surrounding sights, sounds, and tastes of the area's bars, restaurants, shops, hotels, and Art Deco relics. There's a plethora of places to stay, whether you're on a budget or are willing to splurge; and best of all, the beach is free and a great place to crash and watch the sun set after spending the night out in the clubs!

Days ❻ & ❼: Swanky & Annette— aka Fort Lauderdale Beach 𝒶𝒶𝒶

Your dad may have spent Spring Break here with his frat buddies when the Beatles were just a random group of country bumpkins from Liverpool, but if he saw it now, he'd be completely surprised. Sure, the beach is beautiful, clean—no dogs allowed except on a special pet beach nearby—and visible from A1A, but the surrounding area—the infamous Fort Lauderdale Strip—has matured into a sophisticated cafe society with outdoor eateries, bars, and more. If you must enter a beer-drinking contest, however, we're sure you'll find one nearby. See p. 311.

2 South Florida in 2 Weeks

Consider this tour a South Florida sampler. We've custom-built an itinerary that will provide you with a local's-eye view of some of the best diversions So Flo is known for. Whether you're into being a beach bum or a beachcomber, a club hopper or someone who prefers to swing a club, a nature lover or people-watcher—there's something for everyone on this tour.

Days ❶ & ❷: Arrive in Key West 𝒶𝒶𝒶

After arriving in the so-called Conch Republic, or Margaritaville if you will, plan to spend at most a day or two here. A full day on the 4×2-mile island is plenty for exploring, but if you're into doing the Duval Bar Crawl you may want to leave yourself with a day to recover from that inevitable hangover. Focus most of your sightseeing energy on Old Town, where you'll see stunning, restored Victorian-style homes; lush, tropical greenery; and the old Bahama Village. Make sure not to miss the sunset celebration at Mallory Square and, if possible, do dinner at **Blue Heaven** in the Bahama Village. Then hit the Duval Street bars if

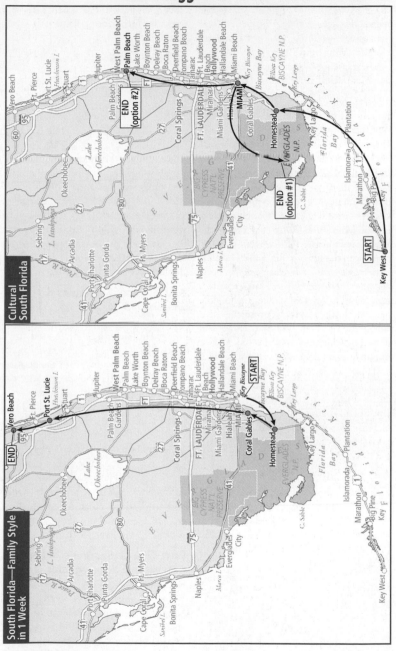

you're so inclined. The next day, either spend the day relaxing at your hotel pool—we recommend the **Gardens Hotel** or **Simonton Court** for a true Key West experience—or explore the Historic Seaport and all its shops and Key West kitsch. See p. 275.

Day ❸: Miami: Coral Gables, Little Havana & South Beach ✪✪✪

Take the 3-hour drive on the Overseas Highway to **Miami**—one of the most scenic drives you'll ever take, albeit sometimes a boring one. If you've seen it before, just fly. Make a pit stop in Coral Gables where you can either get a bite to eat on **Miracle Mile** or cool off in the **Venetian Pool.** If you like what you see, check into the historic **Biltmore Hotel.** If not, make sure to at least see the hotel and then continue on to SW 8th Street, otherwise known as Calle Ocho, the heart of Little Havana. Peruse the cigar stores, the old men playing dominoes in Domino Park and buy an old Cuban phone book at Little Havana to Go. Grab a Cuban coffee at Versailles and then head north to South Beach and watch the cruise ships leave from **Smith & Wollensky.** Spend the night in the trendy South of Fifth area at the **Hotel St. Augustine,** known for its sublime spa bathrooms. See p. 60.

Day ❹: South Beach ✪✪✪

Wake up early and catch the sunrise on the beach. Have breakfast at the Front Porch Café. Stake your claim on the sand and spend the morning on the beach. Hit Lincoln Road for lunch. Try David's Café for a delicious, inexpensive Cuban feast. Shop along Lincoln and Collins avenues before having a cocktail at the **Rose Bar at the Delano Hotel.** Return to your own hotel for a disco nap; wake up around 9pm. Have dinner at **Prime 112,** and then hit the clubs: **Opium, Prive, Mansion, Cameo,** and **SET.** If you're still up for the boogie, head to **Mokai.** Grab a

late night snack at **San Loco Taco** or the **11th St. Diner** and then crash at your hotel.

Day ❺: From South Beach to Fort Lauderdale ✪✪

Have breakfast and watch the club kids coming home from the night before at the Big Pink. Get in the car and take A1A north—the scenic route. Hit the Hollywood Beach Broadwalk, our version of Atlantic City without the casinos. If you're hungry for lunch, have the world's best burger at **Le Tub.** Continue along A1A until you reach the famous Fort Lauderdale strip. Take a break at the world-famous **Elbo Room** and watch the action on the beach. Spend the night at the **Riverside Hotel** on Las Olas Boulevard.

Day ❻: Sand, Seminoles & Santana ✪✪

Hit the famous Fort Lauderdale Beach, where Frankie and Annette used to play beach blanket bingo. Then take a bit of a diversion and head west to the **Seminole Hard Rock Hotel and Casino** where you may catch a concert by a Billboard-charting artist or even Jerry Seinfeld; hit the jackpot on one of the hundreds of slot machines (the hotel claims it pays out $12.9 million daily!); or relax by the pool which is almost as nice, if not nicer, than the one at the Hard Rock Hotel in Vegas. Also check out the **Seminole Okalee Indian Village and Museum** before heading over and out to spot signs of real wildlife in the Everglades. See p. 230.

Days ❼ & ❽: Seminole Indian Reservation & Everglades National Park ✪✪✪

Travel 45 minutes west on I-75 to the Seminole Indian Reservation, which encompasses over 69,000 acres of the Everglades' Big Cypress Swamp. Hop on a swamp buggy at the **Billie Swamp Safari** to see hogs, bison, 'gators, and deer. Continue west to Everglades City, check into the **Ivey House B&B**, and ask owners Sandee and David if they can hook you up with a special, insiders' tour of the 'Glades.

Days ❾ & ❿: The Palm Beaches ✾✾

Skip Boca Raton and head directly to Delray Beach, where its Atlantic Avenue is full of stores, restaurants, bars, and clubs. Check into the **Sundy House** and peruse the hotel's Taru Gardens. The next day, do not miss the **Morikami Museum and Japanese Gardens** before moving on to West Palm Beach where you should check into the **Hotel Biba** and do a little antiques shopping in downtown West Palm. At night, check out the clubs and restaurants in downtown West Palm, on Clematis Street. Make sure to have a beer and enjoy the view at **Bradley's.**

Day ⓫: From Mar-A-Lago to the Moon—Well, Jupiter, at Least ✾✾

Spend the morning driving around Palm Beach proper, making sure to stop and catch a glimpse of Donald Trump's palatial **Mar-A-Lago.** Stop by **Worth Avenue** to see the ladies with little dogs who lunch and shop. It's the Rodeo Drive of South Florida, truly, and you can't miss the people-watching there. For an actual glimpse inside a Palm Beach manse, go to the **Flagler Museum** where you can explore Whitehall, Standard Oil tycoon Henry Flagler's wedding present to his third wife. Go back to reality and head toward Jupiter, the home of Burt Reynolds. Check into the **PGA National Resort and Spa.** See p. 354.

Days ⓬ & ⓭: The Treasure Coast

You may not find gold in your exploration of the Treasure Coast but you will find **Jonathan Dickinson State Park on Hutchinson Island,** where you should rent a canoe and explore the plethora of botanical treasures. If you're into snorkeling and diving and feel like delving deeper, check out the most popular artificial reef in the area, **the USS *Rankin,*** an old WWII ship that was sunk in 1980, located 7 miles east northeast of the St. Lucie Inlet. Check into the Hutchinson Island Marriott Beach Resort and Marina and consider taking the *Loxahatchee Queen* for a 2-hour tour of the area. Next, head to Vero Beach and Sebastian for a taste of old Florida. Sports fans will want to check out Dodgertown where the Los Angeles Dodgers spend their winters. Check into the completely unique **Driftwood Resort** or the swank **Vero Beach Hotel and Club** and do dinner at the **Ocean Grill** if your budget allows. If not, The Beachside Restaurant at the Palm Court Resort is a great spot for blue-plate specials and, for NY-style pizza, **Nino's** can't be beat.

Day ⓮: Lake Okeechobee or Bust?

If you can't extend your trip to include a side trip to Lake Okeechobee (p. 379), consider it for next time. In the meantime, fly home out of either Palm Beach International Airport, 35 miles south of Vero Beach, or the Melbourne International Airport, which is less than 35 miles north of Vero Beach.

3 South Florida, Family Style, in 1 Week

Despite a thriving nightlife and sometimes R-rated (or worse) sensibility—and dress code (or lack thereof)—South Florida is definitely a kid-friendly destination. While we don't recommend you taking the little ones to South Beach, there are tons of other places that are family friendly and won't have the kids screaming that they wish they were at Disney World!

Hollywood South—Celebrities' South Beach (& Beyond)

It's not that ironic that the French Riviera is now billing itself as a European South Beach. Between all the jet-setters, celebrities, rock stars, and magazine stories on the place, it's about time! Some people come to South Florida just for a taste of this fabulous life. This is not an itinerary per se, but the following tips will help you plan a busy social schedule so you don't miss out on a Paris or Diddy sighting.

Haute Hotels. Wherever you decide to stay, it won't matter, because if you're looking for celebrities on South Beach, you'll end up spying most of them by the end of your trip. We suggest you do breakfast at the Blue Door Restaurant at the Delano, where you may catch a glimpse of Jamie Foxx sunbathing by the wading pool. Linger as long as you are able to before heading next door to the Raleigh, where you may find Uma Thurman sipping an iced tea at the pool. Grab some lunch if you're hungry or wait until you go next door to the Shore Club, where Nobu acts as the hotel's resident star magnet, a place where Madonna, Justin Timberlake, and Cameron Diaz always stop when in town. Hit Lincoln Road and see if you can spot J-Lo. If you don't she's probably at the Bal Harbour Shops, so you may want to go there. For early evening cocktails, head to The Setai, where Jay Z, Beyoncé, Bono, and Lenny Kravitz have all partied. Take your drink either at the Champagne or Crustacean bar indoors or outside by the pool. Hit the Ritz Carlton South Beach for a nightcap, where some of the Desperate Housewives have stayed. Off of South Beach, you'll probably spot the likes of Tom Cruise and Katie Holmes, or Britney Spears, either at the Mandarin Oriental

Days ❶ & ❷: Key Biscayne 𝒜𝒜𝒜
The **Ritz-Carlton Key Biscayne** has fabulous children's programs, not to mention pretty cool diversions for adults, too. Spend a day checking out the resorts, and then skip the **Miami Seaquarium**—unless the kids want to swim with the dolphins—and spend the day at the **Marjory Stoneman Douglas Biscayne Nature Center** where the entire family can explore an ancient fossil tidal pool. If there's time left, check out the **Bill Baggs Cape Florida State Park** and rent a hydrobike. See p. 63.

Days ❸ & ❹: Coral Gables 𝒜𝒜𝒜 **& South Miami** 𝒜𝒜
Get an early start and head south to Homestead's legendary **Coral Castle.**

After the kids tire of seeing this wacky attraction, grab lunch at the family-friendly, family-run Mexican mainstay, **El Toro Taco.** On your way to Coral Gables, make a stop at **Miami Metro Zoo or Monkey Jungle** depending on your preference in animals, and then clean off that stinky animal scent with a splash in Coral Gables's resplendent, refreshing **Venetian Pool.** If you're up for it, check out **Vizcaya Museum and Gardens** and/or the **Miami Science Museum.** After working up an appetite, take the kids for a big dinner at **Porcao,** where they'll enjoy holding up their signs when they're ready to eat more meat!

on Brickell Key, the Four Seasons Miami and, on Key Biscayne, the Ritz-Carlton Key Biscayne. For details on Miami hotels, see p. 74.

Stars & Bars. Keeping in mind that you can go to any of these places on any given night, some clubs do have specific nights that are better than others in terms of crowds and celebs. On Monday night, check out Cameo, where Matt Damon actually met his wife, Luciana, who was a cocktail waitress there. Tuesday night, hit one of the hotels. Wednesday night, it's The Forge, where the likes of Lindsay Lohan and Jennifer Lopez hang. Thursday night, check out Skybar and Set. On Friday, it's all about Opium Garden and Prive, where any celeb who's in town will stop by—if not for the evening, at least for one drink. On Saturday, the Pawn Shop Lounge downtown is the place to be, with an '80s soundtrack and celebs such as Colin Farrell partying in the club's Airstream trailer. Mansion on South Beach is pretty hot, too. Sunday afternoon, thankfully, is the hottest party at the Shore Club, where you can lounge by the pool along with the likes of Jessica—or O. J.—Simpson. On any given night you may run into Bono or Farrell at Ted's Hideaway or Mac's Club Deuce, two of Miami's beloved dive bars. For details on Miami's nightlife, see p. 210.

Eating It Up (Stars Eat, Too). Among the places you'll find celebs stuffing their faces: Nobu; Nemo; The Forge; The Restaurant at the Setai; DeVito South Beach; The Blue Door; Barton G. The Restaurant; Prime 112; Azul; Table 8; News Café; China Grill; Tuscan Steak; and, we kid you not, San Loco Taco, the late-night, fast-food Mexican joint across the street from Club Deuce. For more on Miami's dining scene, see p. 113.

Days ❺ to ❼: Miami–Port St. Lucie ☆☆☆

Before leaving Miami, make sure to stop at the **Miami Children's Museum** where the kids can spend a few hours channeling their inner grown up in a bona fide TV and recording studio. If they'd rather see animal antics, head across the causeway to **Jungle Island.** Grab a TV dinner at the G-rated **Big Pink** on South Beach and then hit the road to Vero Beach and check into the **Club-Med Sandpiper** on the St. Lucie River, where there are four different children's clubs for ages 4 months all the way up to 13 years. En route to Vero, you may want to take the kids to West Palm Beach's whimsical **Playmobil Fun Park** or on a safari through **Lion Country Safari** and then grab lunch at Jupiter's legendary **Nick's Tomato Pie.** See p. 359.

Day ❼: Vero Beach ☆☆☆

As if Club Med doesn't have enough for the family to do—or not do—you may want to take the kids out to **Dodgertown,** the place where the L.A. Dodgers spend spring training, or to **Disney's Vero Beach Resort,** which is situated on 71 acres of beach and features that Disney vibe the kids may be in the mood for at this point!

4 Cultural South Florida

When it comes to culture in South Florida, I used to joke that the only semblance of such was the kind found on a Petri dish after swabbing the floor of one of Miami's most popular nightclubs. That's no longer the story. If you're looking for real culture—eclectic, ethnic, and otherwise—we've got that, too, now. Whew.

Days ❶ & ❷: Key West 𝘈𝘈𝘈

In order to completely understand Conch Culture, you have to experience it with a few days in wacky Key West. To fully get it, try to stay in a B&B like La Pensione or a swankier one like The Gardens or Simonton Court. Leave the Hiltons for bigger cities if you must. Then book yourself on the famous Trails of Margaritaville Jimmy Buffet–themed tour of the city. If you're still standing after that, hit all the bars on Duval Street and its side streets making sure not to miss Captain Tony's Saloon and the Green Parrot; and then steal away to the Bahama Village for dinner and drinks amid the cackling roosters in the backyard of the famous Blue Heaven. See p. 275.

Days ❸ & ❹: Key West to Miami 𝘈𝘈

There are all sorts of bizarre spots along the Overseas Highway en route to Miami. You can't miss the gigantic lobster out front of one wacky gift shop, nor can you avoid the pink manatees beckoning you into the various shell and souvenir shops. Very much a part of Keys culture is a stop in Islamorada's famous Tiki Bar, where the rumrunners are potent and the vibe is the quintessence of vacation. When passing through Homestead, you may or may not want to stop at the Coral Castle, the place built by a Latvian man obsessed by his unrequited love, or just continue on to Miami, where you'll check into the quaint and charming Miami River Inn, a vestige of old Florida culture smack in the midst of the city. See p. 104.

Days ❹ to ❺: The Hottest Spots North of Havana 𝘈𝘈𝘈

Don't listen to what people say about Little Havana. If you do it right, it's entirely worth seeing. In fact, we recommend you take the Herencia Hispana Tour that will take you through Miami's most vibrant cultural neighborhood with very knowledgeable guides, who will tell you everything you ever wanted to know about Miami's Cuban culture. After the tour, grab a croquette and *medianoche* (midnight sandwich) at Versailles, where Cuban cafe culture is alive and well. You can also do Little Havana at night if you dig dancing—check out Hoy Como Ayer, especially on Thursdays, for the best in Latin tunes and dancing. See p. 65.

Day ❻: Miami by Design 𝘈𝘈

Definitely not an all-day affair, but nonetheless cool if you're into art and design, Miami's Design District is worth a look-see. While you're there, grab a bite at Sheba, the city's only Ethiopian restaurant, or the organic-chic Michael's Genuine Food & Drink and Grass. After that, don't miss Miami Beach's Bass Museum and North Miami's Museum of Contemporary Art, and South Beach's Wolfsonian museum if you're into history and kitsch. By the time you have this book, we hope the long-awaited, zillion-dollar Miami Beach Performing Arts Center will raise its curtains and make its debut.

Day ❼: Everglades or Palm Beach? You Decide 𝘈𝘈

When it comes to nature and South Florida's fascinating Native American

South Florida Literary Tour

Pompano Beach: Author Elmore Leonard took his mother to a small motel on Pompano Beach, which some say was his inspiration for the Coconut Palms Resort Apartments, to where George Moran, the main character in Leonard's 1982 book *Cat Chaser,* runs.

Dania Beach Pier: Harry Crews used the Dania Pier as a backdrop for a July 4th fireworks display and beauty contest in *Karate Is a Thing of the Spirit.*

Bahia Mar Beach Resort: Travis McGee, the protagonist in John D. MacDonald's 21 novels (including *The Deep Blue Goodbye*), lived at this resort, 801 Seabreeze Blvd. (© 888/802-2442; www.bahiamarhotel.com).

Little Haiti: The place where a no-good former oil burner repairman wanders in Russell Banks' *Continental Drift.*

Flagler Street: Where Brett Halliday's private eye, Michael Shayne, kept his office.

Hialeah Race Course: The inspiration for Damon Runyon's short story *Pick the Winner.* Log onto http://tinyurl.com/52552y.

Cardozo Hotel: Elmore Leonard's favorite backdrop—as seen in *Get Shorty, La Brava,* and *Rum Punch*—was this hotel, 1300 Ocean Dr., Miami Beach (© 800/782-6500; www.cardozohotel.com).

Barnacle State Historic Site: James W. Hall's *Hard Aground* transforms the Barnacle into Mangrove House, a place with a sinister history. See p. 174.

Domino Park: Ana Menendez's *In Cuba I Was a German Shepherd* reminisces about Little Havana's most hopping spot, at the southwest corner of 15th Avenue and 8th Street.

Tobacco Road: Miami's oldest bar gets is name from the 1932 novel by Erskine Caldwell. See p. 145.

culture, the Everglades are the place to be. Besides the kitschy 'gator wrestling and airboat rides, there is still a thriving Native American community that lives and works within the remarkable Everglades. If you're afraid of getting bit by mosquitoes, or if nature's just not your thing, head up to Palm Beach, where all things natural give way to Botox and silicone. Check out the fascinating Norton Museum of Art and the Flagler Museum, where you can view old railroad cars, and Whitehall, the so-called Taj Mahal of the South.

5

Getting to Know Miami

Apropos jokes about bad drivers, Grandma forgetting to shut off her turn signal, and traffic nightmares aside, Miami is a fascinating city to explore, be it by foot, bike, scooter, boat, or car. Because of its larger-than-life persona, Miami may seem a lot bigger than it really is, but although the city comprises many different neighborhoods, it's really not that difficult to learn the lay of the land. Much like the bodies beautiful on Ocean Drive, the Magic City is a tidy package that's a little less than 2,000 square miles.

1 Orientation

ARRIVING

Originally carved out of scrubland in 1928 by Pan American Airlines, **Miami International Airport (MIA)** has become 2nd in the United States for international passenger traffic and 10th in the world for total passengers. Despite the heavy traffic, the airport is quite user friendly and not as much of a hassle as you'd think. You can change money or use your ATM card at Bank of America, located near the exit. Visitor information is available 24 hours a day at the **Miami International Airport Main Visitor Counter,** Concourse E, second level (© **305/876-7000**). Information is also available at **www.miami-airport.com.** Because MIA is the busiest airport in South Florida, travelers may want to consider flying into the less crowded **Fort Lauderdale Hollywood International Airport (FLL)** (© **954/359-1200**), which is closer to north Miami than MIA, or the **Palm Beach International Airport (PBI)** (© **561/471-7420**), which is about 1½ hours from Miami.

GETTING INTO TOWN

Miami International Airport is about 6 miles west of downtown and about 10 miles from the beaches, so it's likely you can get from the plane to your hotel room in less than half an hour. Of course, if you're arriving from an international destination, it will take more time to go through Customs and Immigration.

BY CAR   All the major car-rental firms operate off-site branches reached via shuttles from the airline terminals. See the "Rentals" section, under "Getting Around," on p. 67, for a list of major rental companies in Miami. Signs at the airport's exit clearly point the way to various parts of the city, but the car-rental firm should also give you directions to your destination. If you're arriving late at night, you might want to take a taxi to your hotel and have the car delivered to you the next day.

BY TAXI   Taxis line up in front of a dispatcher's desk outside the airport's arrivals terminals. Most cabs are metered, though some have flat rates to popular destinations. The fare should be about $25 to Coral Gables, $20 to downtown, and $32 to South Beach, plus tip, which should be about 15% (add more for each bag the driver handles).

Words to Live By

I figure marriage is kind of like Miami; it's hot and stormy, and occasionally a little dangerous . . . but if it's really so awful, why is there still so much traffic?
—Sarah Jessica Parker's character, Gwen Marcus, in *Miami Rhapsody*

Depending on traffic, the ride to Coral Gables or downtown takes about 15 to 20 minutes, and to South Beach, 20 to 25 minutes.

BY VAN OR LIMO   Group limousines (multipassenger vans) circle the arrivals area looking for fares. Destinations are posted on the front of each van, and a flat rate is charged for door to-door service to the area marked.

SuperShuttle (© **305/871-2000;** www.supershuttle.com) is one of the largest airport operators, charging between $10 and $40 per person for a ride within the county. Its vans operate 24 hours a day and accept American Express, MasterCard, and Visa. This is a cheaper alternative to a cab (if you are traveling alone or with one other person), but be prepared to be in the van for quite awhile, as you may have to make several stops to drop passengers off before you reach your own destination. SuperShuttle also has begun service from Palm Beach International Airport to the surrounding communities. The door-to-door, shared-ride service operates from the airport to Stuart, Fort Pierce, Palm Beach, and Broward counties.

Private limousine arrangements can be made in advance through your local travel agent. A one-way meet-and-greet service should cost about $50. Limo services include **City Limousine** (© **800/819-LIMO**) and **DLS Limousine Service** (© **888/988-9567**).

BY PUBLIC TRANSPORTATION   Public transportation in South Florida is a major hassle bordering on a nightmare. Painfully slow and unreliable, buses heading downtown leave the airport only once per hour (from the arrivals level), and connections are spotty, at best. It could take about 1½ hours to get to South Beach via public transportation. Journeys to downtown and Coral Gables, however, are more direct. The fare is $1.50, plus an additional 50¢ for a transfer.

VISITOR INFORMATION

The most up-to-date information is provided by the **Greater Miami Convention and Visitor's Bureau,** 701 Brickell Ave., Suite 700, Miami, FL 33131 (© **800/933-8448** or 305/539-3000; fax 305/530-3113). Several chambers of commerce in Greater Miami will send out information on their particular neighborhoods; for addresses and numbers, see "Visitor Information" in chapter 3.

If you arrive at the Miami International Airport, you can pick up visitor information at the airport's main visitor counter on the second floor of Concourse E. It's open 24 hours a day.

Always check local newspapers for special events during your visit. The city's only daily, the *Miami Herald,* is a good source for current-events listings, particularly the "Weekend" section in Friday's edition. Even better is the free weekly alternative paper the *Miami New Times,* available in bright red boxes throughout the city.

Information on everything from dining to entertainment in Miami is available on the Internet at www.miami.citysearch.com, www.digitalcity.com/southflorida, www.miaminewtimes.com, and www.herald.com.

CITY LAYOUT

Miami seems confusing at first, but quickly becomes easy to navigate. The small cluster of buildings that make up the downtown area is at the geographical heart of the city. In relation to downtown, the airport is northwest, the beaches are east, Coconut Grove is south, Coral Gables is west, and the rest of the city is north.

FINDING AN ADDRESS   Miami is divided into dozens of areas with official and unofficial boundaries. Street numbering in the city of Miami is fairly straightforward, but you must first be familiar with the numbering system. The mainland is divided into four sections (NE, NW, SE, and SW) by the intersection of Flagler Street and Miami Avenue. Flagler divides Miami from north to south, and Miami Avenue divides the city from east to west. It's helpful to remember that avenues generally run north-south, while streets go east-west. Street numbers (1st St., 2nd St., and so forth) start from here and increase as you go farther out from this intersection, as do numbers of avenues, places, courts, terraces, and lanes. Streets in Hialeah are the exceptions to this pattern; they are listed separately in map indexes.

Getting around the barrier islands that make up Miami Beach is easier than moving around the mainland. Street numbering starts with 1st Street, near Miami Beach's southern tip, and goes up to 192nd Street, in the northern part of Sunny Isles. As in the city of Miami, some streets in Miami Beach have numbers as well as names. When listed in this book, both name and number are given.

The numbered streets in Miami Beach are not the geographical equivalents of those on the mainland, but they are close. For example, the 79th Street Causeway runs into 71st Street on Miami Beach.

STREET MAPS   It's easy to get lost in sprawling Miami, so a reliable map is essential. The **Trakker Map of Miami** is a four-color accordion map that encompasses all of Dade County. Some maps of Miami list streets according to area, so you'll have to know which part of the city you are looking for before the street can be found.

THE NEIGHBORHOODS IN BRIEF

South Beach—The Art Deco District
South Beach's 10 miles of beach are alive with a frenetic, circuslike atmosphere and are center stage for a motley crew of characters, from eccentric locals, seniors, snowbirds, and college students to gender benders, celebrities, club kids, and curiosity seekers. Individuality is as widely accepted on South Beach as Visa and MasterCard.

Bolstered by a Caribbean-chic cafe society and a sexually charged, tragically hip nightlife, people-watching on South Beach (1st St.–23rd St.) is almost as good as a front-row seat at a Milan fashion show. But although the beautiful people do flock to South Beach, the models aren't the only sights

worth drooling over. The thriving Art Deco District within South Beach has the largest concentration of Art Deco architecture in the world (in 1979, much of South Beach was listed in the National Register of Historic Places). The pastel-hued structures are supermodels in their own right—only *these* models improve with age.

Miami Beach   In the fabulous '50s, Miami Beach was America's true Riviera. The stomping ground of choice for the Rat Pack and notorious mobsters such as Al Capone, its huge self-contained resort hotels were vacations unto themselves, providing a full day's worth of meals, activities, and entertainment. Then in the 1960s and 1970s, people who fell in love with Miami began to buy apartments rather than rent hotel rooms. Tourism declined, and many area hotels fell into disrepair.

However, since the late 1980s and South Beach's renaissance, Miami Beach has experienced a tide of revitalization. Huge beach hotels are finding their niche with new international tourist markets and are attracting large convention crowds. New generations of Americans are quickly rediscovering the qualities that originally made Miami Beach so popular, and they are finding out that the sand and surf now come with a thriving international city.

Before Miami Beach turns into Surfside, there's North Beach, where there are uncrowded beaches, some restaurants, and examples of Miami Modernism architecture. For information on North Beach and its slow renaissance, go to www.gonorthbeach.com.

Surfside, Bal Harbour, and **Sunny Isles** make up the north part of the beach (island). Hotels, motels, restaurants, and beaches line Collins Avenue and, with some outstanding exceptions, the farther north one goes, the cheaper lodging becomes. Excellent prices, location, and facilities make Surfside and Sunny Isles attractive places to stay, although, despite a slow-going renaissance, they are still a little rough around the edges. Revitalization is in the works for these areas, and, while it's highly unlikely they will ever become as chic as South Beach, there is potential for this, especially as South Beach falls prey to the inevitable spoiler: commercialism. Keep in mind that beachfront properties are at a premium, so many of the area's moderately priced hotels have been converted to condominiums, leaving fewer and fewer affordable places to stay.

In exclusive and ritzy Bal Harbour, few hotels remain amid the many beachfront condominium towers. Instead, fancy homes, tucked away on the bay, hide behind gated communities, and the Rodeo Drive of Miami (known as the Bal Harbour Shops) attracts shoppers who don't flinch at four-, five-, and six-figure price tags.

Note that **North Miami Beach,** a residential area near the Dade-Broward County line (north of 163rd St.; part of N. Dade County), is a misnomer. It is actually northwest of Miami Beach, on the mainland, and has no beaches, though it does have some of Miami's better restaurants and shops. Located within North Miami Beach is the posh residential community of **Aventura,** best known for its high-priced condos, the Fairmont Turnberry Isle Resort, and the Aventura Mall.

Note: South Beach, the historic Art Deco District, is treated as a separate neighborhood from Miami Beach.

Key Biscayne Miami's forested and secluded Key Biscayne is technically one of the first islands in the Florida Keys. However, this island is nothing like its southern neighbors. Located south of Miami Beach, off the shores of Coconut Grove, Key Biscayne is protected from the troubles of the mainland by the long Rickenbacker Causeway and its $1.25 toll.

Largely an exclusive residential community with million-dollar homes and sweeping water views, Key Biscayne also offers visitors great public beaches, a top (read: pricey) resort hotel, world class tennis facilities, and a few decent restaurants. Hobie Beach, adjacent to the causeway, is the city's premier spot for windsurfing, sailboarding, and jet-skiing (see "Miami's Beaches" and "Watersports" in chapter 8). On the island's southern tip, Bill Baggs State Park has great beaches, bike paths, and dense forests for picnicking and partying.

Downtown Miami's downtown boasts one of the world's most beautiful cityscapes. Unfortunately, that's about all it offers—for now. During the day, a vibrant community of students, businesspeople, and merchants makes its way through the bustling streets, where vendors sell fresh-cut pineapples and mangos while young consumers on shopping sprees lug bags and boxes. However, at night, downtown is mostly desolate (except for NE 11th St., where there is a burgeoning nightlife scene) and not a place where you'd want to get lost. The downtown area does have a mall (Bayside Marketplace, where many cruise passengers come to browse), some culture (Metro-Dade Cultural Center), and a few decent restaurants, as well as the sprawling American Airlines Arena (home to the Miami Heat). A downtown revitalization project in the works promises a cultural arts center, urban-chic dwellings and lofts, and an assortment of hip boutiques, eateries, and bars, all to bring downtown back to a life it never really had. The city has even rebranded the downtown area with a new ad campaign, intentionally misspelling it as DWNTN to inexplicably appeal to hipsters. We don't get it either. **The Downtown Miami Partnership** offers guided historic walking tours daily at 10:30am (© **305/379-7070**). For more information on downtown, go to www.downtownmiami.com.

Design District With restaurants springing up between galleries and furniture stores galore, the Design District is, as locals say, the new South Beach, adding a touch of New York's SoHo to an area formerly known as downtown Miami's "Don't Go." The district, which is a hotbed for furniture-import companies, interior designers, architects, and more, has also become a player in Miami's ever-changing nightlife. Its bars, lounges, clubs, and restaurants—including one of Miami's best, Michael's Genuine Food and Drink, ranging from überchic and retro to progressive and indie, have helped the area become hipster central for South Beach expatriates and artsy bohemian types. In anticipation of its growing popularity, the district has also banded together to create an up-to-date website, www.designmiami.com, which includes a calendar of events, such as the internationally lauded Art Basel, which attracts the who's who of the art world. The district is loosely defined as the area bounded by NE 2nd Avenue, NE 5th Avenue East and West, and NW 36th Street to the south.

Biscayne Corridor From downtown, near Bayside, to the 70s (affectionately known as the Upper East Side), where trendy curio shops and upscale restaurants are slowly opening, Biscayne Boulevard is aspiring to reclaim itself as a safe thoroughfare where tourists can wine, dine, and shop. Once known for sketchy, dilapidated 1950s- and 1960s-era hotels that had fallen on hard times, residents fleeing the high prices of the beaches in search of affordable housing are renovating Biscayne block by block, trying to make this famous boulevard worthy of a Sunday drive.

Impressions

The wonderful thing about Miami is that you don't have to make anything up. You don't have to have an imagination at all. All you have to do is read the newspaper here.

—Dave Barry

⌐Fun Fact The Mistress of Miami

From 10,000 B.C. to about 1875, much of Miami was a swamp until an unsuspecting woman named Julia Tuttle arrived to collect her inheritance—a large swath of swamp in the Miami area. Over the next 20 years, Tuttle acquired much more property throughout the Miami area and prepared it for the major development that exists today. Following Tuttle, Henry Morrison Flagler arrived in Miami around 1895. A developer and Standard Oil cohort of J. D. Rockefeller, Flagler had no intention of traveling down to Miami's swampland and instead focused on building a railroad that began at the northern tip of Florida and ended in Palm Beach. A hopeful Tuttle contacted Flagler with a proposal asking him to extend his railroad down to Miami in exchange for half of her property. Flagler declined the offer until a cold front froze out most of northern Florida, and, ultimately, all the tourists. It was then that Flagler decided to see Miami for himself. What he found was a warm tropical paradise, and, ultimately, a partner in Tuttle. Train service to Miami began in April 1896 and the swampy city has never been the same.

Little Havana If you've never been to Cuba, just visit this small section of Miami and you'll come pretty close. The sounds, tastes, and rhythms are very reminiscent of Cuba's capital city, and some say you don't have to speak a word of English to live an independent life here—even street signs are in Spanish and English.

Cuban coffee shops, tailor and furniture stores, and inexpensive restaurants line "Calle Ocho" (pronounced "*Kah*-yeh *Oh*-choh"), SW 8th Street, the region's main thoroughfare. In Little Havana, salsa and merengue beats ring loudly from old record stores while old men in *guayaberas* (loose-fitting cotton short-sleeved shirts) smoke cigars over their daily game of dominoes. The spotlight focused on the neighborhood during the Elián González situation in 2000, but the area was previously noted for the groups of artists and nocturnal types who had moved their galleries and performance spaces here, sparking culturally charged neobohemian nightlife.

Coral Gables "The City Beautiful," created by George Merrick in the early 1920s, is one of Miami's first planned developments. Houses here were built in a Mediterranean style along lush, tree-lined streets that open onto beautifully carved plazas, many with centerpiece fountains. The best architectural examples of the era have Spanish-style tiled roofs and are built from Miami oolite, native limestone commonly called "coral rock." The Gables's European-flaired shopping and commerce center is home to many thriving corporations. Coral Gables also has landmark hotels, great golfing, upscale shopping to rival Bal Harbour, and some of the city's best restaurants, headed by renowned chefs.

Coconut Grove An arty, hippie hangout in the psychedelic '60s, Coconut Grove once had residents who dressed in swirling tie-dyed garb. Nowadays, they prefer the uniform color schemes of the Gap. Chain stores, theme restaurants, a megaplex, and bars galore make Coconut Grove a commercial success, but this gentrification has pushed most alternative types out. Ritzier types have now resurfaced here, thanks, in part, to the antiboho Ritz-Carlton Coconut

Grove (p. 108). The intersection of Grand Avenue, Main Highway, and McFarlane Road pierces the area's heart. Right in the center of it all is Coco Walk and the Shops at Mayfair, filled with boutiques, eateries, and bars. Sidewalks here are often crowded, especially at night, when University of Miami students come out to play.

Southern Miami–Dade County To locals, South Miami is both a specific area, southwest of Coral Gables, and a general region that encompasses all of southern Dade County, including Kendall, Perrine, Cutler Ridge, and Homestead. For the purposes of clarity, this book has grouped all these southern suburbs under the rubric "Southern Miami–Dade County." The area is heavily residential and packed with strip malls amid a few remaining plots of farmland. Tourists don't usually stay in these parts, unless they are on their way to the Everglades or the Keys. However, southern Miami–Dade County contains many of the city's top attractions (see chapter 8), meaning that you're likely to spend at least some of your time in Miami here.

2 Getting Around

Officially, Miami Dade County has opted for a "unified, multimodal transportation network," which basically means you can get around the city by train, bus, and taxi. However, in practice, the network doesn't work very well. Things have improved somewhat thanks to the $17 billion Peoples' Transportation Plan, which has offered a full range of transportation services at several community-based centers throughout the county, but, unless you are going from downtown Miami to a not-too-distant spot, you are better off in a rental car or taxi.

With the exception of downtown Coconut Grove and South Beach, Miami is not a walker's city. Because it is so spread out, most attractions are too far apart to make walking between them feasible. In fact, most Miamians are so used to driving that they do so even when going just a few blocks.

BY PUBLIC TRANSPORTATION

BY RAIL   Two rail lines, operated by the **Metro-Dade Transit Agency** (© 305/770-3131 for information; www.co.miami-dade.fl.us/mdta), run in concert with each other.

Metrorail, the city's modern high-speed commuter train, is a 21-mile elevated line that travels north-south, between downtown Miami and the southern suburbs. Locals like to refer to this semi-useless rail system as Metro*fail.* If you are staying in Coral Gables or Coconut Grove, you can park your car at a nearby station and ride the rails downtown. However, that's about it. There are plans to extend the system to service Miami International Airport, but until those tracks are built, these trains don't go most places tourists go, with the exception of Vizcaya (p. 176) in Coconut Grove. Metrorail operates daily from about 6am to midnight. The fare is $1.50.

Metromover, a 4½-mile elevated line, circles the downtown area and connects with Metrorail at the Government Center stop. Riding on rubber tires, the single-car train winds past many of the area's most important attractions and its shopping and business districts. You may not go very far on the Metromover, but you will get a beautiful perspective from the towering height of the suspended rails. System hours are daily from about 6am to midnight, and the ride is free.

BY BUS   Miami's suburban layout is not conducive to getting around by bus. Lines operate and maps are available, but instead of getting to know the city, you'll find that relying on bus transportation will acquaint you only with how it feels to wait at bus stops. In short, a bus ride in Miami is grueling. You can get a bus map by mail, either from the Greater Miami Convention and Visitor's Bureau (see "Visitor Information," earlier in this chapter) or by writing the Metro-Dade Transit System, 3300 NW 32nd Ave., Miami, FL 33142. In Miami, call © **305/770-3131** for public-transit information. The fare is $1.50.

BY CAR

Tales circulate about vacationers who have visited Miami without a car, but they are very few indeed. If you are counting on exploring the city, even to a modest degree, a car is essential. Miami's restaurants, hotels, and attractions are far from one another, so any other form of transportation is relatively impractical. You won't need a car, however, if you are spending your entire vacation at a resort, are traveling directly to the Port of Miami for a cruise, or are here for a short stay centered on one area of the city, such as South Beach, where everything is within walking distance and parking is a costly nightmare.

When driving across a causeway or through downtown, allow extra time to reach your destination because of frequent drawbridge openings. Some bridges open about every half-hour for large sailing vessels to make their way through the wide bays and canals that crisscross the city, stalling traffic for several minutes.

RENTALS   It seems as though every car-rental company, big and small, has at least one office in Miami. Consequently, the city is one of the cheapest places in the world to rent a car. Many firms regularly advertise prices in the neighborhood of $150 per week for their economy cars. You should also check with your airline: There are often special discounts when you book a flight and reserve your rental car simultaneously. A minimum age, generally 25, is usually required of renters; some rental agencies have also set maximum ages! A national car-rental broker, **Car Rental Referral Service** (© **800/404-4482**), can often find companies willing to rent to drivers between the ages of 21 and 24 and can also get discounts from major companies as well as some regional ones.

National car-rental companies, with toll-free numbers, include **Alamo, Avis, Budget, Dollar, Hertz, National,** and **Thrifty.** One excellent company that has offices in every conceivable part of town and offers extremely competitive rates is **Enterprise.** Comparison shop before you make any decisions—car-rental prices can fluctuate more than airfares. For car rental contact information, see p. 391.

Many car-rental companies also offer cellular phones or electronic map rentals. It might be wise to opt for these additional safety features (the phone will definitely come in handy if you get lost), although the cost can be exorbitant.

Finally, think about splurging on a convertible. Not only are convertibles one of the best ways to see the beautiful surroundings, but they're also an ideal way to perfect a tan!

PARKING   Always keep plenty of quarters on hand to feed hungry meters, most of which have been removed in favor of those pesky parking payment stations where you feed a machine and get a printed receipt to display on your dash. Or, on Miami Beach, stop by the chamber of commerce at 1920 Meridian Ave. or any Publix grocery store to buy a magnetic **parking card** in denominations of $10, $20, or $25. Parking is usually plentiful (except on South Beach and Coconut Grove), but when it's not, be careful: Fines for illegal parking can be stiff, starting at $18 for an expired meter and going way up from there.

In addition to parking garages, valet services are commonplace and often used. Because parking is such a premium in bustling South Beach as well as in Coconut Grove, prices tend to be jacked up—especially at night and when there are special events (day or night). You can expect to pay an average of $5 to $15 for parking in these areas.

LOCAL DRIVING RULES   Florida law allows drivers to make a right turn on a red light after a complete stop, unless otherwise indicated. In addition, all passengers are required to wear seat belts, and children under 3 must be securely fastened in government-approved car seats.

BY TAXI

If you're not planning on traveling much within the city (and especially if you plan on spending your vacation within the confines of South Beach's Art Deco District), an occasional taxi is a good alternative to renting a car and dealing with the parking hassles that come with renting your own car. Taxi meters start at about $2.50 for the first quarter-mile and cost around $2.40 for each additional mile. You can blame the rate hikes on the gas crunch. There are standard flat-rate charges for frequently traveled routes—for example, Miami Beach's Convention Center to Coconut Grove will cost about $25.

Major cab companies include **Yellow Cab** (© **305/444-4444**) and, on Miami Beach, **Central** (© **305/532-5555**).

BY BIKE

Miami is a biker's paradise, especially on Miami Beach, where the hard-packed sand and boardwalks make it an easy and scenic route. However, unless you are a former New York City bike messenger, you won't want to use a bicycle as your main means of transportation.

For more information on bicycles, including where to rent the best ones, see "More Ways to Play, Indoors & Out," in chapter 8.

FAST FACTS: Miami

Airport   See "Orientation," earlier in this chapter.

American Express   You'll find American Express offices in downtown Miami at 100 N. Biscayne Blvd. (© **305/358-7350**; Mon–Fri 9am–5pm); 9700 Collins Ave., Bal Harbour (© **305/865-5959**; Mon–Sat 10am–6pm); and 32 Miracle Mile, Coral Gables (© **305/446-3381**; Mon–Fri 9am–5pm and Sat 10am–4pm). To report lost or stolen traveler's checks, call © **800/221-7282**.

Area Code   The original area code for Miami and all of Dade County is 305. That is still the code for older phone numbers, but all phone numbers assigned since July 1998 have the area code 786 (SUN). For all local calls, even if you're just calling across the street, you must dial the area code (305 or 786) first. Even though the Keys still share the Dade County area code of 305, calls to there from Miami are considered long distance and must be preceded by 1-305. (Within the Keys, simply dial the seven-digit number.) The area code for Fort Lauderdale is 954; for Palm Beach, Boca Raton, Vero Beach, and Port St. Lucie, it's 561.

Business Hours Banking hours vary, but most banks are open weekdays from 9am to 3pm. Several stay open until 5pm or so at least 1 day during the week, and most banks feature automated teller machines (ATMs) for 24-hour banking. Most stores are open daily from 10am to 6pm; however, there are many exceptions (see chapter 9). As far as business offices are concerned, Miami is generally a 9-to-5 town.

Car Rentals See "Getting Around," above.

Climate See "When to Go," in chapter 3.

Curfew Although not strictly enforced, there is an alleged curfew in effect for minors after 11pm on weeknights and midnight on weekends in all of Miami-Dade County. After those hours, children younger than 17 cannot be out on the streets or driving unless accompanied by a parent or on their way to work. Somehow, however, they still manage to sneak out and congregate in popular areas such as Coconut Grove and South Beach.

Dentists **A&E Dental Associates,** 11400 N. Kendall Dr., Mega Bank Building (© **305/271-7777**), offers 'round-the-clock care and accepts MasterCard and Visa.

Doctors In an emergency, call an ambulance by dialing © **911** (a free call) from any phone. The Dade County Medical Association sponsors a **Physician Referral Service** (© **305/324-8717**), weekdays from 9am to 5pm. **Health South Doctors' Hospital,** 5000 University Dr., Coral Gables (© **305/666-2111**), is a 285-bed acute-care hospital with a 24-hour physician-staffed emergency department.

Driving Rules See "Getting Around," above.

Drugstores See "Pharmacies," below.

Emergencies To reach the police, an ambulance, or the fire department, dial © **911** from any phone. No coins are needed. Emergency hotlines include **Crisis Intervention** (© **305/358-HELP** or 305/358-4357) and the **Poison Information Center** (© **800/222-1222**).

Eyeglasses **Pearle Vision Center,** 7901 Biscayne Blvd. (© **305/754-5144**), can usually fill prescriptions in about an hour.

Hospitals See "Doctors," above.

Information See "Visitor Information," earlier in this chapter.

Internet Access Internet access is available at **Kafka's Cyber Cafe,** 1464 Washington Ave., South Beach (© **305/673-9669**); the **South Beach Internet Cafe,** 1106 Collins Ave. (© **305/532-4331**); and, no joke, the swank all-in-one **Mobil Station,** at 2500 NW 87th Ave., Doral (© **305/477-2501**).

Laundry & Dry Cleaning For dry cleaning, self-service machines, and a wash-and-fold service by the pound, call **All Laundry Service,** 5701 NW 7th St. (© **305/261-8175**); it's open daily from 7am to 10pm. **Clean Machine Laundry,** 226 12th St., South Beach (© **305/534-9429**), is convenient to South Beach's Art Deco hotels and is open 24 hours a day. **Coral Gables Laundry & Dry Cleaning,** 250 Minorca Ave., Coral Gables (© **305/446-6458**), has been dry cleaning, altering, and laundering since 1930. It offers a lifesaving same-day service and is open weekdays from 7am to 7pm and Saturday from 8am to 3pm.

Liquor Laws Only adults 21 or older may legally purchase or consume alcohol in the state of Florida. Minors are usually permitted in bars, as long as the bars also serve food. Liquor laws are strictly enforced; if you look young, carry identification. Beer and wine are sold in most supermarkets and convenience stores. The city of Miami's liquor stores are closed on Sunday. Liquor stores in the city of Miami Beach are open daily.

Lost Property If you lost something at the airport, call the **Airport Lost and Found** office (© 305/876-7377). If you lost something on the bus, Metrorail, or Metromover, call **Metro-Dade Transit Agency** (© 305/770-3131). If you lost something anywhere else, phone the **Dade County Police Lost and Found** (© 305/375-3366). You may also want to fill out a police report for insurance purposes.

Luggage Storage & Lockers In addition to the baggage check at Miami International Airport, most hotels offer luggage-storage facilities. If you are taking a cruise from the Port of Miami, bags can be stored in your ship's departure terminal.

Newspapers & Magazines The *Miami Herald* is the city's only English-language daily. It is especially known for its extensive Latin American coverage and has a decent Friday "Weekend" entertainment guide. The most respected alternative weekly is the giveaway tabloid called *New Times,* which contains up-to-date listings and reviews of food, films, theater, music, and whatever else is happening in town. Also free, if you can find it, is *Ocean Drive,* an oversize glossy magazine that's limited on text (no literary value) and heavy on ads and society photos. It's what you should read if you want to know who's who and where to go for fun; it's available at a number of chic South Beach boutiques and restaurants. It is also available at newsstands.

For a large selection of foreign-language newspapers and magazines, check with any of the large bookstores or try **News Cafe,** 800 Ocean Dr., South Beach (© 305/538-6397). Adjacent to the **Van Dyke Cafe,** 846 Lincoln Rd., South Beach (© 305/534-3600), is a fantastic newsstand with magazines and newspapers from all over the world. Also check out **Eddie's News,** 1096 Normandy Dr., Miami Beach (© 305/866-2661), and **Worldwide News,** 1629 NE 163rd St., North Miami Beach (© 305/940-4090).

Pharmacies **Walgreens Pharmacy** has dozens of locations all over town, including 8550 Coral Way (© 305/221-9271), in Coral Gables; 1845 Alton Rd. (© 305/531-8868), in South Beach; and 6700 Collins Ave. (© 305/861-6742), in Miami Beach. The branch at 5731 Bird Rd. at SW 40th Street (© 305/666-0757) is open 24 hours, as is **CVS,** 6460 S. Dixie Hwy., in South Miami (© 305/661-0778).

Photographic Needs **One Hour Photo,** in the Bayside Marketplace (© 305/377-FOTO), is pricey (about $20 to develop and print a roll of 36 pictures), but they're open Monday to Saturday from 10am to 10pm, and Sunday from noon to 8pm. Walgreens (see above, under "Pharmacies") or Eckerd will develop film for the next day for about $10.

Police For emergencies, dial © **911** from any phone. No coins are needed for this call. For other police matters, call © 305/595-6263.

Post Office The **Main Post Office,** 2200 Milam Dairy Rd., Miami, FL 33152 (© **800/275-8777),** is located west of the Miami International Airport. Conveniently located post offices include 1300 Washington Ave. in South Beach and 3191 Grand Ave. in Coconut Grove. There is one central number for all post offices: © **800/275-8777.**

Radio On the AM dial, 610 (WIOD), 790 (WNWS), 1230 (WJNO), and 1340 (WPBR) are all talk. There is no all-news station in town, although 940 (WINZ) gives traffic updates and headline news in between its talk shows. WDBF (1420) is a good big-band station, and WPBG (1290) features golden oldies. Switching to the FM dial, the two most popular R&B stations are WFDR/99 Jamz (99.1) and Hot 105 (105.1). The best rock stations on the FM dial are WPYM/93 Rock (93.1), WBGG/Big 106 (105.9), and the progressive college station WVUM (90.5). WKIS (99.9) is the top country station. Top-40 music can be heard on WHYI (100.3), and hip-hop on Mega 103 (103.5). For more hip-hop and dance music, Power 96 (96.5) WPOW will help to get your groove on. WGTR (97.3) plays easy listening, WDNA (88.9) has the best Latin jazz and multiethnic sounds, and public radio can be heard either on WXEL (90.7) or WLRN (91.3).

Religious Services Miami houses of worship are as varied as the city's population and include St. Patrick Catholic Church, 3716 Garden Ave., Miami Beach (© **305/531-1124);** Coral Gables Baptist Church, 5501 Granada Blvd. (© **305/665-4072);** Temple Judea, 5500 Granada Blvd., Coral Gables (© **305/667-5657);** Coconut Grove United Methodist, 2850 SW 27th Ave. (© **305/443-0880);** Christ Episcopal Church, 3481 Hibiscus St., Coconut Grove (© **305/442-8542);** Plymouth Congregational Church, 3400 Devon Rd., at Main Highway, Coconut Grove (© **305/444-6521);** Masjid Al-Ansar (Muslim), 5245 NW 7th Ave., Miami (© **305/757-8741);** and Buddhist Temple of Miami, 15200 SW 240th St., Homestead (© **305/245-2702).**

Restrooms Stores rarely let customers use their restrooms, and many restaurants offer their facilities only for their patrons. However, most malls have restrooms, as do many fast-food restaurants. Public beaches and large parks often provide toilets, though in some places you have to pay or tip an attendant. Most large hotels have clean restrooms in their lobbies.

Safety As always, use your common sense and be aware of your surroundings at all times. Don't walk alone at night, and be extra wary when walking or driving though downtown Miami and surrounding areas.

Reacting to several highly publicized crimes against tourists several years ago, both local and state governments have taken steps to help protect visitors. These measures include special highly visible police units patrolling the airport and surrounding neighborhoods, and better signs on the state's most touristtraveled routes.

Spas & Massage There are a number of great spa packages at some of the ritzier hotels, but those without spas often have relationships with on-call massage therapists, which can be arranged by asking the concierge to make an appointment for an in-room session. Popular day spas include the **Russian Turkish Baths,** 5445 Collins Ave. at the Castle Hotel (© **305/867-8313),** otherwise known as "The Schvitz," where the old guard meets the new in eucalyptus-scented Turkish steam rooms and aroma baths bolstered by marble columns. **Browne's Beauty Lounge,** 841 Lincoln Rd., Miami Beach (𝄐 **305/532-8703**), has expanded from a small second-floor salon into a full-service, 5,250-square-foot spa, offering massages, waxing, manicures, and a sublime signature hot-rock massage. **Le Spa Miami,** 150 8th St., Miami Beach (𝄐 **305/674-6744**), is one of the best day spas in the area, exclusively using Lancôme products and featuring a laundry list of facials, body treatments, makeup applications, waxing, manicures, pedicures, and even photo shoots. Best known for introducing the super-popular bare-it-all Brazilian bikini wax to the United States, the **J Sisters,** 663 Lincoln Rd., Miami Beach (𝄐 **305/672-7142**), have brought their depilating expertise to Miami from New York so that the likes of Gwyneth and J-Lo can take care of business while in town.

As far as hotel spas go, my three favorites are at the Standard on South Beach, the Mandarin Oriental in Miami, and the Ritz-Carlton in Key Biscayne.

The Spa at Mandarin Oriental is where the likes of Jacko, J-Lo, and Diddy are pampered with treatments such as the 4-hour Ultimate Spa Indulgence that includes a welcome foot ritual, purifying herbal linen wrap with hot stones, facial cleanse, body exfoliation, body wrap with fresh algae and nourishing mud, Ayurvedic holistic massage, heated volcanic stones or oil-pouring Shirodhara, herbal tea, two-course lunch, aromatherapy facial, holistic hand and nail treatment, foot and nail treatment, yoga, Oriental bath soak, and choice of Thai massage or shiatsu. You needn't be a celebrity to experience this spa's stellar treatment.

The Ritz-Carlton Key Biscayne Spa has 20,000 square feet of space overlooking the Atlantic Ocean. It features unheard-of treatments such as the Rum Molasses Waterfall treatment (a combination massage/hair treatment), the Key Lime Coconut Body Scrub, and the Everglades Grass Body Wrap.

Hip hotelier Andre Balazs pulled out all the stops when renovating the old-school, Borscht Belt–style Lido Spa and transforming it into South Beach's very own branch of L.A.'s hip **Standard Hotel.** While Tinseltown's Standards are high, the South Beach version breaks new ground in town as a bona fide spa hotel complete with hundreds of treatments, including an authentic Turkish hammam, the Wall of Sound Shower, a cedar sauna room, and more.

Taxes A 6% state sales tax (plus .5% local tax, for a total of 6.5% in Miami-Dade County [from Homestead to North Miami Beach]) is added on at the register for all goods and services purchased in Florida. In addition, most municipalities levy special taxes on restaurants and hotels. In Surfside, hotel taxes total 10.5%; in Bal Harbour, 9.5%; in Miami Beach (including South Beach), 11.5%; and in the rest of Dade County, a whopping 12.5%. In Miami Beach, Surfside, and Bal Harbour, the resort (hotel) tax also applies to hotel restaurants and restaurants with liquor licenses.

Taxis See "Getting Around," earlier in this chapter.

Television The local stations are channel 4, WFOR (CBS); channel 6, WTVJ (NBC); channel 7, WSVN (FOX); channel 10, WPLG (ABC); channel 17, WLRN

(PBS); channel 23, WLTV (independent); and channel 33, WBFS (independent). Channel 39 is the CW (WBZL), and channel 33 is UPN (WBFS).

Time Zone Miami, like New York, is in the Eastern Standard Time (EST) zone. Between the second Sunday of March and the first Sunday of November, daylight saving time is adopted, and clocks are set 1 hour ahead. America's eastern seaboard is 5 hours behind Greenwich Mean Time. To find out what time it is, call © **305/324-8811.**

Transit Information For Metrorail or Metromover schedule information, phone © **305/770-3131** or surf over to www.co.miami-dade.fl.us/mdta.

Weather Hurricane season in Miami runs June through November. For an up-to-date recording of current weather conditions and forecast reports, call © **305/229-4522.** Also see "When to Go" in chapter 3 for more information on the weather.

6

Where to Stay in Miami

As much a part of the landscape as the palm trees, many of Miami's hotels are on display as if they were contestants in a beauty pageant. The city's long-lasting status on the destination A-list has given rise to an ever-increasing number of upscale hotels, and no place in Miami has seen a greater increase in construction than Miami Beach. Since the area's renaissance, which began in the late 1980s, the beach has turned what used to be a beachfront retirement community into a sand-swept hot spot for the Gucci and Prada set. Contrary to popular belief, however, the beach does not discriminate, and it's the juxtaposition of the chic elite and the hoi polloi that contributes to its allure.

While the increasing demand for rooms on South Beach means increasing costs, you can still find a decent room at a fair price. In fact, most hotels in the Art Deco District are less Ritz-Carlton than they are Holiday Inn, unless, of course, they've been renovated (many hotels in this area were built in the 1930s for the middle class). Unless you plan your vacation entirely in and around your hotel, most of the cheaper Deco hotels are adequate and a wise choice for those who plan to use the room only to sleep. Smart vacationers can almost name their price if they're willing to live without a few luxuries, such as an oceanfront view.

Many of the old hotels from the 1930s, 1940s, and 1950s have been totally renovated, giving way to dozens of "boutique" (small, swank, and, for the most part,

independently owned) hotels. Keep in mind that when a hotel claims that it was just renovated, it can mean that they've completely gutted the building—or just applied a coat of fresh paint. Always ask what specific changes were made during a renovation, and be sure to ask if a hotel will be undergoing construction while you're there. You should also find out how near your room will be to the center of the nightlife crowd; trying to sleep directly on Ocean Drive or Collins and Washington avenues, especially during the weekend, is next to impossible, unless your lullaby of choice happens to include throbbing salsa and bass beats.

The best hotel options in each price category and those that have been fully upgraded recently are listed below. You should also know that along South Beach's Collins Avenue, there are dozens of hotels and motels—in all price categories—so there's bound to be a vacancy somewhere. If you do try the walk-in routine, don't forget to ask to see a room first. A few dollars extra could mean all the difference between flea and fabulous.

While South Beach may be the nucleus of all things hyped and hip, it's not the only place with hotels. The advantage to staying on South Beach as opposed to, say, Coral Gables or Coconut Grove, is that the beaches are within walking distance, the nightlife and restaurant options are aplenty, and, basically, everything you need is right there. However, staying there is definitely not for everyone. If you're wary, don't worry: South

Beach is centrally located and only about a 15- to 30-minute drive from most other parts of Miami.

For a less expensive stay that's only a 10-minute cab ride from South Beach, Miami Beach proper (the area north of 23rd St. and Collins Ave. all the way up to 163rd St. and Collins Ave.) offers a slew of reasonable stays, right on the beach, that won't cost you your kids' college education fund.

What *will* cost you a small fortune are the luxury hotels in the city's financial Brickell Avenue district, the area of choice for expense-account business travelers and camera-shy celebrities trying to avoid the South Beach spotlight.

For a less frenetic, more relaxed, and more tropical experience, the resorts on Key Biscayne exude an island feel, even though, across the water, a cosmopolitan vibe beckons, thanks to the shimmering, spectacular Miami skyline.

Those who'd rather bag the beach in favor of shopping bags will enjoy North Miami Beach's proximity to the Aventura Mall. For Miami with an old-world European flair, Coral Gables and its charming hotels and exquisite restaurants provide a more prim and proper, well-heeled perspective of Miami than the trendy boutique and condo hotels on South Beach.

SEASONS & RATES South Florida's tourist season is well-defined, beginning in mid-November and lasting until Easter. Hotel prices escalate until about March, after which they begin to decline. During the off season, hotel rates are typically 30% to 50% lower than their winter highs. But timing isn't everything. Rates also depend on your hotel's proximity to the beach and how much ocean you can see from your window. Small motels a block or two from the water can be up to 40% cheaper than similar properties right on the sand.

The rates listed below are broken down into two broad categories: winter (generally, Thanksgiving through Easter) and off season (about mid-May through Aug). The months in between, the shoulder season, should fall somewhere between the highs and lows, while rates always go up on holidays. Remember, too, that state and city taxes can add as much as 12.5% to your bill in some parts of Miami. Some hotels, especially those in South Beach, also tack on additional service charges, and don't forget that parking is a pricey endeavor.

PRICE CATEGORIES The hotels below are divided first by area and then by price (**very expensive, expensive, moderate,** or **inexpensive**). Prices are based on published rates (or rack rates) for a standard double room during the high season. You should also check with the reservations agent, since many rooms are available above and below the category ranges listed below, and ask about packages, since it's often possible to get a better deal than these "official" rates. Most important, always call the hotel to confirm rates, which may be subject to change without notice because of special events, holidays, or blackout dates.

LONG-TERM STAYS If you plan to visit Miami for a month, a season, or more, think about renting a condominium apartment or a room in a long-term hotel. Long-term accommodations exist in every price category, from budget to deluxe, and in general are extremely reasonable, especially during the off season. Check with the reservation services below, or write a short note to the chamber of commerce in the area where you plan to stay. In addition, many local real estate agents handle short-term rentals (meaning less than a year).

RESERVATION SERVICES Central Reservation Service (© 800/950-0232 or 305/274-6832; www.reservation-services.com) works with many of Miami's hotels and can often secure discounts of up to 40%. It also gives advice on specific locales, especially in Miami Beach and downtown. During holiday time, there may be a 3-to-5-day minimum stay required to use their services. Call for more information.

For bed-and-breakfast information throughout the state, contact **Florida** **Bed and Breakfast Inns** (© **800/524-1880;** www.florida-inns.com). For information on the ubiquitous boutique hotels, check out the Greater Miami Convention and Visitor's Bureau's new website, www.miamiboutiquehotels.com.

1 South Beach

Choosing a hotel on South Beach is similar to deciding whether you'd rather pay $2 for french fries at Denny's or $12 for the same fries—but let's call them *pomme frites*—in a pricey haute-cuisine restaurant. It's all about atmosphere. The rooms of some hotels may *look* ultrachic, but they are as comfortable as sleeping on a concrete slab. Once you decide how much atmosphere you want, the choice will be easier. Fortunately, for every chichi hotel in South Beach—and there are many—there are just as many moderately priced, more casual options.

Prices mentioned here are rack rates—that is, the price you would be quoted if you walked up to the front desk and inquired about rates. The actual price you will end up paying will usually be less than this—especially if a travel agent makes the reservations for you. Many hotels on South Beach have chosen to go with a low-to-high rate representing the hotel's complete pricing range. It pays to try to negotiate the price of a room. In some of the trendier hotels, however, negotiating is highly unfashionable and not well regarded. In other words, your attempt at negotiation will either be met with a blank stare or a snippy refusal. It never hurts to try, though.

If status is important to you, as it is to many South Beach visitors, then you will be quite pleased with the number of haute hotels in the area. But the times may be a-changin': Courtyard by Marriott (© **800/321-2211** or 305/604-8887) maintains a 90-room, moderately priced hotel on a seedy stretch of Washington Avenue, smack in the middle of Clubland, a horror to many a South Beach trend seeker.

Note: Art Deco hotels, while pleasing to the eye, may be a bit run-down inside. It's par for the course on South Beach, where appearances are, at times, deceiving.

To locate the hotels in this section, see the "South Beach Accommodations" map (p. 79).

VERY EXPENSIVE

The Angler's Resort ✹✹✹   Opened in 2007, the Angler's isn't your typical South Beach boutique hotel in that here, *service*—not surface—is paramount. Located 2 blocks from the beach, the hotel is a unique collection of four very different buildings—two completely restored and two brand new buildings offering a variety of accommodations from suites and duplexes to triplex villas. All rooms feature the typical luxury comforts of Wi-Fi, flatscreen TVs and iPod. Not so typical: one remote control works on all of these features—even the internal and external lights. An outdoor pool is surrounded by gardens and a stellar restaurant, La Maison d'Azur, a South Beach meets St. Tropez seafood brasserie complete with DJ, stellar shellfish, caviar, and over 80 wines by the glass. For those who'd rather do the beach than the pool, stop by the front desk to pick up a beach goodie bag complete with sunscreen, toys, water, snacks, and even the latest best-selling novel. Novel, indeed.

660 Washington Ave., South Beach, FL 33139. © **305/534-9600.** Fax 305/532-3099 www.theanglersresort.com. 49 fully furnished residences including suites and villas. Winter studio suites: $225–$495, duplex suites: $500–$1200.

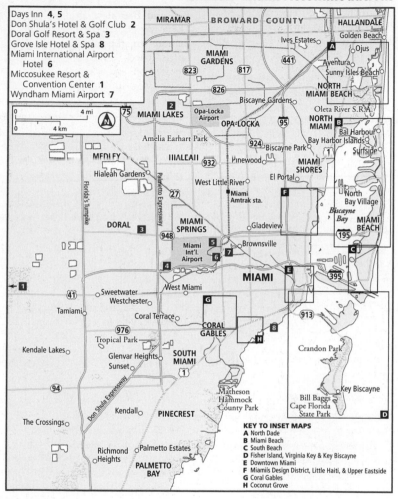

Days Inn **4, 5**
Don Shula's Hotel & Golf Club **2**
Doral Golf Resort & Spa **3**
Grove Isle Hotel & Spa **8**
Miami International Airport Hotel **6**
Miccosukee Resort & Convention Center **1**
Wyndham Miami Airport **7**

KEY TO INSET MAPS
A North Dade
B Miami Beach
C South Beach
D Fisher Island, Virginia Key & Key Biscayne
E Downtown Miami
F Miami's Design District, Little Haiti, & Upper Eastside
G Coral Gables
H Coconut Grove

Valet parking. Pet-friendly environment. **Amenities:** Restaurant with expansive terrace cafe; private rooftop terraces, gardens, or outdoor water experiences; poolside dining cabana; designated beach concession and lounge area; indoor and poolside spa services; 24-hr. concierge service; room service; complimentary wireless Internet. *In room:* A/C; Flatscreen TV/DVD; iPod docking station; minibar; hair dryer; safe.

Bentley Hotel   The biggest coup the Bentley Hotel pulls off is its ability to remain immune to the throngs of pedestrians on the well-traveled Ocean Drive. A private front entrance leads, via elevator, to the main lobby. Inside this enclave of Old World luxury you will find a charming ambience and an overly accommodating, professional staff. The hotel's 53 suites are both hotel rooms and condos; some of them can be rented year-round. Rooms come complete with marble floors, well-stocked kitchens, and roomy bathrooms with steam showers. Try not to get a corner room, though, or you will learn more about your neighbors than you'd ever want to. Because

Checking into Hotel Bars

While South Beach is known for its trendy club scene, hotel bars all over Miami are also very much a part of the nightlife. Among the hottest hotel bars are the **Lobby Bar** at The Setai, **Skybar** and the **Nobu Lounge** at The Shore Club, the **Rose Bar** at the Delano, the **Bond St.** Lounge at the Townhouse, **Amadeus Bar** at the Ritz-Carlton Coconut Grove, the **M Bar** at the Mandarin Oriental, and **Bahia** at the Four Seasons. See chapter 10 for more details on the above bars.

it is located on South Beach's bustling strip of neon and nightlife, the Bentley, despite its efforts to stand apart from the rest of its neighbors, isn't impervious to noise. However, if you want luxe in the midst of all the action, the Bentley is a great choice.

510 Ocean Dr., South Beach, FL 33139. ℰ 800/236-8510 or 305/538-1700. Fax 305/532-4865. www.thebentleyhotel. com. 53 units. Winter $310–$1,200 double; off season $220–$900 double. AE, DC, DISC, MC, V. **Amenities:** Rooftop pool; concierge; 24-hr. room service; dry cleaning. *In room:* A/C, TV/DVD player, fax, dataport, kitchen, minibar, coffeemaker, hair dryer.

Casa Tua   This outrageous boutique offers custom-tailored amenities (from toiletries to snacks) for each of its guests, who fill out a detailed profile when booking one of Casa Tua's five suites. Styled like a glorious Mediterranean beach house, Casa Tua also has a posh restaurant with an Italian-accented menu and a second-floor lounge for afternoon tea and evening cocktails. The hotel's management is very cagey as far as hotel details are concerned, expressing a deep concern for "keeping its clientele extremely exclusive" and, essentially, by word of mouth. Enough said, I suppose. Rather than fork over the money to stay here—there's no pool anyway—I do suggest that you absolutely splurge at Casa Tua, the restaurant (p. 116), which happens to be one of South Beach's most exquisite.

1700 James Ave., Miami Beach, FL 33139. ℰ 305/673-1010. 5 suites. $750 and up. Call for details.

Delano 🛈   Though Madonna and Beyoncé may choose The Setai over the Delano these days, it doesn't mean South Beach's original see-and-be-seen hotel is over just yet. The stunning pool area, Rose Bar, Agua Spa, and Blue Door restaurant are still studded with the bold-faced and the beautiful, but today the Delano, a place where smiles from staffers were as rare as snow in Miami, is somewhat kinder and gentler. The fact that Delano's parent company, Morgans Hotel Group, scrapped plans to expand the Delano in favor of opening a less expensive Delano-esque hotel across the street speaks volumes. But it certainly is still amusing to look at—with 40-foot sheer white billowing curtains hanging outside, mirrors everywhere, Adirondack chairs, and faux fur–covered beds. Rooms that were once done up sanitarium style, sterile yet terribly trendy, just received a revamp that boasts a splash of color and reworked bathrooms that went from spartan to spacious.

1685 Collins Ave., South Beach, FL 33139. ℰ 800/555-5001 or 305/672-2000. Fax 305/532-0099. www.delano-hotel. com. 195 units, including 1 penthouse. Winter $445–$795 standard, $1,200–$2,550 suite, $2,200–$3,500 bungalow or 2-bedroom, $3,500–$5,500 penthouse; off season $405–$715 standard, $1150–$2,250 suite, $1,700–$3,200 bungalow or 2-bedroom, $3,500–$5,000 penthouse. Additional person $25. AE, DC, DISC, MC, V. Valet parking $34. **Amenities:** 3 restaurants (featuring the acclaimed Blue Door); bar; large outdoor pool; state-of-the-art gym; spa; children's programs; concierge; business center; room service; in-room massage; same-day laundry and dry-cleaning services. *In room:* A/C, TV/VCR, CD player, Wi-Fi, minibar, hair dryer, safe.

South Beach Accommodations

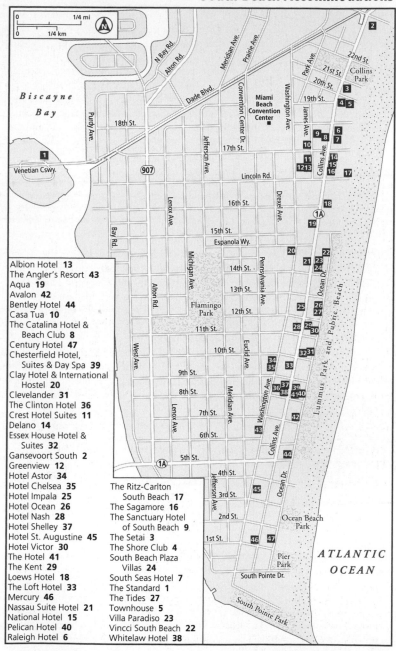

Albion Hotel **13**
The Angler's Resort **43**
Aqua **19**
Avalon **42**
Bentley Hotel **44**
Casa Tua **10**
The Catalina Hotel &
 Beach Club **8**
Century Hotel **47**
Chesterfield Hotel,
 Suites & Day Spa **39**
Clay Hotel & International
 Hostel **20**
Clevelander **31**
The Clinton Hotel **36**
Crest Hotel Suites **11**
Delano **14**
Essex House Hotel &
 Suites **32**
Gansevoort South **2**
Greenview **12**
Hotel Astor **34**
Hotel Chelsea **35**
Hotel Impala **25**
Hotel Ocean **26**
Hotel Nash **28**
Hotel Shelley **37**
Hotel St. Augustine **45**
Hotel Victor **30**
The Hotel **41**
The Kent **29**
Loews Hotel **18**
The Loft Hotel **33**
Mercury **46**
Nassau Suite Hotel **21**
National Hotel **15**
Pelican Hotel **40**
Raleigh Hotel **6**

The Ritz-Carlton
 South Beach **17**
The Sagamore **16**
The Sanctuary Hotel
 of South Beach **9**
The Setai **3**
The Shore Club **4**
South Beach Plaza
 Villas **24**
South Seas Hotel **7**
The Standard **1**
The Tides **27**
Townhouse **5**
Villa Paradiso **23**
Vincci South Beach **22**
Whitelaw Hotel **38**

Fisher Island Club 🎭🎭🎭 *Finds*   Located on an exclusive island just off Miami Beach, this hotel is a luxurious fusion of *Fantasy Island, Lifestyles of the Rich and Famous,* and *Survivor.* Just minutes from South Beach, it's still worlds away. The only way to get there is by private ferry, which shuttles guests to and from the mainland every 15 to 20 minutes. It can be a hassle, but it does run on a very regular schedule. The ferry lets residents on first, so if there's no room after all the Bentleys roll on, you'll have to wait for the next one. Don't worry if you are carless—golf carts are the island's preferred mode of transportation. Rooms vary in size and shape, and cottages come with hot tubs. There's also a world-class spa, restaurants, tennis, golf, and pretty much everything to entertain the island's offbeat millionaires—you know, the kind who tug their Gucci-clad pooches around in their Rolls Royce golf carts.

1 Fisher Island Dr., Fisher Island, FL 33190. Ⓒ 800/537-3708 or 305/535-6020. Fax 305/535-6003. www.fisherisland-florida.com. 60 units. Winter $405–$495 double, $890–$2,040 suite or cottage; off season $325–$395 double, $450–$1,630 suite or cottage. Golf, tennis, and spa packages available seasonally. 20% gratuity added to all food and beverages. AE, DC, MC, V. **Amenities:** 3 restaurants; 3 bars; P. B. Dye Golf Course; 18 tennis courts; world-class spa; 2 marinas; concierge; secretarial service; limited room service; babysitting; laundry service; dry cleaning; airport transportation. *In room:* A/C, TV/VCR, minibar, coffeemaker, hair dryer.

Gansevoort South 🎭🎭   As of this writing, this was understandably the "It" place of the 2008/2009 season. One of NYC's hippest hotels opened on South Beach in January 2008 much to the delight of hipsters, jet-setters, and the scene-obsessed. This 334-room hotel features the flagship David Barton Gym and Spa, a lounge, restaurants by Philippe Chow, and, inexplicably, a shark tank with 27 types of fish and sharks that spans 50 feet of the terminally trendy lobby. A 26,000 rooftop playground (complete with a 110-ft. elevated swimming pool, Plunge bar, and lounge) offers divine views of the ocean, the bay, and downtown. On the main level is a 40,000-square-foot semicircular oceanfront pool plaza with infinity-edge pool, teak decking, and cabanas. Room furniture screams hot pink, magenta, and yellow, set against charcoal gray suede walls dotted with pictures of 40s pinup girls. Most rooms have balconies overlooking the ocean.

2377 Collins Ave., South Beach, FL 33139. Ⓒ 305/604-1000. Fax 305/604-6886. www.gansevoortsouth.com. 334 units. AE, DC, DISC, MC, V. On-site valet parking. **Amenities:** 2 restaurants, bar and lounge; pool plaza; beach club; rooftop pool; fitness center; spa; concierge; salon; 24-hr. room service. *In room:* A/C, TV/DVD, DVD/CD player, complimentary wireless Internet, direct DID and fax lines, iPod docks, minibar, hair dryer, safe.

Hotel Victor 🎭🎭   A victory for Ocean Drive, a street that hasn't seen such a swank stay since The Tides, which is going the hotel/condo route, Hotel Victor is a hyperluxe, 91-room boutique see-and-be-seen hotel designed by Parisian Jacques Garcia—this is his first hotel foray in the U.S. Best known for his design work at Paris's tragically hip Hotel Costes and for the discriminating Sultan of Brunei, Garcia has lent his exquisite taste to this hotel located on notoriously tacky Ocean Drive. The hotel's cabana-dotted pool and bistro Vix have become command central for hipsters and celebrities—especially on Thursday nights. Directly across from the ocean, Hotel Victor stands apart from the rest of the cookie-cutter minimalist Miami hotels, breaking from bare minimalism and daring to go bold with color and rich fabrics. Deluxe rooms are just that, all with ocean views, ebony-lacquered furniture, a full—not mini—bar, flatscreen plasma TVs and massive white-marbled bathrooms with infinity-edge bathtubs and rain-head shower heads.

1144 Ocean Dr., South Beach, FL 33139. Ⓒ 305/428-1234. Fax 305/421-6281. www.hotelvictorsouthbeach.com. 91 units. Winter $470–$745 double, $1,005–$1,045 suite; off season $305–$650 double, $1,005–$1,045 suite. AE, DC,

Turkish Delightful Spa

The Hotel Victor's Turkish Spa is the hotel's hottest spot—literally, with a large unisex steam room, Turkish hammam, and heated marble slabs. *Insider tip:* Shaunie O'Neal, Shaquille's wife, teamed up with the spa to introduce its newest treatment, the "Miami Heat" ritual, a 75-minute full-body massage to relax and restore overactive bodies (and, at $200, to drain your bank account as well).

DISC, MC, V. Valet parking $25. **Amenities:** 2 restaurants; 4 bars; outdoor pool; 6,000-ft. fitness center, spa, and Turkish hammam; concierge; room service, book and music library. *In room:* A/C, TV/DVD, stereo/CD player, Wi-Fi, minibar, hair dryer.

Loews Hotel *&* *Kids*   The Loews is one of the largest hotels on South Beach, consuming an unprecedented 900 feet of oceanfront. This 790-room behemoth is considered an eyesore by many, an architectural triumph by others. Rooms are a bit boxy and bland, nothing to rave about, but are clean and have new carpets and bedspreads to erase signs of wear and tear from the hotel's heavy traffic. The best rooms do not face very congested Collins Avenue, since rooms that do tend to be quite noisy. If you can steer your way past all the conventioneers in the lobby, you can escape to the equally massive pool (with an undisputedly gorgeous, landscaped entrance that's more Maui than Miami). In addition to children's fare such as the Loews Loves Kids program, the hotel hosts fun activities for adults, such as Dive in Movies at the pool, salsa lessons, and bingo. Emeril Lagasse opened Miami's first-ever Emeril's restaurant here, and a new sprawling spa debuted in 2007.

1601 Collins Ave., South Beach, FL 33139. © 800/23-LOEWS or 305/604-1601. www.loewshotels.com. 790 units. Winter from $459 double; off season from $289 double. AE, DC, DISC, MC, V. Valet parking $30. Pets accepted. **Amenities:** 3 restaurants; 3 bars; coffee bar; sprawling outdoor pool; health club; spa; Jacuzzi; sauna; watersports rentals; children's programs; concierge; business center; 24-hr. room service; babysitting; dry cleaning. *In room:* A/C, TV, high-speed Internet access, minibar, coffeemaker, hair dryer.

National Hotel *&*   Sceney it's not, but scenic? Absolutely. With its towering ceilings, sultry furnishings, and massive gilded mirrors, the elegant 1940s-style National is a Deco darling. At 11 stories, the main building offers grand views of the ocean. Guest rooms and suites were designed as a tranquil and elegant refuge from bustling South Beach. Rooms are divided into two distinctive buildings: the **Historic Tower** and the **Cabana Wing,** which feature their own balconies overlooking the spectacular Infinity Pool. While all the rooms in the main hotel are comfortable and plush, the best rooms are the 32 ultramodern poolside cabana rooms. The hotel's historic Deco lobby is a rarity in a town where all vestiges of the good old days have given way to sterile minimalism. The pool, however, is the hotel's crown jewel. It's Miami's longest pool (205 ft.) and almost too sleek (rivaling even the Delano's pool) for splashing.

1677 Collins Ave., South Beach, FL 33139. © 800/327-8370 or 305/532-2311. Fax 305/534-1426. www.national hotel.com. 152 units. Winter $380–$480 double; off season $270–$350 double. AE, DC, DISC, MC, V. Valet parking $25. **Amenities:** Restaurant; 2 bars; large outdoor pool; exercise room; watersports equipment/rentals; concierge; 24-hr. room service; laundry service; dry cleaning. *In room:* A/C, TV/VCR, stereo, minibar, hair dryer.

The Ritz-Carlton South Beach *&&&* *Kids*   Far from ostentatious, The Ritz-Carlton South Beach moves away from gilded opulence in favor of the more soothing pastel-washed touches of Deco. Though South Beach is better known for its trendy boutique hotels, The Ritz-Carlton provides comfort to those who might prefer 100% cotton Frette sheets and goose-down pillows to high-style minimalism. The best rooms, by far, are the 72 poolside and oceanview lanai rooms. There's also a tanning butler who will spritz you with SPF and water whenever you want. With its impeccable service, an elevated pool with unobstructed views of the Atlantic and a weekend DJ, an impressive stretch of sand with a fabulous beach club, and a world-class 13,000-square-foot spa and wellness center, The Ritz-Carlton kicks sand in the faces of some smaller hotels that think they're doing *you* a favor by allowing you to sleep there. Parents love the Ritz Kids program for kids ages 5 through 12, and for gourmands there's the Ritz's amazing Sunday champagne brunch.

1 Lincoln Rd., South Beach, FL 33139. (*C*) 800/241-3333 or 786/276-4000. Fax 786/276-4001. www.ritzcarlton.com. 375 units. Winter $739 double, $1,009 suite; off season $359 double, $479 suite. AE, DISC, MC, V. Valet parking $30. **Amenities:** 3 restaurants; 3 bars; outdoor heated pool; health club; spa; extensive watersports rentals; children's program; 24-hr. business center; shopping boutique; salon; 24-hr. room service; babysitting; overnight laundry service; beach service. *In room:* A/C, TV, dataport, minibar, hair dryer, iron, safe.

The Sagamore 🏵🏵🏵 Just two doors down from the Delano Hotel is The Sagamore, fabulous in its own right, with an ultramodern lobby-cum-art-gallery-cum-restaurant that's infinitely warmer than your typical pop-art exhibit at the Museum of Modern Art. The hotel doesn't take itself too seriously and boasts a tongue-in-cheeky sense of humor that was evidenced when it hosted a Lox and Botox party—no, we're not kidding. Although the lobby and its requisite restaurant, bar, and lounge areas have become command central for the international chic elite and celebrities, The Sagamore's all-suite, apartment-like rooms are havens from the hype, with all the cushy comforts of home and then some. The sprawling outdoor lawn dotted with cabanas with plasma TVs screening everything from Japanese anime to digital art, pool, and beachfront makes you realize you're not in Kansas anymore. A new branch of Miami's coiffeur to the stars, Rik Rak, opened in one of the outdoor bungalows.

1671 Collins Ave., South Beach, FL 33139. (*C*) 87/SAGAMORE or 305/535-8088. Fax 305/535-8185. www.sagamore hotel.com. 93 units. Winter $355–$1,050 suite; off season $215–$595 suite. AE, DC, DISC, MC, V. Valet parking $20. **Amenities:** Restaurant, bar; pool bar; pool; fitness center; spa; concierge; salon; room service. *In room:* A/C, TV/VCR/DVD, CD player, wireless Internet, full kitchen, minibar, coffeemaker, hair dryer, iron, safe.

The Sanctuary Hotel of South Beach 🏵 Set a bit off the beaten path is this modern, all-suite resident hotel (meaning people can actually rent or buy rooms and live here) that takes luxury very seriously even if it resembles a souped-up motel, with its ground-floor rooms accessible only from a communal outdoor courtyard area. Flying into town? Let the Sanctuary's Bentley pick you up in pure bling-bling style. But don't mistake the flashy car as a sign that the hotel is tacky. It's just the opposite. Soothingly modern, all rooms have full state-of-the-art Italian kitchens, flat plasma-screen televisions, and Wi-Fi. In addition, bathrooms come with Jacuzzi tubs, and in-room fridges are stocked with everything you specify before checking into the hotel. A roof-deck "bedroom" allows you to relax in the sun or slink around in the wading pool. Star chef Douglas Rodriguez recently opened Ola, a fashionable Latin eatery and hot spot situated smack in the middle of the very posh, albeit tiny, lobby.

1745 James Ave., South Beach, FL 33139. (*C*) 305/673-5455. Fax 305/673-3113. www.sanctuarysobe.com. 30 units. Winter $375–$1,500 suite; off season $215–$1,050 suite. AE, DC, DISC, MC, V. Valet parking $18. **Amenities:** Restaurant; bar; pool bar; rooftop pool; fitness center; spa; concierge; room service. *In room:* A/C, TV/VCR/DVD, CD player, dataport, full kitchen, minibar, coffeemaker, hair dryer, iron, safe.

The Setai 🎖🎖🎖   With bank-busting room rates, dinner tabs coming in at around $200 per person, martinis at $26, and a celebrity clientele who doesn't have to ask how much, the Zen-like, Asian-inspired Setai is truly for that 1% of society who can afford it. But if you want to splurge, this is where to do it. All of the suites—some are actually condos participating in the condo-hotel program—are gorgeous apartments with floor-to-ceiling windows, full kitchens, and Jacuzzi bathtubs bigger than a small swimming pool. There are 75 regular hotel rooms that are just 550 square feet compared to the suites' 1,300 to 3,500 square feet. All are adorned in sleek Asian decor with over-the-top comforts including Lavazza espresso makers, Aqua di Parma bathroom amenities, and washer/dryers. The garden area with reflecting pools is lovely, but not as cool as the pool area with a bar serving $26 burgers to celebrity clientele. The Restaurant, its proper name, is authentically Asian, with stainless-steel tandoori ovens, but with steep prices and small portions you may as well buy a ticket to Asia.

2001 Collins Ave., South Beach, FL 33139. (℃) **305/520-6000.** Fax 305/520-6600. www.setai.com. 135 units. Winter $950 studio suite, $25,000 penthouse; off season $475 studio suite, price available on request for penthouse. AE, DC, DISC, MC, V. Valet parking $30. **Amenities:** 2 restaurants; 3 bars; 3 pools; fitness center; spa; concierge; 24-hr. room service. *In room:* A/C, TV/DVD, CD player, complimentary Internet access, full kitchen in 1- and 2-bedroom suites only, minibar, coffeemaker, hair dryer, iron, safe.

The Shore Club 🎖   In the fickle world of hot hotels, The Shore Club secures its place at the top, thanks to Florida's only Nobu sushi restaurant and a celebrity clientele that would fill up an entire issue of *Us Weekly.* Because this hotel is infinitely more cavernous than its hipster neighbor, the Delano (see above), publicity-shy celebrities such as Janet Jackson and Denzel Washington have been known to call it their home away from home—there are indeed places for them to hide. An outpost of L.A.'s celebrity-laden SkyBar reigns supreme with a Marrakech-meets-Miami motif that stretches throughout the hotel's sprawling pool, patio, and garden areas. Beware of surly doormen if you're not a hotel guest. There's also a branch of L.A.'s—and Robert DeNiro's—pricey pasta spot Ago. Rooms (80 % of which have an ocean view) are loaded with state-of-the-art amenities and, frankly, have a bit more personality than those at the Delano.

1901 Collins Ave., Miami Beach, FL 33139. (℃) **877/640-9500** or 305/695-3100. Fax 305/695-3299. www. shoreclub.com. 309 units, including 8 bungalows. Winter $405–$715 double, $825–$1,300 suite, $2,200–$3,500 bungalow; off season $405–$715 double, $725–$1,125 suite, $1,700–$3,200 bungalow. AE, DC, MC, V. Valet parking $34. **Amenities:** 2 restaurants; 4 bars; 2 outdoor swimming pools; spa; concierge; 24-hr. room service. *In room:* A/C, TV, stereo/CD player, On Command System with digitally downloaded movies, high-speed Internet access, minibar.

The Tides 🎖🎖🎖   This 12-story Art Deco masterpiece reminiscent of a gleaming ocean liner, with porthole windows received a massive makeover by trend-setting designer Kelly Wearstler and is now a condo/hotel. Rooms have been newly washed in warm earth tones—a stark yet welcome contrast from its former Delano-esque all white. Also, all rooms are at least twice the size of a typical South Beach hotel room and have a breathtaking panoramic view of the ocean. The penthouses on the ninth and tenth floors are situated at the highest point on Ocean Drive, allowing for a priceless panoramic view of the ocean, the skyline, and the beach. Recent renovations to the one lackluster pool, including poolside cabanas and landscaping, have helped to bring it up to posh par. The hotel's restaurant, La Marea, is located in the lobby, and is good, but very pricey. A full selection of spa services is available in rooms and poolside.

1220 Ocean Dr., South Beach, FL 33139. © **800/439-4095** or 305/604-5070. Fax 305/503-3275. www.tidessouth beach.com. 45 elegantly appointed suites. Winter $695 studio suites, $3,500–$7,500 penthouse suites; off season $595 studio suites, $3,500–$7,500 penthouse suites. Additional guests (more than 2) $100. AE, DC, DISC, MC, V. Valet parking $32. Pets $150 1-time fee including new "Paws" program. **Amenities:** La Marea Restaurant, Lobby Lounge and Coral Bar; outdoor heated pool with poolside spa cabanas; fitness room; concierge; 24-hr. room service; 24-hr. "personal assistant" service, in-room massage; laundry service; dry cleaning; beach lounge service. *In room:* A/C, TV/VCR, stereo/CD player with selection of music, video rentals dataport, minibar, hair dryer, iron, safe.

Vincci South Beach 𝄐𝄐   This swank, $76 million, 80-suite, five-story hotel was a Regent for about 5 minutes before it was taken over by Vincci. With two entrances on Ocean Drive and Collins Avenue, the beach and nightlife are literally at your doorsteps. Every suite has floor-to-ceiling soundproof windows, which provide spectacular views. Bathrooms are huge with marble floors and a large shower with wall sprays and rain shower. Feather beds, duvets, and goose-down pillows make it hard to leave the room, as does the Bose surround sound and two flatscreens. A stunning glass-paneled-bottom pool provides prime viewing of the lounge scene below at Table 8 (an 8,000-sq.-ft. eatery imported from L.A.). The open-air fitness center with all the latest equipment is a refreshing (temperature-controlled) change from the usual stuffy gyms.

1458 Ocean Dr., South Beach, FL 33139. © **305/674-4554.** Fax 305/674-4553.www.vinccisouthbeach.com. 83 units. Winter $355–$1,050 suite; off season $215–$695 suite. AE, DC, DISC, MC, V. Valet parking $30. **Amenities:** Restaurant; lounge; pool; spa and fitness center; 24-hr. concierge; 24-hr. room service. *In room:* A/C, TV/DVD player, CD player, Wi-Fi, minibar, coffeemaker, hair dryer, iron, safe.

EXPENSIVE

Albion Hotel 𝄐   An architectural masterpiece, originally designed in 1939 by internationally acclaimed architect Igor Polevitzky (of Havana's legendary Hotel Nacional fame), this sleek, modern, nautical-style hotel was once the local headquarters for Abbie Hoffman and the Students for a Democratic Society during the 1972 Democratic National Convention in Miami. Though the Albion has fallen off the hipster radar somewhat and is in desperate need of a sprucing up of its lobby and pool areas, its location 2 blocks from the beach is key. Rooms have been fully renovated—no longer are they sterile and industrial chic, but much warmer and with color, taking a little of the edge off. While there is no restaurant in the hotel, for lighter fare, the mezzanine-level Pantry provides snacks and continental breakfast items. The Albion is more of a hotel for quiet, hip intellectual types rather than those who prefer to be on parade.

1650 James Ave. (at Lincoln Rd.), South Beach, FL 33139. © **877/RUBELLS** or 305/913-1000. Fax 305/674-0507. www.rubellhotels.com. 100 units. Winter $250–$395 double; off season $175–$205 double. AE, DC, DISC, MC, V. Valet parking $25. Pets accepted. **Amenities:** Bar; large outdoor heated pool; small exercise room; concierge; business and secretarial services; in-room massage; babysitting; dry cleaning; airport limo service. *In room:* A/C, TV/VCR, stereo w/CD and cassette player, dataport, complimentary Wi-Fi, minibar, hair dryer, iron.

Century Hotel 𝄐𝄐   Located in South Beach's trendy South of Fifth area, The Century was the hotel of choice for artists, celebrities, musicians, and a slew of quirky, eccentric, Warholian types—before the area became hip. Practically hidden at the southern tip of South Beach, the Century is a 1939 Hohauser masterpiece, which has been restored and fully modernized, with rooms featuring funky decor, hardwood floors, and a stellar marble bathroom with glass shower. There's no pool, but the beach is literally across the street, and the hotel is within walking distance of some of the hottest restaurants and bars in town. If you're one of those who is too cool to stay with the mainstream at The Shore Club, staying at the Century is like telling people you live in the coolest apartment building in the hippest neighborhood.

Hotel Dining

Although travelers don't necessarily choose a hotel by its dining options, a number of Miami's best restaurants can be found inside hotels. Some of the city's most hailed cuisine can be had at the Setai's **Restaurant,** Delano's **Blue Door** (p. 114), **Casa Tua's** eponymous eatery (p. 116), Loews Hotel's **Emeril's Miami Beach** (p. 117, The Hotel's **Wish** (p. 121), and Mandarin Oriental's **Azul** (p. 137). **Nobu** (p. 118), a New York import at The Shore Club, is the only one that doesn't take reservations unless you're a bona fide celebrity. See chapter 7 for reviews of these and other hotel restaurants.

140 Ocean Dr., South Beach, FL 33139. (C) **888/982-3688** or 305/674-8855. Fax 305/538-5733. www.centurysouth beach.com. 26 units. Year round $95–$350. Rate includes continental breakfast. AE, DC, DISC, MC, V. Valet parking $25. **Amenities:** 24-hr. concierge; In room: A/C, TV/VCR, stereo w/CD player, dataport, minibar, hair dryer, iron, safe.

The Hotel 𝒦𝒦𝒦   Kitschy fashion designer Todd Oldham whimsically restored this 1939 gem (formerly the Tiffany Hotel) as he would have restored a vintage piece of couture. He laced it with lush, cool colors, hand-cut mirrors, and glass mosaics from his ready-to-wear factory, and then added artisan detailing, terrazzo floors, and port-hole windows. The small, soundproof rooms are very comfortable and incredibly stylish, though the bathrooms are a bit cramped. Nevertheless, the showers are irresistible, with fantastic rain-head shower heads. There's no need to pay more for an oceanfront view here—go up to the rooftop, where the hip and funky Spire Bar and pool are located, and you'll have an amazing view of the Atlantic. The hotel's restaurant, Wish (p. 121), is one of South Beach's best.

801 Collins Ave., South Beach, FL 33139. (C) **877/843-4683** or 305/531-2222. Fax 305/531-3222. www.thehotelof southbeach.com. 53 units. Winter $285–$335 double, $425 suite; off season $215–$265 double, $355 suite. AE, DC, DISC, MC, V. Valet parking $18. **Amenities:** Restaurant; bar; pool bar; small pool; health club; concierge; business center; room service. In room: A/C, TV/VCR, stereo system with CD and cassette players, video library, dataport, minibar, coffeemaker, hair dryer.

Hotel Astor 𝒦𝒦   One of the hottest hotels on South Beach closed for renovations in 2006 and reopened in late 2007 with highly stylized rooms by designer Sam Robin who added handcrafted furniture, whangee-wood floors, Sisal carpets, and blond oak and whangee-wood cabinetry. Other new additions to the hotel include a nightlife butler who will guide you through South Beach's crazy club scene, a new restaurant, and a spa lap pool.

956 Washington Ave., South Beach, FL 33139. (C) **800/270-4981** or 305/531-8081. Fax 305/531-3193. www.hotel astor.com. 40 units. Winter $155–$220 double, $340–$700 suite; off season $125–$170 double, $220–$500 suite. AE, DC, MC, V. Valet parking $20. **Amenities:** Restaurant; 2 bars; pool; access to nearby health club; 24-hr. concierge service; secretarial services; room service; in-room massage; babysitting; laundry service; dry cleaning. In room: A/C, TV, dataport, minibar, fridge, hair dryer, safe.

Hotel Impala 𝒦 *Finds*   This charming Mediterranean hideaway is one of the area's best, and it's just beautiful, from the Greco-Roman frescos and friezes to an intimate garden that is perfumed with the scents of hanging lilies and gardenias. Rooms have super-cushy sleigh beds, Sisal floors, wrought-iron fixtures, imported Belgian cotton linens, wood furniture, and fabulous-looking, but also incredibly small, bathrooms done up in stainless steel and coral rock. The two smallest rooms here are nos. 102

and 206; otherwise, the rooms are pretty roomy and cushy. Adjacent to the hotel is Spiga (p. 128), an intimate, excellent Italian restaurant that is reasonably priced. Enclaves like this one are rare on South Beach. Rates include complimentary continental breakfast and access to Nikki Beach Club.

1228 Collins Ave., South Beach, FL 33139. (C) **800/646-7252** or 305/673-2021. Fax 305/673-5984. www.hotel impalamiamibeach.com. 17 units. Winter $195–$225 double, $325–$425 suite; off season $145–$195 double, $250–$325 suite. Rates include continental breakfast. AE, DC, MC, V. Valet parking $20. Small pets permitted. **Amenities:** Restaurant; concierge; room service. *In room:* A/C, TV/VCR, stereo/CD player, complimentary videos, high-speed Internet access, hair dryer.

Hotel Nash ☆ Bridging the gap between the hypertrendy and schlocky hotels often found on South Beach, the Hotel Nash is a rarity in that it boasts both style and substance. Located a block from the beach and behind the infamous Versace mansion, the Nash is housed in a 1930s Deco structure, which received an $11 million renovation. The result is a soothing, almost therapeutic hotel in which the scents of aromatherapy seep into every room and public space on the property. Walk through an aromatic indoor garden (of jasmine, bougainvillea, star anise, and cypress), or wade in one of three tiny yet intimate pools—two highlights of this beautiful hotel. Rooms overlook either the city or the Versace mansion observatory. Don't expect to see any celebrities here—the Hotel Nash is not about scene. In fact, it's not even on the hipster radar as far as hangouts are concerned, which, for some, is a blissful thing.

1120 Collins Ave., Miami Beach, FL 33139. (C) **305/674-7800.** Fax 305/538-8288. www.hotelnash.com. 50 units. Winter $230–$279 double, $325–$525 suite; off season $155–$225 double, $289–$495 suite. Rates change frequently. AE, DC, MC, V. Valet parking $25. **Amenities:** Restaurant; bar; 3 outdoor pools; watersports equipment/ rentals; car service. *In room:* A/C, TV/VCR or DVD player, CD player, dataport, minibar, hair dryer, iron, safe.

Hotel Ocean ☆ This Mediterranean enclave, located smack in the middle of crazy Ocean Drive, remains somehow protected from the disarray, perhaps due to the lovely French-style courtyard, in which live jazz is often performed. The European-style hotel's 27 suites are great, with soundproofed windows, terraces facing the ocean, massive bathrooms with French toiletries, and original fireplaces that add to the coziness, even if you're not likely to use them. Funky and comfy new furniture, wood flooring, and Spanish tile bathrooms with brand new (and sublime) 20-square-foot showers are the latest additions to the hotel's rooms. Room 504 is the hotel's best-kept secret, with ocean view and private balcony for a reasonable $360 a night. The hotel's restaurant, Hosteria Romana II, is known for its superb service, rustic decor, and big plates of Italian food. There's no pool, but since the beach is directly across the street, it really shouldn't stop you from staying at this excellent spot.

1230 Ocean Dr., Miami Beach, FL 33139. (C) **800/783-1725** or 305/672-2579. Fax 305/672-7665. www.hotelocean. com. 27 units. Winter $230–$280 double, $330–$515 suite, $750 penthouse; off season $199–$245 double, $290–$460 suite, $555 penthouse. Rates include continental breakfast. AE, DC, DISC, MC, V. Valet parking $20. Pets accepted for $15 per day. **Amenities:** Half-price admission to nearby health club; concierge; secretarial services; limited room service; babysitting; laundry service; dry cleaning. *In room:* A/C, TV/VCR (with video/CD library), CD player, dataport, minibar (stocked w/guests' personalized order), fridge, hair dryer, iron, safe.

Hotel St. Augustine ☆☆ *Finds* Proving that good things do, indeed, come in small packages is this diminutive, South of Fifth boutique hotel that's part spa, part hotel, and part haven for hipsters seeking refuge from the more mainstream boutique hotel cum hangouts. The lobby is minute, with an equally miniature bar, but at least there is a bar, and the rooms are smallish, but designed like cosmopolitan lofts, with maple wood beds and banquettes, and outstanding, spacious bathrooms with glass-enclosed spa cabinets with steam baths and European engineered multijet spray showers. Seriously, if you're into bathrooms, this is Nirvana. Dimmable lighting in the bathroom and a spa bar that offers aromatherapy oils, cooling eye masks, invigorating shower gels, body buffers, and protective sun products make it hard to leave the room. If we had to vote for best hotel bathroom in town, the St. Augustine would win, hands down.

347 Washington Ave., Miami Beach, FL 33139. © 800/310-7717 or 305/532-0570. Fax 305/532-8493. www.hotel staugustine.com. 24 units. Year-round $155–$175 double. Rates include continental breakfast. AE, DC, MC, V. Self-parking $15. **Amenities:** Bar; discounted use of nearby health club; 24-hr. concierge; video/CD library. *In room:* A/C, TV/VCR, CD player, dataport, minibar, hair dryer, spa bar.

Mercury ✪ *(Finds* Another South of Fifth hot spot, The Mercury is an upscale, modern all-suite resort that combines Mediterranean charm with trendy South Beach flair. The hotel is also attached to (but not affiliated with) two of the beach's best restaurants, Nemo and Shoji Sushi (p. 122 and 123, respectively), which also provide the hotel's room service. A small outdoor heated pool and Jacuzzi are located in a courtyard that's shared with the restaurant (yes, diners can see you swim). Accommodations are ultrastylish, with sleek light-wood furnishings, Mascioni cotton bedding, European kitchens, and spacious bathrooms with spa tubs. If you're able to splurge, the penthouse here is hypercool, with wraparound terrace and massive living and bedroom areas and kitchen. If you're looking to stay in style without the hassle of the South Beach hustle and bustle, this is the place for you.

100 Collins Ave., Miami Beach, FL 33139. © 877/786-2732 or 305/398-3000. Fax 305/398-3001. www.mercury resort.com. 44 units. Seasonal rates $165–$695. AE, DC, MC, V. Valet parking $25. **Amenities:** Heated pool; access to local fitness center (Crunch); Jacuzzi; concierge; room service; laundry service; free airport pickup; Wi-Fi. *In room:* A/C, TV/VCR, entertainment center with stereo w/CD player, fax, dataport, kitchen, minibar, coffeemaker, hair dryer.

Raleigh Hotel ✪✪ The Raleigh is quintessential old school Miami Beach with a modern twist. Polished wood, original terrazzo floors, and an intimate martini bar add to the fabulous atmosphere that's favored by fashion photographers, for whom the hotel's fleur-de-lis pool is the favorite subject. In fact, one look at the pool and you'll expect Esther Williams to splash up in a dramatic, aquatic plié. The entire outdoor area is a stunning oasis that elicits oohs and aahs from even the most jaded jet-setters. Thanks to the hotel's owner Andre Balazs (of New York's Mercer and Los Angeles's Chateau Marmont and Standard hotels fame), rooms have been redone with period furnishings, iPod docking stations, gourmet minibars, and terrazzo floors (those overlooking the pool and ocean are the most peaceful). The massive penthouse is a favorite among visiting celebrities and authors. But it's the Raleigh's warm, romantic Deco atmosphere that lures people away from chillier, neighboring boutique hotels.

1775 Collins Ave., Miami Beach, FL 33139. © 800/848-1775 or 305/534-6300. Fax 305/538-8140. www.raleighhotel. com. 104 units. Winter $495–$925 double, $950–$2750 suite; off season $225–$700 double, $700–$2000 suite. AE, DC, DISC, MC, V. Valet parking $30. **Amenities:** Restaurant; bar; coffee bar; fantastic large outdoor pool; concierge; business services; 24-hr. room service; massage; overnight laundry service. *In room:* A/C, TV/VCR, CD player, Wi-Fi, minibar, fridge, hair dryer, iron, safe.

⌒Fun Fact **Desi Was Here**

During the Raleigh Hotel's opening-night white-tie ball in 1940, a sick band member was replaced by a then-unknown local drummer. You may have heard of him: Desi Arnaz.

The Best Hotel Spas

- **Agua Spa at the Delano,** 1685 Collins Ave., Miami Beach (© 305/673-2900), is resplendently situated on the rooftop of the hotel, overlooking the Atlantic, and features stellar treatments such as the milk-and-honey massage that make it popular with celebs and laywomen alike. Lose yourself in a tub of fragrant oils, algae, or minerals for a 20-minute revitalization, or try the collagen, mud, and hydrating masks.
- **The Ritz-Carlton, Key Biscayne Spa,** 415 Grand Bay Dr., Key Biscayne (© 305/648-5900), is a sublime 20,000-square-foot West Indies–colonial style Eden in which you can treat yourself to over 60 treatments, including the Key Lime Coconut Body Scrub and the Everglades Grass Body Wrap. For a real splurge, the Fountain of Youth treatment is a 6-hour indulgence featuring a facial, massage, manicure, pedicure, shampoo, styling, and lunch served on the oceanview terrace.
- **The Standard,** 40 Island Ave., Miami Beach (© 305/673-1717), is an updated version of an old school, Borscht Belt–style, Miami Beach spa, featuring authentic Turkish hammam, a Wall of Sound Shower, cedar sauna room, and resplendent bayfront pool.
- **Fairmont Turnberry Isle Resort & Club,** 19999 W. Country Club Dr., Aventura (© 305/932-6200), offers a sprawling 25,000-square-foot spa with a massive menu of treatments, Finnish saunas, Turkish steam rooms, turbulent whirlpools, and bracing cold-plunge tubs that are sure to give you an uplifting jolt.
- **Spa Internazionale at Fisher Island,** 1 Fisher Island Dr., Fisher Island (© 800/537-3708), is the city's poshest spa, known for its picturesque

The Standard 𝒢𝒢   The quintessential spa resort, The Standard, owned by Raleigh owner Andre Balazs, is housed in Miami Beach's legendary Lido Spa spot, a place that was swinging back in the days when women still wore bathing caps. Today, the hotel is full of all the modern trappings of a swank spa resort, with a bayfront view and a serene location on the Venetian Causeway—walking distance to all the South Beach craziness. Remnants of the atomic age of the fabulous '50s still exist here—the lobby's white-marble walls, terrazzo floors, and stainless-steel elevators. Add to that a touch of Scandinavian retro modernism. Whitewashed guest rooms are serviced by roaming carts offering herbal teas and aromatherapy footbaths. There's a cedar sauna, a Turkish hammam, tongue-in-cheeky treatments such as the cellulite fighting Standard Spanking and a chlorine-free plunge pool, with a 12-foot-tall waterfall and DJ-spun music piped beneath the water, clothing-optional mud baths, and a waterfront restaurant with glorious waterfront views. Anything but standard.

40 Island Ave., Miami Beach, FL 33139. © 305/673-1717. Fax 305/673-8181. www.standardhotel.com. 105 units. $225–$1250 suite. AE, DC, DISC, MC, V. Valet parking $22. **Amenities:** Restaurant; bar; pool; spa; sauna; concierge. *In room:* A/C, TV/DVD, stereo/CD player, high-speed Internet access, minibar, hair dryer, iron, safe.

setting and the Guinot Paris Hydradermie facial—a 75-minute moisturizing and cleansing facial that leaves the skin silky smooth.

- **The Spa at Mandarin Oriental,** 500 Brickell Key Dr., Miami (© **305/913-8288**), is a luxe, tri-level spa preferred by the likes of Jennifer Lopez, among others, best known for its innovative and restorative treatments inspired by the ancient traditions of Chinese, ayurvedic, European, Balinese, and Thai cultures. The 17 private treatment rooms are done up in bamboo, rice paper, glass, and natural linens, and two of the spa's split-level suites include a personal multijet tub overlooking Biscayne Bay.
- **ESPA at Acqualina,** 17875 Collins Ave., Miami Beach (© **304/918-6844**), the first of its kind in the United States, offers the latest facials, advanced massages, and Ayurvedic experiences. The luxurious two-story spa overlooks the glistening Atlantic Ocean.
- **Sports Club/LA at the Four Seasons,** 1435 Brickell Ave., Miami (© **305/358-3535**). Although this 44,000-square-foot musclehead hangout is a cardio and weight-lifting-obsessed paradise, there's also a spa consisting of 10 treatment rooms including a couple's massage room and wet treatment room with Vichy showers.
- **Spa V at the Hotel Victor,** 1144 Ocean Dr., Miami Beach (© **305/728-6500**), a calming subterranean oasis designed by the world-renowned Jaques Garcia, offers signature European-inspired treatments and the first Turkish-style hammam on South Beach.

MODERATE

Aqua 🅖 *Value* It's been described as the Jetsons meets Jaws, but the Aqua isn't all Hollywood. Animated, yes, but with little emphasis on special effects and more on a friendly staff, Aqua is a good catch for those looking to stay in style without compromising their budget. Rooms are ultramodern in an Ikea sort of way—in other words, cheap chic. There are apartment-like junior suites, suites, and a really fabulous penthouse, but the standard deluxe rooms aren't too shabby either, with decent-size bathrooms and high-tech amenities. It's a favorite among Europeans and young hipsters on a budget. This '50s-style motel has definitely been spruced up and its sun deck, courtyard garden, and small pool are popular hangouts for those who prefer to stay off the nearby sand. A small yet sleek lounge inside is a good place for a quick cocktail, breakfast, or snack.

1530 Collins Ave., Miami Beach, FL 33139. © **305/538-4361.** Fax 305/673-8109. www.aquamiami.com. 45 units. Winter $160 double, $200–$400 suite; off season $95 double, $125–$395 suite. Rates include European-style breakfast buffet. AE, DISC, MC, V. Valet parking $18. **Amenities:** Lounge; bar; small pool. *In room:* A/C, TV, Web TV, CD player, minibar.

(Value) Two Good-Value South Beach Hotels

For a taste of South Beach action without breaking the bank, check out the **South Seas Hotel** (1751 Collins Ave.; ⓒ **800/345-2678** or 305/538-1411; www. southseashotel.com) or the **Avalon** (700 Ocean Dr.; ⓒ **800/933-3306** or 305/538-0133; www.avalonhotel.com). Both offer good deals on their websites for clean, functional rooms. The South Seas common areas may be bland, but the hotel sits on a stretch of Collins between the Delano and Raleigh—a great location if you want to hang at either hotel's happening poolside bar. The Avalon is smack in the middle of Ocean Drive's *Girls Gone Wild* scene; thumping bass and wet T-shirt contests might rage around you, but the hotel maintains an aura of Art Deco calm—as does its excellent restaurant, **A Fish Called Avalon.**

—*Kelly Regan*

The Catalina Hotel & Beach Club 𝒦𝒦   The Catalina is something straight out of an Austin Powers movie. It's groovy, indeed! Stylish but not at all stuffy, the Catalina is perhaps the only hotel in the area that can pull off using red shag carpeting—though it tends to get a bit mangy. The mod squad lobby decor gives way to rooms glazed in white with hints of bright colors featuring Tempur-Pedic Swedish mattresses, 300-thread-count Mascioni sheets, goose-down comforters and pillows, iPods, and, of course, flatscreen TVs. The hotel has a happening bar and lounge scene with a decidedly European jet-set vibe and a splashy beach club where you can get poolside manicures and pedicures. If Catalina is sold out, check out its sister hotel, the **Metropole Suites,** 635 Collins Ave. (ⓒ **305/672-0009;** www.metropolesouthbeach.com), another favorite for hipsters and recording artists. Rates there start at $195 in season and $125 off season.

1732 Collins Ave., South Beach, FL 33139. ⓒ **305/674-1160.** Fax 305/672-8216. www.catalinahotel.com. 136 units. Winter $225–$300 double; off season $125–$250 double. Rates include continental breakfast bar and unlimited happy-hour cocktails daily from 7–8pm. AE, DC, MC, V. Valet parking $30. **Amenities:** Restaurant; bar; pool; laundry services; Japanese koi fishpond; Zen garden. *In room:* A/C, TV/VCR, CD player, Wi-Fi ($15 a day), minibar, hair dryer, iron, safe.

Chesterfield Hotel, Suites and Day Spa 𝒦 *(Finds)*   A great hotel with little attitude, the Chesterfield is like a reasonably priced, high-fashion garment hidden on a rack full of overpriced threads. This charismatic sliver of a property has won the loyalty of fashion industrialists and romantics alike. The very central location (1 block from the ocean) is a plus, especially since the hotel lacks a pool. Most of the rooms are immaculate and reminiscent of a loft apartment; large bathrooms with big, deep tubs are especially enticing. However, some rooms are dark and have not had such upgrades (we have gotten complaints), and are to be avoided; do not hesitate to ask for a room change. We've also gotten complaints about the music coming from the hotel next door, but you have to realize that if you're staying on Collins or Washington avenues, you're going to hear noise: South Beach isn't known for its quiet, peaceful demeanor, but for R&R, try the hotel's new day spa!

841 Collins Ave., South Beach, FL 33139. ⓒ **305/673-3767.** Fax 305/535-9665. www.thechesterfieldhotel.com. 90 units. Winter $175–$245 suite, $395 penthouse; off-season $125–$195 suite, $335 penthouse. Additional person $20. AE, DC, MC, V. Valet parking $30. "Well-behaved" pets accepted. **Amenities:** Restaurants; 2 bars; reduced rates at local gym; day spa; concierge; business services. *In room:* A/C, TV, CD player, high-speed Internet access, minibar, hair dryer, safe.

The Clinton Hotel ⊕   The former president has nothing to do with this chic boutique hotel, but once he gets a gander of the model types who hang here, he may want to endorse it as his own. The Clinton Hotel is one of South Beach's newest renovated standouts, a formerly decrepit building that has benefited from a $12 million renovation that brings a space-age meets South Beach vibe to the area thanks to funky furniture, a somewhat sedate lobby bar, the pricey designer boutique Ona Saez, and a restaurant that has changed hands several times. Although boutique hotels are becoming as dime-a-dozen as, say, Holiday Inns, this one manages to stand out from the rest thanks to its inner sanctum of serenity that includes a sleek (but tiny) pool, private sunning deck, and rooftop spa.

825 Washington Ave., South Beach, FL 33139, ⊙ 305/938-4040. Fax 305/530-1472. www.clintonsouthbeach.com. 00 units. Winter $295–$450 suite; off season $149–$219 suite. AE, DC, DISC, MC, V. Valet parking $22. **Amenities:** Restaurant; bar; coffee and sandwich bar; pool bar; pool; spa and fitness center; concierge; room service. In room: A/C, TV, dataport, minibar, hair dryer, iron, safe.

Crest Hotel Suites ⊕ (Finds   One of South Beach's best-kept secrets, the Crest Hotel has a quietly fashionable, contemporary, relaxed atmosphere with friendly service. Built in 1939, the Crest was restored to preserve its Art Deco architecture, but the interior of the hotel is thoroughly modern, with rooms resembling cosmopolitan apartments. All suites have a living room/dining room area, kitchenette, and executive work space. An indoor/outdoor cafe with terrace and poolside dining isn't besieged with trendy locals, but does attract a younger crowd. Around the corner from the hotel is Lincoln Road, with its sidewalk cafes, gourmet restaurants, theaters, and galleries. In an effort to expand its quiet trendiness, the Crest opened its second hotel, the **South Beach Hotel,** at 236 21st St., in an area that presently isn't so great (though it's on its way up). Until the neighborhood goes through more of a renaissance, this second hotel should be a last resort if you can't get a room elsewhere.

1670 James Ave., Miami Beach, FL 33139. ⊙ 800/531-3880 or 305/531-0321. Fax 305/531-8180. www.crestgroup hotels.com/cresthotelsuites.htm. 64 units. Winter $120–165 double, $211 suite; off season $115 double, $175 suite. Packages available and 10% discount offered if booked on website. AE, MC, V. **Amenities:** Restaurant; cafe; pool; laundry service; dry cleaning. In room: A/C, TV, dataport, kitchenette, fridge, coffeemaker (in select units).

Essex House Hotel and Suites ⊕   The Essex House Hotel was created by Deco pioneer Henry Hohauser in 1938 and has received numerous awards for its authentic restoration. The hotel's whimsically created shiplike architecture rises from the shore with decks that are designed to take in succulent ocean breezes. The sleek Bauhaus interiors add to the distinct charm of the place. All suites feature solid-oak furnishings and have a fridge, wet bar, and Jacuzzi. Although the hotel is right on the pulse of South Beach's constant activity, the new double-glazed, sound-absorbing windows provide an acoustical barrier to the street noise. A spa pool graces the south patio and gardens. In an area where the infamous Al Capone used to play cards, there is now an intimate dining area where complimentary breakfast is served and evening cocktails can be enjoyed.

1001 Collins Ave., Miami Beach, FL 33139. ⊙ 800/553-7739 or 305/534-2700. Fax 305/532-3827. www.essexhotel. com. Winter $159–$269 double; off season $144–$266 double. Rates include breakfast. AE, DC, DISC, MC, V. **Amenities:** Bar; outdoor pool; concierge. In room: A/C, TV, dataport, fridge, coffeemaker, hair dryer, iron.

Greenview ⊕   Art Deco takes a decidedly Parisian turn in this 1939 Hohauser hotel completely renovated in 1994 by Parisian designer Chahan Minassian. The Greenview is located just 2 blocks from the ocean on a quiet corner that's close enough to the action, but far enough away that you'll actually feel secluded from the nearby hyperactivity. Recordings of Edith Piaf and Marlene Dietrich provide background to this elegantly understated hotel, whose jewel-box, living-room-like lobby opens to a serene courtyard. Rooms feature handcrafted furnishings, original Modernist artwork, hardwood floors, and Sisal area rugs, although some are rather tawdry and hostel-like. Hallways are a bit dingy, too, and a far cry from the inviting lobby. The best part about the hotel is the feel-at-home factor, bolstered by the complimentary baker's breakfast and iced tea and chocolate-chip cookies in the afternoon and evening.

1671 Washington Ave. (at Lincoln Rd.), Miami Beach, FL 33139. © **305/531-6588.** Fax 305/531-4580. 42 units. Winter $150–$230 double; off season $95–$175 double. Rates include complimentary baker's breakfast. AE, DC, DISC, MC, V. **Amenities:** Small business center; same-day laundry service. *In room:* A/C, TV.

Hotel Chelsea &
This funky Art Deco property is a boutique hotel with a bit of a twist, with accents and decor based on the Japanese art of feng shui. Soft amber lighting, bamboo floors, full-slate bathrooms, and Japanese-style furniture arranged in a way that's meant to refresh and relax you are what separate the Chelsea from just about any other so-called boutique hotel on South Beach. Complimentary breakfast, reduced rates for yoga classes, free drinks at happy hour, and, in case you've had enough relaxation, free passes to South Beach's hottest nightclubs are added bonuses.

944 Washington Ave. (at 9th St.), Miami Beach, FL 33139. © **305/534-4069.** Fax 305/672-6712. www.thehotel chelsea.com. 42 units. Winter $95–$225 double, $125–$245 king, $165–$300 minisuite; off-season $75–$125 double, $95–$145 king, $115–$165 minisuite excluding special event and holiday time periods; rates are subject to change. Rates include complimentary continental breakfast and complimentary cocktails 7–8pm daily. AE, MC, DC, V. Valet parking $20. **Amenities:** Bar; discounted pass to local gym; concierge; laundry services; discounted passes to Sobe Yoga studio; free pickup from the airport. *In room:* A/C, TV, CD player, dataport, minibar, hair dryer, iron, safe.

The Kent && (Value)
For a funky boutique hotel in the heart of South Beach, The Kent is quite a deal. All rooms feature blond wood floors and ultramodern steel furnishings and accessories, which surprisingly aren't cold, but rather inviting and whimsical. The staff is eager to please and the clientele comes largely from the fashion industry. Frequent photo shoots are coordinated in the lobby and conference room, where full office services are available. The Barbara Hulanicki decor is high on the kitsch factor, heavy on multicolored Lucite with toys and other assorted articles of whimsy, and even if you can't afford to stay in it, the very James Bond-esque Lucite Suite is a must-see. There's no pool or sun deck, but you're only 1 block from the beach here.

1131 Collins Ave., South Beach, FL 33139. © **866/826-KENT** or 305/604-5068. Fax 305/531-0720. www.thekenthotel. com. 54 units. Winter $145–$250 double; off season $79–$250 double. Additional person $15. Rates include continental breakfast bar. AE, DC, DISC, MC, V. Valet parking $16; self-parking $6. **Amenities:** Bar; laundry services; free e-mail access in lobby; garden. *In room:* A/C, TV/VCR, CD player, minibar, hair dryer, iron, safe.

Nassau Suite Hotel &&
Stylish and reasonably priced, this 1937 hotel feels more like a modern apartment building with its 22 suites (studios or one-bedrooms) featuring wood floors, rattan furniture, and fully equipped open kitchens. Beds are all king-size and rather plush, but the bed isn't the room's only place to rest: Each room also has a sitting area that's quite comfortable. Registered as a National Historic Landmark, the Nassau Suite Hotel may exist in an old building, but both rooms and lobby are fully modernized. The Nassau Suite caters to a young, hip crowd of both gay and straight guests. Continental breakfast is available for $5 per person.

1414 Collins Ave., South Beach, FL 33139. © **866/859-4177** or 305/532-0043. Fax 305/534-3133. www.nassau suite.com. 22 units. Winter $150 studio, $190 1-bedroom; off season $120 studio, $160 1-bedroom. AE, DC, DISC, MC,

V. Parking $12. **Amenities:** Access to nearby health club; bike rental; concierge; secretarial services. *In room:* A/C, TV, fax, DSL connection, coffeemaker, hair dryer.

Pelican Hotel 🌟🌟   Owned by the same creative folks behind the Diesel Jeans company, the fashionable Pelican is South Beach's only self-professed "toy-hotel," in which each of its 30 rooms and suites is decorated as outrageously as some of the area's more colorful drag queens. Each room has been designed daringly and rather wittily by Swedish interior decorator Magnus Ehrland. Countless trips to antiques markets, combined with his wild imagination, have turned room no. 309, for instance, into the "Psychedelic(ate) Girl," room no. 201 into the "Executive Fifties" suite, and no. 209 into the "Love, Peace, and Leafforest" room. But the most popular room is the tough-to-score no. 215, or the "Best Whorehouse," which is said to have made even former Hollywood madam Heidi Fleiss red with envy. The Ocean Drive location and the hotel's cafe make the Pelican a very popular people-watching spot.

826 Ocean Dr., Miami Beach, FL 33139. ℂ 800/7-PELICAN or 305/673-3373. Fax 305/673-3255. www.pelicanhotel. com. 30 units. Winter $240–$350 double, $480–$800 oceanfront suite; off season $165–$220 double, $330–$540 oceanfront suite. Valet parking $22. AE, DC, MC, V. **Amenities:** Restaurant; bar; access to area gyms; concierge; business services; room service; same-day laundry service; dry cleaning; complimentary beach chair, towel, and umbrella on the beach; Wi-Fi throughout the hotel. *In room:* A/C, TV, stereo/CD player, On Command movies and music, fridge, hair dryer, iron, safe.

South Beach Plaza Villas 🌟   This charming place and all its lush gardens, villas, suites, rooms, and bungalows stands apart from the rest of South Beach for one reason—it's the first and only entirely nonsmoking hotel in the area. The newly renovated Spanish Mediterranean-style 1930s villas feature wood-planked vaulted ceilings, fireplaces (just what we need here, though it does add to the cozy ambience), modern stainless-steel kitchens, and great lighting. The villas look down upon the spruced up so-called Exotic Hawaiian Gardens and waterfalls. Standard king-sized hotel rooms are nearly the same but without the kitchens. All rooms, of course, have flatscreen TVs, but strangely enough, not all have full length mirrors. If you plan to stay 4 or more nights, check out and check into one of the private bungalows featuring stainless-steel kitchens, bedroom, office, den, and pullout sofa. The bar is a great place for martinis, and the restaurant in the garden serves breakfast, lunch, and dinner.

1411 Collins Ave., South Beach, FL 33139. ℂ 305/531-1331. Fax 305/538-9898. www.brighamgardens.com. 23 units. Winter $100–$199 1-bedroom; off season $70–$110 1-bedroom. Additional person $10. 10% discount on stays of 7 days or longer. AE, MC, V. Pets accepted for $6 a night. **Amenities:** Bar; restaurant; concierge. *In room:* A/C, TV, dataport, fridge, coffeemaker, microwave.

Townhouse 🌟🌟   New York hipster Jonathan Morr felt that Miami Beach had lost touch with the bon vivants who gave the city its original cachet, so he decided to take matters into his own hands. His solution: this 67-room, five-story, so-called shabby-chic hotel. The charm of this hotel is in its clean and simple yet chic design with quirky details: exercise equipment that stands alone in the hallways, free laundry machines in the lobby, and a water bed–lined rooftop. Comfortable, shabby-chic rooms boast L-shaped couches for extra guests (for whom you aren't charged). Though the rooms are all pretty much the same, consider the ones with the partial ocean view. The hotel's basement features the hot sushi spot, Bond St. Lounge (p. 125).

150 20th St., South Beach, FL 33139. ℂ 877/534-3800 or 305/534-3800. Fax 305/534-3811. www.townhousehotel. com. 70 units. Winter $230–$325 double, $395 penthouse; off season $115–$185 double, $395 penthouse. Rates include Parisian-style (coffee and pastry) breakfast. AE, MC, V. Valet parking $25. **Amenities:** Restaurant; bar; workout stations; bike rental; free laundry service; rooftop terrace with water beds. *In room:* A/C, TV/VCR, CD player, dataport, fridge, hair dryer, safe.

Whitelaw Hotel 🌟 With a slogan that reads "Clean sheets, hot water, and stiff drinks," the Whitelaw Hotel stands apart from other boutique hotels with its fierce sense of humor. Only half a block from Ocean Drive, this hotel, like its clientele, is full of distinct personalities, pairing such disparate elements as luxurious Belgian sheets with shag carpeting to create an innovative setting. All-white rooms manage to be homey and plush, and not at all antiseptic, but some guests have complained that their rooms looked more like 1950s kitchens with linoleum floors than anything else. Bathrooms are pretty small and not that well stocked, and towels are sometimes in short supply, but those who stay here aren't really looking for luxury—they just want to party. Complimentary cocktails in the lobby every night from 7 to 8pm contribute to a very social atmosphere.

808 Collins Ave., Miami Beach, FL 33139. ✆ 305/398-7000. Fax 305/398-7010. www.whitelawhotel.com. 49 units. Winter $165–$225 double/king, $250–$300 minisuite; off season $95–$145 double/king, $145–$250 minisuite; during special events, rates are subject to change. Rates include complimentary continental breakfast and free cocktails in the lobby (daily 7–8pm). AE, DC, MC, V. Parking $30. **Amenities:** Lounge; concierge; business services; free airport pickup (to and from MIA); laundry service; complimentary passes to area nightclubs. *In room:* A/C, TV, CD player, Wi-Fi ($15 per day), minibar, hair dryer, safe.

INEXPENSIVE

Clay Hotel & International Hostel (Value 🌟 A member of the International Youth Hostel Federation (IYHF), the Clay occupies a beautiful 1920s-style Spanish Mediterranean building at the corner of historic Española Way. Like other IYHF members, this hostel is open to all ages and is a great place to meet people. The usual smattering of Australians, Europeans, and other budget travelers makes it Miami's best clearinghouse of "insider" travel information. Although a thorough renovation in 1996 made this hostel an incredible value and a step above any others in town, don't expect nightly turndown service or chocolates. But, for a hostel, it's full of extras. Ninety rooms have private bathrooms and 12 VIP rooms have balconies overlooking quaint Española Way. There are also male and female dorm rooms with four to six beds and private bathrooms. You will find occasional movie nights, an outdoor weekend market, and a tour desk with car rental available. Reservations for private rooms are essential in season and recommended year-round.

1438 Washington Ave. (at Española Way), South Beach, FL 33139. ✆ 800/379-2529 or 305/534-2988. Fax 305/673-0346. www.clayhotel.com. 120 units. $42–$88 double; $16–$20 dorm beds. During the off season, pay for 6 nights in advance and get 7th night free. MC, V. Parking $10. **Amenities:** Cafe; access to nearby health club; bike rental; concierge; computer center; coin-op washers and dryers; lockers; kitchen. *In room:* A/C, TV, dataport, fridge, hair dryer.

Clevelander A South Beach institution favored by the beer-swilling set, the Clevelander is best known for its neon- and glass-blocked poolside and bar used in countless photo shoots and Budweiser commercials. As far as its reputation as a hotel, well, it's conveniently located on Ocean Drive and it's dirt cheap considering its location. Unfortunately, the dirt didn't stop there—until a 2008 renovation closed the hotel so it could receive a major facelift in the form of new lobby and guest rooms with Wi-Fi and flatscreens, and, of course, more bars and a rooftop lounge. The makeover won't change the noise level, which on Ocean Drive can be deafening. Party animals don't mind at all. But if your idea of a party doesn't involve drinking challenges and wet-T-shirt contests, visit the Clevelander for a cocktail and stay elsewhere.

1020 Ocean Dr., Miami Beach, FL 33139. ✆ 305/531-3485. Fax 305/534-4707. www.clevelander.com. 60 units. Winter $159–$269 double; off season $129–$209 double. AE, DC, MC, V. Valet parking $20. **Amenities:** Outdoor cafe; bar; outdoor pool; rooftop decks. *In room:* A/C, TV, Wi-Fi.

Impressions

I think South Beach targets vacationers who, if not affluent, would like to feel that way for a little while.

—Rachel Ponce on PBS's *Going Places*

Hotel Shelley 𝕲 The renovated Hotel Shelley has a laid-back beach atmosphere, yet cutting-edge style. The architecturally sound boutique hotel built in 1931 in the heart of the Art Deco district of Miami Beach has reinvented itself with a complete $1.5-million renovation of its 49 guest rooms. Complete with Mascioni 300-thread-count linens, goose-down pillows and comforters, LCD plasma TVs, and custom-built cabinetry, the guest rooms at the Shelley allow you to chill out after a long day at the beach or rock out before a big night of partying. The subtle purple hues in the rooms and public areas are in true Art Deco style. The bar in the lobby offers free drinks from 7 to 8pm every night and VIP passes to area nightclubs. Located on Collins and 1 block from Ocean Drive, this hotel allows you to reach beach, shopping, or nightlife within a few minutes' walk.

844 Collins Ave., Miami Beach, Florida 33139 ℭ **305/531.3341.** Fax 305/535.9665. www.hotelshelley.com. 49 units. Winter $145–$225 double, $165–$245 king, $165–$300 minisuite; off season $75–$125 double, $95–$145 king; $115–$165 minisuite; during special events and holidays, rates are subject to change. Rates include free cocktails in the lobby. AE, DC, MC, V. Parking $30. **Amenities:** Lounge; concierge; laundry service; free airport pickup (to and from MIA); complimentary passes to area nightclubs; Wi-Fi. *In room:* A/C, TV, CD player, dataport, minibar, hair dryer, safe.

The Loft Hotel A boutique hotel along the lines of the Aqua (p. 89)—though less whimsical, enticing, and airy-feeling—this renovated apartment building (which really gives you the feeling of staying in an apartment rather than a hotel) offers 20 suites, all surrounding a tidy, tropically landscaped garden. Rooms are especially spacious, with queen-size beds, breakfast room, conversation area, and hardwood or tile floors. Bathrooms are brand new and, for an old Art Deco building, pretty spacious. This hotel is popular with young, hip European types, just as the Aqua is, but there isn't that much difference between the two hotels other than the fact that the Loft's rooms have fully equipped kitchens while Aqua's rooms don't, and Aqua has a bar/restaurant while the Loft does not. Prices at the Loft are very reasonable and the owners, who also own Villa Paradiso (see below), are extremely accommodating.

952 Collins Ave., Miami Beach, FL 33139. ℭ **305/534-2244.** Fax 305/538-1509. www.thelofthotel.com. 57 units. Winter $139–$179 double; off season $89–$129 double. AE, DC, MC, V. Valet parking $20. **Amenities:** On-site laundry; VIP passes to local nightclubs. *In room:* A/C, TV/VCR, kitchen, hair dryer.

Villa Paradiso 𝕲𝕲 *(Finds* This guesthouse, like South Beach Villas (see above), is more like a cozy apartment house than a hotel. There's no elegant lobby or restaurant, but the amicable staff is happy to give you a room key and advice on what to do. The recently renovated spacious apartments are simple but elegant—hardwood floors, French doors, and stylish wrought-iron furniture—and are remarkably quiet considering their location, a few blocks from Lincoln Road and all of South Beach's best clubs. All have full kitchens, and guests have a choice of either a queen or two double beds or foldout couches for extra friends. Bathrooms have recently been renovated with marble tile. All rooms overlook the hotel's pretty courtyard garden.

1415 Collins Ave., Miami Beach, FL 33139. (℃) **305/532-0616.** Fax 305/673-5874. www.villaparadisohotel.com. 17 units. Winter $100–$165 apartment; off season $75–$129 apartment. Weekly rates are 10% cheaper. Additional person $10. AE, DC, MC, V. Parking nearby $15. Pets (including small "nonbarking" dogs) accepted for $10 with a $100 deposit. **Amenities:** Coin-op washers/dryers. *In room:* A/C, TV, kitchen, fridge, coffeemaker.

2 Miami Beach: Surfside, Bal Harbour & Sunny Isles

The area just north of South Beach, known as Miami Beach, encompasses Surfside, Bal Harbour, and Sunny Isles. Unrestricted by zoning codes throughout the 1950s, 1960s, and especially the 1970s, area developers went crazy, building ever-bigger and more brazen structures, especially north of 41st Street, which is now known as Condo Canyon. Consequently, there's now a glut of medium-quality condos, with a few scattered holdouts of older hotels and motels casting shadows over the newer, swankier stays emerging on the beachfront.

The western section of the neighborhood used to be inundated with Brooklyn's elderly Jewish population during the season. Though the area still maintains a religious preference, visiting tourists from Argentina to Germany, replete with Speedos and thong bikinis, are clearly taking over.

Miami Beach, as described here, runs from 24th Street to 192nd Street, a long strip that varies slightly from end to end. Staying in the southern section, from 24th to 42nd streets, can be a good deal—it's still close to the South Beach scene, but the rates are more affordable. The North Beach area begins at 63rd Street and extends north to the city limit at 87th Terrace and west to Biscayne Bay (at Bay Dr. W.). Bal Harbour and Bay Harbor are at the center of Miami Beach and retain their exclusivity and character. The neighborhoods north and south of here, such as Surfside and Sunny Isles, have nice beaches and some shops, but are a little worn around the edges.

VERY EXPENSIVE

Alexander All-Suite Luxury Hotel *𝒦*   Just a few miles from happening South Beach or ritzy Bal Harbour, the Alexander is pricey, but worth it for the size of the suites and the doting attention. Like staying at a rich grandparent's condo, suites are spacious one- and two-bedroom miniapartments with private balconies overlooking the Atlantic Ocean and Miami's Intracoastal Waterway. Each contains a living room, a fully equipped kitchen, *two* bathrooms (one with just a shower and the other with a shower/tub combo), and a balcony. The hotel itself is well decorated, with sculptures, paintings, antiques, and tapestries, most of which were garnered from the Cornelius Vanderbilt mansion. Two oceanfront pools are surrounded by lush vegetation; one of these "lagoons" is fed by a cascading waterfall. Shula's Steak House, owned by former Dolphins football coach Don Shula, is open for lunch and dinner daily.

5225 Collins Ave., Miami Beach, FL 33140. (℃) **800/327-6121** or 305/865-6500. Fax 305/341-6553. www.alexander hotel.com. 150 units. Winter: 1-bedroom suite $399, 2-bedroom suite $599; Summer: 1-bedroom suite $239, 2-bedroom suite $399 and up. Packages available. AE, MC, V. Parking $25. Very small pets accepted for a $250 nonrefundable deposit for cleaning the suite. **Amenities:** 3 restaurants; 2 bars; 2 large outdoor pools; small fitness center; spa; Jacuzzis; sauna; watersports equipment/rentals; concierge; car rental through concierge; business center and secretarial services; salon; limited room service; in-room massage; laundry service; dry cleaning. *In room:* A/C, TV, VCR (upon request), radio, fax, dataport, Wi-Fi, kitchen, coffeemaker, hair dryer, safe.

EXPENSIVE

Double Tree Ocean Point Resort & Club *𝒦* *Kids*   The 166 all-suite luxury resort is a short drive from Aventura shopping and South Beach nightlife, if, in fact, you feel the need to go elsewhere for entertainment. With Ocean Point, you may not. Rooms are all done up a la condos—with studio, one-, two-, and three-bedroom floor plans. The rooms are quite luxurious, with 220-thread-count linens, a huge bathroom (with Jacuzzi tub), and kitchenettes. The European Health Spa has the usual menu of services as well as informative lectures. Tai chi on the beach and poolside treatments will have you wondering whether working out is such a chore. Kids' programs are impressive as well, as are the well-heeled, savvy staff, landscaped gardens, beach club, and pool with waterfalls.

17375 Collins Ave., Sunny Isles, FL 33160. ℂ 866/623-2678 or 305/940-5422. Fax 786/528-2519. www.ocean pointresort.com. 585 units. Year round $179–$490. AE, DC, MC, V. Valet parking $16. **Amenities:** 2 restaurants; poolside bar and grill; in-suite spa services; game room; concierge; business center; room service; babysitting; child-care center; laundry service; dry cleaning; airport pickup/drop off service. In room: A/C, TV/VCR, CD player, high-speed Internet dataport, fully equipped kitchen, minibar, coffeemaker, microwave, hair dryer, safe, washer/dryer.

The Palms Hotel & Spa ℛ   Although it's a bit off the beaten path, The Palms is a breezy antebellum tropical oasis in which Art Deco meets *Gone With the Wind*. On Thursdays, Fridays, and Saturdays, the hotel offers Yoga Under the Palms, complimentary Yoga sessions taking place in and around the hotel's garden. Rooms have been spruced up beautifully, bordering on boutiquey, with high-tech amenities, and if you're so inclined, you can take advantage of the hotel's Relax and Rejuvenate spa treatments in the comfort of your own room. In 2005, the rooms were given a "soft and cozy" upgrade with Sealy Posturepedic pillow-top mattresses and 300-thread-count linens. A huge outdoor area is landscaped with palms and hibiscus and has a large freshwater pool as its centerpiece. It faces a popular boardwalk for runners and strollers as well as a large beach where watersports equipment is available. A new spa debuted in 2008.

3025 Collins Ave., Miami Beach, FL 33140. ℂ 800/550-0505 or 305/534-0505. Fax 305/534-0515. www.thepalms hotel.com. 243 units. Winter $219–$599 double; $749 suite; off season $159–$579 double; $549 suite. AE, DC, MC, V. Valet parking $25. **Amenities:** Restaurant; poolside bar; lounge; heated pool; bike rental; concierge; tour desk; carrental desk; room service; laundry service; dry cleaning. In room: A/C, TV, CD player, Wi-Fi, minibar, hair dryer, iron, safe.

MODERATE

Bay Harbor Inn and Suites ℛℛ   This charming, quiet inn is just moments from the beach, fine restaurants, and the Bal Harbour Shops. The inn comes in two parts: The more modern section overlooks a swampy river and a heated outdoor pool. On the other side of the street, "townside," is the cozier, antiques-filled portion, where glass-covered bookshelves hold good beach reading. The rooms have a hodgepodge of wood furnishings (mostly Victorian replicas), while suites boast an extra half-bathroom. You can often smell the aroma of cooking from the restaurant below, which is operated by students at Johnson & Wales Culinary Institute.

9660 E. Bay Harbor Dr., Bay Harbor Island, FL 33154. ℂ 305/868-4141. Fax 305/867-9094. www.bayharborinn.com. 45 units. Winter $169–$199 double, $279 suite; off season $129–$159 double, $229 suite. Additional person $10. Rates include continental breakfast. AE, MC, V. Free parking and dockage space. **Amenities:** Restaurant; brunch room; bar; exercise room; concierge; business center; limited room service. In room: A/C, TV, dataport, minibar, hair dryer.

Circa39 Hotel ℛ *Finds*   Some folks like to get away, take a holiday from the neighborhood, which is why Circa39 had the wisdom to open up where it did—close enough to the South Beach action for those who want to play, but far enough away to actually get some sleep when you want it. The 86-room boutique (what else?) hotel known as the Copley Plaza circa 1939, hence the name, has been redone and spruced up with modern amenities such as high-speed Internet access, the requisite bistro conducive to

Miami Beach

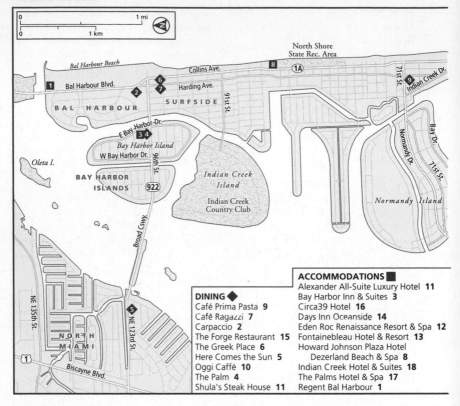

ACCOMMODATIONS ■
Alexander All-Suite Luxury Hotel **11**
Bay Harbor Inn & Suites **3**
Circa39 Hotel **16**
Days Inn Oceanside **14**
Eden Roc Renaissance Resort & Spa **12**
Fontainebleau Hotel & Resort **13**
Howard Johnson Plaza Hotel
  Dezerland Beach & Spa **8**
Indian Creek Hotel & Suites **18**
The Palms Hotel & Spa **17**
Regent Bal Harbour **1**

DINING ◆
Café Prima Pasta **9**
Café Ragazzi **7**
Carpaccio **2**
The Forge Restaurant **15**
The Greek Place **6**
Here Comes the Sun **5**
Oggi Caffé **10**
The Palm **4**
Shula's Steak House **11**

attracting hipsters, pool deck, tropical garden with massage cabanas, and fitness center. If you're looking to stay in a hip hotel but don't want to deal with the hubbub of being smack in the middle of things, this is a great option. Otherwise, consider staying in one of the countless boutiques on South Beach, where you'll get a lot more scene for your buck.

3900 Collins Ave., South Beach, FL 33139. © 877/824-7223 or 305/538-4900. Fax 305/538-4998. www.circa39. com. 82 units. Winter $139–$289 double; off season $119–$189 double. Additional person $25. AE, MC, V. Self-parking $15. Pet friendly. **Amenities:** Breakfast bistro; lounge; outdoor pool, tropical courtyard, concierge, fitness center; laundry service; dry cleaning. *In room:* A/C, TV, high-speed Internet access, minibar, fridge, coffeemaker, hair dryer, iron, safe, radio/clock.

Howard Johnson Plaza Hotel Dezerland Beach and Spa
The Dezerland is where *Happy Days* meets Miami Beach, with its visible homage to hot rods and antique cars. Visitors, many of them German tourists, are welcomed by a 1959 Cadillac stationed by the front door, one of a dozen mint-condition classics around the grounds and lobby. The hotel's Nirvana Spa is a popular Turkish-style bathhouse, but the best part about this place is the cheesy restaurant in which you dine in classic cars. The rooms are still somewhat lackluster, despite the fact that the renovation added new drapes, bedspreads, furniture, and wall coverings. Though named for various

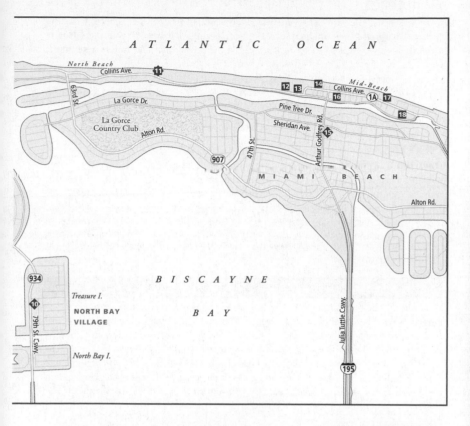

fabulous cars, these, alas, are the Pintos of hotel rooms—nothing more than a typical motel room. The lovely pool, however, has its requisite Cadillac—a mosaic pink one, located at the bottom. For '50s kitsch and car fanatics, this is a fun place to stay; otherwise, you may think you were taken for a ride.

8701 Collins Ave., Miami Beach, FL 33154. © **800/331-9346** in the U.S., 800/331-9347 in Canada, or 305/865-6661. Fax 305/866-2630. www.dezerhotels.com. 225 units. Winter $99–$139 double; off season $69–$99 double. Additional person $10. Special packages and group rates available. AE, DC, DISC, MC, V. **Amenities:** Restaurant; pool; nearby tennis courts; full spa; Jacuzzi; watersports equipment/rentals; tour desk; car-rental desk; shuttle service to Aventura Mall and South Beach (Art Deco Section); coin-op washers/dryers. *In room:* A/C, TV, kitchen in some rooms, fridge (on request), hair dryer, iron, safe.

Indian Creek Hotel and Suites 🅐 *Finds*   Located off the beaten path, the Indian Creek Hotel is a meticulously restored 1936 building with one of the first operating elevators in Miami Beach. Because of its location facing the Indian Creek waterway and its lush landscaping, this place feels like an old-fashioned Key West bed-and-breakfast. The revamped rooms are outfitted in Art Deco furnishings, such as antique writing desks, pretty tropical prints, and small but spotless bathrooms. Just 1 block from a good stretch of sand, the hotel also has a landscaped pool area in the back garden. Although one reader who stayed there complained that the staff was surly, the room was dirty, the lush courtyard was overgrown and he wasn't informed that he needed a parking pass—obtainable at the hotel—the good news is that there is new ownership and things seem to be running more smoothly. The hotel's restaurant, Creek 28, is one of Miami's best kept secrets.

2727 Indian Creek Dr. (1 block west of Collins Ave. and the ocean), Miami Beach, FL 33140. ℂ **800/491-2772** or 305/531-2727. Fax 305/531-5651. www.indiancreekhotel.com. 61 units. Winter $149–$199 double, $269–$289 suite; off season $69–$199 double, $179–$249 suite. Additional person $25. Group packages and summer specials available. AE, DC, DISC, MC, V. **Amenities:** Restaurant; bar; pool; concierge; limited room service. *In room:* A/C, TV/VCR, CD player in suites, wireless Internet, fridge (in suites), hair dryer.

INEXPENSIVE

Days Inn Oceanside *Value* One of the most economical choices for travelers, this hotel has been refurbished in splashy pastels and bright lavenders. It's clean and cheap, and children under 17 stay free. A kosher Chinese restaurant is on the premises.

4299 Collins Ave., Miami Beach, FL 33140. ℂ **800/356-3017** or 305/673-1513. Fax 305/538-0727. 143 units. Winter $119–$299 double; off season $99–229 double. AE, MC, V. Garage and self-parking available at $16 plus tax per day. No Pets accepted. **Amenities:** 2 restaurants; lounge; pool; access to nearby watersports; concierge; room service; laundry service; dry cleaning; free 24/7 lobby coffee. *In room:* A/C, TV, free wireless Internet, fridge (at charge), coffeemakers, iron/ironing board, safe.

3 Key Biscayne

Locals call it the Key, and technically, Key Biscayne is the northernmost island in the Florida Keys, even though it's located in Miami. A relatively unknown area until Richard Nixon bought a home here in the '70s, Key Biscayne, at 1¼ square miles, is an affluent but hardly lively residential and recreational island known for its pricey homes, excellent beaches, and actor Andy Garcia, who makes his home here. The island is far enough from the mainland to make it feel semiprivate, yet close enough to downtown for guests to take advantage of everything Miami has to offer.

For a map of these listings, see p. 149.

VERY EXPENSIVE

The Ritz-Carlton Key Biscayne 🌟🌟🌟 *Kids* The Ritz-Carlton takes Key Biscayne to the height of luxury with 44 acres of tropical gardens, a 20,000-square-foot European-style spa, and a world-class tennis center under the direction of tennis pro Cliff Drysdale. Decorated in British Colonial style, The Ritz-Carlton is straight out of Bermuda, with its impressive flower-laden landscaping. The Ritz Kids programs provide children ages 5 to 12 with fantastic activities, and the 1,200-foot beachfront offers everything from pure relaxation to fishing, boating, or windsurfing. Spacious and luxuriously appointed rooms are elegantly Floridian, featuring large balconies overlooking the ocean or lush gardens. The oceanfront Italian restaurant Cioppino is excellent for formal dining, or if you prefer casual dining, the oceanfront Cantina Beach serves great Mexican food and even a Tequlier—a sommelier for tequila—and a brand new Rum Bar. The hotel's remote location—just a 10-minute drive from the hustle and bustle—makes it a favorite for those (John Travolta, among others) who want to avoid the hubbub.

455 Grand Bay Dr., Key Biscayne, FL 33149. ℂ **800/241-3333** or 305/365-4500. Fax 305/365-4501. www.ritz carlton.com. 402 units. Winter $669 double, $954 suite; off season $289 double, $499 suite. AE, DC, DISC, MC, V. Valet parking (call for fees). **Amenities:** 3 restaurants; 2 bars; 2 outdoor heated pools; tennis center with lessons available; fitness center; spa; watersports equipment; children's programs; concierge; business center; shopping boutique; salon; 24-hr. room service; overnight laundry service. *In room:* A/C, TV, dataport, minibar, hair dryer, safe.

MODERATE

Silver Sands Beach Resort   If Key Biscayne is where you want to be and you don't want to pay the prices of the Ritz next door, consider this quaint one-story motel. Everything is crisp and clean, and the pleasant staff will help with anything you may need, including babysitting. But despite the name, it's certainly no resort. Except for the beach and pool, you'll have to leave the premises for almost everything else, including food. The well-appointed rooms are very beachy, sporting a tropical motif and simple furnishings. Oceanfront suites have the added convenience of full kitchens, with stoves and pantries. You'll sit poolside with an unpretentious set of Latin-American families and Europeans who have come for a long and simple vacation—and get it.

301 Ocean Dr., Key Biscayne, FL 33149. ⓒ **305/361-5441.** Fax 305/361-5477. 56 units. Winter $169–$349 double; off season $129–$309 double. Additional person $30. Weekly rates available. AE, DC, MC, V. Free parking. **Amenities:** Medium-size pool; secretarial services; coin-op washers/dryers. *In room:* A/C, TV, VCR (in some rooms), kitchenette, fridge, coffeemaker, microwave.

4 Downtown

If you've ever read Tom Wolfe's *Bonfire of the Vanities,* you may understand what downtown Miami is all about. If not, it's this simple: Take a wrong turn and you could find yourself in some serious trouble. Desolate and dangerous at night, downtown is trying to change its image, but it's been a long, tedious process. Recently, however, part of the area has experienced a renaissance in terms of nightlife, with several popular dance clubs and bars opening up in the environs of NE 11th Street off Biscayne Boulevard. If you're the kind of person who digs an urban setting, you may enjoy downtown, but if you're looking for shiny, happy Miami, you're in the wrong place (for now). As posh, pricey lofts keep going up faster than the nation's deficit, downtown is about to experience the renaissance it has been waiting for. Keep your eye on this area, and remember that you read it here first: Like orange—or pink, or white, or blue—being the new black, downtown Miami will be the new South Beach.

Most downtown hotels cater primarily to business travelers and cruise passengers. Although business hotels can be expensive, quality and service are of a high standard. Look for discounts and packages on weekends, when offices are closed and rooms often go empty.

VERY EXPENSIVE

Conrad Miami 🏵🏵🏵   Although you won't find ubiquitous Hilton heiresses Paris and Nicky at this business-oriented hotel (they hang out on South Beach), you will find luxury-lovers who have no interest in minimalism or J-Lo spottings. In this 203-room, 36-floor skyscraper located in the heart of Miami's financial district, you may feel as if you're in an office building, but once you walk over the bridge across a sparkling pool, visions of cramped cubicles and bad lighting will immediately disappear. Located on the 26th floor, the lobby is illuminated by a magnificent atrium that shares the attention with a restaurant, lounge, and bar and splits the difference between the 203-guest rooms and the 116 fully serviced luxury apartments. All rooms feature hyper–high-tech amenities and, best of all, INNCOM, a bedside remote that controls all lights, thermostat, and DO NOT DISTURB signs in the room. There's a superbly equipped gym, spa, and two tennis courts.

1395 Brickell Ave., Miami, FL 33131. ℭ 305/503-6500. Fax 305/533-7177. www.conradmiami.com. 203 units. Winter $269–$319 double; off season $159–$239 double. AE, DC, DISC, MC, V. Valet parking $20. **Amenities:** 2 restaurants; 2 bars; rooftop pool; fitness center; full-service spa; outdoor Jacuzzi; concierge; 24-hr. business center; babysitting; laundry service. In room: A/C, TV/VCR/DVD player, dataport, coffeemaker, minibar, hair dryer, iron, safe.

The Four Seasons 🐾🐾🐾 (Kids)   Deciding between the hyperluxe Mandarin Oriental and the equally luxe, albeit somewhat museum-like Four Seasons is almost like trying to tell the difference between Eva and Zsa Zsa Gabor. There are some obvious differences and some similarities, but they're kind of subtle. While the architecturally striking Mandarin is located on the semiprivate Brickell Key, the 70-story Four Seasons resembles an office building and is smack in the middle of the business district. The rooms and suites are plush, and, as with the Mandarin, service is paramount. Most rooms overlook Biscayne Bay, and while all rooms are cushy, thanks to the hotel's signature "untucked" beds, the bland decor leaves a lot to be desired, really. The best rooms are the corner suites with views facing both south and east over the water. There are three gorgeous pools spread out on more than 2 acres with cabanas featuring flatscreen TVs, private bars, and iPod docking stations. There's also a phenomenal kids' program and, for chocoholics, an all-you-can-eat chocolate buffet every Friday and Saturday night for $21 per person. Eat that, Mandarin!

1435 Brickell Ave., Miami, FL 33131. ℭ 305/358-3535. Fax 305/358-7758. www.fourseasons.com/miami.com. 260 units. Winter, $475–$575 double; $675 suite; off season $350–$450 double, $550 suite. AE, DC, DISC, MC, V. Valet parking $30. **Amenities:** 2 restaurants; martini bar; outdoor bar; 3 outdoor pools; The Sports Club/LA fitness center; full-service spa; outdoor Jacuzzi; concierge; 24-hr. business center. In room: A/C, TV, dataport, minibar, hair dryer, iron, safe.

Hotel Inter-Continental Miami 🐾   This hotel presents a serious catch-22: It's got a front-row view of all of Miami Beach, Biscayne Bay, the Miami River, and the Atlantic Ocean, but it is also located in downtown Miami. If it's a view that you want, stay here; but if it's location you want, reconsider. With the decidedly threatening presence of the hyperluxurious Mandarin Oriental just over the Brickell Bridge, the Inter-Continental had no choice but to keep up with the competition. A $34-million renovation renders it downtown-proper's swankiest hotel. It boasts more marble than the Liberace Museum, but it is warmed by bold colors and a fancified Florida flavor. Rooms are a tad nicer than those in a typical chain hotel, with marble bathrooms and sit-in windowsills. A new spa is in the works for late 2008. *Note:* Construction on several new condominiums adjacent to the Inter-Continental may disturb the deafening silence common to downtown Miami.

100 Chopin Plaza, Miami, FL 33131. ℭ 800/327-3005 or 305/577-1000. Fax 305/577-0384. www.icmiamihotel.com. 641 units. Winter $179–$389 double; off season $139–$339 double; year-round $550–$3,000 suite. Additional person $30. Weekend and other packages available. AE, DC, DISC, MC, V. Valet parking $20. **Amenities:** 3 restaurants; 2 lounges; Olympic-size outdoor heated pool; access to nearby golf course; spa; concierge; tour desk; car-rental desk; large business center; shopping arcade; salon and barbershop; 24-hr. room service; coin-op washers/dryers; 24-hr. laundry and dry-cleaning service. In room: A/C, TV/VCR, CD player, minibar, coffeemaker, hair dryer.

Mandarin Oriental, Miami 🐾🐾🐾   Corporate big shots and celebrities not in the mood for the South Beach spotlight have a high-end luxury hotel to stay in while wheeling and dealing their way through Miami. Catering to business travelers, big-time celebrities (J-Lo, Jacko, Will Smith, and so on), and the leisure traveler who doesn't mind spending big bucks, the swank Mandarin Oriental features a waterfront location, residential-style rooms with Asian touches (most with balconies), and upscale dining. The waterfront view of the city is the hotel's best asset. The hotel's two

Downtown Miami

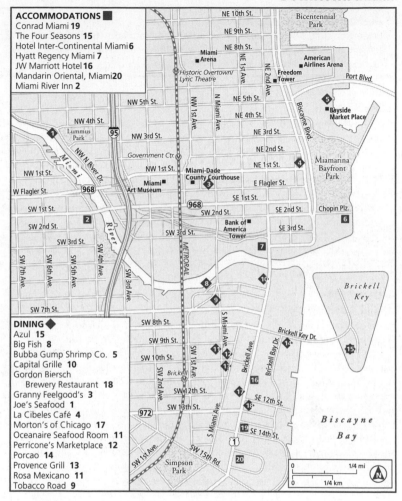

ACCOMMODATIONS ■
Conrad Miami **19**
The Four Seasons **15**
Hotel Inter-Continental Miami **6**
Hyatt Regency Miami **7**
JW Marriott Hotel **16**
Mandarin Oriental, Miami **20**
Miami River Inn **2**

DINING ◆
Azul **15**
Big Fish **8**
Bubba Gump Shrimp Co. **5**
Capital Grille **10**
Gordon Biersch
    Brewery Restaurant **18**
Granny Feelgood's **3**
Joe's Seafood **1**
La Cibeles Café **4**
Morton's of Chicago **17**
Oceanaire Seafood Room **11**
Perricone's Marketplace **12**
Porcao **14**
Provence Grill **13**
Rosa Mexicano **11**
Tobacco Road **9**

restaurants, the high-end Azul (p. 137) and the more casual Café Sambal, are two of Miami's best, as is the 15,000-square-foot spa, in which traditional Thai massages and ayurvedic treatments are the norm. The hotel is also home to a 20,000-foot white-sand beach club with a fabulous Friday night happy hour, complete beach butlers, and beachside cabana treatments, which is nice, considering that the hotel is 15 minutes from the beach.

500 Brickell Key Dr., Miami, FL 33131. ✆ 305/913-8383. Fax 305/913-8300. www.mandarinoriental.com. 326 units. $435–$900 double; $1,3000–$6,500 suite. AE, DC, DISC, MC, V. Valet parking $24 plus tax. **Amenities:** 2 restaurants; 3 bars; Oasis Beach Club; infinity pool, nearby tennis and golf; state-of-the-art fitness center; full-service holistic spa; spa wellness rooms; outdoor Jacuzzi; outdoor jogging trail; South Beach retreat; concierge; business center; 2 shops including Shanghai Tang boutique. *In room:* A/C, TV, dataport, high-speed Internet, minibar, hair dryer, iron, safe, Aromatherapy Associates amenities.

Wanna Be Signin' Something

Celebrity tidbit: Michael Jackson stayed at the **Mandarin Oriental Miami** and felt the need to sign his name to a painting in his suite—despite the fact that he didn't paint it. Amused, the hotel decided to keep it.

EXPENSIVE

Hyatt Regency Miami ☞   The Hyatt Regency is located just off the Miami River in the heart of downtown Miami. It shares space with the Miami Convention Center, the James L. Knight Convention Center Theater, an exhibition hall, and a 5,000-seat auditorium and concert hall. This hotel is perfect for large groups, business travelers, or basketball fanatics in town to see the Miami Heat play at the nearby American Airlines Arena. The People Mover and Metrorail are just blocks away, and water taxis are available at the front steps. Most of the spacious, recently renovated guest rooms have great bathrooms, products, and a balcony with a view of either the city or the bay.

400 SE Second Ave., Miami, FL 33131. ☎ 800/233-1234 or 305/358-1234. Fax 305/374-1728. www.miami.hyatt. com. 612 units. Winter $309–$349 double, suite $369–$409; off season $219–$259 double, $269–$349 suite. AE, DC, DISC, MC, V. Valet parking $18. **Amenities:** Restaurant; outdoor pool; health club; extensive business center. *In room:* A/C, TV, dataport, coffeemaker, hair dryer, safe.

MODERATE

Miami River Inn ☞☞☞ *(Finds)*   The Miami River Inn, listed on the National Register of Historic Places, is a quaint, country-style hideaway (Miami's *only* bed-and-breakfast!), consisting of four cottages smack in the middle of downtown Miami. In fact, it's so hidden that most locals don't even know it exists, which only adds to its panache. Every room has hardwood floors and is uniquely furnished with antiques dating from 1908. In one room, you might find a hand-painted bathtub, a Singer sewing machine, and an armoire from the turn of the 20th century, restored to perfection. Thirty-eight rooms have private bathrooms—4 have a shower only, 6 have a tub only, and 28 have a splendid tub/shower. One- and two-bedroom apartments are available as well. In the foyer, you can peruse a library filled with books about old Miami. It's close to public transportation, restaurants, and museums, and only 5 minutes from the business district.

118 SW South River Dr., Miami, FL 33130. ☎ 800/468-3589 or 305/325-0045. Fax 305/325-9227. www.miami riverinn.com. 38 units. Winter $149–$299 double; off season $89–$139 double. Rates include continental breakfast and parking. Additional person $15. AE, DC, DISC, MC, V. Free parking. Pets accepted for $25 per night. **Amenities:** Small pool; access to nearby gym facilities; Jacuzzi; babysitting; laundry service; dry cleaning; coin-op washers and dryers. *In room:* A/C, TV, hair dryer (upon request), iron/ironing board (upon request).

5 Coral Gables

Translated appropriately as "City Beautiful," the Gables, as it's affectionately known, was one of Miami's original planned communities and is still among the city's prettiest and most pedestrian-friendly, albeit preservation-obsessed, neighborhoods. Pristine with a European flair, Coral Gables is best known for its wide array of excellent upscale restaurants of various ethnicities, as well as a hotly contested (the quiet city didn't want to welcome new traffic) shopping megacomplex with upscale stores such as Nordstrom.

The Biltmore's Oldest Guests

Rumor has it that Al Capone, for whom the Biltmore's Everglades Suite is nick-named, roams the halls here, as do wounded soldiers from the days when this was a post WWII-hospital. Even if you don't stay at the Biltmore, a tour of the property is worth taking (call (C) **305/445-1926** for more information; see p. 182).

If you're looking for luxury, Coral Gables has a number of wonderful hotels, but if you're on a tight budget, you may be better off elsewhere. One well-priced chain in the area is the **Holiday Inn**, 1350 S. Dixie Hwy. ((C) **800/HOLIDAY** or 305/667-5611), with rates between $99 and $199. It's directly across the street from the University of Miami and is popular with families and friends of students.

For a map of these listings, see p. 153.

VERY EXPENSIVE

Biltmore Hotel 𝕽𝕽𝕽   A romantic sense of old-world glamour combined with a rich history permeates the Biltmore as much as the pricey perfume of the guests who stay here. Built in 1926, it's the oldest Coral Gables hotel and is a National Historic Landmark—one of only two operating hotels in Florida to receive that designation. Rising above the Spanish-style estate is a majestic 300-foot copper-clad tower, mod-eled after the Giralda bell tower in Seville and visible throughout the city. Large Moor-ish-style rooms are decorated with tasteful decor, European feather beds, Egyptian cotton duvets, writing desks, and some high-tech amenities. The landmark 23,000-square-foot winding pool now has the requisite hipster accessories—the private cabana, al fresco bar, and restaurant. Always a popular destination for golfers, includ-ing former president Clinton (who stays in the Al Capone suite), the Biltmore is sit-uated on a lush, rolling, 18-hole Donald Ross course that is as challenging as it is beautiful. Sunday brunch is an equal feat—book early.

1200 Anastasia Ave., Coral Gables, FL 33134. (C) **800/727-1926** or 305/445-1926. Fax 305/442-9496. www.biltmore hotel.com. 276 units. Winter $395–$895 double; off season $229–$499 double; year-round $659–$6,500 specialty suites. Additional person $20. Special packages available. AE, DC, DISC, MC, V. Overnight valet parking $25; self-park-ing free. **Amenities:** 4 restaurants; 4 bars; outdoor pool; 18-hole golf course; 10 lit tennis courts; state-of-the-art health club; full-service spa; sauna; concierge; car rental through concierge; elaborate business center; secretarial services; salon; 24-hr. room service; laundry service; dry cleaning; wine cellar. *In room:* A/C, TV, VCR (upon request), fax, dataport, kitchenette (in tower suites), minibar, hair dryer, iron, safe.

Hyatt Regency Coral Gables 𝕽𝕽   High on style, comfort, and price, this Hyatt is part of Coral Gables' Alhambra, an office-hotel complex with a Mediterranean motif. The building itself is gorgeous, designed with pink stone, arched entrances, grand courtyards, and tile roofs. Most recently, the pool and lobby were beautifully renovated. Inside you'll find overstuffed chairs on marble floors surrounded by opu-lent antiques and chandeliers. The large guest rooms are comfortable, if uninspired. A few rooms have balconies. Though the hotel fails to authentically mimic something much older and much farther away, it is attractive in its newness and is an excellent place from which to admire the more historic properties in the neighborhood.

50 Alhambra Plaza, Coral Gables, FL 33134. (C) **800/233-1234** or 305/441-1234. Fax 305/441-0520. www.coral gables.hyatt.com. 242 units. Winter $329–$389 double; off season $159–$179 double; year-round $219–$1,800 1-bedroom suite, $575–$2,050 2-bedroom suite. Additional person $25. Packages and senior discounts available. AE, MC, V. Valet parking $14; self-parking $11. **Amenities:** Restaurant; bar; large outdoor heated pool; nearby golf

course; health club; Jacuzzi; 2 saunas; concierge; business center; limited room service; in-room massage; babysitting; same-day laundry service; dry cleaning. *In room:* A/C, TV, fax (in some rooms), dataport, minibar, coffeemaker, hair dryer, iron, safe.

EXPENSIVE

David William Hotel 🦋🦋   This sister hotel to the Biltmore shares many of the same amenities without the Biltmore's price. Although it's located in a residential area, you can take a shuttle from here to the Biltmore to play a round of golf, enjoy the health club and spa, play tennis, or take a dip in the pool. The luxurious one- and two-bedroom suites are extremely spacious and have eat-in kitchens for extended stays. For a spectacular view of Miami, go up to the roof and have a drink by the pool. The hotel, which has undergone a recent external renovation, is directly across the street from the Granada Golf Course, less than 5 miles from the airport, and only 20 minutes from Miami Beach.

700 Biltmore Way, Coral Gables, FL 33134. ℂ 800/757-8073 or 305/445-7821. Fax 305/913-1933. www.david williamhotel.com. 65 units. Winter $179–$499 double; off season $99–$399 double. AE, DISC, MC, V. Valet parking $12; limited free self-parking. **Amenities:** Restaurant; rooftop pool; room service (dinner only). *In room:* A/C, TV, kitchenette (in deluxe rooms), minibar, coffeemaker, hair dryer, iron, safe.

Hotel St. Michel 🦋🦋🦋   This European-style hotel, in the heart of Coral Gables, is one of the city's most romantic options. The accommodations and hospitality are straight out of Old-World Europe, complete with dark-wood-paneled walls, cozy beds, beautiful antiques, and a quiet elegance that seems startlingly out of place in trendy Miami. Everything here is charming—from the brass elevator and parquet floors to the paddle fans. One-of-a-kind furnishings make each room special. Bathrooms are on the smaller side, but are hardly cramped. All have tub/showers except for two, which have one or the other. If you're picky, request your preference. Guests are treated to fresh fruit upon arrival and enjoy perfect service throughout their stay. The exceptional Restaurant St. Michel is a very romantic dining choice. *Tip:* Ask for the hotel's stay-and-dine specials in which dinner is included in the rate.

162 Alcazar Ave., Coral Gables, FL 33134. ℂ 800/848-HOTEL or 305/444-1666. Fax 305/529-0074. www.hotel stmichel.com. 27 units. Winter $200 double, $250 suite; off season $125 double, $155 suite. Additional person $10. Rates include continental breakfast and fruit basket upon arrival. AE, DC, MC, V. Self-parking $7. **Amenities:** Restaurant; lounge; access to nearby health club; concierge; room service; laundry service; dry cleaning; Wi-Fi in all public areas. *In room:* A/C, TV, dataport, hair dryer, iron/ironing board (upon request).

6 Coconut Grove

This waterfront village hugs the shores of Biscayne Bay, just south of U.S. 1 and about 10 minutes from the beaches. Once a haven for hippies, head shops, and artsy bohemian characters, the Grove succumbed to the inevitable temptations of commercialism and has become a Gap nation, featuring a host of theme restaurants, bars, a megaplex, and lots of stores. Outside the main shopping area, however, you'll find the beautiful remnants of Old Miami in the form of flora, fauna, and, of course, water.

For a map of these listings, see p. 151.

VERY EXPENSIVE

Grand Bay Miami   Grand in size and stature, the place formerly known as the Grand Bay Hotel was "going through a transition" in 2008. It looks like it belongs in Acapulco circa 1980 with its ziggurat structure and tropical landscaping, but once you see the massive bright-red sculpture/structure done by late *Condé Nast* editorial director Alexander

Lieberman in the driveway, you know you're not in Mexico. British singer George Michael filmed his *Careless Whisper* video here because of the sweeping views of Biscayne Bay. Back then, this was *the* hotel to stay at, but not so much now. Still, rooms are nice, with views of the bay and the Coconut Grove Marina. In early 2008, rumors were swirling that the owners of South Beach and St Tropez's Nikki Beach Club would be taking over the hotel as the first-ever Nikki Beach Hotel, which would breathe much-needed life into this once bustling Miami hot spot.

2669 S. Bayshore Dr., Coconut Grove, FL 33133. (C) **305/858-9600.** Fax 305/859-2026. www.grandbaymiami.com. 177 units. Winter $225–$409 suite; off season $120–$209 suite. Additional person $20. AE, DC, MC, V. Valet parking $18. **Amenities:** Restaurant; outdoor pool; 24-hr. health club; Jacuzzi; sauna; concierge; business center; babysitting. *In room:* A/C, TV, CD player, fax, dataport, minibar, coffeemaker, hair dryer, iron, safe.

Grove Isle Hotel and Spa ⟨ Hidden away in the bougainvillea and lushness of the Grove, the Grove Isle Hotel and Spa is off the beaten path on its own lushly land-scaped 20-acre island, just outside the heart of Coconut Grove. The isolated exclusivity of this resort contributes to a country-club vibe, though for the most part, the people here aren't snooty, but just value their privacy and precious relaxation time. Everyone dresses in white and pastels, and if they're not on their way to a set of tennis, they're not in a rush to get anywhere. You'll step into suites that are elegantly furnished with mosquito-netted canopy beds and a patio overlooking the bay. You'll need to reserve early here—rooms go very fast. Baleen (p. 150), a hit-or-miss haute cuisine restaurant, serves fresh seafood and other regional specialties in a spectacular, elegant dining room, or, better yet, outside on the water. The 6,000-square-foot, Indonesian-inspired Spaterre is, er, terre-ific.

4 Grove Isle Dr., Coconut Grove, FL 33133. (C) **800/884-7683** or 305/858-8300. Fax 305/854-6702. www.groveisle. com. 49 units. Winter $689–$849 double, $839–$949 suite; off season $379–$549 double, $589–$675 suite. Rates include breakfast with certain packages only. AE, DC, MC, V. Valet parking $17. **Amenities:** Large outdoor heated pool; 12 outdoor tennis courts; full-service spa; concierge; secretarial services; salon; room service; in-room massage; babysitting; laundry service; dry cleaning. *In room:* A/C, TV/VCR, CD player, dataport, minibar, hair dryer, iron, safe.

Mayfair Hotel and Spa ⟨ Don't be fooled by the hotel's gaudy, Gaudí-esque facade, located within the deserted streets of Mayfair Mall (an outdoor shopping area). Its recent renovation and acquisition by the hip Kimpton Hotel group has given the lobby and interior of the hotel, rooms included, a more modern boutiquey feel with the usual trimmings—Wi-Fi, terry robes, 300-thread-count sheets and plasma TVs. The rooftop deck area has a 60-foot swimming pool, bar, and guest cabanas with—you guessed it—plasma TVs. Since the lobby is in a shopping mall, recreation is confined to the roof, where you'll find a small pool, sauna, and snack bar. NBA players have been known to stay here, as has one of Miami's more public residents, O. J. Simpson. A new restaurant, Ginger Grove, is a hip addition to the hotel, with Asian menu and decor as well as a cool poolside bar.

3000 Florida Ave., Coconut Grove, FL 33133. (C) **800/433-4555** or 305/441-0000. Fax 305/447-9173. www.mayfair hotelandspa.com. 179 units. Winter $379–$679 suite; off season $279–$579 suite; year-round $3,000 penthouse. Packages available. AE, DC, DISC, MC, V. Valet parking $25. Pet-friendly rooms available. **Amenities:** Restaurant; rooftop snack bar; outdoor pool; Jacuzzi; concierge; business center and secretarial services; 24-hr. room service; dry cleaning. *In room:* A/C, TV/DVD player, CD player, fax, dataport, minibar, coffeemaker, hair dryer, safe.

Mutiny Hotel ⟨ En route to the center of the Grove, docked along Sailboat Bay and the marina, lies this revamped hotel best known as the hangout for the *Miami Vice* set—drug kingpins, undercover cops, and other shady characters—during the mid-'80s. Now it caters to a much more legitimate clientele. Service and style are bountiful at the Mutiny, which somehow has avoided the Nouveau-hotel hype and managed to stand on its own quiet merits without becoming part of the scene. The newly converted condos promise to be the best-kept secret in the Grove. The suites' British Colonial motif is warmed up with soft drapes, comfortable mattresses, and regal Old English furnishings. Each suite comes with a large bathroom (executive and two-bedroom suites have two bathrooms), full kitchen complete with china and complimentary coffee, and all the usual amenities associated with this class of hotel. The Mutiny is just a few blocks away from CocoWalk and the shops at Mayfair.

2951 S. Bayshore Dr., Miami, FL 33133. (C) 888/868-8469 or 305/441-2100. Fax 305/441-2822. www.mutinyhotel. com. 120 suites. Winter $229–$799 1- and 2-bedroom suites; off season $199–$599 1- and 2-bedroom suites; year-round $799–$1,799 1- and 2-bedroom penthouses. AE, DC, DISC, MC, V. Valet parking $16. **Amenities:** Restaurant; small outdoor heated pool with whirlpool; health club; spa; concierge; limited room service; babysitting; laundry service; dry cleaning. *In room:* A/C, TV/VCR, dataport, kitchen, coffeemaker, hair dryer.

Ritz-Carlton Coconut Grove   The third and smallest of Miami's Ritz-Carlton hotels is, hands down, the most intimate of its properties, surrounded by 2 acres of tropical gardens and overlooking Biscayne Bay and the Miami skyline. Decorated in an Italian Renaissance design, the hotel's understated luxury is a welcome addition to an area known for its gaudiness. In addition to the usual Ritz-Carlton standard of service and comfort, the hotel has an excellent, extremely elegant restaurant (with footstools for women to put their purses on—how classy!), Biscaya Grill, and a sophisticated wine-tasting scene at the Amadeus Bar.

3300 SW 27th Ave., Coconut Grove, FL 33133. (C) 800/241-3333 or 305/644-4680. Fax 305/644-4681. www.ritzcarlton. com. 115 units. Winter $469 double, $569 suite; off season $249 double, $359 suite. AE, DC, DISC, MC, V. Valet parking $25. **Amenities:** Restaurant; pool grill; 2 bars; outdoor heated pool; fitness center; Boutique Spa; concierge; business center; shopping boutique; 24-hr. room service; babysitting; overnight laundry service. *In room:* A/C, TV, dataport, minibar, hair dryer, safe.

MODERATE

Hampton Inn   This very standard chain hotel is a welcome reprieve in an area otherwise known for very pricey accommodations. The rooms are nothing exciting, but the freebies, like local phone calls, parking, in-room movies, breakfast buffet, and hot drinks around the clock, make this a real steal. Although there is no restaurant or bar, it is close to lots of both—only about half a mile to the heart of the Grove's shopping and retail area and about as far from Coral Gables. Rooms are brand new, sparkling clean, and larger than that of a typical motel. Located at the residential end of Brickell Avenue, it's a quiet, convenient location 15 minutes from South Beach and 5 minutes from Coconut Grove. If you'd rather save your money for dining and entertainment, this is a good bet.

2800 SW 28th Terrace (at U.S. 1 and SW 27th Ave.), Coconut Grove, FL 33133. (C) 305/448-2800. Fax 305/442-8655. www.Hampton-inn.com. 137 units. Winter $179–$209 double; off season $124–$169 double. Rates include continental breakfast buffet and local calls. AE, DC, DISC, MC, V. Free parking. **Amenities:** Large outdoor pool; exercise room; Jacuzzi. *In room:* A/C, TV, microwave and fridge (on request).

7 West Miami/Airport Area

As Miami continues to grow at a rapid pace, expansion has begun westward, where land is plentiful. Several resorts have taken advantage of the space to build world-class tennis courts and golf courses. Although there's no sea to swim in, a plethora of facilities makes up for the lack of an ocean view.

For a map of these listings, see p. 77.

EXPENSIVE

Doral Golf Resort and Spa 𝔊 *Kids*   This sprawling 650-acre resort in a suburban West Miami enclave is all about golf. Doral is where world-class tournaments and the excruciating Blue Monster course have seen even Tiger frustrated. There's also the Great White Course—the Southeast's first desertscape course, designed by The Shark himself, Greg Norman. Repeat guests usually book the season well in advance. Rooms are spacious, all with private balconies, many overlooking a golf course or garden. Rooms reveal a plantation-style decor with lots of wicker and wood and large marble bathrooms. Enhancements to the golf courses, spa suites, and driving range have also brought the resort up to speed with its competition. There's a phenomenal kids program and The Blue Lagoon water park featuring two 80,000-gallon pools with cascading waterfalls, a rock facade, and a 125-foot water slide. For a spa or golf vacation, the Doral is an ideal choice. Otherwise, consider investing your money in a hotel that's better located.

4400 NW 87th Ave., Miami, FL 33178. © 800/71-DORAL or 305/592-2000. Fax 305/594-4682. www.doralresort. com. 693 units. Winter $269 double, $370 suite, $420 1-bedroom suite, $500 2-bedroom suite; off season $119 double, $280 suite, $400 1-bedroom suite, $480 2-bedroom suite. Additional person $35. Golf and spa packages available. AE, DC, DISC, MC, V. Valet parking $17. **Amenities:** 5 restaurants; 6 pools, 1 with a 125-ft. water slide; 5 golf courses; driving range; 10 tennis courts; health club; world-class spa; concierge; business center; room service; babysitting; laundry service; dry cleaning. *In room:* A/C, TV, dataport, minibar, coffeemaker, hair dryer, iron, safe.

Miccosukee Resort and Convention Center 𝔊   Located on the edge of the Everglades, about 30 to 40 minutes west of the airport, the Miccosukee Resort is the closest thing South Florida's got to Las Vegas, but accommodations really are just a step above a Holiday Inn. The Miccosukee tribe was originally part of the lower Creek Nation, which lived in areas now known as Alabama and Georgia. After the final Seminole War in 1858, the last of the Miccosukees settled in the Everglades. Following the lead set recently by many other Native American tribes, they built the resort to accumulate gambling revenue. Although many tourists go out to the resort solely to gamble, it also has expansive meeting and banquet facilities, spa services, great children's programs, entertainment, and excursions to the Florida Everglades. Guest rooms are standard, furnished with custom pieces made exclusively for the resort, but if you're here, you're not likely to spend that much time in your room.

500 SW 177th Ave. (at intersection with SW 8th St.), Miami, FL 33194. © 877/242-6464 or 305/221-8623. Fax 305/925-2556. www.miccosukee.com. 309 units. Year-round $109 double; $135 suite; $325 presidential suite. All rooms sleep up to 3 people; suites sleep 4–6 people. AE, DC, DISC, MC, V. Free parking. **Amenities:** 5 restaurants; 24-hr. deli; indoor heated pool; state-of-the-art health club and spa; game room; 24-hr. room service; laundry service; dry cleaning. *In room:* A/C, TV, in-room movies, dataport, minibar, coffeemaker, hair dryer, some suites have whirlpool and wet bar.

MODERATE

Miami International Airport Hotel 𝔊   I don't know of a nicer airport hotel, and you can't beat the convenience—it's actually in the airport at Concourse E. Every amenity of a first-class tourist hotel is here. The rooms are modern, clean, and spacious, with newly renovated furnishings, mattresses, fixtures, and carpeting. You might think you'd be deafened by the roar of the planes, but all of the rooms have been soundproofed and actually allow in very little noise. In addition, the hotel has modern security systems and is extremely safe. Renovations were made in 2008 to the pool and spa.

Airport Terminal Concourse E (at the intersection of NW 20th St. and Le Jeune Rd.; P.O. Box 997510), Miami, FL 33299-7510. (℃ 800/327-1276 or 305/871-4100. Fax 305/871-0800. www.miahotel.com. 260 units. Winter $199–$219 double; off season $185–$209 double. Additional person $10. AE, DC, MC, V. Parking $15. **Amenities:** Restaurant; cocktail lounge; large rooftop pool; racquetball courts; well-equipped health club; Jacuzzi; sauna; concierge; tour desk; business center; salon; limited room service; laundry service; dry cleaning. *In room:* A/C, TV, dataport, hair dryer, iron.

BARGAIN CHAINS

If you must stay near the airport, consider any of the dozens of moderately priced chain hotels. You'll find one of the cheapest and most recommendable options at either of the **Days Inn** locations at 7250 NW 11th St. or 4767 NW 36th St. (℃ 800/329-7466 for both or 305/888-3661 or 305/261-4230, respectively), each about 2 miles from the airport. The larger property on 36th Street offers slightly cheaper rates with singles starting as low as $69. The 11th Street locale may charge more for weekends, but prices usually start at $99. Prices include free transportation from the airport.

A more luxurious option is the **Wyndham Miami Airport,** at 3900 NW 21st St. (℃ 305/871-3800), with rates from $119 to $250.

8 North Dade County

For a map of these listings, see p. 135.

VERY EXPENSIVE

Acqualina 🍸   Some people are still scratching their heads as to why this luxurious resort opened across the street from a Denny's and T-shirt shops, but once you step inside, you forget that you're even in Miami and feel as if you're on the Italian Riviera. On 4½ beachfront acres with more than 400 feet of Atlantic coastline, Acqualina is a Mediterranean-style resort towering over all the others with its baroque fountains, just 97 impeccably appointed suites, and a branch of NYC's acclaimed Il Mulino restaurant. The ESPA is one of Miami's priciest and poshest spas, and while there are three pools just steps away from the beach, the outdoor area is uninspiring. The hotel's AcquaMarine Program has a splashy array of marine-biology activities for kids and adults. Best of all, the chance of Paris Hilton and Tara Reid partying here is unlikely. In fact, there's really no scene here at all, which for some is just blissful.

17875 Collins Ave., Sunny Isles Beach, FL 33160. (℃ 305/918-8000. Fax 305/918-8100. www.acqualina.com. 97 units. Winter $725–$925 double, $1,175–$2,3000 suite; off season $475–$675 double, $925–$1,800 suite. AE, DC, DISC, MC, V. Valet parking $26. **Amenities:** 3 restaurants; bar; 3 outdoor pools; state-of-the-art spa; 24-hr. concierge; 24-hr. room service; babysitting. *In room:* A/C, TV, CD player, fax, Wi-Fi, minibar, coffeemaker, hair dryer, iron, safe.

Fairmont Turnberry Isle Resort & Club 🍸🍸🍸   One of Miami's classiest—and priciest—resorts (along the lines of the Mandarin Oriental), this gorgeous 300-acre compound has every possible facility for active guests, particularly golfers. You'll pay a lot to stay here thanks to a $100-million renovation of all guest rooms, suites, golf courses, the spa, pool, fitness center, and beach club. The main attractions are two Raymond Floyd courses, available only to members and guests of the hotel, and Bourbon Steak, a restaurant by star chef Michael Mina. A new, seven-story Mediterranean-style wing is surrounded by tropical gardens that are joined by covered marble walkways. The Willow Stream Spa offers an unabridged menu of treatments. A location in the well-manicured residential and shopping area of Aventura appeals to those who want peace, quiet, and a great mall. The only drawback to this hotel is that you'll need to take a shuttle to the beach.

19999 W. Country Club Dr., Aventura, FL 33180. © 800/327-7028 or 305/936-2929. Fax 305/933-6560. www. turnberryisle.com. 392 units. Winter $699–$809 double, $1,999–$4,000 suite; off season $299–$399 double, $599–$1,700 suite; year-round $4,000 grand presidential suite. AE, DC, DISC, MC, V. Valet parking $12; self-parking free. **Amenities:** 6 restaurants; numerous bars and lounges; 2 outdoor pools; 2 golf courses; 2 tennis complexes; state-of-the-art spa; extensive watersports equipment rental; concierge; secretarial services; 24-hr. room service; babysitting. *In room:* A/C, TV/VCR, CD player, fax, dataport, minibar, fridge (upon request), coffeemaker (upon request), hair dryer, iron, safe.

Le Meridien Sunny Isles Beach ★★   This all-suite beachfront resort is Le Meridien's first oceanfront resort in the U.S. It brings a nice touch of European-style glitz and glamour to the area and—sorry, Donald—it trumps the nearby Trump resort in many ways. All rooms—there are 130 one-bedroom suites and 80 two-bedroom suites—feature king-size beds with Egyptian cotton linens, and the latest in technology, not to mention full-size Italian kitchens, washer/dryer, and spa-quality bathrooms. The gorgeous lobby has a bustling 30-seat bar where people usually hang out when waiting for a table at the delicious Bice Italian restaurant. Service throughout the hotel is impeccable. The hotel's 6,000-square-foot spa is also a hot spot for those seeking pampering, but I prefer the pool area, where an infinity-edge beachfront pool stands out like a supermodel in a crowd of circus clowns. A great spot for families looking for a bit more luxury than usual, Le Meridien has planned activities for kids and adults.

18683 Collins Ave., Sunny Isles Beach, FL 33140. © 888/627-8557 or 305/503-6000. Fax 305/503-6001. www.le meridien.com/miami 210 units. Winter $319–$459 double, $539–$1,350 suite; off season $299–$399 double, $439–$619 suite. AE, DC, DISC, MC, V. Valet parking $25. **Amenities:** Restaurant; lounge; bar; outdoor pool spa; watersports equipment; 24-hr. concierge; business center; 24-hr. room service; in-room massage; babysitting; laundry service; dry cleaning. *In room:* A/C, TV/DVD, Wi-Fi, kitchen, minibar, coffeemaker, hair dryer, safe.

Regent Bal Harbour ★★★   Proving too swank even for South Beach, the very regal Regent packed its bags and moved uptown—to a more fitting locale in the chichi shopping hamlet of Bal Harbour. But this is no mall hotel. Until the St. Regis finishes completion in the former Sheraton Bal Harbour, this is the only oceanfront resort in the area—and it's a stunner. The penultimate in luxury, Regent suites are resplendent in mahogany floors, with leather walls, panoramic views of the ocean, bathrooms with 10-foot floor-to-ceiling windows and, my favorite, a free-standing tub overlooking the ocean. Elevators take you directly into your suite, like a luxury apartment building. A Guerlain spa, butler service, spectacular pool and beach area, and world class dining will cost you a pretty penny, but if you're looking to be doted on hand and foot without lifting a finger—except to pay your bill at the end—this is the place.

10295 Collins Ave., Bal Harbour FL 33154. © 800/545-4000 or 305/866-2121. Fax 305/866-2419. www.regenthotels. com/balharbour. 124 units. Winter $750–$900 deluxe, $1,000–$2,500 suite; off season $450–$600 deluxe, $780–$1,550 suite; $8,500 presidential suite; AE, MC, V. Valet parking, luxury car service, private jet/yacht charter. A"ties: Restaurant; bar; outdoor pool, spa; 24-hr. concierge; business center; 24-hr. room service; in-room massage; laundry service; dry cleaning; butler service. *In room:* A/C, 42" flatscreen TV/DVD/CD player, Wi-Fi, minibar, coffeemaker, hair dryer, safe.

Trump International Sonesta Beach Resort *(Overrated)*   Donald, Donald, Donald, what were you thinking when you opened this uninspiring 32-story, 390-room beach resort? Yes, the Trump International sits on a prime piece of beachfront property, but I've seen rooms in Holiday Inns that have more personality than these. Completely bland with no style whatsoever, the Trump International is a folly of massive proportions despite a recent renovation that added a pool and increased the beachfront. With a cavernous, blasé lobby in which you can hear a pin drop, a restaurant that looks like a common room ripped out of an old Catskills resort (and not updated), and views of T-shirt shops and Denny's, this hotel is a travesty. That's really all I can say. And it's not made better with the tacky digital sign out front trying to entice people inside. *Maybe*, with an emphasis on the *maybe*, if there were a casino in here, it would justify a stay. Otherwise, it's just more vanity fare for the egomaniacal developer who seems to think that bigger is always better.

18001 Collins Ave., Sunny Isles Beach, FL 33160. © 800/SONESTA (800/766-3782) or 305/692-5600. Fax 305/ 692-5601. www.trumpsonesta.com. 390 units. Winter $345–$445 double, $445–$1,200 suite; off season $240–$345 double, $310–$875 suite. AE, DC, DISC, MC, V. Valet parking $18. **Amenities:** 2 restaurants; 2 bars and lounges; 2 outdoor pools; full service spa; watersports equipment/rentals; Just Us Kids program (ages 5–12); concierge; business center; 24-hr. room service; babysitting; air-conditioned cabanas on pool and beach. *In room:* A/C, TV, CD player, radio, high-speed Internet access, minibar, coffeemaker, hair dryer, iron, safe, microwave, washer/dryer (suites only).

Where to Dine in Miami

Don't be fooled by the plethora of super-lean model types you're likely to see posing throughout Miami. Contrary to popular belief, dining in this city is as much a sport as the in-line skating on Ocean Drive. With more than 6,000 restaurants to choose from, dining out in Miami has become a passionate pastime for locals and visitors alike. Our star chefs have fused Californian-Asian with Caribbean and Latin elements to create a world-class flavor all its own: *Floribbean*. Think mango chutney splashed over fresh swordfish or a spicy sushi sauce served alongside Peruvian ceviche.

Formerly synonymous with early-bird specials, Miami's new-wave cuisine now rivals that of San Francisco—or even New York. Nouveau Cuban chef Douglas Rodriguez returned to his roots with a fabulous South Beach nouveau Latino eatery. In addition, other stellar chefs, such as Mark Militello, the Food Network's own Michelle Bernstein, Allen Susser, Norman van Aken, Govind Armstrong, and Clay Conley remain firmly planted in the city's culinary scene, fusing local ingredients into edible masterpieces. Florida foodies are bracing themselves for the arrival of Alain Ducasse, sometime when the construction ends on Biscayne Boulevard. This New World cuisine is not only high in calories, it's high in price. But if you can manage to splurge at least once, it'll be worth it.

Thanks to a thriving cafe society in both South Beach and Coconut Grove, you can also enjoy a moderately priced meal and linger for hours without having a waiter hover over you. In Little Havana, you can chow down on a meal that serves about six for less than $10. Since seafood is plentiful, it doesn't have to cost you an arm and a leg to enjoy the appendages of a crab or lobster. Don't be put off by the looks of our recommended seafood shacks in places such as Key Biscayne—oftentimes, these spots get the best and freshest catches.

Whatever you're craving, Miami's got it—with the exception of decent Chinese food and a New York–style slice of pizza. If you're craving a scene with your steak, then South Beach is the place to be. Like many cities in Europe and Latin America, it is fashionable to dine late in South Beach, preferably after 9pm, sometimes as late as midnight. Service on South Beach is notoriously slow and arrogant, but it comes with the turf. (Of course, it is possible to find restaurants that defy the notoriety and actually pride themselves on friendly service.) On the mainland—especially in Coral Gables and, more recently, downtown and on Brickell Avenue—you can also experience fine dining without the pretense.

The biggest complaint when it comes to Miami dining isn't the haughtiness, but rather the dearth of truly moderately priced restaurants, especially in South Beach and Coral Gables. It's either really cheap or really expensive; the in-between somehow gets lost in the culinary shuffle. Quick-service diners don't exist here as they do in other cosmopolitan areas. I've tried to cover a range of cuisine in a range of prices. But with new restaurants opening on a weekly basis, you're bound to find an array of savory dining choices for every budget.

Many restaurants keep extended hours in high season (roughly Dec–Apr) and may close for lunch and/or dinner on Monday when the traffic is slower. Always call ahead, since schedules do change. During the month of August, many Miami restaurants participate in Miami Spice, where three-course lunches and dinners are served at affordable prices. Check out www.miamirestaurant-month.com. Also, always look carefully at your bill—many Miami restaurants add a 15% to 18% gratuity to your total due to the enormous influx of European tourists who are not accustomed to tipping. Keep in mind that this amount is the *suggested* amount and can be adjusted, either higher or lower, depending on your assessment of the service provided. Because of this tipping-included policy, South Beach waitstaff are best known for their lax or inattentive service. *Feel free to adjust it* if you feel your server deserves more or less.

If you want to picnic on the beach or pick up some dessert, check out the gourmet-food shops, green markets, and bakeries listed under "Food" in chapter 9.

1 South Beach

The renaissance of South Beach started in the early '90s and is still continuing as classic cuisine gives in to modern temptation by inevitably fusing with more chic, nouveau developments created by faithful followers and devotees of the Food Network school of cooking. The ultimate result has spawned dozens of first-rate restaurants. In fact, big-name restaurants from across the country have capitalized on South Beach's international appeal and have continued to open branches here with great success. A few old standbys remain from the *Miami Vice* days, but the flock of newcomers dominates the scene, with places going in and out of style as quickly as the tides.

On South Beach, new restaurants are opening and closing as frequently as Emeril says "Bam!" Since it's impossible to list them all, I recommend strolling and browsing. Most restaurants post a copy of their menu outside. With very few exceptions, the places on Ocean Drive are crowded with tourists and priced accordingly. You'll do better to venture a little farther onto the pedestrian-friendly streets just west of Ocean Drive.

VERY EXPENSIVE

Blue Door 𝒦𝒦𝒦 FRENCH BRAZILIAN   It used to be that the Blue Door's greatest claim to fame was that Madonna was part owner. The food was unremarkable, but the eye candy was sickly sweet. When the Material Girl fled, so did others, leaving the Blue Door wide open for anything, as long as it was as fabulous as the hotel in which it sits. This really is quintessential South Beach dining. The most recent incarnation of the restaurant begs for superlatives more flattering than the standard "fabulous." The eye candy is still here, but now you have good reason to focus your eyes on the food rather than who's eating it. Thanks to award-winning Chef Claude Troisgros (rhymes with foie gras)—a star in his own right—the menu frowns upon the ubiquitous fusion moniker in favor of a more classic French approach to tropical spices and ingredients. Caramelized rack of lamb with toasted Moroccan couscous in a passion mint fruit glaze, and beef tenderloin with gorgonzola cream sauce, Beaujolais poached Asian pear, crispy potato, raisins, and green peppercorns are just a few of the Blue Door's tempting offerings, but the menu changes frequently. Service can be snippy,

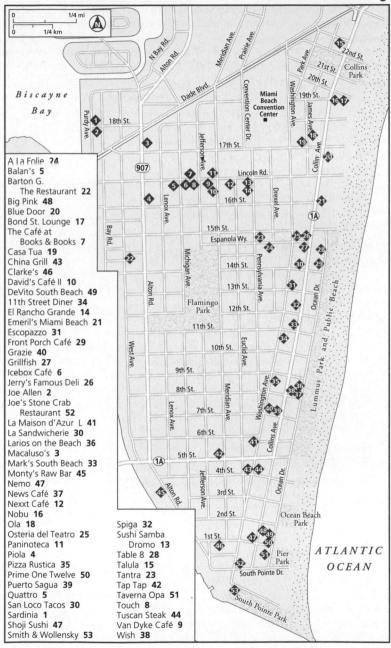

A la Folie **24**
Balan's **5**
Barton G.
   The Restaurant **22**
Big Pink **48**
Blue Door **20**
Bond St. Lounge **17**
The Café at
   Books & Books **7**
Casa Tua **19**
China Grill **43**
Clarke's **46**
David's Café II **10**
DeVito South Beach **49**
11th Street Diner **34**
El Rancho Grande **14**
Emeril's Miami Beach **21**
Escopazzo **31**
Front Porch Café **29**
Grazie **40**
Grillfish **27**
Icebox Café **6**
Jerry's Famous Deli **26**
Joe Allen **2**
Joe's Stone Crab
   Restaurant **52**
La Maison d'Azur L **41**
La Sandwicherie **30**
Larios on the Beach **36**
Macaluso's **3**
Mark's South Beach **33**
Monty's Raw Bar **45**
Nemo **47**
News Café **37**
Nexxt Café **12**
Nobu **16**
Ola **18**
Osteria del Teatro **25**
Paninoteca **11**
Piola **4**
Pizza Rustica **35**
Prime One Twelve **50**
Puerto Sagua **39**
Quattro **5**
San Loco Tacos **30**
Sardinia **1**
Shoji Sushi **47**
Smith & Wollensky **53**

Spiga **32**
Sushi Samba
   Dromo **13**
Table 8 **28**
Talula **15**
Tantra **23**
Tap Tap **42**
Taverna Opa **51**
Touch **8**
Tuscan Steak **44**
Van Dyke Café **9**
Wish **38**

slow, and, at times, downright rude, but the food makes up for what the restaurant lacks in hospitality. Sunday brunch here is one of the most popular in town.

In the Delano Hotel, 1685 Collins Ave., South Beach. ⓒ 305/674-6400. www.chinagrillmgt.com. Reservations recommended for dinner. Main courses $31–$46. AE, DC, MC, V. Daily 7am–4pm and 7pm–midnight (room service menu available for people who are still at the bar after the restaurant has closed, 3–7am); Sun brunch 10:30am–2:30pm.

Casa Tua 🖈🖈 *Finds* ITALIAN The stunning Casa Tua is a sleek and chic, country Italian–style establishment set in a refurbished 1925 Mediterranean-style house-cum-hotel. It has several dining areas, including a resplendent outdoor garden, comfy Ralph Lauren–esque living room, and a communal eat-in kitchen. The lamb chops are stratospheric in price ($42) but sublime in taste and a bargain compared to the $50 milk-fed veal chop. Service is, as always with South Beach eateries, inconsistent, ranging from ultra-professional to absurdly lackadaisical. For these prices, they should be wiping our mouths for us. What used to be a fabulous lounge upstairs is now a members' only club, so don't even try to get in.

1700 James Ave., South Beach. ⓒ 305/673-1010. Reservations required. Main courses $24–$100. AE, DC, MC, V. Mon–Sat 7pm–midnight.

China Grill 🖈 PAN-ASIAN If ever a restaurant could be as cavernous as, say, the Asian continent, this would be it. Formerly a hub of hype and pompous circumstance, China Grill has calmed on the hip meter, but its cuisine is still sizzling, if not better than ever. You'll find an incomparable and dizzying array of amply portioned dishes, including outrageous crispy spinach, wasabi mashed potatoes, and seared rare tuna in spicy Japanese pepper sauce. Keep in mind that China Grill is a family-style restaurant and dishes are meant to be shared. For those who can't stay away from sushi, China Grill also has Dragon, a 40-seat "sushi den" in a private back room with one-of-a-kind rolls such as the Havana Roll, which consists of yellowtail snapper, rum, coconut, avocado, and red tobiko, plus cocktails such as the Lemongrass Saketini. New in 2008: In what was once China Grill's private room is a South Beach branch of the ultra pricey **Kobe Club** (ⓒ 305/673-5370), a 50-seat restaurant devoted to all things meaty, where a "flight" of beef—Kobe, Waygu, American—costs upwards of $350. You really better love meat to spend that money.

404 Washington Ave., South Beach. ⓒ 305/534-2211. Reservations strongly recommended. Main courses $26–$59. AE, DC, MC, V. Mon–Thurs 11:45am–midnight; Fri 11:45am–1am; Sat 6pm–1am; Sun 6pm–midnight.

DeVito South Beach 🖈 ITALIAN CHOPHOUSE The latest production from actor Danny DeVito (and a few bona fide restaurant professionals), this Italian style chophouse is a stunning homage to decor—and DeVito. Brick walls and rich, textured bordello-style paneling are adorned with flat screen TVs playing DeVito's greatest hits, although 1 weekend night they switched it up with James Bond. An elegant, warm interior is matched by an even more elegant price tag—dinner for two can cost upwards of $200 thanks to a heavily sauced, heavily priced menu of steaks and assorted family style dishes including Dover sole, Maine lobster risotto, an excellent calamari appetizer and a gargantuan veal parmigiana that is enough to serve the entire restaurant. The $300 (!) Global Steak Flight is the restaurant's signature dish, with three different kinds of Kobe beef—authentic Japanese Kobe Beef, Australian Wagyu Rollatini and American Kobe Flat Iron. Order wisely here and take advantage of the freebies you get when you sit down—homemade popovers, a selection of salumi, cheese, and veggies.

150 Ocean Dr., South Beach. ℂ 305/531-0911. www.devitosouthbeach.com Reservations strongly recommended. Main courses $16–$300. AE, DC, MC, V. Daily noon–3pm; Sun–Thurs 5pm–midnight; Fri–Sat 5pm–1am.

Emeril's Miami Beach 🦐🦐🦐 CREOLE   This is the real deal. In a city where restaurants pride themselves on celebrity sightings and snooty service, Emeril's is a spicy breath of fresh air. If you've never dined at Emeril's original restaurant(s) in New Orleans and you're craving gourmet Creole cuisine, dine here ASAP. Elaborately designed by David Rockwell, the 8,000-square-foot restaurant is reminiscent of a bustling and cavernous New York City hot spot with chandeliers, massive wine cellars, and a very inviting open kitchen in which Emeril himself sometimes stars. Call the restaurant ahead to find out when he's in town, and book your reservations immediately. Portions are massive and signature dishes include New Orleans barbecue shrimp with a petite rosemary biscuit; Niman Ranch double-cut pork chop with tamarind glaze, caramelized sweet potatoes and green chili mole sauce; and banana cream pie with banana crust, caramel sauce, and chocolate shavings. Service is stellar and should serve as an example to other area restaurants. A 3-hour Sunday Jazz Brunch is worth breaking the diet for, too.

In the Loews Hotel, 1601 Collins Ave., South Beach. ℂ 305/695-4550. www.emerils.com. Reservations required. Main courses $18–$50. AE, MC, V. Sun–Thurs 11:30am–2pm and 5:30–10pm; Fri–Sat 11:30am–2pm and 5:30–11pm.

Escopazzo 🦐🦐🦐 ITALIAN   *Escopazzo* means "I'm going crazy" in Italian, but the only sign of insanity in this primo Northern Italian eatery is the fact that it seats only 90 and it's one of the best restaurants in town. The wine bottles have it better—the restaurant's cellar holds 1,000 bottles of various vintages. In 2007, Escopazzo added "Organic Italian Restaurant" to its title. Not necessary as the ingredients here have always been of the freshest, but for those who need further encouragement, there it is. Should you be so lucky to score a table at this romantic local favorite (choose one in the back dining room that's reminiscent of an Italian courtyard, complete with fountain and faux windows; it's not cheesy at all), you'll have trouble deciding between dishes that will have you swearing off the Olive Garden with your first bite. Standouts are milk and basil dough pasta with baby calamari, chick peas, tomatoes, and arugula, or grass-fed hanger steak with roasted baby organic veggies in a truffle sauce. The hand-rolled pastas and risotto are near perfection. Eating here is like dining with a big Italian family—it's never boring (the menu changes five or six times a year), the service is excellent, and nobody's happy until you are blissfully full.

1311 Washington Ave., South Beach. ℂ 305/674-9450. www.escopazzo.com. Reservations required. Main courses $14–$34. AE, MC, V. Mon–Fri 6pm–midnight; Sat 6pm–1am; Sun 6–11pm.

Joe's Stone Crab Restaurant 🦐 SEAFOOD   Unless you grease the palms of one of the stone-faced maître d's with some stone-cold cash, you'll be waiting for those famous claws for up to 2 hours—if not more. As much a Miami landmark as the beaches themselves, Joe's is a microcosm of the city, attracting everyone from T-shirted locals to a bejeweled Ivana Trump. Whatever you wear, however, will be eclipsed by a kitschy, unglamorous plastic bib that your waiter will tie on you unless you say otherwise. Open only during stone-crab season (Oct–May), Joe's reels in the crowds with the freshest (though some disagree and consider Joe's stash subpar to less assuming area restaurants), meatiest stone crabs and their essential accouterments: creamed spinach and excellent sweet-potato fries. The claws come in medium, large, and jumbo. Some say size doesn't matter; others swear by the jumbo (and more expensive)

Anti-Social? South Beach Loses a Hot Spot

We didn't see it coming. When China Grill's emperor Jeffrey Chodorow took over the arty lobby of the Sagamore with his ode to fashionable fare, the hotel was overrun by hipsters. Beyond all the glitz, glamour, and celebrity, **Social Miami** was a serious restaurant, with a fantastic, creative menu. And now it's gone. The official statement from China Grill Management: "Due to operational differences with hotel ownership, China Grill Management announces it has ceased operations at Social Miami at Sagamore as of Sunday, July 6, 2008. We look forward to relocating the Social concept to another South Florida location in the near future. No other information (or comment) is available at this time." We'll always have fond memories of the place—its chicken lollipops and deviled eggs, especially—a place where lots of big (and not so big) celebs and chefs have passed through. Keep your ears open for news of a reopening, or check Frommers.com for updates.

---

ones. Whatever you choose, pair them with a savory mustard sauce (a perfect mix of mayo and mustard) or hot butter. Not feeling crabby? The fried chicken and liver and onions on the regular menu are actually considered by many as far superior—they're definitely far cheaper—to the crabs. Oh yes, and save room for dessert. The Key lime pie here is the best in town. If you don't feel like waiting, try Joe's Takeaway, which is next door to the restaurant—it's a lot quicker and just as tasty.

11 Washington Ave. (at Biscayne St., just south of 1st St.), South Beach. © 305/673-0365 or 305/673-4611 for takeout. www.joesstonecrab.com. Reservations not accepted. Market price varies but averages $65 for a serving of jumbo crab claws, $45 for large claws. AE, DC, DISC, MC, V. Sun 11:30am–2pm and 4–10pm; Mon–Thurs 11:30am–2pm and 5–10pm; Fri–Sat 11:30am–2pm and 5–11pm. Open mid-Oct to mid-May.

La Maison d'Azur ☆☆☆ SEAFOOD   A brand new seafood brasserie in the spanking new Angler's Hotel, La Maison d'Azur is where South Beach meets St. Tropez (but owned by a congenial French Canadian turned NYC restaurateur). Thank goodness the attitude was left back in France and what remains is stellar service and outstanding fresh French fare. The steak frites are among the best in town, if not *the* best, and for high rollers, there's an unabridged list of caviars and wines by the glass. Soothing lighting and modern French brasserie decor makes for an outstanding dining experience, complete with a DJ imported straight from the Riviera, who spins an assortment of dinner music that's unusually soothing and entertaining. An outdoor garden area is perfect for cool nights. The menu changes often; ask for the chef's recommendations. Among ours: the John Dorie, perfectly filleted and served tableside; the seafood platter that's as tall as the Eiffel Tower, full of oysters, caviar, crab, shrimp and escargot; and for a true indulgence, the foie gras is fantastic. Save room for dessert—the chef makes his own ice cream *and* ice cream cones—don't miss the Nutella-flavored ice cream. *C'est magnifique!*

634 Washington Ave. (between 6th & 7th). Miami Beach FL, 33139. © 305/534-9600. Reservations suggested. Main courses $26–$65. AE, MC, V. Sun–Wed 7am–1am, Thurs–Sat 7am–4am.

Nobu ☆☆☆ SUSHI   When Madonna ate here, no one really noticed. The same thing happened when Justin Timberlake and Cameron Diaz canoodled here. It's not because people were purposely trying not to notice, but because the real star at Nobu is the sushi. The raw facts: Nobu has been hailed as one of the best sushi restaurants in the world, with always-packed eateries in New York, London, and Los Angeles. The Omakase, or Chef's Choice—a multicourse menu entirely up to the chef for $70 per person and up—gets consistent raves. Although you won't wait long for your food to be cooked, you will wait forever to score a table here.

At The Shore Club Hotel, 1901 Collins Ave., South Beach. ℃ 305/695-3232. Reservations only for parties of 6 or more. Main courses $26 and above. AE, MC, V. Sun 7–11pm; Mon–Thurs 7pm–midnight; Fri–Sat 7pm–1am.

Ola 𝕽𝕽 NUEVO LATINO   Star chef Douglas Rodriguez single-handedly created the nouveau Latino and Cubano cuisine in Miami when he founded Lincoln Road's Yuca restaurant in 1989. From there, he skyrocketed to fame (and left Yuca to rot in mediocrity) and became co owner and executive chef at New York City's lauded Patria (leaving Miami restaurant-goers to wallow in their sorrows). But now Rodriguez is back in full force with Ola, which moved from its larger confines in the Deco landmark, The Savoy, to the smaller, chic-er Sanctuary Hotel, serving Spanish tapas and ceviches as well as Rodriguez's very own inimitable culinary concoctions. For those who are addicted to the low-carb craze, you'll find several items on the menu tailored to your diet. But why bother? Latin food is about flavor and carbs, so indulge here (like your wallet will have to).

1745 James Ave. in the Sanctuary Hotel, Miami Beach ℃ 305/673-5455. Reservations recommended. Main courses $21–$50. AE, DC, MC, V. Mon–Thurs 5:30–11pm; Fri–Sat 5:30pm–midnight.

Osteria del Teatro 𝕽𝕽𝕽 ITALIAN   Located in an unassuming storefront beneath the ultrasceney Cameo nightclub, it's hard to believe that Osteria del Teatro is the best Italian bistro on the beach. What it might be lacking in decor is certainly not absent in the elaborate cuisine. Regulars who swear by this place won't even bother looking at the menu; instead they concentrate on the enormous changing list of specials on the blackboard. You will definitely be faced with some tough choices: plump chicken breast sautéed with shallots and sun-dried tomatoes in champagne cream sauce; seafood baked with linguine, garlic, fresh tomatoes, and olive oil in parchment paper; or homemade ravioli stuffed with scallops and crab in lobster sauce. The regulars here are on a first-name basis with the waiters, who always seem to know what you're in the mood for.

1443 Washington Ave. (at Española Way), South Beach. ℃ 305/538-7850. Reservations recommended. Main courses $15–$40. AE, DC, MC, V. Mon–Sat 6pm–midnight. Closed Sept.

Prime One Twelve 𝕽𝕽𝕽 STEAKHOUSE   Part of the ever-expanding culinary empire of Nemo, Big Pink, and Shoji Sushi, Prime One Twelve is the media darling of the exclusive group of restaurants in the hot South of Fifth Street area of South Beach, ranking near the top of the list of highest grossing restaurants in the entire country in 2007. A celebrity-saturated sleek steakhouse ambience and bustling bar (complete with dried strips of bacon in lieu of nuts) play second fiddle to the beef, which is arguably the best in the entire city. The 12-ounce filet mignon is seared to perfection and can be enhanced with optional dipping sauces (for a price)—truffle, garlic herb, foie gras, and chipotle. The 22-ounce bone-in rib-eye is fabulous, as is the gigantic 48-ounce porterhouse. Prime One Twelve also features a Kobe beef hot dog ($20) and a Kobe burger, a $30 version of sheer ecstasy, although fries are extra at $8, as are all the side dishes (the broccoli rabe sautéed in garlic is outstanding, as are the scalloped potatoes)—typical in a steakhouse, but the prices here are hefty. A powerhouse crowd gathers here for lunch and dinner, and reservations are rarer than the yellowfin tuna tartare appetizer, but should you be lucky enough to score such a "prime" reservation, take it without hesitation.

112 Ocean Dr. (in The Browns Hotel), South Beach. ℂ 305/532-8112. www.prime112.com. Reservations recommended. Main courses $20–$88. AE, DISC, MC, V. Mon–Fri 11:30am–3pm and 6:30pm–midnight; Sat–Sun 6:30pm–midnight.

Smith & Wollensky 𝔊 STEAKHOUSE   Although it's a chain steakhouse, Miami Beach's Smith & Wollensky has a waterfront view that separates it from the rest. Inside seating is typical steakhouse—dark woods, and so on—but make sure to request a table by the window so you can watch the cruise ships pass by as they leave the port. Outdoor seating, weather permitting, is resplendent, with a bar that doubles as command central for the happy hour set on Friday nights. The menu here is a lot more basic than the priceless views, almost austere, with a few chicken and fish choices and beef served about a dozen ways. The classic is the sirloin, seared lightly and served naked. The veal chop is of Flintstonian proportion. Mediocre side dishes such as asparagus, baked potato, onion rings, creamed spinach, and hash browns are sold a la carte. Service is erratic, from highly professional to rudely aloof. You'll find much tastier steaks (at comparable prices) at the Forge or Tuscan Steak (p. 132 and 121).

1 Washington Ave. (in South Pointe Park), South Beach. ℂ 305/673-2800. www.smithandwollensky.com. Reservations recommended. Main courses $20–$50. AE, DC, DISC, MC, V. Mon–Sat noon–2am; Sun 11:30am–2am.

Table 8 𝔊 CALIFORNIA CUISINE   Star chef Govind Armstrong, who got his start at the age of 13 with Wolfgang Puck at L.A.'s legendary Spago, opened a branch of this L.A. hot spot on South Beach. Housed what was once the Regent Hotel (now owned by a chain called Vincci), Table 8 is a massive space of all things hip, groovy, swell, and sleek. With 255 seats, the restaurant consists of a main dining room, a private dining room for celebrity and VIP clientele, and a wine room. Can't score reservations? Don't fret! There's also a 40-seat lounge situated beneath the hotel's fabulous glass-bottom pool and featuring a delicious small-plate lounge menu which, in our opinion is better than the actual menu—try the grilled cheese and then tell us what you think! Among chef Armstrong's signature dishes: a salt-roasted porterhouse steak, which the *Robb Report* called the best of the best in one of its coveted "best of" issues and isn't on the menu, so consider that an inside tip.

1458 Ocean Dr. South Beach. ℂ 305/695-4114. www.table8restaurants.com. Reservations recommended. Main courses $26–$52. AE, DC, DISC, MC, V. Sun–Tues 6–11pm, Wed–Sat 6pm–midnight.

Tantra 𝔊 ECLECTIC   Marrakech meets Miami Beach in this truly original, exotic outpost devoted to the ancient Indian tantric philosophy of tempting the senses with all things pleasurable. While Tantra used to be on the South Beach "it" list, it has faded off the radar somewhat in terms of seeing and being seen with the exception of a weekly Monday night bacchanal that goes into the wee hours. But for a meal, Tantra shouldn't be ignored even though the star chefs have left for greener pastures. Begin with your surroundings: a sultry interior of soft grass (yes, it's real; they resod weekly) and starry lights overhead. In the front room by the bar, there are low-lying couches and pillow-lined booths bolstered by drapes that can be closed for privacy. Belly dancers mix with cocktail waitresses singing the praises of Tantra's special aphrodisiac cocktails and offering you a puff of Turkish tobacco from the communal hookah pipe (they insist it's clean, but I'd be wary). A private VIP room off to the side features a hammock and a peaceful spiritual soundtrack. Tantra serves a combination of Middle Eastern, Mediterranean, and Indian dishes that really are divine. Consider the Tantra Love Apple (a ripe tomato layered with Laura Chenel goat cheese and basil oil, garnished with pomegranate seeds) or perhaps the truffle-stuffed organic roast chicken. On the negative side, prices are obscene. Don't come to Tantra looking for a serene vibe to match the setting and menu. Tantra practically turns into a nightclub after dinner, attracting a crowd of party types who can barely afford to pay their rent, never mind a tab here. Fans of *Top Chef Miami* take note: Sandee Birdsong is the executive chef here!

1445 Pennsylvania Ave. (at Española Way), South Beach. ℂ 305/672-4765. www.tantrarestaurant.com. Reservations required. Main courses $25–$55. AE, DC, DISC, MC, V. Daily 7pm–5am. Late night menu 1am to closing.

Touch ℛ ECLECTIC   Despite the presence of the ubiquitous velvet ropes out front and the loud soundtrack inside, Touch is not a nightclub, although it does exude a cheesy Cirque du Soleil vibe with scantily clad acrobats and fire eaters. Located on busy Lincoln Road, Touch works hard to be something of a tropical supper club, complete with faux palm trees. The food is classified by talented chef Sean Brasel as "Modern Influenced Grill," which is basically a fancy term for expensive meat, fish, and chicken dishes. And while they're expensive, the dishes are quite good, especially the Kobe rib eye steak and the smoked margarita salmon cured in—yep, Tequila! Despite the circus-like ambience inside, service is actually quite good. If the noise inside is too loud, and it often is, request a table outside, ensconced safely behind the ropes, where you can watch the passersby try to put their fingers on what, exactly, Touch portends to be.

910 Lincoln Rd., South Beach. ℂ 305/532-8003. www.touchrestaurant.com. Reservations required. Main courses $20–$75. AE, DC, MC, V. Sun–Thurs 7pm–midnight; Fri–Sat 7pm–1am.

Tuscan Steak ℛℛ ITALIAN/STEAKHOUSE   This excellent Northern Italian restaurant, a member of the China Grill scion, is all about meat served Italian style, in large family-style portions. With a rich wood interior, the atmosphere is reminiscent of the dining room of a well-connected family—ornate and very loud. The house salad is a massive undertaking of classic antipasto, filled with shredded slices of salami and pepperoni, chunks of mozzarella, and delicate vinaigrette. Be sure to order the sautéed spinach with garlic and the onion-mashed potatoes with whichever steak you choose. All steaks are big enough for at least three people to share. The house specialty is a delicious T-bone steak served with pungent garlic purée. The bar is usually buzzing, especially on weekends, the background music is straight out of Studio 54, and so is the flashy crowd. Despite the long waits, after one meal here, you'll likely want to kiss the ring of the true boss of this culinary mob scene—the chef.

433 Washington Ave., South Beach. ℂ 305/534-2233. Reservations strongly recommended on weekends. Main courses $15–$78. AE, DISC, MC, V. Sun–Thurs 6–11pm; Fri–Sat 6pm–midnight.

Wish ℛℛℛ ASIAN   Located in the stylish Todd Oldham–designed The Hotel, this is one of the most beautiful, romantic outdoor restaurants in South Beach. Chef Michael Bloise has taken the restaurant to a new level of taste with a fabulous, funky cuisine that Bloise himself calls "unpretentious yet artful." He's spot on. His Asian-inspired dishes are among the most creative in town and include crispy skinned snapper with grilled shrimp, Chinese sausage, Jasmine rice, and Vietnamese tea foam. Desserts are equally creative. Take the PJ and Jay—a dark chocolate peanut butter tart with raspberry jam and peanut butter gelato. And then there are the "electric cocktails," such as the glowing green apple martini served with psychedelic ice cubes. The only thing you'll wish for after you leave here is to go back!

801 Collins Ave., South Beach. ℂ 305/531-2222. Reservations suggested. Main courses $29–$44. AE, DC, MC, V. Mon 11:30am–3pm; Tues–Sun 11:30am–3pm and 6–11pm; Fri–Sat 11:30am–3pm and 6pm–midnight.

EXPENSIVE

Barton G. The Restaurant ⊕ AMERICAN   For those who are jaded by pan-fusion, pan-everything cuisine these days, Barton G. The Restaurant is the culinary antithesis, an homage to gourmet kitsch. Set on a residential block on the west side of South Beach, Barton G., named after its owner, who happens to be one of Miami's best-known, most over-the-top event planners, is a place that looks like a trendy restaurant, but eats like a show. Here, presentation is paramount. Take, for instance, the popcorn shrimp appetizer. This is not your average Red Lobster popcorn shrimp. Served on a plate full of, yes, popcorn, with field greens and the plump, crispy rock shrimp stuffed into an actual popcorn box, this dish is one of many awe-inspiring—and tasty—items you'll find in this, the most unique restaurant in Miami. A grilled sea bass that is light and flavorful is served in a brown paper bag with laundry clips keeping the steam in until your server unclips them and releases the flavor within. Desserts are equally outrageous, including the Chocolate Fun-Do, a mini chocolate fountain overflowing with 4 pounds of Belgian chocolate and tons of dipping delicacies from cake to fruit. A giant plume of cotton candy reminiscent of drag diva Dame Edna's hair is surrounded by three white-, dark-, and milk-chocolate-covered popcorn balls that, when cracked, reveal a sinful chocolate truffle inside. There's nothing ordinary about this seemingly ordinary restaurant, which is why people such as Tom Cruise and Will Smith are regulars. An elegant, well-lit indoor dining room is popular with members of the socialite set, for whom Barton G. has done many an affair, while the bar area and outdoor courtyard is the place to be for younger trend-seekers who appreciate what's on their plates as much as they do who's sitting next to them.

1427 West Ave., South Beach. ℂ 305/672-8881. www.bartong.com Reservations suggested. Main courses $10–$50. AE, DC, DISC, MC, V. Daily 6pm–midnight.

Nemo ⊕ PAN-ASIAN   Located in the chic South Beach area known as SoFi ("South of Fifth St."), Nemo is a funky, high-style eatery with an open kitchen and an outdoor courtyard canopied by trees and lined with an eclectic mix of model types and foodies. Among the reasons to eat in this restaurant, whose name is actually *omen* spelled backward: grilled Indian-spiced pork chop; grilled local mahimahi with citrus and grilled sweet-onion salad, kimchi glaze, basil, and crispy potatoes; and an inspired dessert menu that's not for the faint of calories. Seating inside is comfy-cozy, but borders on cramped. On Sunday mornings, the open kitchen is converted into a buffet counter for the restaurant's unparalleled brunch. Be prepared for a wait, however, and the line tends to spill out onto the street.

100 Collins Ave., South Beach. ℂ 305/532-4550. www.nemorestaurant.com. Reservations recommended. Main courses $29–$75; Sun brunch $29. AE, MC, V. Mon–Sat noon–3pm and 6:30pm–midnight; Sun 11am–3pm and 6pm–midnight. Valet parking $10, or $20 for curbside.

Quattro ⊕⊕ ITALIAN   Not just another Italian restaurant on Lincoln Road, Quattro is a Northern Italian standout thanks to its chefs—29-year-old twin brothers hailing from the Piedmont region of Italy who barely speak English, but speak pasta fluently. Signature dishes on the menu include homemade beef ravioli Piemontese style with butter and sage, barley "risotto" with Taleggio and cracked white pepper, and Mediterranean sea bass baked in a salt crust. The wine list is all Italian and reasonably priced. The room is gorgeous, with dramatic lighting, chandeliers, and an all-glass bar that buzzes with *la dolce vita*. Try the cheese plate if you're not that hungry—it's a meal in itself and features that salami you wished you had smuggled back home the last time you returned from Italy.

1014 Lincoln Rd., South Beach. © 305/531-4833. www.quattromiami.com. Reservations recommended. Main courses $31–$50. AE, MC, V. Sun–Thurs noon–4pm and 6pm–midnight; Fri–Sat noon–4pm and 6pm–1am.

Sardinia 🦀🦀 ITALIAN   A quiet sensation in South Beach terms, Sardinia doesn't need celebrity sightings and publicists to boost their business. And it's not your typical caprese salad and fusilli pasta factory, either. For starters, the cheese and salumi plates will transport you—or at least your palate—to Italy, as will the rest of the innovative menu, consisting of oriechette with wild boar; crunchy fried sweetbreads with Brussels sprouts; and rabbit with Brussels sprouts and beets. Sure, the food's a bit heavy, but it's worth it. As for scene here, it's all about the food, although the bar is always bustling with people waiting for highly coveted tables.

1801 Purdy Ave., South Beach. © 305531-2228. www.sardinia-ristorante.com. Reservations for parties of 6 or more. Main courses $14–$38. AE, MC, V. Mon–Fri noon–midnight, Sat–Sun 6pm–midnight.

Shoji Sushi 🦀 SUSHI   Despite the sushi saturation on South Beach, Shoji stands apart from the typical sashimi-and-California-roll routine with expertly prepared, exquisitely fresh, and innovative top-notch rolls. The sleek sister to its next-door neighbor Nemo, Shoji is known for its authentic Japanese box sushi technique, in which the sushi, rice, and ingredients are packed into a tidy, tasty cake that won't crumble into your lap. Among the rolls I can't seem to get enough of here are the hamachi jalapeño—cilantro, daikon sprout, asparagus, avocado, and jalapeños—and the spicy lobster roll, which consists of mango, avocado, scallion, shiso, salmon egg, and huge chunks of lobster. Wash it all down with the saketinis and my personal fave, the gingertini, which is made with ginger, vodka, triple sec, ginger ale, and pickled ginger juice.

100 Collins Ave., South Beach. © 305/532-4245. www.shojisushi.com. Reservations recommended. Main courses $13–$25. AE, MC, V. Mon–Thurs noon–3pm and 6pm–midnight; Fri noon–3pm and 6pm–1am; Sat–Sun 6pm–1am. Valet parking $15.

Social Miami 🦀🦀 TAPAS/SMALL PLATES   Ever since China Grill's emperor Jeffrey Chodorow took over the arty lobby of the Sagamore Hotel with his latest ode to fashionable fare, the hotel has been overrun by hipsters, especially on Friday and Saturday nights when the restaurant turns into a virtual nightclub of seeing and being seen. But beyond all the glitz, glamour, and celebrity, Social Miami is a serious restaurant, with a fantastic, creative menu. Most menu items are small and meant to be shared—beware that prices add up and if you're on a budget, order cautiously. Among the best items: lobster tacos, deviled crab stuffed eggs, sweet and sour lamb ribs, and Kobe sliders. The menu recently took a turn toward the steakhouse, offering a 28-ounce porterhouse at a whopping $76. Good, but stick to the smaller items. Tables are long and communal and the din of diners is very loud. If you want a quiet(er) experience, avoid Fridays and Saturdays and request a table outside in the hotel's video garden where arty anime is broadcast on large plasma TVs.

In the Sagamore Hotel, 1671 Collins Ave., South Beach. © 786/594-3444. www.chinagrillmgt.com. Reservations recommended. Tapas $11–$19; main courses $22–$76. AE, DC, MC, V. Sun–Wed 6pm–11pm, Thurs–Sat 6pm–1am.

Sushi Samba Dromo & SUSHI/CEVICHE   It's Brazilian, it's Peruvian, it's Japanese, it's super sushi! This multinational New York City import is definitely scene-worthy: It's a hipster's paradise. This stylish, sexy restaurant charges a pretty penny for some exotic sushi rolls such as the $15 soft-shell crab roll, a tasty combo of chives, jalapeño, and crab, and the $12 South Asian roll with shrimp, tomato, cucumber, chives, cilantro, and onions. And while the sushi is top notch, the sashimi ceviches are even better. An assortment of five—your choice of four from either lobster, salmon, yellowtail, tuna, and fluke—is somewhat of a deal at $27, considering the fact that separately each can run you from $9 to $14. Main plates are equally exceptional, and while they have the usual haute dishes of snapper and Chilean sea bass, I'd try the churrasco à Rio Grande, a divine assortment of meats served with rice, beans, collard greens, and chimichurri sauce. Sushi Samba Dromo is one of the area's newer places to be, whether for a sushi roll that may set you back your kid's college fund or for a very potent Pisco Sour or sakegria. Come here for good food and an excellent scene.

600 Lincoln Rd., South Beach. (ℂ) 305/673-5337. Reservations recommended. Main courses $17–$27. AE, MC, V. Mon–Wed noon–midnight; Thurs 11:30am–1am; Fri–Sat noon–2am; Sun brunch 11:30am–3:30pm, dinner 3:30pm–1am.

Talula &&& CREATIVE AMERICAN   Take two star chefs and combine their epicurean efforts, and you've got Talula, one of the most creative, refreshing restaurants to come onto the South Beach scene since Barton G. The Restaurant (p. 122). Owned by husband-and-wife team Andrea Curto-Randazzo, formerly of Wish, and Frank Randazzo, formerly of the now-defunct Gaucho Room, Talula is a blissful marriage of many flavors, as seen in such signature dishes as grilled Sonoma foie gras with caramelized figs, blue-corn cakes, chile syrup, and candied walnuts; and sausage Vidalia onion stuffed grilled center pork chop with garlic-sautéed broccoli rabe, apple smoke bacon, bean ragout, caramelized Granny Smith apple and whole grain mustard sauce. Chef Frank's chophouse specials are also hot-ticket items, including the 14-ounce, 21-day dry-aged rib-eye. Daily specials always include a chopped salad, soup, risotto, and a meat or fish dish. The wine list is well-balanced, featuring 85 vintages from California, Italy, France, Australia, and South America. Wines by the glass are a reasonable, un–South Beach $6 to $10. As to be expected with any restaurant in South Beach, Talula is cool looking, with an unpretentious, warm decor and outdoor garden patio that is a popular spot for the fantastic buffet-style Sunday brunches. An exhibition kitchen is a tempting seating option, with five seats allowing a priceless view of the culinary action.

210 23rd St., South Beach. (ℂ) 305/672-0778. www.talulaonline.com. Reservations recommended. Main courses $18–$36. AE, MC, V. Tues–Thurs noon–2:30pm and 6:30–11pm; Fri noon–2:30pm and 6:30–11:30pm; Sat 6:30–11:30pm; Sun 6–10pm. Happy hour Tues–Sun 5–7pm.

MODERATE

Balan's & MEDITERRANEAN   Balan's provides undeniable evidence that the Brits actually do know a thing or two about cuisine. A direct import from London's Soho, Balan's draws inspiration from various Mediterranean and Asian influences, labeling its cuisine "Mediterrasian." With a brightly colored interior straight out of a mod '60s flick, Balan's is a favorite among the gay and arty crowds, especially on weekends during brunch hours. The moderately priced food is rather good here—especially the sweet-potato soufflé with leeks and roasted garlic; fried goat cheese and portobello mushrooms; and Chilean sea bass with roasted tomato. When in doubt, the restaurant's signature lobster club sandwich is always a good choice. Adding to the ambience is the restaurant's people-watching vantage point on Lincoln Road.

1022 Lincoln Rd. (between Lenox and Michigan), South Beach. (©) 305/534-9191. Reservations accepted, except for weekend brunch. Main courses $7–$25 (breakfast and dinner specials weekdays). AE, DISC, MC, V. Sun–Thurs 8am–midnight; Fri–Sat 8am–1am; Sat–Sun brunch noon–3:30pm.

Big Pink ♠ *Kids* AMERICAN "Real Food for Real People" is the motto to which this restaurant strictly adheres. Set on what used to be a gritty corner of Collins Avenue, Big Pink—owned by the folks at the higher-end Nemo—is quickly identified by a whimsical Pippi Longstocking–type mascot on a sign outside. Scooters and motorcycles line the streets surrounding the place, which is a favorite among beach bums, club kids, and those craving Big Pink's comforting and hugely portioned pizzas, sandwiches, salads, and hamburgers. The fare is above average, at best, and the menu is massive, but it comes with a good dose of kitsch, such as the "gourmet" spin on the classic TV dinner, which is done perfectly, right down to the compartmentalized dessert. Televisions line the bar area, and the family-style table arrangement (there are several booths, too) promotes camaraderie among diners. Outdoor tables are available. Even picky kids will like the food here, and parents can enjoy the family-friendly atmosphere (not the norm for South Beach) without worrying whether their kids are making too much noise.

157 Collins Ave., Miami Beach. (©) 305/532-4700. Main courses $13–$20. AE, DC, MC, V. Mon–Wed 8am–midnight; Thurs 8am–2am; Fri–Sat 8am–5am; Sun 8am–2am.

Bond St. Lounge ♠ SUSHI A New York City import, the sceney Bond St. Lounge is in the basement of the shabby-chic Townhouse Hotel and is packing in hipsters as tightly as the crabmeat in a California roll. Despite its tiny size, Bond St. Lounge's super-fresh nigiri and sashimi, and funky sushi rolls such as the sun-dried tomato and avocado or the arugula crispy potato, are worth cramming in here for. As the evening progresses, however, Bond St. becomes more of a bar scene than a restaurant, but sushi is always available at the bar to accompany your sake Bloody Mary.

Townhouse Hotel, 150 20th St., South Beach. (©) 305/398-1806. Reservations recommended. Sushi $6–$20. AE, MC, V. Daily 6pm–2am.

The Café at Books & Books ♠ AMERICAN Not only does this sidewalk café (with a few tables inside the bookstore) offer some of the best, freshest breakfasts and lunches in town—the egg and tuna salad combo is my favorite as is the amazing homemade hash browns—but gourmet dinners as well. This is not your chain bookstore's pre fab tuna sandwich. Chef Bernie Matz gave star Chef Douglas Rodriguez his start—enough said. Sandwiches, salads, and burgers are good, but after five, the real gourmand comes out in Matz with dishes like a juicy flank steak marinated in espresso and brown sugar, seared, sliced and served with a pineapple and onion salsa and a pair of plantain nests smothered in garlicky mojo. Because it's a bookstore, there's no full bar, just beer and wine only, but regardless, you may be more inspired to go inside and pick up a cookbook instead of a cocktail!

933 Lincoln Rd., South Beach. (©) 305/695-8898. Main courses $5–$25. AE, MC, V. Daily 9am–11pm.

Clarke's ♠ IRISH There's more to this neighborhood pub than pints of Guinness. With a warm, inviting ambience and a gorgeously rich wood bar as the focal point, Clarke's is the only true gastropub in Miami, with excellent fare that goes beyond bangers and mash and delicious burgers, and delves into the gourmet with olive oil yellowtail poached snapper with mushroom confit, tomato marmalade and frisée salad; Sazerac House crab cakes, whose secret recipe hails from owner Laura Cullen's father's New York City landmark, the Sazerac House; and Mom's Montauk-style scallops. If you're not in the mood for full fare, my favorite is the New York–style pretzel, served on a spike with mustard on the side. The vibe here is very friendly, which is why everyone from Miami Heat basketball players and police chiefs to South Beach celebrity types choose Clarke's when they want a low-key night with delicious fare—and even more delicious "dish."

840 1st St., South Beach. ℂ **305/538-9885.** www.clarkesmiamibeach.com. Main courses $6–$27. AE, MC, V. Mon–Sat 5pm–midnight; Sun brunch 11am–3pm, 4pm–midnight.

El Rancho Grande *⋆⋆* MEXICAN
Hidden on a side street off of Lincoln Road, El Rancho Grande is a favorite local cantina that has attracted the likes of Cher and Matt Damon, thanks to its ultrafresh fare and unassuming ambience. With a "Pottery Barn meets Acapulco" decor, El Rancho Grande doesn't hold anything back when it comes to the cuisine. The Aztec soup, a hot-and-spicy blend of chicken and tortilla strips, is one of the best I've had. The salsa here is not at all watery and is freshly made—a tongue-tickling blend of spices, cilantro, tomatoes, onions, and peppers, and the Mexican favorites of burritos, enchiladas, and fajitas are all very well represented. All portions are huge and can be shared or taken home for extra meal mileage. Margaritas are a little weak when frozen and better ordered on the rocks. Expect a wait at the small bar for your table, especially on weekends. Limited outdoor seating is also available.

1626 Pennsylvania Ave., South Beach. ℂ **305/673-0480.** Main courses $10–$19. AE, DC, MC, V. Daily 11am–11pm.

Grillfish *⋆* SEAFOOD
From the beautiful Byzantine-style mural and the gleaming oak bar, you'd think you were eating in a much more expensive restaurant, but Grillfish manages to pay the exorbitant South Beach rent with the help of a loyal following of locals who come for fresh, simple seafood in a relaxed but upscale atmosphere. The servers are friendly and know the menu well. The barroom seafood chowder is full of chunks of shellfish, as well as some fresh whitefish filets in a tomato broth. The small ear of corn included with each entree is about as close as you'll get to any type of vegetable offering, besides the pedestrian salad. Still, at these prices, it's worth a visit to try some local fare, including mako shark, swordfish, tuna, marlin, and wahoo. Most recently, they opened up a pizza restaurant next door called Crust, in case crustaceans aren't your thing.

1444 Collins Ave. (corner of Española Way), South Beach. ℂ **305/538-9908.** www.grillfish.com. Reservations accepted for parties of 6 or more only. Main courses $9–$26. AE, DC, DISC, MC, V. Daily 11:30am–4pm and 5:30pm–midnight.

Jerry's Famous Deli *⋆* DELI
Answering the cries for a real, New York–style deli on South Beach is Jerry's Famous Deli, actually a Los Angeles import, which now occupies the cavernous space that used to house the very decadent gay disco, the Warsaw Ballroom. In a way, Jerry's still channels that same decadence, albeit with a menu that features over 700 monstrously portioned items, from your typical corned beef on rye to your atypical brisket burrito. While the quality of the food is excellent, the service pales in comparison: This 24-hour deli is not a place to go if you're in a rush. The modern cafeteria, complete with full bar and a very Los Angelean nonsmoking policy (which has expanded to all Florida restaurants), is dimly lit with a disco soundtrack that is somewhat reminiscent of its predecessor. People come here to linger over sandwiches

that can feed at least two people, if not more, and should you be craving a Reuben sandwich after a night of clubbing at 5am, Jerry's is command central for that set as well as the original early birders who are first waking at 5am and will have their dinner at 5pm. One thing, though: This is *not* your grandfather's deli, where sandwiches were only a few bucks. Prepare to shell out at least $10 and up for one of Jerry's. What do you expect? It's 21st-century South Beach!

1450 Collins Ave., South Beach. © 305/532-8030. Main courses $7–$30. www.jerrysfamousdeli.com AE, DC, DISC, MC, V. Daily 24 hr.

Joe Allen ✿ *Finds* AMERICAN   It's hard to compete in a city with haute spots everywhere you look, but Joe Allen, a restaurant that has proven itself in both New York and London, has stood up to the challenge by establishing itself off the beaten path in possibly the only area of South Beach that has remained impervious to trendiness and overdevelopment. Located on the bay side of the beach, Joe Allen is conspicuously devoid of neon lights, valet parkers, and fashionable pedestrians. Inside, however, one discovers a hidden jewel: a stark yet elegant interior and no-nonsense, fairly priced, ample-portioned dishes such as meatloaf, pizza, fresh fish, and salads. The scene has a homey feel favored by locals looking to escape the hype without compromising quality.

1787 Purdy Ave./Sunset Harbor Dr. (3 blocks west of Alton Rd.), South Beach. © 305/531-7007. Reservations recommended, especially on weekends. Main courses $15–$25. MC, V. Daily 11:30am–11:30pm.

Larios on the Beach ✿ *Overrated* CUBAN   If you're a fan of singer Gloria Estefan, you will definitely want to check out this restaurant, which she and her husband Emilio co-own; if not, you may want to reconsider, as the place is an absolute mob scene, especially on weekends. The classic Cuban dishes get a so-so rating from the Cubans, but a better one from those who aren't as well versed in the cuisine. The portions here are larger than life, as are some of the restaurant's patrons, who come here for the sidewalk scenery and the well-prepared black beans and rice. Inside, the restaurant turns into a makeshift salsa club, with music blaring over the animated conversations and the sounds of English clashing with Spanish. Because of its locale on Ocean Drive, Larios is a great place to bring someone who's never experienced the Cuban culture or tasted its cuisine.

820 Ocean Dr., South Beach. © 305/532-9577. Reservations recommended. Main courses $8–$30. AE, MC, V. Sun–Thurs 11:30am–midnight; Fri–Sat 11:30am–1am.

Macaluso's ✿✿ ITALIAN   This restaurant epitomizes the Italians' love for—and mastery of—savory, plentiful, down-home Staten Island–style food. While the storefront restaurant is intimate and demure in nature, there's nothing delicate about the bold mix of flavors in every meat and pasta dish here. Catch the fantastic clam pie when in season—the portions are huge. Pricier items vary throughout the season but will likely feature fresh fish handpicked by chef (and owner) Michael, the don of the kitchen, who is so accommodating that he'll take special requests or even bring to your table a complimentary signature meatball. If he doesn't, don't hesitate to ask your waiter for one; he'll be glad to bring it to you. Everyone will recommend favorites such as the rigatoni and broccoli rabe. There are also delicious desserts ranging from homemade anisette cookies to gooey pastries. The wine list is also good. Celeb alert: Macaluso's is where Demi Moore and Ashton Kutcher made their official debut as a couple while in Miami.

1747 Alton Rd., Miami Beach. © 305/604-1811. Main courses $14–$32; pizza $8–$17. MC, V. Tues–Sat 6pm–midnight; Sun 6–11pm. After 10:30pm, only pies are served.

Monty's Raw Bar ✴ (Value) SEAFOOD   This restaurant is the antithesis of South Beach trendiness, with scrappy wood floors and a very casual raw bar set outside around a large swimming pool. The best deal in town is still the all-you-can-eat stone crabs—about $45 for the large ones and $35 for the mediums. That's about the same price that Joe's, located 2 blocks away, charges for just three or four claws. (But don't order stone crabs in summer—they aren't as fresh.) Enjoy the incredible views and off-season fish specialties, including the Maryland she-crab soup, rich and creamy without too much thickener. Other bar snacks such as peel-and-eat shrimp, smoked-fish dip, and Buffalo wings go really well with beer or rum runners. Beware of Friday nights, when the happy-hour crowds convene around (and sometimes in) the pool for post-work revelry.

300 Alton Rd., South Beach. © 305/673-3444. Reservations recommended. Main courses $20–$40. AE, DC, MC, V. Sun–Thurs 5:30–11pm; Fri–Sat 5:30pm–midnight.

Nexxt Café ✴ AMERICAN   Locals joke that this lively, always-packed outdoor cafe should be called Nexxt Year to reflect the awfully slow service that has become its unfortunate trademark. In fact, since the last book was written, I'm still waiting for my Southwestern chicken salad. Service aside, however, Nexxt has made quite a splash on South Beach, attracting an evening crowd looking for nighttime revelry and a morning crowd on the weekends for a standing-room-only brunch sensation. The fresh food comes in lavish portions that could easily feed two; the salads are an especially good bargain. Start your meal with the calamari fritti—they're a lot fresher here than at most other local restaurants—or the popcorn shrimp, which are larger than you might expect. The burgers and sandwiches are similarly big, and the steaks are well worth a taste. They have coffees in tall, grande, and "maxxi." There are also plenty of coffee cocktails, mixed drinks, frozen beverages, and wines, giving this place a nice bar life, too.

700 Lincoln Rd. (off Euclid Ave.), South Beach. © 305/532-6643. Main courses $12–$26. AE, MC, V. Daily 9am–1am.

Spiga ✴✴ (Finds) ITALIAN   If you want a side scene with your spaghetti, don't even think of dining at Spiga, a place that's so low-key that many of South Beach's most ostentatious hipsters have never even heard of it. The complimentary bruschetta with grilled eggplant, served to you at one of the few tables inside or out, is the first of many culinary treats. The simple gnocchi with tomato and basil is a garlicky sensation, not to mention a most filling entree. The fresh asparagus baked in Parmesan cheese is so fresh that gourmands insist that Alice Waters, the queen of organic cooking, had something to do with it, and the red snapper with kalamata olives, fresh tomatoes, capers, and onions is a refreshingly simple departure from the fusion variety that can be found in almost any area restaurant. The place is extremely romantic and vaguely reminiscent of a Florentine trattoria.

Hotel Impala, 1228 Collins Ave., South Beach. © 305/534-0079. Reservations accepted. Main courses $7–$20. AE, DC, MC, V. Daily 6pm–midnight.

Tap Tap ✴ HAITIAN   The whole place looks like an overgrown *tap tap,* a brightly painted jitney common in Haiti. Every inch is painted in vibrant neon hues (blue, pink, purple, and so on), and the atmosphere is always fun. It's where the Haiti-philes and Haitians, from journalists to politicians, hang out. The *lanbi nan citron,* a tart, marinated conch salad, is perfect with a tall tropical drink and maybe some lightly grilled goat tidbits, which are served in a savory brown sauce and are less stringy than typical goat dishes. Another super-satisfying choice is the pumpkin soup, a rich brick-colored purée of subtly seasoned pumpkin with a dash of pepper. An excellent salad of avocado, mango, and watercress is a great finish. Soda junkies should definitely try the watermelon soda. For the ethnophobic, there's a rather tasty vegetable stew, but I strongly recommend the goat—it tastes just like chicken.

819 5th St. (between Jefferson and Meridian aves., next to the Shell Station), South Beach. © 305/672-2898. Reservations accepted. Main courses $6–$20. AE, DC, DISC, MC, V. Mon–Thurs 5–11pm; Fri–Sat 5pm–midnight; Sun 5–10pm. Closed in July.

Van Dyke Cafe 𝒜 AMERICAN News Café's younger, less harried sibling, Van Dyke is a locals' favorite, at which people-watching is also premium, but attitude is practically nonexistent. Like News, the menu here is pretty cut and dried—sandwiches, salads, eggs, and so on, but the Van Dyke's warm, wood-floored interior, upstairs jazz bar, accessible parking, and intense chocolate soufflé make it a less taxing alternative. Also, unlike News, Van Dyke turns into a sizzling nightspot featuring live jazz nearly every night of the week (a $6 cover charge, $11 on weekends, is added to your bill if you sit at a table; the bar's free). Outside there's a vast tree-lined seating area that's ideal for people-watching. Those allergic to or afraid of dogs might reconsider eating here, as Van Dyke is also a canine hot spot.

846 Lincoln Rd., South Beach. © 305/534-3600. Reservations recommended for dinner. Main courses $9–$20. AE, DC, MC, V. Daily 8am–2am.

INEXPENSIVE

Don't miss the South Beach branch of the Gold Coast's fun and tasty **Taverna Opa** (36–40 Ocean Dr., 1 block south of 1st St.; © 305/673-6730) in South Beach. For a review of the restaurant, see p. 216.

A La Folie 𝒜𝒜 FRENCH The Left Bank took a wrong turn and ended up on the quiet(er) end of Española Way in the form of A La Folie. Reflecting the *positive* things about our former allies, A La Folie is an authentic French cafe in which wooden booths and walls full of foreign newspapers and magazines make you have to take a second look at your plane ticket to make sure you're still in Miami. In addition to the affected, über-French waitstaff (not snotty, but aloof), A La Folie features some of the best cafe fare in Miami including delicious, hugely portioned sandwiches such as the French fave croque monsieur, salads, crepes, and, of course, cafe au lait and plenty of wine. Indoor and outdoor seating are equally conducive to whiling away many hours sipping coffee, reading a magazine, and reflecting on that whole Freedom Fry controversy.

516 Española Way, South Beach. © 305/538-4484. Main courses $5–$10. MC, V. Daily 9am–midnight.

David's Café II 𝒜 CUBAN The farthest thing from a trendy spot, David's Cafe's Cuban food is so good, cheap, and available 24 hours a day, that Michael Jackson even sauntered up to the outdoor counter to order a cafe Cubano. Enjoy supercheap breakfasts (two eggs, home fries or grits, coffee, and toast is $4.75), Cuban sandwiches (ham, pork, Swiss, pickles, and mustard), midnight *arroz con pollo,* fantastic cheeseburgers, a wonderful grilled-cheese sandwich, *ropa vieja* Habanera (shredded sirloin and sauce), and pretty much anything you can think of—even, oddly enough, brown rice. Hey, this is South Beach, what can you expect?

1654 Meridian Ave., South Beach. © 305/672-8707. Main courses $4–$20. AE, MC, V. Daily 24 hr.

11th Street Diner AMERICAN   The only real diner on the beach, the 11th Street Diner is the antidote to a late-night run to Denny's. Be forewarned that some of Miami's most colorful characters, especially the drunk ones, convene here at odd hours and your greasy-spoon experience can quickly turn into a three-ring circus. Uprooted from its 1948 Wilkes-Barre, Pennsylvania, foundation, the actual structure was dismantled and rebuilt on a busy—and colorful (a gay bar is right next door so be on the lookout for very flamboyant drag queens)—corner of Washington Avenue. Although it can use a good window cleaning, it remains a popular round-the-clock spot that attracts all walks of life. If you're craving french fries, order them smothered in mozzarella with a side of gravy—a tasty concoction known as disco fries because of its popularity among starving clubbers.

1065 Washington Ave., South Beach. ℂ 305/534-6373. Items $8–$15. AE, MC. Daily 24 hr.

Front Porch Café Ⓡ AMERICAN   Located in an unassuming, rather dreary-looking Art Deco hotel, the Front Porch Café is a relaxed local hangout known for cheap breakfasts. Some of the servers tend to be a bit attitudinal and lackadaisical (many are bartenders or club kids by night), so this isn't the place to be if you're in a hurry, especially on the weekends, when the place is packed all day long and lines are the norm. Enjoy home-style French toast with bananas and walnuts, omelets, fresh fruit salads, pizzas, and classic breakfast pancakes that put IHOP to shame. If you're looking to avoid the tourists and prefer to dine with the locals, Front Porch is where it's at for breakfast, lunch, and even dinner.

In the Penguin Hotel, 1418 Ocean Dr., South Beach. ℂ 305/531-8300. Main courses $5–$20. AE, DC, DISC, MC, V. Daily 8am–10:30pm.

Icebox Café Ⓡ AMERICAN   Locals love this place for its homey comfort food—tuna melts, pot pies, and eggs for breakfast, lunch, and dinner—but Oprah Winfrey singled it out for its desserts, which is really why people raid the Icebox whenever that sweet tooth calls. In the Icebox, you'll discover the best chocolate cake, pound cake, and banana cream pies outside of your grandma's kitchen.

1657 Michigan Ave., South Beach. ℂ 305/538-8448. Main courses and desserts $3–$10. AE, MC, V. Daily 8am–10:30pm.

La Sandwicherie SANDWICHES   You can get mustard, mayo, or oil and vinegar on sandwiches elsewhere in town, but you'd be missing out on all the local flavor. This gourmet sandwich bar, open until the crack of dawn, caters to ravenous club kids, biker types, and the body artists who work in the tattoo parlor next door. For many people, in fact, no night of clubbing is complete without capping it off with a turkey sub from La Sandwicherie.

229 14th St. (behind the Amoco station), South Beach. ℂ 305/532-8934. Sandwiches and salads $6–$12. AE, MC, V. Daily 9am–5am. Delivery 9:30am–11pm.

News Cafe Ⓡ AMERICAN   This South Beach cafe–cum–landmark hasn't fallen off the radar as far as buzz and hype are concerned. The quintessential South Beach experience, News is still au courant, albeit swarming with mostly tourists. Unless it's appallingly hot or rainy out, you should wait for an outside table, which is where you need to be to fully appreciate the experience. Service is abysmal and often arrogant (perhaps because the tip is included), but the menu is reliable, running the gamut from sandwiches and salads to pasta dishes and omelets. My favorite here is the Middle Eastern platter, a dip lover's paradise, with hummus, tahini, tabbouleh, babaganoush, and fresh pita bread. If it's not too busy, feel free to order just a cappuc-cino—your server may snarl, but that's what News is all about; creative types like to bring their laptops and sit here all day (or all night—this place is open 24 hr. a day). If you're by yourself and need something to read, there's an extensive collection of national and international newspapers and magazines at the in-house newsstand.

800 Ocean Dr., South Beach. ⓒ 305/538-6397. Items $5–$20. AE, DC, MC, V. Open 24 hrs.

Paninoteca ⓕ SANDWICHES   A gourmet Italian-style sandwich shop with deli-cious offerings such as grilled veggies and goat cheese on focaccia, the only thing that's not so palatable about Paninoteca is the slow service. Consider takeout or a leisurely, very leisurely, snack. There's also a Coral Gables shop at 264 Miracle Mile, between Ponce de León Boulevard and Salzedo Street, ⓒ **305/443-8388.**

809 Lincoln Rd., South Beach. ⓒ **305/538-0058.** Sandwiches $7–$12. No credit cards. Sun–Thurs 11am–11pm; Fri–Sat 11am–midnight.

Piola ⓕ PIZZA   This hip Italian import miraculously transforms pizza from an eat-out-of-the-box-stuff-a-slice-into-your-mouth experience into a fun, sit-down meal that's hard to beat for the price, quality, and quantity. An unabridged menu of nearly 80 different kinds of pizzas-for-one that are really enough to share between two peo-ple is mind numbing and mouthwatering. I suggest that you order several pizzas, depending on how many people you are dining with (two is more than enough for two, for example). Start with the quattro formaggio pizza—brie, Gorgonzola, Parme-san and mozzarella—and then consider a funkier version, say, smoked salmon and caviar. All pizzas are thin crusted and full of flavor. Waitstaff is extremely friendly, too, but be prepared for a lengthy wait, especially on weekend nights when the movie-going crowds next door spill over for a snack.

1625 Alton Rd., South Beach. ⓒ **305/674-1660.** Reservations accepted. Main courses $7–$15. AE, DC, MC, V. Daily 6pm–1am.

Puerto Sagua ⓕ CUBAN/SPANISH   This brown-walled diner is one of the only old holdouts on South Beach. Its steady stream of regulars ranges from *abuelitos* (lit-tle old grandfathers) to hipsters who stop in after clubbing. It has endured because the food is good, if a little greasy. Some of the less heavy dishes are a super-chunky fish soup with pieces of whole flaky grouper, chicken, and seafood paella, or marinated kingfish. Also good are most of the shrimp dishes, especially the shrimp in garlic sauce, which is served with white rice and salad. This is one of the most reasonably priced places left on the beach for simple, hearty fare. Don't be intimidated by the hunched, older waiters in their white button-down shirts and black pants. Even if you don't speak Spanish, they're usually willing to do charades. Anyway, the extensive menu, which ranges from BLTs to grilled lobsters to yummy fried plantains, is trans-lated into English. Hurry, before another boutique goes up in its place.

700 Collins Ave., South Beach. ⓒ **305/673-1115.** Main courses $6–$24; sandwiches and salads $5–$10. AE, DC, MC, V. Daily 7:30am–2am.

San Loco Tacos ⓕ MEXICAN   There are no talking Chihuahuas to promote this excellent fast-food Mexican joint, but word of human mouth seems to do the trick. The food is served quickly, with no frills attached, but it's done very well and the place is open late—perfect for an after-clubbing bite. The guacamole is very fresh, and the tacos, burritos, enchiladas, and a host of other Mexican munchies are zesty, not skimpy, and really cheap. Salsa is not watered down or prepackaged and comes in mild, medium, or painfully hot. There are a few tables inside, but most people prefer to pick up their chow and take it out with them.

235 14th St., South Beach. © 305/538-3009. Items $2–$7. No credit cards. Sun–Thurs 11am–5am; Fri–Sat 11am–6am.

2 Miami Beach, North Beach, Surfside, Bal Harbour, Sunny Isles & North Miami

The area north of the Art Deco District—from about 21st Street to 163rd Street—had its heyday in the 1950s when huge hotels and gambling halls blocked the view of the ocean. Now, many of the old hotels have been converted into condos or budget lodgings, and the bayfront mansions have been renovated by and for wealthy entrepreneurs, families, and speculators. The area has many more residents, albeit seasonal, than visitors. On the culinary front, the result is a handful of super-expensive, traditional restaurants as well as a number of value-oriented spots.

For a map of these listings, see p. 98.

VERY EXPENSIVE

The Forge Restaurant ☆☆☆ STEAKHOUSE/AMERICAN   English oak paneling and Tiffany glass suggest high prices and haute cuisine, and that's exactly what you get at The Forge. Each elegant dining room possesses its own character and features high ceilings, ornate chandeliers, and European artwork. The atmosphere is elegant but not too stuffy. On Wednesday night (the party night here), however, it's pandemonium as the who's who of Miami society gathers for dinner, dancing, and schmoozing. Like the rest of the menu, appetizers are mostly classics, from Beluga caviar to baked onion soup to shrimp cocktail and escargot. When they're in season, order the stone crabs. For the main course, any of the seafood, chicken, or veal dishes are recommendable, but The Forge is especially known for its award-winning steaks. Its wine selection is equally lauded—ask for a tour of the cellar. *Celeb alert:* None other than Michael Jackson has dined here on numerous occasions and considers The Forge one of his favorite restaurants of all time. Same goes for Sharon Stone, Madonna, Jennifer Lopez, Paris Hilton, Michael Jordan, and, well, you get the picture.

432 Arthur Godfrey Rd. (41st St.), Miami Beach. © 305/538-8533. Reservations recommended. Main courses $25–$60. AE, DC, MC, V. Sun–Thurs 6pm–midnight; Fri–Sat 6pm–1am.

The Palm ☆☆ STEAKHOUSE   As sturdy as the tree that shares its name, the Palm is one of the country's most heralded steakhouses, known for its Jurassic portions and no-nonsense service. Everything here is a la carte, and the prices add up quicker than the cholesterol courses through your veins. Both fish and meat are praiseworthy; the blackened swordfish steak is as hearty and massive as the filet mignon. Prime rib and New York strip are full of flavor as well and cooked to perfection. To complicate matters further, the veal and lamb chops are absolutely divine. For those who like a little surf with their turf, the lobsters here are truly freaks of nature, weighing in at 4 pounds and up. The food is prepared simply, but needs no enhancement. Sharing is encouraged unless you're a linebacker, and even they've been known to split a steak. Side dishes include salads, potatoes, and vegetables; be sure to try the superb creamed spinach. Another, more spacious Palm has sprouted in Coral Gables at The Village of Merrick Park, 4425 Ponce de León Blvd. (© 786/552-7256).

9650 E. Bay Harbor Dr., Bay Harbor Island. © 305/868-7256. Reservations highly recommended. Main courses $20–$50. AE, DC, MC, V. Daily 5–11pm. From Collins Ave., turn west onto 96th St.; at Bal Harbour Shops, go over a small bridge, and turn right onto East Bay Harbor Dr. The restaurant is half a block down on the left.

EXPENSIVE

Carpaccio ☞ ITALIAN   A favored spot for the ladies who lunch, Carpaccio's location in the ritzy Bal Harbour Shops is its tastiest aspect: It's definitely a place to see and be seen. Ask for specials rather than ordering off the regular menu; they're much more interesting—linguine lobster, snapper piccata, and veal chop any style—though they may be a bit pricier. Wear sunglasses to block the blinding glare of all the diamonds.

9700 Collins Ave. (97th St., in Bal Harbour Shops), Bal Harbour. ☎ 305/867-7777. Reservations recommended. Main courses $15–$35; pastas $12–$20. AE, MC, V. Daily 11:30am–11pm.

Timo ☞☞☞ ITALIAN/MEDITERRANEAN   A hip, haute restaurant in Sunny Isles, where, until recently, Tony Roma's was the hottest eatery. Owned by Tim Andriola, former executive chef of Mark's South Beach, Timo is a stylish Italian Mediterranean restaurant catering to mostly North Miami Beach locals who have been yearning for something else besides the fabulous Chef Allen's. Among the specialties, try the handcrafted pastas, including semolina gnocchi with braised oxtail; a traditional Sicilian pasta pie consisting of thin slices of eggplant wrapped around macaroni with crushed red pepper and buffalo mozzarella; and a phenomenal veal scaloppini. Less pricey, less heavy items are also available, such as a delicious ricotta-and-fontina wood-fired pizza with white truffle oil—perfect for lunch or a happy-hour snack. At Timo, a cool bistro-meets-lounge atmosphere gives way to a decidedly cool vibe, something that was always conspicuously lacking at Tony Roma's.

17624 Collins Ave., Sunny Isles. ☎ 305/936-1008. Reservations required. Main courses $11–$27. AE, DC, MC, V. Sun–Thurs 11:30am–3pm and 6–10:30pm; Fri–Sat 11:30am–3pm and 6–11pm.

MODERATE

Cafe Prima Pasta ☞ ITALIAN   Once a small, unknown trattoria on a very trafficky, tacky street, Cafe Prima Pasta has expanded into a place to be for excellent Italian food and quite a bit of fanfare. Because a massive waiting line always spilled out onto the street, the cafe expanded to include ample outdoor seating that is set back from the street noise and traffic, thanks to some creative landscaping. The pasta here is homemade and the kitchen's choice ingredients include ripe, juicy tomatoes; imported olive oil that would cost you a boatload if you bought it in the store; fresh, drippy mozzarella; and fish that tastes as if it has just been caught right out back. The zesty, spicy garlic and oil that is brought out as dip for the bread should be kept with you during your meal, for it doubles as extra seasoning for your food—not that it's necessary. Though tables are packed in, the atmosphere still manages to be romantic. Because of the chef's fancy for garlic, this is a three-Altoid restaurant, so be prepared to pop a few or request that they go light on the garlic.

414 71st St. (half a block east of the Byron movie theater), Miami Beach. ☎ 305/867-0106. Reservations accepted for parties of 6 or more. Main courses $10–$26; pastas $12–$20. MC, V. Mon–Thurs noon–midnight; Fri noon–1am; Sat 1pm–1am; Sun 5pm–midnight.

Cafe Ragazzi ☞☞ ITALIAN   This diminutive Italian cafe, with its rustic decor and a swift, knowledgeable waitstaff, enjoys great success for its tasty, simple pastas. The spicy puttanesca sauce with a subtle hint of fish is perfectly prepared. Also recommended is the salmon with radicchio. You can choose from many decent salads and carpacci, too. Ragazzi has a faithful following of regulars, so be prepared for the crowd spill on the street—especially on weekend nights.

9500 Harding Ave. (on the corner of 95th St.), Surfside. ☎ 305/866-4495. Reservations accepted for parties of 3 or more. Main courses $10–$25 MC, V. Mon–Fri 11:30am–3pm; daily 5–11:30pm.

Oggi Caffe ✦ ITALIAN   Tucked away in a tiny strip mall on the 79th Street Causeway, this neighborhood favorite makes fresh pastas daily. Each one, from the agnolotti stuffed with fresh spinach and ricotta to the wire-thin spaghettini, is tender and tasty. A hearty *pasta e fagiole* is filled with beans and vegetables and could almost be a meal. I also recommend the daily soups, especially the creamy spinach soup when it's on the menu. Though you could fill up on the starters, the entrees, especially the grilled dishes, are superb. The salmon is served on a bed of spinach with a light lemon-butter sauce. The place is small and a bit rushed, but it's worth the slight discomfort for this authentic, moderately priced food. Another Oggi Caffe opened at 7921 NW 2nd St. in downtown Miami and a sister restaurant, Caffe DaVinci, 1009 Kane Concourse in Bay Harbor Islands, just west of Bal Harbour, has been attracting a faithful following for several years.

1740 79th St. Causeway (in the White Star shopping center next to the Bagel Café), North Beach. ⓒ 305/866-1238. Reservations recommended. Main courses $14–$30; pastas $10–$15. AE, DC, MC, V. Mon–Fri 11:30am–2:30pm; daily 6–11pm.

INEXPENSIVE

The Greek Place GREEK   This little hole-in-the-wall diner with sparkling white walls and about 10 wooden stools serves fantastic Greek and American diner-style food. Daily specials like *pastitsio,* chicken *alcyone,* and roast turkey with all the fixings are big lunchtime draws for locals working in the area. Typical Greek dishes like shish kabob, souvlakia, and gyros are cooked to perfection as you wait. Even the hamburger, prime ground beef delicately spiced and freshly grilled, is wonderful.

233 95th St. (between Collins and Harding aves.), Surfside. ⓒ 305/866-9628. Main courses $6–$10. No credit cards. Mon–Fri 10am–5pm; Sat 11am–3pm.

Here Comes the Sun ✦ AMERICAN/HEALTH FOOD   One of Miami's first health-food spots, this bustling grocery-store-turned-diner serves hundreds of plates a night, mostly to blue-haired locals. It's noisy and hectic but worth it. In season, all types pack the place for a $7.95 special, served between 4 and 6:30pm, which includes an entree (you'll pick from more than 20 choices), soup or salad, coffee or tea, and a small frozen yogurt. Fresh grilled fish and chicken entrees are reliable and served with a nice array of vegetables. The miso burgers with "sun sauce" are a vegetarian's dream.

2188 NE 123rd St. (west of the Broad Causeway), North Miami. ⓒ 305/893-5711. Reservations recommended in season. Main courses $8–$18; sandwiches and salads $5–$15 AE, DC, DISC, MC, V. Mon–Sat 11am–8:30pm.

3 North Miami Beach

Although there aren't many hotels in North Dade, the population in the winter months explodes due to the onslaught of seasonal residents from the Northeast. A number of exclusive condominiums and country clubs, including William's Island, Turnberry, and the Jockey Club, breed a demanding clientele, many of whom dine out nightly. That's good news for visitors, who can find superior service and cuisine at value prices.

VERY EXPENSIVE

Chef Allen's ✦✦✦ NEW WORLD   If anyone deserves to have a restaurant named after him, it's Chef Allen Susser, winner of the esteemed James Beard Award for Best American Chef in the Southeast—the Academy Award of cuisine—and practically

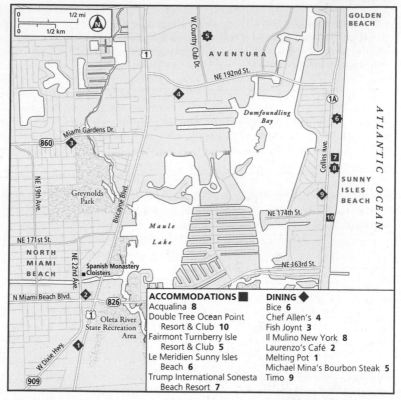

AVENTURA

NE 192nd St.

W Country Club Dr.

Dumfoundling
Bay

ATLANTIC OCEAN

Miami Gardens Dr.

860

Greynolds
Park

Biscayne Blvd.

Maule
Lake

Collins Ave.

SUNNY
ISLES
BEACH

NE 174th St.

NE 171st St.

NE 19th Ave.

NE 22nd Ave.

NORTH
MIAMI
BEACH

Spanish Monastery
Cloisters

NE 163rd St.

N Miami Beach Blvd.

826

Oleta River
State Recreation
Area

W Dixie Hwy.

909

ACCOMMODATIONS ■
Acqualina **8**
Double Tree Ocean Point
  Resort & Club **10**
Fairmont Turnberry Isle
  Resort & Club **5**
Le Meridien Sunny Isles
  Beach **6**
Trump International Sonesta
  Beach Resort **7**

DINING ◆
Bice **6**
Chef Allen's **4**
Fish Joynt **3**
Il Mulino New York **8**
Laurenzo's Café **2**
Melting Pot **1**
Michael Mina's Bourbon Steak **5**
Timo **9**

every other form of praise and honor awarded by the most discriminating palates. Chef Allen, the man, is royalty around here. Chef Allen's, the restaurant, is his province, and foodies are his disciples. His platform? New World cuisine and the harmony of exotic tropical fruits, spices, and vegetables. It is under Chef Allen's magic that ordinary Key limes and mangoes reappear in the forms of succulent salsas and sauces. A traditional antipasto is transformed into a Caribbean one, with papaya-pineapple barbecued shrimp, jerk calamari, and charred rare tuna. Whole yellowtail in coconut milk and curry sauce is a particularly spectacular entree. Unlike other restaurants where location is key, Chef Allen's, located at the rear of a strip mall, could be in the desert and hordes of people would still make the trek.

19088 NE 29th Ave. (at Biscayne Blvd.), Aventura. *C* **305/935-2900.** Reservations recommended. Main courses $25–$45. AE, DC, MC, V. Sun–Thurs 6–10pm; Fri-Sat 6–11pm.

Christine Lee's ★★ CHINESE   This Cantonese restaurant is a 35-year-old Miami staple that serves excellent but overpriced Chinese-style dishes featuring steak, shrimp, and lobster sauce, as well as a good rendition of steak kew, a Cantonese dish with oyster sauce and hot bean paste. Considering the dearth of good Chinese restaurants in Miami, this is a fine choice if you absolutely *must* satisfy your cravings for Chinese, but it will definitely cost you more than it should, especially since it moved to its

Impressions

What's really exciting about Miami is its growth as an international destination. We don't have many restrictions as to what our neighborhoods should look like, and that's reflected in our food . . . It's very open and exciting.
                                                                    —Chef Allen Susser

swank new location at the Gulfstream Racing and Casino. There's another Christine Lee's in Jupiter, at 1200 Town Center Dr. (© **561/624-0404**).

Gulfstream Racing and Casino, 901 S. Federal Hwy., Hallandale. © **954/457-6255.** Reservations recommended. www.christinelees.com Main courses $8–$32. AE, DISC, MC, V. Daily 11:30am–3pm and 4–10:30pm (not open for lunch May–Sept).

Il Mulino New York ⊕ ITALIAN   New York's veritable Greenwich Village Italian hot spot opened in Sunny Isles to mixed reviews. An ornate restaurant located in the even more ornate Acqualina Resort, Il Mulino is a saucy affair with signature fare such as spaghettini Bolognese, a Flintstonian-sized rack of lamb, veal chop, and more. Service ranges from spotty to spectacular, but there's something about the tuxedoed waiters that makes it all so elegant and romantic. But again, there's that sauce issue. When I ate here, my dish was covered in sauce and I forgot what I ordered. I've come to the conclusion, based on the opinions of others who have eaten here, that it's hit or miss. If you're in the mood for fancy Italian food and money's no object, what have you got to lose by trying it, other than your food lost in a sea of sauce?

17875 Collins Ave. (in Acqualina), Sunny Isles. © **305/466-9191.** Reservations recommended. Main courses $24–$60. AE, MC, V. Mon–Thurs 5–10:30pm; Fri–Sat 5–11:30pm.

Michael Mina's Bourbon Steak ⊕⊕ STEAKHOUSE   Although there's no shortage of steakhouses in Miami, there's nothing like this one. Reminiscent of something out of Las Vegas, everything here is massive—from the stunning all-glass wine cellar that takes up an entire wall, to the sheer size of the place at 7,600 square feet. And then there are the prices. But if you don't mind splurging, a meal at the star chef's first and only South Florida location is worth it. Start off with some oysters on the half shell—east coast or west coast, your choice—and then continue with the all-natural farm-raised angus beef, American Kobe beef, or actual Japanese Kobe beef—where a 6-ounce rib-eye will set you back $170! Side dishes are delicious—jalapeño creamed corn ($9), truffled mac and cheese ($12), and a trio of duck fat fries ($8) will not only bust your bank account, but your cholesterol levels, too. A scene of well-heeled Aventura residents—including actor James Caan and perma-tanned man George Hamilton—and elegantly dressed hotel guests compose the equally rich crowd.

1999 West Country Club Dr. (in The Fairmont Turnberry Isle Resort & Club), Aventura. © **786/279-6600.** Reservations recommended. Main courses $29–$190. AE, DC, DISC, MC, V. Mon–Thurs 5–10:30pm; Fri–Sat 5–11:30pm.

EXPENSIVE

Fish Joynt ⊕⊕ SEAFOOD   People craving an out-of-this-world high that won't get them arrested can usually be found lining up at this small neighborhood seafood spot where the frills are on the fish and not the decor. Industrial kitsch is the best description of the Fish Joynt's interior, which tends to be on the loud side, but you don't come here for the decor: Simple, fresh fish is the draw, prepared in a multitude of ways, including the Chilean sea bass in sweet-and-sour glaze or the grouper oreganato.

If you like shrimp, order the shrimp cocktail—the crustaceans are absolutely Jurassic size. Every meal comes with irresistible potato pancakes rather than your average boring baked potato. No matter what you order, however, you're guaranteed to experience a high of sorts, thanks to the stellar quality of this one-of-a-kind fish joint—er, joynt.

2570 NE Miami Gardens Dr., North Miami Beach. ℂ 305/936-8333. Main courses $17–$29. AE, DC, MC, V. Sun–Thurs 5–10pm; Fri–Sat 5–11pm.

MODERATE

Melting Pot FONDUE   Traditional fondue is supplemented by combination meat-and-fish dinners, which are served with one of almost a dozen different sauces. With its lace curtains and cozy booths, the Melting Pot can be quite romantic. To satisfy health-conscious diners, the owners have introduced a more wholesome version of fondue, in which you cook vegetables and meats in a low-fat broth. It tastes good, although this version is less fun than watching drippy cheese flow from the hot pot. Best of all is dessert: chunks of fruit that you dip into a creamy chocolate fondue. No liquor is served here, but the wine list is extensive, and beer is available. For those über-conscious of smelling like your last meal, bring along some perfume, because the eau de fondue scent will stay with you for hours after. A second Melting Pot is located at 11520 SW 72nd St. (Sunset Dr.) in Kendall (ℂ **305/279-8816**).

15700 Biscayne Blvd., North Miami Beach. ℂ 305/947-2228. www.meltingpot.net. Reservations recommended on weekends. Fondues $11–$25. AE, DC, DISC, MC, V. Sun–Thurs 5:30–11pm; Fri–Sat 5:30pm–midnight.

INEXPENSIVE

Laurenzo's Café ITALIAN   This Italian restaurant in the middle of a chaotic grocery store used to be among the city's best, but now, thanks to a mediocre, somewhat dirty-looking buffet and abysmal service, we lament the old Laurenzo's. Stick to buying your own stuff at the grocery and you'll be much better off.

16385 W. Dixie Hwy. (south of the corner of 163rd St.), North Miami Beach. ℂ 305/945-6381. Main courses $4–$10; salads $3–$10. No credit cards. Mon–Fri 8:30am–7:30pm; Sat 8am–7pm; Sun 8am–5pm.

4 Downtown Miami

Downtown Miami is a large sprawling area divided by the Brickell Bridge into two distinct areas: Brickell Avenue and the bayfront area near Biscayne Boulevard. You shouldn't walk from one to the other—it's quite a distance and unsafe at night. Convenient Metromover stops do adjoin the areas, so for a quarter, it's better to hop on the scenic sky tram (closed after midnight). Thanks to the urban renaissance taking place in downtown, a lot more hip, chichi restaurants are starting to pop up. Perhaps one day soon, it'll be safe to walk through the city at night from one hot spot to the next. Wishful thinking, perhaps, but then again, South Beach used to be unsafe as well.

For maps of these listings, see p. 103 and p. 157.

VERY EXPENSIVE

Azul 🌟🌟🌟 GLOBAL FUSION   Azul is one of the most upscale, prettiest—and priciest—waterfront restaurants in town. The views of the city skyline are stunning and rival the food—well, almost. Executive chef Clay Conley, who honed his skills with star chef Todd English, creates a tour de force of international cuisine, inspired by Caribbean, French, Argentine, Asian, and even American flavors. Like a stunning designer gown, the restaurant's decor, with its waterfront view, high ceilings, walls burnished in copper, and silk-covered chairs, is complemented by sparkling jewels—in

Impressions

Miami's cuisine is fearless; there are no boundaries.

—Chef Michelle Bernstein, Azul

this case, the food. Among the standouts: Moroccan-inspired lamb; a miso-marinated duck breast; and, my favorite, "A Study in Tuna": raw tuna, tempura avocado, and Asian sauces with osetra caviar. Downstairs is the Mandarin's more casual, less expensive **Café Sambal,** an Asian eatery serving breakfast, lunch, and dinner with the same priceless views.

At the Mandarin Oriental, 500 Brickell Key Dr., Miami. ℭ **305/913-8254.** Reservations strongly recommended. Main courses $24–$55. AE, DC, DISC, MC, V. Mon–Fri noon–3pm and 7–11pm; Sat 7–11pm.

Capital Grille 𝕉𝕉 STEAKHOUSE   The best of all the chain steakhouses, Capital Grille is a serious power spot. Wine cellars are filled with high-end classics, and the dark-wood paneling, pristine white tablecloths, chandeliers, and marble floors all contribute to the clubby atmosphere. For an appetizer, start with the lobster and crab cakes. If you're not in the mood for beef or lobster, try the pan-seared red snapper and asparagus covered with Hollandaise. You're surrounded by wine cellars filled with about 5,000 bottles of wine—too extensive and rare to list. While some people prefer the more stalwart style and service of Morton's up the block, others find Capital to be a bit livelier. The food's pretty much the same between the two, though I find the steaks at Morton's to be a notch better; however, the atmosphere at the Capital Grille is *much* more inviting. Complimentary valet parking here (as opposed to Morton's, which charges a fee) is another reason to visit this carnivorous capital.

444 Brickell Ave., Miami. ℭ **305/374-4500.** Reservations recommended. Main courses $21–$35. AE, DC, DISC, MC, V. Mon–Thurs 11:30am–3pm and 5–10:30pm; Fri 11:30am–3pm and 5–11pm; Sat 6–11pm; Sun 5–10pm.

Porcao 𝕉𝕉 BRAZILIAN   The name sounds eerily like "pork out," which is what you'll be doing at this exceptional Brazilian *churrascaria* (a Brazilian-style restaurant devoted mostly to meat—it's the Portuguese translation of "steakhouse"). For about $40, you can feast on salads and meat *after* you sample the unlimited gourmet buffet, which includes such fillers as pickled quail eggs, marinated onions, and an entire pig. Do not stuff yourself here, as the next step is the meaty part: Choose as much lamb, filet mignon, chicken hearts, and steak as you like, grilled, skewered, and sliced right at your table. Side dishes also come with the meal, ranging from beans and rice to fried yucca.

801 Brickell Bay Dr., Miami. ℭ **305/373-2777.** Reservations accepted. Prix fixe $43 per adult, $23 per child, all you can eat. AE, DC, MC, V. Daily noon–midnight.

EXPENSIVE

Big Fish 𝕉𝕉 *Finds* SEAFOOD/ITALIAN   This scenic seafood shack on the Miami River is a real catch—if you can find it. Hard to locate but well worth the search, Big Fish's remote locale keeps many people biting. In fact, some Italian options were added to its all-seafood menu in the hopes of luring more people, and that worked, too. Big Fish has a sweeping view of the Miami skyline and some of the freshest catches around. But the spectacular setting may be the real draw, right there on the Miami River where freighters, fishing boats, dinghies, and sometimes yachts slink by to the amusement of faithful diners who no longer have to fish around for a charming, serene seafood

Andiamo Brick Oven Pizza **5**
Brosia **8**
Dogma Grill **3**
Domo Japones **7**
Grass Restaurant & Lounge **10**
Jimmy's East Side Diner **2**
Jumbo's **1**
Karma Car Wash **3**
Michael's Genuine
  Food & Drink **9**
Michy's **4**
Sheba Ethiopian Restaurant **11**
Soyka Restaurant & Café **6**

restaurant. However, you should beware of Friday nights, when Big Fish turns into a big happy-hour scene.

55 SW Miami Avenue Rd. (C) **305/373-1770.** Reservations recommended. Main courses $15–$33. AE, DC, MC, V. Mon–Thurs noon–11pm; Fri–Sat noon–midnight. Cross the Brickell Ave. Bridge heading south and take the 1st right on SW 5th St. The road narrows under a bridge. The restaurant is just on the other side.

Grass Restaurant and Lounge ⟨⟨ ⟨Finds⟩ AMERICAN/ASIAN   What once used to be a snooty, haughtier-than-thou lounge/restaurant is now a welcoming restaurant/lounge, where the priority is excellent, fresh cuisine and not fresh doormen, who have thankfully been weeded out. Signature dishes include ginger lime–marinated grilled mahimahi, grass-fed grilled and smoked beef rib-eye and seared Szechuan pepper–crusted foie gras. The tiki-chic eatery surrounded by vines, bamboo, and cozy banquettes is all outdoors, so it's really weather permitting, but when it's nice out, it's a stunning departure from the rest of Miami's ultramodern restaurants. A soon-to-open indoor dining area and lounge will make this an all-season restaurant, but most importantly, the food's always in season and if you're hungry, you're more than welcome to indulge.

28 NE 40th St. ℂ 305/573-3355. Reservations recommended. Main courses $15–$39. AE, DC, MC, V. Wed–Sat 6pm–11pm; Late night bar menu 11pm–2am.

Michy's 𝕽𝕽 (Finds LATIN   Star chef Michelle Bernstein left the fancy confines of the Mandarin Oriental Miami's Azul to open her own, homey 50-seat eatery on Miami's burgeoning Upper East Side. If you drive too fast, you'll miss the small storefront restaurant, a deceiving facade for a whimsical retro orange-and-blue interior where stellar small plates such as ham-and-blue-cheese croquettes are consumed in massive quantities because they're that good. There's also a zingy ceviche; braised duck with Jerez and peaches; conch escargot style in parsley, butter, and garlic; and, for those whose palates can take it, sautéed sweet breads with bacon and orange juice. There's nothing ordinary about Michy's, except for the fact that a reservation here is nearly impossible to score if not made weeks in advance.

6927 Biscayne Blvd. ℂ 305/759-2001. Reservations recommended. Main courses $15–$30. AE, DC, MC, V. Tues–Thurs noon–3pm and 6–10:30pm; Fri noon–3pm and 6–11pm; Sat 6–11pm; Sun 6–10:30pm.

Oceanaire Seafood Room 𝕽𝕽 SEAFOOD   The first restaurant to open in the Mary Brickell Village, Oceanaire is a pricey ocean-liner–inspired chain seafooder known for freshly caught fare. The elegant streamlined dining room is always abuzz with power types and foodies looking for the freshest fish dishes in town. This is not always the case, but it's not everywhere in Miami where you can indulge in guajillo barbecue salmon with spicy, crispy red onions, and it's not a common site to see Nairagi Marlin on the menu. So if you're in the downtown area and in the mood for serious fish dishes, this is the place. If you want stone crabs or something simpler, save your money and check out Joe's Seafood or Garcia's instead.

900 S. Miami Ave. ℂ 305/372-8862. Reservations recommended. Main courses $15–$30. AE, DC, MC, V. Sun–Thurs 5pm-10pm; Fri–Sat 5–11pm.

Provence Grill 𝕽 FRENCH   This restaurant serves some of the tastiest French meals this side of Toulouse. The brothers Cormouls-Houles have used their prodigious culinary skills to assemble an affordable menu that allows us to know just how the French really live—and they do it, dare we say, with incredible panache. The grilled specialties, from chicken to salmon, are imbued with only the best seasonings and sauces. Sautéed mussels with garlic and chives are fabulous as a meal and as a dipping sauce for the crusty bread. Duck lovers will enjoy the grilled duck filet in a red port sauce. Real culinary adventurers should try the dessert menu—crème brûlée spiced with lavender (a local French favorite) is just one selection—which is truly a delight. A full bar outside brings you back from your French delusions of grandeur to a delightful downtown Miami state of mind and beautiful views of the city skyline.

1001 South Miami Ave., Miami. ℂ 305/373-1940. Reservations recommended on weekends. Main courses $14–$22; appetizers $4.95–$6.95. AE, MC, V. Sun 5:30–10:30pm; Mon–Thurs 11am–3pm and 5:30–10:30pm; Fri 11am–3pm and 5:30–11pm; Sat 5:30–11pm.

Rosa Mexicano 𝕽𝕽 MEXICAN   Also in the Mary Brickell Village, this upscale chain Mexican is always lively and not just because the frozen pomegranate margaritas pack a major punch. A stunning decor with 15-foot waterfall and a great bar scene are two assets, but Rosa's use of serious spices and tableside guacamole preparation, served in a lava rock bowl with homemade tortillas (they make them right there in the middle of the dining room!) make this one of Miami's most talked about in a long time. Among the dishes: Mole de Xico, a Veracruz mole made with mulatto, ancho and pasilla chiles or a choice of Mestizas, a sauce of roasted tomatillos, tomatoes, and chipotles; and Chamorro, a crispy pork shank, slow-roasted for 6 hours, dipped in the deep fryer, and served with mushroom-chipotle cream sauce and red bean-chorizo chili. And did we mention the margaritas and the guacamole? *¡Olé!*

900 S. Miami Ave. ⓒ 786/425-1001. www.rosamexicano.com Reservations recommended. Main courses $13–$30. AE, DC, MC, V. Mon–Fri 11am–3pm; Sun–Thurs 5pm-10pm; Fri–Sat 5–11pm.

Sheba Ethiopian Restaurant ⚅⚅ *Finds* ETHIOPIAN   This Design District find is a fantastic, funky place, not to mention an ideal opportunity to expand your palate. The authentic Ethiopian fare—D'Jaj Bi Zitoune, marinated chicken tenderloins sautéed with green olives and spices; and Doro Wat, Ethiopia's national dish of chicken legs and thighs marinated and seasoned in garlic, ginger, and fenugreek (a Mediterranean-grown spice and herb), and stewed in a spicy Berbere sauce (spicy Ethiopian sauce with cardamom, shallots, peppercorns, and fenugreek)—is outstanding and bursting with flavor. If you like spicy food, you'll love Sheba, whose chefs are not afraid to use generous amounts of peppers, peppercorns, and African spices. The restaurant itself exudes a very cool vibe with dim lighting, authentic African masks and decor, and an awesome world-music soundtrack. The bar scene is abuzz here with local artists, hipsters, and those with more adventurous palates.

4029 N. Miami Ave. ⓒ 305/573-1819. Reservations recommended on weekends. Main courses $12–$26. AE, DC, MC, V. Mon–Sat 11:30am–midnight; Sun 5–11pm.

MODERATE

Brosia ⚅⚅⚅ *Finds* MEDITERRANEAN   Located on a quiet corner in the normally quiet Design District, Brosia is bringing some much-needed life to the area with its outstanding cuisine and spectacular setting. With a chef who schooled under the tutelage of Norman Van Aken's kitchen, Brosia isn't just another trendy bistro; the piri piri shrimp and the lamb skewers with tzaziki sauce are the way to start, continuing to the grilled pork tenderloin with caperberries, cornichons, and grain mustard, with a side of perfectly salted, skinny French fries and roasted garlic asparagus. Seriously out of this world. And it all goes down well with the restaurant's signature sangria—in red or white—we prefer the red, but either one will do. And then there's that courtyard, a serene, spectacular outdoor space with couches, tables, and mosaic tile underneath a large oak tree. There's something about Brosia that's very comforting but you may want to wear comfy pants before you go, because you'll definitely want to eat as much as you can here.

163 NE 39th St., Miami. ⓒ 305/572-1400. www.brosiamiami.com. Reservations recommended. Main courses $12–$28. AE, DC, DISC, MC, V. Mon–Fri 11am–5pm, 5pm–11pm; Sat–Sun 5pm–11pm.

Bubba Gump Shrimp Co. *Kids* SEAFOOD   Inspired by the Tom Hanks megahit *Forrest Gump,* the Bubba Gump Shrimp Co. likens life not to a box of chocolates, but rather to a bucket o' shrimp. Located right on the water, this place offers lots of affordable, oddly named shrimp specials. For starters, try the Run Across America Sampler, which includes Bubba's Far Out Dip and Chips, New Orleans Peel 'n' Eat Shrimp, Texas Wild Wings, and Alabama Fried Shrimp. The Bubba's After the Storm Bucket of Boat Trash will trash your arteries with a deep-fried, albeit tasty, mix of shrimp, slipper lobster, and mahimahi. Lt. Dan's Drunken Shrimp is a delicious concoction of shrimp in bourbon sauce with spicy sausage and garlic mashed potatoes. A number of shrimpless salads and sandwiches are also on the menu. It's a fun place to bring the kids on a sunny afternoon. If you haven't stuffed yourself on shrimp, you may want to try the overly caloric Jenny's Strawberry Dream—pound cake layered with vanilla ice cream, surrounded by Jenny's "special sauce," and topped with fresh strawberry purée and whipped cream.

In Bayside Marketplace, 401 Biscayne Blvd. (at Fourth Ave., north of the port of Miami), Miami. © 305/379-8866. www.bubbagump.com Main courses $8–$20. AE, DC, DISC, MC, V. Sun–Thurs 11am–11pm; Fri–Sat 11am–midnight. Closed Thanksgiving and Christmas.

Domo Japones (R) (Finds) SUSHI   A place where the sake menu is much larger than the food one, Domo Japones is a hipster hangout for Design District denizens who don't feel like schlepping over the causeway for sushi. The food is good, if not limited, with the usual raw fish fare as well as some unusual dishes such as miso cod and duck yaki yudon—don't ask, just try it. The ambience is very downtown, with brick walls, modern art including bare-breasted photographs of some very famous supermodels and an upstairs lounge that's cozy and intimate and, best of all, overlooks the scene below, which borders on buzzing, though hardly booming.

4000 NE Second Ave., Miami. © 305/573-5474. www.domojapones.com. Reservations recommended. Sushi $5–$15. Main courses $14–$23. AE, DC, DISC, MC, V. Mon–Fri noon–3pm; Mon–Wed 6–11pm, Thurs–Sat 6–midnight.

Gordon Biersch Brewery Restaurant CONTINENTAL   Best known for its home-brewed lager beers and strict adherence to the 1516 German Purity Law (which mandates the use of only malt, hops, water, and yeast in the brewing process), Gordon Biersch is always buzzing with locals who cram into every bit of the restaurant's sprawling 10,800 square feet. The food, for a beer hall, is particularly good, but sometimes too exotic. There are the usual suspects—burgers and pizza—offset by heavier dishes such as chicken-and-andouille-sausage gumbo and cashew chicken stir-fry. A popular lunch place for local businesspeople, Gordon Biersch is usually packed on Fridays for happy hour.

1201 Brickell Ave. (next to the JW Marriott), Miami. © 786/425-1130. Main courses $12–$20. AE, DC, MC, V. Sun–Thurs 11:30am–11pm; Fri–Sat 11:30am–midnight.

Granny Feelgood's AMERICAN/HEALTH FOOD   Locals love Granny's for the fresh fish and poultry specials, a line of salads that define greenery and good health, and the always-impeccable service by a family-oriented staff who likes to get to know its clientele. Tourists swinging through downtown on the Metromover or just spinning by can munch healthily on anything from a brown rice and steamed vegetable plate to Granny's famous tuna-salad platter. The chef's identity is a secret, but I happen to know he was trained under local chef extraordinaire Allen Susser and also did a stint on nearby Fisher Island's swank members-only restaurant, so the cuisine here will most definitely please the palate. Granny Feelgood's sells its own line of vitamins and herbal products as well.

25 W. Flagler St., Miami. © 305/377-9600. Reservations not accepted. Main courses $9–$15. AE, MC, V. Mon–Fri 7am–5pm.

Joe's Seafood (R) (Finds) SEAFOOD   A good catch on the banks of the Miami River, Joe's Seafood (not to be confused with Joe's Stone Crab) has a great waterfront setting and a fairly simple, yet tasty menu of fresh fish cooked in a number of ways—grilled, broiled, fried, or, the best in my opinion, in garlic or green sauce. Meals are quite the deal here, all served with green salad or grouper soup, and yellow rice or french fries. The complimentary fish-spread appetizer is also a nice touch. Because of this, not to mention the great, gritty ambience that takes you away from neon, neo-Miami in favor of the old seafaring days, there's usually a wait for a table. If so, try **Garcia's** right next door—it may as well be Joe's twin—best known for inexpensive, delicious stone crabs and famous conch fritters. They also recently opened an upstairs bar and lounge overlooking the river.

400–404 NW N. River Dr., Miami. ℂ 305/381-9329. Reservations recommended. Main courses $14–$23. AE, DC, DISC, MC, V. Sun–Thurs 11am–10pm; Fri–Sat 11am–11pm.

Michael's Genuine Food and Drink ✸✸✸ NEW AMERICAN
My favorite restaurant to open in 2007, Michael's is owned and operated by chef Michael Schwartz, formerly of Nemo fame. The sleek, yet unassuming dining room and serene courtyard seating are constantly abuzz with Design District hipsters and foodies alike. The food is stellar, a fresh mix of all organic products, some from Schwartz's own stash, including eggs from his own hens. With an emphasis on products sourced from local growers and farmers, the menu, which changes daily, is divided into small, medium, large, and extra large plates, all rather reasonably priced and extremely hard to choose from. There are also excellent pizzas, such as the exotic mushroom pizza with cave-aged gruyere, caramelized onion, fresh thyme, and truffle oil; a roasted Berkshire pork shoulder with Anson Mills cheese grits, pickled onion and parsley sauce; and my personal favorite: the $4 bar menu, featuring crispy hominy with chile and lime, deviled eggs, kimchi and chicken liver crostini. There's something for everyone here—that is, except a reservation. Book early for Michael's as it's always crowded. Genuinely.

130 NE 40th St., Miami. ℂ **305/573-5550**. Reservations recommended. Main courses $4–$39. AE, DC, DISC, MC, V. Mon–Fri 11:30am–3pm; Mon–Thurs 5:30pm–11pm; Fri 5:30pm–midnight; Sat 6pm–midnight; Sun 5:30–10pm.

Perricone's Marketplace ✸ ITALIAN
A large selection of groceries and wine, plus an outdoor porch and patio for dining, makes this one of the most welcoming spots downtown. Its rustic setting in the midst of downtown is a fantastic respite from city life. Sunday offers buffet brunches and all-you-can-eat dinners, too. But the place is most popular on weekdays at noon, when the "suits" show up for delectable sandwiches, quick and delicious pastas, and hearty salads.

15 SE 10th St. (corner of S. Miami Ave.), Miami. ℂ **305/374-9693**. Sandwiches $5.95 and up; pastas $13 and up. AE, MC, V. Sun and Mon 7am–10pm; Tues–Sat 7am–11pm.

Soyka Restaurant & Café ✸ AMERICAN
Brought to us by the same man who owns the News and Van Dyke cafes in South Beach, Soyka is a much-needed addition (though it's easy to miss) to the seedy area known as the Biscayne Corridor. The motif inside is industrial chic, reminiscent of a souped-up warehouse you might find in New York. Lunches focus on burgers, sandwiches, and wood-fired oven pizzas. Dinners include simple fare, such as an excellent, massive Cobb salad, or more elaborate dishes such as the delicious turkey Salisbury steak. The bar area provides a few comfy couches and bar stools and tables at which to dine, if you prefer not to sit in the open dining room. A children's menu is available for both lunch and dinner. A lively crowd of bohemian Design District types, professionals, and singles gather here for a taste of urban life. On weekends, the place is packed and very loud. Do not expect an after-dinner stroll around the neighborhood—it's still too dangerous for pedestrian traffic. Head over the causeway to South Beach and stroll there.

5556 NE 4th Court (Design District, off Biscayne Blvd. and 55th St.), Miami. ⓒ **305/759-3117.** Reservations recommended for parties of 8 or more. Main courses $8–$26. AE, MC, V. Restaurant Sun–Thurs 11am–11pm; Fri–Sat 11am–midnight. Happy hour Mon–Fri 4–7pm. Bar Sun–Thurs 11am–midnight; Fri–Sat 11am–1am.

INEXPENSIVE

Andiamo Brick Oven Pizza ⊛ PIZZA   Leave it to visionary Mark Soyka (News Cafe, Van Dyke Cafe, Soyka) to turn a retro-style 1960s carwash into one of the city's best pizza places. The brick-oven pizzas are to die for, whether you choose the simple Andiamo pie (tomato sauce, mozzarella, and basil) or the designer combos of pancetta and caramelized onions; hot and sweet sausage with broccoli rabe; or portobello mushrooms with truffle oil and goat cheese. Pizzas come in three sizes—10-, 13-, and 16-inch. Though the pizza is undeniably delicious here, the most talked-about aspect of Andiamo is the fact that while you're washing down slice after slice, you can get your car washed and detailed at Leo's, the space's original and still-existing occupant out back.

5600 Biscayne Blvd., Miami. ⓒ **305/762-5751.** Main courses $3–$15. MC, V. Sun–Thurs 11am–11pm; Fri–Sat 11am–midnight.

Dogma Grill ⊛⊛ HOT DOGS   A little bit of L.A. comes to a gritty stretch of Biscayne Boulevard in the form of this very tongue-and-cheeky hot-dog stand whose motto is "A Frank Philosophy." The brainchild of a former MTV executive, Dogma will change the way you view hot dogs, offering a plethora of choices, from your typical chili dog to Chicago style with celery salt, hot peppers, onions, and relish. The tropical version with pineapple is a bit funky but fitting for this stand, which attracts a very colorful, arty crowd from the nearby Design District. The buns here are softer than feather pillows, and the hot dogs are grilled to perfection. Try the garlic fries and the lemonade, too. Two new locations of Dogma opened, one across the street from the Museum of Contemporary Art at 899 NE 125th St. in North Miami and the other on South Beach at 1500 Washington Ave.

7030 Biscayne Blvd., Miami. ⓒ **305/759-3433.** Main courses $3–$4. No credit cards. Daily 11am–9pm.

Jimmy's East Side Diner ⊛ DINER   The only thing wrong with this quintessential, consummate greasy-spoon diner is that it's not open 24 hours. Other than that, for the cheapest breakfasts in town, not to mention lunches and early dinners, Jimmy's is a dream come true. Try the banana pancakes, corned beef hash, roasted chicken, or Philly cheese steak. Located on the newly hip Upper East Side of Biscayne Boulevard, Jimmy's is a very neighborhoody place where late Bee Gee Maurice Gibb used to dine every Sunday. Adding to the aging regulars is a new, eclectic contingency of hung-over hipsters for whom Jimmy's is a sweet—and cheap—morning-after salvation.

7201 Biscayne Blvd., Miami. ⓒ **305/759-3433.** Main courses $3–$11. No credit cards. Daily 7am–4pm.

Jumbo's ⊛⊛⊛ *Finds* SOUL FOOD   Open 24 hours daily, this Miami institution is the kind of place where you'll see everyone from Rastafarian musicians and cab drivers to Lenny Kravitz. It's in a shady neighborhood—Carol City—so if you go there, you're going for only one reason—Jumbo's. Family owned for more than 50 years, Jumbo's is known for its world-famous fried shrimp, fried chicken, catfish fingers, and collard greens. Their motto—"Life is to be enjoyed, not to be endured . . . Making friends is our business" is spot on. The service is friendly and fun, and there's history here, too. Jumbo's is the first restaurant in Miami to integrate in 1966, and the first to hire African-American employees in 1967.

7501 NW 7th Ave., Miami. ⓒ **305/751-1127.** Main courses $5–$15. AE, DC, MC, V. Daily 24 hr.

Karma Car Wash *Finds* TAPAS   The funkiest thing to hit Biscayne Boulevard since Dogma, this carwash-cum-tapas and wine bar is a big hit with the locals who love their SUVs as much as their hot spots. Put your car in for a wash and relax on the outdoor patio, reminiscent of your best friend's backyard, where you can sip from an impressive number of micro beers, wines, and coffees, and snack on delicious tapas, from cheese plates to chorizo. DJs and cocktail parties make it a happening spot from Thursday on, and while we don't encourage you to drink and drive, of course, there's never been a better excuse to shine your car (it's pricey, but they do a spotless job!) while waxing social at the same time.

7010 Biscayne Blvd., Miami. *C* 305/759-1392. Tapas $5–$15. AE, DC, MC, V. Tapas bar/cafe Wed–Sat 8am–1am. Car wash daily 8am–8pm.

La Cibeles Café *Value* CUBAN   This typical Latin diner serves some of the best food in town. Just by looking at the line that runs out the door every afternoon between noon and 2pm, you can see that you're not the first to discover it. For about $5, you can have a huge and filling meal. Pay attention to the daily lunch specials and go with them. A *pechuga* (pounded, tender chicken breast) is smothered in sautéed onions and served with rice and beans and a salad. The trout and the roast pork are both very good. When available, try the *ropa vieja,* a shredded-beef dish delicately spiced and served with peas and rice.

105 NE Third Ave. (1 block west of Biscayne Blvd.), Miami. *C* 305/577-3454. No credit cards. Main courses $5–$10. Mon–Sat 7:30am–7:30pm.

Latin American Cafeteria *** CUBAN   The name may sound a bit generic, but this no-frills indoor-outdoor cafeteria has the best Cuban sandwiches in the entire city. They're big enough for lunch and a doggie-bagged dinner, too. Service is fast, prices are cheap, but be forewarned: English is truly a second language at this chain, so have patience—it's worth it.

6820 SW 40th St., Miami. *C* 305/663-2600. Main courses $5–$10. AE, MC, V. Daily 7:30am–11pm.

Tobacco Road AMERICAN   Miami's oldest bar (95 years and counting) is a bluesy, Route 66–inspired institution favored by barflies, professionals, and anyone else who wishes to indulge in good and greasy bar fare—chicken wings, nachos, and so on—at reasonable prices in a down-home, gritty-but-charming atmosphere. The burgers are also good—particularly the Death Burger, a deliciously unhealthful combo of choice sirloin topped with grilled onions, jalapeños, and pepper-jack cheese (bring on the Tums!). Also a live-music venue, the Road, as it's known by locals, is well traveled, especially during Friday's happy hour and Tuesday's Lobster Night, when 100 1¼-pound lobsters go for only $13 apiece.

626 S. Miami Ave. *C* 305/374-1198. www.tobacco-road.com. Main courses $7–$10; nightly specials $12–$15. AE, DC, MC, V. Mon–Sat 11:30am–5am; Sun noon–5am. Cover $5–$6 Fri–Sat nights.

5 Little Havana

The main artery of Little Havana is a busy commercial strip called Southwest 8th Street, or *Calle Ocho.* Auto-body shops, cigar factories, and furniture stores line this street, and on every corner there seems to be a pass-through window serving superstrong Cuban coffee and snacks. In addition, many of the Cuban, Dominican, Nicaraguan, Peruvian, and other Latin American immigrants have opened full-scale restaurants ranging from intimate candlelit establishments to bustling stand-up lunch counters.

EXPENSIVE

Casa Juancho 🎭🎭 SPANISH   A generous taste of Spain comes to Miami in the form of the cavernous Casa Juancho, which looks like it escaped from a production of *Don Quixote*. The numerous dining rooms are decorated with traditional Spanish furnishings and enlivened nightly by strolling Spanish musicians who tend to be annoying and expect tips—do not encourage them to play at your table; you'll hear them loud and clear from other tables, trust me. Try not to be frustrated with the older staff members who don't speak English or respond quickly to your subtle glance—the food is worth the frustration. Your best bet is to order lots of tapas, small dishes of Spanish finger food. Some of the best include mixed seafood vinaigrette, fresh shrimp in hot garlic sauce, and fried calamari rings. A few entrees stand out, such as roast suckling pig, baby eels in garlic and olive oil, and Iberian-style snapper.

2436 SW 8th St. (just east of SW 27th Ave.), Little Havana. ℂ 305/642-2452. www.casajuancho.com. Reservations recommended but not accepted on Fri–Sat after 8pm. Main courses $20–$38; tapas $6–$15. AE, DC, DISC, MC, V. Sun–Thurs noon–midnight; Fri–Sat noon–1am.

MODERATE

Hy-Vong 🎭🎭 VIETNAMESE   This place is a must in Little Havana, so expect to wait hours for a table and don't even think of mumbling a complaint. This Vietnamese cuisine combines the best of Asian and French cooking with spectacular results. Food at Hy-Vong is elegantly simple and super spicy. Appetizers include small, tightly packed Vietnamese spring rolls, and kimchi, a spicy, fermented cabbage (they ran out of it on my last visit, because I got there too late—so get there early!). Star entrees include pastry-enclosed chicken with watercress cream-cheese sauce and fish in tangy mango sauce. Unfortunately, service here is not at all friendly or stellar—in fact, it borders on abysmal, but once you finally get your food, all will be forgotten.

Cuban Coffee

Despite the more than dozen Starbucks that dot the Miami landscape, locals still rely on the many Cuban cafeterias for their daily caffeine fix. Beware of the many establishments throughout Miami that serve espresso masked as Cuban coffee. For the real deal, go to the most popular—and most animated—Cuban cafeterias: **La Carreta** and **Versailles** (see below).

Cuban coffee is a longstanding tradition in Miami. You'll find it served from the takeout windows of hundreds of *cafeterías* or *loncherías* around town, especially in Little Havana, Downtown, Hialeah, and the beaches. Depending on where you are and what you want, you'll spend between 40¢ and $1.50 per cup.

The best *café cubano* has a rich layer of foam on top formed when the hot espresso shoots from the machine into the sugar below. The result is the caramelly, sweet, potent concoction that's a favorite of locals of all nationalities.

To partake, you've just got to learn how to ask for it *en español*.

From Ceviche to Picadillo: Latin Cuisine at a Glance

In Little Havana for dinner? Many restaurants list menu items in English for the benefit of *norteamericano* diners. In case they don't, though, here are translations and suggestions for filling and delicious meals:

Arroz con pollo: Roast chicken served with saffron-seasoned yellow rice and diced vegetables.

Café cubano: Very strong black coffee, served in thimble-size cups with lots of sugar. It's a real eye-opener.

Camarones: Shrimp.

Ceviche: Raw fish seasoned with spice and vegetables and marinated in vinegar and citrus to "cook" it.

Croquetas: Golden-fried croquettes of ham, chicken, or fish.

Paella: A Spanish dish of chicken, sausage, seafood, and pork mixed with saffron rice and peas.

Palomilla: Thinly sliced beef, similar to American minute steak, usually served with onions, parsley, and a mountain of french fries.

Pan cubano: Long, white crusty Cuban bread. Ask for it *tostado*(toasted and flattened on a grill with lots of butter.

Picadillo: A rich stew of ground meat, brown gravy, peas, pimientos, raisins, and olives.

Plátano: A deep-fried, soft, mildly sweet banana.

Pollo asado: Roasted chicken with onions and a crispy skin.

Ropa vieja: A shredded beef stew whose name literally means "old clothes."

Sopa de pollo: Chicken soup, usually with noodles or rice.

Tapas: A general name for Spanish-style hors d'oeuvres, served in grazing-size portions.

Enjoy the wait with a traditional Vietnamese beer and lots of company. Outside this tiny storefront restaurant, you'll meet interesting students, musicians, and foodies who come for the large, delicious portions.

3458 SW 8th St. (between 34th and 35th aves.), Little Havana. © **305/446-3674.** Reservations accepted for parties of 5 or more. Main courses $7–$20. AE, DISC, MC, V. Sun–Thurs 6–11pm; Fri–Sat 6–11:30pm. Closed 2 weeks in Aug.

INEXPENSIVE

La Carreta ⭐ CUBAN   This cavernous family-style restaurant is filled with relics of an old farm and college kids eating *medianoches* (midnight sandwiches with ham, cheese, and pickles) after partying all night. Waitresses are brusque but efficient and will help Anglos along who may not know the lingo. The menu is vast and very authentic, but is known for its sandwiches and smaller items. Try the *sopa de pollo*, a rich golden stock loaded with chunks of chicken and fresh vegetables, or the *ropa vieja*, a shredded beef stew in thick brown sauce. Because of its immense popularity and low prices, La Carreta has opened seven branches throughout Miami, including a counter in the Miami airport. Check the White Pages for other locations.

3632 SW 8th St., Little Havana. © **305/444-7501.** Main courses $5–$22. AE, DC, DISC, MC, V. Daily 24 hr.

Versailles ⚘⚘ CUBAN   Versailles is the meeting place of Miami's Cuban power brokers, who meet daily over café con leche to discuss the future of the Cuban exiles' fate. A glorified diner, the place sparkles with glass, chandeliers, murals, and mirrors meant to evoke the French palace. There's nothing fancy here—nothing French, either—just straightforward food from the home country. The menu is a veritable survey of Cuban cooking and includes specialties such as Moors and Christians (flavorful black beans with white rice), *ropa vieja* (shredded beef stew), and fried whole fish. Versailles is the place to come for mucho helpings of Cuban kitsch. With its late hours, it's also the perfect place to come after spending your night in Little Havana.

3555 SW 8th St., Little Havana. ⓒ 305/444-0240. Main courses $5–$20; soup and salad $2–$10. DC, DISC, MC, V. Mon–Thurs 8am–2am; Fri 8am–3am; Sat 8am–4:30am; Sun 9am–1am.

6 Key Biscayne

Key Biscayne has some of the world's nicest beaches, hotels, and parks, yet it is not known for great food. Locals, or "Key rats" as they're known, tend to go off-island for meals or takeout, but here are some of the best on-the-island choices.

EXPENSIVE

Rusty Pelican ⚘ SEAFOOD   The Pelican's private tropical walkway leads over a lush waterfall into one of the most romantic dining rooms in the city, located right on beautiful blue-green Biscayne Bay. The restaurant's windows look out over the water onto the sparkling stalagmites of Miami's magnificent downtown. Inside, quiet wicker paddle fans whirl overhead and saltwater fish swim in pretty tableside aquariums. The restaurant's surf-and-turf menu features conservatively prepared prime steaks, veal, shrimp, and lobster. The food is good, but the atmosphere—the reason why you're here—is even better, especially at sunset, when the view over the city is magical.

3201 Rickenbacker Causeway, Key Biscayne. ⓒ 305/361-3818. Reservations recommended. Main courses $16–$30. AE, DC, MC, V. Sun–Thurs 11:30am–4pm and 5–11pm; Fri–Sat 11:30am–4pm and 5pm–midnight.

Stefano's ITALIAN   For its cheesy mid-'80s ambience, Stefano's has no match. Its restaurant and disco share the same strobe-lit atmosphere. Food is traditional and reliable, if a little pricey. You'll find an older country-club crowd here in the evenings, enjoying steaks, pastas, and seafood. Among the best entrees are the flavorful *risotto frutti di mare* (saffron risotto with shrimp, clams, mussels, and calamari) and the very cheesy lasagna. After 7:30pm, the band starts playing American pop and Latin favorites. Some nights you feel as if you've accidentally happened upon your long-lost cousin's wedding, as you watch the parade of taffeta dresses and tipsy uncles.

24 Crandon Blvd., Key Biscayne. ⓒ 305/361-7007. Reservations recommended on weekends. Main courses $11–$32. AE, DC, MC, V. Sun–Thurs 5–11pm; Fri–Sat 5pm–5am. Disco open later Sun–Thurs.

INEXPENSIVE

Bayside Seafood Hut ⚘ *Finds* SEAFOOD   Known by locals as "the Hut," this ramshackle restaurant and bar is a laid-back outdoor Tiki hut and terrace that serves pretty good sandwiches and fish platters on paper plates. A blackboard lists the latest catches, which can be prepared blackened, fried, broiled, or in a garlic sauce. The fish dip is wonderfully smoky and moist, if a little heavy on mayonnaise. Local fishers and yachties share this rustic outpost with equal enthusiasm and loyalty. A completely new, air-conditioned area for those who can't stand the heat is a welcome addition, as

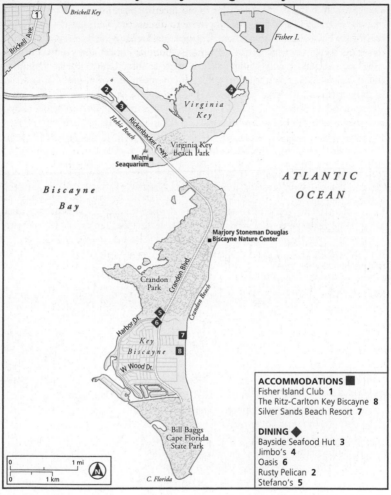

ACCOMMODATIONS ■
Fisher Island Club **1**
The Ritz-Carlton Key Biscayne **8**
Silver Sands Beach Resort **7**

DINING ◆
Bayside Seafood Hut **3**
Jimbo's **4**
Oasis **6**
Rusty Pelican **2**
Stefano's **5**

is the new deck and the spruced-up decor. But behind it all, it's nothing fancier than a hut—if it were anything else, it wouldn't be nearly as appealing.

3501 Rickenbacker Causeway, Key Biscayne. (✆ **305/361-0808.** Reservations accepted for parties of 15 or more. Appetizers, salads, and sandwiches $5–$15; platters $7–$13. AE, MC, V. Daily 10am until closing (which varies).

Jimbo's *Finds* SEAFOOD   Locals like to keep quiet about Jimbo's, a ramshackle seafood shack that started as a gathering spot for fishermen and has since become the quintessential South Florida watering hole, snack bar, and hangout for those in the know. If ever Miami had a backwoods, this is it, right down to the smoldering garbage can, stray dogs, and chickens. Do *not* get dressed up to come here—you will get dirty. Go to the bathroom before you get here, too, because the porta-potties are absolutely rancid. Grab yourself a dollar can of beer (there's only beer, water, and soda, but you are allowed to bring your own choice of drink if you want) from the cooler and take in the view of the tropical lagoon where they shot *Flipper.* You may even see a manatee or two. Vacant shacks that served as backdrops for films such as *True Lies* surround this hidden enclave, which attracts everyone from shrimpers and politicians to well-oiled beach bums. Oddly enough, there's even a bocce court here, and the owner, Jimbo, may challenge you to a game. Play if you must, but word has it he never loses. Jimbo's smoked fish—marlin or salmon—is the best in town, but be forewarned: There are no utensils or napkins. When I asked for some, the woman said, "Lady, this is a place where you eat with your hands." I couldn't have said it better.

Off the Rickenbacker Causeway at Sewerline Rd., Virginia Key. ℂ 305/361-7026. Smoked fish about $8 a pound. No credit cards. Mon–Fri 6am–6:30pm; Sat–Sun 6am–7:30pm. Head south on the main road toward Key Biscayne, make a left just after the MAST Academy (there will be a sign that says VIRGINIA KEY); tell the person in the tollbooth you're going to Jimbo's, and he'll point you in the right direction.

Oasis *(Value* CUBAN   Everyone, from the city's mayor to the local handymen, meet for delicious paella and Cuban sandwiches at this little shack. They gather outside, around the little takeout window, or inside at the few tables for super-powerful *cafecitos* and rich *croquetas.* It's slightly dingy, but the food is good and cheap.

19 Harbor Dr. (on corner of Crandon), Key Biscayne. ℂ 305/361-5709. Main courses $4–$15; sandwiches $3–$7. No credit cards. Daily 6am–9pm.

7 Coconut Grove

Coconut Grove was long known as the artists' haven of Miami, but the rush of developers trying to cash in on the laid-back charm of this old settlement has turned it into something of an overgrown mall. Still, there are several great dining spots both in and out of the confines of Mayfair or CocoWalk.

VERY EXPENSIVE

Baleen ✹✹✹ SEAFOOD/MEDITERRANEAN   While the prices aren't lean, the cuisine here is worth every pricey, precious penny. Oversize crab cakes, oak-smoked diver scallops, and steakhouse-quality meats are among Baleen's excellent offerings. The lobster bisque is the best on Biscayne Bay. Everything here is a la carte, so order wisely, as it tends to add up quicker than you can put your fork down. The restaurant's spectacular waterfront setting makes Baleen a true knockout. Request one of the few tables that are actually on the water's edge; lit with Tiki torches and an illuminated backdrop of Biscayne Bay, Baleen is the kind of restaurant where a reality show like *The Bachelor* would use for a scene when the happy couple expresses their love for each other.

4 Grove Isle Dr. (in the Grove Isle Hotel), Coconut Grove. ℂ 305/858-8300. Reservations recommended. Main courses $18–$50. AE, DC, MC, V. Sun–Wed 7am–10pm; Thurs–Sat 7am–11pm.

Christabelle's Quarter ✹ CREOLE   Although this restaurant intends to appear as if it was shipped right from the French Quarter, because it's in mainstream Coconut Grove, it feels more like an exhibit in EPCOT's World Showcase. And that's not a bad thing. After leaving post-Katrina New Orleans for Miami, chef Alex Patout set up shop in the kitchen here as investors pumped in millions of dollars to recreate this French Quarter masterpiece (visually speaking). The cuisine, unfortunately, pales in comparison to the ornate wrought iron railings, brick walls, chandeliers, and stained glass ceiling and dome. Sure, you can order a variety of gumbos, crab cakes, oysters, and étoufée, but when it comes to high-priced Creole cuisine, we'd rather eat at

Coconut Grove

ACCOMMODATIONS ■
Grand Bay Miami **9**
Hampton Inn **10**
Mayfair Hotel & Spa **6**
Mutiny Hotel **7**
Ritz-Carlton Coconut Grove **8**

DINING ◆
Anokha **2**
Café Tu Tu Tango **5**
Christabelle's Quarter **3**
Le Bouchon du Grove **4**
Señor Frog's **1**

Emeril's. Because of that, Patout left the restaurant in October 2007. Owners said the food was too heavy and planned to lighten the dishes up. Not sure how they're going to do that with Creole cuisine, but stay tuned. For entertainment purposes, however, Christabelle's reigns, with live Dixie jazz bands, jazz brunches and, because it's Miami, not New Orleans, a gorgeous upstairs bar, complete with DJ, bouncers, and dreaded cover charge. *Les bonnes temps,* indeed.

3159 Commodore Plaza (between Main Hwy. and Grand Ave.), Coconut Grove. ⓒ **786517-5299.** Main courses $15–$50. AE, DC, MC, V. Mon–Fri 11:30am–3pm; Daily 5:30–midnight; Sun jazz brunch 11:30am–3pm.

EXPENSIVE

Anokha ⓡⓡⓡ INDIAN   This is the best Indian restaurant in Miami. Anokha's motto is "A guest is equal to God and should be treated as such," and they do stick to it. The food here is from the gods, with fantastic tandooris, curries, and stews. The restaurant's setting at the end of a quiet stretch of Coconut Grove is especially enticing because it prevents throngs of pedestrians from overtaking what some people consider to be a diamond in the rough.

3195 Commodore Plaza (between Main Hwy. and Grand Ave.), Coconut Grove. ⓒ **786/552-1030.** Main courses $13–$40. AE, DC, MC, V. Sun and Tues–Wed 6–10:30pm; Thurs–Sat 6–11:30pm.

Getting Back Into the Grove

Aging hippies may recall **Coconut Grove** as a hub of all things peace and love. When the '60s ended, the beatniks made The Grove a retro-fab kind of town. Then came the '80s, and the Grove was as dead as Joplin and Hendrix. The '90s saw a resurgence with **CocoWalk,** whose sole purpose was to attract tourists, locals, and college students to its open air debauchery, which still continues with **Fat Tuesday's** (✆ **305/534-1328**) and **Hooters** (✆ **305/442-7283**). Cafe Tu Tu Tango changed things a bit with its then-unique tapas-only menu and excellent sangria, but it closed in 2008. So did Dan Marino's, a sports pub and grill owned by the former Miami Dolphin. Unbelievably, so did the Cheesecake Factory. Today, Hooters is alive and well, as is Fat Tuesday's, and in the old Marino's/Cheesecake Factory space is a **Chili's** (✆ **305/772-5472**). It's nothing innovative or spectacular, but it may suit this town well, like an old Crosby, Stills & Nash song.

Le Bouchon du Grove ✿ FRENCH   This very authentic, exceptional bistro is French right down to the waitstaff, who may speak only French to you, forgetting they're in the heart of Coconut Grove, U.S.A. But it matters not. The food, prepared by an animated French (what else?) chef, is good. It used to be superb, but it has fallen off a bit. Still, a delicious starter that's always reliable is the wonderful *gratinée lyonnaise* (traditional French onion soup). Fish is brought in fresh daily; try the Chilean sea bass *(filet de loup poele)* when it's in season. Though slightly heavy on the oil, it is delivered with succulent artichokes, tomato confit, and seasoned roasted garlic and it is a gastronomic triumph. The *carre d'agneau roti* (roasted rack of lamb with Provence herbs) is served warm and tender, with a perfect amount of seasoning. There's also an excellent selection of pricey, but drinkable, French and American red and white wines.

3430 Main Hwy., Coconut Grove. ✆ **305/448-6060.** Reservations recommended. Main courses $18–$26. AE, MC, V. Mon–Thurs 10am–3pm and 5–11pm; Fri 10am–3pm and 5pm–midnight; Sat 8am–3pm and 5pm–midnight; Sun 8am–3pm and 5–11pm.

MODERATE

Señor Frogs MEXICAN   Filled with a collegiate crowd, this restaurant is known for a raucous good time, a mariachi band, and powerful margaritas. The food at this rocking cantina is a bit too cheesy, but it's tasty, if not exactly authentic. The mole enchiladas, with 14 different kinds of mild chiles mixed with chocolate, is as flavorful as any I've tasted. Almost everything is served with rice and beans in quantities so large that few diners are able to finish their portions.

3480 Main Hwy., Coconut Grove. ✆ **305/448-0999.** Reservations not accepted. Main courses $15–$30. AE, DC, MC, V. Mon–Sat 11:30am–2am; Sun 11:30am–1am.

8 Coral Gables

Coral Gables is a foodie's paradise—a city in which you certainly won't go hungry. What Starbucks is to most major cities, excellent gourmet and ethnic restaurants are to Coral Gables, where there's a restaurant on every corner, and everywhere in between.

Coral Gables

ACCOMMODATIONS ■
Biltmore Hotel **1**
David William Hotel **2**
Hotel St. Michel **7**
Hyatt Regency Coral Gables **10**

DINING ◆
Brasserie Les Halles **9**
Caffe Abbracci **4**
Christy's **13**
Daily Bread Marketplace **3**
House of India **11**
John Martin's **6**
Miss Saigon Bistro **8**
Ortanique on the Mile **5**
Palme d'Or **1**
Pascal's on Ponce **12**

VERY EXPENSIVE

Christy's ☆☆ STEAKHOUSE/AMERICAN　Power is palpable at this old-school English-style Miami steakhouse where a rock star can be sitting at one table, an ex-president at another. When we say rock star, we mean aging rock star à la Rod Stewart, though. This isn't your flashy South Beach scenery. But Christy's is the kind of place where conversations are at a hush and no one seems to care whom they're sitting next to. The selling point here, rather, is the corn-fed beef and calves' liver, not to mention the broiled lamb chops, prime rib of beef with horseradish sauce, teriyaki-marinated filet mignon, and perfectly tossed Caesar salad. Baked sweet potatoes and a sublime blackout cake are also yours for the taking. For a little drama, order the baked Alaska. It livens up the staid place. Just like a fine wine or the typical Christy's customer, the meat here is aged a long time. A landmark since 1978, Christy's has thrived amid the comings and goings of neighboring nouveau Coral Gables restaurants. It's located on a nondescript corner, and you'll know you've arrived at the right place if you can count the Rolls-Royces parked out front.

3101 Ponce de León Blvd., Coral Gables. © **305/446-1400.** www.christysrestaurant.com. Reservations recommended. Main courses $20–$48. AE, DC, MC, V. Mon–Thurs 11:30am–10pm; Fri 11:30am–11pm; Sat 5–11pm; Sun 5–10pm.

Impressions

Miami is the same place that New Orleans was a hundred years ago in the emergence of different cultures. It's fascinating because in the same way North Americans have come to understand the difference between Northern Italian and Southern Italian, we're coming to understand the difference between Peruvian, Venezuelan, and Brazilian cuisine.

—Chef Norman Van Aken

Palme d'Or ✿✿✿ FRENCH   What once used to be an überstuffy restaurant suitable for the regal Biltmore Hotel has tried to hippify itself, if you will, by adopting a modernized French menu conducive to chic, albeit less formal, dining. While I haven't exactly seen the hipsters flocking here, at least the menu is more fun than before, because you are allowed to custom design your own menu, choosing from over 20 dishes which you are encouraged to mix and match. A four-course, custom-made tasting meal costs about $54. Not bad for a place that used to be known for only the upper tax-bracketed. Although some of the food is funky—foam mushroom bisque, squab breast, and rabbit, for example, it's all pretty seductive and, at these accessible prices, worth trying at least once for the experience.

The Biltmore Hotel, 1200 Anastasia Ave., Coral Gables. ✆ 305/445-1926. Reservations recommended. Main courses $15–$30; tasting menus $42–$66. AE, DISC, MC, V. Tues–Sat 6–10:30pm.

Pascal's on Ponce ✿✿✿ FRENCH   Straight from the tutelage of world-renowned chef Alain Ducasse, chef Pascal Oudin has established himself as a star student at his very own restaurant that takes French food to another level. Diver sea scallops topped with beef short rib, young fennel, carrot Vichy, and fava beans; and filet mignon with escargot provençal are just a few outstanding examples of how Oudin combines classical French techniques with the ingredients of the Americas.

2611 Ponce de León Blvd., Coral Gables. ✆ 305/444-2024. www.pascalmiami.com Reservations recommended. Main courses $26–$36. AE, DISC, MC, V. Sun–Thurs 6–10pm; Fri–Sat 6–11pm; Mon–Thurs 11:30am–3pm.

EXPENSIVE

Caffe Abbracci ✿✿ ITALIAN   You'll understand why this restaurant's name means "hugs" in Italian the moment you enter the dark, romantic enclave: Your appetite will be embraced by the savory scents of fantastic Italian cuisine wafting through the restaurant. The homemade black-and-red ravioli filled with lobster in pink sauce, risotto with porcini and portobello mushrooms, and the house specialty—grilled veal chop topped with tricolor salad—are irresistible and perhaps the culinary equivalent of a warm, embracing hug. A cozy bar and lounge were added recently to further encourage the warm and fuzzy feelings.

318 Aragon Ave. (1 block north of Miracle Mile, between Salzedo St. and Le Jeune Rd.), Coral Gables. ✆ 305/441-0700. Reservations recommended for dinner. Main courses $15–$40; pastas $15–$30. AE, DC, MC, V. Sun 6–11:30pm; Mon–Thurs 11:30am–3pm and 6–11:30pm; Fri 11:30am–3pm and 6pm–12:30am; Sat 6pm–12:30am.

Ortanique on the Mile ✿✿✿ NEW WORLD CARIBBEAN   You'll be greeted as you enter with soft, spiderlike lights and canopied mosquito netting that will make you wonder whether you're on a secluded island or inside one of King Tut's temples. Chef Cindy Hutson has truly perfected her tantalizing New World Caribbean cuisine that also graces the menus of her two other Ortaniques in Washington, D.C. and Las Vegas. For starters, an absolute must is the pumpkin bisque with a hint of pepper sherry. Afterward, move on to the tropical mango salad with fresh marinated sable hearts of palm, julienne mango, baby field greens, toasted Caribbean candied pecans, and passion-fruit vinaigrette. For an entree, I recommend the pan-sautéed Bahamian black grouper marinated in teriyaki and sesame oil. It's served with an *ortanique* (an orangelike fruit) orange liqueur sauce and topped with steamed seasoned chayote, zucchini, and carrots on a lemon-orange boniato–sweet plantain mash. For dessert, try the chocolate mango tower—layers of brownie, chocolate mango mousse, meringue, and sponge cake, accompanied by mango sorbet and tropical-fruit salsa. Entrees may not be cheap, but they're a lot less than airfare to the islands, which is where most, if not all, of the ingredients hail from.

278 Miracle Mile (next to Actor's Playhouse), Coral Gables. © 305/446-7710. Reservations requested. Main courses $19–$40. AE, DC, MC, V. Mon–Tues 6–10pm; Wed–Sat 6–11pm; Sun 5:30–9:30pm.

MODERATE

House of India INDIAN   House of India's curries, kormas, and kabobs are very good, but the restaurant's well-priced, all-you-can-eat lunch buffet is unsurpassed. All the favorites are on display, including tandoori chicken, naan, various meat and vegetarian curries, as well as rice and dal (lentils). This place isn't fancy and could use a good scrub-down (in fact, I've heard it described as a "greasy spoon"), but the service is excellent and the food is good enough to keep you from staring at your surroundings.

22 Merrick Way (near Douglas and Coral Way, 1 block north of Miracle Mile), Coral Gables. © 305/444-2348. Reservations recommended. Main courses $8–$17. AE, DC, DISC, MC, V. Sun–Thurs 11:30am–3pm and 5–10pm; Fri–Sat 11:30am–3pm and 5–11pm.

John Martin's ⋒ IRISH PUB   Forest-green and dark-wood walls provide a very intimate, publike atmosphere in which local businesspeople and barflies alike come to hoist a pint or two. The menu offers some tasty British specialties (not necessarily an oxymoron!), such as bangers and mash and shepherd's pie, as well as Irish lamb stew and corned beef and cabbage.

Of course, to wash it down, you'll want to try one of the ales on tap or one of the more than 20 single-malt scotches. The crowd is upscale and chatty, as is the young waitstaff. Check out happy hour on weeknights, plus the Sunday brunch with loads of hand-carved meats and seafood.

253 Miracle Mile, Coral Gables. © 305/445-3777. Reservations recommended on weekends. Main courses $9–$20; sandwiches and salads $5–$16. AE, DC, DISC, MC, V. Sun–Thurs 11:30am–midnight; Fri–Sat 11:30am–2am.

Red Fish Grill ⋒ SEAFOOD   Hidden away at the edge of the saltwater lagoon in lush and tropical Matheson Hammock Park, Red Fish Grill is a decent seafood restaurant, but people don't come here for the food. Judging by the ambience alone, the restaurant deserves four stars, but because the food is just okay (fish is either greasy or dry), it only gets one. But that's okay. Romantic, hard to find, and truly reminiscent of Old Miami, Red Fish Grill makes up for its lack of flavor with its hard-to-beat, majestic setting.

In Matheson Hammock Park, 9610 Old Cutler Rd., Coral Gables. © 305/668-8788. www.redfishgrill.net Reservations accepted. Main courses $15–$32. AE, DC, DISC, MC, V. Tues–Thurs 6–10pm; Fri–Sun 5–10pm. Enter Matheson Hammock Park; stay on the main road until you see the restaurant's parking lot.

INEXPENSIVE

Daily Bread Marketplace GREEK   This place is great for takeout food and homemade breads. The falafel and gyro sandwiches are large, fresh, and filling. The spinach pie for less than $1 is also recommended, though it's short on spinach and heavy on pastry. Salads and spreads, including luscious tabbouleh, hummus, and eggplant, are also worth a go. To eat in or take out, the Middle Eastern fare here is a real treat, especially in an area so filled with fancy French and Cuban fare. Plus, you can pick up groceries such as grape leaves, fresh olives, couscous, fresh nuts, and pita bread.

2400 SW 27th St. (off U.S. 1 under the monorail), Coral Gables. (C) 305/856-0363 or 305/856-0366. Sandwiches and salads $4–$10. MC, V. Mon–Sat 9am–8pm; Sun 11am–5pm.

Miss Saigon Bistro 🌟🌟 VIETNAMESE   Unlike Andrew Lloyd Webber's bombastic Broadway show, this Miss Saigon is small, quiet, and not at all flashy. Servers at this family-run restaurant—among them, Rick, the owners' son—will graciously recommend dishes or even have something custom-made for you. If you're lucky, Rick may even sing you an aria with a voice ironically tailored to Webber shows. The menu is varied and reasonably priced, and the portions are huge—large enough to share. Noodle dishes and soup bowls are hearty and flavorful; caramelized prawns are fantastic, as is the whole snapper with lemon grass and ginger sauce. Despite the fact that there are few tables inside and a hungry crowd usually gathers outside in the street, you won't be rushed through your meal, which is worth savoring. There is also a new, much larger location at 9503 S. Dixie Hwy., in South Miami's Pinecrest (© 305/661-2911).

148 Giralda Ave. (at Ponce de León and 37th Ave.), Coral Gables. (C) 305/446-8006. Main courses $9–$22. AE, DC, DISC, MC, V. Mon and Wed–Thurs 11:30am–3pm and 5:30–10pm; Tues 11:30am–3pm and 6:30–10pm; Fri 11:30am–3pm and 5:30–11pm; Sat 5:30–11pm; Sun 5:30–10pm.

9 South Miami & West Miami

Though mostly residential, these areas nonetheless have several eating establishments worth the drive.

EXPENSIVE

Chispa 🌟🌟🌟 CONTEMPORARY LATIN   Simply put, Chispa rocks. The brainchild of star chef Robin Haas (formerly of Baleen), this cavernous, stylish nouveau Latin restaurant will blow you away. If you've ever tasted the delicious, greasy croquetas at any Cuban bodega, wait until you try Chispa's gourmet version—a magnificent shrimp-and-black-eyed-pea croqueta that renders the greasy ones good for hangovers only. For a real Cuban experience, try Sergio's spit-roasted young suckling pig. A slew of fantastic seafood ceviches, an unparalleled mahimahi with sour orange aioli, and those addictive shrimp-and-black-eyed-pea croquetas with wood-roasted mushrooms atop a seared cornmeal stew prove that there is indeed a way to be creative with Cuban food. A 40-foot bar and massive booths seating 8 to 10 people make Chispa a great place for large groups. The acoustics, however, need to be improved, as it's louder than a Celia Cruz tribute in here.

11500 NW 41st St. (C) 305/591-7166. Reservations strongly recommended. Main courses $19–$34. AE, DC, MC, V. Sun–Thurs 11:30am–2:30pm and 5:30–10:30pm; Fri–Sat 5:30–11:30pm.

Greater Miami Dining

Baleen **9**
Casa Juancho **8**
Chispa **1**
Crepe Maker Café **12**
Hy Vong **7**
Kon Chau **2**
La Carreta **5**
Latin American Cafeteria **4**
Red Fish Grill **10**
Shorty's **11**
The Tea Room at Cauley Square **13**
Tropical Chinese **3**
Versailles **6**

KEY TO INSET MAPS
A North Dade
B Miami Beach
C South Beach
D Fisher Island, Virginia Key & Key Biscayne
E Downtown Miami
F Miamis Design District, Little Haiti, & Upper Eastside
G Coral Gables
H Coconut Grove

ATLANTIC OCEAN

0   4 mi
0   4 km

Tropical Chinese &&& CHINESE   This strip-mall restaurant, way out in West Miami–Dade, is hailed as the best Chinese restaurant in the city. While the food is indeed very good—certainly more interesting than at your typical beef-and-broccoli place—it still seems overpriced. Garlic spinach and prawns in a clay pot are delicious, with the perfect mix of garlic cloves, mushrooms, and fresh spinach. But this isn't your typical Chinese takeout. It's not cheap. Unlike most Chinese restaurants, the dishes here are not large enough to share. Sunday-afternoon dim sum is extremely popular, and lines often snake around the shopping center.

7991 Bird Rd., West Miami. © **305/262-7576.** Reservations highly recommended on weekends. Main courses $10–$25. AE, DC, MC, V. Mon–Fri 11:30am–10:30pm; Sat 11am–11:30pm; Sun 10:30am–10pm. Take U.S. 1 to Bird Rd. and go west on Bird, all the way down to 78th Ave. The restaurant is between 78th and 79th on the north side of Bird Rd.

INEXPENSIVE

Crepe Maker Café & *Kids* CREPES/FRENCH   Create your own delicious crepes at this little French cafe. You can choose from ham, tuna, black olives, red peppers, capers, artichoke hearts, and pine nuts. Some of the best include a Philly cheesesteak with mushrooms, and a classic chicken *cordon bleu*. Delicious dessert crepes include ice cream, strawberries, peaches, walnuts, and pineapples. Enjoy your crepe fresh off the griddle at the counter or from a bar stool. The soups are delicious. Kids can run around in a small play area.

8269 SW 124th St., South Miami. © **305/233-4458** or 305/233-1113. Crepes $1.50–$8.50. AE, DC, MC, V. Sun–Thurs 11:30am–9:30pm; Fri–Sat 11:30am–10:30pm. Take U.S. 1 south to 124th St. and make a left. The restaurant is on the north side of the street, across from the park.

El Toro Taco Family Restaurant &&& *Finds* MEXICAN   Until I discovered this Mexican oasis in the midst of South Florida farmland, I never had a good enough reason to leave my quasi-cosmopolitan confines in Miami for rural Homestead, way down south. I've put major mileage on my car since I first stumbled upon this 96-seat family-run restaurant a few years ago, when I was lost and very hungry. Fabulous (and I mean fabulous) Mexican fare—tacos, enchiladas, and burritos drenched with the freshest and zestiest salsa this side of Baja—is what you'll find here in abundance. It may sound odd to travel from a big city with tons of restaurants to farm country for Mexican food, but trust me: It's so cheap and delicious, it's worth the trip.

1 S. Krome Ave., Homestead. © **305/245-8182.** Main courses $1.75–$12. DISC, MC, V. Tues–Sun 10am–9pm; Fri–Sat 10am–10pm. Take 836 W. (Dolphin Expwy.) toward Miami International Airport. Take Florida Tpk. S. ramp toward Florida City/Key West. Take U.S. 41/SW 8th St. exit (exit 25) and turn left onto SW 8th St. Take SW 8th St. to Krome Ave. (⅕ mile) and turn left.

Kon Chau & CHINESE/DIM SUM   Don't be put off by the rather unappealing shopping center in which this cheap dim-sum place is located. If you want fancy plastic chopsticks and fancy prices, go up the block to Tropical Chinese (see above). If you want delicious dim sum at ridiculously low prices, Kon Chau is where you'll find it. A simple checklist allows you to choose as many items as you want, from savory steamed shrimp dumplings to airy pork buns, for as little as $1 apiece, all day long. There are also regular dishes if you don't want dim sum.

8376 Bird Rd., West Miami. © **305/553-7799.** Items $1 and up. MC, V. Mon–Sat 11am–9:45pm; Sun 10am–9:30pm. Take Bird Rd. west to 83rd St. The restaurant is between 83rd and 84th sts. on the south side of the road, in a Dunkin' Donuts shopping center.

Shorty's 🅡 BARBECUE   A Miami tradition since 1951, this honky-tonk of a log cabin still serves some of the best ribs and chicken in South Florida. People line up for the smoke-flavored, slow-cooked meat that's so tender it seems to fall off the bone. The secret, however, is to ask for your order with sweet sauce. The regular stuff tastes bland and bottled. All of the side dishes, including the coleslaw, corn on the cob, and baked beans, look commercial but complete the experience. This is a jeans-and-T-shirt kind of place, but you may want to wear jeans with an elastic waistband, as overeating is not uncommon.

9200 S. Dixie Hwy. (between U.S. 1 and Dadeland Blvd.), South Miami. 🄲 305/670-7732. Main courses $5–$9. DISC, MC, V. Sun–Thurs 11am–10pm; Fri–Sat 11am–11pm.

The Tea Room at Cauley Square 🅡 ENGLISH TEA   Do stop in for a spot of tea at this cozy tearoom in historic Cauley Square, off U.S. 1. The little lace-curtained room is an unusual sight in this heavily industrial area better known for its warehouses than its doilies. Try one of the simple sandwiches, such as the turkey club with potato salad and a small lettuce garnish, or onion soup—rich brown broth and stringy cheese. The Ambrosia with finger sandwiches is an interesting choice: a blend of pineapple, mandarin oranges, miniature marshmallows, and sour cream served with finger sandwiches or banana-nut bread. Daily specials (such as spinach-and-mushroom quiche) and delectable desserts are musts before you begin your explorations of the old antiques and art shops in this little enclave of civility down south. Oh, and remember to put your pinky up while sipping your tea.

12310 SW 224th St. (at Cauley Sq.), South Miami. 🄲 305/258-0044. Sandwiches and salads $7–$12; soups $3–$4. AE, DISC, MC, V. Daily 11am–4pm. Take 836 W. (Dolphin Expwy.) toward Miami International Airport. Take Palmetto Expwy. S. ramp toward Coral Way. Merge onto 826 S. Follow signs to Florida Tpk. toward Homestead. Take the turnpike south and exit at Caribbean Blvd. (exit 12). Go about 1 mile on Caribbean Blvd. and turn left on S. Dixie Hwy. and then right at SW 224th St. Then turn left onto Old Dixie Hwy. and take a slight right onto SW 224th St. The restaurant is at Cauley Square Center.

White Lion Cafe 🅡 AMERICAN   The quintessence of a quaint off-the-beaten-path eatery in not-so-quaint Miami, the White Lion Cafe is a hidden gem serving southern-style blue-plate specials, including delicious meat loaf and fried chicken. There's also an extensive entertainment calendar here, with everything from live jazz to karaoke. If you're in the Homestead area en route to or coming from the Keys, it's definitely worth a stop here, where time seems to stand still, at least until the band starts playing.

146 NW 7th St., Homestead. 🄲 305/248-1076. www.whitelioncafe.com. Main courses $10–$20. AE, DISC, MC, V. Daily 5pm until "the fat lady sings." Take the 836 East to the 826 South, at Exit 6 make a left and head West on 8th St. (Campbell Dr.), after crossing Krome Ave. take a left at 1st Ave. (the very next light), and turn right on 7th St. The cafe is on the left.

8

What to See & Do in Miami

If there's one thing Miami doesn't have, it's an identity crisis. Multiple personalities, maybe, but hardly a crisis. In fact, it's the city's vibrant, multifaceted personality that attracts millions each year from all over the world. South Beach may be on the top of many Miami to-do lists, but the rest of the city, a fascinating assemblage of multicultural neighborhoods, should not be overlooked. Once considered "God's Waiting Room," the Magic City now attracts an eclectic mix of old and young, celebs and plebes, American and international, and geek and chic with an equally varied roster of activities.

For starters, Miami boasts some of the world's most natural beauty, with dazzling blue waters, fine sandy beaches, and lush tropical parks. The city's man-made brilliance, in the form of crayon-colored architecture, never seems to fade in Miami's unique Art Deco district. For cultural variation, you can experience the tastes, sounds, and rhythms of Cuba in Little Havana.

As in any metropolis, though, some areas aren't as great as others. Downtown Miami, for instance, is still in the throes of a major, albeit slow, renaissance, in which the sketchier warehouse sections of the city are being transformed into hubs of all things hip. In contrast to this development, however, are the still poverty-stricken areas of downtown such as Overtown, Liberty City, and Little Haiti (though Overtown is striving to transform itself into the Overtown Historic Village, showcasing its landmarks such as the famous Lyric Theater and the home of DA Dorsey, Miami's first African-American millionaire). While I obviously advise you to exercise caution when exploring the less-traveled parts of the city, I would also be remiss in telling you to bypass them completely.

Lose yourself in the city's nature and its neighborhoods and, best of all, its people—a sassy collection of artists and intellectuals, beach bums and international transplants, dolled-up drag queens and bodies beautiful. No wonder celebrities love to vacation here—the spotlight is on the city and its residents. Also, unlike most stars, Miami is always ready for its close-up. With so much to do and see, Miami is a virtual amusement park that's bound to entertain all those who pass through its palm-lined gates.

1 Miami's Beaches

Perhaps Miami's most popular attraction is its incredible 35-mile stretch of beachfront, which runs from the tip of South Beach north to Sunny Isles and circles Key Biscayne and the numerous other pristine islands dotting the Atlantic. The characteristics of Miami's many beaches are as varied as the city's population: There are beaches for swimming, socializing, or serenity; for families, seniors, or gay singles; some to make you forget you're in the city, others darkened by huge condominiums. Whatever

Bal Harbour Beach **2**
Bill Baggs Cape Florida State Park **9**
Crandon Park Beach **8**
85th Street Beach **3**
Haulover Beach **1**
Hobie Beach **6**
Lummus Park Beach **4**
Matheson Hammock Park Beach **10**
12th Street Beach **5**
Virginia Key **7**

type of beach vacation you're looking for, you'll find it in one of Miami's two distinct beach areas: Miami Beach and Key Biscayne.

MIAMI BEACH'S BEACHES Collins Avenue fronts more than a dozen miles of white-sand beach and blue-green waters from 1st to 192nd streets. Although most of this stretch is lined with a solid wall of hotels and condos, beach access is plentiful. There are lots of public beaches here, wide and well maintained, complete with lifeguards, bathroom facilities, concession stands, and metered parking (bring lots of quarters). Except for a thin strip close to the water, most of the sand is hard-packed—the result of a $10 million Army Corps of Engineers Beach Rebuilding Project meant to protect buildings from the effects of eroding sand.

In general, the beaches on this barrier island (all on the eastern, oceanside of the island) become less crowded the farther north you go. A wooden boardwalk runs along the hotel side of the beach from 21st to 46th streets—about 1½ miles—offering a terrific sun-and-surf experience without getting sand in your shoes. Miami's lifeguard-protected public beaches include 21st Street, at the beginning of the boardwalk; 35th Street, popular with an older crowd; 46th Street, next to the Fontainebleau Hilton; 53rd Street, a narrower, more sedate beach; 64th Street, one of the quietest strips around; and 72nd Street, a local old-timers' spot.

Fun Fact **From Desert Island to Fantasy Island**

Miami Beach wasn't always a beachfront playground. In fact, it was a deserted island until the late 1800s, when a developer started a coconut farm there. That action sparked an interest in many other developers, including John Collins (for whom Collins Ave. is named), who began growing avocados. Other visionaries admired Collins's success and eventually joined him, establishing a ferry service and dredging parts of the bay to make the island more accessible. In 1921, Collins built a 2½-mile bridge linking downtown Miami to Miami Beach, creating excellent accessibility *and* the longest wooden bridge in the world. Today Miami Beach has six links to the mainland.

KEY BISCAYNE'S BEACHES   If Miami Beach doesn't provide the privacy you're looking for, try Virginia Key and Key Biscayne. Crossing the Rickenbacker Causeway ($1 toll), however, can be a lengthy process, especially on weekends, when beach bums and tan-o-rexics flock to the Key. The 5 miles of public beach there, however, are blessed with softer sand and are less developed and more laid-back than the hotel-laden strips to the north.

THE BEST BEACHES

- **Best Party Beach:** In Key Biscayne, **Crandon Park Beach,** on Crandon Boulevard, is National Lampoon's *Vacation* on the sand. It's got a diverse crowd consisting of dedicated beach bums and lots of leisure-seeking families, set to a soundtrack of salsa, disco, and reggae music blaring from a number of competing stereos. With 3 miles of oceanfront beach, bathrooms, changing facilities, 493 acres of park, 75 grills, three parking lots, several soccer and softball fields, and a public 18-hole championship golf course, Crandon is like a theme park on the sand. More recently, they added Eco-Adventure Tours, including kayaking and snorkeling. For more information, call © **305/365-3018.** It's open daily from 8am to sunset.

- **Best Beach for People-Watching: Lummus Park Beach,** aka Glitter Beach, runs along Ocean Drive from about 6th to 14th streets on South Beach. It's the best place to go if you're seeking entertainment as well as a great tan. On any day of the week, you might spy models primping for a photo shoot, nearly naked (topless is legal here) sun-worshippers avoiding tan lines, and an assembly line of washboard abs off of which you could (but shouldn't) bounce your bottle of sunscreen. Bathrooms and changing facilities are available on the beach, but don't expect to have a Cindy Crawford encounter in one of these. Most people tend to prefer using the somewhat drier, cleaner bathrooms of the restaurants on Ocean Drive.

- **Best Beach for Communing with Nature: Bill Baggs Cape Florida State Park** is the pot of gold at the end of Key Biscayne, with over a mile of unfettered beach, a historic lighthouse, and nature trails that take you back to the days when South Florida was a tropical wilderness.

- **Best Swimming Beach:** The **85th Street Beach,** along Collins Avenue, is the best place to swim away from the maddening crowds. It's one of Miami's only stretches of sand with no condos or hotels looming over sunbathers. Lifeguards patrol the area throughout the day and bathrooms are available, though they are not exactly the benchmark of cleanliness.

- **Best Windsurfing Beach: Hobie Beach,** on the side of the causeway leading to Key Biscayne, is not really a beach, but an inlet with predictable winds and a number of places where you can rent windsurf boards. Bathrooms are available but not exactly the cleanest.
- **Best Shell-Hunting Beach:** You'll find plenty of colorful shells at **Bal Harbour Beach,** Collins Avenue at 96th Street. There's also an exercise course and good shade—but no lifeguards, bathrooms, or changing facilities.
- **Best (Ahem) All-Around Tanning Beach:** For that all-over tan, head to **Haulover Beach,** just north of the Bal Harbour border, and join nudists from around the world in a top-to-bottom tanning session. Should you choose to keep your swimsuit on, however, there are changing rooms and bathrooms.
- **Best Surfing Beach: Haulover Beach,** just over the causeway from Bal Harbour, seems to get Miami's biggest swells. Go early to avoid getting mauled by the aggressive young locals prepping for Maui. Rancid bathrooms are available if you absolutely must. Surfers also like the southern tip of South Beach, not necessarily for the waves, but for the surfers themselves.
- **Best Scenic Beach: Matheson Hammock Park Beach,** at 9610 Old Cutler Rd. in South Miami (© **305/665-5475**), is the epitome of tranquillity. And while it's scenic, it's not too much of a scene. It's a great beach for those seeking "alone time." Bathrooms and changing facilities are available.
- **Best Family Beach:** Because of its man-made lagoon, which is fed naturally by the tidal movement of the adjacent Biscayne Bay, the waters of **Matheson Hammock Park Beach** are extremely calm, not to mention safe and secluded enough for families to keep an eye on the kids. Clean bathrooms are a plus.
- **Best Beach for Seclusion: Virginia Key** on Key Biscayne is where people go when they don't want to be found. It's also incredibly picturesque. Bathrooms are decent.
- **Best for Gay Beachgoers:** South Beach's **12th Street Beach** is *the* place to be for Miami's best gay beach scene. Here you'll see strutting, kibitzing, and gossiping among some of Miami's most beautiful gay population. You might even find yourself lucky enough to happen upon a feisty South Beach party while you're soaking up some rays here. If you can hold it, skip the public bathroom and head over to the Palace on Ocean Drive and use their bathroom.

2 The Art Deco District (South Beach)

"You know what they used to say? 'Who's Art?'" recalls Art Deco revivalist Dona Zemo. "You'd say, 'This is an Art Deco building,' and they'd say, 'Really, who is Art?' These people thought 'Art Deco' was some guy's name."

How things have changed. This guy Art has become one of the most popular Florida attractions since, well, that mouse named Mickey. The district is roughly bounded by the Atlantic Ocean on the east, Alton Road on the west, 6th Street to the south, and Dade Boulevard (along the Collins Canal) to the north.

Simply put, Art Deco is a style of architecture that, in its heyday of the 1920s and 1930s, used to be considered ultramodern. Today, fans of the style consider it retro fabulous. But while some people may not consider the style fabulous, it's undoubtedly retro. According to the experts, Art Deco made its debut in 1925 at an exposition in Paris in which it set a stylistic tone, with buildings based on early neoclassical styles with the application of exotic motifs such as flora, fauna, and fountains based on

Finds **Walking by Design**

The Miami Design Preservation League offers several tours of Miami Beach's historic architecture, all of which leave from the Art Deco Welcome Center at 1001 Ocean Dr. in Miami Beach. A self-guided audio tour (available daily 10am–4pm) turns the streets into a virtual outdoor museum, taking you through Miami Beach's Art Deco district at your own leisure, with tours in several languages for just $15 for adults, $10 for seniors. Guided tours conducted by local historians and architects offer an in-depth look at the structures and their history. The 90-minute Ocean Drive and Beyond tour (offered Wed and Sat at 10:30am) takes you through the district, pointing out the differences between Mediterranean Revival and Art Deco for $20 for adults, $15 for seniors. If you're not blinded by neon, the Thursday night Art Deco District Up-to-Date Tour (leaving at 6:30pm) will whisk you around for a 90-minute walk, making note of how certain local hot spots were architecturally famous way before the likes of Madonna and Co. entered the scene. The cost is $20 for adults, $15 for seniors. For more information on tours or reservations, call ℭ 305/672-2014 (www.mdpl.org).

geometric patterns. In Miami, Art Deco is marked by the pastel-hued buildings that line South Beach and Miami Beach. But it's a lot more than just color. If you look carefully, you will see the intricacies and impressive craftsmanship that went into each building back in Miami in the '20s, '30s, '40s, and today, thanks to intensive restoration.

Most of the finest examples of the whimsical Art Deco style are concentrated along three parallel streets—Ocean Drive, Collins Avenue, and Washington Avenue—from about 6th to 23rd streets.

After years of neglect and calls for the wholesale demolition of its buildings, South Beach got a new lease on life in 1979. Under the leadership of Barbara Baer Capitman, a dedicated crusader for the Art Deco region, and the Miami Design Preservation League, founded by Baer Capitman and five friends, an area made up of an estimated 800 buildings was granted a listing on the National Register of Historic Places. Designers then began highlighting long-lost architectural details with soft sherbet shades of peach, periwinkle, turquoise, and purple. Developers soon moved in, and the full-scale refurbishment of the area's hotels was underway.

Not everyone was pleased, though. Former Miami Beach commissioner Abe Resnick said, "I love old buildings. But these Art Deco buildings are 40, 50 years old. They aren't historic. They aren't special. We shouldn't be forced to keep them." But Miami Beach kept those buildings, and Resnick lost his seat on the commission.

Today hundreds of new establishments—hotels, restaurants, and nightclubs—have renovated these older, historic buildings, putting South Beach on the cutting edge of Miami's cultural and nightlife scene.

EXPLORING THE AREA

If you're touring this unique neighborhood on your own, start at the **Art Deco Welcome Center,** 1001 Ocean Dr. (ℭ **305/531-3484**), which is run by the Miami Design Preservation League. The only beachside building across from the Clevelander Hotel and bar, the center gives away lots of informational material, including maps

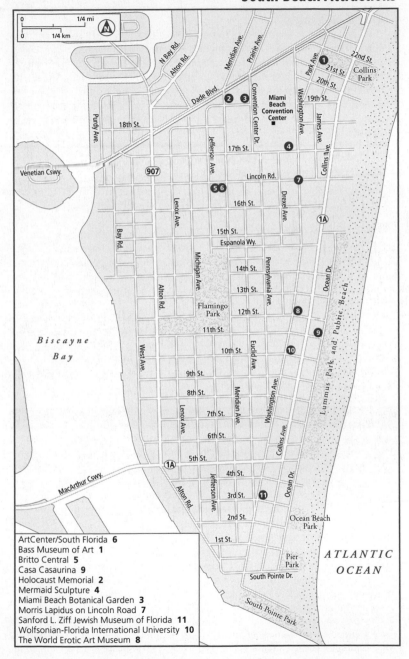

South Beach Attractions

0   1/4 mi
0   1/4 km

N Bay Rd.
Alton Rd.
Meridian Ave.
Prairie Ave.
Park Ave.
22nd St.
1
21st St.
20th St.
Collins Park
Dade Blvd.
2 **3**
Miami Beach Convention Center
Washington Ave.
19th St.
James Ave.
Collins Ave.
Purdy Ave.
18th St.
Jefferson Ave.
17th St.
Convention Center Dr.
4
Venetian Cswy.
907
Lincoln Rd.
7
5 6
16th St.
Drexel Ave.
1A
Lenox Ave.
15th St.
Espanola Wy.
Bay Rd.
Michigan Ave.
14th St.
Pennsylvania Ave.
13th St.
Ocean Dr.
Alton Rd.
Flamingo Park
12th St.
8
11th St.
9
Biscayne Bay
West Ave.
10th St.
Euclid Ave.
10
9th St.
8th St.
Washington Ave.
Meridian Ave.
Lenox Ave.
7th St.
6th St.
Collins Ave.
Lummus Park and Public Beach
1A
5th St.
MacArthur Cswy.
Alton Rd.
Jefferson Ave.
4th St.
3rd St.
11
2nd St.
Ocean Dr.
Ocean Beach Park
1st St.

ArtCenter/South Florida **6**
Bass Museum of Art **1**
Britto Central **5**
Casa Casaurina **9**
Holocaust Memorial **2**
Mermaid Sculpture **4**
Miami Beach Botanical Garden **3**
Morris Lapidus on Lincoln Road **7**
Sanford L. Ziff Jewish Museum of Florida **11**
Wolfsonian-Florida International University **10**
The World Erotic Art Museum **8**

Pier Park
South Pointe Dr.

ATLANTIC OCEAN

South Pointe Park

Miami or Madrid?

On a tiny street in South Beach, there's a piece of Spain that's so vibrant, you almost feel as if you're in Madonna's La Isla Bonita video. In 1925, Miami Beach developer NBT Roney hired architect Robert Taylor to design a Spanish village on the property he just purchased on a street called Española Way. Today, the historic Mediterranean-revival-style Spanish Village—or Plaza De España—envisioned by Roney and complete with fountain, stretches from Washington Avenue to Drexel Avenue and features charming boutiques, cafes, and a weekend market.

and pamphlets, and runs guided tours around the neighborhood. Art Deco books (including *The Art Deco Guide,* an informative compendium of all the buildings here), T-shirts, postcards, mugs, and other paraphernalia are for sale. It's open daily from 10am to 7:30pm.

Take a stroll along **Ocean Drive** for the best view of sidewalk cafes, bars, colorful hotels, and even more colorful people. Another great place for a walk is **Lincoln Road,** which is lined with boutiques, large chain stores, cafes, and funky art and antiques stores. The Community Church, at the corner of Lincoln Road and Drexel Avenue, was the neighborhood's first church and is one of its oldest surviving buildings, dating from 1921.

Or, if you prefer to cruise South Beach in a tiny yellow buggy—part scooter, part golf cart, consider **GoCar,** 1661 James Ave. (© **888/462-2755;** www.gocartours. com), a three-wheeled vehicle for two that comes with a GPS device that not only tracks and tells you where to go, but prompts a recorded tour that kicks on with every site you cruise by. Cost is $49 for the first hour, $39 for the second hour, and $29 for the third hour, or $150 for the entire day.

3 Miami's Museum & Art Scene

Miami has never been known as a cultural mecca as far as museums are concerned, though its reputation is improving thanks to the international attention brought to the scene by such esteemed fairs as Switzerland's Art Basel, which comes to Miami for a week every December. Though several exhibition spaces have made forays into collecting nationally acclaimed work, limited support and political infighting have made it a difficult proposition. Recently, however, things have changed as museums such as the Wolfsonian, the Museum of Contemporary Art, the Bass Museum of Art, and the Miami Art Museum have gotten on the bandwagon, boasting collections and exhibitions high on the list of art aficionados. It's now safe to say that world-class exhibitions start here. Listed below are the most lauded museums that have become a part of the city's cultural heritage and are as diverse as the city itself. Art lovers should check local listings for periodic gallery walks. Please note that many art museums and galleries are closed in the summer so call ahead so you won't be disappointed.

The focal point of December's enormously popular Art Basel is **Collins Park Cultural Center,** which comprises a trio of arts buildings on Collins Park and Park Avenue (off Collins Ave.), bounded by 21st to 23rd streets—the newly expanded Bass Museum of Art (see below), the new Arquitectonica-designed home of the Miami City Ballet, and the Miami Beach Regional Library, an ultramodern building designed

Roadside Attractions

The following examples of public art and prized architecture are great photo opportunities and worth visiting if you're in the area.

- **Casa Casaurina, aka Versace Mansion (Amsterdam Palace):** Morbid curiosity has led hordes of people—tourists and locals—to this, once the only private home (now a country club) on Ocean Drive. If you can get past the fact that the late designer was murdered on the steps of this palatial estate, you should definitely observe the intricate Italian architecture that makes this house stand out from its streamlined deco neighbors. Built in the 1930s as a replica of Christopher Columbus's son's palace in Santo Domingo, the house was originally called Casa Casaurina (House of the Pine), but was rechristened the Amsterdam Palace in 1935 when George Amsterdam purchased it. While there were rumors that the mansion was to be turned into a Versace museum, it was, instead, purchased by a private citizen from Texas. Located at the northwest corner of Ocean Drive and 11th Street, South Beach.
- **Mermaid Sculpture:** A pop-art masterpiece designed by Roy Lichtenstein, this sculpture captures the buoyant spirit of Miami Beach and its environs. It's in front of the Jackie Gleason Theater of the Performing Arts, at 1700 Washington Ave., Miami Beach.
- **Morris Lapidus on Lincoln Road:** Famed designer/architect, the late Morris Lapidus—the "high priest of high kitsch"—who is best known for the Fontainebleau Hotel, created a series of sculptures that are angular, whimsical, and quirky, competing with the equally amusing mix of pedestrians who flock to Lincoln Road. In addition to the sculptures on Lincoln Road (at Washington Ave.), which you can't miss, Lapidus also created the Colony Theater, 1040 Lincoln Rd., which was built by Paramount in 1943; the 1928 Sterling Building, 927 Lincoln Rd., whose glass blocks and blue neon are required evening viewing; and the Lincoln Theater, 555 Lincoln Rd., which features a remarkable tropical bas-relief.

by architect Robert A. M. Stern, with a special focus on the arts. The Library Café is on the library's first floor, serving coffee and pastries and exuding that cafe society ambience. Collins Park, the former site of the Miami Beach Library, returned to its original incarnation as an open space extending to the Atlantic, but it is also now the site of large sculpture installations and cultural activities planned jointly by the organizations that share the space.

ArtCenter/South Florida 𝒢ℛ   Not exactly a museum in the classic sense of the word, ArtCenter/South Florida is a multichambered space where local artists display their works in all media—from photography and sculpture to video and just about anything else that might exemplify their artistic nature. Admission is free, and it's quite fun to mosey through the space viewing the various artists at work in their studios. Of course, all the art is for sale, but there's no pressure to buy. If you call ahead,

---

(Finds   Eyeing the Storm

For Weather Channel fanatics and those who are just curious, the National Hurricane Center offers free tours before and after hurricane season, from January 15 through May 15, explaining everything from keeping track of storms to the history of some of the nation's most notorious and devastating hurricanes. Reservations required. Florida International University, 11691 SW 17th St., South Florida. (C) **305/229-4470.** Free admission.

---

you can schedule a guided tour of all the studios, which will give you extra insight into the exhibits. Otherwise, just wander and enjoy.

800–924 Lincoln Rd. (at Meridian Ave.), South Beach. (C) 305/674-8278. www.artcentersf.org. Free admission. Daily 11am–10pm.

Bass Museum of Art ✹✹✹   The Bass Museum of Art has expanded and received a dramatically new look, rendering it Miami's most progressive art museum. World-renowned Japanese architect Arata Isozaki designed the magnificent new facility, which has triple the former exhibition space, and added an outdoor sculpture terrace, a museum cafe and courtyard, and a museum shop, among other improvements. In addition to providing space in which to show the permanent collection, exhibitions of a scale and quality not previously seen in Miami will now be featured at the Bass. The museum's permanent collection includes European paintings from the 15th through the early 20th centuries, with special emphasis on northern European art of the Renaissance and baroque periods, including Dutch and Flemish masters. Past exhibitions have included the works of Picasso, Frida Kahlo, and Francois Marie Banier. The museum also has a lab, The New Information Workshop, making it possible for all aspiring artists to create their own masterpieces on computers for free or a nominal charge.

2121 Park Ave. (1 block west of Collins Ave.), South Beach. (C) 305/673-7530. www.bassmuseum.org. Admission $8 adults, $6 students and seniors, free for children 6 and under. Free 2nd Thurs of the month 6–9pm. Tues–Wed and Fri–Sat 10am–5pm; Thurs 10am–9pm; Sun 11am–5pm.

Diaspora Vibe Art Gallery ✹✹   This culturally charged art complex is a funky artist hangout and is the home to some of the greatest artworks of Miami's diverse Caribbean, Latin American, and African-American cultures. The gallery has two seasons of shows, often focusing on emerging artists. During the winter, three artists are selected by the gallery to travel to and exhibit their works in Paris. On the last Friday of every month, from May through October, the gallery holds its fabulous cocktail-infused "Final Fridays." A new artist's work is spotlighted inside, while outside in the courtyard are live music performances and readings of poetry and folk tales. Delicious Caribbean cuisine is also served while the who's who of Miami's cognoscenti gather here to recharge their cultural batteries.

3938 N. Miami Ave., Miami. (C) 305/573-4046. www.diasporavibe.com. Free admission. "Final Fridays" events $15. Tues–Sat 11am–6pm; "Final Fridays" events May–Oct last Fri of the month 7–11pm.

Holocaust Memorial ✹✹✹   This heart-wrenching memorial is hard to miss and would be a shame to overlook. The powerful centerpiece, Kenneth Triester's *Sculpture of Love & Anguish,* depicts victims of the concentration camps crawling up a giant yearning hand stretching up to the sky, marked with an Auschwitz number tattoo.

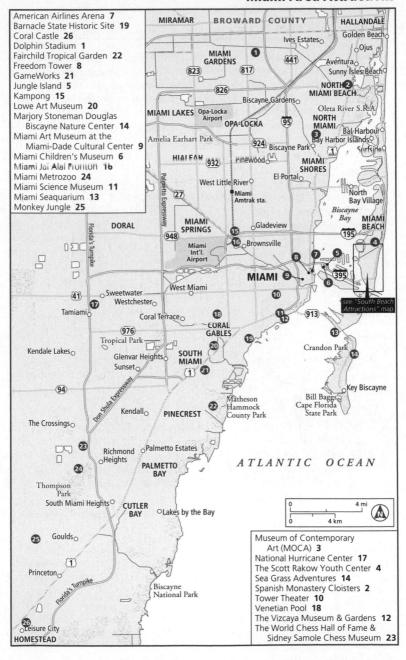

Miami Area Attractions

American Airlines Arena **7**
Barnacle State Historic Site **19**
Coral Castle **26**
Dolphin Stadium **1**
Fairchild Tropical Garden **22**
Freedom Tower **8**
GameWorks **21**
Jungle Island **5**
Kampong **15**
Lowe Art Museum **20**
Marjory Stoneman Douglas
  Biscayne Nature Center **14**
Miami Art Museum at the
  Miami-Dade Cultural Center **9**
Miami Children's Museum **6**
Miami Jai Alai Fronton **16**
Miami Metrozoo **24**
Miami Science Museum **11**
Miami Seaquarium **13**
Monkey Jungle **25**

Museum of Contemporary
  Art (MOCA) **3**
National Hurricane Center **17**
The Scott Rakow Youth Center **4**
Sea Grass Adventures **14**
Spanish Monastery Cloisters **2**
Tower Theater **10**
Venetian Pool **18**
The Vizcaya Museum & Gardens **12**
The World Chess Hall of Fame &
  Sidney Samole Chess Museum **23**

ATLANTIC OCEAN

Miami Art Galleries

Miami's finest art galleries are located within walking distance of one another in Coral Gables along Ponce de León Boulevard, extending from U.S. 1 to Bird Road. Still others are clustered in Bal Harbour's ritzy shopping district, on 96th Street off of Collins Avenue, right near the Bal Harbour Shops. Unfortunately, South Beach's Lincoln Road, which once had dozens of galleries, now has only a few—a result of soaring rents.

Also check out the burgeoning art scene in the Design District, north of downtown just west of Biscayne Boulevard around 40th Street. Listed below is a selection of galleries both in and out of these areas.

If you happen to be in town on the first Friday of the month, you should take the free trolley tour of the Coral Gables Art District. The tour runs from 7 to 10pm; meet at the Douglas Road Metrorail or at any of the other participating galleries in the area. Also check out www.artcircuits.com/c_cg.html for a map of the walking area.

Barbara Gillman Gallery   This gallery's ongoing exhibit of jazz photographer Herman Leonard's fantastic black-and-white photographs of legends such as Billie Holiday and Frank Sinatra has been so popular that it hasn't changed in years. In addition to the works of Leonard and other renowned artists such as Andres Serrano, Andy Warhol, and James Rosenquist, the gallery displays the work of new local talent. 2320 N. Miami Ave., Design District. © 305/573-1920.

Britto Central   Some people liken local Brazilian artist Romero Britto to Andy Warhol because of his colorful, whimsical paintings of young children

Along the reflecting pool is the story of the Holocaust, told in cut marble slabs. Inside the center of the memorial is a tableau that is one of the most solemn and moving tributes to the millions of Jews who lost their lives in the Holocaust I've seen. You can walk through an open hallway lined with photographs and the names of concentration camps and their victims. From the street you'll see the outstretched arm, but do stop and tour the sculpture at ground level. 1933 Meridian Ave. (at Dade Blvd.), South Beach. © 305/538-1663. www.holocaustmmb.org. Free admission. Daily 9am–9pm.

Lowe Art Museum 🏛🏛   Located on the University of Miami campus, the Lowe Art Museum has a dazzling collection of 8,000 works that include American paintings, Latin American art, Navajo and Pueblo Indian textiles, and Renaissance and baroque art. Traveling exhibits, such as *Wine Spectator* magazine's classic posters of the Belle Epoque, also stop here. For the most part, the Lowe is known for its collection of Greek and Roman antiquities, and, as compared to the more modern MOCA, Bass, and Miami Art Museum, features mostly European and international art hailing back to ancient times. University of Miami, 1301 Stanford Dr. (at Ponce de León Blvd.), Coral Gables. © 305/284-3603. www.lowe museum.org. Admission $7 adults, $5 seniors and students with ID. Donation day is first Tues of the month. Tues–Wed and Fri–Sat 10am–5pm; Thurs noon–7pm; Sun noon–5pm.

and animals, among other things. Serious art lovers, however, consider Britto's cartoonish works more along the lines of a second-rate Walt Disney. You decide. 818 Lincoln Rd., South Beach. © 305/531-8821.

Diana Lowenstein Fine Arts One of Miami's preeminent modern art collectors, Lowenstein's gallery in the burgeoning Wynwood area of downtown Miami is a hot spot for serious collectors and admirers. 2043 N. Miami Ave., Miami. © 305/576-1804.

Elite Fine Art Touted as one of the finest galleries in Miami, Elite features modern and contemporary Latin American painters and sculptors such as Angel Hurtado, Olga Sinclair, and Gina Pellon, among others. 3140 Ponce de León Blvd., Coral Gables. © 305/448-3800.

Evelyn S. Poole Ltd. Known as the finest of the fine antiques collections, the Poole assortment of European 17th-, 18th-, and 19th-century decorative furniture and accessories is housed in 5,000 square feet of space in the newly revived Decorator's Row. 3925 N. Miami Ave., Miami. © 305/573-7463.

Tower Theater This renovated movie theater in Little Havana features highly regarded Cuban art such as Carlos Navarro's Cosas Cubanas (Cuban Things). 1508 SW 8th St., Little Havana. © 305/237-6180.

Wallflower Gallery *(Finds* Funky, eclectic, and reminiscent of Andy Warhol's Factory, the Wallflower Gallery features an assortment of exhibits from local artists from erotica to exotica and everything in between. Performance art and live music are also featured here. 10 NE 3rd St., Miami. © 305/579-0069.

Miami Art Museum at the Miami-Dade Cultural Center ✸✸✸ The Miami Art Museum (MAM) features an eclectic mix of modern and contemporary works by such artists as Eric Fischl, Max Beckmann, Jim Dine, and Stuart Davis. Rotating exhibitions span ages and styles, and often focus on Latin American or Caribbean artists. JAM at MAM is the museum's popular happy hour, which takes place on the third Thursday of the month and is tied in to a particular exhibit. Almost as artistic as the works inside the museum is the composite sketch of the people—young and old—who attend these events.

The Miami-Dade Cultural Center, where the museum is housed, is a fortresslike complex designed by Phillip Johnson. In addition to the acclaimed Miami Art Museum, the center houses the main branch of the Miami-Dade Public Library, which sometimes features art and cultural exhibits, and the Historical Museum of Southern Florida, which highlights the fascinating history of the area. Unfortunately, the plaza onto which the complex opens is home to many of those in downtown Miami's homeless population, which makes it a bit off-putting but not dangerous. As of press time, work began on Museum Park, an underused 29-acre property on the bay in downtown Miami that will become MAM's new home. The 125,000-square-foot Museum Park will include a sculpture garden and spacious galleries. Estimated completion is sometime in 2009.

Checkmate

The World Chess Hall of Fame and Sidney Samole Chess Museum, 13755 SW 119th Ave. in South Miami (© 786/242-4255; www.chessmuseum.org; Thurs–Sat 10:30am–5pm and Sun 1–5pm; adults $5, students $3), is eye-catching, housed in a 45-foot-tall chessboardlike structure and featuring an interactive history of chess; an introduction to famous and celebrity players; computer-simulated, fully participatory games and challenges; tournament spaces; rare artifacts; an IBM Deep Blue feature; and a short film called *Chess Experience.*

101 W. Flagler St., Miami. © 305/375-3000. www.miamiartmuseum.org. Admission $5 adults, $2.50 seniors and students, free for children 11 and under. Tues–Fri 10am–5pm; 3rd Thurs of each month 10am–9pm; Sat–Sun noon–5pm. Closed major holidays. From I-95 south, exit at Orange Bowl–NW 8th St. and continue south to NW 2nd St.; turn left at NW 2nd St. and go 1½ blocks to NW 2nd Ave.; turn right.

Miami Children's Museum ✮✮ *Kids* The Children's Museum, across the Mac-Arthur Causeway from Jungle Island, is a modern, albeit odd-looking, 56,500-square-foot facility that includes 12 galleries, classrooms, a parent/teacher resource center, a Kid Smart educational gift shop, a 200-seat auditorium, and a Subway restaurant. The museum offers hundreds of bilingual, interactive exhibits as well as programs, classes, and learning materials related to arts, culture, community, and communication. Even as an adult, I have to say I was tempted to participate in some kids-only activities and exhibitions, such as the miniature Bank of America and Publix Supermarket, and a re-creation of the NBC 6 television studio. There's also a re-creation of a Carnival cruise ship and even a port stop in a re-created Brazil. Perhaps the coolest thing of all is the World Music Studio in which aspiring rock stars can lay down a few tracks and play instruments.

980 MacArthur Causeway, Miami Beach. © 305/373-5437. www.miamichildrensmuseum.org. Admission $10 adults and children, $5 for city residents. Daily 10am–6pm.

Miami Science Museum ✮✮ *Kids* The Miami Science Museum features more than 140 hands-on exhibits that explore the mysteries of the universe. Live demonstrations and collections of rare natural history specimens make a visit here fun and informative. Many of the demos involve audience participation, which can be lots of fun for willing and able kids and adults alike. There is also the Wildlife Center, with more than 175 live reptiles and birds of prey. The adjacent Space Transit Planetarium projects astronomy and laser shows as well as interactive demonstrations of upcoming computer technology and cyberspace features. Call or visit the website for a list of upcoming exhibits and laser shows.

3280 S. Miami Ave. (just south of the Rickenbacker Causeway), Coconut Grove. © 305/646-4200. www.miamisci.org. Admission $20 adults, $18 seniors and students, $13 children 3–12, free for children 2 and under. Laser shows, $7 adults, $4 seniors and children 3–12. Daily 10am–6pm, 10am–10pm 1st Fri of every month; call for show times (last show is at 4pm weekdays and 5pm weekends). Closed Thanksgiving and Christmas.

Museum of Contemporary Art (MOCA) ✮✮✮ MOCA boasts an impressive collection of internationally acclaimed art with a local flavor. It is also known for its forward thinking and ability to discover and highlight new artists. A high-tech screening facility allows for film presentations to complement the exhibitions. You can see works by Jasper Johns, Roy Lichtenstein, Larry Rivers, Duane Michaels, and Claes Oldenberg; plus, there are special exhibitions by such artists as Yoko Ono, Sigmar Polke, John Baldessari, and Goya. Guided tours are offered in English, Spanish, French, Creole, Portuguese, German, and Italian. The MOCA Annex at the Goldman Warehouse in the gritty, yet burgeoning Wynwood Arts District, 404 NW 26th St., is used to exhibit portions of the museum's permanent collection and projects by emerging artists.

770 NE 125th St., North Miami. © 305/893-6211. Fax 305/891-1472. www.mocanomi.org. Admission $5 adults, $3 seniors and students with ID, free for children 12 and under. Tues by donation. Tues–Sat 11am–5pm; Sun noon–5pm. Closed major holidays.

Ruboll Family Art Collection *★★★ (Finds* This impressive collection, owned by the Miami hotelier family the Rubells, is housed in a two-story, 40,000-square-foot former Drug Enforcement Agency warehouse in a sketchy area north of downtown Miami. The building looks like a fortress, which is fitting: Inside is a priceless collection of more than 1,000 works of contemporary art by the likes of Keith Haring, Damien Hirst, Julian Schnabel, Jean-Michel Basquiat, Paul McCarthy, Charles Ray, and Cindy Sherman. But be forewarned: Some of the art is extremely graphic and may be off-putting to some. The gallery changes exhibitions twice yearly, and there is a seasonal program of lectures, artists' talks, and performances by prominent artists.

95 NW 29th St. (on the corner of NW 1st Ave. near the Design District), Miami. © 305/573-6090. www.rubellfamily collection.com. Admission $10 adults, $5 seniors and students. Wed–Sun 10am–6pm.

Sanford L. Ziff Jewish Museum of Florida *★* Chronicling over 230 years of Jewish heritage and experiences in Florida, the Jewish Museum presents a fascinating look at religion and culture through films, lectures, and exhibits such as "Mosaic: Jewish Life in Florida," which features over 500 photos and artifacts documenting the Jewish experience in Florida since 1763. Housed in a former synagogue, the museum also delves into the Jewish roots of Latin America.

301 Washington Ave., South Beach. © 305/672-5044. www.jewishmuseum.com. Admission $6 adults, $5 seniors and students, $12 families. Free admission Sat. Tues–Sun 10am–5pm. Closed Jewish holidays.

Wolfsonian-Florida International University *★★★ (Finds* Mitchell Wolfson, Jr., heir to a family fortune built on movie theaters, was known as an eccentric, but I'd call him a pack rat. A premier collector of propaganda and advertising art, Wolfson was spending so much money storing his booty that he decided to buy the warehouse that was housing it. It ultimately held more than 70,000 of his items, from controversial Nazi propaganda to King Farouk of Egypt's match collection. Thrown in the eclectic mix are also zany works from great modernists such as Charles Eames and Marcel Duchamp. He then gave this incredibly diverse collection to Florida International University. The former 1927 storage facility has been transformed into a museum that is the envy of curators around the world. The museum is unquestionably fascinating and hosts lectures and rather swinging events surrounding particular exhibits. The Dynamo, the museum's cafe and shop, is a fun and funky spot serving coffee, wine, beer, and nibbles, whose focal point is a large library shelving system from the late–19th century, donated by Samson Management, designed by Bernard R. Green, and crafted of iron by the Snead & Company Iron Works. The design represents the first modular book-stacking system ever created. Leave it to the Wolfsonian to make even its restaurant a piece of work!

1001 Washington Ave., South Beach. ℂ 305/531-1001. www.wolfsonian.org. Admission $7 adults, $5 seniors, students with ID, and children 6–12. Mon–Tues and Fri–Sat 11am–6pm; Thurs 11am–9pm; Sun noon–5pm.

The World Erotic Art Museum 🔦 The Hustler store across the street has nothing on this wacky, X-rated museum. Opened in 2005 by 70-year-old-grandmother Naomi Wilzig, the museum features Wilzig's collection of more than 4,000 pieces of erotic art, including Kama Sutra temple carvings from India, peek-a-boo Victorian figurines that flash their booties, and a prop from the sexual thriller *A Clockwork Orange*. The 12,000-square-foot museum is located above Mansion, a club that's no stranger to erotic art—that is, performance art. This is a great place to spend an hour or two on a rainy day, and more than anything, the stuff is more amusing than sexy or racy.

1205 Washington Ave., South Beach. ℂ 305/532-9336. www.weam.com. Admission $15; under 18 years not admitted. Daily 11am–midnight.

4 Historic Homes & Sites

South Beach's well-touted Art Deco District is but one of many colorful neighborhoods that can boast dazzling architecture. The rediscovery of the entire Biscayne Corridor (from downtown to about 80th St. and Biscayne Blvd.) has given light to a host of ancillary neighborhoods on either side, which are filled with Mediterranean-style homes and Frank Lloyd Wright gems. Coral Gables is home to many large and beautiful homes, mansions, and churches that reflect architecture from the 1920s, 1930s, and 1940s. Some of the homes, or portions of their structures, have been created from coral rock and shells. The Biltmore Hotel is also filled with history; see p. 105 for information on touring it.

Barnacle State Historic Site 🔦🔦 The former home of naval architect and early settler Ralph Middleton Munroe is now a museum in the heart of Coconut Grove. It's the oldest house in Miami and it rests on its original foundation, which sits on 5 acres of natural hardwood forest and landscaped lawns. The house's quiet surroundings, wide porches, and period furnishings illustrate how Miami's first snowbird lived in the days before condomania and luxury hotels. Enthusiastic and knowledgeable state park employees provide a wealth of historical information to those interested in quiet, low-tech attractions such as this one. On Wednesdays from 6pm-7:30pm they have sunset yoga by the sea. Call for details on the fabulous monthly moonlight concerts during which folk, blues, or classical music is presented and picnicking is encouraged.

3485 Main Hwy. (1 block south of Commodore Plaza), Coconut Grove. ℂ 305/448-9445. Fax 305/448-7484. Admission $1. Concerts $5, free for children 9 and under. Fri–Mon 9am–4pm. Tours Fri–Mon at 10am, 11:30am, 1pm, and 2:30pm. From downtown Miami, take U.S. 1 south to 27th Ave., make a left, and continue to S. Bayshore Dr.; then make a right, follow to the intersection of Main Hwy., and turn left.

A Glimpse into the Past

Coconut Grove's link to the Bahamas dates from before the turn of the 20th century, when islanders came to the area to work in a newly opened hotel called the Peacock Inn. Bahamian-style wooden homes built by these early settlers still stand on Charles Street. Goombay, the lively annual Bahamian festival, celebrates the Grove's Caribbean link and has become one of the largest black-heritage street festivals in America. (See p. 34 for more information.)

Freedom Tower

Driving north on Biscayne Boulevard in downtown Miami, some may be distracted by the traffic, the neon lights coming from the Bayside Marketplace, or the behemoth cruise ships docked at the port. But perhaps the most dramatic presence on this heavily trafficked stretch of downtown is the Freedom Tower, 600 Biscayne Blvd. at NE 6th Street, built in 1925 and modeled after the Giralda Tower in Spain. Once home to the now-defunct *Miami Daily News* and *Metropolis* newspapers, the Freedom Tower was sold in 1957 to the U.S. General Services Administration, which used the building to process over 500,000 Cubans fleeing the island once Castro took over.

Considered the Ellis Island of the Cuban Exile community, Miami's Freedom Tower has remained largely vacant over the years (the government left the building in 1974) despite hopes and unfulfilled plans to turn it into a museum reflecting its historical significance. Most recently, the building was donated to Miami Dade College by the Terra Group, a condo development company, for use as a museum, cultural center, and classroom space—as long as they allow them to build a 62-story condo behind it.

Coral Castle ⟨★⟩ *(Finds* There's plenty of competition, but Coral Castle is probably the strangest attraction in Florida. In 1923, the story goes, a 26-year-old crazed Latvian, suffering from the unrequited love of a 16-year-old who left him at the altar, immigrated to South Miami and spent the next 25 years of his life carving huge boulders into a prehistoric-looking roofless "castle." It seems impossible that one rather short man could have done all this, but there are scores of affidavits on display from neighbors who swear it happened. Apparently, experts have studied this phenomenon to help figure out how the great pyramids and Stonehenge were built. Rocker Billy Idol was said to have been inspired by this place to write his song "Sweet 16." An interesting 25-minute audio tour guides you through the spot, now on the National Register of Historic Places. Although Coral Castle is overpriced and undermaintained, it's worth a visit when you're in the area, which is about 37 miles from Miami.

28655 S. Dixie Hwy., Homestead. ⟨©⟩ **305/248-6345.** www.coralcastle.com. Admission $9.75 adults, $6.50 seniors, $5 children 7–12. Daily 7am–8pm. Take 836 West (Dolphin Expwy.) toward Miami International Airport. Merge onto 826 South (Palmetto Expwy.) and take it to the Florida Tpk. toward Homestead. Take the 288th St. exit (#5) and then take a right on South Dixie Hwy., a left on SW 157th Ave., and then a sharp left back onto South Dixie Hwy. Coral Castle is on the left side of the street.

Spanish Monastery Cloisters ⟨★★★⟩ *(Finds* Did you know that the alleged oldest building in the Western Hemisphere dates from 1133 and is located in Miami? The Spanish Monastery Cloisters were first erected in Segovia, Spain. Centuries later, newspaper magnate William Randolph Hearst purchased and brought them to America in pieces. The carefully numbered stones were quarantined for years until they were finally reassembled on the present site in 1954. It has often been used as a backdrop for weddings, movies, and commercials, and is a very popular tourist attraction.

16711 W. Dixie Hwy. (at NE 167th St.), North Miami Beach. ⟨©⟩ **305/945-1461.** www.spanishmonastery.com. Admission $5 adults, $2.50 seniors and students with ID, $1 children 3–12. Mon–Fri 10am–4pm; Sun 1–5pm. Call ahead because the monastery closes for special events without notice.

Digging Miami

Until the controversial discovery of the archaeological site known as the Miami River Circle, the oldest existing artifacts in the city were presumed to have existed in the closets of Miami's retirement homes. In September 1998, during a routine archeological investigation on the mouth of the Miami River, several unusual and unique features were discovered cut into the bedrock: a prehistoric circular structure, 38 feet in diameter, with intentional markings of the cardinal directions as well as a 5-foot-long shark and two stone axes, suggesting the circle had ceremonial significance to Miami's earliest inhabitants—the Tequesta Indians. Radiocarbon tests confirm that the circle is about 2,000 years old.

While some have theorized that the circle is a calendar or Miami's own version of Stonehenge, most scholars believe that the discovery represents the foundation of a circular structure, perhaps a council house or a chief's house. Expert scientists, archeologists, and scholars who have made visits to the site indicate that the circle is of local, regional, and national significance. Local preservationists formed an organization, Save the Miami Circle, to ensure that developers don't raze the circle to make way for condominiums. For now, the circle remains put, albeit surrounded by cranes constructing mega-condos, and the mystery continues. See http://starkimages.homestead.com/miamicircle.html for more information.

Venetian Pool 𝒦𝒦𝒦 *Kids*   Miami's most beautiful and unusual swimming pool, dating from 1924, is hidden behind pastel stucco walls and is honored with a listing in the National Register of Historic Places. Underground artesian wells feed the free-form lagoon, which is shaded by three-story Spanish porticos and has both fountains and waterfalls. It can be cold in the winter months. During summer, the pool's 800,000 gallons of water are drained and refilled nightly, thanks to an underground aquifer, ensuring a cool, *clean* swim. Visitors are free to swim and sunbathe here, just as Esther Williams and Johnny Weissmuller did decades ago. For a modest fee, you or your children can learn to swim during special summer programs.

2701 DeSoto Blvd. (at Toledo St.), Coral Gables. ℂ 305/460-5356. www.venetianpool.com. Admission Nov–Mar $5.50 for those 13 and older, $3.50 for children 12 and under; Apr–Oct $10 for those 13 and older, $6.75 for children 12 and under. Children must be at least 3 years old and provide proof of age with birth certificate, or 38 in. tall to enter. Daily hours are at least 11am–4:30pm but are often longer. Call for more information.

The Vizcaya Museum and Gardens 𝒦𝒦𝒦   Sometimes referred to as the "Hearst Castle of the East," this magnificent villa is more Gatsbyesque than anything else you'll find in Miami. It was built in 1916 as a winter retreat for James Deering, cofounder and former vice president of International Harvester. The industrialist was fascinated by 16th-century art and architecture, and his ornate mansion, which took 1,000 artisans 5 years to build, became a celebration of that period. If you love antiques, this place is a dream come true, packed with European relics and works of art from the 16th to the 19th centuries. Most of the original furnishings, including dishes and paintings, are still intact. You will see very early versions of a telephone switchboard, central vacuum-cleaning system, elevators, and fire sprinklers. A free guided tour of the 34 furnished rooms on the first floor takes about 45 minutes. The second floor, which consists mostly of bedrooms, is open to tour on your own. The spectacularly opulent villa wraps itself around a central courtyard. Outside, lush formal gardens, accented with statuary, balustrades, and decorative urns, front an enormous swath of Biscayne Bay. Definitely take the tour of the rooms, but immediately thereafter, you will want to wander and get lost in the resplendent gardens.

3251 S. Miami Ave. (just south of Rickenbacker Causeway), North Coconut Grove. (C) 305/250-9133. www.vizcaya museum.com. Admission $12 adults, $9 seniors, $5 children 6–12, free for children 5 and under. Villa daily 9:30am–5pm (ticket booth closes at 4:30pm); gardens daily 9:30am–5:30pm.

5 Nature Preserves, Parks & Gardens

The Miami area is a great place for outdoor types, with beaches, parks, nature preserves, and gardens galore. For information on South Florida's two national parks, the Everglades and Biscayne National Park, see chapter 11.

The **Amelia Earhart Park,** 401 E. 65th St., Hialeah ((C) **305/685-8389**), is the only real reason to travel to industrial, traffic-riddled Hialeah. The park has five lakes stocked with bass and bream for fishing, playgrounds, picnic facilities, a skate park, and a big red barn that houses cows, sheep, and goats for petting and ponies for riding. There's also the Bill Graham Farm Village, a re-created Miami-Dade County homestead housing a country store and dozens of old-time farm activities such as horseshoeing, sugarcane processing, and more. Parking is free on weekdays and $4 per car on weekends. The park is open daily from 9am to sunset, but all the attractions close at about 4pm. To drive here, take I-95 north to the NW 103rd Street exit, go west to East 4th Avenue, and then turn right. Parking is 1½ miles down the street. Depending on traffic, Hialeah is about a half-hour from downtown Miami.

At the historic **Bill Baggs Cape Florida State Park** (★, 1200 Crandon Blvd. ((C) **305/ 361-5811**), at the southern tip of Key Biscayne about 20 minutes from downtown Miami, you can explore the unfettered wilds and enjoy some of the most secluded beaches in Miami. There's also a historic lighthouse that was built in 1825, which is the oldest lighthouse in South Florida. The lighthouse was damaged during the Second Seminole War (1836) and again in 1861 during the Civil War. Out of commission for awhile, it was restored to working lighthouse condition in 1978 by the U.S. Coast Guard. A rental shack leases bikes, hydrobikes, kayaks, and many more water toys. It's a great place to picnic, and a newly constructed restaurant serves homemade Latin food, including great fish soups and sandwiches. Just be careful that the raccoons don't get your lunch—the furry black-eyed beasts are everywhere. Wildlife aside, however, Bill Baggs has been consistently rated as one of the top 10 beaches in the U.S. for its 1¼ miles of wide, sandy beaches and its secluded, serene atmosphere. Admission is $5 per car with up to eight people (or $3 for a car with only one person; $1 to enter by foot or bicycle). Open daily from 8am to sunset. Tours of the lighthouse are available every Thursday through Monday at 10am and 1pm. Arrive at least half an hour early to sign up—there is room for only 10 people on each tour. Take I-95 to the Rickenbacker Causeway and take that all the way to the end.

Fairchild Tropical Garden (★★★, at 10901 Old Cutler Rd. in Coral Gables ((C) **305/667-1651;** www.ftg.org), is the largest of its kind in the continental United States. A veritable rainforest of both rare and exotic plants, as well as 11 lakes and countless meadows, are spread across 83 acres. Palmettos, vine pergola, palm glades, and other unique species create a scenic, lush environment. More than 100 species of birds have been spotted at the garden (ask for a checklist at the front gate), and it's home to a variety of animals. You should not miss the 30-minute narrated tram tour (tours leave on the hour 10am–3pm weekdays and 10am–4pm weekends) to learn about the various flowers and trees on the grounds. There is also a museum, a cafe, a picnic area, and a gift shop with edible gifts and fantastic books on gardening and cooking. Fairchild often hosts major art exhibits by the likes of Dale Chihuly and Roy Lichtenstein. The 2-acre rainforest exhibit, *Windows to the Tropics,* will save you a trip to the Amazon. Expect to spend a minimum of 2 hours here.

Admission is $20 for adults, $15 for seniors, $10 for children ages 3 to 12, and free for children 2 and under. Open daily, except Christmas, from 9:30am to 4:30pm. Take I-95 south to U.S. 1, turn left onto Le Jeune Road, and follow it straight to the traffic circle; from there, take Old Cutler Road 2 miles to the park.

On Biscayne Bay in Coconut Grove (4013 Douglas Rd.; www.ntbg.org/gardens/ kampong.php), the **Kampong** 𝒜𝒜 is a 7-acre botanical garden with a stunning array of flowering trees and tropical fruit trees, including mango, avocado, and pomelos. In the early 1900s, noted plant explorer David Fairchild traveled the world seeking rare plants of economic and aesthetic value, which might be cultivated in the United States. In 1928, Fairchild and his wife, Marian—the daughter of Alexander Graham Bell—decided to build a residence here (now listed on the National Register of Historic Places) surrounded by some of his findings, and named it after the Malaysian word *kampong,* meaning "home in a garden." In the 1960s, the Fairchilds sold the Kampong to Catherine Hauberg Sweeney, who donated it to the National Tropical Botanical Garden to promote and preserve this South Florida treasure. It's a must-see for those interested in horticulture. Admission and tours are by appointment only, from Monday to Friday. For tour and price information, call ℂ **305/442-7169** from 9am to 5pm Monday through Friday. Take U.S. 1 to Douglas Road (SW 37th Ave.). Go east on Douglas Road for about a mile. The Kampong will be on your left.

Named after the late champion of the Everglades, the **Marjory Stoneman Douglas Biscayne Nature Center** 𝒜, 6767 Crandon Blvd., Key Biscayne (ℂ **305/361-6767;** www.biscaynenaturecenter.org), is housed in a $4-million facility and offers hands-on marine exploration, hikes through coastal hammocks, bike trips, and beach walks. Local environmentalists and historians lead intriguing trips through the local habitat. Call to reserve a spot on a regularly scheduled weekend tour or program. Be sure to wear comfortable, closed-toe shoes for hikes through wet or rocky terrain. Open daily 10am to 4pm. Admission to the park is $4 per person; admission to the nature center is free. Special programs and tours cost $10 per person. Call for weekend programs. To get there, take I-95 to the Rickenbacker Causeway Exit (#1) and take the causeway all the way until it becomes Crandon Boulevard. The center is on the east side of the street (the Atlantic Ocean side) and about 25 minutes from downtown Miami.

Because so many people are focused on the beach itself, the **Miami Beach Botanical Garden,** 2000 Convention Center Dr., Miami Beach (ℂ **305/673-7256**), remains a secret garden. The lush, tropical 4½-acre garden is a fabulous natural retreat from the hustle and bustle of the silicone-enhanced city. Open Tuesday through Sunday from 9am to 5pm; admission is free.

The **Oleta River State Recreation Area** 𝒜𝒜, 3400 NE 163rd St., North Miami (ℂ **305/919-1846**), consists of 993 acres—the largest urban park in the state—on

Biscayne Bay. The beauty of the Oleta River, combined with the fact that you're essentially in the middle of a city, makes this park especially worth visiting. With miles of bicycle and canoe trails, a sandy swimming beach, kayak and mountain bike rental shop, Blue Marlin Fish House Restaurant, shaded picnic pavilions, and a fishing pier, Oleta River State Recreation Area allows for an outstanding outdoor recreational experience cloistered from the confines of the big city. There are 14 air-conditioned cabins on the premises, which sleep four people. The cost is $45 per night, and guests are required to bring their own linens. Bathrooms and showers are outside, as is a fire circle with a grill for cooking. For reservations, call © **800/326-3521.** Open daily from 8am to sunset. Admission for pedestrians and cyclists is $1 per person. By car: Driver plus car costs $3; driver plus one to seven passengers and car costs $5. Take 1 95 to exit 17 (S.R. 826 E.) and go all the way east until just before the causeway. The park entrance is on your right. Driving time from downtown Miami is about a half-hour.

A testament to Miami's unusual climate, the **Preston B. Bird and Mary Heinlein Fruit and Spice Park** ⟨R⟩, 24801 SW 187th Ave., Homestead (© **305/247-5727;** www.fruitandspicepark.org), harbors rare fruit trees that cannot survive elsewhere in the country. If a volunteer is available, you'll learn some fascinating things about this 30-acre living plant museum, where the most exotic varieties of fruits and spices— akee, mango, Ugli fruits, carambola, and breadfruit—grow on strange-looking trees with unpronounceable names. There are also original coral rock buildings dating back to 1912. The Strawberry Folk Festival in February and an art festival here in January are among the park's most popular—and populated—events. The best part? You're free to take anything that has *naturally* fallen to the ground (no picking here). You'll also find samples of interesting fruits and jellies made from the park's bounty, as well as exotic ingredients and cookbooks in the gift store.

Admission to the spice park is $6 for adults and $1.50 for children 12. It's open daily from 10am to 5pm; closed on Christmas. Tours are included in the price of admission and are offered at 11am, 1:30pm, and 3pm. Take U.S. 1 south, turn right on SW 248th Street, and go straight for 5 miles to SW 187th Avenue. The drive from Miami should take 45 minutes to an hour.

Tropical Park, 7900 SW 40th St. in West Miami (© **305/226-8315**), has it all. Enjoy a game of tennis or racquetball for a minimal fee, swim and sun yourself on the secluded little lake, rent bikes, or try horseback riding. You can use the fishing pond for free, and they'll even supply you with the rods and bait. If you catch anything, however, you're on your own. Open daily from 7am to 10pm; admission is free. To get there, go west on Bird Road until you reach the overpass for the Palmetto Expressway (826). The park is on the left side immediately after the overpass.

6 Sightseeing Cruises & Organized Tours

BOAT & CRUISE-SHIP TOURS

You don't need a boating license or a zillion-dollar yacht to explore Miami by boat. Thanks to several enterprising companies, boat tours are easy to find, affordable, and an excellent way to see the city from a more liquid perspective.

Celebration Cruising ⟨R⟩   Dinner cruises, sunset sails, and a 2-hour air-conditioned cruise will take you past Millionaires' Row and the Venetian Islands (see "Venice in Miami," below). There's a food stand and cash bar. Tours are bilingual. There are also powerboat tours and various lunch and dinner cruise packages.

Moments Venice in Miami

You don't have to endure jet lag and time-zone differences to enjoy the beauty of Italy. Located just off Miami Beach, Florida's own Venetian Islands (NE 15th St. and Dade Blvd.) were joined together in 1926 by a bascule bridge known as the **Venetian Causeway.** A series of 12 bridges connecting the Venetian Islands and stretching between Miami and Miami Beach feature octagonal concrete entrance towers, which give you a great view of the water. The oldest causeway in metropolitan Miami, the Venetian is rickety in a charming way, with fantastic views of the city and the mammoth cruise ships docked at the port, not to mention glimpses of some of Miami's most beautiful waterfront homes. Bikers and joggers especially love the Venetian Causeway, thanks to its limited traffic and beautiful scenery.

Bayside Marketplace Marina, 401 Biscayne Blvd., Downtown. © 305/373-7001. www.celebrationcruising.com. $18–$40, free for children 12 and under. Millionaires Row tour daily 11am and 1, 3, 5, and 7pm. Evening party cruise (music and cash bar) Fri–Sat 9–11pm.

Heritage Miami II Topsail Schooner   This relaxing ride aboard Miami's only tall ship is a fun way to see the city, since it's on a schooner (as opposed to the other tour company's cruising boats), which gives you more of a feel of the water. The 2-hour cruise passes by Villa Vizcaya, Coconut Grove, and Key Biscayne, and puts you in sight of Miami's spectacular skyline and island homes. Call ahead to confirm the ship's schedule. On Friday, Saturday, and Sunday evenings, there are 1-hour tours to see the lights of the city, for $15 per person.

Bayside Marketplace Marina, 401 Biscayne Blvd., Downtown. © 305/442-9697. www.heritageschooner.com. Tickets for day tours $20 adults, $15 children 12 and under; hour-long evening trips at 6:30 and 8pm $15 adults, $10 children. Sept–May only. Tours leave Mon–Thurs at 1:30, 4, and 6:30pm; Fri–Sun at 1:30, 4, 6:30, 9, 10, and 11pm.

Miami Beach Architecture Cruise &   Sail a 32-foot catamaran with Randall Robinson, executive director of the North Beach Development Corp., and learn all about Miami Modern (MiMo) architecture on this engaging 90-minute cruise. Sure, you'll see stars' homes—Ricky Martin, Jennifer Lopez, and the Bee Gees—but more interesting than who lives there is who built the places.

Boat departs from 65th St. and Indian Creek Dr, Miami Beach. © 305/865-4147. Tickets $30. Cruises leave at 5:30pm Fri in the summer and 4pm Fri in the winter.

Miami Duck Tours   Hands down, this is the corniest, kookiest tour in the entire city. In fact, the company prefers to call these tours the "Quackiest" way to visit Miami and the beaches. Whatever you call it, it's weird. The *Watson Willy* is the first of several Miami Duck Tours "vesicles," not a body part, but a hybrid name that means part vessel, part vehicle (technical name: Hydra Terra Amphibious Vehicle). Each "vesicle" seats 49 guests, plus a captain and tour guide, and leaves from Watson Island behind Jungle Island, traveling through downtown Miami and South Beach. If you're image conscious, you may want to reconsider traveling down Ocean Drive in a duck. That's right, a duck, which is what the "vesicle" looks like. After driving the streets in the duck, you'll end up cruising Biscayne Bay, past all the swank houses. Embarrassing or downright hilarious, Miami Duck Tours is definitely unique.

1665 Washington Ave. South Beach. (℃ 877/DUCK-TIX. www.ducktoursmiami.com. Tickets $32 adults, $26 seniors and military, $18 children 12 and under.

Tropical Boat Tours   Private boat trips on 22-foot powerboats are a fantastic way to explore the bays and waterways of Miami, if you can afford it. There are also beautiful yachts and catamarans for rent. Tour Biscayne Bay or even go as far as Bimini in the Bahamas. Among the best tours: "Islands of the Rich and Famous," in which you cruise past Star Island, Hibiscus Island, Fisher Island, and Palm Island. Keep your eyes open—Star Island resident Rosie O'Donnell always goes jet-skiing out by these boats. A sunset cruise of Miami is also highly recommended. We hear that Tropical Boat Tours are a popular activity among visiting celebrities who relish their privacy—even on the high seas.

(℃ 786/218-3030. www.tropicalboat.com. Trips $145–$1,400.

SIGHTSEEING TOURS

Miami Nice Excursion Travel and Service ℛ   Pick your destination and the Miami Nice tours will take you by bus to the Everglades, Fort Lauderdale, South Beach, the Seaquarium, Key West, Cape Canaveral, or wherever else you desire. The best trip for first-timers is the City Tour, a comprehensive tour of the entire city and its various neighborhoods. If you've got the time, you will definitely want to add on a side trip to the Everglades and/or Key West (though I suggest exploring the Everglades on your own). Included in most Miami trips is a fairly comprehensive city tour narrated by a knowledgeable guide. The company is one of the oldest in town.

18801 Collins Ave., Miami Beach. (℃ 305/949-9180. www.miaminicetours.com. Tours $25–$160 adults, $25–$140 children 3–9. Mon–Sat 7am–10pm. Call ahead for directions to various pickup areas.

SPECIALIZED TOURS

In addition to tours listed below, a great option for seeing the city is a tour led by **Dr. Paul George.** Dr. George is a history teacher at Miami-Dade Community College and a historian at the Historical Museum of Southern Florida. He also happens to be "Mr. Miami." There's a variety of tours (including the "Mystery, Mayhem and Vice Crime Tour," detailed below), all fascinating to South Florida buffs. Tours focus on neighborhoods such as Little Havana, Brickell Avenue, or Key Biscayne, and on themes such as Miami cemeteries and the Miami River. There are also eco-history coach, walking and bike tours. The often-long-winded discussions can be a bit much

Vintage Miami

Although it's hardly Napa Valley, Miami does have an actual winery: Schnebly Redland's Winery, 30205 SW 217th Ave., Homestead (℃ **888/717-WINE;** www.schneblywinery.com), which recently debuted its $1.5-million tasting room in which you can sample from various vintages. I've tried some and while they're too fruity for my taste, it's still worth a trip down just to see the press deck where fruit becomes juice and eventually wine. There's live music and extended hours on Saturday and Sunday, and if you like what you taste, you can buy any four bottles of wine for $65. Open 10am to 5pm Monday to Friday, 10am to 8pm Saturday, and noon to 7pm Sunday.

for those who just want a quick look around, but Dr. George certainly knows his stuff. The cost is $25 to $42, and reservations are required (© **305/375-1621;** www.hmsf. org/programs-adult.htm). Tours leave from the Historical Museum at 101 W. Flagler St., downtown. Call for a schedule.

Biltmore Hotel Tour 🎯🎯🎯 *(Value)*   Take advantage of these free, 55-minute Sunday walking tours to enjoy the hotel's history and beautiful grounds. Starting in the upstairs lobby, the tour will even take you to Everglades Suite, when available, home to dignitaries and heads of state and a sanctuary for celebrities. Call ahead to confirm.
1200 Anastasia Ave., Coral Gables. © **305/445-1926.** www.biltmorehotel.com. Free admission. Tours depart Sun at 1:30, 2:30, and 3:30pm.

Eco-Adventure Tours 🎯🎯🎯   For the eco-conscious traveler, the Miami-Dade Parks and Recreation Department offers guided nature, adventure, and historic tours involving biking, canoeing, snorkeling, hiking, and bird-watching all over the city. Contact them for more information.
© **305/365-3018.** www.miamidade.gov/parks/fun-eco_adventures.asp.

Herencia Hispana Tour   For those looking to immerse themselves in Miami's rich Latin-American culture, the Herencia Hispana Tour is the ideal way to explore it all. Hop on a bus and zoom past such hotbeds of Latin activity as downtown's Flagler Street, the unavoidable Elián González house, Little Havana's Domino Park and Tower Theater, among others. Not just a sightseeing tour, this one includes two very knowledgeable, albeit corny, guides who know just when to infuse a necessary dose of humor into the Elián saga, a segment of history that some people may not consider so amusing.
Tours depart at 9, 9:30, and 10am every Sat in Oct from the Steven P. Clark Government Center, 111 NW 1st St. © **305/770-3131.** www.co.miami-dade.fl.us/transit/hispanicher.asp. Tours (which are in Spanish or English, but you must specify which one you require) are free, but advanced reservations are required.

Little Havana Walking Tour 🎯🎯🎯   Dr. Paul George will guide you through Little Havana, pointing out the significance of South Florida bungalow architecture, the Tower Theater, old-fashioned hand rollers at a cigar factory and more. Visit Cuban Memorial Boulevard and observe the monuments that speak to the exile presence in Miami. See the home of Miami's first mayor.
© **305/375-1621.** $25. www.hmsf.org.

Miami Design Preservation League 🎯🎯   On Thursday evenings and Saturday mornings, the Design Preservation League sponsors walking tours that provide a fascinating inside look at the city's historic Art Deco District. Tourgoers meet for a 1½-hour walk through some of America's most exuberantly "architectured" buildings. The league led the fight to designate this area a National Historic District and is proud to share the splendid locale with visitors. Also see p. 164 for more information.
Art Deco Welcome Center, 1001 Ocean Dr., South Beach. © **305/672-2014.** www.mdpl.org. Walking tours $20 per person. Tours leave Wed and Sat at 10:30am and Thurs at 6:30pm. Self-guided audio tours also available daily for $15. No reservations necessary, but arrive 15 minutes early. Call ahead for updated schedules.

Miami SkyLift Balloon   For a view above the cranes—500 ft. above, specifically— this 73-foot tall balloon takes 30 people above the Miami skyline for a 15-minute ride. Check the weather reports, because the balloon doesn't fly in high winds.

Balloon is at the Mildred and Claude Pepper fountain at Bayfront Park. © **305/995-5815.** www.miamiskylift.com. $15 adults, $8.50 kids 3-12.

Mystery, Mayhem and Vice Crime Bus Tour 𝔏𝔏𝔏 Visit the past by video and bus to Miami-Dade's most celebrated crimes and criminals from the 1800s to the present, including some sites where the 80s TV series Miami Vice was filmed. From the murder spree of the Ashley Gang to the most notorious murders and crimes of our century, including the murder of designer Gianni Versace, historian Paul George conducts a most fascinating 3-hour tour of scandalous proportions.

Held twice a year, usually in Apr and Oct; leaves from the Dade Cultural Center, 101 W. Flagler St., Miami. Tickets $39. Advance reservations required; call © **305/375-1621.**

Redland Tropical Trail Tours 𝔏𝔏𝔏 Check out South Florida farmlands—yes, they do exist in an area near Homestead called The Redlands—on this tour featuring a circuit of stops, tastings, and sightseeing that will take you from gardens and jungles to an orchid farm, an actual working winery (see below), fruit stand, and more. There's no cost to follow the trail with a map (available on the website) on your own, but call for pricing information for certain attractions found on the trail.

© **305/245-9180.** www.redlandtrail.com.

7 Watersports

There are many ways to get well acquainted with Miami's wet look. Choose your own adventure from the suggestions listed below.

BOATING

Private rental outfits include **Boat Rental Plus,** 2400 Collins Ave., Miami Beach (© **305/534-4307**), where 50-horsepower, 18-foot powerboats rent for some of the best prices on the beach. There's a 2-hour minimum, and rates go from $100 to $500, including taxes and gas. They also have great specials on Sunday. Cruising is permitted only in and around Biscayne Bay (ocean access is prohibited), and renters must be 21 or older to rent a boat. The rental office is at 23rd Street, on the inland waterway in Miami Beach. It's open daily from 10am to sunset. If you want a specific type of boat, call ahead to reserve. Otherwise, show up and take what's available.

Club Nautico of Coconut Grove, 2560 S. Bayshore Dr. (© **305/858-6258;** www.clubnauticousa.com), rents high-quality powerboats for fishing, water-skiing, diving, and cruising in the bay or ocean. All boats are Coast Guard–equipped, with VHF radios and safety gear. Rates start at $359 for 4 hours and $469 for 8 hours; prices go up as the boats get larger. You can also rent by the hour at $125. Club Nautico is open daily from 8am to 6pm (weather permitting). Other locations include the Crandon Park Marina, 4000 Crandon Blvd., Key Biscayne (© **305/361-9217**), with the same rates and hours as the Coconut Grove location; and the Miami Beach Marina, Pier E, 300 Alton Rd., South Beach (© **305/673-2502**). Nautico on Miami Beach is open daily from 9am to 5pm.

JET SKIS/WAVERUNNERS

Don't miss a chance to tour the islands on the back of your own powerful watercraft. Bravery is, however, a prerequisite, as Miami's waterways are full of speeding jet-skiers and boaters who think they're in the Indy 500. Many beachfront concessionaires rent a variety of these popular (and loud) water scooters. The latest models are fast and

A Whole New World

Every Columbus Day, Biscayne Bay becomes a veritable mob scene of boaters celebrating the discovery of another day off of work. The unofficial Columbus Day Regatta has become a tradition in which people take to the water for a day of boating, sunning, and, literally, the bare necessities, as they often strip down to their birthday suits in an eye-opening display of their appreciation for Columbus's discovery of the nude, er, new world.

smooth. **American Watersports,** at the Miami Beach Marina, 300 Alton Rd. (© **305/ 538-7549;** www.jetskiz.com), is the area's most popular spot for jet-ski rental. Rates begin at $65 for a half-hour and $120 for an hour. They also offer fun jet ski tours past celebrity homes for $140 for the first hour and $70 for the second, with a 2-hour minimum.

KAYAKING

The **Blue Moon Outdoor Center** rents kayaks at 3400 NE 163rd St. in Oleta River Park (© **305/957-3040;** www.bluemoonmiami.com). The outfitters here give explorers a map to take with them and quick instructions on how to work the paddles and boats. They also operate very scenic 4-hour guided tours through rivers with mangroves and islands—fewer than 10 people on the tour costs $45 per person; more than 10 people costs $35 per person. These must be booked in advance. Hourly and half-day rentals available for single, tandem, and canoe. Price ranges from $12 to $45. Guided eco-tours are also available with advance reservation for $45 to $55 per person. While you are on the paddling route, make sure to stop at the Blue Marlin Fish House for some smoked fish. They also rent mountain bikes. Open daily from 9am to sunset. Special event tours at night, including a full moon kayak tour are also available.

SAILING

You can rent sailboats and catamarans through the beachfront concessions desks of several top resorts, such as the Doral Golf Resort and Spa (p. 109).

Aquatic Rental Center, on Key Biscayne in the Crandon Marina (next to Sundays on the Bay), 4000 Crandon Blvd., Key Biscayne (© **305/361-0328** days, 305/279-7424 evenings; www.arcmiami.com), can also get you out on the water. A 22-foot sailboat rents for $80 for 2 hours, $135 for a half-day, and $195 for a full day. A Sunfish sailboat for two people rents at $30 per hour. If you've always had a dream to win the America's Cup but can't sail, the able teachers here will get you started. They offer a 10-hour course over 5 days for $350 for one person, or $450 for you and a buddy.

SCUBA DIVING & SNORKELING

In 1981, the U.S. government began a wide-scale project designed to increase the number of habitats available to marine organisms. One of the program's major accomplishments has been the creation of nearby artificial reefs, which have attracted all kinds of tropical plants, fish, and animals. In addition, Biscayne National Park (p. 244) offers a protected marine environment just south of downtown.

Several dive shops around the city offer organized weekend outings, either to the reefs or to one of more than a dozen old shipwrecks around Miami's shores. Check "Divers" in the Yellow Pages for rental equipment and for a full list of undersea tour operators.

Diver's Paradise of Key Biscayne, 4000 Crandon Blvd. (© **305/361-3483;** www.keydivers.com), offers one dive expedition per day during the week and two per day on the weekends to the more than 30 wrecks and artificial reefs off the coast of Miami Beach and Key Biscayne. You can take a 3-day certification course for $499, which includes all the dives and gear. If you already have your C-card, a dive trip costs about $100 if you need equipment and $55 if you bring your own gear. It's open Tuesday through Friday from 10am to 6pm and Saturday and Sunday from 8am to 6pm. Call ahead for times and locations of dives. For snorkeling, they will set you up with equipment and maps on where to see the best underwater sights. Rental for mask, fins, and snorkel is $50.

South Beach Divers, 850 Washington Ave., Miami Beach (© **305/531-6110;** www.southbeachdivers.com), will also be happy to tell you where to go under the sea and will provide you with scuba rental equipment as well for $65. You can rent snorkel gear for $20. They also do dive trips to Key Largo three times a week and do dives off Miami on Sunday at $100 for a two-tank dive.

The most amusing and apropos South Beach diving spot has to be the **Jose Cuervo Underwater Bar,** located 150 yards southeast of the Second Street lifeguard station—a 22-ton concrete margarita bar that was sunk on May 5, 2000. Nicknamed "Sinko De Mayo," the site is designed with a dive flag roof, six bar stools, and a protective wall of tetrahedrons. For more information, go to www.sinkodemayo.com.

WINDSURFING

Many hotels rent windsurfers to their guests, but if yours doesn't have a watersports concession stand, head for Key Biscayne. **Sailboards Miami,** Rickenbacker Causeway, Key Biscayne (© **305/361-SAIL;** www.sailboardsmiami.com), operates out of two big yellow trucks on Windsurfer Beach, the most popular windsurfing spot in the city (though our pick for best is Hobie Beach). For those who've never ridden a board but want to try it, they offer a 2-hour lesson for $69 that's guaranteed to turn you into a wave warrior, or you get your money back. After that, you can rent a board for $25 to $30 an hour. If you want to make a day of it, a 10-hour prepaid card costs $180. These cards reduce the price by about $70 for the day. You can use the card year-round, until the time on it runs out. Open Tuesday through Sunday from 10am to 5:30pm. Make your first right after the tollbooth (at the beginning of the causeway—you can't miss it) to find the outfitters. They also rent kayaks.

8 More Ways to Play, Indoors & Out

The cement promenade on the southern tip of South Beach is a great place to ride. Biking up the beach (either on the beach or along the beach on a cement pathway—which is a lot easier!) is great for surf, sun, sand, exercise, and people-watching—just be sure to keep your eyes on the road, as the scenery can be most distracting. Most of the big beach hotels rent bicycles, as does the **Miami Beach Bicycle Center,** 601 5th St., South Beach (© **305/674-0150;** www.bikemiamibeach.com), which charges $8 per hour or $24 for up to 24 hours. It's open Monday through Saturday from 10am to 7pm, Sunday from 10am to 5pm.

Bikers can also enjoy more than 130 miles of paved paths throughout Miami. The beautiful and quiet streets of Coral Gables and Coconut Grove (several bike trails are spread throughout these neighborhoods) are great for bicyclists, where old trees form canopies over wide, flat roads lined with grand homes and quaint street markers.

A Berry Good Time

South Florida's farming region has been steadily shrinking in the face of industrial expansion, but you'll still find several spots where you can get back to nature while indulging in a local gastronomic delight—picking your own produce at the "U-Pic-'Em" farms that dot South Dade's landscape. Depending on what's in season, you can get everything from fresh herbs and vegetables to a mélange of citrus fruits and berries. During berry season—January through April—it's not uncommon to see hardy pickers leaving the groves with hands and faces that are stained a tale-telling crimson and garnished with happy smiles. On your way through South Dade, keep an eye out for the bright red U-Pic signs.

There are also a number of fantastic fruit stands in the region. **Burr's Berry Farms,** 12741 SW 216th St. (© **305/251-0145**), located in the township of Goulds, about an hour from downtown Miami, has created a sensation with its fabulous strawberry milkshakes. To get there, go south on U.S. 1 and turn right on SW 216th St. The fruit stand is about 1 mile west. It's open daily from 9am to 5:30pm.

For fresh fruit in a tasty pastry or tart, head over to **Knaus Berry Farm,** at 15980 SW 248th St. (© **305/247-0668**), in an area known as the Redlands. Some people erroneously call this farm an Amish farm, but in actuality, it's run by a sect of German Baptists. The stand offers items ranging from fresh flowers to homemade ice cream, but be sure to indulge in one of their famous homemade cinnamon buns. Be prepared to wait in a long line to stock up—people flock here from as far away as Palm Beach. Head south on U.S. 1 and turn right on 248th St. The stand is 2½ miles farther on the left side. Open Monday through Saturday from 8am to 5:30pm.

The terrain in Key Biscayne is perfect for biking, especially along the park and beach roads. If you don't mind the sound of cars whooshing by your bike lane, **Rickenbacker Causeway** is also fantastic, since it is one of the only bikeable inclines in Miami from which you get fantastic elevated views of the city and waterways. However, be warned that this is a grueling ride, especially going up the causeway. **Key Cycling,** 61 Harbor Dr., Key Biscayne (© **305/361-0061;** www.keycycling.com), rents mountain bikes for $5 per hour (2-hr. minimum) or $15 a day. It's open Tuesday through Friday from 10am to 7pm, Monday and Saturday from 10am to 6pm, and Sunday from 10am to 3pm.

If you want to avoid the traffic altogether, head out to **Shark Valley** in the Everglades National Park—one of South Florida's most scenic bicycle trails and a favorite haunt of city-weary locals. For more information on Shark Valley and the Everglades, see chapter 11.

For a decent list of trail suggestions throughout South Florida, visit www.geocities.com/floutdoorzone/bike.html. *Biking note:* Children under the age of 16 are required by Florida law to wear a helmet, which can be purchased at any bike store or retail outlet selling biking supplies.

FISHING   Fishing licenses are required in Florida. If you go out with one of the fishing charter boats listed below, you are automatically accredited because the companies are. If you go out on your own, however, you must have a Florida fishing license, which costs $17 for Florida residents and $30 for nonresidents. Call © **888/ FISH-FLO** or visit www.wildlifelicense.com for more information.

Some of the best surf casting in the city can be had at **Haulover Beach Park** at Collins Avenue and 105th Street, where there's a bait-and-tackle shop right on the pier. **South Pointe Park,** at the southern tip of Miami Beach, is another popular fishing spot and features a long pier, comfortable benches, and a great view of the ships passing through Government Cut, the deep channel made when the port of Miami was dug.

You can also do some deep-sea fishing in the Miami area. One bargain outfitter, the **Kelley Fishing Fleet,** at the Haulover Marina, 10800 Collins Ave. (at 108th St.), Miami Beach (© **305/945-3801;** www.miamibeachfishing.com), has half-day, full-day, and night fishing aboard diesel-powered "party boats." The fleet's emphasis on drifting is geared toward trolling and bottom fishing for snapper, sailfish, and mackerel. Half-day and night-fishing trips are $31 for adults and $22 for children up to 10 years old, and full-day trips are $49 for adults and $39 for children; prices are $5 cheaper if you have your own rod. Daily departures are scheduled at 9am and 1:45 and 8pm; reservations are recommended.

Also at the Haulover Marina is the charter boat *Helen C* (10800 Collins Ave.; © **305/947-4081;** www.fishmiamibeach.com). Although there's no shortage of private charter boats here, Capt. Dawn Mergelsberg is a good pick, since she puts individuals together to get a full boat. Her *Helen* is a twin engine 55-footer, equipped for big-game "monster" fish such as marlin, tuna, dolphin fish, shark, and sailfish. The cost is $140 per person. Private, full-day trips are available for groups of six people per vessel and cost $999; half-days are $700. Group rates and specials are also available. Sailings are scheduled for 8am to noon and 1 to 5pm daily; call for reservations. Children are welcome.

For a serious fishing charter, Captain Charlie Hotchkiss' **Sea Dancer** (© **305/733-5126;** www.seadancercharter.com) offers a first class experience on a 38" Luhrs boat complete with tuna tower and air conditioned cabin. If you're all about big game— marlin, dolphin, tuna, wahoo, swordfish, and sailfish—this is the charter for you.

⌒Tips A Fisherman's Friend

The Biscayne Bay area is prime tarpon fishing country and a pretty good spot for a lot of other trophy sportfish: snook, bonefish, dolphin fish, swordfish, and sailfish. For a fee, local guides are happy to show you the hot spots and make sure you reel one in. One such guide is **Capt. David Parsons** (© **305/968-9603;** www.fishingmiamiflorida.com), who owns a great 36-foot boat, *Hakuna Matada*. He knows where the fish are biting and will take you from Biscayne Bay to the Atlantic Ocean in search of the best catch of the day for $700 for four people (swordfish can be caught at nighttime only; those trips are also $700), including rods, gear, and bait. All you bring is food/drink. Capt. Parsons also leads trips to Bimini for those who want to explore the fishing in the Bahamas.

Catch and release or filet your catch to take home. Auto transportation is available to wherever the boat may be docked. Rates are $700 for a half day and $1,100 for a full day.

Key Biscayne offers deep-sea fishing to those willing to get their hands dirty and pay a bundle. The competition among the boats is fierce, but the prices are basically the same, no matter which you choose. The going rate is about $400 to $450 for a half-day and $600 to $700 for a full day of fishing. These rates are usually for a party of up to six, and the boats supply you with rods and bait as well as instruction for first-timers. Some will also take you out to the Upper Keys if the fish aren't biting in Miami.

You might also consider the following boats, all of which sail out of the Key Biscayne marina and are in relatively good shape and nicer than most out there: *Sunny Boy* (✆ 305/361-2217), *Top Hatt* (✆ 305/361-2528), and *L & H* (✆ 305/361-9318). Call for reservations.

Bridge fishing in Biscayne Bay is also popular in Miami; you'll see people with poles over almost every waterway. But look carefully for signs telling you whether it's legal to do so wherever you are: Some bridges forbid fishing.

GAMBLING   Although gambling is technically illegal in Miami, there are plenty of loopholes that allow all kinds of wagering. Gamblers can try their luck at offshore casinos or on shore at bingo, jai alai, card rooms, horse tracks, dog races, and Native American reservations. You can also drive up to Broward County, where the Seminole Hard Rock Hotel and Casino (www.seminolehardrock.com) and the new Gulfstream Park Casino and Racing (www.gulfstreampark.com) in Hallandale both offer slots and poker.

Despite the Hard Rock in Hollywood's behemoth presence on the gambling circuit, some people prefer the less flashy **Miccosukee Indian Gaming,** 500 SW 177th Ave. (off S.R. 41, in West Miami on the outskirts of the Everglades; ✆ 800/741-4600 or 305/222-4600), where a touch of Vegas meets west Miami. This tacky casino isn't Caesar's Palace, but you can play tab slots, high-speed bingo (watch out for the serious blue-haired players who will scoff if you make too much noise or if you win before they do), and even poker (with a $10 maximum pot). With more than 85,000 square feet of playing space, the complex even provides overnight accommodations for those who can't get enough of the thrill and don't want to make the approximately 1-hour trip back to downtown Miami. Take the Florida Turnpike south toward Florida City/Key West. Take the SW 8th Street exit (#25) and turn left onto SW 8th Street. Drive for about 3½ miles and then turn left onto Krome Avenue, and left again at 177th Street; you can't miss it.

Recently, many of Miami's sketchier gambling-cruise operators have been shut down. The classiest and most legitimate gambling cruise still in business is the *Aquasino,* which docks at the Miami Beach Marina. This 228-foot yacht has more than 200 slot machines, 22 blackjack tables, craps, poker, baccarat, roulette, a sportsbook room with 42-inch plasma TVs, a full blown gourmet buffet, and several lounges. Live DJs on the upper deck and Vegas-style entertainment keeps the non gamblers busy, too. Price, $40, includes free parking at the marina, complimentary cocktail, gourmet buffet and more drinks—if you're gambling. Ships sail Monday and Tuesday 7:30pm to 12:30am, Wednesday to Friday noon to 5pm and 7:30pm to 12:30am, Saturday 11am to 4:30pm and 7:30pm to 1:30am, and Sunday 11am to 4:30pm and 7:30pm to 12:30am. Call ✆ 305/532-0021 or www.aquasinosouthbeach.com for updated schedules. You must be 21 or older to sail.

GOLF   There are more than 50 private and public golf courses in the Miami area. Contact the **Greater Miami Convention and Visitor's Bureau** (© **800/933-8448;** www.miamiandbeaches.com) for a list of courses and costs.

The best hotel courses in Miami are found at the **Doral Golf Resort and Spa** (p. 109), home of the legendary Blue Monster course, as well as the Gold Course, designed by Raymond Floyd; the Great White Shark Course; and the Silver Course, refinished by Jerry Pate.

Other hotels with excellent golf courses include the **Fairmont Turnberry Isle Resort & Club** (p. 110), with two Robert Trent Jones, Sr.–designed courses for guests and members, and the **Biltmore Hotel** (p. 105), which is my pick for best public golf course because of its modest greens fees and an 18-hole par 71 course located on the hotel's spectacular grounds. It must be good: Despite his penchant for privacy, former president Bill Clinton prefers teeing off at this course more than any other in Miami!

Otherwise, the following represent some of the area's best public courses. **Crandon Park Golf Course,** formerly known as the Links, 6700 Crandon Blvd., Key Biscayne (© **305/361-9129**), is the number-one-ranked municipal course in the state and one of the top five in the country. The park is situated on 200 bayfront acres and offers a pro shop, rentals, lessons, carts, and a lighted driving range. The course is open daily from dawn to dusk; greens fees (including cart) are $56.50 for nonresidents and includes cart. Special twilight rates are also available.

One of the most popular courses among real enthusiasts is the **Doral Park Golf and Country Club,** 5001 NW 104th Ave., West Miami (© **305/591-8800**); it's not related to the Doral Hotel or spa. Call to book in advance, since this challenging, semiprivate 18-holer is extremely popular with locals. The course is open from 6:30am to 6pm during the winter and until 7pm during the summer. Cart and greens fees vary, so call © **305/592-2000,** ext. 2104, for information.

Known as one of the best in the city, the **Country Club of Miami,** 6801 Miami Gardens Dr., at NW 68th Avenue, North Miami (© **305/829-8456;** www.golfmiami cc.com), has three 18-hole courses of varying degrees of difficulty. You'll encounter lush fairways, rolling greens, and some history, to boot. The west course, designed in 1961 by Robert Trent Jones, Sr., and updated in the 1990s by the PGA, was where Jack Nicklaus played his first professional tournament and Lee Trevino won his first professional championship. The course is open daily from 7am to sunset. Cart and greens fees are $12.50–$38 depending on season and tee times. Special twilight rates are available.

The recently renovated **Miami Beach Golf Club,** 2301 Alton Rd., South Beach (© **305/532-3350;** www.miamibeachgolfclub.com), is a gorgeous, 79-year-old course that, par for the, er, course in Miami Beach, received a $10-million face-lift. Miami Heat players and Matt Damon have been known to tee off here. Greens fees range from $90 to $200 depending on the season.

Golfers looking for some cheap practice time will appreciate **Haulover Beach Park,** 10800 Collins Ave., Miami Beach (© **305/940-6719**), in a pretty bayside location. The longest hole on this par-27 course is 125 yards. It's open daily from 7:30am to 6pm during the winter, and until 7:30pm during the summer. Greens fees are $7 per person during the winter and summer.

IN-LINE SKATING   Miami's consistently flat terrain makes in-line skating a breeze. Lincoln Road, for example, is a virtual skating rink as bladers compete with bikers and walkers for a slab of slate. But the city's heavy traffic and construction do make it tough to find long routes suitable for blading.

Because of the popularity of blading and skateboarding, the city passed a law prohibiting skating on the west side (the cafe-lined strip) of Ocean Drive in the evenings, as well as a law that all bladers must skate slowly and safely. Also, if you're going to partake of the sport, remember to keep a pair of sandals or sneakers with you, since many area shops won't allow you inside with skates on.

Despite all the rules, you can still have fun, and the following rental outfit can help chart an interesting course for you and supply you with all the necessary gear. In South Beach, **Fritz's Skate Shop**, 730 Lincoln Rd. Mall (© **305/532-1954**), rents top-quality skates, including safety pads, for $10 per hour, $24 per day, and $69 per week. They provide free lessons at 10:30am on Sunday when you rent equipment, or they can hook you up with an instructor for private lessons. The shop also stocks lots of gear and clothing.

SWIMMING   There is no shortage of water in the Miami area. See the Venetian Pool listing (p. 176) and the "Miami's Beaches" section on p. 160 for descriptions of good swimming options.

TENNIS   Hundreds of tennis courts in South Florida are open to the public for a minimal fee. Most courts operate on a first-come, first-served basis and are open from sunrise to sunset. For information and directions, call the **City of Miami Beach Recreation, Culture, and Parks Department** (© **305/673-7730**) or the **City of Miami Parks and Recreation Department** (© **305/575-5256**). Of the 590 public tennis courts throughout Miami, the three hard courts and seven clay courts at the **Crandon Tennis Center,** 6702 Crandon Blvd. (© **305/361-5263**), are the best and most beautiful. Because of this, they often get crowded on weekends. You'll play on the same courts as Lendl, Graf, Evert, McEnroe, Federer, the Williams sisters and other greats; this is also the venue for one of the world's biggest annual tennis events, the Sony Ericsson Open. There's a pleasant, if limited, pro shop, plus many good pros. Only four courts are lit at night, but if you reserve at least 24 to 48 hours in advance, you can usually take your pick. Hard courts cost $3 person per hour during the day, $5 per person per hour at night. Clay courts cost $6 per person per hour during the day. There are no night hours on the clay courts. The courts are open Monday through Friday from 8am to 9pm, Saturday and Sunday until 6pm.

Other courts are pretty run of the mill and can be found in most neighborhoods. I do, however, recommend the **Miami Beach public courts at Flamingo Park,** 1001 12th St. in South Beach (© **305/673-7761**), where there are 19 clay courts that cost $4 per person an hour for Miami Beach residents and $8 per person an hour for nonresidents. It's first come, first served. Open 8am to 9pm Monday through Friday, 8am to 8pm Saturday and Sunday.

Hotels with the best tennis facilities are the Biltmore, Fairmont Turnberry Isle Resort and Spa, Doral Resort and Spa, and Inn and Spa at Fisher Island.

HEALTH CLUBS

Being situated in a very body-conscious city, many of Miami's hotels have state-of-the-art gyms. **Sports Club/LA** at the Four Seasons, among others. Guests of hotels with health clubs can usually use the equipment for free. Although many of Miami's full-service hotels have fitness centers and may be convenient, you can't always count on them in less-upscale establishments or in the small Art Deco District hotels. Instead, you may want to turn to the several health clubs around the city that will take in nonmembers on a daily basis. For **Bally's Total Fitness,** dial © **800/777-1117** to

On Location in Miami

With its warm weather, picturesque skylines, and gorgeous sunsets, Miami is the perfect setting for making movies.

Since the earliest days of the film industry, Miami has had a starring role in some of America's most celebrated celluloid classics, from the Marx Brothers' first feature, *The Cocoanuts* (1929), to the 1941 classic, *Citizen Kane*, which used the spectacular South Florida coastline as the setting for Kane's own Hearst Castle, Xanadu. As the film industry evolved and productions became more elaborate, Miami was twice seized by a suave international man of intrigue known as Bond, James Bond, in *Dr. No, Live and Let Die,* and *Goldfinger.* In the past 5 years, there were over 60 major motion pictures filmed in Miami–Dade County, from action flicks like the hideous *Miami Vice* remake, *True Lies,* and *Any Given Sunday* to comedies such as *There's Something About Mary* and dramas such as *Random Hearts* to action flicks like *Bad Boys II.*

At any given time of day—or night—actors, directors, and film crews can be spotted on the sands and streets of Miami working on what may be the next blockbuster to hit the big screen. Watching a film being shot is fun, free entertainment. Unfortunately, filming schedules are not publicized, so keep an eye out for CREW signs posted throughout the city and check with hotel personnel, who are usually up-to-date on who's in town shooting what. Who knows? You could be discovered!

find the clubs closest to where you'll be staying. (There are no outlets on the beaches; most are in South Miami.) One of the most popular clubs, which welcomes walk-in guests is **Crunch,** 1253 Washington Ave., South Beach (© **305/674-8222**), where you might work out on the top-of-the-line equipment with Cindy Crawford, Madonna, or any of a number of supermodels when they're in town. Use of the facility is $25 daily or $75 weekly. It keeps late hours, especially in season, when it's often open until midnight. The newest member of the fitness club on South Beach is **Equinox Fitness,** 520 Collins Ave. (© **305/673-1172;** www.equinoxfitness.com), a huge space complete with every piece of fitness equipment you can imagine or haven't yet imagined. Fees vary for out-of-town guests so call and inquire.

9 Spectator Sports

Check the *Miami Herald's* sports section for a daily listing of local events and the paper's Friday "Weekend" section for comprehensive coverage and in-depth reports. For last-minute tickets, call the venue directly, since many season ticket holders sell singles and return unused tickets. Expensive tickets are available from brokers or individuals listed in the classified sections of the local papers. Some tickets are also available through **Ticketmaster** (© **305/358-5885;** www.ticketmaster.com).

BASEBALL   The 2003 World Champion **Florida Marlins** shocked the sports world in 1997 when it became the youngest expansion team to win a World Series, but then floundered as its star players were sold off by former owner Wayne Huizenga. The team shocked the sports world again in 2003 by winning the World Series, and turned many of Miami's apathetic sports fans into major-league ball fans. The Marlins are not that good anymore after trading its best players, and rumor has it that the team is looking to move to another state. The Maine Marlins? Sounds fishy. Anyway, if you're interested in catching a game, be warned: The summer heat in Miami can be unbearable, even in the evenings.

Home games are held at **Dolphin Stadium,** 2269 NW 199th St., North Miami Beach (② **305/623-6200**). Tickets cost from $4 to $50. Box office hours are Monday to Friday from 8:30am to 5:30pm and before games; tickets are also available through Ticketmaster. The team currently holds spring training in Melbourne, Florida.

BASKETBALL   The **Miami Heat** (② **786/777-1000**), once again led by celebrity coach Pat Riley and featuring star player Shaquille O'Neal, is one of Miami's hottest tickets, especially since the team won the NBA championship in 2006. Courtside seats are full of visiting celebrities. The season lasts from October to April, with most games beginning at 7:30pm. The team plays in the brand-new waterfront **American Airlines Arena,** downtown on Biscayne Boulevard. Tickets are $14 to $100 or much more. Box office hours are Monday through Friday from 10am to 5pm (until 8pm on game nights); tickets are also available through Ticketmaster (② **305/358-5885**).

FOOTBALL   Miami's golden boys are the **Miami Dolphins,** the city's most recognizable team, followed by thousands of "dolfans." The team plays at least eight home games during the season, between September and December, at **Dolphin Stadium,** 2269 NW 199th St., North Miami Beach (② **305/620-2578**). Tickets cost between $20 and much, much more. The box office is open Monday through Friday from 8:30am to 5:30pm; tickets are also available through Ticketmaster (② **305/358-5885;** www.ticketmaster.com).

HORSE RACING   Located on the Dade–Broward County border in Hallandale (just north of North Miami Beach/Aventura) is **Gulfstream Park Casino and Racing,** at U.S. 1 and Hallandale Beach Boulevard (② **305/931-7223;** www.gulfstream park.com), South Florida's very own version of the Kentucky Derby, but without the hats. This horse track is a haven for serious gamblers and voyeurs alike. Large purses and important races are commonplace at this sprawling suburban course, and the track is typically crowded, especially after receiving a multimillion-dollar face-lift that has added to the park a brand-new flashy casino, nightclubs, and restaurants. Admission and parking are free unless you want to go to Gulfstream's dance club Serenata, where there's a $20 cover after 10pm on Thursday, Friday, and Saturday. January through March, post times are 1:30pm on weekdays and 1pm on weekends. It's closed Tuesday. And while not exactly racing, a newish event that takes place on the sands of South Beach is the **Miami Beach Polo Cup,** featuring hard-core sand-kicking polo matches, a parade of the ponies down the beach, and chic parties. General admission to matches throughout the weekend is free to the public, while VIP tickets are available for those seeking more than a view from the sidelines and for coveted events outside of the arena. Visit www.miamipolo.com.

ICE HOCKEY   The young **Florida Panthers** (② **954/835-7000**) have already made history. In the 1994–95 season, the team played in the Stanley Cup finals, and it has amassed a legion of loving fans. Much to the disappointment of Miamians, the Panthers moved to a new venue in Sunrise, the next county north of Miami-Dade, more than an hour from downtown Miami. Call for directions and ticket information.

Jai Alai Explained

Jai alai originated in the Basque country of northern Spain, where players used church walls as their courts. The game looks very much like lacrosse, actually, with rules similar to handball or tennis. The game is played on a court with numbered lines. What makes the game totally unique, however, is the requirement that the ball must be returned in one continuous motion. The server must bounce the ball behind the serving line and, with the basket, must hurl the ball to the front wall, with the aim being that, upon rebound, the ball will bounce between lines four and seven. If it doesn't, it is an under- or overserve and the other team receives a point.

JAI ALAI   Jai alai, sort of a Spanish-style indoor lacrosse, was introduced to Miami in 1924 and is regularly played in two Miami-area frontons (the buildings in which jai alai is played). Although the sport has roots stemming from ancient Egypt, the game, as it's now played, was invented by Basque peasants in the Pyrenees Mountains during the 17th century. Players use *cesetas,* curved wicker baskets strapped to their wrists, to hurl balls, called *pelotas,* at speeds that sometimes exceed 170 mph. Spectators, who are protected behind a wall of glass, place bets on the evening's players. The Florida Gaming Corporation owns the jai alai operations throughout the state, making betting on this sport as legal as buying a lottery ticket.

The **Miami Jai Alai Fronton,** 3500 NW 37th Ave., at NW 35th Street (© **305/ 633-6400**), is America's oldest fronton, dating from 1926. It schedules 13 games per night, which typically last 10 to 20 minutes, but can occasionally go much longer. Admission is free. There are year-round games. On Wednesday, Thursday, and Sunday, there are matinees only, which run from noon to 5:30pm. Friday, Saturday, and Monday, there are matinees in addition to evening games, from 7pm to midnight. The fronton is closed on Tuesday. This is the main location where jai alai is played in Miami. The other South Florida jai alai venue is in Dania, near the Fort Lauderdale–Hollywood International Airport. See p. 313 for more information on **Dania Jai Alai.**

10 Animal Parks

For a tropical climate, Miami's got a lot of nontropical animals to see, and we're not talking about the motorists on I-95. Everything from dolphins and alligators to lions, tigers, and bears call Miami home (most in parks, some in nature). Call the parks to inquire about discount packages or coupons, which may be offered at area retail stores or in local papers.

Jungle Island ⊛ 𝘒𝘪𝘥𝘴   This Miami institution took flight from its lush, natural South Miami environment and headed north in the winter of 2003 to a new, overly fabricated, disappointing $46-million home on Watson Island, along the MacArthur Causeway near Miami Beach. While the island doubles as a protected bird sanctuary, the jungle's former digs (in a coral rock structure built around 1900 in the heart of South Miami) had a lot more charm and kitsch. The overpriced 19-acre park features an Everglades exhibit, a petting zoo, and several theaters, jungle trails, and aviaries.

A Japanese Garden

If you ask someone what Japanese influences can be found in Miami, they'll likely point to Nobu, Sushi Siam, Sushi Rock Café, and even Benihana. But back in the '50s, well before sushi became trendy, Kiyoshi Ichimura became obsessed with Miami and started sending people and objects from Tokyo, including carpenters, gardeners, and a landscape architect, to design and construct the San-Ai-An Japanese Garden. Originally located in the Jungle Island space, the garden was dismantled during construction and re-created adjacent to the park. The completed 1-acre garden was renamed Ichimura Miami Japan Garden in honor of its original benefactor, and its sculptures and Japanese artifacts are managed by a coalition of city organizations. Japanese holidays and festivals are celebrated here.

Watch your heads because flying above are hundreds of parrots, macaws, peacocks, cockatoos, and flamingos. Be sure to check out the Crocosaurus, a 20-foot-long saltwater crocodile that hangs out in the park's Serpentarium. Also a pleasant surprise here is the Ichimura Miami Japan Garden (see "A Japanese Garden," above). Continuous shows star roller-skating cockatoos, card-playing macaws, and numerous stunt-happy parrots. There are also tortoises, iguanas, and a rare albino alligator on exhibit. The park's website sometimes offers downloadable discount coupons, so take a look before you visit because you definitely won't want to pay full price for this park, which has nerve to charge for parking. If you do get your money's worth and see all the shows and exhibits, expect to spend upward of 4 hours here. *Note:* The former South Miami site of (Parrot) Jungle Island is now known as **Pinecrest Gardens**, 11000 Red Rd. (✆ **305/669-6942**), which features a petting zoo, mini–water park, lake, natural hammocks, and Banyan caves. Open daily from 8am until sunset; admission is free.

1111 Parrot Jungle Trail, Watson Island (on the north side of MacArthur Causeway/I-395). ✆ **305/372-3822**. www.parrotjungle.com. Admission $30 adults, $26 seniors and military, $23 children 3–10. Parking $7 per vehicle. Daily 10am–6pm. From I-95, take I-395 E. (MacArthur Causeway); make a right on Parrot Jungle Trail, which is the first exit after the bridge. Follow the road around and under the causeway to the parking garage on the left side.

Miami Metrozoo ✵✵ (Kids)   This 290-acre, sparsely landscaped complex is quite a distance from Miami proper and the beaches—about 45 minutes—but worth the trip. Isolated and never really crowded, it's also completely cageless—animals are kept at bay by cleverly designed moats. This is a fantastic spot to take younger kids (the older ones seem bored and unstimulated here); there's a wonderful petting zoo and play area, and the zoo offers several daily programs designed to educate and entertain. Mufasa and Simba (of Disney fame) were modeled on a couple of Metrozoo's lions. Other residents include two rare white Bengal tigers, a Komodo dragon, rare koala bears, a number of kangaroos, and an African meerkat. The air-conditioned Zoofari Monorail tour offers visitors a nice overview of the park. The zoo is always upgrading its facilities, including the impressive aviary. A cool exhibit is The Samburu Giraffe Feeding Station, where, for $2, you get to feed the giraffes veggies. Opened in late 2008, Tropical America, featuring jaguars, anacondas, giant river otters, harpy eagles, sting ray touch tanks, air-conditioned buildings, and a unique display of a forest before and during flood times. At 27 acres and $35 million, the exhibit is massive and makes Metrozoo the third Zoo in the country to have Giant River Otters, its keystone species. Private tours and overnights are also available for those who really want to commune with nature. *Note:* The distance between animal habitats can be great, so you'll do *a lot* of walking here. There are benches and shaded gazebos strategically positioned throughout the zoo so you can rest when you need to. Also, because the zoo can be miserably hot during summer months, plan these visits in the early morning or late afternoon. Expect to spend about 3 hours here.

12400 SW 152nd St., South Miami. © 305/251-0400. www.miamimetrozoo.com. Admission $14 adults, $13 seniors, $10 children 3–12. Daily 9:30am–5:30pm (ticket booth closes at 4pm). Free parking. From U.S. 1 south, turn right on SW 152nd St. and follow signs about 3 miles to the entrance.

Miami Seaquarium *Kids Overrated*   If you've been to Orlando's SeaWorld, you may be disappointed with Miami's version, which is considerably smaller and not as well maintained. It's hardly a sprawling seaquarium, but you will want to arrive early to enjoy the effects of its mild splash. You'll need at least 3 hours to tour the 35-acre oceanarium and see all four daily shows, starring a number of showy ocean mammals. You can cut your visit to 2 hours if you limit your shows to the better, albeit corny, *Flipper Show* and *Killer Whale Show.* The highly regarded Dolphin Encounter allows visitors to touch and swim with dolphins in the Flipper Lagoon. The program costs $139 per person participating, $40 per observer, and is offered at daily at 12:15 and 3:15pm. Children must be at least 52 inches tall to participate. Reservations are necessary for this program. Call © **305/365-2501** in advance for reservations. The Seaquarium took a major hit during 2005's Hurricane Wilma and reopened in early 2006, restoring all the damage to the park's most popular attractions, such as Discovery Bay and Shark Channel. The Seaquarium also debuted a new sea lion show.

4400 Rickenbacker Causeway (south side), en route to Key Biscayne. © 305/361-5705. www.miamiseaquarium. com. Admission $32 adults, $25 children 3–9, free for children 2 and under. Daily 9:30am–6pm (ticket booth closes at 4pm). Parking $7.

Monkey Jungle *Overrated*   Personally, I think this place is nasty. It reeks, the monkeys are either sleeping or in heat, and it's really far from the city, even farther than the zoo. But if primates are your thing and you'd rather pass on the zoo, you'll be in paradise. You'll see rare Brazilian golden lion tamarins and Asian macaques. There are no cages to restrain the antics of the monkeys as they swing, chatter, and play their way into your heart. Screened-in trails wind through acres of "jungle," and daily shows feature the talents of the park's most progressive pupils. People who come here are not monkeying around—many of the park's frequent visitors are scientists and anthropologists. In fact, an interesting archaeological exhibition excavated from a Monkey Jungle sinkhole displays 10,000-year-old artifacts, including human teeth and animal bones. A somewhat amusing attraction here, if you can call it that, is the Wild Monkey Swimming Pool, a show in which you get to watch monkeys diving for food. If you can stand the humidity, the smell, and the bugs (flies, mosquitoes, and so on), expect to spend about 2 hours here. The park's website sometimes offers downloadable discount coupons, so if you have Internet access, take a look before you visit.

14805 SW 216th St., South Miami. © 305/235-1611. www.monkeyjungle.com. Admission $26 adults, $24 seniors and active-duty military, $20 children 4–12. Daily 9:30am–5pm (tickets sold until 4pm). Take U.S. 1 south to SW 216th St., or from Florida Tpk., take exit 11 and follow the signs.

Sea Grass Adventures *Value Kids*   Even better than the Seaquarium is Sea Grass Adventures, in which a naturalist from the Marjory Stoneman Douglas Biscayne Nature Center introduces ($10 per person) kids and adults to an amazing variety of creatures that live in the sea grass beds of the Bear Cut Nature Preserve near Crandon Beach on Key Biscayne. You will be able to wade in the water with your guide and catch an assortment of sea life in nets provided by the guides. At the end of the program, participants gather on the beach while the guide explains what everyone has just caught, passing the creatures around in miniature viewing tanks. Call for available dates, times, and reservations.

Marjory Stoneman Douglas Biscayne Nature Center, 6767 Crandon Blvd., Key Biscayne. ℂ 305/361-6767. Free admission to the center. Daily 10am–4pm.

11 Video Arcades & Entertainment Centers

GameWorks *Kids* At Steven Spielberg's SEGA GameWorks in the Shops at Sunset Place, you'll see people fighting off dinosaurs from *Jurassic Park,* racing in the Indy 500, swooshing down a snowy ski trail, throwing darts, and shooting pool in this multilevel playground. The young and the young at heart will find a good combination of vintage arcade games, high-tech videos, virtual-reality arenas, pool tables, food, and cocktails in this playground occupying more than 33,000 square feet. Bring lots—and we mean lots—of change.

5701 Sunset Dr., South Miami. ℂ 305/667-4263. www.gameworks.com. Sun–Mon 11am–11pm; Tues–Thurs noon–11pm; Fri–Sat 11am–2am. Games 50¢–$5.

The Scott Rakow Youth Center *Kids* This center is a hidden treasure on Miami Beach. The two-story facility boasts an ice-skating rink, bowling alleys, a basketball court, gymnasium equipment, and full-time supervision for kids in the fourth grade and up. Call for a complete schedule of organized events. The only drag is that it's not open to adults (except on Sun, family day).

2700 Sheridan Ave., Miami Beach. ℂ 305/673-7767. Admission is $9 adults, $6 for children 9–17. Sat–Sun 9am–5pm.

Miami Shopping

Miami is one of the world's premier shopping cities; more than 10 million visitors come every year and typically spend in excess of $13 billion. People come to Miami from all over—from Latin America to Hong Kong—in search of some products that are all-American (in other words, Levi's, Nike, and such).

So if you're not into sunbathing and outdoor activities, or you just can't take the heat, you'll be in good company in one of Miami's many malls—and you are not likely to emerge empty-handed. In addition to the strip malls, Miami offers a choice of megamalls, from the upscale Village of Merrick Park and the mammoth Aventura Mall to the ritzy Bal Harbour Shops and touristy, yet scenic, Bayside Marketplace (just to name a few).

Miami also offers more unique shopping spots, such as the up-and-coming area near downtown known as the Biscayne Corridor, where funky boutiques dare to defy the Gap, and Little Havana, where you can buy hand-rolled cigars and *guayabera* shirts (loose-fitting cotton or gauzy shirts).

You may want to order the Greater Miami Convention and Visitors Bureau's "Shop Miami: A Guide to a Tropical Shopping Adventure." Although it is limited to details on the bureau's paying members, it provides some good advice and otherwise unpublished discount offers. The glossy little pamphlet is printed in English, Spanish, and Portuguese and provides information about transportation from hotels, translation services, and shipping. Call © **800/283-2707** or 305/539-3000 for more information.

1 The Shopping Scene

Below you'll find descriptions of some of the more popular retail areas, where many stores are conveniently clustered together to make browsing easier.

As a general rule, shop hours are Monday through Saturday from 10am to 6pm, and Sunday from noon to 5pm. Many stores stay open late (until 9pm or so) 1 night of the week, usually Thursday. Shops in Coconut Grove are open until 9pm Sunday through Thursday, and even later on Friday and Saturday. South Beach's stores also stay open later—as late as midnight. Department stores and shopping malls keep longer hours as well, with most staying open from 10am to 9 or 10pm Monday through Saturday, noon to 6pm on Sunday. With all these variations, you may want to call specific stores to find out their hours.

The 6.5% state and local sales tax is added to the price of all nonfood purchases. Food and beverage in hotels and restaurants are subject to the resort tax, which is 3% in Miami/South Beach and Bal Harbour, 4% in Surfside, and 2% in the rest of Miami–Dade County.

Most Miami stores can wrap your purchase and ship it anywhere in the world via United Parcel Service (UPS). If they can't, you can send it yourself, either through FedEx (© 800/463-3339), UPS (© 800/742-5877), or through the U.S. Mail (see "Fast Facts: Miami" on p. 68).

SHOPPING AREAS

Most of Miami's shopping happens at the many megamalls scattered from one end of the county to the other; however, there is also some excellent boutique shopping and browsing to be done in the following areas (see "The Neighborhoods in Brief" on p. 62 for more information):

AVENTURA   On Biscayne Boulevard between Miami Gardens Drive and the county line at Hallandale Beach Boulevard is a 2-mile stretch of major retail stores including Best Buy, Borders, DSW, Bed Bath and Beyond, Loehmann's, Circuit City, Linens 'n Things, Marshall's, Sports Authority, and more. Also here is the mammoth Aventura Mall, housing a fabulous collection of shops and restaurants.

BISCAYNE CORRIDOR ✿   Amid the ramshackle old motels of yesteryear exist several funky, kitschy, and arty boutiques along the stretch of Biscayne Boulevard from 50th Street to about 79th Street known as the Biscayne Corridor. Everything from hand-painted tank tops to expensive Juicy Couture sweat suits can be found here, but it's not just about fashion: Several furniture stores selling antiques and modern pieces exist along here as well, so look carefully, as you may find something here that would cause the appraisers on *Antiques Road Show* to lose their wigs. For more mainstream creature comforts—Target, Circuit City, PetSmart, Loehmann's, Marshall's, and West Elm—a new complex called The Shops at Midtown Miami has opened on a gritty, yet, developing street at North Miami Avenue and NE 36th Street.

Impressions

Someday . . . Miami will become the great center of South American trade.

—Julia Tuttle, Miami's founder, 1896

CALLE OCHO   For a taste of Little Havana, take a walk down 8th Street between SW 27th Avenue and SW 12th Avenue, where you'll find some lively streetlife and many shops selling cigars, baked goods, shoes, furniture, and record stores specializing in Latin music. For help, take your Spanish dictionary.

COCONUT GROVE   Downtown Coconut Grove, centered on Main Highway and Grand Avenue, and branching onto the adjoining streets, is one of Miami's most pedestrian-friendly zones. The Grove's wide sidewalks, lined with cafes and boutiques, can provide hours of browsing pleasure. Coconut Grove is best known for its chain stores (Gap, Banana Republic, and so on) and some funky holdovers from the days when the Grove was a bit more bohemian, plus excellent sidewalk cafes centered on CocoWalk and the Streets of Mayfair.

DOWNTOWN MIAMI   If you're looking for discounts on all types of goods—especially watches, fabric, buttons, lace, shoes, luggage, and leather—Flagler Street, just west of Biscayne Boulevard, is the best place to start. I wouldn't necessarily recommend buying expensive items here, as many stores seem to be on the shady side and do not understand the word *warranty*. However, you can still have fun here as long as you are a savvy shopper and don't mind haggling. Most signs are printed in

English, Spanish, and Portuguese; however, many shopkeepers may not be entirely fluent in English. Mary Brickell Village, a 192,000-square-foot urban entertainment center west of Brickell Avenue and straddling South Miami Avenue between 9th and 10th streets downtown, opened in 2006. Although everything was not yet open at the time of this writing, the $80-million complex will eventually consist of a slew of trendy restaurants, boutiques, and the requisite Starbucks—a sure sign that a neighborhood has been revitalized.

MIRACLE MILE (CORAL GABLES)   Actually only a half-mile long, this central shopping street was an integral part of George Merrick's original city plan. Today the strip still enjoys popularity, especially for its bridal stores, ladies' shops, haberdashers, and gift shops. Recently, newer chain stores, such as Barnes & Noble, Old Navy, and Starbucks, have been appearing on the Mile. The hyperupscale **Village of Merrick Park,** a mammoth, 850,000-square-foot outdoor shopping complex between Ponce de León Boulevard and Le Jeune Road, just off the Mile, houses Nordstrom, Neiman Marcus, Armani, Gucci, Jimmy Choo, and Yves St. Laurent, to name a few.

SOUTH BEACH   Slowly but surely, South Beach has come into its own as far as shopping is concerned. While the requisite stores such as the Gap and Banana Republic have anchored here, several higher-end stores have also opened on the southern blocks of Collins Avenue, which has become the Madison Avenue of Miami. For the hippest clothing boutiques (including Armani Exchange, Ralph Lauren, Versace, Benetton, Levi's, Barneys Co-Op, Diesel, Guess, Club Monaco, Kenneth Cole, and Nicole Miller, among others), stroll along this pretty strip of the Art Deco District.

For those who are interested in a little more fun with their shopping, consider South Beach's legendary Lincoln Road. This pedestrian mall, originally designed in 1957 by Morris Lapidus, recently underwent a multimillion-dollar renovation, restoring it to its former glory. Here shoppers find an array of clothing, books, tchotchkes, and art, as well as a menagerie of sidewalk cafes flanked on one end by a multiplex movie theater and, at the other, by the Atlantic Ocean.

2 Shopping A to Z

ANTIQUES & COLLECTIBLES

Miami's antiques shops are scattered in small pockets around the city. Many that feature lower-priced furniture can be found in North Miami, in the 1600 block of NE 123rd Street, near West Dixie Highway. About a dozen shops sell china, silver, glass, furniture, and paintings. But you'll find the bulk of the better antiques in Coral Gables and in Southwest Miami along Bird Road between 64th and 66th avenues and between 72nd and 74th avenues. For international collections from Bali to France, check out the burgeoning scene in the Design District centered on NE 40th Street west of First Avenue. Miami also hosts several large antiques shows each year. In October and November, the most prestigious one—the **Antique Show**—hits the Miami Beach Convention Center (© 305/673-7311). Exhibitors from all over come to display their wares, including jewelry. There's also a decent monthly show at the **Coconut Grove Convention Center** (© **305/579-3312**). Miami's huge concentration of Art Deco buildings from the '20s and '30s makes this the place to find the best selections of Deco furnishings and decorations. A word to the serious collectors: Dania Beach, up in Broward County (see chapter 13), about half an hour from downtown Miami, is the best place for antiques (it's known as the antiques capital of South Florida), so you may want to consider browsing in Miami and shopping up there.

Alhambra Antiques   This fabulous store specializes in 18th- and 19th-century European antiques, accessories, lighting, and art. Exhibits open to the public—and for sale—include post-Impressionist female artists from the early 20th century. The store prides itself on the fact that they do not use outsourced buyers or wholesalers. Every piece in the store has been purchased by the owners on their quarterly trips to Europe. Every Saturday they offer free wine and cheese while you peruse. 2850 Salzedo St., Coral Gables. ℂ 305/446-1688.

Architectural Antiques   A great place to browse—if you don't mind a little dust— this huge warehouse has an impressive stash of ironwork, bronzes, paintings, lamps, furniture, and sculptures which have been salvaged from estates worldwide. Don't be surprised to find odd items, too, like an old British phone booth or a pair of gargoyles off an ancient church. 2520 SW 28th Lane (just west of U.S. 1), Miami. ℂ 305/285-1330.

Industrian   What's a retro-fabulous Charles Eames chair doing sitting next to an ultramodern 21st-century, Jetsonian piece of furniture? The answer is Industrian, where vintage and new furniture live in harmony. 5580 NE 4th Court, Miami. ℂ 305/754-6070.

Miami Twice   While they are not technically antiques yet, the Old Florida furniture and decorations from the '30s, '40s, and '50s are great fun (and collectible). In addition to loads of Deco memorabilia, there are also vintage clothes, shoes, and jewelry. 6562 SW 40th St., South Miami. ℂ 305/666-0127. Fax 305/661-1142.

Modernism Gallery   Specializing in 20th-century furnishings from Gilbert Rohde, Noguchi, and Heywood Wakefield, this shop has some of the most beautiful examples of Deco goods from France and the United States. If they don't have what you're looking for, ask. They possess the amazing ability to find the rarest items. 800 Douglas Rd., Suite 101., Coral Gables. ℂ 888/217-2760 or 305/442-8743.

Senzatempo *(Finds*   If the names Charles Eames, George Nelson, or Gio Ponti mean anything to you, this is where you'll want to visit. There's retro, Euro-fabulous designer furniture and decorative arts from 1930 to 1960 here, as well as collectible watches, timepieces, and clocks. 1655 Meridian Ave., 2nd floor (at Lincoln Rd.), South Beach. ℂ 305/534-5588. www.senzatempo.com.

Stone Age Antiques *(Finds*   Movie posters, military memorabilia, tribal masks, cowboy hats—you name it, they probably have it, but nautical antiques are their specialty. Looking for a certain ship's wheel? Stone Age most likely has it. 3236 NW S. River Dr. at NW 32nd St. N. Miami. ℂ 305/633-5114. www.stoneage-antiques.com.

ART GALLERIES

See p. 170 for a list of some of the art galleries in the greater Miami area.

BOOKS

You can find local branches of **Barnes & Noble** at 152 Miracle Mile (ℂ 305/446-4152), 5701 Sunset Dr. (ℂ 305/662-4770), 18711 NE Biscayne Blvd. (ℂ 305/935-9770), 7710 N. Kendall Dr. (ℂ 305/598-7292), and 12405 N. Kendall Dr. (ℂ 305/598-7727). **Borders** can be found at 9205 S. Dixie Hwy. (ℂ 305/665-8800), 11401 NW 12th St. (ℂ 305/597-8866), 3390 Mary St. (ℂ 305/447-1655), 19925 Biscayne Blvd. (ℂ 305/935-0027), and 8811 SW 107th Ave. (ℂ 305/271-7457).

Books & Books   A dedicated following turns out to browse at this warm and wonderful little independent shop. Enjoy the upstairs antiquarian room, which specializes in art books and first editions. If that's not enough intellectual stimulation for you, the shop hosts free lectures from noted authors, experts, and personalities almost nightly, from Monica Lewinsky to Martin Amis. At another location (933 Lincoln Rd., South Beach; ℂ **305/532-3222**), you'll rub elbows with tanned and buffed South Beach bookworms sipping cappuccinos at the Russian Bear Cafe inside the store. This branch stocks a large selection of gay literature and also features lectures. And if you happen to be at the ritzy Bal Harbour Shops and not in the mood to do the Gucci thing, there's another Books & Books here, too (ℂ **305/864-4241**). 265 Aragon Ave., Coral Gables. ℂ 305/442-4408. www.booksandbooks.com.

Kafka's Cyberkafe   Check your e-mail and surf the Web while you sip a latte or snack on a sandwich or pastry with friendly neighborhood regulars. This popular used bookstore also stocks a wide range of foreign and domestic magazines and caters to an international-youth-hostel-type crowd. 1464 Washington Ave., South Beach. ℂ 305/673-9669.

CIGARS

Although it is illegal to bring Cuban cigars into the United States, somehow, forbidden *Cohibas* show up at every dinner party and nightclub in town. Not that I condone it, but if you hang around the cigar smokers in town, no doubt one will be able to tell you where you can get some of the highly prized contraband. Be careful, however, of counterfeits, which are typically Dominican cigars posing as Cubans. Cuban cigars are illegal and unless you go down a sketchy alley to buy one from a dealer (think of it as shady as a drug deal), you are going to be smoking Dominican ones.

The stores listed below sell excellent hand-rolled cigars made with domestic- and foreign-grown tobacco. Many of the *viejitos* (old men) got their training in Cuba working for the government-owned factories in the heyday of Cuban cigars.

El Credito Cigars   This tiny storefront shop employs about 45 veteran Cuban rollers who sit all day rolling the very popular torpedoes and other critically acclaimed blends. They're usually back-ordered, but it's worth stopping in: They will sell you a box and show you around. 1106 SW 8th St., Little Havana. ℂ 305/858-4162.

Mike's Cigars Distributor's Inc. *(Finds)*   Mike's may have abandoned its old digs for a bigger, newer location, but it's one of the oldest and best smoke shops in town. Since 1950, Mike's has been selling the best from Honduras, the Dominican Republic, and Jamaica, as well as the very hot local brand, La Gloria Cubana. Many say it has the best prices, too. Mike's has the biggest selection of cigars in town and the employees speak English. 1030 Kane Concourse (at 96th St.), Bay Harbor Island. ℂ 305/866-2277. www.mikescigars.com.

COSMETICS, FRAGRANCES, BEAUTY PRODUCTS & A SALON

Brownes & Co. Apothecary *(Finds)*   Designed to look like an old-fashioned apothecary, this recently expanded beauty emporium combines the best selection of makeup and hair products—MAC, Shu Uemura, Kiehl's, Stila, Molton Brown, Francois Nars, and Dr. Hauschka, just to name a few—with lots of delicious-smelling bath and body stuff, plus a full-service beauty salon. Feel free to browse and sample here, as perfume-spritzing salespeople won't bother you. If you do need help, the staff is a collection of experts when it comes to beauty and hair products. Upstairs is the Browne's Beauty Lounge, in which you can get fabulously coiffed, colored, buffed, and waxed by the experts at the store's renowned salon, Some Like It Hot. For those of you looking for that J-Lo glow, she shops here, so ask one of the staff to point you in the right direction. 841 Lincoln Rd., South Beach. ℂ 305-532-8703. www.brownesbeauty.com.

Sephora　The Disney World of makeup, Sephora offers a dizzying array of cosmetics, perfumes, and styling products. Unlike Brownes & Co., however, personal service and attentiveness is at a minimum. Because there are so many products, shopping here can be a harrowing experience. Three locations: 721 Collins Ave., South Beach (ℂ 305/532-0904); 19575 Biscayne Blvd., Aventura (ℂ 305/931-9579); or in the Dadeland Mall, 7535 SW 88th St., Miami (ℂ 305/740-3445).

FASHION: CLOTHING & ACCESSORIES

Miami didn't become a fashion capital until—believe it or not—the pastel-hued, Armani-clad cops on *Miami Vice* had their close-ups on the tube. Before that, Miami was all about old men in white patent leather shoes and well-tanned women in bikinis. How things have changed! Miami is now a fashion mecca in its own right, with some of the same high-end stores you'd find on Rue de Fauborg St. Honore in Paris or Bond Street in London. You'll find all the chichi labels, including Prada and Gucci, right here at the posh Bal Harbour Shops. For funkier frocks, South Beach is the place, where designers such as Nicole Miller, Ralph Lauren and Giorgio Armani compete for window shoppers with local up-and-coming designers, some of whom design for drag queens and club kids only. The strip on Collins Avenue between 7th and 10th streets has become quite upscale, including such shops as Armani Exchange and Intermix, along with the inescapable Gap and Banana Republic. Of course, there's also more mainstream (and affordable) shopping in the plethora of malls and outdoor shopping and entertainment complexes that are sprinkled throughout the city (see "Malls," below).

UNISEX

Atrium　Young Hollywood always makes Atrium a stop on their South Beach shopping list. With designer brands at designer prices, don't be surprised if you see that $200 white T-shirt on an Olsen twin in the latest issue of *Us Weekly.* 1925 Collins Ave., South Beach. ℂ 305/695-0757.

Barneys Co-Op　Finally, an outpost of posh Barneys New York opens on South Beach, only this time, it's more "affordable." Hooey. If you think a T-shirt for $150 is affordable, then this store is for you. Otherwise, Barneys Co-Op is always great for browsing and marveling over the fashion victims who actually do pay such absurd prices for a cotton T-shirt. 832 Collins Ave., South Beach. ℂ 305/421-2010.

Base USA　A hipster hangout, featuring clothing that's fashionable, and, of course, pricey. Base is also known for its cool and funky CD collection (all for sale, of course), coffee table books and nice smelling candles. 939 Lincoln Rd., South Beach. ℂ 305/531-4982.

Diesel Jeans　Yet another store where the label conscious can drop hundreds on denim. If you're not in the market for $200 jeans, Diesel carries some cool accessories such as ski caps, which really come in handy in Miami. 801 Washington Ave., South Beach. ℂ 305/535-9655.

En Avance　If you couldn't get into Mynt or Opium last night, consider plunking down some major pocket change for the au courant labels that En Avance is known for. One outfit bought here and the doormen have no ground to stand on when it comes to high-fashion dress codes. 734 Lincoln Rd., South Beach. ℂ 305/534-0337.

Urban Outfitters   It took a while for this urban outpost to hit Miami, but once it did, it became a favorite for the young hipster set who favor T-shirts that say "Princess" instead of Prada. Cheapish, utilitarian, and funky, Urban Outfitters is an excellent place to pick up a pair of used jeans or some funky tchotchkes for your apartment. Two locations: 653 Collins Ave., South Beach (✆ 305/535-9726); or Shops at Sunset, 5701 SW 72nd St., South Miami (✆ 305/663-1536).

Y-3   A collaboration between couture designer Yohji Yamamoto and Adidas, Y-3 chose Miami's Design District as its first freestanding store ever, but bigger news than that is that it's the district's first-ever clothing store, featuring a full range of funky men's and women's apparel, shoes and accessories. The two-story store prides itself on fusing style and sport and often hosts very fabulous art and culture events. 150 NE 40th St., Design District. ✆ 305/535-9726 or 305/573-1603. www.y-3.com.

> **Impressions**
>
> *We're the only city that has big-butt mannequins.*
>
> —Anna Maria Diaz-Balart, Miami-based fashion designer

WOMEN'S

Belinda's Designs   This German designer makes some of the most beautiful and intricate teddies, nightgowns, and wedding dresses. The styles are a little too Stevie Nicks for me, but the creations are absolutely worth admiring. The prices are appropriately high. 917 Washington Ave., South Beach. ✆ 305/532-0068.

HiHo Batik   Hand-painted tank tops, adorable accessories, and funky jewelry including Hello Kitty is what you'll discover in this tiny Biscayne Corridor storefront. 6909 Biscayne Blvd., Miami. ✆ 305/754-8890.

Intermix   Pretty young things can get all dolled up thanks to Intermix's fun assortment of hip women's fashions, from Stella McCartney's pricey rhinestone T-shirts to the latest jeans worn by everyone at the MTV Awards. 634 Collins Ave., South Beach. ✆ 305/531-5950.

La Perla   The only store in Florida that specializes in superluxurious Italian intimate apparel. Of course, you could fly to Milan for the price of a few bras and a nightgown, but you can't find better quality. 342 San Lorenzo Ave., Coral Gables. ✆ 305/864-2070.

Morgan Miller   A dream come true for shoe lovers, Morgan Miller is a design-your-own shoe boutique where you pick everything from heel to toe—Swarovski crystals, gold chains, bamboo rings—and the experts put it all together for you. Prices range from $150 to $500. Aventura Mall, 19575 Biscayne Blvd. ✆ 305/932-3451. www.morganmillershoes.com.

Place Vendome   This shop is for cheap and funky club clothes from zebra-print pants to bright, shiny tops. Two locations: 934 Lincoln Rd., South Beach ✆ 305/673-4005, and Aventura Mall, North Miami Beach ✆ 305/932-8931.

Rebel   Fashionable and funky clothing for mom and daughter is what you'll find in this fabulous Biscayne Corridor boutique that carries labels not found anywhere else. Super-friendly help is a bonus, too. 6669 Biscayne Blvd., Miami. ✆ 305/758-2369.

Scoop   Here's the real scoop: The Shore Club hotel boutique hails from New York City and is the shop of choice for celebs like Cameron Diaz, who just walks in and doesn't have to ask the price of the latest from Diane Von Furstenberg, Helmut Lang, Marc Jacobs, Paul Smith, Malo, and Jimmy Choo. The Shore Club, 1901 Collins Ave. ✆ 305/532-5929.

MEN'S

Giorgio's European Clothing   One of the finest custom men's stores in Miami, Giorgio's features an extensive line of Italian suits and all the latest by Canelli. 350 Miracle Mile, Coral Gables. ℂ 305/448-4302.

La Casa de las Guayaberas *(Finds* Miami's premier purveyor of the traditional yet retro-hip Cuban shirt known as the *guayabera*—a loose-fitting, pleated, button-down shirt—was founded by Ramon Puig, who emigrated to Miami over 40 years ago. He still uses the same scissors he did back then, only now he's joined by a team of seamstresses who hand-sew 20 shirts a day in all colors and styles. Prices range from $15 to $375. 5840 SW 8th St., Little Havana. ℂ 305/266-9683.

Original Penguin Store   Remember the Izod alligator? Forget it for a second and consider this, the hippest retro men's line since, well, Izod, featuring sweaters, polo shirts, T's and more sporting a, well, penguin logo. 925 Lincoln Rd., South Beach. ℂ 305/673-0722.

CHILDREN'S

Most department stores have extensive children's sections. But if you can't find what you are looking for, consider one of the many Baby Gaps or Gap Kids outlets around town or try one of the specialty boutiques listed here.

Genius Jones   In addition to the requisite, adorable and pricey kids' threads, Genius Jones has high-end kids' furniture by the likes of Agatha Ruiz de la Prada, David Netto, and other brands that will set you back some serious bucks. 635 1661 Michigan Ave., South Beach. ℂ 305/534-7622.

Kidding Around   Pricey kids' boutique with name-brand clothes, toys, and furniture. The Falls, 8888 SW 136th St. South Miami. ℂ 305/253-0708.

ACCESSORIES

Me & Ro Jewelery   This store carries fun and funky baubles (not cheap) as seen on Debra Messing, Sarah Jessica Parker, and Julia Roberts. The Shore Club, 1901 Collins Ave., South Beach. ℂ 305/672-3566.

SEE   This fantastic eyewear store features an enormous selection of stylish specs all priced between $169 and $239, including your prescription. The staff is patient and knowledgeable. 921 Lincoln Rd., South Beach. ℂ 305/672-6622.

Simons and Green   Fantastic sterling silver jewelry, leather goods, and other assorted high-end tchotchkes and gift items are what you'll find in this quaint mainstay on South Miami's Sunset Drive. 5843 Sunset Dr., South Miami. ℂ 305/667-1692.

FOOD

There are dozens of ethnic markets in Miami, from Cuban *bodegas* (little grocery stores) to Jamaican import shops and Guyanese produce stands. Check the phone book under grocers for listings. I've listed a few of the biggest and best markets in town that sell prepared foods as well as staple items. On Saturday mornings, vendors set up stands loaded with papayas, melons, tomatoes, and citrus, as well as cookies, ice creams, and sandwiches on South Beach's Lincoln Road.

Epicure   This is the closest thing Miami Beach has to the famed Balducci's or Dean & DeLuca. Here, you'll find not only fine wines, cheeses, meats, fish, and juices, but some of the best produce, such as portobello mushrooms the size of a yarmulke. This neighborhood landmark is best known for supplying the Jewish residents of the beach with all their Jewish favorites, such as matzo ball soup, gefilte fish, and deli items. Prices are steep, but generally worth it. The cakes in particular are rich and decadent, and a rather large one doesn't cost more than $10. 1656 Alton Rd., Miami Beach. (C) 305/672-1861.

Gardner's Market Anything a gourmet or novice cook could desire can be found here. One of the oldest and best grocery stores in Miami, Gardner's now has three locations, all of which offer great takeout and the freshest produce. 7301 Red Rd., South Miami ((C) 305/667-9953); 8287 SW 124th St., Pinecrest ((C) 305/255-2468); 3117 Bird Ave., Miami ((C) 305/476-9900).

Joe's Takeaway If you don't want to wait 2 hours to get your paws on Joe's Stone Crab's meaty claws, let Joe's, Miami's stone-crab institution (p. 117), ship you stone crabs anywhere in the country, but only during the season, which runs from mid-October through mid-May. 11 Washington Ave., South Beach. (C) 800/780-CRAB or 305/673-0365.

La Brioche Doree This tiny storefront off 41st Street is packed most mornings with French expatriates and visitors who crave the real thing. There are luscious pastries and breads, plus soup and sandwiches at lunch. No one makes a better croissant. 4017 Prairie Ave., Miami Beach. (C) 305/538-4770.

Laurenzo's Italian Supermarket and Farmer's Market Anything Italian you want—homemade ravioli, hand-cut imported Romano cheese, plus fresh fish and meats—can be found here. Laurenzo's also offers one of the most comprehensive wine selections in the city. Be sure to see the neighboring store full of just-picked herbs, salad greens, and vegetables from around the world. A daily Farmer's Market is open from 7am to 6pm. Incredible daily specials lure thrifty shoppers from all over the city. 16385 and 16445 W. Dixie Hwy., North Miami Beach. (C) 305/945-6381 or 305/944-5052.

Morning Call Bakery You'll be happy to pay upward of $6 a loaf when you sink your teeth into these inimitable Old World–style breads. Also, most of the locations have a to-die-for prepared-food counter serving up everything from chicken curry salad to hummus and potpies. Pastries and cakes are as gorgeous as they are delicious. 5868 SW 72nd St., Miami. (C) 305/667-9333.

JEWELRY

For name designers like Gucci and Tiffany & Co., go to the Bal Harbour Shops (see "Malls," below).

The International Jewelry Exchange At least 50 reputable jewelers hustle their wares from individual counters at one of the city's most active jewelry centers. Haggle your brains out for excellent prices on timeless antiques from Tiffany's, Cartier, or Bulgari, or on unique designs you can create yourself. Stop by Dahlia's Unique booth and ask for Dorie. She'll give you a good deal. 19275 Biscayne Blvd. (in the Fashion Island), North Miami Beach. (C) 305/931-3383.

Seybold Buchwald's Jewelers Jewelers who specialize in an assortment of goods (diamonds, gems, watches, rings, and such) gather here daily to sell diamonds and gold. With 300 jewelry stores located inside this independently owned and operated multilevel treasure chest, the glare is blinding as you enter. You'll be sure to see handsome and up-to-date designs, but not too many bargains. 36 NE 1st St., Downtown. (C) 305/374-7922.

MALLS

There are so many malls in Miami and more being built all the time that it would be impossible to mention them all. What follows is a list of the biggest and most popular.

You can find any number of nationally known department stores including Saks Fifth Avenue, Macy's, Bloomingdale's, Sears, and JCPenney in the Miami malls listed below. Miami's own, Burdines, is now a Macy's, too, located at 22 E. Flagler St., Downtown and 1675 Meridian Ave. (just off Lincoln Rd.) in South Beach.

Aventura Mall (Kids)   A multimillion-dollar makeover has made this spot one of the premier places to shop in South Florida. With more than 2.3 million square feet of space, this airy, Mediterranean-style mall has a 24-screen movie theater and more than 250 stores, including megastores JCPenney, Nordstrom, Macy's, Bloomingdale's, Sears, and Burdines. The mall offers moderate- to high-priced merchandise and is extremely popular with families. A large indoor playground, Adventurer's Cove, is a great spot for kids, and the mall frequently offers activities and entertainment for children. There are numerous theme restaurants and a food court that eschews the usual suspects in favor of local operations. 19501 Biscayne Blvd. (at 197th St. near the Dade–Broward County line), Aventura. ℂ 305/935-1110. www.shopaventuramall.com.

Bal Harbour Shops   One of the most prestigious fashion meccas in the country, Bal Harbour offers the best-quality goods from the finest names. Giorgio Armani, Dolce & Gabbana, Christian Dior, Fendi, Joan & David, Harry Winston, Pucci, Krizia, Rodier, Gucci, Brooks Brothers, Waterford, Cartier, H. Stern, Tourneau, and many others are sandwiched between Neiman Marcus and a newly expanded Saks Fifth Avenue. Well-dressed shoppers stroll in a pleasant open-air emporium featuring several good cafes, covered walkways, and lush greenery. Parking costs $1 an hour with a validated ticket. *Tip:* You can stamp your own at the entrance to Saks Fifth Avenue, even if you don't make a purchase. 9700 Collins Ave. (on 97th St., opposite the Sheraton Bal Harbour Hotel), Bal Harbour. ℂ 305/866-0311. www.balharbourshops.com.

Bayside Marketplace   A popular stop for cruise-ship passengers, this touristy waterfront marketplace is filled with the usual suspects of chain stores as well as a slew of tacky gift shops and carts hawking assorted junk in the heart of downtown Miami. The second-floor food court is stocked with dozens of fast-food choices and bars. Most of the restaurants and bars stay open later than the stores. There's Lomardi's, Bubba Gump Shrimp Co., Hooters, Hard Rock Cafe, Fat Tuesday, Captain Joe's Seafood, and Let's Make a Daiquiri. Parking is $1 per hour. While we wouldn't recommend you necessarily drop big money at Bayside, you should go by just for the view (of Biscayne Bay and the Miami skyline) alone. In June you can watch the Opsail sailboat show, and in February, the Miami Sailboat Show, where sailboats dock in the area and make the view even nicer. Beware of the adjacent amphitheater known as Bayfront Park, which usually hosts large-scale concerts and festivals, causing major pedestrian and vehicle traffic jams. 401 Biscayne Blvd., Downtown. ℂ 305/577-3344. www.baysidemarketplace.com.

CocoWalk   CocoWalk is a lovely outdoor Mediterranean-style mall with the usual fare of Americana: Gap, Banana Republic, and so on. Its open-air style architecture is inviting not only for shoppers but also for friends or spouses of shoppers who'd prefer to sit at an outdoor cafe while said shopper is busy in the fitting room. A multiplex movie theater is also here, which comes in handy when there are big sales going on and the stores are mobbed. 3015 Grand Ave., Coconut Grove. ℂ 305/444-0777. www.cocowalk.com.

Dadeland Mall   One of the county's first malls, Dadeland features more than 175 specialty shops, anchored by four large department stores: Macy's, JCPenney, Nordstrom, and Saks Fifth Avenue. The mall also boasts the country's largest Limited/Express store. Sixteen restaurants serve from the adjacent Treats Food Court. New retail stores are constantly springing up around this centerpiece of South Miami suburbia. If you're not in the area, however, the mall is not worth the trek. Additionally, many non-Spanish-speaking people are put off by Dadeland because of the predominance of Spanish-speaking store employees. 7535 N. Kendall Dr. (intersection of U.S. 1 and SW 88th St., 15 min. south of Downtown), Kendall. ✆ 305/665-6226.

Dolphin Mall   As if Miami needed another mall, this $250-million megamall is similar to Broward County's monstrous Sawgrass Mills outlet, albeit without the luxury stores. The 1.4-million-square-foot outlet mall features outlets such as Off Fifth (Saks Fifth Avenue), plus several discount shops, and a 28-screen movie theater. Florida Tpk. at S.R. 836, West Miami. ✆ 305/365-7446. www.shopdolphinmall.com.

The Falls   Traffic to this mall borders on brutal, but once you get there, you'll feel a slight sense of serenity. Tropical waterfalls are the setting for this outdoor shopping center with dozens of moderately priced and slightly upscale shops. Miami's first Bloomingdale's is here, as are Polo, Ralph Lauren, Caswell-Massey, and more than 60 other specialty shops. A recent renovation added Macy's, Crate & Barrel, Brooks Brothers, and Pottery Barn, among others. If you are planning to visit any of the nearby attractions, which include Metrozoo and Monkey Jungle, check with customer service for information on discount packages. 8888 Howard Dr. (at the intersection of U.S. 1 and 136th St., about 3 miles south of Dadeland Mall), Kendall. ✆ 305/255-4570. www.shopthefalls.com.

Sawgrass Mills   Just as some people need to take a tranquilizer to fly, others need one to traipse through this mammoth mall—the largest outlet mall in the country. Depending on what type of shopper you are, this experience can either be blissful or overwhelming. If you've got the patience, it is worth setting aside a day to do the entire place. Though it's located in Broward County, it is a phenomenon that attracts thousands of tourists and locals sniffing out bargains. In 2006, the mall debuted its swank new luxe section, the Colonnade Outlets, featuring outlet versions of Coach, Miss Sixty USA, Salvatore Ferragamo and other luxury outlets offering savings of up to 70%. When driving, take I-95 north to 595 west to Flamingo Road. Exit and turn right, driving 2 miles to Sunrise Boulevard. You can't miss this monster on the left. Parking is free, but don't forget where you parked your car or you might spend a day looking for it. 12801 W. Sunrise Blvd., Sunrise (west of Fort Lauderdale). ✆ 954/846-2300. www.millscorp.com.

Shops at Sunset Place   Completed in early 1999 at a cost of over $140 million, this sprawling outdoor shopping complex offers more than just shopping. Visitors experience high-tech special effects, such as daily tropical storms (minus the rain) and the electronic chatter of birds and crickets. In addition to a 24-screen movie complex and an IMAX theater, there's a GameWorks (Steven Spielberg's Disney-esque playground for kids and adults), a Virgin Records store, and a NikeTown as well as mall standards such as Victoria's Secret, Gap, Urban Outfitters, bebe, and so on. 5701 Sunset Dr. (at 57th Ave. and U.S. 1, near Red Rd.), South Miami. ✆ 305/663-0482.

Streets of Mayfair   This sleepy, desolate, labyrinthine shopping area conceals a movie theater, several top-quality shops, a bookstore, restaurants, art galleries, bars, and nightclubs. It was meant to compete with the CocoWalk shopping complex (just across the street), but its structure is very mazelike. Though it is open air, it is not wide open like CocoWalk and pales in comparison to that more populated neighbor. 2911 Grand Ave. (just east of Commodore Plaza), Coconut Grove. ℂ 305/448-1700.

Village of Merrick Park   Giving Bal Harbour Shops a literal run for its money is this Coral Gables Mediterranean-style outdoor mall consisting of extremely high-end stores such as Jimmy Choo, Sonia Rykiel, Neiman Marcus, Miami's very first Nordstrom, and upscale eateries such as The Palm. In fact, the owner of Bal Harbour Shops was so paranoid he'd lose his business to Merrick Park that he shoveled a ton of cash in an ad campaign making sure people wouldn't forget that Bal Harbour was here first. People who can afford it won't be forgetting about either anytime soon. 4425 Ponce de León Blvd., Coral Gables. ℂ 305/529-0200.

MUSIC STORES

Casino Records Inc.   The young, hip salespeople here speak English and tend to be music buffs. This store has the largest selection of Latin music in Miami, including pop icons such as Willy Chirino, Gloria Estefan, Albita, and local boy Nil Lara. Their slogan translates to: "If we don't have it, forget it." Believe me, they've got it. 1208 SW 8th St., Little Havana. ℂ 305/856-6888.

Yesterday and Today Records *(Finds)*   This is Miami's most unique and well-stocked store for vinyl—you know, the audio dinosaur that went out with the Victrola? Y & T, as it's known, is a collector's heaven, featuring every genre of music imaginable on every format. Chances are, you could find some eight-track tapes, too. 7902 NW 36th St., Miami. ℂ 305/468-0311.

SPORTS EQUIPMENT

People-watching seems to be the number-one sport in South Florida, but for the more athletic pursuits, consider the shops listed below. One of the area's largest sports-equipment chains is the **Sports Authority**, with at least six locations throughout the county. Check the White Pages for details.

Alf's Golf Shop   This is the best pro shop around. The knowledgeable staff can help you with equipment for golfers of every level, and the neighboring golf course offers discounts to Alf's clients. There are three locations. 524 Arthur Godfrey Rd., Miami Beach (ℂ 305/673-6568); 15369 S. Dixie Hwy., Miami (ℂ 305/378-6086); and 2600 NW 87th Ave., Pinecrest, in South Miami (ℂ 305/470-0032).

Bass Pro Shops Outdoor World   Fishing and sports enthusiasts must head north to Broward County to see this huge retail complex, which offers demonstrations in such sports as fly-fishing and archery, classes in marine safety, and every conceivable gadget you could ask for. 200 Gulf Stream Way (west side of I-95), Dania Beach. ℂ 954/929-7710.

Edwin Watts Golf Shops   One of 30 Edwin Watts shops throughout the Southeast, this full-service golf retail shop is one of the most popular in Miami. You can find it all here, including clothing, pro-line equipment, gloves, bags, balls, videos, and books. Plus, you can get coupons for discounted greens fees on many courses. 15100 N. Biscayne Blvd., North Miami Beach. ℂ 305/944-2925.

Island Water Sports   You'll find everything from booties to gloves to baggies and tanks. Check in here before you rent that WaveRunner or windsurfer. 16231 Biscayne Blvd., North Miami. ℂ 305/944-0104.

South Beach Dive and Surf Shop   Prices are slightly higher at this beach location, but you'll find the hottest styles and equipment. They also offer surfboard rental. Free surf report at © **305/534-7873.** 850 Washington Ave., South Beach. © **305/673-5900.**

THRIFT STORES/RESALE SHOPS

C. Madeleines's   The best vintage store in town, brands from Gucci, Pucci, Fiorucci, and even Chanel and Balenciaga are usually snatched up by the likes of Jessica Simpson, Lenny Kravitz, or their stylists, who call this fashion emporium home. 13702 Biscayne Blvd., N. Miami. © **305/945-0010.**

The Children's Exchange *(Kids*   Selling everything from layettes to overalls, this pleasant little shop is chock-full of good Florida-style stuff for kids to wear to the beach and in the heat. 1415 Sunset Dr., Coral Gables. © **305/666-6235.**

Douglas Gardens Jewish Home and Hospital Thrift Shop   Prices here are no longer the major bargain they once were, but for housewares and books, you can do all right. Call to see if they are offering any specials for seniors or students. 5713 NW 27th Ave., North Miami Beach. © **305/638-1900.**

Rags to Riches   This is an old-time consignment shop where you might find some decent rags, and maybe even some riches. Though not as upscale as it used to be, this place is still a good spot for costume jewelry and shoes. 12577 Biscayne Blvd., North Miami. © **305/891-8981.**

Red White & Blue Thrift Store *(Finds*   Miami's best-kept secret is this mammoth thrift store that is meticulously organized and well stocked. You've got to search for great stuff, but it is there. There are especially good deals on children's clothes and housewares. 12640 NE 6th Ave., North Miami. © **305/893-1104.**

10

Miami After Dark

With all the hype, you'd expect Miami to have long outlived its 15 minutes of fame by now. But you'd be wrong. Miami's nightlife, in South Beach *and,* slowly but surely, downtown, is hotter than ever before—and still getting hotter. Practically every club in the area has installed closely guarded velvet ropes to create an air of exclusivity. Don't be fooled or intimidated by them—*anyone* can go clubbing in the Magic City, and throughout this chapter, I've provided tips to ensure that you gain entry to your desired venue.

South Beach is certainly Miami's uncontested nocturnal nucleus, but more and more diverse areas, such as the Design District, South Miami, and even Little Havana, are increasingly providing fun alternatives without the ludicrous cover charges, "fashionably late" hours of operation (things don't typically get started on South Beach until after 11pm), the lack of sufficient self-parking, and outrageous drink prices that are standard in South Beach.

While South Beach dances to a more electronic beat, other parts of Miami dance to a Latin beat—from salsa and merengue to tango and cha cha. However, if you're looking for a less frenetic good time, Miami's bar scene has something for everyone, from haute hotel bars to sleek, loungey watering holes.

Parts of downtown, such as the Biscayne Corridor, the Miami River, and the Design District, are undergoing a trendy makeover à la New York City's Meatpacking District. Cool lounges, bars, and clubs are popping up and providing the "in" crowds with a newer, more urban-chic nocturnal pasture.

But if the possibility of a celebrity sighting in one of the city's lounges, bars, or clubs doesn't fulfill your cultural needs, Miami also provides a variety of first-rate diversions in theater, music, and dance, including a world-class ballet (under the aegis of Edward Villella), a recognized symphony, and a talented opera company. The new Cesar Pelli–designed, $446-million Carnival Center for the Performing Arts, which, at the time of this writing was about to be renamed the Adrienne Arsht Center for the Performing Arts of Miami-Dade County after the philanthropist gave $30 million to the financially troubled center, is the focal point for the arts, created to prove to the world that Miami isn't as shallow and devoid of culture as people once thought.

For up-to-date listing information, and to make sure the club of the moment hasn't expired, check the *Miami Herald*'s "Weekend" section, which runs on Friday, or the more comprehensive listings in *New Times,* Miami's free alternative weekly, available each Wednesday; or visit www.miami.citysearch.com online.

Impressions

Miami is where neon goes to die.

—Lenny Bruce

1 Bars & Lounges

There are countless bars and lounges in and around Miami (most require proof that you are 21 or older to enter), with the highest concentration on trendy South Beach. The selection here is a mere sample. Keep in mind that many of the popular bars— and the easiest to get into—are in hotels (with a few notable exceptions—see below). For a clubbier scene, if you don't mind making your way through hordes of inebriated club kids, a stroll on Washington Avenue will provide you with ample insight into what's hot and what's not. Just hold on to your bags. It's not dangerous, but, occasionally, a few shady types manage to slip into the crowd. Another very important tip when in a club: *Never put your drink down out of your sight*—there have been unfortunate incidents in which drinks have been spiked with illegal chemical substances. For a less hard-core, more collegiate nightlife, head to Coconut Grove. Oh, yes, and when going out in South Beach, make sure to take a so-called disco nap, as things don't get going until at least 11pm. If you go earlier, be prepared to face an empty bar or club. Off of South Beach and in hotel bars in general, the hours are fashionably earlier, with the action starting as early as, say, 7pm.

The Abbey   Dark, dank, and hard to find, this local microbrewery is a favorite for locals looking to escape the $15 candy-flavored martini scene. Best of all, there's never a cover and it's always open until 5am, perfect for those pesky and insatiable hops cravings that pop up at 3 or 4am. 1115 16th St., South Beach. © 305/538-8110.

Automatic Slim's   This is *the* bar where Ozzie and Harriet types become more like Ozzy and Sharon. As South Beach's most popular unpretentious bar, Automatic Slim's is indeed a slim space of bar, but it packs people in, thanks to an exhaustive list of cheap(er) drinks, lack of attitude, great rock music, and a decor that can only be described as white trash–chic. 1216 Washington Ave., South Beach. © 305/695-0795.

Blue   A very laid-back, very local scene set to a sultry soundtrack of deep soul and house music has Miami's hipsters feeling the blues here on a nightly basis from 10pm to 5am. Before you whip out the St. John's wort, dive into this so-not-trendy-it's-trendy lounge, in which the pervasive color blue will actually heighten your spirits as an eclectic haze of models, locals, and lounge lizards gather to commiserate over their dreaded trendy status. 222 Española Way (between Washington and Collins aves.), South Beach. © 305/534-1009.

Clarke's   Ever since this classy Irish pub and restaurant opened in the chichi South of Fifth Street area in 2005, it became command central for everyone from Shaquille O'Neal and the Miami Beach police chief to local moguls and club kids looking for cold beer and, surprisingly, a gourmet menu consisting of shepherd's pie, seared scallops, and the best burger in the 'hood. My personal favorite, however, is the New York–style pretzel served on a spike with a side of mustard. 840 1st St., South Beach © 305/538-9885.

Impressions

There are two shifts in South Beach. There's nine to five. And then there's nine to five.

—South Beach artist Stewart Stewart

Clevelander   If wet-T-shirt contests and a fraternity party atmosphere are your thing, this Ocean Drive mainstay is your kind of place. Popular with tourists and locals who like to pretend they're tourists, the Clevelander, which was closed for a year of much-needed renovations (adding even more bars, as if they need them!), attracts a lively, sporty crowd of only adults (the burly bouncers *will* confiscate fake IDs) who have no interest in being part of a scene, but, rather, like to take in the very revealing scenery. A great time to check out the Clevelander is on a weekend afternoon, when beach Barbies and Kens line the bar for a post-tanning beer or frozen cocktail. 1020 Ocean Dr., South Beach. ✆ 305/531-3485.

The Florida Room   The Delano's new subterranean speakeasy, the Florida Room is the antithesis of the hotel in which it resides. Designed by Lenny Kravitz's firm, this dimly chandelier-lit den features old-school Florida–meets–swank cruise-ship lounge decor. It's a place of 200 maximum capacity where everyone from young hipsters and swank sophisticates to The Golden Girls would go for a fancy night out. Rue McClanahan's feisty, randy Blanche would be right at home climbing atop the Lucite piano to channel Michelle Pfeiffer in The Fabulous Baker Boys. 1685 Collins Ave. in the Delano hotel, Miami Beach. ✆ 305/673-2000. (Door policy tends to be a bit exclusive, bordering on snooty.)

Forge   The Forge bar hosts an unusual mix of the uptight and those who wear their clothes too tight. It's also where surgically altered ladies look for their cigar-chomping sugar daddies in a setting that somehow reminds me of *Dynasty.* Call well in advance if you want to watch the parade of characters from a dinner table. The Forge owners also own **Glass,** a ritzier nightclub (which is attached to the club) that debuted in 2006 (they say it's a private club, but if you dine at the restaurant or are acquainted with someone in the know, you can get in). 432 41st St., Miami Beach. ✆ 305/538-8533. (Door policy tends to be a bit exclusive; dress up and you should have no problem.)

Fox's Sherron Inn *(Finds*   The spirit of Frank Sinatra is alive and well at this dark and smoky watering hole that dates back to 1946. Everything down to the vinyl booths and the red lights make Fox's a retro fabulous dive bar. Cheap drinks, couples cozily huddling in booths, and a seasoned staff of bartenders and barflies make Fox's the perfect place to retreat from the trenches of trendiness. Oh, and the food's actually good here, too. 6030 S. Dixie Hwy. (at 62nd Ave.), South Miami. ✆ 305/661-9201.

Laundry Bar   This is the only place in Miami where it's okay to let friends drink and dry. Laundry Bar features working washers, dryers, a fully stocked bar, and several other distractions to help make doing your laundry a fun rather than a dreaded chore. It's also one of the only bars on South Beach open from 7am to 5am daily. And although it's most popular with the gay community, Laundry Bar draws a mixed crowd; on weekends, the place is packed like an overloaded washing machine. Daily happy hours (4–9pm) with two-for-one drinks allow you to save your change for the washing machines. 721 N. Lincoln Lane (behind Burdines off Lincoln Rd.), South Beach. ✆ 305/ 531-7700.

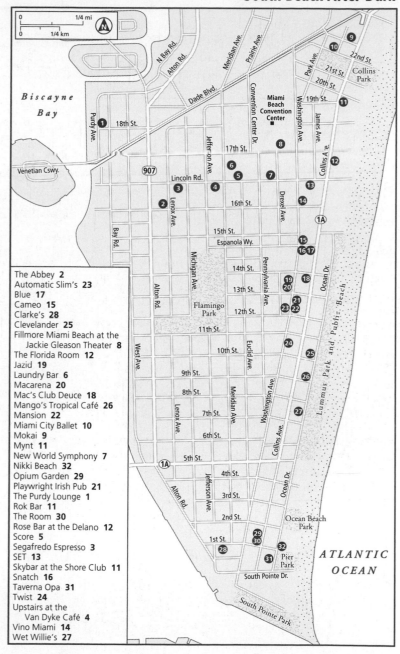

The Abbey **2**
Automatic Slim's **23**
Blue **17**
Cameo **15**
Clarke's **28**
Clevelander **25**
Fillmore Miami Beach at the
 Jackie Gleason Theater **8**
The Florida Room **12**
Jazid **19**
Laundry Bar **6**
Macarena **20**
Mac's Club Deuce **18**
Mango's Tropical Café **26**
Mansion **22**
Miami City Ballet **10**
Mokai **9**
Mynt **11**
New World Symphony **7**
Nikki Beach **32**
Opium Garden **29**
Playwright Irish Pub **21**
The Purdy Lounge **1**
Rok Bar **11**
The Room **30**
Rose Bar at the Delano **12**
Score **5**
Segafredo Espresso **3**
SET **13**
Skybar at the Shore Club **11**
Snatch **16**
Taverna Opa **31**
Twist **24**
Upstairs at the
 Van Dyke Café **4**
Vino Miami **14**
Wet Willie's **27**

Moments Stargazing

The most popular places for celebrity sightings include Mynt, Opium Garden, SkyBar, poolside at the Shore Club or the Delano, and, when it comes to J-Lo, somewhere on the beach around 20th Street. Miami Heat basketball games are also star magnets.

Macarena 🔍🔍 This Macarena has long outlived its passé line-dance namesake and is rather hip, actually, looked after by a young crew of Spanish imports whose families own several popular restaurants in Madrid. Show up before 10pm and you're sure to get a table. After that time, especially on weekends, it's standing room only. The gorgeous Euro crowd shows up for foot-stomping flamenco (every Wed and Fri—call for show times). Try some of the terrific sangria, made with slices of fresh fruit and a subtle tinge of sweet soda. 1334 Washington Ave., South Beach. ℂ 305/531-3440. www.macarena web.com.

Mac's Club Deuce Standing amid an oasis of trendiness, Mac's Club Deuce is the quintessential dive bar, with cheap drinks and a cast of characters ranging from your typical barfly to your atypical drag queen. It's got a well-stocked jukebox, friendly bartenders, and a pool table. Best of all, it's an insomniac's dream, open daily from 8am to 5am. 222 14th St., South Beach. ℂ 305/673-9537.

Mokai Trendy, yes, but tragically so? Not at all. This chic, cozy lounge is the brainchild of several South Beach nightlife impresarios who know how to attract the A-list. Reminiscent of an après-ski bar in Aspen, Mokai's stone walls, dim lighting, and plush leather couches are upscale reminders that elegant slumming doesn't come cheap. Drink prices are expectedly high, but it's the price you pay for hanging out with celebrities, such as the stars of Entourage who hang out here to jam, or the visiting DJs who spin everything from Bar Mitzvah kitsch to deep house. 235 23rd St., South Beach. ℂ 305/531-4166. www.mokaimiami.com.

Mynt A massive 6,000-square-foot place, Mynt is nothing more than a huge living room in which models, celebrities, and assorted hangers-on bask in the green glow to the beat of very loud lounge and dance music. If you want to dance—or move, for that matter—this is not the place in which to do so. It's all about striking a pose in here. Unless you know the person at the door, be prepared to be ridiculed, emasculated, and socially shattered, as you may be forced to wait outside upward of an hour. If that's the case, forget it; it's not worth it. Wait next door at the Greek place for a celebrity sighting, since you'll have a better chance of seeing people from there instead of just waiting in the melee at the door. 1921 Collins Ave., South Beach. ℂ 786/276-6132. Cover $10–$20.

Playwright Irish Pub Bono came here once when U2 was in town, not because it's such an authentic Irish pub, but because the bar was showing some European soccer match—and serves pints of Guinness. A great pre- or post-club spot, Playwright is one of the few places in town that also features live music from time to time. 1265 Washington Ave, South Beach. ℂ 305/534-0667.

The Purdy Lounge With the exception of a wall of lava lamps, Purdy is not unlike your best friend's basement, featuring a pool table and a slew of board games such as Operation to keep the attention-deficit-disordered from getting bored. It even has a bingo and spelling-bee night! Because it's a no-nonsense bar with relatively cheap cocktails (by South Beach standards), Purdy gets away with not having a star DJ or fancy bass-heavy Bose sound system. A CD player somehow does the trick. With no cover and no attitude, a line is inevitable (it gets crowded inside), so be prepared to wait. Saturday night has become the preferred night for locals, while Friday night's happy hour draws a young professional crowd on the prowl. 1811 Purdy Ave./Sunset Harbor, South Beach. (C) 305/531-4622.

Rok Bar   Larger-than-life rocker Tommy Lee has assembled a motley Miami crew at this paradox of a bar that combines down-'n'-dirty rock 'n' roll with the swank comforts of a chic lounge. The place is claustrophobic, with limited seating (unless you're Pamela Anderson, forget about scoring a table), high-priced drinks, and an oxymoronic soundtrack of Lynyrd Skynyrd, Michael Jackson, and Kid Rock. 1905 Collins Ave., South Beach. (C) 305/538-7171.

The Room   It's beer and wine only at this South of Fifth hideaway where locals and NY expats (there are a few Rooms in NYC) come to get away from the insanity just a few blocks away. The beer selection is comprehensive with brews from almost everywhere in the world. The wine is not so great, but there's no whining here at this tiny, industrial-style, candlelit spot that doesn't have a DJ—just a CD player spinning indie tunes—or those pesky Paris Hilton sightings. 100 Collins Ave, South Beach. (C) 305/531-6061.

Rose Bar at the Delano   If every rose has its thorn, the thorn at this painfully chic hotel bar is the excruciatingly high price of cocktails. Otherwise, the crowd here is full of the so-called glitterati and other assorted poseurs who view life through (Italian-made) rose-colored glasses. 1685 Collins Ave., South Beach. (C) 305/672-2000.

Segafredo Espresso   Although Segafredo is technically a cafe, it has become an integral part of Miami's nightlife as command central for Euros who miss that very special brand of European cafe society. Not in the mood for a club or bar, but want to hear great music, sip a few cocktails, snack on delicious sandwiches and pizza, and sit outside and people-watch? This is the place. European lounge music, tons of outdoor tables on a prime corner of Lincoln Road, and always a mob scene make 'Fredo one of my—and many other Miamians'—favorite nocturnal diversions. 1040 Lincoln Rd., South Beach. (C) 305/673-0047.

Skybar at The Shore Club   Skybar lives up to its name in terms of loftiness; something this place has perfected better than anyone else, whether at its original L.A. location or the sprawling South Beach location at The Shore Club. If you're not a hotel guest, not Beyoncé, or not on the "list," or if you're a guy with several other guys and no girls, forget about it. For those of you who can't get in, the Skybar is basically the entire backyard area of The Shore Club, consisting of several areas, including the Moroccan-themed garden area, the hip-hop-themed indoor Red Room, the Sand Bar by the beach, and the Rum Bar by the pool. Sunday afternoon pool parties are a magnet for celebs and locals alike. Popular on any given night, Skybar is yet another brilliant example of how hotelier Ian Schrager has managed to control the hipsters in a most Pavlovian way. At The Shore Club, 1901 Collins Ave., South Beach. (C) 305/695-3100.

Snatch   Despite its unfortunate name, this trendy rock 'n' roll–themed bar and its upstairs VIP lounge, Suite, are two of the hottest spots in town. As much as we'd like to think Snatch is hot because it has a working mechanical bull, it's who rides the bull that makes the place sizzling. Everyone from scantily clad cocktail waitresses and supermodels to Axl Rose have been on that bull. But you don't have to channel John

Swank Hotel Bars

Long gone are the days of the old-school Holiday Inn lounges. In fact, some hotels seem to spend more money on their bars than they do on their bedding. That aside, hotel bar-hopping is very popular in Miami. The newest hotel in town, the swanker-than-thou **Setai,** has the prettiest and most expensive bars, including their "Champagne and Crustacean Bar." Here's my list of the rest of the best:

Rose Bar at the Delano (p. 215): For seeing and being seen.

SkyBar at The Shore Club (p. 215): Also for seeing and being seen.

Metro Kitchen + Bar at Hotel Astor (p. 85): To bask in a flattering light with a sophisticated, not snotty, crowd. Call ✆ **305/672-7217** for Metro reservations.

Bond St. Lounge at the Townhouse Hotel (p. 125): A tiny bar/lounge that also serves food. A New York import, it's known for excellent sushi and a hip, chic, jet-set crowd.

Raleigh Bar at the Raleigh Hotel (p. 87): A true throwback to the days of deco set to the tunes of Edith Piaf, Tony Bennett, Sinatra, and more, and run by Crispy, one of Miami's best-known bartenders (ask for her original concoction, the Frescita).

Travolta or Debra Winger in *Urban Cowboy* to have fun here. It's wild, loud, and packed from Thursday to Monday nights. Get there early or you won't get in. 1437 Washington Ave., South Beach. ✆ 305/604-3644.

Taverna Opa   Although this Greek taverna (also located in Hollywood and Fort Lauderdale) calls itself a restaurant, I consider it more of a raucous dance club that just happens to serve excellent Greek food. How many restaurants do you know of that allow patrons to dance suggestively with waiters on tables, throw napkins in the air as if they were confetti, and guzzle ouzo straight from the bottle, all to the tune of some very loud, jazzed-up Greek dance music? Get here early, as the place is always packed—and I mean *packed* as in standing room only. Although there is an outdoor bar, the real fun and scenery are indoors in the dining room, where the tables double as dance floors and some very animated characters channel their best Zorbas. Be prepared for a big, fat Greek hangover the next day. 36 Ocean Dr., South Beach. ✆ 305/673-6730.

Transit Lounge   It's hard to locate, but once you do find Transit Lounge, you'll be happy you did. Reminiscent of what locals describe as "a real big-city lounge," Transit is cavernous, featuring a huge bar, tons of cozy couches and tables, board games, a funky crowd, and, hallelujah, live music. 1729 SW 1st Ave., Miami. ✆ 305/377-4628.

Vino Miami   Vino is the city's *only* bona fide wine bar, with a collection of more than 300 bottles and 60 wines by the glass, mostly from boutique and unheard-of wineries around the world. Decorated as if it came straight out of a West Elm catalogue, this chic, Manhattanesque wine bar is known for many things, especially the fact that it's a chill lounge in which the age-30-and-over set can hang out, have audible conversations, sip wine, and even enjoy cheeses, fondues, and delicious desserts. Vino also has monthly wine-tasting events with experts hailing from around the world. 1601 Washington Ave., South Beach. © 305/532-1860.

Wet Willie's   With such telling drinks as Call a Cab, this beachfront oasis is not the place to go if you have a long drive ahead of you. A well-liked pre- and post-beach hangout, Wet Willie's inspires serious drinking. Popular with the Harley-Davidson set, tourists, and beachcombers, this bar is best known for its rooftop patio (get there early if you plan to get a seat) and its half-nude bikini beauties. 760 Ocean Dr., South Beach. © 305/532-5650.

2 Dance Clubs, Live Music, the Gay & Lesbian Scene & Latin Clubs

DANCE CLUBS

Clubs are as much a cottage industry in Miami as is, say, cheese in Wisconsin. Clubland, as it is known, is a way of life for some. On any given night in Miami, there's something going on—no excuses are needed to throw a party here. Short of throwing a glamorous event for the grand opening of a new gas station, Miami is very party hearty, celebrating everything from the fact that it's Tuesday night to the debut of a hot new DJ. Within this very bizarre after-dark community, a colorful assortment of characters emerges, from (a)typical nine-to-fivers to shady characters who have reinvented themselves as hot shots on the club circuit. While this "see and be seen" scene may not be your cup of Absolut, it's certainly never boring.

The club music played on Miami's ever-evolving social circuit is good enough to get even the most rhythmically challenged wallflowers dancing. For aspiring DJs, a branch of the renowned **Scratch DJ Academy,** 642 6th St. (© **305/535-2599**), opened; for $300 a session, you, too, can become a master of the turntables.

To keep things fresh in Clubland, local promoters throw one-nighters, which are essentially parties with various themes or motifs, from funk to fashion. Because these change so often, we can't possibly list them here. Word of mouth, local advertising, and listings in the free weekly *New Times,* www.miami.citysearch.com, or the "Weekend" section of the *Miami Herald* are the best ways to find out about these ever-changing events.

Before you get all decked out to hit the town as soon as the sun sets, consider the fact that Miami is a very late town. Things generally don't get started here before 11pm. The Catch-22 is that if you don't arrive on South Beach early enough, you may find yourself driving around aimlessly for parking, as it is very limited outside of absurd $20 valet charges. Municipal lots fill up quickly, so your best bet is to arrive on South Beach somewhat early and kill time by strolling around, having something to eat, or sipping a cocktail in a hotel bar. Another advantage of arriving a bit earlier than the crowds is that some clubs don't charge a cover before 11pm or midnight, which could save you a wad of cash over time. Most clubs are open every night of the week, though some are open only Thursday to Sunday and others are open only Monday through Saturday. Call ahead to get the most up-to-date information possible: Things change very quickly around here, and a call in advance can help you make sure that the dance club you're planning to go to hasn't become a video arcade. Cover charges are very haphazard, too. If you're not on the ubiquitous guest list (ask your concierge to put you on the list—he or she usually has the ability to do so, which won't help you with the wait to get in, but will eliminate the cover charge), you may have to fork over a ridiculous $20 to walk

> ⎛*Tips* **Ground Rules: Stepping Out in Miami**
>
> * Nightlife on South Beach doesn't really get going until after 11pm. As a result, you may want to consider taking what is known as a disco nap so that you'll be fully charged until the wee hours.
> * If you're unsure of what to wear out on South Beach, your safest bet is anything black.
> * Do *not* try to tip the doormen manning the velvet ropes. That will only make you look desperate, and you'll find yourself standing outside for what will seem like an ungodly amount of time. Instead, try to land your name on the ever-present guest list by calling the club early in the day yourself or, better yet, having the concierge at your hotel do it for you. If you don't have connections and you find yourself without a concierge, then act assertive, not surly, at the velvet rope, and your patience will usually be rewarded with admittance. If all else fails—for men, especially—surround yourself with a few leggy model types and you'll be noticed quicker.
> * If you are a man going out with a group of men, unless you're going to a gay bar, you will most likely not get into any South Beach hot spot unless you are with women.
> * Finally, have fun. It may look like serious business when you're on the outside, but once you're in, it's another story. Attacking Clubland with a sense of humor is the best approach to a successful, memorable evening out.

past the ropes. Don't fret, though. There are many clubs and bars that have no cover charge—they just make up for it by charging $15 for a martini!

Bongo's Cuban Café   Gloria Estefan's latest hit in the restaurant business pays homage to the sights, sounds, and cuisine of pre-Castro Cuba. Bongo's is a mammoth restaurant attached to the American Airlines Arena in downtown Miami. On Friday after 11pm and Saturday after 11:30pm, it's transformed from a friendly family restaurant into the city's hottest 21-and-over salsa nightclub. Cover charges can be hefty, but consider it your ticket to an astounding show of some of the best salsa dancers in the city. Prepare yourself for standing room only. Salsa lessons are also available for those with two left feet. At the American Airlines Arena, 601 Biscayne Blvd., Downtown Miami. ℂ **786/ 777-2100.** Cover Fri $10 for guys only; Sat $20 for all.

Cameo ⨁   Still haunted by the ghost of clubs past, the space formerly known as cro-bar has undergone much-needed renovations and reopened as Cameo, its original incarnation. It's expected to once again boomerang to the top of the see-and-be-seen list with a supersonic sound system, star DJs, and plenty of VIP seating. Cameo also has a club-within-a-club upstairs known as Vice. Open Thursday through Monday from 10pm to 5am. 1445 Washington Ave., South Beach. ℂ **305/531-8225.** www.crobarmiami. com. Cover Thurs, Sun, Mon $20; Fri–Sat $25.

Club Space ⨁   Clubland hits the mainland with this cavernous downtown warehouse of a club. With more than 30,000 square feet of dance space, you can spin around à la Stevie Nicks (albeit to a techno beat) without having to worry about banging into someone. On Saturday and Sunday nights, the party usually extends to the next morning, sometimes as late as 10am. It's quite a sight to see club kids rushing off to work straight from Space on a Monday morning. Known as the venue of choice for world-renowned DJs, Club Space sometimes charges ludicrous admission fees to cover its hefty price tags. *Note:* Club Space doesn't really get going until around 3am. Call for more information, as it doesn't have a concrete schedule. 34 NE 11th St., Miami. ℭ 305/372-9378. Cover $0–$20.

Mansion A product of the same team that's behind the utterly addictive Opium Garden (see below) is a massive multilevel lounge that, according to the owners and promoters, is entirely "VIP," meaning you'd best know someone to get in or else you'll be among the masses outside and not even close to the manse.

Live DJs, models, and celebrities galore—ubiquitous Paris Hilton, Tara Reid, Shannen Doherty, N*Sync, and more—not to mention high ceilings, wood floors, brick walls, and a decidedly nonsmoky interior—make this Mansion, despite its cheesy name, a *must* on the list of see-and-be-scenesters. Open Tuesday through Sunday from 11pm to 5am. 1235 Washington Ave., South Beach. ℭ 305/531-5535. Cover varies, $10–$40.

Nikki Beach What the Playboy Mansion is to L.A., the Nikki Beach Club is to South Beach, but if you want a locals scene, you won't find it here. The allure is mostly for visiting tourists who love to gawk at their fellow half-naked ladies and men actually venturing into the daylight on Sunday (around 4pm, which is ungodly in this town) to see, be seen, and, at times, be obscene. At night, it's very "Brady Bunch goes to Hawaii," with a sexy Tiki hut/Polynesian theme style, albeit rated R. Also located within this bastion of hedonism is the second floor Club Nikki, formerly Pearl restaurant, for those who want to dance on an actual dance floor and not sand. In late 2007, Nikki expanded into Coconut Grove with Nikki Coconut Grove adjacent to the Sonesta Bayfront Hotel at 2889 McFarlane Rd. Nikki Beach Hotel and Resort's Executive Chef Brian Molloy has been tapped to open the new location after opening the club's Mexico and Marbella branches. Nikki Coconut Grove will offer the Aperitif Party every day from 4 to 7pm as well as full dinner. Nikki Coconut Grove will also include a street level, European-style deli café that will serve breakfast, lunch, and specialty coffee. After the opening, Chef de Cuisine Tommy Nguyen will take over and oversee the launch of "Amazing Sundays"—a brunch that will include a five- to seven-course experience and a la carte menu. Beginning in February, special "Themed Nights" will take food and wine enthusiasts on a culinary journey of wine-producing regions. 101 Ocean Dr., South Beach. ℭ 305/538-1111. Cover $10–$20.

Opium Garden Housed in a massive open-air space, Opium Garden is a highly addictive nocturnal habit for those looking for a combination of sexy dance music; scantily clad dancers; celebrities such as J-Lo, Janet Jackson, Lenny Kravitz, and P. Diddy; and, for the masochists out there, an oppressive door policy and two sets of velvet ropes set up to keep those deemed unworthy out of this see-and-be-sceney den of iniquity. Opium has a sushi restaurant (decent) and an ultra-VIP, celeb-saturated lounge, Prive, whose separate door policy makes the aforementioned seem like a romp in the sand. 136 Collins Ave., South Beach. ℭ 305/531-5535. Cover $20.

Winter Music Conference

Every March, Miami is besieged by the most unconventional conventioneers the city has ever seen. These fiercely dedicated souls descend upon the city in a very audible way, with dark circles under their eyes and bleeps, blips, and scratches that can wake the dead. No, we're not talking about a Star Trek convention, but, rather, the Winter Music Conference (WMC), the world's biggest and most important gathering of DJs, remixers, agents, artists, and pretty much anyone who makes a dime off of the booming electronic music industry hailing from more than 60 countries from all over the world. But unlike most conventions, this one is completely interactive and open to the paying public as South Beach and Miami's hottest clubs transform into showcases for the various audio wares. For 5 consecutive days and nights, DJs, artists, and software producers play for audiences comprised of A&R reps, talent scouts, and locals just along for the ride. Parties take place everywhere, from hotel pools to street corners. There's always something going on every hour on the hour, and most people who really get into the throes of the WMC get little or no sleep. Energy drinks become more important than water, and, for the most part, if you see people popping pills, they're not likely to be vitamins.

At any rate, the WMC is worth checking out if you get ecstatic over names such as Hex Hector, Paul Oakenfold, Ultra Nate, Chris Cox, and Mark Ronson, among many, many others. For more information on WMC events, go to www.wmcon.com. And for those who just yearn to be the next big DJ, the **Scratch DJ Academy,** 642 6th St., South Beach (℃ **305/535-2599;** www. scratch.com) is now open and ready to teach you the turntables for a whopping $300 per 70-minute course. But just think, top DJs these days make in excess of $300,000 per gig, so it may be worth the investment!

Parkwest Nightclub   A 6,000-foot dance and lounge palace, Parkwest features the usual top-of-the-line sound system and an unusual LED wall, the only one of its size in South Florida. With five bars—two of the most popular are Stero and Rehab, the club's indy-rock inspired dance lounge featuring antique gas pumps, celebrity mug shots, three bars, two levels and 2,500 square feet—VIP areas, and lounge seating throughout the space, Parkwest is for the hardcore club goer. 30 NE 11th St. Downtown Miami. ℃ 305/350-7444. Cover $20.

Pawn Shop Lounge   This former Pawn Shop is far from shabby or schlocky, but it is, perhaps, the kitschiest spot in Miami in which *Sanford and Son* meets South Beach. In addition to a full-blown big yellow school bus that doubles as a cocktail lounge, Pawn Shop boasts an Airstream Trailer in which the likes of Colin Farrell and Paris Hilton have kicked back on the couch and looked out the window at the ensuing insanity on the dance floor. Or relax in a seat located in the jetliner fuselage—actual plane seats that are surprisingly more comfy than in cattle class. Pawn Shop throws unusual parties such as the one that featured an impersonator of Larry Wilcox, "The white guy from CHiPs," and the one when Hilton debuted her album by taking over the DJ booth and screaming "I hate techno, so turn this *&* off." Alan T., the door personality—there's no other word for him—is one of the club's best attractions. Be sure to tell him we say hello. 1222 NE 2nd Ave. ⓒ 305/373-3511. Cover $10–$20.

SET   The Opium Group's undisputed "it" child, SET is *the* place to be, at least at the time of this writing. A luxurious lounge with chandeliers and design mag-worth decor is always full of trendsetters, celebs, and wannabes. Where you really want to be, however, is upstairs, in the private VIP room, where Britney Spears was seen downing purple hooter shots. A classy place that doesn't designate the behavior of its patrons, SET is also known for a ruthless door policy. Ask your hotel concierge to get you in or you may find yourself standing on the wrong side of the velvet ropes wasting precious vacation time. 320 Lincoln Rd. South Beach. ⓒ 305/531-2800. www.setmiami.com Cover $20.

SoHo Lounge *(Finds)*   This multilevel, multifaceted Design District club is tons of fun if you are into either '80s music or electroclash. Cheap drinks; a sprawling outdoor patio; and several different nooks, crannies, bars, and dance areas are available for perusal. The best area in the entire club is the two-story dance floor in which a big screen shows everything from *Tron* to anime. Music ranges from the '80s greatest hits to more obscure music from Europe. One of the best venues in town for live music, SoHo Lounge has hosted the likes of Peaches and Electro-cute, and if those names don't ring a bell, consider going to SoHo to become acquainted with them. 175 NE 36th St., Design District. ⓒ 305/576-1988. Cover $0–$10.

The White Room *(Finds)*   Yet another cavernous, warehousey cocktail hall featuring 6,0000 square feet of outdoor space and 4,500 square feet of indoor space where the long-running Brit-pop, hipster happy one-nighter Pop Life takes up residence every Saturday. 1306 N. Miami Ave., Downtown Miami. ⓒ 305/005-5050. Cover $0–$10.

LIVE MUSIC

Unfortunately, Miami's live music scene is not thriving. Instead of local bands garnering devoted fans, local DJs are more admired, skyrocketing much more easily to fame—thanks to the city's lauded dance-club scene. However, there are still several places that strive to bring Miami up to speed as far as live music is concerned. You just have to look—and listen—for it a bit more carefully. The following is a list of places where you can, from time to time, catch some live acts.

Arturo Sandoval Jazz Club *(Finds)*   The legendary Grammy Award–winning Cuban jazz great, who often plays here, opened this retro-fabulous supper club, where equally great musicians from Roberta Flack to Willie Chorino play on a weekly basis. An extensive menu featuring some of Sandoval's Latin-flavored favorites is also available.

Rock 'n' Bowl

A new kind of nightlife debuted in South Beach in 2005 in the form of **Lucky Strike Lanes**, 1691 Michigan Ave., South Beach (ⓒ 305/532-0307; www.bowl luckystrike.com), which keeps you off the streets, but in the gutters. Low lighting, glow-in-the-dark pins, and loud music keep things rolling day and night from 11am until 2am. If you're not in the mood to bowl, the restaurant and bar are always hopping, too. Games are $4.95 to $7.95 depending on the time you're there or $55 to $75 an hour; shoes are an extra $4. After 9pm, you have to be 21 and older to enter.

6701 Collins Ave. (in the Deauville Beach Resort), Miami Beach. © 305/865-5775. www.arturosandoval
jazzclub.com. Cover $15–$50.

Churchill's Hideaway *(Finds*   British expatriate Dave Daniels couldn't live in Miami
without a true English-style pub, so he opened Churchill's Hideaway, the city's premier space for live rock music. Filthy and located in a rather unsavory neighborhood,
Churchill's is committed to promoting and extending the lifeline of the lagging local
music scene. A fun no-frills crowd hangs out here. Bring earplugs with you, as it is
deafening once the music starts. Monday is open-mic night, while Wednesday is
reserved for ladies' wrestling. 5501 NE 2nd Ave., Little Haiti. © 305/757-1807. www.churchills
pub.com. Cover $0–$6.

Jazid *(Finds*   Smoky, sultry, and illuminated by flickering candelabra, Jazid is the kind
of place where you'd expect to hear Sade's "Smooth Operator" on constant rotation.
Instead, however, you'll hear live jazz (sometimes acid jazz), soul, and funk. An eclectic mix of mellow folk convenes here for a much-needed respite from the surrounding
Washington Avenue mayhem. 1342 Washington Ave., South Beach. © 305/673-9372. Cover $10.

Studio A *(Finds*   A favorite among indie music fans, downtown's Studio A is a cross
between a South Beach hotspot (check out the chandeliers) and New York's sadly
defunct punk hangout CBGB with an impressive roster of bands you'd read about in
Blender Magazine—Lady Sovereign and The Brazilian Girls, among many others. In
other words, if you're looking for mainstream music, you won't find it here. 60 NE 11th
St., Miami. © 305/358-7625. Cover $0–$20.

Tobacco Road   Al Capone used to hang out here when it was a speakeasy. Now
locals flock here to see local bands perform, as well as national acts such as George
Clinton and the P-Funk All-Stars, Koko Taylor, and the Radiators. Tobacco Road (the
proud owner of Miami's very first liquor license) is small and gritty, and meant to be
that way. Escape the smoke and sweat in the backyard patio, where air is a welcome
commodity. The downright cheap nightly specials, such as the $11 lobster on Tues-
day, are quite good and served until 2am; the bar is open until 5am. 626 S. Miami Ave.
(over the Miami Ave. Bridge near Brickell Ave.), downtown. © 305/374-1198. Cover Thurs–Sat $5–$10.

Upstairs at the Van Dyke Cafe *(Finds*   The cafe's jazz bar, located on the second
floor, resembles a classy speakeasy in which local jazz performers play to an intimate,
enthusiastic crowd of mostly adults and sophisticated young things, who often hud-
dle at the small tables until the wee hours. 846 Lincoln Rd., South Beach. © 305/534-3600.
Cover Sun–Thurs $5, Fri–Sat $10 for a seat; no cover at the bar.

THE GAY & LESBIAN SCENE

Miami and the beaches have long been host to what is called a "first-tier" gay community. Similar to the Big Apple, the Bay Area, or LaLa land, Miami has had a large alternative community since the days when Anita Bryant used her citrus power to boycott
the rise in political activism in the early '70s. Well, things have changed and Miami-
Dade now has a gay-rights ordinance.

Newcomers intending to party in any bar, whether downtown or certainly on the
beach, will want to check ahead for the schedule, as all clubs must have a gay or lesbian night to pay their rent. Miami Beach, in fact, is a capital of the gay circuit party
scene, rivaling San Francisco, Palm Springs, and even the mighty Sydney, Australia,
for tourist dollars. However, ever since South Beach got bit by the hip-hop bug, many
of Miami's gays have been crossing county lines into Fort Lauderdale, where there are,
surprisingly, many more gay establishments.

Laundry Bar   A full-service Laundromat has everyone coming clean at this gay-friendly bar off of Lincoln Road, where Thursdays and Saturdays are particularly packed with people willing and ready to air their dirty laundry. 721 Lincoln Lane, South Beach. ℭ 305/531-7700.

Score   There's a reason this Lincoln Road hotbed of gay activity is called Score. In addition to the huge pick-up scene, Score offers a multitude of bars, dance floors, lounge areas, and outdoor tables, in case you need to come up for air. Sunday afternoon tea dances are legendary. 727 Lincoln Rd., South Beach. ℭ 305/535-1111.

Twist   One of the most popular bars (and hideaways) on South Beach, this recently expanded bar (which is literally right across the street from the police station) has a casual yet lively atmosphere. 1057 Washington Ave., South Beach. ℭ 305/538-9478.

LATIN CLUBS

Considering that Hispanics make up a large part of Miami's population and that there's a huge influx of Spanish-speaking visitors, it's no surprise that there are some great Latin nightclubs in the city. Plus, with the meteoric rise of the international music scene based in Miami, many international stars come through the offices of MTV Latino, SONY International, and a multitude of Latin TV studios based in Miami—and they're all looking for a good club scene on weekends. Most of the Anglo clubs also reserve at least 1 night a week for Latin rhythms.

Casa Panza *Finds*   This *casa* is one of Little Havana's liveliest and most popular nightspots. Every Tuesday, Thursday, and Saturday night, Casa Panza, in the heart of Little Havana, becomes the House of Flamenco, with shows at 8 and 11pm. You can either enjoy a flamenco show or strap on your own dancing shoes and participate in the celebration. Enjoy a fantastic Spanish meal before the show, or just a glass of sangria before you start stomping. Open until 4am, Casa Panza is a hotspot for young Latin club kids and, occasionally, a few older folks who are so taken by the music and the scene that they've failed to realize it's well past their bedtime. 1620 SW 8th St. (Calle Ocho), Little Havana. ℭ 305/643-5343.

Hoy Como Ayer   Formerly known as Cafe Nostalgia, the Little Havana hangout dedicated to reminiscing about Old Cuba, Hoy Como Ayer is like the Brady Bunch of Latin hangouts—while it was extremely popular with old-timers in its Cafe Nostalgia incarnation, it is now experiencing a resurgence among the younger generation seeking its own brand of nostalgia. Its Thursday night party, Fuacata (slang for "Pow!"), is a magnet for Latin hipsters, featuring classic Cuban music mixed in with modern DJ-spun sound effects. Open Thursday to Sunday from 9pm to 4am. 2212 SW 8th St. (Calle Ocho), Little Havana. ℭ 305/541-2631. Cover Thurs–Sun $10.

La Covacha *Finds*   This hut, located virtually in the middle of nowhere (West Miami), is the hottest Latin joint in the entire city. Sunday features the best in Latin rock, with local and international acts. But the shack is really jumping on weekend nights, when the place is open until 5am. Friday is *the* night here, so much so that the owners had to place a red velvet rope out front to maintain some semblance of order. It's an amusing sight—a velvet rope guarding a shack—but once you get in, you'll understand the need for it. Do not wear silk here, as you *will* sweat. 10730 NW 25th St. (at NW 107th Ave.), West Miami. ℭ 305/594-3717. Cover $0–$10.

Mango's Tropical Café   Claustrophobic types do not want to go near Mango's—ever. One of the most popular spots on Ocean Drive, this outdoor enclave of Latin

The Rhythm Is Gonna Get You

Are you feeling shy about hitting a Latin club because you fear your two left feet will stand out? Then take a few lessons from one of the following dance companies or dance teachers. They offer individual and group lessons to dancers of any origin who are willing to learn. These folks have made it their mission to teach merengue and flamenco to non-Latinos and Latino left-foots, and are among the most reliable, consistent, and popular ones in Miami. So what are you waiting for?

Thursday and Friday nights at **Bongo's Cuban Café** (American Airlines Arena, 601 Biscayne Blvd., downtown; ℭ **786/777-2100**) are amazing showcases for some of the city's best salsa dancers, but amateurs need not be intimidated, thanks to the instructors at Latin Groove Dance Studios, who are on hand to help you with your two left feet. Lessons are free.

At **Ballet Flamenco La Rosa** (in the Performing Arts Network [PAN] building, 13126 W. Dixie Hwy., North Miami; ℭ **305/899-7730**), you can learn to flamenco, salsa, or merengue. This is the only professional flamenco company in the area. $15 per class.

Nobody teaches salsa like **Luz Pinto** (ℭ **305/868-9418**). She teaches 7 days a week and, trust me, with her you'll learn cool turns easily. She charges $45 for a private lesson for up to four people, and $10 per person for a group lesson. She also teaches group classes at PAN on Miami Beach. Although she teaches everything from classic and hip wedding dances and from ballroom to merengue, her specialty is Casino-style salsa, popularized in the 1950s in Cuba, Luz's homeland. You will be impressed with how well and quickly Luz can teach you to have fun and feel great dancing. Call her for more information. **Angel Arroyo** has been teaching salsa to the clueless out of his home (at 16467 NE 27th Ave., North Miami Beach; ℭ **305/949-7799**) for the past 10 years. Just $10 will buy you an hour's time. He traditionally teaches Monday and Wednesday nights, but call ahead to check for any schedule changes.

liveliness shakes with the intensity of a Richter-busting earthquake. Mango's is *Cabaret,* Latin style. Nightly live Brazilian and other Latin music, not to mention scantily clad male and female dancers, draws huge gawking crowds in from the sidewalk. But pay attention to the music, if you can: Incognito international musicians often lose their anonymity and jam with the house band on stage. Open daily from 11am to 5am. 900 Ocean Dr., South Beach. ℭ 305/673-4422. Cover $5–$15.

3 The Performing Arts

Highbrows and culture vultures complain that there is a dearth of decent cultural offerings in Miami. What do locals tell them? Go back to New York! In all seriousness, however, in recent years, Miami's performing arts scene has improved greatly. The city's Broadway Series features Tony Award–winning shows (the touring versions, of course), which aren't always Broadway caliber, but usually pretty good and not nearly as pricey. Local arts groups such as the Miami Light Project, a not-for-profit cultural organization that presents live performances by innovative dance, music, and theater artists, have had huge success in attracting big-name artists such as Nina Simone and Philip Glass to Miami. Also, a burgeoning bohemian movement in Little Havana has given way to performance spaces that are nightclubs in their own right.

THEATER

The **Actors' Playhouse,** a musical theater at the newly restored Miracle Theater at 280 Miracle Mile, Coral Gables (℃ **305/444-9293;** www.actorsplayhouse.org), is a grand 1948 Art Deco movie palace with a 600-seat main theater and a smaller theater/rehearsal hall that hosts a number of excellent musicals for children throughout the year. In addition to these two theaters, the Playhouse recently added a 300-seat children's balcony theater. Tickets run from $27 to $40.

The **Coconut Grove Playhouse,** 3500 Main Hwy., Coconut Grove (℃ **305/442-4000;** www.cgplayhouse.org), is also a former movie house, built in 1927 in an ornate Spanish rococo style. Because of budget issues, the Playhouse's 2007 season was canceled, but the place has such a faithful following that city leaders and locals have worked to save the landmark, which promises to have its curtains up in the near future.

The **Gables Stage,** at the Biltmore Hotel (p. 105), Anastasia Avenue, Coral Gables (℃ **305/445-1119**), stages at least one Shakespearean play, one classic, and one contemporary piece a year. This well-regarded theater usually tries to secure the rights to a national or local premiere as well. Tickets cost $35 for adults, and $15 and $32, respectively, for students and seniors.

The **Jerry Herman Ring Theatre** is on the main campus of the University of Miami in Coral Gables (℃ **305/284-3355**). The University's Department of Theater Arts uses this stage for advanced-student productions of comedies, dramas, and musicals. Faculty and guest actors are regularly featured, as are contemporary works by local playwrights. Performances are usually scheduled Tuesday through Saturday during the academic year. In the summer, don't miss "Summer Shorts," a selection of superb one act plays. Tickets sell for $14 to $16.

The **New Theater,** 4120 Laguna St., Coral Gables (℃ **305/443-5909**), prides itself on showing renowned works from America and Europe. As the name implies, you'll find mostly contemporary plays, with a few classics thrown in. Performances are staged Thursday through Sunday year-round. Tickets are $35 on Thursday, $40 on Friday and Saturday, and $35 to $40 on Sunday. If tickets are available on the day of the performance—and they usually are—students pay half-price.

CLASSICAL MUSIC

In addition to a number of local orchestras and operas (see below), which regularly offer quality music and world-renowned guest artists, each year brings a slew of classical-music special events and touring artists to Miami. The **Concert Association of Florida** (**CAF;** ℃ **877/433-3200**) produces one of the most important and longest-running series. Known for more than a quarter of a century for its high-caliber, star-packed schedules, CAF regularly arranges the best "serious" music concerts for the city. Season after season, the schedules are punctuated by world-renowned dance companies and seasoned virtuosi such as Itzhak Perlman, Andre Watts, and Kathleen Battle. Since CAF does not have its own space, performances are usually scheduled in the Miami-Dade County Auditorium or the Jackie Gleason Theater of the Performing Arts (see "Major Venues," below). The season lasts October through April, and ticket prices range from $20 to $70.

Florida Philharmonic Orchestra   South Florida's premier symphony orchestra, under the direction of James Judd, presents a full season of classical and pops programs interspersed with several children's and contemporary popular music performances. The Philharmonic performs downtown in the Gusman Center for the Performing Arts and at the Miami-Dade County Auditorium (see "Major Venues," below). 4120 Leguna St., Coral Gables. (C) 800/226-1812. Tickets $15–$60. When extra tickets are available, students are admitted free on day of performance.

Miami Chamber Symphony   This professional orchestra is a small, subscription-series orchestra that's not affiliated with any major arts organizations and is therefore an inexpensive alternative to the high-priced classical venues. Renowned international soloists perform regularly here. The season runs October to May, and most concerts are held in the Gusman Concert Hall, on the University of Miami campus. 5690 N. Kendall Dr., Kendall. (C) 305/284-6477. Tickets $12–$30.

New World Symphony   This organization, led by artistic director Michael Tilson Thomas, is a stepping stone for gifted young musicians seeking professional careers. The orchestra specializes in innovative, energetic performances, and often features renowned guest soloists and conductors. The season lasts from October to May, during which time there are many free concerts. 541 Lincoln Rd., South Beach. (C) 305/673-3331. www.nws.org. Tickets free–$58. Rush tickets (remaining tickets sold 1 hr. before performance) $20. Students $10 (1 hr. before concerts; limited seating).

OPERA

Florida Grand Opera   Around for more than 60 years, this company regularly features singers from top houses in both America and Europe. All productions are sung in their original language and staged with projected English supertitles. Tickets become scarce when Placido Domingo or another opera luminary comes to town. The season runs roughly from November to April, with five performances each week. In 2007, the opera moved into more upscale headquarters in the Sanford and Dolores Ziff Ballet Opera House at the **Arsht Center** (Carnival Center) for the Performing Arts. Box office: 1300 Biscayne Blvd. Miami. (C) 305/949-6722. www.fgo.org. Tickets $24–$125. Student discounts available.

DANCE

Several local dance companies train and perform in the Greater Miami area. In addition, top traveling troupes regularly stop at the venues listed below. Keep your eyes open for special events and guest artists.

Ballet Flamenco La Rosa   For a taste of local Latin flavor, see this lively troupe perform impressive flamenco and other styles of Latin dance on Miami stages. (They also teach Latin dancing—see "The Rhythm Is Gonna Get You," above.) 13126 W. Dixie Hwy., North Miami, (C) 305/899-7729. Tickets $25 at door; $20 in advance; $18 for students and seniors.

Miami City Ballet   This artistically acclaimed and innovative company, directed by Edward Villella, features a repertoire of more than 60 ballets, many by George Balanchine, and has had more than 20 world premieres. The company's three-story center features eight rehearsal rooms, a ballet school, a boutique, and ticket offices. The City Ballet season runs from September to April. Ophelia and Juan Jr. Roca Center, Collins Ave. and 22nd St., South Beach. (C) 305/929-7000 or 305/929-7010 for box office. Tickets $17–$50.

MAJOR VENUES

The **Colony Theater,** on Lincoln Road in South Beach (© 305/674-1040), which has become an architectural showpiece of the Art Deco District, opened in 2006 after a $4.3-million renovation that added wing and fly space, improved access for those with disabilities, and restored the lobby to its original Art Deco look.

At the **Miami-Dade County Auditorium,** West Flagler Street at 29th Avenue, Southwest Miami (© 305/547-5414), performers gripe about the lack of space, but for patrons, this 2,430-seat auditorium is the only Miami space in which you can hear the opera—for now. A multimillion-dollar performing arts center downtown has been in the works for years (see below), but for now, the Auditorium is home to the city's Florida Grand Opera, and it also stages productions by the Concert Association of Florida, many programs in Spanish, and a variety of other shows.

At the 1,700-seat **Gusman Center for the Performing Arts,** 174 E. Flagler St., downtown Miami (© 305/372-0925), seating is tight, and so is funding, but the sound is superb. In addition to hosting the Florida Philharmonic Orchestra and the Miami Film Festival, the elegant Gusman Center features pop concerts, plays, film screenings, and special events. The auditorium was built as the Olympia Theater in 1926, and its ornate palace interior is typical of that era, complete with fancy columns, a huge pipe organ, and twinkling "stars" on the ceiling.

Not to be confused with the Gusman Center (above), the **Gusman Concert Hall,** 1314 Miller Dr. at 14th Street, Coral Gables (© 305/284-6477), is a roomy 600-seat hall that gives a stage to the Miami Chamber Symphony and a varied program of university recitals.

The newly revamped **Fillmore Miami Beach** at the **Jackie Gleason Theater,** located in South Beach at Washington Avenue and 17th Street (© 305/673-7300; www.gleasontheater.com), may be a mouthful, but when it comes to live music, it truly rocks. In addition to its very modern Hard Rock meets Miami Beach décor, complete with requisite bars, chandeliers, and an homage to the original legendary Fillmore in San Francisco, Fillmore, which was taken over by Live Nation, brings major talent to the beach, from Kid Rock and Fall Out Boy to comediennes Sara Silverman and Lisa Lampanelli. Fillmore also hosts various awards shows, from the Food Network Awards to the Fox Sports Awards.

Last, but definitely not least, **The Arsht Center for the Performing Arts** (formerly Carnival Center), 1300 Biscayne Blvd. (© 786/468-2000), opened in late 2006 after a whopping $446-million tab. The 2,400-seat **Sanford and Dolores Ziff Ballet Opera House** and the 2,200-seat **Knight Concert Hall** are Miami venues for the **Concert Association of Florida, Florida Grand Opera, Miami City Ballet,** and **New World Symphony,** as well as premier venues for a wide array of local, national, and international performances, ranging from Broadway musicals and visiting classical artists to world and urban music, Latin concerts, and popular entertainment from many cultures. The **Studio Theater,** a flexible black-box space designed for up to 200 seats, hosts intimate performances of contemporary theater, dance, music, cabaret, and other entertainment. The **Peacock Education Center** acts as a catalyst for arts education and enrichment programs for children and adults. Finally, the **Plaza for the Arts** is a magnificent setting for outdoor entertainment, social celebrations, and informal community gatherings.

Designed by world-renowned architect Cesar Pelli, it is the focal point of a planned Arts, Media, and Entertainment District in mid-Miami. The complex is wrapped in limestone, slate, decorative stone, stainless steel, glass curtain walls, and tropical land-scaping, and was completed in mid-2006. The biggest joke in town, however, is that after spending all that money, the planners forgot to include parking facilities. As a result, valet parking is available for $10 to $20 or you can park at the Marriott nearby, but it's truly a pain, so to make things easy, just take a cab. It'll cost you the same and you won't have to deal with traipsing across Biscayne Boulevard in your fine theater threads. For more information, check out the website at www.carnivalcenter.org.

4 Cinemas, the Literary Scene, Spectator Sports & a Video Arcade

CINEMAS

In addition to the annual Miami Film Festival in February and other, smaller film events, Miami has nearly as many multiplex cinemas as it does palm trees. But if 40 screens of *Jurassic Park III* aren't your idea of a day at the movies, consider the follow-ing artsy theaters, known for showing lots of subtitled, foreign films as well as those that get bumped off the big screen by the *Jurassic Parks* of the celluloid world.

Bill Cosford Cinema, at the University of Miami, is on the second floor of the memorial building off Campo Sano Avenue (© **305/284-4861**). This well-endowed little theater has been revamped and boasts high-tech projectors, air-conditioning, and a new decor. It sponsors independent films as well as lectures by visiting filmmakers and movie stars. It also hosts the African American Film Festival, a Student Film Fes-tival, and collaborations with the Fort Lauderdale Festival (a very small film festival). Admission is $6; seniors pay $3.

Miami Beach Cinematheque, 508 Española Way (© **305/673-4567;** www.mb cinema.com), is the kind of place where people who call movies "films" like to hang out, with comfy couches and very arty, foreign, domestic, and classic flicks. Admission ranges from $8 to $10.

THE LITERARY SCENE

Books & Books, in Coral Gables at 265 Aragon Ave. and in Miami Beach at 933 Lin-coln Rd., hosts readings almost every night and is known for attracting such top authors as Colleen McCullough, Jamaica Kincaid, and Martin Amis. For details on their free readings, call © **305/442-4408.** (Also see p. 201 for more information on the shop.)

To hear more about what's happening on Miami's literary scene, tune into the "Cover to Cover" radio show, broadcast at 8pm on Mondays on public radio station WLRN (91.3 FM).

SPECTATOR SPORTS

For information on watching baseball, basketball, football, horse racing, ice hockey, and jai alai (many of these games are at night), see "Spectator Sports" on p. 191.

VIDEO ARCADE

GameWorks *(Kids* At Steven Spielberg's SEGA GameWorks in the Shops at Sunset Place, you'll see people fighting off dinosaurs from *Jurassic Park,* racing in the Indy 500, swooshing down a snowy ski trail, throwing darts, and shooting pool in this mul-tilevel playground. The young and the young-at-heart will find a good combination of vintage arcade games, high-tech videos, virtual-reality arenas, pool tables, food, and cocktails in this playground occupying more than 33,000 square feet. Bring lots—and we mean lots—of change. Open Sunday and Monday from 11am to 11pm; Tuesday through Thursday from noon to 11pm; and Friday and Saturday from 11am to 2am. 5701 Sunset Dr., South Miami. © 305/667-4263. www.gameworks.com. Games 50¢–$5.

5 Late-Night Bites

Although some dining spots in Miami stop serving at 10pm, many are open very late or even around the clock—especially on weekends. So, if it's 4am and you need a quick bite after clubbing, don't fret. There are a vast number of pizza places lining Washington Avenue in South Beach that are open past 6am. Especially good are **La Sandwichorie,** 229 14th St. (behind the Amoco station; © **305/532-8934**), which serves up a great late-night sandwich until 5am; and its next-door neighbor **San Loco Tacos** (235 14th St.; © **305/538-3009**), which slings tacos until 5am on weeknights and 6am on weekends. Another place of note for night owls is the **News Café,** 800 Ocean Dr. (© **305/538-6397**), a trendy and well-priced cafe that has an enormous menu offering great all-day breakfasts, Middle Eastern platters, fruit bowls, or steak and potatoes—and everything is served 24 hours a day. If you're craving a corned beef on rye at 5am, **Jerry's Famous Deli,** 1450 Collins Ave. (© **305/534-3244**), is open 24/7. If your night out was at one of the Latin clubs around town, stop in at **Versailles,** 3555 SW 8th St. (© **305/444-0240**), in Little Havana. What else but a Cuban *medianoche* (midnight sandwich) will do? It's not open all night, but its hours extend well past midnight—usually until 3 or 4am on weekends—to cater to gangs of revelers, young and old.

For a more thorough listing of Miami's most notable restaurants, see chapter 7.

11

The Everglades & Biscayne National Park

President Harry S. Truman once declared the Everglades "an irreplaceable primitive area." While those words don't exactly do justice to the Everglades and the surrounding Biscayne National Park, he clarified what he said: "Here are no lofty peaks seeking the sky, no mighty glaciers or rushing streams wearing away the uplifted land. Here is land, tranquil in its quiet beauty, serving not as the source of water, but as the last receiver of it. To its natural abundance we owe the spectacular plant and animal life that distinguishes this place from all others in our country."

There's no better reality show than the one that exists in the Everglades. Up-close-and-personal views of alligators, crocodiles, and bona fide wildlife—not the kind you'd find on, say, South Beach, after midnight—make for an interesting, photo-opportunistic experience that's worthy of a show on Animal Planet.

Tourists in South Florida shouldn't leave the area without taking time to see some of the wild plant and animal life in the swampy Everglades and the underwater treasures of Biscayne National Park.

1 A Glimpse of Everglades National Park ★★

35 miles SW of Miami

Before visiting it, my conception of the Everglades was that it was one big swamp swarming with ominous creatures, like something from the programming geeks at the SciFi Network. For someone who'd rather endure an endless series of root canals than audition for a role on *Survivor* (the closest I'd ever been to nature was sleep-away camp), the Everglades might as well have been the *Never*glades—that is, until I finally decided to venture there. To my surprise, and contrary to popular belief, the Everglades isn't really a swamp at all, but one of the country's most fascinating natural resources.

For first-timers or those with dubious athletic skills, the best way to see the 'Glades is probably via airboats, which aren't actually allowed in the park proper, but cut through the saw grass on the park's outskirts, taking you past countless birds, alligators, crocodiles, deer, and raccoons. A walk on one of the park's many trails will provide you with a different vantage point: up-close interaction with an assortment of tame wildlife. But the absolutely best way to see the 'Glades is via canoe, which allows you to get incredibly close to nature. Whichever method you choose, I guarantee that you will marvel at the sheer beauty of the Everglades. Despite the multitude of mosquito bites (the bugs seem to be immune to repellent—wear long pants and cover your arms), an Everglades experience will definitely contribute to a newfound appreciation for Florida's natural (and beautiful) wonderland.

This vast and unusual ecosystem is actually a shallow, 40-mile-wide, slow-moving river. Rarely more than knee-deep, the water is the lifeblood of this wilderness, and the subtle shifts in water level dictate the life cycles of the native plants and animals. In 1947, 1.5 million acres—less than 20% of the Everglades' wilderness—were established as Everglades National Park. At that time, few lawmakers understood how neighboring ecosystems relate to each other. Consequently, the park is heavily affected by surrounding territories and is at the butt end of every environmental insult that occurs upstream in Miami.

> ### Lazy River
> It takes a month for 1 gallon of water to move through Everglades National Park.

While there has been a marked decrease in the indigenous wildlife here, Everglades National Park nevertheless remains one of the few places where you can see dozens of endangered species in their natural habitat, including the swallowtail butterfly, American crocodile, leatherback turtle, southern bald eagle, West Indian manatee, and Florida panther.

Take your time on the trails, and a hypnotic beauty begins to unfold. Follow the rustling of a bush, and you might see a small green tree frog or tiny brown anole lizard, with its bright-red spotted throat. Crane your neck to see around a bend, and discover a delicate, brightly painted mule-ear orchid.

The slow and subtle splendor of this exotic land may not be immediately appealing to kids raised on video games and rapid-fire commercials, but they'll certainly remember the experience and thank you for it later. Your kids will find plenty of dramatic fun around the park, such as airboat rides, hiking, and biking, to keep them satisfied for at least a day.

JUST THE FACTS

GETTING THERE & ACCESS POINTS   Although the Everglades may seem overwhelmingly large and unapproachable, it's easy to get to the park's two main areas—the northern section, accessible via Shark Valley and Everglades City, and the southern section, accessible through the Ernest F. Coe Visitor Center, near Homestead and Florida City.

Northern Entrances   A popular day trip for Miamians, **Shark Valley,** a 15-mile paved loop road (with an observation tower in the middle of the loop) overlooking the pulsating heart of the Everglades, is the easiest and most scenic way to explore the national park. Just 25 miles west of the Florida Turnpike, Shark Valley is best reached via the Tamiami Trail, South Florida's pre-turnpike, two-lane road, which cuts across the southern part of the state along the park's northern border. Roadside attractions (boat rides and alligator farms, for example) along the Tamiami Trail are operated by the Miccosukee Indian Village and are worth a quick, fun stop. An excellent tram tour (leaving from the Shark Valley Visitor Center) goes deep into the park along a trail that's also terrific for biking. Shark Valley is about an hour's drive from Miami.

A little less than 10 miles west along the Tamiami Trail from Shark Valley, you'll discover **Big Cypress National Preserve,** in which stretches of vibrant green cypress and pine trees make for a fabulous Kodak moment. If you pick up S.R. 29 and head south from the Tamiami Trail, you'll hit a modified version of civilization in the form of Everglades City (where the Everglades meet the Gulf of Mexico), where there's another entrance to the park and the **Gulf Coast Visitor Center.** From Miami to Shark Valley:

The Everglades

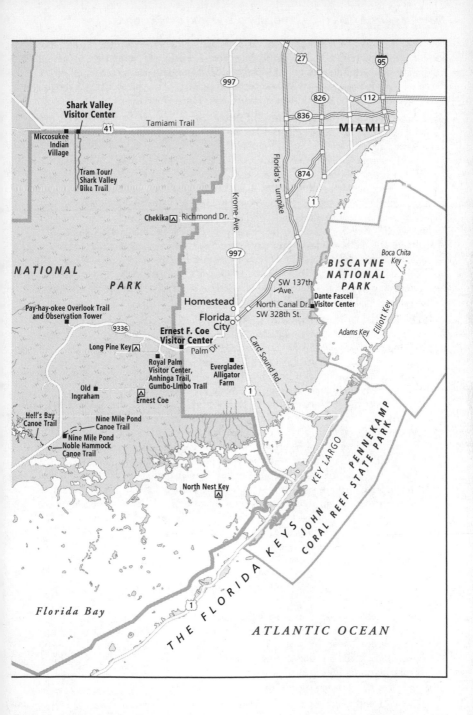

Shark Valley
Visitor Center

Miccosukee
Indian
Village

Tamiami Trail

Tram Tour/
Shark Valley
Dike Trail

MIAMI

27

95

997

41

826

836

112

874

Florida's Turnpike

1

Chekika   Richmond Dr.

Krome Ave.

997

NATIONAL

PARK

Pay-hay-okee Overlook Trail
and Observation Tower

9336

Long Pine Key

Old
Ingraham

Hell's Bay
Canoe Trail

Nine Mile Pond
Canoe Trail

Nine Mile Pond

Noble Hammock
Canoe Trail

North Nest Key

SW 137th
Ave.

North Canal Dr.
SW 328th St.

BISCAYNE
NATIONAL
PARK

Boca Chita
Key

Dante Fascell
Visitor Center

Elliott Key

Adams Key

Homestead

Florida
City

Ernest F. Coe
Visitor Center

Palm Dr.

Royal Palm
Visitor Center,
Anhinga Trail,
Gumbo-Limbo Trail

Ernest Coe

Everglades
Alligator
Farm

Card Sound Rd

1

KEY LARGO

PENNEKAMP

JOHN

CORAL REEF STATE PARK

THE FLORIDA KEYS

1

Florida Bay

ATLANTIC OCEAN

233

Go west on I-395 to S.R. 821 South (the Florida Tpk.). Take the U.S. 41/SW 8th Street (Tamiami Trail) exit. The Shark Valley entrance is just 25 miles west. To get to Everglades City, continue west on the Tamiami Trail and head south on S.R. 29. Everglades City is approximately a 2½-hour drive from Miami, but because it is scenic, it may take longer if you stop or slow down to view your surroundings.

Southern Entrance (via Homestead & Florida City)   If you're in a rush to hit the 'Glades and don't care about the scenic route, this is your best bet. Just southeast of Homestead and Florida City, off S.R. 9336, the southern access to the park will bring you directly to the Ernest F. Coe Visitor Center. Right inside the park, 3 miles beyond the Ernest F. Coe Visitor Center, is the Royal Palm Visitor Center, which is the starting point for the two most popular walking trails, Gumbo Limbo and Anhinga, where you'll witness a plethora of birds and wildlife roaming freely, unperturbed by human voyeurs. Thirteen miles west of the Ernest F. Coe Visitor Center, you'll hit Pa-hay-okee Overlook Trail, which is worth a trek across the boardwalk to reach the observation tower, over which vultures and hawks hover protectively amid a resplendent, picturesque, bird's-eye view of the Everglades. From Miami to the southern entrance: Go west on I-395 to S.R. 821 South (Florida Tpk.), which will end in Florida City. Take the first right through the center of town (you can't miss it) and follow signs to the park entrance on S.R. 9336. The Ernest F. Coe Visitor Center is about 1½ hours from Miami.

VISITOR CENTERS & INFORMATION   General inquiries and specific questions should be directed to **Everglades National Park Headquarters,** 40001 S.R. 9336, Homestead, FL 33034 (© **305/242-7700**). Ask for a copy of *Parks and Preserves,* a free newspaper that's filled with up-to-date information about goings-on in the Everglades. Headquarters is staffed by helpful phone operators daily from 8:30am to 4:30pm. You can also try www.nps.gov/ever/visit/index.htm.

Note that all hours listed are for the high season, generally November through May. During the slow summer months, many offices and outfitters keep abbreviated hours. Always call ahead to confirm hours of operation.

The **Ernest F. Coe Visitor Center,** located at the Park Headquarters entrance, west of Homestead and Florida City, is the best place to gather information for your trip. In addition to details on tours and boat rentals, and free brochures outlining trails, wildlife, and activities, you will find state-of-the-art educational displays, films, and interactive exhibits. A gift shop sells postcards, film, an impressive selection of books about the Everglades, unusual gift items, and a supply of your most important gear: insect repellent. The shop is open daily from 8am to 5pm.

The **Royal Palm Visitor Center,** a small nature museum located 3 miles past the park's main entrance, is a smaller information center. The museum is not great (its displays are equipped with recordings about the park's ecosystem), but the center is the departure point for the popular Anhinga and Gumbo Limbo trails. The center is open daily from 8am to 4pm.

Knowledgeable rangers, who provide brochures and personal insight into the park's activities, also staff the **Flamingo Visitor Center,** 38 miles from the main entrance, at the park's southern access, with natural-history exhibits and information on visitor services, and the **Shark Valley Visitor Center,** at the park's northern entrance. Both are open daily from 8:30am to 5pm.

ENTRANCE FEES, PERMITS & REGULATIONS   Permits and passes can be purchased only at the main park or Shark Valley entrance station. Even if you are just visiting the park for an afternoon, you'll need to buy a 7-day permit, which costs $10 per

Glades in the Spotlight

ABC's canceled television series *Invasion* may have been shot mostly on a set in Los Angeles, but its creator, Shaun Cassidy, a Florida resident and, yes, *that* Shaun Cassidy, has been to the Everglades and is as intrigued as the rest of us. "It's a very primordial place," Cassidy said in a magazine interview. "There are a lot of species that have existed there that have not existed anywhere else. It's a place that was cut off from the rest of the world for a very long time."

vehicle. Pedestrians and cyclists are charged $5 each. An Everglades Park Pass, valid for a year's worth of unlimited admissions, is available for $25. You may also purchase a 12-month National Parks Pass for $50, which is valid for entrance into any U.S. national park. U.S. citizens age 62 and older pay only $10 for a Golden Age Passport that's valid for life. A Golden Access Passport is available free to U.S. citizens with disabilities.

Permits are required for campers to stay overnight either in the backcountry or at the primitive campsites. See "Camping in the Everglades," on p. 240.

Those who want to fish without a charter captain must obtain a standard State of Florida saltwater fishing license. These are available in the park at Flamingo Lodge (if it's open, see p. 238) or at any tackle shop or sporting goods store nearby. Nonresidents pay $30 for a 7-day license or $17 for a 3-day license. Florida residents pay $17 for an annual fishing license. Snook and crawfish licenses must be purchased separately at a cost of $2 each.

Charter captains carry vessel licenses that cover all paying passengers, but ask to be sure. Freshwater fishing licenses are available at various bait-and-tackle stores outside the park at the same rates as those offered inside the park. A good one nearby is **Don's Bait & Tackle,** 30710 S. Federal Hwy., right on U.S. 1 in Homestead (© **305/247-6616**). *Note:* Most of the area's freshwater fishing, limited to murky canals and artificial lakes near housing developments, is hardly worth the trouble when so much good saltwater fishing is available.

SEASONS   There are two distinct seasons in the Everglades: high season and mosquito season. High season is also dry season and lasts from late November to May. Most winters here are warm, sunny, and breezy—a good combination for keeping the bugs away. This is the best time to visit because low water levels attract the largest variety of wading birds and their predators. As the dry season wanes, wildlife follows the receding water; by the end of May, the only living things you are sure to spot will make you itch. The worst, called "no-see-ums," are not even swattable. If you choose to visit during the buggy season, be vigilant in applying bug spray. Also, realize that many establishments and operators either close or curtail offerings in summer, so always call ahead to check schedules.

RANGER PROGRAMS   More than 50 ranger programs, free with entry, are offered each month during high season and give visitors an opportunity to gain an expert's perspective. Ranger-led walks and talks are offered year-round from Royal Palm Visitor Center, and at the Flamingo and Gulf Coast visitor centers, as well as Shark Valley Visitor Center during winter months. Park rangers tend to be helpful, well informed, and good humored. Some programs occur regularly, such as Royal Palm Visitor Center's Glade Glimpses, a walking tour on which rangers point out flora and fauna and discuss issues affecting the Everglades' survival. Tours are scheduled at

Warning!

High levels of mercury have been found in Everglades' bass and in some fish species in northern Florida Bay. Do not eat bass caught north of the Main Park Road. Do not eat bass caught south of the Main Park Road more than once a week. Children and pregnant women should not eat any bass. The following salt-water species caught in northern Florida Bay should not be consumed more than once per week by adults or once per month by women of child-bearing age and children: spotted sea trout, gaff-topsail, catfish, bluefish, crevalle jack, or ladyfish.

1:30pm daily. The Anhinga Amble, a similar program that takes place on the Anhinga Trail, starts at 10:30am daily. Since times, programs, and locations vary from month to month, check the schedule, available at any of the visitor centers.

SAFETY   There are many dangers inherent in this vast wilderness area. *Always* let someone know your itinerary before you set out on an extended hike. It's mandatory that you file an itinerary when camping overnight in the backcountry (which you can do when you apply for your overnight permit at either the Flamingo Visitor Center or the Gulf Coast Visitor Center). When you're on the water, watch for weather changes; severe thunderstorms and high winds often develop rapidly. Swimming is not recommended because of the presence of alligators, sharks, and barracudas. Watch out for the region's four indigenous poisonous snakes: diamondback and pygmy rattlesnakes, coral snakes (identifiable by their colorful rings), and water moccasins (which swim on the surface of the water). Bring insect repellent to ward off mosquitoes and biting flies. First aid is available from park rangers. The nearest hospital is in Homestead, 10 miles from the park's main entrance.

SEEING THE HIGHLIGHTS

Shark Valley, a 15-mile paved road (ideal for biking) through the Everglades, provides a fine introduction to the wonders of the park, but don't plan on spending more than a few hours here. Bicycling and taking a guided tram tour (p. 240) are fantastic ways to cover the highlights.

If you want to see a greater array of plant and animal life, make sure that you venture into the park through the main entrance, pick up a trail map, and dedicate at least a day to exploring from there.

Stop first along the Anhinga and Gumbo Limbo trails, which start right next to each other, 3 miles from the park's main entrance. These trails provide a thorough introduction to Everglades' flora and fauna and are highly recommended to first-time visitors. Each is a .5-mile round-trip. **Gumbo Limbo Trail** (my pick for best walking trail in the Everglades) meanders through a gorgeous, shaded, junglelike hammock of gumbo-limbo trees, royal palms, ferns, orchids, air plants, and a general blanket of vegetation, though it doesn't put you in close contact with much wildlife. **Anhinga Trail** is one of the most popular trails in the park because of its abundance of wildlife: There's more water and wildlife in this area than in most parts of the Everglades, especially during dry season. Alligators, lizards, turtles, river otters, herons, egrets, and other animals abound, making this one of the best trails for seeing wildlife. Arrive early to spot the widest selection of exotic birds, such as the Anhinga bird, the trail's namesake, a large black fishing bird so accustomed to humans that many of them build their nests in plain view. Take your time—at least an hour is recommended for each trail. Both are wheelchair accessible. If you treat the trails and modern boardwalk as pathways to get through quickly, rather than destinations to experience and savor, you'll miss out on the still beauty and hidden treasures that await you.

To get closer to nature, a few hours in a canoe along any of the trails allows paddlers the chance to sense the park's fluid motion and to become a part of the ecosphere. Visitors who choose this option end up feeling more like explorers than observers. (See "Sports & Outdoor Activities," below.)

No matter which option you choose (and there are many), I strongly recommend staying for the 7pm program, available during high season at the Long Pine Key Amphitheater. This ranger-led talk and slide show will give you a detailed overview of the park's history, natural resources, wildlife, and threats to its survival.

SPORTS & OUTDOOR ACTIVITIES

BIKING   The relatively flat, 38-mile paved **Main Park Road** is great for biking because of the multitude of hardwood hammocks (treelike islands or dense stands of hardwood trees that grow only a few inches above land) and a dwarf cypress forest (stunted and thinly distributed cypress trees, which grow in poor soil on drier land).

Shark Valley, however, is the best biking trail by far. If the park isn't flooded from excess rain (which it often is, especially in spring), this is South Florida's most scenic bicycle trail. Many locals haul their bikes out to the 'Glades for a relaxing day of wilderness-trail riding. You'll share the flat, paved road only with other bikers, trams, and a menagerie of wildlife. (Don't be surprised to see a gator lounging in the sun or a deer munching on some grass. Otters, turtles, alligators, and snakes are common companions in the Shark Valley area.) There are no shortcuts, so if you become tired or are unable to complete the entire 15-mile trip, turn around and return on the same road. Allow 2 to 3 hours to bike the entire loop.

Those who love to mountain-bike and who prefer solitude might check out the **Southern Glades Trail,** a 14-mile unpaved trail lined with native trees and teeming with wildlife, such as deer, alligators, and the occasional snake. The remote trail runs along the C-111 canal, off S.R. 9336 and SW 217th Street.

Bicycles are available from **Shark Valley Tram Tours,** at the park's Shark Valley entrance (© **305/221-8455;** www.sharkvalleytramtours.com), for $6.25 per hour; rentals can be picked up anytime between 8:30am and 3pm and must be returned by 4pm.

BIRD-WATCHING   More than 350 species of birds make their home in the Everglades. Tropical birds from the Caribbean and temperate species from North America can be found here, along with exotics that have flown in from more distant regions. Eco and Mrazek ponds, located near Flamingo, are two of the best places for birding, especially in early morning or late afternoon in the dry winter months. Pick up a free birding checklist from one of the visitor centers (p. 234) and inquire about what's been spotted in recent days.

CANOEING   Canoeing through the Everglades may be one of the most serene, surprisingly diverse adventures you'll ever have. From a canoe (where you're incredibly close to the water level), your vantage point is priceless. Canoers in the 'Glades can coexist with the gators and birds in a way no one else can; the creatures behave as if you're part of the ecosystem—something that won't happen on an airboat. A ranger-guided boat tour is your best bet and costs $27 per adult, $14 per child. As always, a ranger will help you understand the surroundings and what you're seeing. They

don't take reservations, but for more information on the various boat tours, call
© **239/695-2591.**

Everglades National Park's longest "trails" are designed for boat and canoe travel,
and many are marked as clearly as walking trails. The **Noble Hammock Canoe Trail,**
a 2-mile loop, takes 1 to 2 hours and is recommended for beginners. The **Hell's Bay
Canoe Trail,** a 3- to 6-mile course for hardier paddlers, takes 2 to 6 hours, depending
on how far you choose to go. Fans of this trail like to say, "It's hell to get in and hell
to get out." Park rangers can recommend other trails that best suit your abilities, time
limitations, and interests.

You can rent a canoe at **Everglades Adventures** (© **239/695-3299;** www.everglades
adventures.com) at the Ivey House B&B (p. 241) for $50 for 24 hours, $35 per full day
(any 8-hr. period), or for $25 per half-day (1–5pm only). Kayaks and tandem kayaks are
also available. The concessionaire will shuttle your party to the trail head of your choice
and pick you up afterward. Rental facilities are open daily from 6am to 8pm.

Overnight canoe rentals are available for $50 to $60. During ideal weather conditions (stay away during bug season!), you can paddle right out to the Gulf and camp
on the beach. However, Gulf waters at beach sites can be extremely rough, and people in small watercraft such as a canoe should exercise caution.

You can also take a canoe tour from the Parks Docks on Chokoloskee Causeway on
S.R. 29, ½ mile south of the traffic circle at the ranger station in Everglades City. Call
Everglades National Park Boat Tours (© **800/445-7724**) for information.

FISHING   About a third of Everglades National Park is open water. Freshwater fishing is popular in brackish **Nine-mile Pond** (25 miles from the main entrance) and
other spots along the Main Park Road, but because of the high mercury levels found
in the Everglades, freshwater fishers are warned not to eat their catch. Before casting,
check in at a visitor center, as many of the park's lakes are preserved for observation
only. Fishing licenses are required; see p. 235 for more information.

Saltwater anglers will find snapper and sea trout plentiful. Charter boats and guides
are available at Flamingo Lodge, Marina, and Outpost Resort (see below). Phone for
information and reservations.

MOTORBOATING   Motorboating around the Everglades seems like a great way to
see plants and animals in remote habitats, and, indeed, it's an interesting and fulfill-
ing experience as you throttle into nature. However, environmentalists are taking
stock of the damage inflicted by motorboats (especially airboats) on the delicate
ecosystem. If you choose to motor, remember that most of the areas near land are "no
wake" zones and that, for the protection of nesting birds, landing is prohibited on
most of the little mangrove islands. Motorboating is allowed in certain areas, such as
Florida Bay, the backcountry toward Everglades City, and the Ten Thousand Islands
area. In all the freshwater lakes, however, motorboats are prohibited if they're above 5
horsepower. There's a long list of restrictions and restricted areas, so get a copy of the
park's boating rules from Park Headquarters before setting out.

The Everglades' only marina—accommodating about 50 boats with electric and
water hookups—is **Flamingo Lodge, Marina, and Outpost Resort,** which suffered
terrible damage from Hurricanes Katrina and Wilma in 2005 and is *still* in the process
of being restored. As of this writing, they're still closed; call to confirm. If they
open, reservations are made through the marina store (© **239/695-3101**). Skiffs with
15-horsepower motors are available for rent. These low-power boats cost about $90 per
day, $65 per half-day (any 5-hr. period), and $22 per hour. A $125 deposit is required.

ORGANIZED TOURS

AIRBOAT TOURS   Shallow-draft, fan-powered airboats were invented in the Ever-glades by frog hunters who were tired of poling through the brushes. Airboats cut through the saw grass and are sort of like hydraulic boats; at high-enough speeds, a boat actually rises above the saw grass and into the air. Even though airboats are the most efficient (not to mention fast and fun!) way to get around, they are not permit-ted in the park—these shallow-bottom runabouts tend to inflict severe damage on animals and plants. Just outside the boundaries of the Everglades, however, you'll find a number of outfitters offering rides. *Tip:* Consider bringing earplugs, as these high-speed boats are loud. Sometimes they give you plugs, but bring a pair just in case.

One of the best airboat outfitters is **Gator Park,** 12 miles west of the Florida Turn-pike at 24050 SW Eighth St. (© **305/559-2255;** www.gatorpark.com), which, despite its touristy name, happens to be one of the most informative and entertaining airboat-tour operators around, not to mention the only one to give out free earplugs. Some of the guides deserve a medal for getting into the water and poking around a massive alligator, even though they're not really supposed to. After the boat ride, there's a free interactive wildlife show that features alligator wrestling and several other frightening acts involving scorpions. Take note of the gorgeous peacocks that live in the trees here. Admission for the boat ride and show is $20 for adults, $10 for chil-dren 6 to 11; prices are cheaper if you purchase tickets online. Airboats depart every 20 minutes. Gator Park is open daily from 9am to 7pm.

Another outfitter I recommend is **Coopertown Airboat Tours** (© **305/226-6048;** www.coopertownairboats.com), located about 11 miles west of the Florida Turnpike on the Tamiami Trail (U.S. 41) in a town that boasts a total population of eight humans! The super-friendly staff has helped the company garner the title of "Florida's Best" by the *Miami Herald* for 40 years in a row. You never know what you're going to see, but with great guides, you're sure to see *something* of interest on the 40-minute, 9-mile round-trip tours. There's also a restaurant and a small gator farm on the prem-ises. Airboat rides cost $18 for adults, $9 for children 7 to 11. The company is open daily from 8am to 6pm; tours leave frequently.

Thirty-minute Airboat rides are also offered at the **Miccosukee Indian Village,** just west of the Shark Valley entrance on U.S. 41/Tamiami Trail and MM 70 (© **305/ 223-8380;** www.miccosukeetours.com). The price is $10 per person, with cheaper rates online. However, be warned and advised: I am not recommending this particu-lar outfit over others—it's merely the one closest to the Shark Valley entrance. As always, the quality of your tour is only as good as the quality of your tour guide, and, unfortunately, I've gotten some complaints about the Miccosukee tours.

The **Everglades Alligator Farm,** 4 miles south of Palm Drive on SW 192nd Avenue (© **305/247-2628;** www.everglades.com), offers half-hour guided airboat tours daily from 9am until 6pm. The price, which includes admission to the park, is $19 for adults and $12 for children 4 to 11.

Another reputable company is **Captain Doug's,** located 35 miles south of Naples and 1 mile past the bridge in Everglades City (© **800/282-9194**).

CANOE TOURS   A fabulous way to explore the Everglades backcountry is via canoe. Slink through the mangroves, slide across saw-grass prairies, and even walk the sands of the unfettered Ten Thousand Islands. Expert guides will lead you in the right direction. Contact **Everglades Adventures** (© **239/695-3299;** www.evergladesadventures.com) at the Ivey House B&B (p. 241).

ECO-TOURS   Although it's fascinating to explore on your own, it would be a shame for you to tour the Everglades without a clue about what you're seeing. It's a lot more than saw grass and alligators in the backcountry, which is why **Everglades Adventures** (© **239/695-3299**), located within the Ivey House B&B (p. 241), is there to guide and entertain you, as well as explain such key issues as the differences between alligators and crocodiles, or between swamps and the Everglades.

MOTORBOAT TOURS   Both Florida Bay and backcountry tours are offered Thursday through Monday at the **Flamingo Lodge, Marina, and Outpost Resort.** Florida Bay tours cruise nearby estuaries and sandbars, while six-passenger backcountry boats visit smaller sloughs. Passengers can expect to see birds and a variety of other animals (I once saw a raccoon and some wild pigs). Both are available in 1½- and 2-hour versions that cost $12 or $18 for adults, $7 or $12 for children 6 to 13. Tours depart throughout the day; reservations are recommended. Charter-fishing and sightseeing boats can also be booked through the resort's main reservation number (© **239/695-3101**). *Note:* The Flamingo Lodge is closed as we go to print but may reopen. Call © **239/695-3101** for updates.

TRAM TOURS   At the park's Shark Valley entrance, open-air tram buses take visitors on 2-hour naturalist-led tours that delve 7½ miles into the wilderness and are the best quick introduction you can get to the Everglades. At the trail's midsection, passengers can disembark and climb a 65-foot observation tower with good views of the 'Glades (though the tower on the Pa-hay-okee Trail is better). Visitors will see plenty of wildlife and endless acres of saw grass. Tours run December through April, daily on the hour between 9am and 4pm, and May through November at 9:30am, 11am, 1pm, and 3pm. They're sometimes stalled by flooding or particularly heavy mosquito infestation. Reservations are recommended from December to March. The cost is $15 for adults, $14 for seniors, and $8.75 for children under 13. For further information, contact **Shark Valley Tram Tours** (© **305/221-8455;** www.sharkvalleytramtours.com).

WHERE TO STAY

The only lodging in the park proper is Flamingo Lodge. At the time of this writing, however, Flamingo Lodge's overnight facilities were closed for business after taking a whopping in 2005 from Hurricanes Katrina and Wilma. A 2006 *Miami Herald* article reported that the lodge was being redone. "We think this opens up the opportunity to rethink Flamingo Lodge overall," said park planner Fred Herling. The National Park Service, however, ruled out building a new, large hotel unless private interests chip in. Until they all agree on what to do with the rebuilding, however, Flamingo Lodge remains closed to sleepovers. However, a few accommodations just outside the park are even cheaper. A $45-million casino hotel, **Miccosukee Resort** (© **877/242-6464;** www.miccosukee.com), is adjacent to the Miccosukee bingo and gaming hall on the northern edge of the park. Although bugs can be a major nuisance, especially in the warm months, camping (the best way to fully experience South Florida's wilderness) is really the way to go in this very primitive environment.

CAMPING IN THE EVERGLADES

Campgrounds are available year-round in Flamingo and Long Pine Key. Both have drinking water, picnic tables, charcoal grills, restrooms, and tent and trailer pads, and they welcome RVs (Flamingo allows up to 40-ft. vehicles, while Long Pine Key accepts up to 60-footers), though there are no electrical hookups. Flamingo has cold-water showers; Long Pine Key does not have showers or hookups for showers. Private ground fires are not permitted, but supervised campfire programs are conducted during winter months. Long Pine Key and Flamingo are popular and require reservations in advance, which can be made through the National Park Reservations Service (© **800/365-CAMP**; www.nps.gov/ever/visit/camping.htm). Campsites are $16 per night with a 14-day consecutive-stay limit, and a maximum of 30 days a year.

Camping is also available year-round in the **backcountry** (those remote areas accessible only by boat, foot, or canoe—basically most of the park), on a first-come, first-served basis. Campers must register with park rangers and get a free permit in person or by phone no less than 24 hours before the start of their trip. For more information, contact the **Gulf Coast Visitor Center** (© **239/695-3311**) or the **Flamingo Visitor Center** (© **239/695-2945**), which are the only two places that give out these permits. Once you have one, camping sites cost $16 (with a maximum of 8 people per site), or $30 for a group site (maximum of 15 people). Campers can use only designated campsites, which are plentiful and well marked on visitor maps.

Many backcountry sites are **chickee huts**—covered wooden platforms (with toilets) on stilts. They're accessible only by canoe and can accommodate free-standing tents (without stakes). Ground sites are located along interior bays and rivers, and beach camping is also popular. In summer especially, mosquito repellent is necessary gear.

LODGING IN EVERGLADES CITY

Since Everglades City is 35 miles southeast of Naples and 83 miles west of Miami, many visitors choose to explore this western entrance to Everglades National Park, located off the Tamiami Trail, on S.R. 29. An annual seafood festival held the first weekend in February is a major event that draws hordes of people. Everglades City (the gateway to the Ten Thousand Islands), where the 'Glades meet the Gulf of Mexico, is the closest thing you'll get to civilization in South Florida's swampy frontier, with a few tourist traps—er, shops—a restaurant, and two bed-and-breakfasts.

Everglades Spa and Lodge *Finds*   This very cute B&B is right on the money, as far as kitsch is concerned—it's a fabulous retreat from the lush greenery of the swampy Everglades to the even more lush greenery of money. The place is located in a building that was formerly the first bank established, in 1923, in Collier County, and though money is this place's premise, it won't cost you too much to stay here. Rooms are clean and comfy, all with bathrooms and are located on the floor where banking used to be done until 1962. Unlike a real bank, however, the knowledgeable staff at the inn is happy to give free advice on what to do in the area. A day spa on the premises provides all the necessary pampering after a long day exploring the swamps. A bonus is the expanded breakfast served in the rooms, offering a bounty of fresh fruits, muffins, cereals, juices, granola, coffees, and teas.

201 W. Broadway, Everglades City, FL 34139. © **239/695-3151**. Spa © 239/695-1006. Fax 239/695-3335. www.banksoftheeverglades.com. 6 units. $110–$130 double; $125–$135 efficiency, suite. Rates include continental breakfast delivered to your door. AE, DISC, MC, V. **Amenities:** Free use of bikes; wireless Internet; Everglades excursions available. *In room:* A/C, TV.

Ivey House B&B *Finds*   The first certified Green Lodging in Collier County, The Ivey House offers a variety of accommodations: The Ivey House Inn features spacious rooms with private bathrooms, TVs, phones, and a view of the courtyard pool and waterfall; the Ivey House Lodge, housed in what used to be a recreational center for the men who built the Tamiami Trail, features 10 small rooms with communal bathrooms (one each for women and men), no TVs or phones; and the Ivey House Cottage offers two bedrooms, a full kitchen, a private bathroom, and a screened-in porch. Owners Sandee and David Harraden are extremely knowledgeable about the Everglades and assist guests by providing a variety of daily excursions. Rates include a full breakfast served from 6:30 to 10am. A full hot breakfast is provided during peak season. Box lunches are available year round for $10.50. *Note:* There is no smoking in any of the buildings.

107 Camellia St., Everglades City, FL 34139. ✆ **877/567-0679** or 239/695-3299. Fax 239/695-4155. www.ivey house.com. 28 units. Winter Rates: $100–$200 inn; $60–$105 lodge; $175–$235 cottage (2-night minimum); 2-night minimum in all facilities during Everglades Seafood Festival in Feb. Off season $75–$85 inn; $60–$65 lodge; $135 cottage. MC, V. **Amenities:** Restaurant, pool; Wi-Fi available; Everglades excursions available. *In room:* A/C, TV, kitchen (in cottages), fridge (in inn and cottages).

Rod & Gun Lodge 🐾 Set on the banks of the sleepy Baron River, this rustic, old white-clapboard house has plenty of history and all kinds of activities for sports enthusiasts, including a pool, bike rentals, a tennis center, and nearby boat rentals and private fishing guides. Hoover vacationed here after his 1928 election victory, and Truman flew in to sign Everglades National Park into existence in 1947 and stayed over as well. Other guests have included Richard Nixon, Burt Reynolds, and Mick Jagger. The public rooms are beautifully paneled and hung with tarpon, wild boar, deer antlers, and other trophies. Guest rooms in this single-story building are unfussy but perfectly comfortable. All have porches looking out on the river. Out by the pool, a screened veranda with ceiling fans is a pleasant place for a libation. The excellent seafood restaurant serves breakfast, lunch, and dinner. The entire property is nonsmoking.

Riverside Dr. and Broadway (P.O. Box 190), Everglades City, FL 34139. ✆ **239/695-2101.** 17 units. Winter $145 double; off season $110 double. No credit cards. Closed after July 4 for the summer. **Amenities:** Restaurant; pool; tennis courts; bike rental. *In room:* A/C, TV.

LODGING IN HOMESTEAD & FLORIDA CITY

Homestead and Florida City, two adjacent towns that were almost blown off the map by Hurricane Andrew in 1992, have come back better than before. About 10 miles from the park's main entrance, along U.S. 1, 35 miles south of Miami, these somewhat rural towns offer several budget options, including chain hotels. There is a **Days Inn** (✆ **305/245-1260**) in Homestead and a **Hampton Inn** (✆ **800/426-7866** or 305/ 247-8833) right off the turnpike in Florida City. The best options are listed below.

Best Western Gateway to the Keys This standard two-story motel provides contemporary style and comfort about 10 miles from the park's main entrance. A decent-size pool and a small spa make it attractive to some. Each standard room has bright, tropical bedspreads and oversize picture windows. The suites have convenient extras such as a microwave, coffeemaker, extra sink, and small fridge. Clean and conveniently located, the only drawback is that, in season, there is often a 3-day minimum-stay requirement. You would do best to call the local reservation line instead of the toll-free number—on several occasions, the hotel has made an exception to the rule, while the central reservation line could not.

411 S. Krome Ave. (U.S. 1), Florida City, FL 33034. ✆ **800/528-1234** or 305/246-5100. Fax 305/242-0056. www.best western.com. 114 units. $100–$150 double. Rates include continental breakfast. During races and the very high season, there may be a 3-night minimum stay. AE, DC, DISC, MC, V. **Amenities:** Pool; spa; laundry service; dry cleaning. *In room:* A/C, TV, dataport, fridge, coffeemaker, hair dryer.

Everglades International Hostel ✦   This is what a hostel *should* be. Sure, I've seen cleaner, more modern ones, but the feeling of camaraderie here is what hostels are all about. Located in a 1930s boardinghouse, this hostel has dorm rooms as well as doubles (all with shared bathrooms), a great kitchen, a washer/dryer, high-speed Internet access, bike rentals, and a garden (with tents, forts, and an outdoor chess board). The friendly, amazingly accommodating staff here provides tons of helpful information and runs sightseeing/canoe trips to the Everglades. *Note:* Some rooms here are cheaper than the rates listed below, but do not have air-conditioning.

20 SW 2nd Ave., Florida City, FL 33034. ✆ 800/372-3874 or 305/248-1122. www.evergladeshostel.com. $22–$26 dorm bed; $60–$65 private double; $50–$55 semi-private room; $16 per person garden camping. MC, V. **Amenities:** Bike rental; tours; laundry facilities; Internet access; kitchen. *In room:* A/C (in some)

WHERE TO DINE IN & AROUND THE PARK

You won't find fancy nouvelle cuisine in this suburbanized farm country, but there are plenty of fast-food chains along U.S. 1 and a few old favorites worth a taste.

Here for nearly a quarter of a century, **El Toro Taco Family Restaurant,** 1 S. Krome Ave., near Mowry and Campbell drives, Homestead (✆ **305/245-8182**), opens daily at 9:30am and stays crowded until at least 9pm most days. The fresh grilled meats, tacos, burritos, salsas, guacamole, and stews are all mild and delicious. No matter how big your appetite, it's hard to spend more than $12 per person at this Mexican outpost. Bring your own beer or wine. See p. 158 for a full review.

Housed in a one-story, windowless building that looks something like a medieval fort, the **Capri Restaurant,** 935 N. Krome Ave., Florida City (✆ **305/247-1542**), has been serving hearty Italian-American fare since 1958. Great pastas and salads complement a menu of meat and fish dishes; portions are big. Lunch and dinner are served Monday through Friday until 9:30pm and Saturday until 10:30pm. The **White Lion Café,** 146 NW Seventh St., Homestead (✆ **305/248-1076**), is a quaint home-and-gardens-cum-cafe with live blues, jazz, and swing music at night, and a menu with items like Dirty Little Shrimp and Poor Man's Steak, which is actually delicious meatloaf with mushrooms, gravy, mashed potatoes, and veggies for just $11. Dinner is served Tuesday through Saturday from 5pm until "the fat lady sings."

The **Miccosukee Restaurant,** just west of the Shark Valley entrance on the Tamiami Trail/U.S. 41 (✆ **305/223-8380**), serves authentic pumpkin bread, fry bread, and fish, and not-so-authentic Native American interpretations of tacos and fried chicken. It's worth a stop for brunch, lunch, or dinner.

Near the Miccosukee reservation is the **Pit Bar-B-Q,** 16400 SW Eighth St. (✆ **305/226-2272**), a total pit of a place known for some of the best smoked ribs, barbecued chicken, and corn bread this side of the Deep South. It's open daily from 11am to 8pm.

In Everglades City, the **Oyster House,** on Chokoloskee Causeway, S.R. (the locals call it Hwy.) 29 South (✆ **239/695-2073**), is a large but homey seafood restaurant with modest prices, excellent service, and a fantastic view of the Ten Thousand Islands. Try the hush puppies.

Once inside the Everglades, you'll want to eat at the only restaurant within the boundaries of this huge park, the **Flamingo Restaurant** (✆ **239/695-3101**). Located in the Flamingo Lodge, Marina, and Outpost Resort (p. 238), this is a very civilized and affordable establishment. All of Flamingo took a beating from 2005's ruthless Hurricanes Katrina and Wilma, and the restaurant, like the lodge, was closed at the time of this writing. The restaurant was slated to reopen in late 2008—but call first.

2 Biscayne National Park (★

35 miles S of Miami, 21 miles E of Everglades National Park

With only about 500,000 visitors each year (mostly boaters and divers), the unusual Biscayne National Park is one of the least-crowded parks in the country. Perhaps that's because the park is a little more difficult than most to access—more than 95% of its 181,500 acres is underwater.

The park's significance was first formally acknowledged in 1968 when, in an unprecedented move (and despite intense pressure from developers), President Lyndon B. Johnson signed a bill to conserve the barrier islands off South Florida's east coast as a national monument—a protected status just a rung below national park. After being twice enlarged, once in 1974 and again in 1980, the waters and land surrounding the northernmost coral reef in North America became a full-fledged national park—the largest of its kind in the country.

To be fully appreciated, Biscayne National Park should be thought of as more preserve than destination. Use your time here to explore underwater life, but also to relax. The park's small mainland mangrove shoreline and keys are best explored by boat. Its extensive reef system is renowned by divers and snorkelers worldwide.

The park consists of 44 islands, but only a few of them are open to visitors. The most popular is **Elliott Key,** which has campsites and a visitor center plus freshwater showers (cold water only), restrooms, trails, and a buoyed swim area. It's about 9 miles from **Convoy Point,** the park's official headquarters on land. During Columbus Day weekend, there is a very popular regatta for which a lively crowd of party people gathers—sometimes in the nude—to celebrate the long weekend. If you'd prefer to rough it a little more, the 29-acre island known as **Boca Chita Key,** once an exclusive haven for yachters, has now become a popular spot for all manner of boaters. Visitors can camp and tour the island's restored historic buildings, including the county's second-largest lighthouse and a tiny chapel.

JUST THE FACTS

GETTING THERE & ACCESS POINTS   Convoy Point, the park's mainland entrance, is 9 miles east of Homestead. To reach the park from Miami, take the Florida Turnpike to the Tallahassee Road (SW 137th Ave.) exit. Turn left, then left again at North Canal Drive (SW 328th St.), and follow signs to the park. Another option is to rent a speedboat in Miami and cruise south for about 1½ hours. If you're coming from U.S. 1, whether you're heading north or south, turn east at North Canal Drive (SW 328th St.). The entrance is approximately 9 miles away. The rest of the park is accessible only by boat.

Because most of Biscayne National Park is accessible only to boaters, mooring buoys abound, since it is illegal to anchor on coral. When no buoys are available, boaters must anchor on sand or on the docks surrounding the small harbor off Boca Chita. Boats can also dock here overnight for $15. Even the most experienced boaters should carry updated nautical charts of the area, which are available at Convoy Point's Dante Fascell Visitor Center. The waters are often murky, making the abundant reefs and sandbars difficult to detect—and there are more interesting ways to spend a day than waiting for the tide to rise. There's a boat launch at adjacent Homestead Bayfront Park and 66 slips on Elliott Key, available free on a first-come, first-served basis.

Round-trip transportation to and from the visitor center to Elliott Key costs $36 (plus tax) round-trip per person and takes about an hour. This is a convenient option, ensuring that you don't get lost on some deserted island by boating there yourself. Call ℂ **305/230-1100** for the seasonal schedule.

VISITOR CENTERS & INFORMATION   Dante Fascell Visitor Center, often referred to by its older name, **Convoy Point Visitor Center,** 9700 SW 328th St., Homestead, FL 33033-5634, at the park's main entrance (ℂ **305/230-7275;** fax 305/ 230-1190; www.nps.gov/bisc), is the natural starting point for any venture into the park without a boat. It provides comprehensive information about the park; on request, rangers will show you a short video on the park, its natural surroundings, and what you may see. The center is open daily from 9am to 5pm.

For information on transportation, glass-bottom boat tours, and snorkeling and scuba diving expeditions, contact the park concessionaire, **Biscayne National Underwater Park, Inc.,** P.O. Box 1270, Homestead, FL 33030 (ℂ **305/230-1100;** fax 305/230-1120; www.nps.gov/bisc). It's open daily from 8:30am to 5pm.

ENTRANCE FEES & PERMITS   Entering Biscayne National Park is free. There is a $15 overnight docking fee at both Boca Chita Key Harbor and Elliott Key Harbor ($7.50 per night for holders of Golden Age or Golden Access passports), which includes a campsite. Campsites are $10 for those staying without a boat. Group camping costs $25 a day and covers up to six tents and 25 people. See p. 235 for information on fishing permits. Backcountry camping permits are free and can be picked up from the Dante Fascell Visitor Center. For more information on fees and permits, call the park ranger at ℂ **305/230-1144.**

SEEING THE HIGHLIGHTS

Since the park is primarily underwater, the only way to truly experience it is with snorkel or scuba gear. Beneath the surface of Biscayne National Park, the aquatic universe pulses with multicolored life: abounding bright parrotfish and angelfish, gently rocking sea fans, and coral labyrinths. (See "Snorkeling & Scuba Diving," below, for more information.) Afterward, take a picnic out to Elliott Key and taste the crisp salt air blowing off the Atlantic. Or head to Boca Chita, an intriguing island that was once the private playground of wealthy yachters.

SPORTS & OUTDOOR ACTIVITIES

CANOEING & KAYAKING   Biscayne National Park affords excellent canoeing, both along the coast and across the open water to nearby mangroves and artificial islands dotting the longest uninterrupted shoreline in the state of Florida. Since tides can be strong, only experienced canoeists should attempt to paddle far from shore. If you do plan to go far, first obtain a tide table from the visitor center and paddle with the current. Free ranger-led canoe tours are scheduled from 9am to noon on the second and fourth Saturdays of the month between January 10 and April 24; phone for information. You can rent a canoe at the park's concession stand for $12 an hour. Two-person kayaks go for $16 an hour. Call ℂ **305/230-1100** for reservations, information, ranger tours, and boat rentals.

FISHING   Ocean fishing is excellent year-round at Biscayne National Park; many people cast their lines from the breakwater jetty at Convoy Point. A fishing license is required; see p. 235 for more information. Bait is not available in Biscayne National Park, but is sold in adjacent Homestead Bayfront Park. Stone crabs and Florida lobsters can be found here, but you're allowed to catch these only on the ocean side when they're in season. There are strict limits on size, season, number, and method of take (including spear fishing) for both freshwater and saltwater fishing. The latest regulations are available at most marinas, bait-and-tackle shops, and the park's visitor centers, or you can contact the **Florida Fish and Wildlife Conservation Commission,** Bryant Building, 620 S. Meridian St., Tallahassee, FL 32399-1600 (© **850/488-0331**).

HIKING & EXPLORING   Since the majority of this park is underwater, hiking is not the main attraction here, but there are some interesting sights and trails nonetheless. At Convoy Point, you can walk along the 370-foot boardwalk and along the half-mile jetty that serves as a breakwater for the park's harbor. From here, you can usually see brown pelicans, little blue herons, snowy egrets, and a few exotic fish.

Elliott Key is accessible only by boat, but once you're there, you have two good trail options. True to its name, the Loop Trail makes a 1.5-mile circle from the bayside visitor center, through a hardwood hammock and mangroves, to an elevated oceanside boardwalk. You'll likely see land crabs scurrying around the mangrove roots.

Reopened in 1998, Boca Chita Key was once a playground for wealthy tycoons, and it still has the peaceful beauty that attracted elite anglers from cold climates. Many of the historic buildings are still intact, including an ornamental lighthouse that was never put to use. Take advantage of the tours, usually led by a park ranger and available every Sunday in winter only at 1:30pm. The tour, including the boat trip, takes about 3 hours. The price is $25 for adults, $20 for seniors, and $17 for children 11 and under. However, call in advance to see whether the sea is calm enough for the trip—the boats won't run in rough waters. See "Glass-Bottom Boat Tours," below, for information about the daily 10am excursions.

SNORKELING & SCUBA DIVING   The clear, warm waters of Biscayne National Park are packed with colorful tropical fish that swim in the offshore reefs. If you don't have your own gear, or if you don't want to lug it to the park, you can rent or buy snorkeling and scuba gear at the full-service dive shop at Convoy Point. Rates are in line with those at mainland dive shops.

The best way to see the park from underwater is to take a snorkeling or diving tour operated by **Biscayne National Underwater Park, Inc.** (© **305/230-1100;** www. nps.gov/bisc). Snorkeling tours depart at 1:30pm daily, last about 3 hours, and cost $35 per person, including equipment. There are also weekend two-tank dives for certified divers; the price is $54, including two tanks and weights. Make your reservations in advance. The shop is open daily from 9am to 5pm.

Before entering the water, be sure to apply waterproof sun block—once you begin to explore, it's easy to lose track of time, and the Florida sun is brutal, even during winter.

SWIMMING   You can swim off the protected beaches of Elliott Key, Boca Chita Key, and adjacent Homestead Bayfront Park, but none of these match the width or softness of other South Florida beaches. Check the water conditions before heading into the sea: The strong currents that make this a popular destination for windsurfers and sailors can be dangerous, even for strong swimmers. Homestead Bayfront Park is really just a marina next to Biscayne National Park, but it does have a beach and picnic facilities, as well as fishing areas and a playground. It's located at Convoy Point, 9698 SW 328th St., Homestead (© **305/230-3034**).

GLASS-BOTTOM BOAT TOURS

If you prefer not to dive, the best way to see the sights is on a glass-bottom boat. **Biscayne National Underwater Park, Inc.** (© **305/230-1100;** www.nps.gov/bisc), has daily trips to view some of the country's most beautiful coral reefs and tropical fish. Boats depart year-round from Convoy Point at 10am and stay out for about 3 hours. At $25 for adults, $20 for seniors, and $17 for children 12 and under, the scenic and informative tours are well worth the price. Boats carry fewer than 50 passengers; reservations are almost always necessary.

WHERE TO STAY

Besides campsites, there are no facilities available for overnight guests to this watery park. Most noncamping visitors come for an afternoon, on their way to the Keys, and stay overnight in nearby Homestead, where there are many national chain hotels and other affordable lodgings; see p. 242 for more information.

Although you won't find hotels or lodges in Biscayne National Park, it does have some of the state's most pristine campsites. Since they are inaccessible by motor vehicle, you'll be sure to avoid the mass of RVs so prevalent in many of the state's other campgrounds. The sites on Elliott Key and Boca Chita can be reached only by boat. If you don't have your own boat, call © **305/230-1100** to arrange a drop-off. Transportation to Elliott Key from the visitor center costs $36 (plus tax) plus $2.50 gas fee round-trip per person. They do not provide transportation to Boca Chita, so you'll have to rent a boat. Boca Chita has only saltwater toilets (no showers or sinks); Elliot Key has freshwater, cold-water showers and toilets, but is otherwise no less primitive. If you didn't pay for the overnight docking fee, campsites are $10.

With a backcountry permit, available free from the visitor center, you can pitch your tent somewhere even more private. Ask for a map and be sure to bring plenty of bug spray. Sites cost $10 a night for up to six persons staying in one or two tents. Backcountry camping is allowed only on Elliott Key, which is a very popular spot (accessible only by boat) for boaters and campers. It is approximately 9 miles from the Dante Fascell Visitor Center and offers hiking trails, fresh water, boat slips, showers, and restrooms. While there, don't miss the Old Road, a 7-mile tropical hammock trail that runs the length of Elliott Key. This trail is one of the few places left in the world to see the highly endangered Schaus swallowtail butterfly, recognizable by its black wings with diagonal yellow bands. These butterflies are usually out from late April to July.

12

The Keys & the Dry Tortugas

The drive from Miami to the Keys is a slow descent into an unusual but breathtaking American ecosystem: On either side of you, for miles ahead, lies nothing but emerald waters. (On weekends, however, you will also see plenty of traffic.) Strung out across the Atlantic Ocean like loose strands of cultured pearls, more than 400 islands make up this 150-mile-long necklace.

Despite the usually calm landscape, these rocky islands can be treacherous, as tropical storms, hurricanes, and tornadoes are always possibilities. The exposed coast poses dangers to those on land as well as at sea.

When Spanish explorers Juan Ponce de León and Antonio de Herrera sailed amid these craggy, dangerous rocks in 1513, they and their men dubbed the string of islands Los Martires (The Martyrs) because they thought the rocks looked like men suffering in the surf. It wasn't until the early 1800s that rugged and ambitious pioneers, who amassed great wealth by salvaging cargo from ships sunk nearby, settled the larger islands (legend has it that these shipwrecks were sometimes caused by "wreckers," who removed navigational markers from the shallows to lure unwitting captains aground). At the height of the salvaging mania (in the 1830s), Key West boasted the highest per-capita income in the country.

However, wars, fires, hurricanes, mosquitoes, and the Depression took their toll on these resilient islands in the early part of the 20th century, causing wild swings between fortune and poverty. In 1938, the spectacular Overseas Highway (U.S. 1) was finally completed atop the ruins of Henry Flagler's railroad (which was destroyed by a hurricane in 1935, leaving only bits and pieces still found today), opening the region to tourists, who had never before been able to drive to this sea-bound destination. These days, the highway connects more than 30 of the populated islands in the Keys. The hundreds of small, undeveloped islands that surround these "mainline" keys are known locally as the "backcountry" and are home to dozens of exotic animals and plants. Therein lie some of the most renowned outdoor sporting opportunities, from bonefishing to spear fishing and—at appropriate times of the year—diving for lobsters and stone crabs. To get to the backcountry, you must take to the water—a vital part of any trip to the Keys. Whether you fish, snorkel, dive, or cruise, include some time on a boat in your itinerary; otherwise, you haven't truly seen the Keys.

Of course, people go to the Keys for the peaceful waters and year-round warmth, but the sea and the teeming life beneath and around it are the main attractions here: Countless species of brilliantly colored fish can be found swimming above the ocean's floor, and you'll discover a stunning abundance of tropical and exotic plants, birds, and reptiles.

The warm, shallow waters (deeper and rougher on the eastern/Atlantic side of the Keys) nurture living coral that supports a complex, delicate ecosystem of plants and animals—sponges, anemones, jellyfish, crabs, rays, sharks, turtles, snails, lobsters, and thousands of types of fish. This vibrant underwater habitat thrives on one of the only living tropical reefs on the entire North American continent. As a result, anglers, divers, snorkelers, and watersports enthusiasts of all kinds come to explore.

Heavy traffic has taken its toll on this fragile ecoscape, but conservation efforts are underway (traffic laws are strictly enforced on Deer Key, for example, due to deer crossings that have been contained, thanks to newly installed fences). In fact, environmental efforts in the Keys exceed those in many other high-traffic visitor destinations.

Although the atmosphere throughout the Keys is that of a laid-back beach town, don't expect many impressive beaches here, especially after the damaging effects of recent hurricane seasons. Nice beaches are mostly found in a few private resorts, though there are some small, sandy strips in John Pennekamp Coral Reef State Park, Bahia Honda State Park, and Key West. One great exception is Sombrero Beach, in Marathon (p. 253), which is well maintained by Monroe County and is larger and considerably nicer than other beaches in the Keys. Sombrero Beach has a beachfront park, picnic facilities, a playground, and a protected cove for children.

The Keys are divided into three sections, both geographically and in this chapter. The Upper and Middle Keys are closest to the Florida mainland, so they are popular with weekend warriors who come by boat or car to fish or relax in such towns as Key Largo, Islamorada, and Marathon. Farther on, just beyond the impressive Seven-mile Bridge (which actually measures 6½ miles), are the Lower Keys, a small, unspoiled swath of islands teeming with wildlife. Here, in the protected regions of the Lower Keys, is where you're most likely to catch sight of the area's many endangered animals—with patience, you may spot the rare eagle, egret, or Key deer. You should also keep an eye out for alligators, turtles, rabbits, and a huge variety of birds.

Key West, the most renowned—and last—island in the Lower Keys, is literally at the end of the road. The southernmost point in the continental United States (made famous by Ernest Hemingway), this tiny island is the most popular destination in the Florida Keys, overrun with cruise-ship passengers and day-trippers, as well as franchises and T-shirt shops. More than 1.6 million visitors pass through it each year. Still, this "Conch Republic" has a tightly knit community of permanent residents who cling fiercely to their live-and-let-live attitude—an atmosphere that has made Key West famously popular with painters, writers, and free spirits despite the recent influx of money-hungry developers who want to turn Key West into Palm Beach south.

The last section in this chapter is devoted to the Dry Tortugas, a national park located 68 nautical miles from Key West.

Tips Don't Be Fooled

Avoid the many "tourist information centers" that dot the main highway. Most are private companies hired to lure visitors to specific lodgings or outfitters (anything that says FREE DISNEY TICKETS or something like that is probably a scam or timeshare racket). You're better off sticking with the official, not-for-profit centers (the legit ones usually don't advertise on the turnpike) that are extremely well located and staffed.

The Florida Keys

EXPLORING THE KEYS BY CAR

After you've left the Florida Turnpike and landed on U.S. 1, which is also known as the Overseas Highway (see "Getting There" under "Essentials," below), you'll have no trouble negotiating these narrow islands, since only one main road connects the Keys. The scenic, lazy drive from Miami can be very enjoyable if you have the patience to linger and explore the diverse towns and islands along the way. If you have the time, I recommend allowing at least 2 days to work your way down to Key West, and 3 or more days once there.

Most of U.S. 1 is a narrow two-lane highway, with some wider passing zones along the way. The speed limit is usually 55 mph (35–45 mph on Big Pine Key and in some commercial areas). Despite the protests of island residents, there has been talk of expanding the highway, but plans have not been finalized. Even on the narrow road,

---

Moments Sweet Home Alabama (Jack's)

On its own, there's not much to the waterfront shack that is **Alabama Jack's, 5800 Card Sound Rd., Card Sound (① 305/248-8741)**. The bar serves beer and wine only, and the restaurant specializes in delicious, albeit greasy, bar fare. But this quintessential Old Floridian dive, located in a historic fishing village called Card Sound between Homestead and Key Largo, is a colorful must on the drive south, especially on Sunday, when bikers mix with barflies, anglers, line dancers, and Southern belles who look as if they just got off the *Hee Haw* set in all their fabulous frills. Live country music resurrects the legendary Johnny Cash and Co. Pull up a bar stool, order a cold one, and take in the sights—in the bay and at the bar. The views of the mangroves are spectacular. To get here, pick up Card Sound Road (the old Rte. 1) a few miles after you pass Homestead, heading toward Key Largo. Alabama Jack's is on the right side and can't be missed.

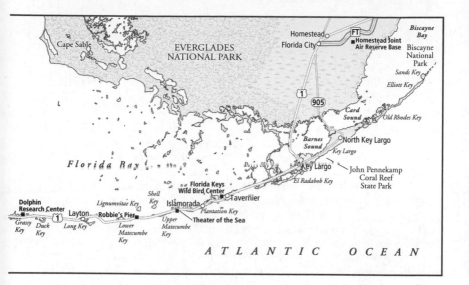

you can usually get from downtown Miami to Key Largo in just over an hour. If you're determined to drive straight through to Key West, allow at least 3½ hours. Weekend travel is another matter entirely: When the roads are jammed with travelers from the mainland, the trip can take upward of 5 to 6 hours (when there's an accident, traffic is at an absolute standstill). If at all possible, I strongly urge you to avoid driving anywhere in the Keys on Friday afternoon or Sunday evening.

To find an address in the Keys, don't bother looking for building numbers; most addresses (except in Key West and parts of Marathon) are delineated by mile markers (MM), small green signs on the roadside that announce the distance from Key West. The markers start at no. 127, just south of the Florida mainland. The zero marker is in Key West, at the corner of Whitehead and Fleming streets. Addresses in this chapter are accompanied by a mile marker (MM) designation when appropriate.

1 The Upper & Middle Keys: Key Largo ★★ to Marathon ★

58 miles SW of Miami

The Upper Keys are a popular year-round refuge for South Floridians, who take advantage of the islands' proximity to the mainland. This is the fishing and diving capital of America, and the swarms of outfitters and billboards never let you forget it.

Key Largo, once called Rock Harbor but renamed to capitalize on the success of the 1948 Humphrey Bogart film (which wasn't actually filmed here), is the largest key and is more developed than its neighbors to the south. Dozens of chain hotels, restaurants, and tourist information centers service the water enthusiasts who come to explore the nation's first underwater state park, **John Pennekamp Coral Reef State Park,** and its adjacent marine sanctuary. **Islamorada,** the unofficial capital of the Upper Keys, has the area's best atmosphere, food, fishing, entertainment, and lodging. It's an unofficial "party capital" for mainlanders seeking a quick tropical excursion. Here (Islamorada is actually composed of four islands) nature lovers can enjoy walking trails, historic exploration, and big-purse fishing tournaments. For a more tranquil, less party-hearty Keys experience, all other keys besides Key West and Islamorada are better choices. **Marathon,** smack in the middle of the Florida Keys, is known as the heart of the Keys and is one of the most populated. It is part fishing village, part tourist center, and part nature preserve. This area's highly developed infrastructure includes resort hotels, a commercial airport, and a highway that expands to four lanes.

ESSENTIALS

GETTING THERE   From Miami International Airport (there is also an airport in Marathon), take Le Jeune Road (NW 42nd Ave.) to Route 836 West. Follow signs to the Florida Turnpike South, about 7 miles. The turnpike extension connects with U.S. 1 in Florida City. Continue south on U.S. 1. For a scenic option, take Card Sound Road south of Florida City, a backcountry drive that reconnects with U.S. 1 in upper Key Largo. The view from Card Sound Bridge is spectacular and well worth the $1 toll.

If you're coming from Florida's west coast, take Alligator Alley to the Miami exit and then turn south onto the turnpike extension. The turnpike ends in Florida City, at which time you will be dumped directly onto the two-lane U.S. 1, which leads to the Keys. Have plenty of quarters (at least $10 worth, round-trip) for the tolls.

The **TransFloridian** luxury motorcoach (© **954/523-0859;** www.transfloridian. com) will take you down to the Keys in a 26-foot luxury car with reclining leather seats, plenty of legroom, wireless Internet service, in-seat power ports for electronic devices, personal headphone jacks, multichannel audio entertainment, overhead DVD monitors, and service by onboard attendants. Transportation from Miami, Fort Lauderdale, or Orlando to and from the Florida Keys ranges from $45–$200.

Greyhound (© **800/231-2222;** www.greyhound.com) has three buses leaving Miami for Key West every day, with stops in Key Largo, Tavernier, Islamorada, Marathon, Big Pine Key, Cudjoe Key, Sugarloaf, and Big Coppit on the way south. Prices range from $13 to $37 one-way and $26 to $75 round-trip; the trip takes from 1 hour and 40 minutes to 4 hours and 40 minutes, depending on how far south you're going. Seats fill quickly in season, so come early. It's first come, first served.

Once you've arrived in the Keys, pilot **Dan Baker** (© **305/731-0000**) offers 18- to 20-minute helicopter tours of the Middle Keys and Marathon areas, departing from Florida Keys Marathon Airport, MM (mile marker) 52.2 (bay side). Up to four passengers can be accommodated on each tour, depending on weight. Cost is $75 per person for four, $100 per person for three, and $150 per person for two.

VISITOR INFORMATION   Make sure you get your information from an official not-for-profit center. The **Key Largo Chamber of Commerce,** U.S. 1 at MM 106, Key Largo, FL 33037 (© **800/822-1088** or 305/451-1414; fax 305/451-4726; www.keylargo.org), runs an excellent facility, with free direct-dial phones and plenty of brochures. Headquartered in a handsome clapboard house, the chamber operates as an information clearinghouse for all of the Keys and is open daily from 9am to 6pm.

The **Islamorada Chamber of Commerce,** housed in a little red caboose, U.S. 1 at MM 82.5, P.O. Box 915, Islamorada, FL 33036 (© **800/322-5397** or 305/664-4503; fax 305/664-4289; www.islamoradachamber.com), offers maps and literature on the Upper Keys.

You can't miss the big, blue visitor center at MM 53.5, **Greater Marathon Chamber of Commerce,** 12222 Overseas Hwy., Marathon, FL 33050 (© **800/262-7284** or 305/743-5417; fax 305/289-0183; www.floridakeysmarathon.com). Here you can receive free information on local events, festivals, attractions, dining, and lodging.

OUTDOOR SIGHTS & ACTIVITIES

Anne's Beach (MM 73.5, on Lower Matecumbe Key, at the southwest end of Islamorada) is really more picnic spot than full-fledged beach, but die-hard tanners still congregate on this lovely but tiny strip of coarse sand that was damaged beyond recognition during the series of storms in 1998. The place has been spruced up a bit, but the public bathrooms there are rancid and need some attention.

A better choice for real beaching is **Sombrero Beach** 𝒢𝒢, in Marathon at the end of Sombrero Beach Road (near MM 50). This wide swath of uncluttered beachfront actually benefited from Hurricane George in 1998, with generous deposits of extra sand and a face-lift courtesy of the Monroe County Tourist Development Council. More than 90 feet of sand is dotted with palms, Australian pines, and royal poincianas, as well as with grills, clean restrooms, and Tiki huts for relaxing in the shade. It's also a popular nesting spot for turtles that lay their eggs at night.

If you're interested in seeing the Keys in their natural, premodern development state, you must venture off the highway and take to the water. Two backcountry islands that offer a glimpse of the "real" Keys are **Indian Key** and **Lignumvitae Key** 𝒢𝒢𝒢. Visitors come here to relax and enjoy the islands' colorful birds and lush hammocks (elevated pieces of land above a marsh).

Named for the lignum vitae ("wood of life") trees found there, Lignumvitae Key supports a virgin tropical forest, the kind that once thrived on most of the Upper Keys. Over the years, human settlers imported "exotic" plants and animals to the Keys, irrevocably changing the botanical makeup of many backcountry islands and threatening much of the indigenous wildlife. Over the past 25 years, however, the Florida Department of Natural Resources has successfully removed most of the exotic vegetation from this key, leaving the 280-acre site much as it existed in the 18th century. The island also holds the Matheson House, a historic structure built in 1919 that has survived numerous hurricanes. You can go inside, but it's interesting only if you appreciate the coral rock of which the house is made. It's now a museum dedicated to the history, nature, and topography of the area. More interesting are the Botanical Gardens, which surround the house and are a state preserve. Lignumvitae Key has a visitor center at MM 88.5 (© **305/664-2540**).

Indian Key, a much smaller island on the Atlantic side of Islamorada, was occupied by Native Americans for thousands of years before European settlers arrived. The 10-acre historic site was also the original seat of Dade County before the Civil War. Interestingly, from an archaeological standpoint, you can see the ruins of the previous settlement and tour the lush grounds on well-marked trails (off Indian Key Fill, Overseas Hwy., MM 79). For more information on Indian Key, call the Florida Park Service (© **305/664-4815**) or check out www.abfla.com/parks/indiankey/indiankey.html.

If you want to see both islands, plan to spend at least half a day. You can rent your own powerboat from **Robbie's Rent-A-Boat,** U.S. 1 at MM 77.5 (on the bay side), on Islamorada. It's then a $1 admission fee to each island, which includes an informative hour-long guided tour by park rangers. This is a good option if you're a confident boater. I also recommend Robbie's **ferry service.** A visit to Lignumvitae Key costs $20 for adults and $12 for kids 12 and under, which includes the $1 park admission. The ferry used to go to Indian Key, too (a trip to both islands cost $25), but it is closed for renovations until late 2008 or early 2009. The ferry is a more economical, easier way to enjoy the beauty of the islands when you aren't negotiating the shallow reefs along the way. The runabouts, which carry up to six people, depart from

Robbie's Pier (p. 256) Thursday through Monday at 10am and 2pm for Lignumvitae Key. In high season, you may need to book 2 days before departure. Robbie's also does eco-tours, 2-hour trips through passages among the sea grass beds that rim the many protected shallow bays. You'll get to cruise among the hundreds of small, uninhabited mangrove and hardwood hammock islands, which host an amazing variety of wildlife and create the island network of the Florida Bay. Call ℭ **305/664-4815** for information from the park service; or call ℭ **305/664-9814** or visit www.robbies.com for Robbie's.

Crane Point Hammock ★★ (Finds (Kids   Crane Point Hammock is a little-known but worthwhile stop, especially for those interested in the rich botanical and archaeological history of the Keys. This privately owned, 64-acre nature area is considered one of the most important historic sites in the Keys. It contains what is probably the last virgin thatch-palm hammock in North America, as well as a rainforest exhibit and an archaeological site with prehistoric Indian and Bahamian artifacts.

Also headquarters for the Florida Keys Land and Sea Trust, the hammock's impressive nature museum has simple, informative displays of the Keys' wildlife, including a walk-through replica of a coral-reef cave and life-size dioramas with tropical birds and Key deer. Kids can participate in art projects, see 6-foot-long iguanas, climb through a scaled-down pirate ship, and touch a variety of indigenous aquatic and landlubber creatures.

5550 Overseas Hwy. (MM 50), Marathon. ℭ 305/743-9100. www.cranepoint.net. Admission $8 adults, $7 seniors over 65, $5 students, free for children 5 and under. Mon–Sat 9am–5pm; Sun noon–5pm.

Pigeon Key ★★   At the curve of the old bridge on Pigeon Key is an intriguing historic site that has been under renovation since late 1993. This 5-acre island once had the camp for the crew that built the old railway in the early 20th century, which later served as housing for the bridge builders. From here, the vista includes the vestiges of Henry Flagler's old Seven-mile Bridge and the one on which traffic presently soars, as well as many old wooden cottages and a truly tranquil stretch of lush foliage and sea. If you miss the shuttle tour from the Pigeon Key visitor center or would rather walk or bike to the site, it's about 2½ miles. Either way, you may want to bring a picnic to enjoy after a brief self-guided walking tour of the Key and a museum visit to what has become an homage to Flagler's railroad, featuring artifacts and photographs of the old bridge. An informative 28-minute video of the island's history is shown every hour starting at 10am. Parking is available at the Knight's Key end of the bridge, at MM 48, or at the visitor center at MM 47, on the ocean side.

East end of the Seven-mile Bridge near MM 47, Marathon. ℭ 305/743-5999. www.pigeonkey.net Admission $11 adults, $8.50 children 12 and under. Prices include shuttle transportation from the visitor center. Daily 10am–3pm; shuttle tours run hourly 10am–4pm.

Seven-mile Bridge ★★★   A stop at the Seven-mile Bridge is a rewarding and relaxing break on the drive south. Built alongside the ruins of oil magnate Henry Flagler's incredible Overseas Railroad, the "new" bridge (between MMs 40 and 47) is considered an architectural feat. The apex of the wide-arched span, completed in 1985 at a cost of more than $45 million, is the highest point in the Keys. The new bridge and its now-defunct neighbor provide excellent vantage points from which to view the stunning waters of the Keys. In the daytime, you may want to walk, jog, or bike along the scenic 4-mile stretch of old bridge. Or you may join local anglers, who catch barracuda,

---

Fun Fact **Bridge Mix**

The Seven-mile Bridge is the longest fragmented (unconnected pieces) bridge in the world. Completed in 1985, it was constructed parallel to the original bridge, part of Henry Flagler's Florida East Coast Railroad, which served as the original link to the Lower Keys. Some people may recognize the remnants of the old bridge from the Arnold Schwarzenegger movie *True Lies*. Others fearfully contemplate a wrong turn leading them to the old bridge instead of the new one. Not to worry: The old bridge is closed to cars and has been transformed into the world's longest fishing pier.

---

yellowtail, and dolphin (the fish, not the mammal) on what is known as "the longest fishing pier in the world." Parking is available on both sides of the bridge. Between MMs 40 and 47 on U.S. 1. (C) 305/289-0025.

VISITING WITH THE ANIMALS
Dolphin Research Center ☆☆☆ *Kids*   If you've always wanted to touch, swim, or play with dolphins, this is the place to do it. Of the three such centers in the continental United States (all located in the Keys), the Dolphin Research Center is the most organized and informative. Although some people argue that training dolphins is cruel and selfish, this is one of the most respected of the institutions that study and protect the mammals. Knowledgeable trainers at the center will also tell you that the dolphins need stimulation and enjoy human contact. They certainly seem to. They nuzzle and seem to smile and kiss the lucky few who get to swim with them in the daily program. The "family" of 15 dolphins swims in a 90,000-square-foot natural saltwater pool carved out of the shoreline.

If you can't get into the swim program, you can still watch the frequent shows, sign up for a class in hand signals, or feed the dolphins from docks. Because the Dolphin Encounter swimming program is the most popular, reservations must be made at least a month in advance. The cost is $180 per person. If you're not brave enough to swim with the dolphins or if you have a child under 12 (not permitted to swim with dolphins), try the Dolphin Splash program, in which participants stand on an elevated platform from which they can "meet and greet" the critters. A height requirement of 44 inches is enforced, and an adult must hold up children shorter than the required height. Cost for this program is $130 per person (free for children 2 and under).

Note: Swimming with dolphins has both its critics and its supporters. You may want to visit the Whale and Dolphin Conservation Society's website at www.wdcs.org. For more information about responsible travel in general, check out www.treadlightly.org and www.ecotourism.org.

U.S. 1 at MM 59 (on the bay side), Marathon. (C) 305/289-1121. www.dolphins.org. Admission $20 adults, $17 seniors, $14 children 4–12. Daily 9am–4pm. Educational walking tours 5 times daily: 10 and 11am, 12:30, 2, and 3:30pm.

Florida Keys Wild Bird Center ☆   Wander through lush canopies of mangroves on wooden walkways to see some of the Keys' most famous residents—the large variety of native birds, including broad-wing hawks, great blue and white herons, roseate spoonbills, cattle egrets, and pelicans. This not-for-profit center operates as a hospital for the many birds that have been injured by accident or disease. In 2002, the World

Parrot Mission was established here, focusing on caring for parrots and educating the public about the birds. Visit at feeding time, usually about 3:30pm, when you can watch the dedicated staff feed the hundreds of hungry birds.

U.S. 1 at MM 93.6 (bay side), Tavernier. ⓒ 305/852-4486. www.fkwbc.org. Donations suggested. Daily 8:30am–6pm.

Robbie's Pier ⭑⭑⭑ *(Value*   One of the best and definitely one of the cheapest attractions in the Upper Keys is the famed Robbie's Pier. Here the fierce steely tarpons, a prized catch for backcountry anglers, have been gathering for the past 20 years. You may recognize these prehistoric-looking giants that grow up to 200 pounds; many are displayed as trophies and mounted on local restaurant walls. To see them live, head to Robbie's Pier, where tens and sometimes hundreds of these behemoths circle the shallow waters waiting for you to feed them. Robbie's Pier also offers ranger-led boat tours and guided kayak tours to Indian Key (closed until late 2007), where you can go snorkeling or just bask in the glory of your surroundings.

U.S. 1 at MM 77.5, Islamorada. ⓒ 305/664-9814. www.robbies.com. Admission $1. Bucket of fish $2. Daily 8am–5pm. Look for the HUNGRY TARPON restaurant sign on the right after the Indian Key channel.

Theater of the Sea ⭑ *(Kids*   Established in 1946, the Theater of the Sea is one of the world's oldest marine zoos. Recently refurbished, the park's dolphin and sea-lion shows are entertaining and informative, especially for children. If you want to swim with dolphins and haven't booked well in advance, you may be able to get into this place with just a few hours' notice, as opposed to the more rigid Dolphin Research Center in Marathon (see above). While the Dolphin Research Center is a legitimate, scientific establishment, Theater of the Sea is more like a theme-park attraction. That's not to say the dolphins are mistreated, but it's not as educational and professional as the Dolphin Research Center. Theater of the Sea also permits you to swim with sea lions and stingrays. (Children 4 and under cannot participate.) There are twice-daily 4-hour adventure and snorkel cruises that cost $69 for adults and $45 for children ages 3 to 12, during which you can learn about the history and ecology of the marine environment.

U.S. 1 at MM 84.5, Islamorada. ⓒ 305/664-2431. www.theaterofthesea.com. Admission $24 adults, $16 children 3–12. Dolphin swim $150; sea-lion swim $100; stingray swim $50. Reservations are a must. Daily 10am–5pm (ticket office closes at 4pm).

TWO EXCEPTIONAL STATE PARKS

One of the best places to discover the diverse ecosystem of the Upper Keys is its most famous park, **John Pennekamp Coral Reef State Park** ⭑⭑⭑, located on U.S. 1 at MM 102.5, in Key Largo (ⓒ 305/451-1202; www.pennekamppark.com). Named for a former *Miami Herald* editor and conservationist, the 188-square-mile park is the nation's first undersea preserve: It's a sanctuary for part of the only living coral reef in the continental United States. The original plans for Everglades National Park included this part of the reef within its boundaries, but opposition from local homeowners made its inclusion politically impossible.

Because the water is extremely shallow, the 40 species of coral and more than 650 species of fish here are accessible to divers, snorkelers, and glass-bottomed boat passengers. To experience this park, visitors must get in the water—you can't see the reef from the shore. Your first stop should be the visitor center, which has a mammoth 30,000-gallon saltwater aquarium that re-creates a reef ecosystem. At the adjacent dive shop, you can rent snorkeling and diving equipment and join one of the boat trips that depart for the reef throughout the day. Visitors can also rent motorboats, sail-boats, sailboards, and canoes. The 2-hour glass-bottomed boat tour is the best way to see the coral reefs if you don't want to get wet. Watch for the lobsters and other sea life residing in the fairly shallow ridge walls beneath the coastal waters. *Remember:* These are protected waters, so you can't remove anything from them.

Canoeing around the park's narrow mangrove channels and tidal creeks is also pop-ular. You can go on your own in a rented canoe or, in winter, sign up for a tour led by a local naturalist. Hikers have two short trails from which to choose: a boardwalk through the mangroves, and a dirt trail through a tropical hardwood hammock. Ranger-led walks are usually scheduled daily from the end of November to April. Call ℂ 305/451-1202 for schedule information and reservations.

Park admission is $3.50 per vehicle for one occupant; for two or more, it's $6 per vehicle, plus 50¢ per passenger. Pedestrians and bicyclists pay $1.50 each. On busy weekends, there's often a line of cars waiting to get into the park. On your way in, ask the ranger for a map. Glass-bottomed boat tours cost $22 for adults and $15 for chil-dren 11 and under. Snorkeling tours are $29 for adults and $24 for children 17 and under, including equipment. Sailing and snorkeling tours are $34 for adults and $29 for children 17 and under, including equipment. Canoes rent for $12 per hour. For experienced boaters only, four different sizes of reef boats (powerboats) rent for $160 to $210 for 4 hours, and $259 to $359 for a full day; call ℂ 305/451-6325 for infor-mation. Fishing boats range from $135 to $359. A minimum $400 deposit (more, depending on boat size) is required. The park's boat-rental office is open daily from 8am to 5pm (last boat rented at 3pm); phone for tour and dive times. Reservations are recommended for all of the above. Also see below for more options on diving, fish-ing, and snorkeling off these reefs.

Long Key State Recreation Area 𝕶𝕶𝕶, U.S. 1 at MM 68, Long Key (ℂ 305/ 664-4815; www.abfla.com/parks/longkey/longkey.html), is one of the best places in the Middle Keys for hiking, camping, snorkeling, and canoeing. This 965-acre site is situated atop the remains of an ancient coral reef. At the entrance gate, ask for a free flyer describing the local trails and wildlife.

Three nature trails can be explored via foot or canoe. The Golden Orb Trail is a 40-minute walk through mostly plants, the Layton Trail is a 15-minute walk along the bay, and the Long Key Canoe Trail glides along a shallow-water lagoon. The excellent 1.5-mile canoe trail is short and sweet, allowing visitors to loop around the mangroves in about an hour. Long Key is also a great spot to stop for a picnic if you get hungry on your way to Key West. Campsites are available along the Atlantic Ocean. The swimming and saltwater fishing (license required) are top-notch here, as is the snor-keling, which is shallow and on the shoreline of the Atlantic. For novices, educational programs on the aforementioned are available, too.

Railroad builder Henry Flagler created the Long Key Fishing Club here in 1906, and the waters surrounding the park are still popular with game fishers. In summer, sea turtles lumber onto the protected coast to lay their eggs. Educational programs are available to view this phenomenon.

Admission is $4 per car, plus 50¢ per person (except for the Layton Trail, which is free). The recreation area is open daily from 8am to sunset. You can rent canoes at the trail head for about $5 per hour or $10 a day. The nearest place to rent snorkel equip-ment is **Holiday Isle,** 84001 U.S. 1, Islamorada (ℂ 800/327-7070).

The 10 "Keymandments"

The Keys have always attracted independent spirits, from Ernest Hemingway and Tennessee Williams to Jimmy Buffett, Zane Grey, and local hero Mel Fisher. Writers, artists, and freethinkers have long drifted down here to escape.

Although you'll generally find a very laid-back and tolerant code of behavior in the Keys, some rules do exist. Be sure to respect the 10 "Keymandments" while you're here, or suffer the consequences.

- Don't anchor on a reef. (Reefs are alive.)
- Don't feed the animals. (They'll want to follow you home.)
- Don't trash our place (or we'll send Bubba to trash yours).
- Don't touch the coral. (After all, you don't even know them. Some pose a mild risk of injury to you as well.)
- Don't speed (especially on Big Pine Key, where deer reside and tar-and-feathering is still practiced).
- Don't catch more fish than you can eat. (Better yet, let them go. Some of them support schools.)
- Don't collect conch. (This species is protected by Bubba.)
- Don't disturb the birds' nests. (They find it very annoying.)
- Don't damage the sea grass (and don't even think about making a skirt out of it).
- Don't drink and drive on land or sea. (There's nothing funny about it.)

WATERSPORTS FROM A TO Z

There are literally hundreds of outfitters in the Keys who will arrange all kinds of water activities, from cave dives to parasailing. If those recommended below are booked up or unreachable, ask the local chamber of commerce for a list of qualified members.

BOATING In addition to the rental shops in the state parks, you'll find dozens of outfitters along U.S. 1 offering a range of runabouts and skiffs for boaters of any experience level. **Captain Pip's,** U.S. 1 at MM 47.5, Marathon (© 800/707-1692 or 305/743-4403; www.captainpips.com), charges $145 to $300 per day. Overnight accommodations are available and include a free boat rental: 2-night minimum $210 to $425; weekly $1,115 to $2,495. Rooms are Key West comfortable and charming, with ceiling fans, tile floors, and pine paneling. But the best part is that every room comes with an 18- to 21-foot boat for your use during your stay. **Robbie's Rent-a-Boat,** U.S. 1 at MM 77.5, Islamorada (© 305/664-9814; www.robbies.com), rents 18- to 26-foot motorboats with engines ranging from 60 to 130 horsepower. Boat rentals are $135 to $185 for a half-day, and $185 to $235 for a full day.

CANOEING & KAYAKING I can think of no better way to explore the uninhabited backcountry on the Gulf side of the Keys than by kayak or canoe, since you can reach places that big boats just can't get to because of their large draft. Manatees will sometimes cuddle up to the boats, thinking them to be another friendly species.

Many area hotels rent kayaks and canoes to guests, as do the outfitters listed here. **Florida Bay Outfitters,** U.S. 1 at MM 104, Key Largo (© **305/451-3018;** www. kayakfloridakeys.com), rents canoes and sea kayaks for use in and around John Pennekamp Coral Reef State Park for $35 to $45 for a half-day, $50 to $60 for a full day. At **Coral Reef Park Co.,** U.S. 1 at MM 102.5, Key Largo (© **305/451-1621**), you can rent canoes and kayaks for $12 per hour; most canoes are sit-on-tops. **Florida Keys Kayak and Sail,** U.S. 1 at MM 75.5, Islamorada (© **305/664-4878;** www.florida keyskayakandski), at Robbie's Pier, offers backcountry tours, botanical-preserve tours of Lignumvitae Key, historic-site tours of Indian Key, and sunset tours through the mangrove tunnels and saltwater flats. Tour rates are from $39 to $49; rental rates range from $15 per hour to $45 per day for a single kayak, and $20 per hour to $60 per day for a double kayak. **Reflections Nature Tours** (© **305/872-4668;** www.floridakeyskayak tours.com) is a small mobile company that specializes in kayak tours through the Lower Keys. Guided kayak excursions cost $50 per person for a 3-hour tour, $40 per person for a 2-hour full-moon tour. The 3-hour custom tours start at $125 for one person and $195 for two people. All tours are by appointment only. Nature lovers can slip through the silent backcountry waters off Key West and the Lower Keys in a kayak, discovering the flora and fauna that make up the unique Keys ecosystem, on **Blue Planet Kayak Tours'** (© **305/294-8087;** www.blue-planet-kayak.com) starlight tour. All excursions are led by an environmental scientist. The starlight tours last between 2½ and 3 hours. No previous kayaking experience is necessary. Cost for the guided kayak adventure is $40 per person.

DIVING & SNORKELING Just 6 miles off Key Largo is a U.S. Navy Landing Ship Dock, the latest artificial wreck site to hit the Keys—or, rather, to be submerged 130 feet *below* the Keys.

The **Florida Keys Dive Center,** U.S. 1 at MM 90.5, Tavernier (© **305/852-4599;** www.floridakeysdivectr.com), takes snorkelers and divers to the reefs of John Pennekamp Coral Reef State Park and environs every day. PADI (Professional Association of Diving Instructors) training courses are available for the uninitiated. While some people have complained that employees are rude here, others disagree; I suggest you decide for yourself. Tours leave at 8am and 12:30pm; the cost is $35 per person to snorkel (plus $10 rental fee for mask, snorkel, and fins), and $50 per person to dive (plus an extra $24 if you need to rent all the gear).

At **Hall's Dive Center & Career Institute,** U.S. 1 at MM 48.5, Marathon (© **305/ 743-5929;** www.hallsdiving.com), snorkelers and divers can dive at Looe Key, Sombrero Reef, Delta Shoal, Content Key, or Coffins Patch. Tours are scheduled daily at 9am and 1pm. You'll spend 1 hour at each of two sites per tour. It's $45 per person to snorkel (gear included) and $55 per person to dive (tanks $8.50 each).

FISHING **Robbie's Partyboats & Charters,** U.S. 1 at MM 77.5, Islamorada (© **305/664-8070** or 305/664-8498; www.robbies.com), located at Robbie's Marina on Lower Matecumbe Key, offers day and night deep-sea and reef-fishing trips aboard a 65-foot party boat. Big-game fishing charters are also available, and "splits" are arranged for solo fishers. Party-boat fishing costs about $35 for a half-day morning tour ($3 for rod and reel rental); it's $20 extra if you want to go back out on an afternoon tour. Charters run about $700 for a half-day, $900 for a full day; splits begin at $120 per person. Phone for information and reservations.

Acquaint Yourself

Fans of stone crabs can get further acquainted with the seasonal crustaceans on 3-hour tours offered by **Keys Fisheries,** aboard 40- to 50-foot vessels that leave from Marathon. The tour includes views of fishermen as they collect crabs from traps and process their claws. The $450 cost includes up to six passengers and up to 6 pounds of fresh claws iced for travel or prepared at a dockside restaurant. Stone-crab season is October 15 to May 15. Call ✆ **305/743-4353** or check www.keysfisheries.com for more information.

Bud n' Mary's Fishing Marina, U.S. 1 at MM 79.8, Islamorada (✆ **800/742-7945** or 305/664-2461; www.budnmarys.com), one of the largest marinas between Miami and Key West, is packed with sailors offering backcountry fishing charters. This is the place to go if you want to stalk tarpon, bonefish, and snapper. If the seas are not too rough, deep-sea and coral fishing trips can also be arranged. Charters cost $500 to $550 for a half-day, $750 to $800 for a full day; splits begin at $125 per person.

WHERE TO STAY

U.S. 1 is lined with chain hotels in all price ranges. In the Upper Keys, the best moderately priced option is the **Key Largo Ramada,** off U.S. 1 at MM 100, Key Largo (✆ **800/THE-KEYS** or 305/451-3939), which has three pools and a casino boat, and is just 3 miles from John Pennekamp Coral Reef State Park. Another good Upper Keys option is **Days Inn Oceanfront Resort,** U.S. 1 at MM 82.5 (✆ **800/DAYS-INN** or 305/664-3681). In the Middle Keys, the **Wellesley Inn,** 13351 Overseas Hwy., MM 54 in Marathon (✆ **305/743-8550**), offers reasonably priced oceanside rooms.

Since the real beauty of the Keys lies mostly beyond the highways, there is no better way to see this area than by boat. So why not stay in a floating hotel? Especially if you're traveling with a group, houseboats can be economical. To rent a houseboat, contact **Houseboat Vacations,** 85944 Overseas Hwy., Islamorada (✆ **305/664-4009;** www.thefloridakeys.com/houseboats). Rates are from $847 to $1,012 for 3 nights. Boats accommodate up to eight people.

For land options, consider the recommendations below.

VERY EXPENSIVE

Cheeca Lodge & Spa ★★★ (Kids)   Located on 27 lush acres of beachfront, this rambling resort sports one of the only golf courses in the Upper Keys. Rooms have the amenities of a world-class resort in a very laid-back setting. You may not feel compelled to leave the sprawling grounds, but it's good to know that the hotel is conveniently situated near excellent restaurants and colorful nightlife. All rooms are spacious, and many have balconies; the nicer ones overlook the ocean and have large marble bathrooms. Units by the golf course have showers, not tubs, and overlook man-made lagoons. The luxurious Avanyu Spa features a gorgeous private spa pool with waterfalls and lush landscaping. Camp Cheeca's organized activities are fabulous for kids. The $39 daily resort fee may seem steep at first, but it's worth it, including tennis, golf, fishing rods, beach cabanas, kayaks, paddle boats, valet parking, Internet access, exercise classes, bottled water, housekeeping gratuity, local calls, daily newspaper, and fax services.

U.S. 1 at MM 82 (P.O. Box 527), Islamorada, FL 33036. (C) **305/664-4651.** Fax 305/664-2893. www.cheeca.com. 199 units. Winter $319–$369 deluxe double, $529–$848 deluxe suite; off season $269–$369 deluxe double, $479–$748 deluxe suite. AE, DC, DISC, MC, V. **Amenities:** 2 restaurants; 2 lounges (1 poolside); 2 outdoor heated pools; saltwater lagoon; 9-hole golf course; 6 lit hard tennis courts; full-service spa; 5 Jacuzzi hot tubs; watersports equipment rental; bike rental; children's nature programs; concierge; limited room service; in-room massage; babysitting; laundry services; dry cleaning. *In room:* A/C, TV/DVD, CD player, dataport, kitchenette (in suites), minibar, coffeemaker, hair dryer, iron, robe.

Hawk's Cay Resort *★★★ Kids*   Set on its own 60-acre island in the Middle Keys, when it comes to activities, this resort is far superior to Cheeca Lodge. In addition to sailing, fishing, snorkeling, and water-skiing, guests have the unique opportunity to interact directly with dolphins in the resort's natural saltwater lagoon. (You'll need to reserve a spot well in advance for this.) Guest rooms are large, with spacious bathrooms, island-style furniture, and private balconies with ocean or tropical views. There are also 225 hyperposh villas modeled after the kitschy 1950s concept of the "boatel." The 7,000-square-foot Calm Waters Spa provides stellar treatments. Organized children's activities include marine- and ecology-inspired programs. A $30 million renovation in 2008 included a veranda and a new lobby incorporating direct water views, a bar, and lounge as well as a vastly expanded main featuring new landscaping, multitiered sun terrace and private butlered cabanas. Fine dining options include a Latininspired steakhouse and Rum Bar featuring live music. *Note:* As we go to print, this property is still undergoing major construction that should be completed by September 2008. Call ahead to confirm.

61 Hawk's Cay Blvd. at MM 61, Duck Key, FL 33050. (C) **888/814-9104** or 305/743-7000. Fax 305/743-5215. www.hawkscay.com. 472 units, including 295 2- and 3-bedroom villas. Winter $329–$539 double, $549–$1,300 suite, $519–$1,400 villa; off season $279–$459 double, $479–$900 suite, $449–$1,000 villa. Packages available. AE, DC, DISC, MC, V. **Amenities:** 5 restaurants; lounge; 5 outdoor heated pool; adults-only private pool; nearby golf course (transportation available); 8 tennis courts (6 hard, 2 clay, 2 lit); exercise room; full-service spa; Jacuzzi; watersports equipment rental; bike rental; children's programs ($28–$35 per child); game room; concierge; room service. *In room:* A/C, TV/VCR, DVD (in villas), fridge, coffeemaker, hair dryer, iron.

EXPENSIVE

Casa Morada *★★★ Finds*   The closest thing to a boutique hotel in the Florida Keys, Casa Morada is the brainchild of a trio of New York women who used to work for hip hotelier Ian Schrager. This 16-suite property is a hipster haven tucked away off a sleepy street and radiates serenity and style in an area where serenity is aplenty, but style is elusive. Sitting on 1.7 acres of prime bayfront, the hotel features limestone grotto, freshwater pool, and poolside beverage service. Each of the cool rooms has either a private garden or a terrace—request the one with the open-air Jacuzzi that faces the bay. While the decor is decidedly island, think St. Barts rather than, say, Gilligan's. There's no onsite restaurant, a complimentary breakfast is served daily, and there's free yoga Wednesday through Sunday at 8:30 am. Enjoy free use of bikes, bocce balls, and board games. Despite the games, this place is not recommended for kids.

Dol-Fans Beware

Swimming with dolphins has both its critics and its supporters. You may want to visit the Whale and Dolphin Conservation Society's website at www.wdcs. org. For more information about responsible travel in general, check out www.treadlightly.org and www.ecotourism.org.

136 Madeira Rd., Islamorada, FL 33036. ⓒ **888/881-3030** or 305/664-0044. Fax 305/664-0674. www.casamorada. com. 16 units. Winter $299–$649; off season $299–$489. Rates include continental breakfast. AE, DISC, MC, V. From U.S. 1 S., at MM 82.2, turn right onto Madeira Rd. and continue to the end of the street. The hotel is on the right. **Amenities:** Freshwater pool; complimentary bike use; bocce ball. *In room:* A/C, TV/DVD, CD player, minibar, hair dryer, safe.

Jules' Undersea Lodge ★★★ *Finds*   Staying here is certainly an experience of a lifetime—if you're brave enough to take the plunge. Originally built as a research lab, this small underwater compartment, which rests on pillars on the ocean floor, now operates as a two-room hotel. As expensive as it is unusual, Jules' is most popular with diving honeymooners. To get inside, guests swim 21 feet under the structure and pop up into the unit through a 4×6-foot "moon pool" that gurgles soothingly all night long. The 30-foot-deep underwater suite consists of two separate bedrooms that share a common living area. Room service will deliver your meals, daily newspapers, and even a late-night pizza in waterproof containers, at no extra charge. If you don't have time or a desire to spend the night, you can hang out and explore the lodge for 3 hours for $125 to $165 per person

51 Shoreland Dr., Key Largo, FL 33037. ⓒ **305/451-2353.** Fax 305/451-4789. www.jul.com. 2 units. $375–$475 per person. Rates include breakfast and dinner, as well as all equipment and unlimited scuba diving in the lagoon for certified divers. Packages available. AE, DISC, MC, V. From U.S. 1 S., at MM 103.2, turn left onto Transylvania Ave., across from the Central Plaza shopping mall. **Amenities:** Entertainment center; dining area. *In room:* A/C, kitchenette.

Kona Kai Resort & Gallery ★★ *Finds*   This little haven is an exquisite, adults-only waterfront property right on Florida Bay—a choice location that offers a stunning sunset view overlooking Everglades National Park. Highly stylized, modern rooms and suites dot the lush 2-acre property, lined with native vegetation and fruit-bearing trees from which you're free to sample. An orchid house has more than 350 flowers. Lounge chairs, hammocks, a freshwater pool (heated in winter and cooled in summer) with fresh fruit poolside daily, a Jacuzzi, and a private beach that's larger than the Marriott's are available for those who want to relax. For the more adventurous, the owners will organize excursions to the Everglades and the backcountry. Kayaks, paddleboats, and tennis are included at no extra charge. Smoking is not permitted indoors. For meals, you'll need to visit a nearby restaurant—three are within walking distance and the exceptional staff will give you inside tips—and discounts—to their favorite local eateries and watering holes. An art gallery doubles as the lobby and guests get a 10% discount.

97802 Overseas Hwy. (U.S. 1 at MM 97.8), Key Largo, FL 33037. ⓒ **800/365-7829** or 305/852-7200. Fax 305/852-4629. www.konakairesort.com. 11 units. Winter $327–$587 double and 1-bedroom suite, $736 2-bedroom suite; off season $208–$389 double and 1-bedroom suite, $528 2-bedroom suite. AE, DISC, MC, V. Closed Sept. Children 15 and under not permitted. **Amenities:** Beachfront heated/cooled pool & Jacuzzi; lit tennis court; watersports equipment; concierge; in-room massage and facials; beachside ping pong; shuffleboard; boat dockage, Wi-Fi. *In room:* A/C, TV/DVD, DVD library, CD player with a selection of CDs by local recording artists, full kitchen (suites only), fridge, hair dryer, daily newspaper, coffee/tea, no phone.

The Moorings ★★★ *Finds*   You'll never see another soul on this 18-acre resort, a former coconut plantation, if you choose not to. There isn't even maid service unless you request it. The romantic whitewashed units, from cozy cottages to three-bedroom houses, are spacious and modestly decorated. Most have washers and dryers, and all have CD players and DVD players; ask when you book. The real reason to come to this resort is to relax on the 1,000-plus-foot beach (one of the only real beaches around). You'll also find a hard tennis court and a few kayaks and sailboards, but no motorized water vehicles in the waters surrounding the hotel, making it completely tranquil. There's no room service or restaurant, but Morada Bay and Pierre's across the street are excellent. This is a place for people who like each other a lot. Leave the kids at home unless they're extremely well-behaved and not easily bored.

123 Beach Rd. near MM 81.5 on the ocean side, Islamorada, FL 33036. (*C*) 305/664-4708. Fax 305/664-4242. www. mooringsvillage.com. 18 units. Winter $275 small cottage, $425 1-bedroom house, $3,675–$9,100 weekly oceanfront house; off season $250 small cottage, $395 1-bedroom house, $3,150–$7,700 weekly oceanfront house. 2-night minimum for smaller cottages; 1-week minimum for larger cottages and oceanfront house. AE, MC, V. **Amenities:** Large outdoor heated pool; tennis court; spa, watersports equipment, private beach. *In room:* A/C, TV/DVD, CD player, kitchen, coffeemaker, microwave, hair dryer, washer/dryer.

Tranquility Bay Beach House Resort *Kids* The newest luxury resort in the lower Keys, Tranquility Bay sits on a tropically landscaped 12 acres on the Gulf of Mexico. You'll feel like you're in your own beach house, with gorgeous two- and three-bedroom suites all with water views. All of the subtly decorated rooms come equipped with everything a techno-savvy beach bum needs—even washers and dryers. Best of all, every room has spacious porches with French doors, wooden deck chairs, and 180-degree views of the water. The restaurant, Butterfly Café, is just as fine, with seasonal seafood menus. A private spa, Island Spice, helps you relax, but, really, this is one of the most relaxing resorts in all the Keys. Grounds sport lagoon pools, gazebos, a great lawn, and a beachfront Tiki bar. There are also activities, from adventure fishing and snorkeling to an adventure kids' club. *Note:* This is a nonsmoking resort. Smoking isn't even permitted on porches, only in designated areas.

2600 Overseas Hwy., Marathon, FL 33036. (*C*) **305/259-0888.** Fax 305/289-0667. www.tranquilitybay.com. 87 units. Winter $399–$539; off season $279–$509. AE, DC, MC, V. **Amenities:** Large outdoor heated pool; fitness center; spa; watersports equipment rental. *In room:* A/C, TV/DVD, CD player, Wi-Fi, kitchen, coffeemaker, microwave, hair dryer.

MODERATE

Banana Bay Resort & Marina *Finds* It doesn't look like much from the sign-cluttered Overseas Highway, but once you enter the lush grounds of Banana Bay, you'll realize you're in one of the most bucolic and best-run properties in the Upper Keys. The resort is a beachfront maze of two-story buildings hidden among banyans and palms, with moderately sized rooms, many with private balconies. A recreational activity area has horseshoe pits, a bocce court, barbecue grills, and a giant lawn chessboard. The kitschy restaurant serves three meals a day, indoors and poolside. The hotel also rents bikes, boats, WaveRunners, kayaks, day-sailing dinghies, and bait and tackle. Another surprising amenity is Pretty Joe Rock, the hotel's private island, available for long weekends and weekly rentals. On it is a two-bedroom, two-bathroom cottage that's ideal for romantic escapes. Banana Bay is family friendly, but for an adults-only resort, there's **Banana Bay Resort** at 2319 N. Roosevelt Blvd., in Key West ((*C*) **305/296-6925**), which doesn't allow children.

U.S. 1 at MM 49.5, Marathon, FL 33050. (*C*) **800/BANANA-1** or 305/743-3500. Fax 305/743-2670. www.banana bay.com. 60 units. Spring $185–$245 double; off season $105–$225 double. Rates include continental breakfast. 3- and 7-night honeymoon and wedding packages available. AE, DC, DISC, MC, V. **Amenities:** Restaurant; bar; pool; tennis courts; Jacuzzi; boat/waverunner/kayak/bike rentals; small beach; marina; fishing charters; barbecue pit; snorkeling area; self-service laundry. *In room:* A/C, TV, fridge, hair dryer, iron.

Conch Key Cottages *Finds* Here's your chance to play castaway in the Keys. Occupying its own private microisland just off U.S. 1, Conch Key Cottages is a comfortable hideaway, a place to get away from it all. The cottages offer solitude, with the exception of one or two interesting eateries. The units, which were built at different times over the past 40 years, overlook their own stretch of natural, but very small, private beach. They have screened-in porches, cozy bedrooms, bathrooms, hammocks, barbecue grills, and two-person kayaks. The two-bedroom cottages are the most spacious and are well designed, practically tailor-made for couples or families. On the other side of the pool is a handful of efficiency apartments that are similarly outfitted but don't enjoy beach frontage.

Private Island off U.S. 1 at MM 62.3, Marathon Florida, 33050 Tel 800/330-1577 or 305/289-1377. Fax 305/743-8661. www.conchkeycottages.com. 12 cottages. Dec 15–Sept 7 $139–$349 for up to 6 people. Sept 8–Dec 14 $85- $199 for up to 4 people. AE, DISC ,MC, V. **Amenities:** Pool, sandy beach, dockage, complimentary kayaks, Internet. *In cottages:* A/C, TV, full kitchens, no phones.

Faro Blanco Marine Resort　Spanning both sides of the Overseas Highway and set entirely on waterfront property, this huge, two-shore marina-and-hotel complex was closed and undergoing a complete renovation at press time. It should reopen in winter 2009 as the Faro Blanco Resort & Yacht Club. It will offer something for every taste, but we hope it remains newly charming in a vintage Florida way and not in a nouveau, trendy Florida way.

1996 Overseas Hwy., U.S. 1 at MM 48.5, Marathon, FL 33050. ℂ **800/759-3276** or 305/743-9018. Fax 305/866-5235. www.spottswood.com.

Holiday Isle Resort　Holiday Isle attracts a spring-break kind of crowd year-round, a crowd that tends not to care about the rooms themselves—and has no qualms cramming an entire fraternity into a single unit for budget reasons. The famous **Tiki Bar,** which is allegedly being torn down to make room for condo units—much to the dismay of many a marathon drinker—claims to have invented the Rum Runner drink (151-proof rum, blackberry brandy, banana liqueur, grenadine, and lime juice), and there's no reason to doubt it. It's the Tiki Bar that brings the people, really. Hordes of partiers are attracted to the resort's nonstop merrymaking, live music, and beachfront bars. As a result, some of the accommodations can be noisy. Rooms are bare-bones; despite the ocean views, they're pretty awful and need a good scrub-down—especially the units that lead to the filthy, sandy Tiki Bar. But, really, isn't that why you're here in the first place?

U.S. 1 at MM 84, Islamorada, FL 33036. ℂ **800/327-7070** or 305/664-2321. Fax 305/664-2703. www.holidayisle. com. 178 units. Winter $144–$294 double, $274–$450 suite; off season $119–$199 double, $245–$425 suite. AE, DISC, MC, V. **Amenities:** 5 restaurants; 12 bars; 3 outdoor heated pools; kids' pool; Jacuzzi; watersports equipment rentals; kids' programs; laundry facilities. *In room:* A/C, TV, fridge, hair dryer.

Lime Tree Bay Resort Motel ⍟　The only place to stay in the tiny town of Layton (pop. 183), Lime Tree is midway between Islamorada and Marathon and is situated on a pretty piece of waterfront graced with hundreds of mature palm trees and tropical foliage. It prides itself on its promise of no hustle, no valets, and, most amusingly, no bartenders in Hawaiian shirts! Motel rooms and efficiencies have tiny bathrooms with showers, but are clean and well maintained. The best deal is the two-bedroom bay-view cottage: A spacious living area with new furnishings leads to a large private deck overlooking the Gulf. There's also a full kitchen and two full bathrooms. Fifteen efficiencies and suites have kitchenettes. Pretty cool in its own right is the Zane Grey Suite (named after the famous author and screenwriter, who lived right around the corner), a two-bedroom, one-bathroom unit with the best views and a second-story location with private stairs.

U.S. 1 at MM 68.5, Layton, Long Key, FL 33001. ℂ **800/723-4519** or 305/664-4740. Fax 305/664-0750. www.lime treebayresort.com. 30 units. Winter $105–$159 double, $165–$345 suite; $185–$215 cottage; off season $95–$139 double, $149–$163 suite, $200–$315 cottage. AE, DC, DISC, MC, V. **Amenities:** Restaurant; small outdoor pool; tennis court; Jacuzzi; watersports equipment rental. *In room:* A/C, TV, dataport, kitchenette (in some).

Pines and Palms 𝒢𝒢𝒢 *Finds*   Looking for a beachfront cottage or, better yet, an oceanfront villa, but don't want to spend your future child's college fund? This is the place. Cheery, cozy cottages, Atlantic views, and a private beachfront with hammocks and a pool give way to a relaxed, tropical paradise. Service is friendly and accommodating. All rooms and cottages have full kitchens and balconies, and are ideal for extended stays. Although there's no restaurant on-site, the staff will be happy to bring a Weber barbecue to your patio so you can grill out by the beach. Because of its popularity, Pines and Palms usually has a 2-night minimum.

MM 80.4 (ocean side), Islamorada, FL 33036. © **800/624-0964** or 305/664-4343. www.pinesandpalms.com. 25 units. $99–$219 double; $129–$299 suite; $159–$459 cottage; $399–$579 villa. AE, MC, V. **Amenities:** Oceanfront heated freshwater pool; bikes and kayaks available for rent; coin-op washers and dryers. *In room:* A/C, kitchen (in most), fridge, coffeemaker.

INEXPENSIVE

Ragged Edge Resort 𝒢𝒢   This small oceanfront property's Tahitian-style units are spread along more than half a dozen gorgeous, grassy waterfront acres. All are immaculately clean and comfortable, and most are outfitted with full kitchens and tasteful furnishings. There's no bar, restaurant, or staff to speak of, but the retreat's affable owner is happy to lend bicycles and give advice on the area's offerings. A large dock attracts boaters and a variety of local and migratory birds. An outdoor heated freshwater pool is a bonus for those months when the temperature gets a bit chilly.

243 Treasure Harbor Rd. (near MM 86.5), Islamorada, FL 33036. © **800/436-2023** or 305/852-5389. www.ragged-edge.com. 11 units. $62–$99 double; $100–$249 suite. AE, MC, V. **Amenities:** Outdoor pool; free use of bikes; coin-op washers and dryers. *In room:* A/C, kitchen (in most), fridge, coffeemaker.

CAMPING

John Pennekamp Coral Reef State Park 𝒢𝒢   One of Florida's best parks, Pennekamp has 47 well-separated campsites, half of which are available by advance reservation. The tent sites are small but equipped with restrooms, hot water, and showers. Note that the local environment provides fertile breeding grounds for insects, particularly in late summer, so bring repellent. Two man-made beaches and a small lagoon nearby attract many large wading birds. Reservations are held until 5pm; the park must be notified of late arrival by phone on the check-in date. Pennekamp opens at 8am and closes around sundown.

U.S. 1 at MM 102.5 (P.O. Box 487), Key Largo, FL 33037. © **305/451-1202.** www.pennekamppark.com. 47 campsites. Reservations can be made in advance by calling Reserve America (© 800/326-3521). $31.49 (with electricity) per site. Park entry $4 per vehicle with driver (50¢ for each additional person). Yearly permits and passes available. AE, DISC, MC, V. No pets.

Long Key State Park 𝒢   The Upper Keys' other main state park is more secluded than its northern neighbor—and more popular. All sites are located oceanside and surrounded by narrow rows of trees and nearby restroom facilities. Reserve well in advance, especially in winter.

U.S. 1 at MM 67.5 (P.O. Box 776), Long Key, FL 33001. © **305/664-4815.** www.abfla.com/parks/longkey/longkey.html. 60 sites. $26 per site for 1–4 people; $3.25 per vehicle. AE, DISC, MC, V. No pets.

WHERE TO DINE

Although not known as a culinary hot spot (though always improving), the Upper and Middle Keys do have some excellent restaurants, most of which specialize in seafood. There's good news for those who missed the landmark **Green Turtle Inn,** 81219 Overseas Hwy. at MM 81.2 (© **305/664-2006**), while it was closed. Chef Dawn

Sieber of Kaiyo fame has put the finishing touches on her version of the much-loved, quintessential Keys restaurant. It now features classic and contemporary Florida cuisine, a full bar and tasting station, custom catering, gourmet to go, and a Green Turtle product line, all in a beautiful, laid-back rustic environment. Her restaurant is to be flanked by an art gallery and sportsfishing outfitter, making it a one-stop shop for locals and fun-loving tourists who have put Islamorada on the map.

Often visitors (especially those who fish) take advantage of accommodations that have kitchen facilities and cook their own meals. Some restaurants will even clean and cook your catch, for a fee.

VERY EXPENSIVE

Atlantic's Edge ★★ SEAFOOD/REGIONAL   Ask for a table by the oceanfront window at this elegant seafood restaurant. Although the service and food are generally first rate, don't get dressed up—sports coats for men are fine, but not necessary. You can choose from an innovative menu of fresh fish, steak, chicken, and pastas. Signature dishes include spiny lobster dumplings; crispy arepitas with smoked mozzarella, chorizo, and caramelized apples; and honey lavender–glazed duck breast. Service can sometimes be less than efficient, but it is always courteous and professional.

In the Cheeca Lodge, U.S. 1 at MM 82, Islamorada. **(*)** **305/664-4651.** Reservations recommended. Main courses $20–$48. AE, DC, DISC, MC, V. Daily 6–10pm.

Kaiyo ★★★ JAPANESE/SUSHI   This funky, colorful restaurant looks out of place in an area where most eateries are housed in shanty shacks, and its exquisite, modern sushi is a first for Islamorada—but the food is so good, people from all over South Florida plan trips around a meal at Kaiyo. The brainchild of Chef Dawn Sieber, former executive chef at Cheeca Lodge, Kaiyo isn't your typical sushi restaurant, but rather one that fuses Florida's fine ingredients with some of the freshest raw fish this side of Tokyo. Signature sushi items, such as the spicy volcano conch roll and the Key lime lobster roll, are outstanding, as are the farm-raised raw oysters and farmed baby-conch tempura. A hip, modern interior is an amusing contrast to the casually dressed, Key-ed up diners, and service here is of five-star caliber—something not typically found in the laid-back Keys. Before you say that you came to the Keys not for trendy sushi, but for fresh fish and conch fritters, do have a meal at Kaiyo. It *will* change the way you view Keys cuisine.

81701 Old Hwy., U.S. 1 at MM 82, Islamorada. **(*)** **305/664-5556.** www.kaiyokeys.com. Reservations recommended. Main courses $12–$20; sushi $4.50–$15. AE, DC, MC, V. Mon–Sat noon–10pm.

Pierre's ★★★ FRENCH   The two-story British West Indies–style plantation home that houses this exquisite French restaurant is only part of the dramatic effect of a memorable dinner at Pierre's. Inside, you'll find more design drama—in a good way, of course—in the form of an eclectic mix of Moroccan, Indian, and African artifacts. Lighting is dim, with candlelight and Tiki torches outside, and it's completely romantic—especially outdoors on the second-floor veranda overlooking the water. The food challenges the setting, with amazing flavors and gorgeous presentation. The tempura lobster tail with hearts of palm hash, soy glaze, and wasabi crème fraîche, and the potato-crusted black grouper with creamy sweet-potato orzo, Osetra caviar, and baby frisée are to die for. Desserts are equally divine and if you can't decide what to have, order the Trilogy of Desserts and sample bread pudding, crème brûlée, and chai tea mousse. After dinner, head downstairs to the Green Flash Lounge, where you'll find a laid-back cocktail scene, with locals and visitors marveling at the exquisite, priceless setting.

U.S. 1 at MM 81.6 (bay side), Islamorada. ℂ 305/664-3225. www.pierres-restaurant.com. Main courses $34–$40. AE, MC, V. Sun–Thurs 5:30–10pm; Fri–Sat 5:30–11pm.

EXPENSIVE

Barracuda Grill 𝑘𝑘 SEAFOOD   Owned by Lance Hill and his wife, Jan, a former sous-chef at Little Palm Island (p. 272), this small, casual spot serves excellent seafood, steaks, and chops. Some favorites here are the Caicos gold conch, braised pork shank, and mangrove snapper and mango. Try the appetizer of tipsy olives, marinated in gin or vodka, to kick-start your meal. For fans of spicy food, go for the red-hot calamari. Decorated with barracuda-themed art, the restaurant also features a well-priced American wine list with lots of California vintages.

U.S. 1 at MM 49.5 (bay side), Marathon. ℂ 305/743-3314. Main courses $15–$30. AE, MC, V. Mon–Sat 6–10pm.

Butterfly Café 𝑘𝑘𝑘 SEAFOOD   Housed in the stunning Tranquility Bay resort, Butterfly Café is the newest gourmet hot spot in the Lower Keys with water views and a stellar menu of fresh local seafood. Among the dishes not to miss: sugarcane-spiced glazed dolphin with mango-ginger salsa, and Cuban spiced grilled double-cut pork chops with mango-lime mojo and spiced macadamia basmati rice. Service is very friendly and knowledgeable, and desserts are to die for. Save room for the sticky toffee pudding and nutty-crust Key lime pie with white chocolate mousse. Open for breakfast, lunch, and dinner, but Sunday brunch is especially spectacular. Don't miss the tropical French toast.

2600 Overseas Hwy., in the Tranquility Bay Resort, Marathon. ℂ 305/289-0888. www.tranquilitybay.com. Main courses $19–$35. AE, MC, V. Daily 7–10am and 11:30am–10pm. Sun brunch 10:30am–2:30pm.

Green Turtle Inn 𝑘𝑘𝑘 SEAFOOD   The legend is back, but this time with a gourmet market and cuisine cooked with locally farmed vegetables and microgreens. While it may not be a throwback to the old Florida Keys, Green Turtle, reopened by Dawn Sieber, who subsequently left "for a change of scenery," remains a must stop for anyone looking for a fabulous dining experience. Some old menu items remain—like the famous beer battered basket of turtle fries and the luscious conch chowder. But the new menu items are nothing to sneer at either. Small plates including braised Florida lobster with tomato chive and sage, butchers tenderloin "Dianne" with Yukon gold potato mash, and whitewater clams in Thai green curry coconut sauce with Key lime and basil are enough for an excellent main course, but don't miss entrees such as local snapper wrapped in shredded filo, tomato, feta, olive and basil salad, and whatever you do, do not miss the chocolate turtle mud ice cream pie. After dinner check out the art gallery and gourmet shop.

81219 Overseas Hwy., mile marker 81.2, Islamorada. ℂ 305/664-2006. Main courses $19–$26. AE, MC, V. Daily 7–10am and 11:30am–10pm.

Marker 88 𝑘𝑘𝑘 SEAFOOD/REGIONAL   An institution in the Upper Keys, Marker 88 has been pleasing locals and visitors since it opened in the 1970s. New chefs and owners have infused a new life into the place and the menu, which still utilizes fresh fruits, local ingredients, and fish caught in the Keys' waters. Among the menu highlights are the yellowtail Rangoon, sautéed and topped with black currant gelee and cinnamon, and served with fresh tropical fruits; and yellowtail Martinique, sautéed and topped with sweet basil, grilled bananas, and garlic butter. The waitresses, who are pleasant enough, require a bit of patience, but the food—not to mention the spectacular Gulf views—is worth it.

U.S. 1 at MM 88 (bay side), Islamorada. © **305/852-9315**. www.marker88.info. Reservations suggested. Main courses $16–$39. AE, DC, DISC, MC, V. Tues–Sun 5–11pm. Closed Sept.

MODERATE

Lorelei Restaurant and Cabana Bar ⊛ SEAFOOD/BAR FOOD   Don't resist the siren call of the enormous roadside mermaid—you won't be dashed onto the rocks. This big old fish house and bar, with excellent views of the bay, is a great place for a snack, a meal, or a beer. A good-value menu focuses mainly on seafood; in season, lobster is the way to go. Other fare includes the standard clam chowder, fried shrimp, and doughy conch fritters. Salads and soups are hearty and satisfying. For those tired of fish, the menu offers a few beef options. The outside bar has live music every evening, and you can order snacks and light meals from a limited menu.

U.S. 1 at MM 82, Islamorada. © **305/664-4656**. Reservations not usually required. Main courses $10–$26. AE, DC, DISC, MC, V. Daily 7am–10:30pm. Outside bar serves breakfast 7–11am; lunch/appetizer menu 11am–9pm. Bar closes at midnight.

INEXPENSIVE

Calypso's Seafood Grill ⊛⊛ *Finds* SEAFOOD   With a motto proudly declaring "Yes, we know the music is loud and the food is spicy. That's the way we like it!" you know you're in a typical Keys eatery. Thankfully the food is anything but, with inventive seafood dishes in a casual and rustic waterside setting. Among the house specialties: cracked conch and superb steamed clams, but if you're not too hot out there, try the She-Crab soup. It's exceptional. The prices are surprisingly reasonable, but the service may be a bit more laid-back than you're used to. And don't be dismayed by the paper plates—Calypso's is one of Key Largo's most exceptional restaurants, so much that owner/chef Todd Lollis has opened a second restaurant in the area, Big Fish, 99010 Overseas Hwy. (© **305/453-0820**), which is a bit easier to find but no less stellar.

1 Seagate Blvd. (near MM 99.5), Key Largo. © **305/451-0600**. Main courses $10–$20. MC, V. Wed–Mon 11:30am–10pm; Fri–Sat 11:30am–11pm. From the south, turn right at the blinking yellow lights near MM 99.5 to Ocean Bay Dr. and then turn right. Look for the blue vinyl-sided building on the left.

Harriette's Restaurant ⊛ BREAKFAST   This little yellow shack packs in a major crowd for breakfast, thanks to friendly service, old-school greasy spoon–style fare and colossal homemade biscuits and muffins. Despite the grease factor, Harriette's realizes some people want to eat healthy—you're in the Keys, though, go nuts—and offers South Beach Diet and Atkins menu items as well.

MM 95.7, Key Largo. © **305/852-8689**. Breakfast $5–$7. Cash Only. Daily 6am–2pm.

Islamorada Fish Company ⊛⊛ SEAFOOD   Pick up a cooler of stone crab claws in season (mid-Oct to Apr), or try the great fried-fish sandwiches. A few hundred yards up the road (at MM 81.6) is Islamorada Fish Company Restaurant & Bakery, the newer establishment, which looks like an average diner but has fantastic seafood, pastas, and breakfasts. Locals gather here for politics and gossip as well as delicious grits, oatmeal, omelets, and pastries. Keep your eyes open while dining outside—the last time I was here, baby manatees were floating around, waiting for their close-ups.

U.S. 1 at MM 81.5 (up the street from Cheeca Lodge), Islamorada. © **800/258-2559** or 305/664-9271. www.islamoradafishco.com. Reservations not accepted. Main courses $10–$37. DISC, MC, V. Sun–Thurs 11am–9pm; Fri–Sat 11am–10pm.

Snapper's 𝒢 SEAFOOD A locals' waterfront favorite, Snapper's serves fresh seafood caught by local fisherman—or by you, if you dare! The blackened mahimahi is exceptional and a bargain, complete with salad, vegetable, and choice of starch. There's also live music nightly and a lively, colorful—and deliciously casual—crowd.

139 Seaside Ave. at MM 94.5, Key Largo. © 305/852-5956. www.islamoradafishco.com. Main courses $10–$25. DISC, MC, V. Sun–Thurs 11am–9pm; Fri–Sat 11am–10pm.

THE UPPER & MIDDLE KEYS AFTER DARK

Nightlife in the Upper Keys tends to start before the sun goes down, often at noon, since most people—visitors and locals alike—are on vacation. Also, many anglers and sports-minded folk go to bed early.

Hog Heaven, MM 85.3, just off the main road on the ocean side, Islamorada (© 305/664-9669), opened in the early 1990s, the joint venture of young locals tired of tourist traps. This whitewashed biker bar is a welcome respite from the neon-colored cocktail circuit. It has a waterside view and diversions such as big-screen TVs and video games. The food isn't bad, either. The atmosphere is cliquish since most patrons are regulars, so start up a game of pool to break the ice. Open daily from 11am to 4am.

No trip to the Keys is complete without a stop at the **Tiki Bar at the Holiday Isle Resort** (p. 264), U.S. 1 at MM 84, Islamorada (© 305/664-2321). Hundreds of revelers visit this oceanside spot for drinks and dancing at any time of day, but the live rock starts at 8:30pm. The thatched-roof Tiki Bar draws a mix of thirsty people, all in pursuit of a good time. In the afternoon and early evening (when everyone is either sunburned, drunk, or just happy to be dancing to live reggae), head for **Kokomo's,** next door. It often closes at 7:30pm on weekends (5:30pm on weekdays), so arrive early. For information, call the Holiday Isle Resort. Rumor has it that greedy developers are going to raze the Tiki Bar to make way for million-dollar condos, but loyal boozehounds are raising hell over it and some are even trying to have the Tiki Bar declared a Florida landmark! Call ahead to make sure it's still open.

Locals and tourists mingle at the outdoor cabana bar at **Lorelei** (see "Where to Dine," above). Most evenings after 5pm, you'll find local bands playing on a thatched-roof stage—mainly rock or reggae, and sometimes blues.

Woody's Saloon and Restaurant, U.S. 1 at MM 82, Islamorada (© 305/664-4335), is a lively, wacky, loud, raunchy, local legend of a place serving up mediocre pizzas, buck-naked strippers, and live bands almost every night. The house band, Big Dick and the Extenders, showcases a 300-pound Native American who does a lewd, rude, and crude routine of politically incorrect jokes and songs starting at 9pm Tuesday through Sunday. He is a legend. By the way, don't think you're lucky if you're offered the front table: It's the target seat for Big Dick's haranguing. Avoid the lame karaoke performance on Sunday and Monday evenings. There's a small cover on most nights. Drink specials, contests, and the legendary Big Dick keep this place packed until 4am almost every night. *Note:* This place is not for the faint of heart, but more for those from the Howard Stern school of nightlife.

For a more subdued atmosphere, try the handsome stained-glass and mahogany-wood bar and club at **Zane Grey's,** on the second floor of World Wide Sportsman, MM 81.5 (© 305/664-4244). Outside, enjoy a view of the calm waters of the bay; inside, soak up the history of real longtime anglers. It's open from 11am to at least 11pm (later on weekends). Call to find out who's playing on Friday and Saturday nights, when there's live entertainment and no cover.

2 The Lower Keys: Big Pine Key to Coppitt Key

128 miles SW of Miami

Unlike their neighbors to the north and south, the Lower Keys (including Big Pine, Sugarloaf, and Summerland) are devoid of rowdy spring-break crowds, boast few T-shirt and trinket shops, and have almost no late-night bars. What they do offer are the very best opportunities to enjoy the vast natural resources on land and water that make the area so rich. Stay overnight in the Lower Keys, rent a boat, and explore the reefs—it might be the most memorable part of your trip.

ESSENTIALS

GETTING THERE   See "Essentials" for the Upper and Middle Keys (p. 252) and continue south on U.S. 1. The Lower Keys start at the end of the Seven-mile Bridge. There are also airports in Marathon and Key West.

VISITOR INFORMATION   Big Pine and Lower Keys Chamber of Commerce, ocean side of U.S. 1 at MM 31 (P.O. Box 430511), Big Pine Key, FL 33043 (© 800/ 872-3722 or 305/872-2411; fax 305/872-0752; www.lowerkeyschamber.com), is open Monday through Friday from 9am to 5pm, and Saturday from 9am to 3pm. The pleasant staff will help with anything a traveler may need. Call, write, or stop in for a comprehensive, detailed information packet.

WHAT TO SEE & DO

Once the centerpiece (these days, it's Big Pine Key) of the Lower Keys and still a great asset is **Bahia Honda State Park**⚘, U.S. 1 at MM 37.5, Big Pine Key (© 305/872-2353; www.bahiahondapark.com), which, even after the violent storms of 2005, has one of the most beautiful coastlines in South Florida. Bahia (pronounced "*Bah*-ya") Honda is a great place for hiking, bird-watching, swimming, snorkeling, and fishing. The 524-acre park encompasses a wide variety of ecosystems, including coastal mangroves, beach dunes, and tropical hammocks. There are miles of trails packed with unusual plants and animals, plus a small white-sand beach. Shaded seaside picnic areas are fitted with tables and grills. Although the beach is never wider than 5 feet, even at low tide, this is the Lower Keys' best beach area.

True to its name (Spanish for "deep bay"), the park has relatively deep waters close to shore—perfect for snorkeling and diving. Easy offshore snorkeling here gives even novices a chance to lie suspended in warm water and simply observe diverse marine life passing by. Or else head to the stunning reefs at Looe Key, where the coral and fish are more vibrant than anywhere else in the United States. Snorkeling trips go from the Bahia Honda concessions to Looe Key National Marine Sanctuary (4 miles offshore). They depart twice daily March through September and cost $29 for adults, $24 for children 6 to 14, and $6 for equipment rental. Call © **305/872-3210** for a schedule.

Entry to the park is $5 per vehicle (plus 50¢ per person), $1.50 per pedestrian or bicyclist, free for children 5 and under. If you're alone in a car, you'll pay only $2.50. Open daily from 8am to sunset.

The most famous residents of the Lower Keys are the tiny Key deer. Of the estimated 300 existing in the world, two-thirds live on Big Pine Key's **National Key Deer Refuge**⚘. To get your bearings, stop by the rangers' office at the Winn-Dixie Shopping Plaza, near MM 30.5 off U.S. 1. They'll give you an informative brochure and map of the area. The refuge is open Monday through Friday from 8am to 5pm.

If the office is closed, head out to the **Blue Hole,** a former rock quarry now filled with the fresh water that's vital to the deer's survival. To get there, turn right at Big Pine Key's only traffic light onto Key Deer Boulevard (take the left fork immediately after the turn) and continue 1½ miles to the observation-site parking lot, on your left. The .5-mile **Watson Hammock Trail,** about three-tenths of a mile past the Blue Hole, is the refuge's only marked footpath. The deer are more active in cool hours, so try coming out to the path in the early morning or late evening to catch a glimpse of these gentle dog-size creatures. There is an observation deck from which you can watch and photograph the protected species. Refuge lands are open daily from a half-hour before sunrise to a half-hour after sunset. Don't be surprised to see a lazy alligator warming itself in the sun, particularly in outlying areas around the Blue Hole. If you do see a gator, do not go near it, do not touch it, and do not provoke it. Keep your distance; if you must get a photo, use a zoom lens. Also, whatever you do, do not feed the deer—it will threaten their survival. Call the **park office** (© 305/872-2239) to find out about the infrequent free tours of the refuge, scheduled throughout the year.

OUTDOOR ACTIVITIES

BIKING   The Lower Keys are a great place to get off busy U.S. 1 to explore the beautiful back roads. On Big Pine Key, cruise along Key Deer Boulevard (at MM 30). Those with fat tires can ride into the National Key Deer Refuge. Many lodgings offer bike rentals.

BIRD-WATCHING   A stopping point for migratory birds on the Eastern Flyway, the Lower Keys are populated with many West Indian bird species, especially in spring and fall. The small, vegetated islands of the Keys are the only nesting sites in the U.S. for the white-crowned pigeon. They're also some of the few breeding places for the reddish egret, roseate spoonbill, mangrove cuckoo, and black-whiskered vireo. Look for them on Bahia Honda Key and the many uninhabited islands nearby.

BOATING   Dozens of shops rent powerboats for fishing and reef exploring. Most also rent tackle, sell bait, and have charter captains available. For instance, **Florida Keys Boat Rental** (© 305/664-2003; www.keysboat.com), offers an impressive selection of boats from $125 to $450 half-day and $105 to $650 for a full day. They also offer kayaks and paddle boats for eco tours.

CANOEING & KAYAKING   The Overseas Highway (U.S. 1) touches on only a few dozen of the many hundreds of islands that make up the Keys. To really see the Lower Keys, rent a kayak or canoe—perfect for these shallow waters. **Reflections Kayak Nature Tours,** operating out of the Old Wooden Bridge Fishing Camp, 1791 Bogie Dr., Mile Marker 30, Big Pine Key (© 305/872-4668; www.floridakeyskayak tours.com), offers fully outfitted backcountry wildlife tours, either on your own or with an expert. The expert, U.S.C.G. licensed Captain Bill Keogh, literally wrote the book on the subject. "The Florida Keys Paddling Guide" written by Bill in 2004 covers all the unique ecosystems and inhabitants as well as launches and favorite routes from Key Biscayne to the Dry Tortugas National Park. The 3-hour kayak tours cost $50 per person. An extended 4-hour backcountry tour for two to six people costs $125 per person and uses a mothership to ferry kayaks and paddlers to the remote reaches of the refuge. Reservations required.

FISHING   A day spent fishing, either in the shallow backcountry or in the deep sea, is a great way to ensure a fresh-fish dinner, or you can release your catch and just appreciate the challenge. Whichever you choose, **Strike Zone Charters,** U.S. 1 at MM 29.5, Big Pine Key (© 305/872-9863), is the charter service to call. Prices for fishing boats start at $500 for a half-day and $650 for a full day with a $50 fuel surcharge added to the cost. If you have enough anglers to share the price (they take up to six people), it isn't too steep. The outfitter may also be able to match you with other interested visitors. Strike Zone also offers daily trips to Looe Key National Marine Sanctuary on a glass-bottom boat. The 2-hour trip costs $25 for viewing, $30 for snorkeling, and $40 for scuba diving. Strike Zone's 5-hour **Eco Island** excursion offers a vivid history of the Keys from the glass-bottom boat. The tour stops for snorkeling, light tackle fishing and eventually docks at an island for their famous island fish cookout. Cost is $49 per person, including mask, snorkel, fins, vests, rods, reel, bait, fishing licenses, food, and all soft drinks.

HIKING   You can hike throughout the flat, marshy Keys on both marked trails and meandering coastlines. The best places to trek through nature are **Bahia Honda State Park,** at MM 29.5, and **National Key Deer Refuge,** at MM 30 (for more information on both, see "What to See & Do," above). Bahia Honda Park has a free brochure describing an excellent self-guided tour along the Silver Palm Nature Trail. You'll traverse hammocks, mangroves, and sand dunes, and cross a lagoon. The walk (less than a mile) explores a great cross section of the natural habitat in the Lower Keys and can be done in less than half an hour.

SNORKELING & SCUBA DIVING   Snorkelers and divers should not miss the Keys' most dramatic reefs at the **Looe Key National Marine Sanctuary.** Here you'll see more than 150 varieties of hard and soft coral—some centuries old—as well as every type of tropical fish, including gold and blue parrotfish, moray eels, barracudas, French angels, and tarpon. **Looe Key Dive Center,** U.S. 1 at MM 27.5, Ramrod Key (© 305/872-2215; www.diveflakeys.com), offers a mind-blowing 5-hour tour aboard a 45-foot catamaran with two shallow 1-hour dives for snorkelers and scuba divers. Snorkelers pay $40; divers pay $80. Equipment is available for rental for $10. On Wednesday and Saturday, you can do a fascinating dive to the *Adolphus Busch, Sr.,* a shipwreck off Looe Key in 100 feet of water, for $80. (See "What to See & Do," above, for other diving options.)

WHERE TO STAY

There are a number of cheap, fairly unappealing fish shacks along the highway for those who want bare-bones accommodations. So far, there are no national hotel chains in the Lower Keys. For information on lodging in cabins or trailers at local campgrounds, see "Camping," below.

VERY EXPENSIVE

Little Palm Island Resort & Spa ★★★   This exclusive island escape—host to presidents, royalty, and even Howard Stern—is not just a place to stay while in the Lower Keys; it is a destination all its own. Built on a private 5½-acre island, it's accessible only by boat or seaplane. Guests stay in thatched-roof duplexes amid lush foliage and flowering tropical plants—and gentle Key deer, which are to this island what cats are to Key West. Many villas have ocean views and private decks with hammocks. Inside, the romantic suites have all the comforts of a swank beach cottage, but without phones, TVs, or alarm clocks. Mosquitoes can be a problem, even in winter. (Bring spray and lightweight, long-sleeved clothing.) Known for a stellar spa and innovative and pricey food, Little Palm also hosts visitors just for dinner, brunch, or lunch. If you're staying on the island, opt for the full American plan, which includes three meals a day.

Launch is on the ocean side of U.S. 1 at MM 28.5, Little Torch Key, FL 33042. (℡ 800/343-8567 or 305/872-2524. Fax 305/872-4843. www.littlepalmisland.com. 30 units. Winter $840–$1,695 double; off season $640–$1,595 double. Rates include transportation to and from the island and unlimited (nonmotorized) watersports. Meal plans include 2 meals daily for $125 per person per day, 3 meals at $140 per person. AE, DC, DISC, MC, V. No children 15 and under. **Amenities:** Restaurant; bar; 2 pools (1 outdoor with small waterfall, 1 indoor); health club; spa; extensive watersports equipment rental; concierge; courtesy van from Key West or Marathon airport; ferry service to and from the mainland; limited room service; in-room massage; laundry service; dry cleaning; jogging trail. *In room:* A/C, dataport, minibar, coffeemaker, hair dryer, Jacuzzi, no phone.

INEXPENSIVE

Parmer's Resort 𝒢 Parmer's, a fixture here for more than 20 years, is well known for its charming hospitality and helpful staff. This downscale resort offers modest but comfortable cottages, each of them unique. Some are waterfront, many have kitchenettes, and others are just a bedroom. The Wahoo room (no. 26), a one-bedroom efficiency, is especially nice, with a small sitting area that faces the water. All units have been recently updated and are very clean. Many can be combined to accommodate families. The hotel's waterfront location, not to mention the fact that it's only a half-hour from lively Key West, almost makes up for the fact that you must pay extra for maid service.

565 Barry Ave. (P.O. Box 430665), near MM 28.5, Little Torch Key, FL 33043. (℡ 305/872-2157. Fax 305/872-2014. www.parmersresort.com. 45 units. Winter $134–$194 double, from $174 efficiency; off season $99–$129 double, from $129 efficiency. Rates include continental breakfast. AE, DISC, MC, V. From U.S. 1, turn right onto Barry Ave. Resort is ½-mile down on the right. **Amenities:** Heated pool; kayak rental; bike rental; coin-op washers and dryers; boat ramp. *In room:* A/C, TV.

CAMPING

Bahia Honda State Park 𝒢𝒢𝒢 (℡ 800/326-3521; www.abfla.com/parks/bahia-honda/bahiahonda.html) offers some of the best camping in the Keys. It is as loaded with facilities and activities as it is with campers. But don't be discouraged by its popularity—this park encompasses more than 500 acres of land, 80 campsites spread throughout three areas, and three spacious and comfortable duplex cabins. Cabins hold up to eight guests each and come complete with linens, kitchenettes, wraparound terraces, barbecue pits, and rocking chairs. For one to four people, camping costs about $25 per person without electricity and $26 with electricity. Depending on the season, cabin prices range from $75 to $120.

Another excellent value can be found at the **KOA Sugarloaf Key Resort** 𝒢𝒢, near MM 20. This oceanside facility has 200 fully equipped sites, with water, electricity, and sewer, which rent for about $94 a night (no-hookup sites cost about $84). Or you can pitch a tent on the 5 acres of waterfront property. This place is especially nice because of its private beaches and access to diving, snorkeling, and boating; its grounds are also well maintained. In addition, the resort rents travel trailers: The 25-foot Dutchman sleeps six and costs about $120 a day. For details, contact the resort at P.O. Box 420469, Summerland Key, FL 33042 (℡ 800/562-7731 or 305/745-3549; fax 305/745-9889; www.koa.com).

WHERE TO DINE

There aren't many fine-dining options in the Lower Keys, with the exception of the **Dining Room at Little Palm Island** (p. 272), MM 285, Little Torch Key (℡ 305/872-2551), where you'll be wowed with gourmet French Caribbean fare that looks like a meal but tastes like a vacation. You need to take a ferry to this chichi private island, where you can indulge at the exquisite oceanside restaurant even if you're not staying over.

MODERATE

Mangrove Mama's Restaurant SEAFOOD/CARIBBEAN   As the dedicated locals who come daily for happy hour will tell you, this is a true Lower Keys institution and a dive in the best sense of the word (the restaurant is a shack that used to have a gas pump as well as a grill). Guests share the property with stray cats and some miniature horses out back. It's run down, but in a charming Keys sort of way—they serve beer in a jelly glass. A handful of simple tables, inside and out, are shaded by banana trees and palm fronds. Fish is the menu's mainstay, although soups, salads, sandwiches, and omelets are also good. Grilled-chicken and club sandwiches are tasty alternatives to fish, as are meatless chef's salads and spicy barbecued baby back ribs. The restaurant is under new ownership, which some say has let the place slip a bit, though they still rock their Sunday brunch with amazing crab benedict.

U.S. 1 at MM 20, Sugarloaf Key. ℂ 305/745-3030. Main courses $10–$20; lunch $6–$10; brunch $5–$15. MC, V. Daily 11am–3pm and 5:30–10pm.

INEXPENSIVE

Coco's Kitchen 🔆 CUBAN/AMERICAN   This tiny storefront has been dishing out black beans, rice, and shredded beef for more than 10 years. The owners, who actually from Nicaragua, cook not only superior Cuban food, but local specialties, Italian dishes, and Caribbean choices. Specialties include fried shrimp, whole fried yellowtail, and Cuban-style roast pork (available only on Sat). The best bet is the daily special, which may be roasted pork or fresh grouper, served with rice and beans or salad and crispy fries. Top off the huge, cheap meal with a rich caramel-soaked flan.

283 Key Deer Blvd. (in the Winn-Dixie Shopping Center), Big Pine Key. ℂ 305/872-4495. Main courses $6–$15; breakfast $2–$10. MC, V. Mon–Sat 7am–7:30pm. Turn right at the traffic light near MM 30.5; stay in the left lane.

No Name Pub PUB FOOD/PIZZA   This funky old bar out in the boondocks serves snacks and sandwiches until 11pm on most nights, and drinks until midnight. Pizzas are tasty—try one topped with local shrimp. Or consider a bowl of chili with all the fixings. Everything is served on paper plates. Locals hang out at the rustic bar, one of the Keys' oldest bars, drinking beer and listening to a jukebox heavy with 1980s tunes.

¼-mile south of No Name Bridge on N. Watson Blvd., Big Pine Key. ℂ 305/872-9115. Pizzas $6–$18; subs $5. MC, V. Daily 11am–11pm. Turn right at Big Pine's only traffic light (near MM 30.5) onto Key Deer Blvd. Turn right on Watson Blvd. At the stop sign, turn left. Look for a small wooden sign on the left marking the spot.

THE LOWER KEYS AFTER DARK

Although the mellow islands of the Lower Keys aren't exactly known for wild nightlife, there are some friendly bars and restaurants where locals and tourists gather to hang out and drink. One of the most scenic is **Paradise Waterfont,** Barry Avenue near MM 28.5 (ℂ **305/872-9989**), the only waterfront restaurant between Key West and Marathon. The place is enclosed with windows looking out onto the water where there's a shark pond for those who are curious. Delicious food is served from 10:30am until 10pm and the bar closes around midnight. The place even has its own brand of wine, which is currently being marketed in France, of all places. Paradise attracts an odd mix of bikers and blue-hairs daily, and is a great place to overhear local gossip and colorful metaphors. Pool tables are the main attraction, but there's also live music some nights. The drinks are reasonably priced, and the food isn't too bad, either. For another fun bar scene, see the **No Name Pub,** listed above in "Where to Dine."

3 Key West ★★★

159 miles SW of Miami

There are two schools of thought on Key West—one is that it has become way too commercial, and the other is that it's still a place where you don't have to worry about being prim, proper, or even well-groomed. I think it's a bizarre fusion of both—a fascinating look at small-town America where people truly live by the (off)beat of their own drum, albeit one with a Coach outlet, Banana Republic, Starbucks, and, most recently, a handful of multimillion-dollar condo developments thrown in to bring you back to reality. The locals, or "conchs" (pronounced "conks"), and the developers here have been at odds for years. This once low-key island has been thoroughly commercialized—there's a Hard Rock Cafe smack in the middle of Duval Street, and thousands of cruise-ship passengers descend on Mallory Square each day. It's definitely not the seedy town Hemingway and his cronies once called their own. Or is it?

Laid-back Key West still exists, but it's now found in different places: the backyard of a popular guesthouse, for example, or an art gallery, a secret garden, a clothing-optional bar, or the hip hangouts of Bahama Village. Fortunately, there are plenty of these, and Key West's greatest historic charm is found just off the beaten path. Don't be afraid to explore these residential areas, as conchs are notoriously friendly. In fact, exploring the side streets always seems to yield a new discovery. Of course, there are always the calm waters of the Atlantic and the Gulf of Mexico all around.

The heart of town offers party people a good time—that is, if your idea of a good time is the smell of stale beer, loud music, and hardly shy revelers. Here you'll find good restaurants, fun bars, live music, rickshaw rides, and lots of shopping. Key West is still very gay-centric, except during spring break. Same-sex couples that walk hand in hand are the norm here; if you're not open-minded and prefer to avoid this scene, look for the ubiquitous rainbow flag hanging outside gay establishments and you'll know what to expect. For the most part, however, the scene is extremely mixed and colorful. If partying isn't your thing, then avoid Duval Street—the Bourbon Street of South Florida—at all costs. Instead, take in the scenery at a dockside bar or oceanside Jacuzzi. Whatever you do, don't bother with a watch or tie—this is the home of the perennial vacation.

ESSENTIALS

GETTING THERE   For directions by car, see "Essentials" (p. 252) for the Upper and Middle Keys and continue south on U.S. 1. When entering Key West, stay in the far-right lane onto North Roosevelt Boulevard, which becomes Truman Avenue in Old Town. Continue for a few blocks and you'll find yourself on **Duval Street** ★, in the heart of the city. If you stay to the left, you'll also reach the city center after passing the airport and the remnants of historic houseboat row, where a motley collection of boats once made up one of Key West's most interesting neighborhoods.

Several regional airlines fly nonstop (about 55 min.) from Miami to Key West; fares are about $120 to $300 round-trip. **American Eagle** (© 800/433-7300), **Continental** (© 800/525-0280), **Delta** (© 800/221-1212), and **US Airways Express** (© 800/428-4322) land at **Key West International Airport,** South Roosevelt Boulevard (© 305/296-5439), on the southeastern corner of the island.

Key West

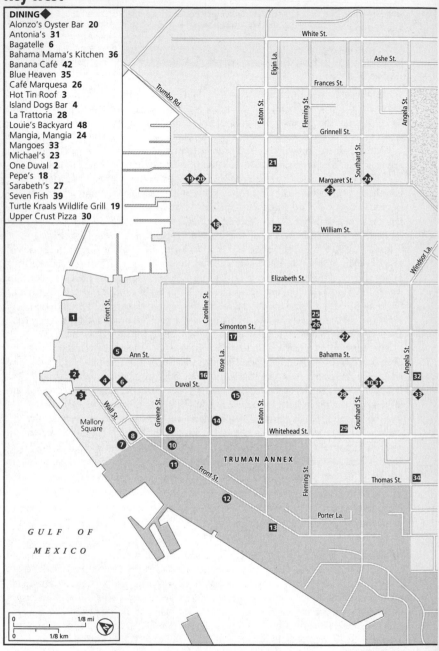

DINING ◆

Alonzo's Oyster Bar **20**
Antonia's **31**
Bagatelle **6**
Bahama Mama's Kitchen **36**
Banana Café **42**
Blue Heaven **35**
Café Marquesa **26**
Hot Tin Roof **3**
Island Dogs Bar **4**
La Trattoria **28**
Louie's Backyard **48**
Mangia, Mangia **24**
Mangoes **33**
Michael's **23**
One Duval **2**
Pepe's **18**
Sarabeth's **27**
Seven Fish **39**
Turtle Kraals Wildlife Grill **19**
Upper Crust Pizza **30**

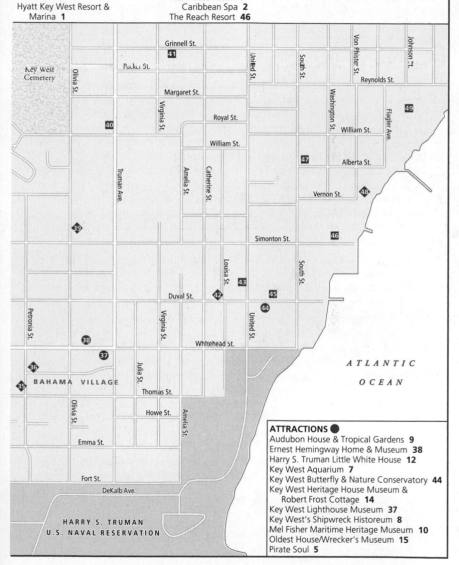

ACCOMMODATIONS ■
Ambrosia Key West **25**
Angelina Guest House **34**
Big Ruby's **29**
Casa Marina Resort & Beach Club **49**
Curry Mansion Inn **16**
The Gardens Hotel **32**
The Grand **41**
Hyatt Key West Resort &
  Marina **1**

Island City House Hotel **22**
Key West International
  Hostel & Seashell Motel **47**
La Pensione **40**
Marquesa Hotel **26**
Ocean Key Resort & Spa **3**
Pearl's Rainbow **43**
Pier House Resort &
  Caribbean Spa **2**
The Reach Resort **46**

Simonton Court **17**
Southernmost Point Guest House **45**
Weatherstation Inn **13**
Westin Key West Resort & Marina **11**
Westwinds Inn **21**

Key West Cemetery

Grinnell St.
Olivia St.
Pucker St.
Margaret St.
Virginia St.
Royal St.
William St.
Truman Ave.
Amelia St.
Catherine St.
United St.
South St.
Von Phister St.
Johnson St.
Reynolds St.
Washington St.
William St.
Flagler Ave.
Alberta St.
Vernon St.
Simonton St.
Louisa St.
Duval St.
South St.
United St.
Petronia St.
Virginia St.
Whitehead St.
Julia St.
BAHAMA VILLAGE
Thomas St.
Olivia St.
Howe St.
Amelia St.
Emma St.
Fort St.
DeKalb Ave.

**HARRY S. TRUMAN
U.S. NAVAL RESERVATION**

*ATLANTIC
OCEAN*

ATTRACTIONS ●
Audubon House & Tropical Gardens **9**
Ernest Hemingway Home & Museum **38**
Harry S. Truman Little White House **12**
Key West Aquarium **7**
Key West Butterfly & Nature Conservatory **44**
Key West Heritage House Museum &
  Robert Frost Cottage **14**
Key West Lighthouse Museum **37**
Key West's Shipwreck Historeum **8**
Mel Fisher Maritime Heritage Museum **10**
Oldest House/Wrecker's Museum **15**
Pirate Soul **5**

Greyhound (© 800/231-2222; www.greyhound.com) has buses leaving Miami for Key West every day for about $40 one-way and $76 round-trip. Seats fill up in season, so come early. The ride takes about 4½ hours.

You can also get to Key West from Miami via the **Key West Express** (© 866/KW-FERRY; www.keywestexpress.us), a 155-foot-long catamaran that travels from Miami to Key West at 40 miles per hour. The Big Cat features two enclosed cabins, sun seated deck, observation deck, Satellite TV, and full galley and bar. The boat leaves daily from the dock next to the Miami Seaquarium and your ticket price of $100 round trip per person includes free parking.

GETTING AROUND   Old Town Key West has limited parking, narrow streets, and congested traffic, so driving is more of a pain than a convenience. Unless you're staying in one of the more remote accommodations, consider trading in your car for a bicycle. The island is small and flat as a board, which makes it easy to negotiate, especially away from the crowded downtown area. Many tourists choose to cruise by moped, an option that can make navigating the streets risky, especially since there are no helmet laws in Key West. Hundreds of visitors are seriously injured each year, so be careful and spend the extra few bucks to rent a helmet.

Rates for simple one-speed cruisers start at about $10 per day. Mopeds start at about $20 for 2 hours, $35 per day, and $100 per week. The best shops include the **Bicycle Center,** 523 Truman Ave. (© **305/294-4556**); the **Moped Hospital,** 601 Truman Ave. (© **305/296-3344**); and **Tropical Bicycles & Scooter Rentals,** 1300 Duval St. (© **305/294-8136**). The **Bike Shop,** 1110 Truman Ave. (© **305/294-1073**), rents cruisers for $12 per day, $60 per week; a $150 deposit is required.

PARKING   Parking in Key West's Old Town is particularly limited, but there is a well-placed **municipal parking lot** at Simonton and Angela streets, just behind the firehouse and police station. If you've brought a car, you may want to stash it here while you enjoy the very walkable downtown part of Key West.

VISITOR INFORMATION   The **Key West Chamber of Commerce,** 402 Wall St., Key West, FL 33040 (© **800/527-8539** or 305/294-2587; www.keywestchamber.com), provides both general and specialized information. The lobby is open daily from 8:30am to 6pm; phones are answered from 8am to 8pm. The **Key West Visitor Center** (© **800/LAST-KEY**) is the area's best for information on accommodations, goings-on, and restaurants; it's open Monday through Friday from 8am to 5:30pm, Saturday and Sunday from 8:30am to 5pm. Gay travelers may want to call the **Key West Business Guild** (© **305/294-4603**), which represents more than 50 guesthouses and B&Bs, as well as many other gay-owned businesses (ask for its color brochure).

While you're in one of the above offices, be sure to pick up a free copy of *Sharon Wells' Walking & Biking Guide to Historic Key West.* Though I still couldn't find all the spots I wanted to in the Key West Cemetery (p. 281) while using the guide, it was helpful for historic descriptions throughout town. Sharon Wells also leads guided walking tours around the island. For information, call her at © **305/294-8380** or go to www.seekeywest.com.

ORIENTATION   A mere 2×4-mile island, Key West is simple to navigate, even though there's no real order to the arrangement of streets and avenues. As you enter town on U.S. 1 (Roosevelt Blvd.), you will see most of the moderate chain hotels and fast-food restaurants. The better restaurants, shops, and outfitters are crammed onto Duval Street, the main thoroughfare of Key West's Old Town. On surrounding streets, many inns and lodges are set in picturesque Victorian/Bahamian homes. On the southern side of the island is the coral-beach area and some of the larger resort hotels.

The area called Bahama Village is the furthest thing from a tourist trap, but can be a bit spotty at night if you aren't familiar with the area. With several newly opened, trendy restaurants and guesthouses, this hippie-ish neighborhood, complete with street-roaming chickens and cats, is the roughest and most urban you'll find in the Keys. You might see a few drug deals happening on street corners, but they're nothing to be overly concerned about: It looks worse than it is, and resident business owners tend to keep a vigilant eye on the neighborhood. The area is actually quite funky and should be a welcome diversion from the Duvalian mainstream.

SEEING THE SIGHTS

Key West's greenest attraction, the **Florida Keys Eco-Discovery Center,** opened in early 2007. Overlooking the waterfront at the Truman Annex (© **301/608-3040**), the Center features 6,000 square feet of interactive exhibits depicting Florida Keys underwater and upland habitats—with emphasis on the ecosystem of North America's only living contiguous barrier coral reef, which parallels the Keys.

Before shelling out big bucks for any of the dozens of worthwhile attractions in Key West, I recommend getting an overview on either of the two comprehensive island tours, the **Conch Tour Train** or the **Old Town Trolley** (p. 283 for both). There are simply too many attractions and historic houses to list. I've highlighted my favorites below, but I encourage you to seek out others.

Audubon House & Tropical Gardens ⟨★★⟩   This well-preserved 19th-century home stands as a prime example of early Key West architecture. Named after renowned painter and bird expert John James Audubon, who is said to have visited the house in 1832, the graceful two-story structure is a peaceful retreat from the bustle of Old Town. Included in the price of admission is a self-guided, half-hour audio tour that spotlights rare Audubon prints, gorgeous antiques, historic photos, and lush tropical gardens. With voices of several characters from the house's past, the tour never gets boring—though it is a bit hokey at times. Even if you don't want to explore the grounds and home, check out the impressive gift shop, which sells a variety of fine mementos at reasonable prices.

205 Whitehead St. (between Greene and Caroline sts.). © **305/294-2116**. www.audubonhouse.com. Admission $11 adults, $5 children 6–12, $6.50 children 12-17. Daily 9:30am–5pm (last entry at 4:30pm).

East Martello Museum and Gallery   Adjacent to the airport, the East Martello Museum is in a Civil War–era brick fort that itself is worth a visit. The museum contains a bizarre variety of exhibits that collectively do a thorough job of interpreting the city's intriguing past. Historic artifacts include model ships, a deep-sea diver's wooden air pump, a crude raft from a Cuban "boat lift," a supposedly haunted doll, and a horse-drawn hearse. Exhibits illustrate the Keys' history of salvaging, sponging, and cigar making. After seeing the galleries (which should take 45–60 min.), climb a steep spiral staircase to the top of the lookout tower for good views over the island and ocean. A member of the Key West Art and Historical Society, East Martello has two cousins: the **Key West Museum of Art and History,** 281 Front St. (© **305/295-6616**), and the **Key West Lighthouse Museum** (p. 281).

3501 S. Roosevelt Blvd. © **305/296-3913**. www.kwahs.com/martello.htm. Admission $6 adults, $5 seniors, $3 children 8–12. Daily 9:30am–4:30pm (last entry at 4pm).

Ernest Hemingway Home and Museum ℛ   Hemingway's particularly handsome stone Spanish colonial house, built in 1851, was one of the first on the island to be fitted with indoor plumbing and a built-in fireplace. It also has the first swimming pool built on Key West (look for the penny that Hemingway pressed into the cement near the pool). The author owned the home from 1931 until his death in 1961, and lived here with about 50 cats, whose descendants, including the famed six-toed felines, still roam the premises. It was during those years that the Nobel Prize–winning author wrote some of his most famous works, including *For Whom the Bell Tolls, A Farewell to Arms,* and *The Snows of Kilimanjaro.* Fans may want to take the optional half-hour house tour to see his study as well as rooms with glass cabinets that store certain artifacts, books, and pieces of mail addressed to him. It's interesting (to an extent) and included in the price of admission. If you don't take the tour or have no interest in Hemingway, the price of admission is really a waste of money, except for the lovely architecture and garden. If you're feline-phobic, beware: There are cats everywhere. Guided tours are given every 15 minutes and expect to spend an hour on the property.

907 Whitehead St. (between Truman Ave. and Olivia St.). ℗ **305/294-1136.** Fax 305/294-2755. www.hemingway-home.com. Admission $11 adults, $6 children. Daily 9am–5pm. Limited parking.

Harry S. Truman Little White House ℛℛ   President Truman used to refer to the White House as the "Great White Jail." On temporary leave from the Big House, Truman discovered the serenity of Key West and made his escape to what became known as the Little White House, which is open to the public for touring. The house is fully restored; the exhibits document Truman's time in the Keys. Tours run every 15 minutes and last between 45 and 50 minutes. For fans of all things Oval Office–related, there's a presidential gift shop on the premises.

Impressions

I've a notion to move the Capitol to Key West and just stay.

—President Harry S. Truman

---

111 Front St. ℗ **305/294-9911.** www.trumanlittle whitehouse.com. Admission $11 adults, $5 children 11 and under. Daily 9am–4:30pm.

Key West Aquarium ℛℛ *Kids*   The oldest attraction on the island, the Key West Aquarium is a modest but fascinating place. A long hallway of eye-level displays showcases dozens of varieties of fish and crustaceans. Kids can touch sea cucumbers and sea anemones in a shallow tank. If possible, catch one of the free guided tours—you can witness the dramatic feeding frenzy of the sharks, tarpon, barracudas, stingrays, and turtles. Expect to spend 1 to 1½ hours here.

1 Whitehead St. (at Mallory Sq.). ℗ **305/296-2051.** www.keywestaquarium.com. Admission $11 adults, $5 children 4–12. Website offers tickets for $1 cheaper. Tickets good for 2 consecutive days. Look for discount coupons at local hotels, at Duval St. kiosks, and from trolley and train tours. Daily 10am–6pm; tours at 11am and 1, 3, and 4pm.

Key West Butterfly & Nature Conservatory ℛℛ *Kids*   Housed in a 13,000-square-foot pavilion, this attraction has nature lovers flitting with excitement, thanks to the 5,000-square-foot, glass-enclosed butterfly aviary as well as a gallery, learning center, and gift shop exploring all aspects of the butterfly world. Inside, more than 1,500 butterflies and 3,500 plants, including rare orchids, and even fish and turtles, coexist in a controlled climate. You'll walk freely among the butterflies, so if you have even the slightest fear of the creatures, consider twice before entering. Expect to spend about an hour inside.

1316 Duval St. ℂ 305/296-2988. www.keywestbutterfly.com. Admission $10 adults, $8.50 seniors, $7.50 children 4–12. Daily 9am–5pm; last ticket sold at 4:30pm.

Key West Cemetery ✪✪✪ *Finds*   This funky cemetery is the epitome of quirky Key West: irreverent and humorous. Many tombs are stacked several high, condominium style, since the rocky soil made digging 6 feet under nearly impossible for early settlers. Epitaphs reflect residents' lighthearted attitudes toward life and death. I TOLD YOU I WAS SICK is one of the more famous, as is the tongue-in-cheek widow's inscription AT LEAST I KNOW WHERE HE'S SLEEPING TONIGHT. Pick up a copy of *Sharon Wells' Walking & Biking Guide to Historic Key West* (p. 278). Some of the inscriptions are hard to find even with the free walking-tour guide, but this place is fun to explore.
Entrance at the corner of Margaret and Angela sts. Free admission. Daily dawn–dusk.

Key West Heritage House Museum and Robert Frost Cottage ✪ *Finds*   For a glimpse into one of the oldest houses in Key West, check out the Heritage House Museum, the former 1834 home of Jesse Porter, a Key West preservationist who hosted the likes of Robert Frost, Tennessee Williams, Gloria Swanson, and Tallulah Bankhead in his home-cum-salon. Furnished with 19th-century antiques, the house is a fascinating look at 19th- and early-20th-century Key West. Guided tours are informative and entertaining, sort of an antique version of an *E! True Hollywood Story.*
410 Caroline St. ℂ 305/296-3573 for tour reservations. www.heritagehousemuseum.org. Guided tour $7, self-guided tour $5. Mon–Sat 10am–4pm.

Key West Lighthouse Museum ✪   When the Key West Lighthouse opened in 1848, it signaled the end of a profitable era for the pirate salvagers who looted reef-stricken ships. The story of this and other area lighthouses is illustrated in a small museum that was formerly the keeper's quarters. It's worth mustering the energy to climb the 88 claustrophobic steps to the top, where you'll be rewarded with magnificent panoramic views of Key West and the ocean.
938 Whitehead St. ℂ 305/294-0012. Admission $10 adults, $9 seniors and locals, $5 children 7–12. Daily 9:30am–4:30pm.

Key West's Shipwreck Historeum   You'll see more impressive artifacts at nearby Mel Fisher's museum, but for the morbidly curious, shipwrecks should rank right up there with car wrecks. For those of you who can't help but look, this museum is the place to be for everything you ever wanted to know about shipwrecks and more. See movies, artifacts, and a real-life wrecker, who will be more than happy to indulge your curiosity about the wrecking industry that preoccupied the early pioneers of Key West. Depending on your level of interest, you can expect to spend up to 2 hours here.
1 Whitehead St. (at Mallory Sq.). ℂ 305/292-8990. Fax 305/292-5536. www.shipwreckhistoreum.com. Admission $11 adults, $5 children 4–12. Website sells tickets for $1 cheaper. Shows daily every half-hour 9:45am–4:45pm.

Mel Fisher Maritime Heritage Museum ✪✪   This museum honors local hero Mel Fisher, whose death in 1998 was mourned throughout South Florida and who, along with a crew of other salvagers, found a multimillion-dollar treasure trove in 1985 aboard the wreck of the Spanish galleon *Nuestra Señora de Atocha.* If you're into diving, pirates, and sunken treasures, check out this small museum, full of doubloons, pieces of eight, emeralds, and solid-gold bars (one of them you can lift!). A 1700 English merchant slave ship, the only tangible evidence of the transatlantic slave trade, is on view on the museum's second floor. An exhibition telling the story of more than

Going, Going, Gone: Where to Catch the Famous Key West Sunset

A tradition in Key West, the Sunset Celebration can be relaxing or overwhelming, depending on your vantage point. If you're in town, you must check out this ritual at least once. Every evening, locals and visitors gather at the docks behind Mallory Square (at the westernmost end of Whitehead St.) to celebrate the day gone by. Secure a spot on the docks early to experience the carnival of portrait artists, acrobats, food vendors, animal acts, and other performers trading on the island's bohemian image. But the carnival atmosphere isn't for everyone: In season, the crowd can be overwhelming, especially when the cruise ships are in port. Also, hold on to your bags and wallets, as the tight crowds make Mallory Square at sunset prime pickpocket territory.

A more refined choice is the Westin's **Sunset Deck** (© 305/294-4000), a luxurious second-floor bar on Front Street, right next door to Mallory Square. From the civilized calm of a casual bar, you can look down on the mayhem with a drink in hand.

Also near the Mallory madness is the bar at the **Ocean Key Resort**, at the very tip of Duval Street (© 800/328-9815 or 305/296-7701). This long open-air pier serves drinks and decent bar food against a dramatic pink-and-yellow-streaked sky.

For the very best potent cocktails and great bar food on an outside patio or enclosed lounge, try **Pier House Resort and Caribbean Spa's Havana Docks**, 1 Duval St. (© 305/296-4600). There's usually live music and a lively gathering of visitors enjoying this island's bounty. The bar is right on the water and makes a prime sunset-viewing spot.

1,400 African slaves captured in Cuban waters and brought to Key West for sanctuary is the museum's latest, most fascinating exhibit to date.

200 Greene St. © 305/294-2633. www.melfisher.org. Admission $11 adults, $9.50 seniors, $6 children 6–12. Daily 9:30am–5pm. Take U.S. 1 to Whitehead St. and turn left on Greene.

Oldest House/Wrecker's Museum ⊛   Dating from 1829, this old New England Bahama House has survived pirates, hurricanes, fires, warfare, and economic ups and downs. The one-and-a-half-story home was designed by a ship's carpenter and incorporates many features from maritime architecture, including portholes and a ship's hatch designed for ventilation before the advent of air-conditioning. Especially interesting is the detached kitchen building outfitted with a brick "beehive" oven and vintage cooking utensils. Although not a must-see on the Key West tour, history and architecture buffs will appreciate the finely preserved details and the glimpse of a slower, easier time in the island's life.

322 Duval St. © 305/294-9502. Admission $5 adults, $1 children 6–12. Thurs–Sat 10am–2pm.

Pirate Soul ⊛ Kids   Thanks to Johnny Depp and Disney's Pirates of the Caribbean, pirates have never been hotter. This museum is dedicated to everything about the legendary seafaring rogues, featuring more than 500 artifacts from the golden age of piracy, as well as animatronics and interactive exhibits. Among the highlights is the only authentic pirate treasure chest in America, originally belonging to Captain Thomas Tew, and Blackbeard's original blunderbuss. As with any kitschy museum, there's a store where you can buy all sorts of gear, from eye patches to bath products sporting the Jolly Roger. If you find yourself thirsty or hungry, Rum Barrel is the museum's homage to grub and grog.

524 Front St. ✆ 305/292-1113. www.piratesoul.com. Admission $15 adults, $9 children 6–12. Tickets are cheaper on the website. Daily 9am–7pm.

ORGANIZED TOURS

BY TRAM & TROLLEY-BUS   Yes, it's more than a bit hokey to sit on this 60-foot tram of yellow cars, but it's worth it—at least once. The city's whole story is packed into a neat, 90-minute package on the **Conch Tour Train,** which covers the island and all its rich, raunchy history. In operation since 1958, the cars are open-air, which can make the ride uncomfortable in bad weather. The engine of the "train" is a propane-powered Jeep disguised as a locomotive. Tours depart from both Mallory Square and the Welcome Center, near where U.S. 1 becomes North Roosevelt Boulevard, on the less-developed side of the island. For information, call ✆ **305/294-5161** or go to www. conchtourtrain.com. The cost is $27 for adults, $13 for children 4 to 12. Tickets are cheaper on the website. Daily departures are every half-hour from 9am to 4:30pm.

The **Old Town Trolley** is the choice in bad weather or if you're staying at one of the hotels on its route. Humorous drivers maintain a running commentary as the enclosed trolley loops around the island's streets past all the major sights. Trolley buses depart from Mallory Square and other points around the island, including many area hotels. For details, call ✆ **305/296-6688** or visit www.trolleytours.com. Tours are $27 for adults, $13 for children 4 to 12. Tickets are cheaper on the website. Departures are daily every half-hour (though not always on the half-hour) from 9am to 4:30pm.

Whichever you choose, both of these historic, trivia-packed tours are well worth the price of tickets.

⟨Moments A Great Escape

Many people complain that Key West's quirky, quaint panache has been lost to the vulture of capitalism, evidenced by the glut of T-shirt shops and tacky bars. But that's not entirely so. For a quiet respite, visit the **Key West Tropical Forest Botanical Gardens** (✆ 305/296-1504; www.keywestbotanicalgarden.org), a little-known slice of serenity tucked between the Aqueduct Authority plant and the Key West Golf Course. The 11-acre gardens—maintained by volunteers and funded by donations—contain the last hardwood hammock in Key West, plus a colorful representation of wildflowers, butterflies, and birds. Over 60 endangered botanical species are alive and well here. A genetically cloned tree is one of the many sites at "the only frost-free tropical moist garden in the continental United States." Located at Botanical Garden Way and College Road, Stock Island. Free admission but a donation of $5 is suggested. Open daily from 8am to sunset. Follow College Road; then turn right just past Bayshore Manor.

Literary Key West

Counting Ernest Hemingway and Tennessee Williams among your denizens would give any city the right to call itself a literary mecca. But over the years, tiny Key West has been home—or at least home away from home—to dozens of literary types who are drawn to some combination of its gentle pace, tropical atmosphere, and lighthearted mood (not to mention its lingering reputation for an oft-ribald lifestyle). Writers have long known that more than a few muses prowl the tree-laden streets of Key West.

Robert Frost first visited Key West in 1934 and wintered here for the remainder of his life. In the early 20th century, writers such as John Dewey, Archibald MacLeish, John Dos Passos, Wallace Stevens, and S. J. Perelman were drawn to the island. Even as Key West boomed and busted and boomed again, and despite the island's growing popularity with world travelers, writers continued to move to Key West or to visit it with such regularity that they were deemed honorary "conchs." Novelists Phil Caputo, Tom McGuane, Jim Harrison, John Hersey, Alison Lurie, and Robert Stone were among these.

Of course, one of Key West's favorite sons also earned a spot in the annals of local literary history. Famous for his good-time, tropical-laced music, Jimmy Buffett was also a surprisingly well-received novelist in the 1990s. Although Buffett now makes the infinitely ritzier Palm Beach his Florida home, his presence is still felt in virtually every corner of Key West.

But it is Nobel Prize winner and avid outdoorsman Ernest Hemingway who is most identified with Key West. Much of the island has changed since he lived here from 1931 to 1961. Even the famous Sloppy Joe's bar, which Hemingway frequented mostly from 1933 to 1937, has changed locations (reportedly without closing—customers picked up their drinks and whatever else they could carry from the bar and brought it all down the block to the new location, and service resumed with barely a blink!). Fortunately, the Ernest Hemingway Home and Museum (p. 280) has been lovingly preserved. But to get the best feel for what Hemingway loved most about Key West, visit the docks at Garrison Bight. It is from here that Hemingway and his many famous (and infamous) friends and contemporaries departed for Caribbean ports of call and for sport upon the sea.

Key West pays homage to its literary legacy with the annual Key West Literary Seminar in January. For information, call © **888/293-9291** or visit www.keywestliteraryseminar.org.

BY AIR   Proclaimed by the mayor as "the official air force of the Conch Republic," **Island Airplane Tours,** at Key West Airport, 3469 S. Roosevelt Blvd. (© **305/294-8687**), offers windy rides in its open-cockpit 1940 Waco biplanes that take you over the reefs and around the islands. Thrill-seekers will also enjoy a spin in the company's S2-B aerobatics airplane, which does loops, rolls, and sideways figure eights. Company owner Fred Cabanas was decorated in 1991, after he spotted a Cuban airman defecting to the United States in a Russian-built MIG fighter. Sightseeing flights cost $50 to $200, depending on duration.

BY BOAT   The catamaran *The Pride of Key West* and the glass-bottom boat *Fireball,* both at Zero Duval St. (© 305/296-6293), depart on daytime coral-reef tours and evening sunset cruises (call for times). Reef trips cost $35 per person; sunset cruises are $37 per person. Kids ages 5 through 12 sail on all cruises for $15.

The schooner *Western Union* (© 305/292-9830; www.schoonerwesternunion. com) was built in 1939 and served as a cable-repair vessel until it was designated the flagship of the city of Key West and began day, sunset, and charter sailings. Sunset sailings are especially memorable and include entertainment, cocktails, and a cannon fire. Prices vary; inquire for details.

A new boat tour combines Florida Keys sunsets with delectable Keys cuisine. **Sunset Culinaire Tours** (© 305/296-098; www.sunsetculinaire.com) is a cruise aboard the vessel *RB's Lady* and includes a tour of Key West harbor as the sun sinks below the horizon, and a gourmet dinner prepared by chef Brian Kirkpatrick. The vessel departs from Sunset Marina, off U.S. 1 at 5555 College Rd., at 5:30pm nightly. Boarding time is 5pm and cost is $75 per person.

OTHER TOURS   **Sharon Wells** (© 305/294-8380; www.seekeywest.com) leads a slew of great tours throughout the island, focusing on things as diverse as literature, architecture, and places connected with the island's gay and lesbian culture.

For a lively look at Key West, try the **Key West Pub Crawl** (© 305/744-9804; www.keywestwalkingtours.com), a tour of the island's most famous bars. It's given on Tuesday and Friday nights at 8pm, lasts 2½ hours, costs $30, and includes five (!) drinks. Another fun option is the 1-mile, 90-minute **ghost tour** (© 305/294-WALK; www.hauntedtours.com), leaving daily at 8pm from the Holiday Inn La Concha, 430 Duval St. Cost is $15 for adults and $10 for children 11 and under. This spooky and interesting tour gives participants insight into many old island legends.

Key West's **Goosebumps & Ghosts Rock-N-Walk Tour** (© 305/766-3356) departs twice nightly from the Pegasus Hotel, 501 Southard St. at the corner of Duval, and it's amusingly creepy. Led by a costumed angel and devil, the tour combines theatrics, history, and fun into a 75-minute stroll to haunting sites in the island city's Old Town district. Among the tales recounted along the way are those about railroad baron Henry Flagler's cursed second wife, the bizarre count whose obsessive love for a doomed Cuban girl extended well beyond her death, and the evil doll that haunted a Key West artist. The tour is at 7pm and 9pm nightly. Cost is $17 per person for adults and $8 for children when booked direct or through the concierges at most island properties. Reservations are required since space is limited.

Since the early 1940s, Key West has been a haven for gay luminaries such as Tennessee Williams and Broadway legend Jerry Herman. A tour of **Gay Key West,** created by the Key West Business Guild, showcases the history, contributions, and landmarks associated with the island's flourishing gay and lesbian culture. Highlights include Williams' house, the art gallery owned by Key West's first gay mayor, and a variety of guesthouses whose gay owners fueled the island's architectural-restoration movement. The 70-minute tour takes place Saturday at 11am, starting and ending at City of Key West parking lot, corner of Simonton Street and Angela Street. Look for the trolley with the rainbow flags. The cost is $25. Call © 305/294-4603.

OUTDOOR ACTIVITIES

BEACHES   Unlike the rest of the Keys, Key West actually has a few small beaches, although they don't compare with the state's wide natural wonders up the coast; the Keys' beaches are typically narrow and rocky. Here are your options: Smathers Beach,

Parrotheads on Parade

For Jimmy Buffett fans, or Parrotheads, as they're also known, **Trails of Margaritaville** (© **305/292-2040**; www.trailsofmargaritaville.com) is an amusing, 90-minute walking tour providing fans with an officially sanctioned peek at the stamping grounds of Buffett's carefree days in Key West back in the 1970s. Decked out in full Parrothead regalia—Hawaiian shirts and parrot hats—the informative and often hilarious guides lead you past the hangouts and other high points of Buffett's Key West, spinning yarns about the musician and Key West in general. The 2-hour tour departs daily at 4pm from **Captain Tony's Saloon**, 428 Greene St., where Buffett used to hang out and perform, and ends at—you guessed it—Margaritaville Cafe, on Duval Street. The tour conveniently goes during happy hour, when most bars serve two-for-one drinks. Tickets are $20 for adults, $15 for locals with ID, and $10 for children 6 to 10. Bring cash or traveler's checks; no credit cards are accepted. Reservations are required at least 2 days in advance. *Note:* If you're not a huge fan of Jimmy Buffett, you might want to skip this tour, as the price is relatively steep and you probably won't be as interested in these attractions as die-hard types.

off South Roosevelt Boulevard west of the airport; Higgs Beach, along Atlantic Boulevard between White Street and Reynolds Road; and Fort Zachary Beach, located off the western end of Southard Boulevard.

A magnet for partying teenagers, **Smathers Beach** is Key West's largest and most overpopulated. Despite the number of rowdy teens, the beach is actually quite clean and looks lovely since its renovation in the spring of 2000. If you go early enough in the morning, you may notice people sleeping on the beach from the night before.

Higgs Beach is a favorite among Key West's gay crowds, but what many people don't know is that beneath the sand is an unmarked cemetery of African slaves who died while waiting for freedom. Higgs has a playground and tennis courts, and is near the minute Rest Beach, which is actually hidden by the White Street pier.

Although there is an entrance fee ($3 per car, plus more for each passenger), I recommend **Fort Zachary Beach,** since it has a great historic fort, a Civil War museum, and a large picnic area with tables, barbecue grills, restrooms, and showers. Large trees scattered across 87 acres provide shade for those who are reluctant to bake in the sun.

BIKING & MOPEDING   A popular mode of transportation for locals and visitors, bikes and mopeds are available at many rental outlets in the city (p. 278). Escape the hectic downtown scene and explore the island's scenic side streets by heading away from Duval Street toward South Roosevelt Boulevard and the beachside enclaves along the way.

DIVING   One of the area's largest scuba schools, **Dive Key West, Inc.,** 3128 N. Roosevelt Blvd. (© **800/426-0707** or 305/296-3823; www.divekeywest.com), offers instruction at all levels; its dive boats take participants to scuba and snorkel sites on nearby reefs.

Key West Marine Park (© **305/294-3100**), the newest dive park along the island's Atlantic shore, incorporates no-motor "swim-only" lanes marked by buoys, providing swimmers and snorkelers with a safe way to explore the waters around Key West. The park's boundaries stretch from the foot of Duval Street to Higgs Beach.

Wreck dives and night dives are two of the special offerings of **Lost Reef Adventures,** 261 Margaret St. (© **800/952-2749** or 305/296-9737). Regularly scheduled runs and private charters can be arranged. Phone for departure information.

For a map of the Florida **Keys Shipwreck Heritage Trail,** an entire network of wrecks from Key Largo to Key West, go to http://floridakeys.noaa.gov/ sanctuary_resources/shipwreck_trail/welcome.html.

Also see **Mosquito Coast Outfitters,** under "Kayaking," below.

FISHING   As any angler will tell you, there's no fishing like Keys fishing. Key West has it all: bonefish, tarpon, dolphin, tuna, grouper, cobia, and more—sharks, too.

Step aboard a small exposed skiff for an incredibly diverse day of fishing. In the morning, you can head offshore for sailfish or dolphin (the fish, not the mammal), and then by afternoon get closer to land for a shot at tarpon, permit, grouper, or snapper. Here in Key West, you can probably pick up more cobia—one of the best fighting and eating fish around—than anywhere else in the world. For a real fight, ask your skipper to go for the tarpon—the greatest fighting fish there is, famous for its dramatic "tail walk" on the water after it's hooked. Shark fishing is also popular.

You'll find plenty of competition among the charter-fishing boats in and around Mallory Square. You can negotiate a good deal at **Charter Boat Row,** 1801 N. Roosevelt Ave. (across from the Shell station), home to more than 30 charter-fishing and party boats. Just show up to arrange your outing, or call **Garrison Bight Marina** (© **305/292-8167**) for details.

The advantage of the smaller, more expensive charter boats is that you can call the shots. They'll take you where you want to go, to fish for what you want to catch. These "light tackles" are also easier to maneuver, which means you can go to backcountry spots for tarpon and bonefish, as well as out to the open ocean for tuna and dolphin fish. You'll really be able to feel the fish, and you'll get some good fights, too. Larger boats, for up to six or seven people, are cheaper and are best for kingfish, billfish, and sailfish. Consider Capt. Vinnie Argiro's **Heavy Hitters Charters** (© **305/745-6665**) if you want a light-tackle experience. For a larger boat, try Capt. Henry Otto's 44-foot *Sunday,* docked at the Hyatt in Key West (© **305/294-7052**).

The huge commercial party boats are more for sightseeing than serious angling, though you can be lucky enough to get a few bites at one of the fishing holes. One especially good deal is the *Gulfstream III* (© **305/296-8494**; www.keywestparty boat.com), an all-day charter that goes out daily from 11am to 4:30pm. You'll pay $45 for adults, $35 for kids under 12, plus $3 for a rod and reel. This 65-foot party boat usually has at least 30 other anglers. Bring your own cooler or buy snacks onboard. Beer and wine are allowed.

Serious anglers should consider the light-tackle boats that leave from **Oceanside Marina,** on Stock Island at 5950 Peninsula Ave., 1½ miles off U.S. 1 (© **305/294-4676**). It's a 20-minute drive from Old Town on the Atlantic side. There are more

---

Tips Reel Deals

When looking for the best deals on fishing excursions, know that the bookers from the kiosks in town generally take 20% of a captain's fee in addition to an extra monthly fee. You can usually save yourself money by booking directly with a captain or by going straight to one of the docks.

than 30 light-tackle guides, which range from flatbed, backcountry skiffs to 28-foot open boats. There are also a few larger charters and a party boat that goes to the Dry Tortugas. Call for details.

For a light-tackle outing with a very colorful Key West flair, call **Capt. Bruce Cronin** (© **305/294-4929;** www.fishbruce.com) or **Capt. Kenny Harris** (© **305/ 294-8843**), two of the more famous (and pricey) captains working these docks for more than 20 years. You'll pay from $750 for a full day, usually about 8am to 4pm, and from $500 for a half-day.

GOLF   A relative newcomer in terms of local recreation, golf is gaining in popularity here, as it is in many visitor destinations. The area's only public golf club is **Key West Golf Club** (© **305/294-5232;** www.keywestgolf.com), an 18-hole course at the entrance to the island of Key West at MM 4.5 (turn onto College Rd. to the course entrance). Designed by Rees Jones, the course has plenty of mangroves and water hazards on its 6,526 yards. It's open to the public and has a new pro shop. Call ahead for tee-time reservations. Rates are $90 per player during off season and $160 in season, or $65 off season and $90 in season after 2:30pm, including cart.

KAYAKING   Housed in a woodsy wine bar, **Mosquito Coast Outfitters,** 1017 Duval St. (© **305/294-7178;** www.mosquitocoast.net), operates a first-rate kayaking and snorkeling tour every day as long as the weather is mild. The tours depart at 9am sharp and return around 3pm. Included in the $60 price are snacks, soft drinks, and a guided tour of the mangrove-studded islands of Sugar Key or Geiger Key, just north of Key West. The tour is primarily for kayaking, but you'll have the opportunity to get in the water for snorkeling, if you're interested. A new 2-hour tour called the Doggie Paddle Tour allows you to bring your furry friend along.

SHOPPING

You'll find all kinds of unique gifts and souvenirs in Key West, from coconut postcards to Key lime pies. On Duval Street, T-shirt shops outnumber almost any other business. If you must get a wearable memento, be careful of unscrupulous salespeople. Despite efforts to curtail the practice, many shops have been known to rip off unwitting shoppers. It pays to check the prices and the exchange rate before signing any sales slips. You are entitled to a written estimate of any T-shirt work before you pay for it.

At Mallory Square, you'll find the **Clinton Street Market,** an overly air-conditioned mall of kiosks and stalls designed for the many cruise-ship passengers who never venture beyond this super-commercial zone. There are some delicious coffee and candy shops, and some high-priced hats and shoes. There's also a free and clean restroom.

Once the main industry of Key West, cigar making is enjoying renewed success at the handful of factories that survived the slow years. Stroll through **Cigar Alley** (while on Greene St., go 2 blocks west and you'll hit Cigar Alley, also known as Pirate's Alley), where you will find *viejitos* (little old men) rolling fat stogies just as they used to do in their homeland across the Florida Straits. Stop at the **Conch Republic Cigar Factory,** 512 Greene St. (© **305/295-9036**), for an excellent selection of imported and locally rolled smokes, including the famous El Hemingway. Remember, buying or selling Cuban-made cigars is illegal. Shops advertising "Cuban cigars" are usually referring to domestic cigars made from tobacco grown from seeds that were brought from Cuba decades ago. To be fair, though, many premium cigars today are grown from Cuban seed tobacco—only it is grown in Latin America and the Caribbean, not Cuba.

If you're looking for local or Caribbean art, you'll find nearly a dozen galleries and shops clustered on Duval Street between Catherine and Fleming streets. There are also some excellent shops scattered on the side streets. One worth seeking out is the **Haitian Art Co.,** 600 Frances St. (© **305/296-8932**), where you can browse through room upon room of original paintings from well-known and obscure Haitian artists, in a range of prices from a few dollars to a few thousand. Also check out **Cuba, Cuba!** at 814 Duval St. (© **305/295-9442;** www.cubacubastore.com), where you'll see paintings, sculpture, and photos by Cuban artists, as well as books and art from the island.

A favorite stop in the Keys is the deliciously fragrant **Key West Aloe,** 524 Front St., between Simonton and Duval streets (© **305/294-5592**). Since 1971, this shop has been selling a simple line of bath products—including lotions, shampoos, and soothing balms—for those who want a reminder of the tropical breezes once they're back home. At the main shop (open until 8pm), you can find great gift baskets, tropical perfumes, and candies and cookies, too. In addition to frangipani, vanilla, and hibiscus scents, sample Key West for Men, a unique and alluringly musky bestseller.

For foodies, the **Key Lime Pie Co.** (© **305/294-6567**) is so popular for its pies, cookies, and pretty much anything made with Key lime (candles, soaps, lotions) that there are two locations on the tiny island. One is at 701 Caroline St.; the other is at 424 Greene St. From sweet to spicy, **Peppers of Key West,** 602 Greene St. (© **305/295-9333;** www.peppersofkeywest.com), is a hot-sauce-lover's heaven, with hundreds of variations, from mild to brutally spicy. Grab a seat at the tasting bar and be prepared to let your taste buds sizzle. *Tip:* Bring beer and they'll let you taste some of their secret sauces!

Literature and music buffs will appreciate the many bookshops and record stores on the island. **Key West Island Bookstore,** 513 Fleming St. (© **305/294-2904**), carries new, used, and rare books, and specializes in fiction by residents of the Keys, including Ernest Hemingway, Tennessee Williams, Shel Silverstein, Ann Beattie, Richard Wilbur, and John Hersey. The bookstore is open daily from 10am to 9pm.

For anything else, from bed linens to candlesticks to clothing, go to downtown's oldest and most renowned department store, **Fast Buck Freddie's,** 500 Duval St. (© **305/294-2007**). For the same merchandise at reduced prices, try **Half Buck Freddie's** 𝕘, 726 Caroline St. (© **305/294-2007**), where you can shop for out-of-season bargains and "rejects" from the main store.

Also check out **KW Light Gallery,** 534 Fleming St. (© **305/294-0566**), for high-quality contemporary photography as well as historic images and other artwork relating to the Keys or to the concept of light and its varied interpretations. The gallery is open Thursday through Tuesday from 10am to 6pm (10am–4pm in summer).

WHERE TO STAY

You'll find a wide variety of places to stay in Key West, from resorts with all the amenities to seaside motels, quaint bed-and-breakfasts, and clothing-optional guesthouses. Unless you're in town during Key West's most popular holidays—Fantasy Fest (around Halloween), where Mardi Gras meets South Florida for the NC-17 set and most hotels have outrageous rates and 5-night minimums; Hemingway Days (in July), where Papa is seemingly and eerily alive and well; and Christmas and New Year's—or for a big fishing tournament (many are held Oct–Dec) or a boat-racing tourney, you can almost always find a place to stay at the last minute. However, you may want to book early, especially in winter, when prime properties fill up and many require 2- or

3-night minimum stays. Prices at these times are extremely high. Finding a decent room for less than $100 a night is a real trick.

Another suggestion, and my recommendation, is to call **Vacation Key West** (© **800/595-5397** or 305/295-9500; www.vacationkw.com), a wholesaler that offers discounts of 20% to 30% and is skilled at finding last-minute deals. It represents mostly larger hotels and motels, but can also place visitors in guesthouses. The phones are answered Monday through Friday from 9am to 6pm, and Saturday from 11am to 2pm. **Key West Innkeepers Association** (© **800/492-1911** or 305/292-3600) can also help you find lodging in any price range from among its members and affiliates.

Gay travelers may want to call the **Key West Business Guild** (© **305/294-4603**), which represents more than 50 guesthouses and B&Bs in town, as well as many other gay-owned businesses. Be advised that most gay guesthouses have a clothing-optional policy. One of the most elegant and popular is **Big Ruby's,** 409 Applerouth Lane (© **800/477-7829** or 305/296-2323; www.bigrubys.com), located on a little alley just off Duval Street. Rates start at $171 double in peak season and $119 off season. A low cluster of buildings surrounds a lush courtyard where a hearty breakfast is served each morning and wine is poured at dusk. The all-male guests hang out by the pool, tanning in the buff.

For women only, **Pearl's Rainbow,** 525 United St. (© **800/74-WOMYN** or 305/292-1450; www.pearlsrainbow.com), is a large, fairly well-maintained guesthouse with lots of privacy and amenities, including two pools and two hot tubs. Rates range from $99 to $379.

VERY EXPENSIVE

Beachside Resort & Conference Center ⟨⟨⟨ Key West's newest luxury resort, this one has the advantage of a star chef, Norman Van Aken, who has two restaurants on the premises—Town and Tavern. In addition to gourmet cuisine, the resort has hyperluxe one-, two-, and three-bedroom suites as well as king bedrooms, all adorned with oversized balconies with waterfront views, open gourmet kitchens, marble Jacuzzi tubs, and, on the third floor, private sundecks. At the waterfront pool, you'll find private cabanas, and casual cuisine and cocktails at Blue Bar. Although the resort is located on busy Roosevelt Boulevard, home to chain motels and restaurants, you'll feel like you're in another world once you enter the premises.

3841 N. Roosevelt Blvd. Key West, FL 33040 © 800/546-0885 or 305/296-8100. Fax 305/293-0205 www.spottswood.com/hotels/beachside. 222 units. Winter $539 double, $739–$1,889 suite; off season $299 double, $499–$1649 suite. AE, DC, MC, V. **Amenities:** 6,000-sq.-ft. events facility, transportation to and from downtown Key West, private helicopter pad, 3 restaurants, 2 bars, heated pool, private cabanas, private beach on the Gulf of Mexico, 12-slip private marina; 24hr. concierge that can facilitate almost anything, including: watersports equipment rental, moped/bike rental, in-room massage, babysitting, dry cleaning services. In room: A/C, LCD flatscreen TVs with satellite, Wi-Fi, full gourmet kitchen in all suites that can be stocked with personal preferences, coffeemaker, hair dryer, iron, washer/dryer in all suites, Frette Linens, L'Occitane bath products.

The Gardens Hotel ⟨⟨⟨ *Finds* At last, the true garden of Eden has been located—and it's on Angela Street in Key West. Once a private residence, the Gardens Hotel (whose main house is listed on the National Register of Historic Places) is hidden amid exotic botanical gardens. Behind the greenery is a Bahamian-style hideaway with luxuriously appointed rooms in the main house, garden and courtyard rooms in the carriage house, and one ultrasecluded cottage. Though the place is within walking distance of frenetic Duval Street, you may not want to leave. A pretty free-form pool is centered in the courtyard, where a Tiki bar serves libations. The Jacuzzi is hidden

Green Gardens

The Gardens Hotel is one of the first "Florida Green Lodging Hotels" (www. floridagreenlodging.org) in the Keys, meaning the hotel has installed energy-efficient light bulbs throughout the property, uses all "green" cleaning products, eliminated plastics and styrofoam use, recycles, and raises room temperatures to 78 degrees when not in use, among other eco-friendly efforts.

behind foliage. Guest rooms have hardwood floors, brass and iron beds, and marble bathrooms. Winding brick pathways leading to secluded seating areas in the private gardens make for an idyllic getaway. *Note:* If you plan to party, do not stay here—guests tend to be on the quieter, more sophisticated side.

526 Angela St., Key West, FL 33040. ⓒ 800/526-2664 or 305/294-2661. Fax 305/292-1007. www.gardenshotel. com. 17 units. Winter $300–$415 double, $495–$620 suite; off season $160–$200 double, $225–$395 suite. Rates include continental breakfast. AE, DC, MC, V. **Amenities:** Bar; pool. *In room:* A/C, TV, hair dryer, safe.

Ocean Key Resort and Spa ⍟ You can't beat the location of this 100-room resort, at the foot of Mallory Square, the epicenter of the sunset ritual. Ocean Key also features a Gulf-side heated pool and the lively Sunset Pier, where guests can wind down with cocktails and live music. Guest rooms are huge and luxuriously appointed, with living and dining areas, oversize Jacuzzis, and views of the Gulf, the harbor, or Mallory Square and Duval Street. The two-bedroom suite is 1,200 square feet and has a full kitchen, three beds, and a large private balcony. The property is adorned in classic Key West decor, from the tile floors and hand-painted furniture to the pastel art. The Indonesian-inspired Spa Terre is perhaps the best in town. The resort's restaurant, Hot Tin Roof (p. 297), is one of Key West's best.

Zero Duval St. (near Mallory Docks), Key West, FL 33040. ⓒ 800/328-9815 or 305/296-7701. Fax 305/292-2198. www.oceankey.com. 100 units. Winter $379–$679 double, $479–$1,149 suite; off season $239–$439 double, $319–$639 suite. AE, DC, MC, V. **Amenities:** 2 restaurants; 3 bars; heated pool; watersports equipment rental; moped/bike rental; concierge; room service; in-room massage; babysitting; laundry services. *In room:* A/C, TV, Wi-Fi, minibar, coffeemaker, hair dryer, iron.

Pier House Resort and Caribbean Spa ⍟ If you're looking for something a bit more intimate than The Reach Resort (see below), Pier House is an ideal choice. Its location—at the foot of Duval Street and just steps from Mallory Docks—is the envy of every hotel on the island. Set back from the busy street, on a short strip of private beach, this place is a welcome oasis of calm. The accommodations vary tremendously, from simple business-style rooms to romantic quarters complete with stereos and whirlpool tubs. Although every unit has either a balcony or a patio, not all overlook the water. My favorites, in the two-story spa building, don't have any view at all. But what they lack in scenery, they make up for in opulence: Each well-appointed spa room has a sitting area and a huge Jacuzzi bathroom.

1 Duval St. (near Mallory Docks), Key West, FL 33040. ⓒ 800/327-8340 or 305/296-4600. Fax 305/296-9085. www.pierhouse.com. 142 units. Winter $309–$529 double, $479–$3,000 suite; off season $229–$369 double, $389–$2,000 suite. AE, DC, MC, V. **Amenities:** 3 restaurants; 3 bars; heated pool; full-service spa and fitness center; 2 Jacuzzis; sauna; watersports equipment rental; moped/bike rental; concierge; limited room service; in-room massage; babysitting; laundry services. *In room:* A/C, TV, dataport, minibar, coffeemaker, hair dryer, iron.

The Reach Resort ⍟⍟ The Reach, which was closed for the better part of 2006 and 2007 for renovations, is ideally located on a 450-foot private, natural sand beach;

it's just a 5-minute walk from the center of the Duval Street action. The guest rooms are large and, at press time, were all being redone in modern tropical decor with the usual trappings of modernity—wireless Internet, plasma TV, and WebTV. All have sliding-glass doors that open onto balconies, and some have ocean views. A massive array of watersports are available right on the premises, and unlike most area resorts which are small-ish, this one seems infinitely larger and, in many ways, worlds away from the rest of Key West.

1435 Simonton St., Key West, FL 33040. © 800/874-4118 or 800/996-3426 for reservations. Fax 305/296-2830. www.reachresort.com. 150 units. Winter $319–$489 double; off season $189–$389 double. AE, DC, DISC, MC, V. **Amenities:** 2 restaurants; bar; outdoor heated pool; nearby tennis and golf; health club; spa; watersports equipment rental; bike rental; concierge; tour desk; business center; salon; 24-hr. room service; in-room massage; babysitting; dry cleaning. *In room:* A/C, TV, dataport, minibar, fridge, coffeemaker, hair dryer, iron.

Westin Key West Resort and Marina &&   Ideally situated at the very end of Duval Street in the middle of Old Town's action, the Westin Key West (formerly the Hilton) is a prime spot from which to enjoy sunsets as well as that hard-to-find, quietly elegant ambience that's so lacking in most big resorts here. The rooms are large and well appointed, with all the modern conveniences and that Westin signature Heavenly Bed. Choose a suite in the main building if you want a Jacuzzi in your living room. Otherwise, the marina building has great views. The secluded beach is great for an escape from the Duval Street frenzy. For $20 per person, you can also enjoy the Westin's private Sunset Key beach, accessible only by the hotel's launch at the marina. Bistro 245, the elegant dining room, serves ample breakfasts and a huge Sunday brunch.

Westin's gorgeous **Sunset Key Guest Cottages** &&&, with whitewashed interiors and fabulous views, are 500 yards offshore on Sunset Key and are accessible only by private launch. Check in at the Westin Key West and take a 10-minute cruise to the island, where there are no cars—only a beach, restaurant, bar, and free-form pool with whirlpool jets. Cottages are equipped with full kitchens; high-tech entertainment centers; and one, two, or three massive bedrooms. Sunset Key guests have access to all watersports at the Westin.

245 Front St. (at the end of Duval St.), Key West, FL 33040. © 800/221-2424 or 305/294-4000. Fax 305/294-4086. www.starwoodhotels.com. 215 units, including cottages. Winter $389–$550 double, $469–$1,149 suite, $745–$2,000 Sunset Key Cottage, up to 5 people; off season $229–$459 double, $359–$1,059 suite, $625–$1,545 Sunset Key Cottage, up to 5 people. Private chef: $75 per person plus additional chef/hotel fees, tax, and gratuities. AE, DC, DISC, MC, V. Valet parking $10; self-parking $7. **Amenities:** 2 restaurants; pool bar; outdoor heated pool; health club; Jacuzzi; watersports equipment rental; bike rental; game room; concierge; business center; limited room service; in-room massage; self-service laundry; dry cleaning; full-service marina. *In room:* A/C, TV, dataport, minibar, coffeemaker, hair dryer, iron.

EXPENSIVE

Casa Marina Resort & Beach Club &   This hotel, formerly the Wyndham Casa Marina, is in the throes of a much-needed transition from old and ratty Key West to new, sleek, and modern Key West. Luxury resort outfit LXR took over the place in 2006 and was pumping millions into this supremely located resort spanning 1,100 feet of private beach. Newly designed rooms have a fresher, softer look than before, with vibrant pastel walls, tropical-print furnishings, crown molding, and soft carpets. One- and two-bedroom oceanview suites have stellar views and separate living areas. In addition to the beach itself, there are also two outdoor pools, a full-service spa, and an outdoor restaurant. Because of its location somewhat off the beaten path from the main streets in Key West, Casa Marina is an ideal haunt for couples and romance seekers looking for a more private, tropical experience.

1500 Reynolds St., Key West, FL 33040. ℭ **888/397-6342** or 305/296-3535. Fax 305/296-4633. www.casamarina resort.com. 311 units. Winter $449–$509 double, $489–$699 suite; off season $259–$299 double, $379–$609 suite. AE, DC, MC, V. **Amenities:** Restaurant; bar; 2 pools; lighted tennis court; spa; bike and scooter rental; concierge. *In room:* A/C, TV, high-speed Internet, minibar, hair dryer, iron, safe.

Curry Mansion Inn ★★ *Finds*

This charismatic inn is the former home of the island's first millionaire, a once-penniless Bahamian immigrant who made a fortune as a pirate. Owned today by Al and Edith Amsterdam, the Curry Mansion is now on the National Register of Historic Places, but you won't feel like you're staying in a museum—it's rather like a wonderfully warm home. Rooms are very sparsely decorated, with wicker furniture, four-poster beds, and pink walls—call it Key West minimalism meets Victorian. The dining room is reminiscent of a Victorian dollhouse, with elegant table settings and rich wood floors and furnishings. Every morning, there's a delicious European-style breakfast buffet; at night, cocktail parties are held. There's also a really nice patio, on which, from time to time, there's live entertainment.

511 Caroline St., Key West, FL 33040. ℭ **800/253-3466** or 305/294-5349. Fax 305/294-4093. www.currymansion. com. 28 units. Winter $240–$300 double, $315–$365 suite; off season $195–$235 double, $260–$285 suite. Rates include breakfast buffet. AE, DC, MC, V. No children 11 and under. **Amenities:** Dining room; pool; bike rental; concierge. *In room:* A/C, TV, minibar.

Hyatt Key West Resort & Marina ★

After a $9 million renovation, the Hyatt is now up to speed with other luxe resorts in the area. Ideally situated on the bay, the Hyatt features a waterfront pool, small beach area and guestrooms with white porcelain tile floors, flatscreens, and fabulous bathrooms. New spa cabanas allow outdoor treatments and a restaurant overlooking the water is great for dinner, but spotty on breakfast service. Located right near Duval Street and next door to several lively bars, the Hyatt offers the best of both worlds when it comes to Key West: relaxation—and partying.

601 Front St., Key West, FL 33040. ℭ **800/55-HYATT** or 305/809-1234. Fax 305/809-4050. www.keywest.hyatt.com. 118 rooms. Winter $485–$550 double, off season $335–$450. AE, DC, DISC, MC, V. **Amenities:** Restaurant; bar; pool; fitness center; spa; water activities; private sailboat; private sunbathing beach; meeting and conference space. *In room:* A/C, private balcony, plasma TV, wireless Internet, dataport, minibar, hair dryer, in-room safe, coffee maker.

Island City House Hotel ★★

A small resort unto itself, the Island City House consists of three separate buildings that share a common junglelike patio and pool. The first building, unimaginatively called the Island City House building, is a historic three-story wooden structure with wraparound verandas on every floor. The warmly outfitted interiors here include wood floors and many antiques. The tile bathrooms could use more counter space, but eccentricities are part of this hotel's charm. The unpainted wooden Cigar House has particularly large bedrooms, similar in ambience to those in the Island City House. The Arch House is the least appealing of the three buildings, but still recommended. Built of Dade County pine, this house's cozy bedrooms are furnished in wicker and rattan, and come with small kitchens and bathrooms.

411 William St., Key West, FL 33040. ℭ **800/634-8230** or 305/294-5702. Fax 305/294-1289. www.islandcityhouse. com. 24 units. Winter $190–$240 1-bedroom suite, $285–$350 2-bedroom suite; off season $120–$185 1-bedroom suite, $195–$250 2-bedroom suite. Rates include breakfast. AE, DC, DISC, MC, V. **Amenities:** Outdoor heated pool; access to nearby health club; Jacuzzi; bike rental; concierge; in-room massage; babysitting; laundry service; dry cleaning; self-service laundry. *In room:* A/C, TV, kitchen, coffeemaker, hair dryer.

Marquesa Hotel ★★★ *Finds*

The Marquesa offers the charm of a small historic hotel coupled with the amenities of a large resort. It encompasses four buildings, two pools, and a three-stage waterfall that cascades into a lily pond. Two of the hotel's buildings are luxuriously restored Victorian homes outfitted with plush antiques and contemporary furniture. The rooms in the two newly constructed buildings are even more opulent; many have four-poster wrought-iron beds with bright floral spreads. The bathrooms in the new buildings are lush and spacious; those in the older buildings are also nice, but not nearly as huge and luxe. The decor is simple, elegant, and spotless. The hotel also boasts one of Key West's most elegant restaurants, Café Marquesa.

600 Fleming St. (at Simonton St.), Key West, FL 33040. © **800/869-4631** or 305/292-1919. Fax 305/294-2121. www.marquesa.com. 27 units. Winter $250–$340 double, $400–$450 suite; off season $190–$270 double, $300–$330 suite. AE, DC, MC, V. No children 11 and under. **Amenities:** Restaurant; 2 outdoor pools (1 heated); access to nearby health club; bike rental; concierge; limited room service. *In room:* A/C, TV, CD player, dataport, minibar, hair dryer, iron, safe.

Simonton Court ✦✦✦ *Finds*   This is my favorite stay in Key West—too bad it's always booked. Once a cigar factory, Simonton Court features meticulously appointed restored historic cottages and suites amidst sparkling pools and luxuriant private gardens. There are several options to choose from: bed and breakfast, cottages, guesthouse, mansion, and inn. Some cottages even have their own pools. There's no restaurant here, but the well informed concierge will help you with reservations anywhere no matter what you crave. What I really crave, however, is a standing reservation here. People love the place so much, they book years in advance. Once you stay here, if you're lucky, you'll understand why.

320 Simonton St., Key West, FL 33040. © **800/944-2687** or 305/294-6386. Fax 305/293-8446. www.simonton court.com. 30 units. Winter $195–$395 double in mansion; cottage $275–$495; inn $195–$395; manor house $285–$425; townhouse $200–$515; off season $145–$265 double in mansion; cottage $155–$375; inn $145–$265; $215–$315 manor house; townhouse $155–$395. Rates include continental breakfast. AE, DISC, MC, V. **Amenities:** Outdoor pool; concierge. *In room:* A/C, TV/VCR, hair dryer.

Weatherstation Inn ✦ *Finds*   Originally built in 1912 as a weather station, this beautifully restored, meticulously maintained, Renaissance-style inn is just 2 blocks from Duval Street but seems worlds away. It's situated on the tropical grounds of the former Old Navy Yard, now an exclusive and private gated community. Presidents Truman, Eisenhower, and JFK all visited the station. Spacious and uncluttered, each guest room is uniquely furnished to complement the interior architecture: hardwood floors, tall sash windows, and high ceilings. The large, modern bathrooms are especially appealing. The staff is both friendly and accommodating.

57 Front St., Key West, FL 33040. © **800/815-2707** or 305/294-7277. Fax 305/294-0544. www.weatherstationinn. com. 8 units. Winter $215–$335 double; off season $170–$235 double. Rates include continental breakfast. AE, DISC, MC, V. **Amenities:** Outdoor pool; concierge. *In room:* A/C, TV/VCR, hair dryer.

MODERATE

Ambrosia Key West ✦✦ *Finds*   Despite countless visits each year to the tiny island of Key West, I discover yet another hidden treasure every time I go back. Ambrosia is one of them, a private compound set on 2 lush acres just a block from Duval Street. Three lagoon-style pools, suites, townhouses, and a cottage are spread around the grounds. Townhouses have living rooms, kitchens, and spiral staircases leading to master suites with vaulted ceilings and private decks. The cottage, overlooking a dip pool, is a perfect family retreat, with two bedrooms, two bathrooms, a living room, and a kitchen. All rooms have private entrances, most with French doors opening onto a variety of intimate outdoor spaces, including private verandas; patios; and gardens with sculptures, fountains, and pools. Fantastic service, bolstered by the philosophy that it's better to have high occupancy than high rates, explains why Ambrosia has a 90% year-round occupancy—a record in seasonal Key West.

622 Fleming St., Key West, FL 33040. ☏ **800/535-9838** or 305/296-9838. Fax 305/296-2425. www.ambrosiakey west.com. 20 units. Winter $279–$609 suite; off season $169–$389 suite. Rates include breakfast. AE, DISC, MC, V. Off- and on-street parking. Pets accepted. **Amenities:** 3 outdoor heated pools. *In room:* A/C, TV, CD player, kitchens (in some), fridge, coffeemaker, hair dryer, iron.

Doubletree Grand Key Resort ⚜ *Finds* If you don't mind staying on the quiet "other" side of the island, a 10-minute cab ride away from Duval Street, the Double-tree is an excellent choice, not to mention excellent value. An ecologically conscious resort, the hotel has been renovated with eco-sensitive materials as well as an interior created to conserve energy, reduce waste, and preserve the area's natural resources. Rooms are clean and comfortable, with some looking onto the spacious pool area, which is surrounded by an unsightly empty lot of mangroves and marshes. The newest addition is a welcome one—a Beach Club located off-property at Smathers Beach, where the hotel has established a hut with chairs, towels, and umbrellas. Watersports are available here, as is a free shuttle to transport guests back and forth.

3990 S. Roosevelt Blvd., Key West, FL 33040. ☏ **888/310-1540** or 305/293-1818. Fax 305/296-6962. www.double treekeywest.com. 216 units. Winter $245–$259 double, $295–$485 suite; off season $179–$194 double, $229–$369 suite. AE, DISC, MC, V. Free parking. **Amenities:** Restaurant; Tiki bar and lounge; pool; gym; concierge; meeting rooms; limited room service. *In room:* A/C, TV/WebTV, dataport, minibar, coffeemaker, hair dryer, iron, safe.

La Pensione ⚜⚜ This classic B&B, set in a stunning 1891 home, is a total charmer. The comfortable rooms all have air-conditioning, ceiling fans, and king-size beds. Many also have French doors opening onto spacious verandas. Although the rooms have no TVs, the distractions of Duval Street, only steps away, should keep you adequately occupied. Breakfast, which includes Belgian waffles, fresh fruit, and a vari-ety of breads or muffins, can be taken on the wraparound porch or at the communal dining table. Recent guests, however, have informed us that service here is not as friendly as it used to be and that the inn's location on U.S. 1 isn't so hot when it comes to the noise and traffic levels.

809 Truman Ave. (between Windsor and Margaret sts.), Key West, FL 33040. ☏ **800/893-1193** or 305/292-9923. Fax 305/296-6509. www.lapensione.com. 9 units. Winter $168–$328 double; off season $118–$168 double. Rates include breakfast. Discount of 10% for readers who mention this book. AE, DC, DISC, MC, V. No children. **Amenities:** Out-door pool; bike rental; wireless Internet. *In room:* A/C.

Southernmost Point Guest House ⚜⚜ *Finds* *Kids* One of the few inns that actu-ally welcomes children and pets, this romantic guesthouse is a real find. The antisep-tically clean rooms are not as fancy as the house's ornate 1885 exterior, but each is unique and includes some combination of basic beds and a hodgepodge of furnish-ings, such as futon couches and high-back wicker chairs. Room no. 5 is best, with a private porch, ocean view, and windows that let in lots of light. Every unit comes with fresh flowers, wine, and a full decanter of sherry. Mona Santiago, the kind, laid-back owner, provides chairs and towels for the beach, which is just a block away. Guests can help themselves to free wine as they soak in the 14-seat hot tub. Kids will enjoy the backyard swings and the pet rabbits.

1327 Duval St., Key West, FL 33040. ☏ **305/294-0715.** Fax 305/296-0641. www.southernmostpoint.com. 6 units. Winter $120–$200 double, $260–$290 suite; off season $75–$120 double, $165–$175 suite. Rates include breakfast. AE, MC, V. Pets accepted ($5 in summer, $10 in winter). **Amenities:** Garden pool; hot tub; laundry facilities; barbe-cue grills. *In room:* A/C, TV/VCR, fridge, coffeemaker, hair dryer, iron.

Westwinds Inn ⚜ A close second to staying in your own private 19th-century, tin-roofed clapboard house is this tranquil inn, just 4 blocks from Duval Street in the historic seaport district. Lush landscaping keeps the place extremely private and secluded; at times, you'll feel as if you're alone. Two pools, one heated in winter, are offset by alcoves, fountains, and the well-maintained whitewashed inn, which is actually composed of five separate buildings. Rooms are Key West comfortable, with private bathrooms, wicker furnishings, and fans. All are nonsmoking.

914 Eaton St., Key West, FL 33040. (℃) 800/788-4150 or 305/296-4440. Fax 305/293-0931. www.westwindskey west.com. 22 units. Winter $165–$220 double, $225–$240 suite; off season $80–$175 double, $140–$195 suite. Rates include continental breakfast. DISC, MC, V. No children 11 and under. **Amenities:** 2 pools (1 heated); bike rental; self-service laundry. *In room:* A/C, TV (in some), kitchenette (in some).

INEXPENSIVE

Angelina Guest House 🜲🜲 This former bordello and gambling-hall-turned-youth-hostel type guesthouse is about the cheapest in town—and it's conveniently located near a hot hippie restaurant called Blue Heaven (p. 300). Though the neighborhood is definitely urban, it's generally safe and full of character. Accommodations are furnished uniquely in a modest style. Two rooms have full kitchens, one has a microwave and small fridge, and all but three have private bathrooms. A gorgeous lagoon-style heated pool with waterfall and tropical landscaping is an excellent addition. Even better are the poolside hammocks—get out there early, as they go quickly! Even though the Angelina is sparse (perfect for bohemian types who don't mind a little grit), it's a great place to crash if you're traveling on the cheap.

302 Angela St. (at Thomas St.), Key West, FL 33040. (℃) 888/303-4480 or 305/294-4480. Fax 305/272-0681. www. angelinaguesthouse.com. 13 units. Winter $99–$199 double; off season $69–$139 double. Rates include continental breakfast. DISC, MC, V. **Amenities:** Outdoor heated pool; concierge. *In room:* A/C, no phone.

The Grand 🜲🜲 *Finds* Don't expect cabbies or locals to know about this well-kept secret, located in a modest residential section of Old Town, about 5 blocks from Duval Street. It's got almost everything you could want, including a very moderate price tag. Proprietors Jim Brown and Jeffrey Daubman provide any and all services for her appreciative guests. All units have private bathrooms, air-conditioning, and private entrances. The best deal is room no. 2; it's small and lacks a closet, but it has a porch and the most privacy. Suites are a real steal, too: The large two-room units come with kitchenettes. This place is undoubtedly the best bargain in town.

1116 Grinnell St. (between Virginia and Catherine sts.), Key West, FL 33040. (℃) 888/947-2630 or 305/294-0590. Fax 305/294-0477. www.thegrandguesthouse.com. 10 units. Winter $168–$208 double, $228–$268 suite; off season $108–$148 double, $128–$168 suite. Rates include expanded continental breakfast and free parking. DISC, MC, V. **Amenities:** Bike/scooter rental; full concierge. *In room:* A/C and ceiling fans, cable TV, wireless Internet, fridge, phone.

Key West International Hostel & Seashell Motel This well-run hostel is a 3-minute walk to the beach and Old Town. Very busy with European backpackers, it's a great place to meet people. The dorm rooms are dark, grimy, and sparse, but livable if you're desperate for a cheap stay. There are all-male, all-female, and coed dorm rooms for couples. The higher-priced private motel rooms are a good deal, especially those equipped with kitchens. Amenities include a pool table under a Tiki roof; bike rentals; cheap food at breakfast, lunch, and dinner; and discounted prices for snorkeling, diving, and sunset cruises. There's also free wireless Internet access throughout the property.

718 South St., Key West, FL 33040. (℃) 800/51-HOSTEL or 305/296-5719. Fax 305/296-0672. www.keywest hostel.com. 92 dorm beds, 10 motel rooms. Year-round $28 dorm room members, $31 dorm room nonmembers. Winter $75–$105 motel room, off season $55–$85 motel room. MC, V. Free parking. **Amenities:** Bike rental; kitchen. *In room:* Motel rooms have A/C, TV, fridge, coffeemaker, hair dryer; dorm rooms have A/C only.

WHERE TO DINE

With its share of the usual drive-through fast-food franchises—mostly up on Roosevelt Boulevard—and Duval Street succumbing to the lure of a Hard Rock Cafe, you might be surprised to learn that, over the years, an upscale and high-quality dining scene has begun to thrive in Key West. Just wander Old Town or the newly spruced-up Bahama Village and browse menus after you've exhausted my list of picks below.

If you don't feel like venturing out, call **We Deliver** (© 305/293-0078), a service that will bring anything you want from any of the area's restaurants or stores for a small fee ($3–$6); it's available from 3 to 11pm. If you're staying in a condominium or efficiency, you may want to stock your fridge with groceries, beer, wine, and snacks from the area's oldest grocer, **Fausto's Food Palace.** Open since 1926, Fausto's has two locations: 1105 White St. and 522 Fleming St. The Fleming Street location will deliver with a minimum $25 order (© **305/294-5221** or 305/296-5663).

VERY EXPENSIVE

Café Marquesa ✿✿✿ CONTEMPORARY AMERICAN   If you're looking for fabulous dining (and service) in Key West, this is the place. The intimate, 50-seat restaurant is something to look at, but it's really the food that you'll want to admire. Specialties include macadamia-crusted yellowtail snapper; prosciutto-wrapped black Angus filet, and roast duck breast with red curry coconut sauce. If you're looking to splurge, this is the place.

In the Marquesa Hotel, 600 Fleming St. © **305/292-1919**. Reservations highly recommended. Main courses $25–$38. AE, DC, MC, V. Summer daily 7–11pm; winter daily 6–11pm.

Hot Tin Roof ✿✿✿ FUSION   Ever hear of conch fusion cuisine? Neither did I, until I experienced it firsthand at Hot Tin Roof, Ocean Key Resort's chichi restaurant, which transforms South American, Asian, French, and Keys cuisine into an experience unlike any other in this part of the world. The vibrant 3,000-square-foot space features both indoor and outdoor deck seating overlooking the harbor. Live jazz/fusion adds to the stunning environment—it's the epitome of casual elegance. Signature dishes include an irresistible lobster with garlic, chiles, and Cuban mojo sauce and macadamia crusted grouper with yellow curry sauce, and chocolate-lava cake that makes this tin roof very hot, to say the least, especially for Key West. Last time I ate here, Meryl Streep was sitting next to me with her family, looking as impressed as she was impressive.

In the Ocean Key Resort, Zero Duval St. © **305/296-7701**. Reservations highly recommended. Main courses $20–$40. AE, DC, MC, V. Daily 7:30–11am and 5–10pm.

Louie's Backyard ✿✿ CARIBBEAN   Nestled amid blooming bougainvillea on a lush slice of the Gulf, Louie's remains one of the most romantic restaurants on earth. It's off the beaten path, which makes it even more romantic. Famed chef Norman Van Aiken of Norman's in Miami brought his talents farther south and started what has become one of the finest dining spots in the Keys. As a result, this is one of the hardest places to score a reservation: Either call way in advance or hope that your hotel concierge has some pull. Try the sweet and sour sweetbreads with sticky rice, or the grilled chile-rubbed Berkshire pork chop that is to die for. After dinner, sit at the dockside bar and watch the waves crash, almost touching your feet, while enjoying a cocktail at sunset. You can't go wrong with the fresh catch of the day, or any seafood dish, for that matter. The weekend brunches are also great. And a ritual for many in Key

298 CHAPTER 12 · THE KEYS & THE DRY TORTUGAS

West are sunset cocktails at the oceanfront Tiki bar. If you can't stay for dinner, go for lunch; this is one dining experience you won't want to miss.

700 Waddell Ave. ℂ 305/294-1061. www.louiesbackyard.com. Reservations highly recommended. Main courses $25–$35; lunch $10–$20. AE, DC, MC, V. Daily 11:30am–3pm and 6–10:30pm.

One Duval 𝒢𝒢𝒢 CARIBBEAN The waterfront setting of this restaurant at the Pier House Resort is beautiful, but you may be too distracted to notice the views when you taste the food. One of the best restaurants in Key West, One Duval blends the ingredients of the Caribbean and Florida with an innovative twist. For starters, the crabmeat stuffed in phyllo is outstanding, and the goat-cheese soufflé is incredibly hedonistic. For main courses, try the macadamia nut–crusted mahimahi or the lobster thermidor stuffed with crabmeat. The Key lime pie with meringue is a must-have. Service is friendly and professional; this is not the kind of restaurant where waiters will rush you. Eat first, and then sit back and digest the views so you don't miss any of this fine restaurant's offerings.

In the Pier House Resort, 1 Duval St. ℂ 305/296-4600. Reservations highly recommended. Main courses $25–$36. AE, DC, MC, V. Daily 6–10:30pm.

Tavern N Town 𝒢𝒢𝒢 FLORIBBEAN Star chef Norman Van Aken abandoned ship in Miami in favor of a swank new resort in Key West, and it's only appropriate. Van Aken got his start at Louie's Backyard and now he returns to his roots with his signature Floribbean cuisine that kicks Keys cuisines up a few price notches. Tavern and Town are two separate eateries within a bilevel space—Van Aken calls it a hyphen-ated restaurant, with Tavern featuring tapas and small plates and Town a more world class dining experience, but both equally good—and pricey. An open theater kitchen shows action, but the real show is on your plate. At Tavern, try the picadillo empanadas with pimento and tomato compote and cumin line crema, or a Key West yellowtail with garlicky mashed potatoes with hearts of palm slaw. Over at Town, try Black grouper in a Japanese konbu broth and Mongolian barbecued veal chop, which are a far cry from Duval Street's chicken fingers and conch fritters. But if it's a splurge you are looking for, there's no better place in Key West to do so.

In the Beachside Resort, 3841 N. Roosevelt Blvd. ℂ 305/296-8100. Reservations highly recommended. Main courses $32–$47. AE, DC, MC, V. Tavern, daily 8am–10:30pm; Town 6pm–11pm.

EXPENSIVE

Antonia's 𝒢𝒢 REGIONAL ITALIAN The food is great, but the atmosphere a bit fussy for Key West. If you don't have a reservation in season, don't even bother. Still, if you don't mind paying high prices for dishes that go for much less elsewhere, try this old favorite. From the perfectly seasoned homemade focaccia to an exemplary crème brûlée, this elegant little standout is amazingly consistent. The menu includes a small selection of classics: linguine with shrimp; delicious, pillowy gnocchi; *zuppa di pesce* (fish soup); and veal Marsala. And don't miss the outstanding warm goat cheese soufflé served with pan-seared asparagus, baby green beans, carrots, and Bel-gian endive over a roasted tomato vinaigrette. You can't go wrong with any of the handmade pastas. And the owners, Antonia Berto and Phillip Smith, travel to Italy every year to research recipes, so you can be sure you're getting an authentic taste of Italy in small-town Key West.

615 Duval St. ℂ 305/294-6565. Fax 305/294-3888. www.antoniaskeywest.com. Reservations suggested. Main courses $20–$30; pastas $15–$30. AE, DC, MC, V. Daily 6–11pm.

Bagatelle ✸✸✸ SEAFOOD/TROPICAL Reserve a seat at the elegant second-floor veranda overlooking Duval Street's mayhem. From the calm above, you may want to start your meal with the zingy conch ceviche or the sashimi-like seared sesame tuna rolled in black peppercorns. The best chicken and beef dishes are given a tropical treatment: grilled with papaya, ginger, and soy. The Jamaican curry chicken is a favorite.

115 Duval St. ⓒ **305/296-6609.** www.bagatelle-keywest.com. Reservations recommended. Main courses $15–$25; lunch $5–$15. AE, DISC, MC, V. Sun–Thurs 11:30am–10pm; Fri–Sat 11:30am–11pm.

La Trattoria ✸ ITALIAN Have a true Italian feast in a relaxed atmosphere. Each dish here is prepared and presented according to old Italian tradition. Try the delicious bread-crumb–stuffed mushroom caps; they're firm yet tender. The stuffed eggplant with ricotta and roasted peppers is light and flavorful. Or have the seafood salad of shrimp, calamari, and mussels, fish-market fresh and tasty. The pasta dishes are also great—go for the penne Venezia, with mushrooms, sun-dried tomatoes, and crabmeat. For dessert, don't skip the homemade tiramisu; it's light yet full-flavored. The dining room is spacious but still intimate, and the waiters are friendly. Before you leave, visit Virgilio's, a cocktail lounge with live jazz until 2am.

524 Duval St. ⓒ **305/296-1075.** www.latrattoria.us. Main courses $16–$38; pasta $14–$24. AE, DC, DISC, MC, V. Daily 5:30–11pm.

Mangoes ✸✸✸ FLORIBBEAN This restaurant's large brick patio, shaded by overgrown banyan trees, is so alluring to passersby that it's packed almost every night of the week. Many people don't realize how pricey the meals can be here, because, upon first glance, it looks like a casual Duval Street cafe. Appetizers include grilled shrimp cocktail with spicy mango chutney. Crispy curried chicken and local snapper with passion-fruit sauce are typical among the entrees, but the garlic and lime pinks—a half-pound of Key West pink shrimp seasoned and grilled with a roasted garlic and Key lime glaze—is the menu's best offering by far. Even though it's right on touristy Duval Street, Mangoes enjoys a good reputation among locals and stands out from the rest of the places offering greasy bar fare. For a cool, locals' loungey scene, check out the back bar inside.

700 Duval St. (at Angela St.). ⓒ **305/292-4606.** www.mangoeskeywest.com. Reservations recommended for parties of 6 or more. Main courses $15–$30; pizzas $10–$15; lunch $7–$18. AE, DC, DISC, MC, V. Daily 11am–midnight; pizza until 1am.

Michael's ✸✸✸ (Finds) STEAK Tucked away in a residential neighborhood, Michael's is a meaty oasis in a big sea of fish. With steaks flown in daily from Chicago, this is *the* steakhouse for when you're craving meat, from New York strip to porterhouse. Unlike most steakhouses, Michael's exudes a relaxed, tropical ambience with a fabulous indoor/outdoor setting that's romantic but not stuffy. A fantastic fondue menu makes for a tasty snack or even a meal, complemented by an excellent, reasonably priced wine list. Sure, Michael's is on the pricier side, but it's not every day that you can enjoy slabs of beef from Chicago in a warm, tropical setting.

532 Margaret St. ⓒ **305/295-1300.** www.michaelskeywest.com. Reservations recommended. Main courses $15–$35. AE, DC, DISC, MC, V. Daily 5–11pm.

Seven Fish ✸✸✸ (Finds) SEAFOOD "Simple, good food" is Seven Fish's motto, but this hidden little secret is much more than simple. One of the most popular restaurants with locals, Seven Fish is a chic seafood spot serving some of the best fish dishes on the island. Crab and shiitake-mushroom pasta, fish of the day, and gnocchi with blue cheese and sautéed fish are among the dishes to choose from. For dessert, do not miss the Key lime cake over tart lime curd with fresh berries.

632 Olivia St. ℂ 305/296-2777. www.7fish.com. Reservations recommended. Main courses $15–$25. AE, MC, V. Wed–Mon 6–10pm.

MODERATE

Alonzo's Oyster Bar ℱ SEAFOOD   Alonzo's serves good seafood in a casual setting. It's on the ground floor of the A&B Lobster House, at the end of Front Street in the marina; if you want to dress up, go upstairs for the "fine dining." To start your meal, try the steamed beer shrimp—tantalizingly fresh jumbo shrimp in a sauce of garlic, Old Bay seasoning, beer, and cayenne pepper. A house specialty is white-clam chili, a delicious mix of tender clams, white beans, and potatoes served with a dollop of sour cream. The staff is cheerful and informative, and the service is very good.

231 Margaret St. ℂ 305/294-5880. www.alonzosoysterbar.com. Main courses $11–$17; appetizers $5–$8. MC, V. Daily 11am–11pm.

Banana Café ℱℱℱ Finds FRENCH   Although neither as elaborate as Cafe des Artistes nor as casual as Blue Heaven, Banana Café is open for three meals a day and benefits from a French-country-cafe look and feel. The upscale local eatery discovered by savvy visitors on the less-congested end of Duval Street has retained its loyal clientele with affordable prices and delightful, light preparations. The crepes are legendary on the island for breakfast or lunch; the fresh ingredients and French-themed menu bring daytime diners back for the casual, classy, tropical-influenced dinner menu. There's live jazz every Thursday night.

1211 Duval St. ℂ 305/294-7227. Main courses $5–$25; breakfast and lunch $2–$10. AE, DC, MC, V. Daily 8am–11pm.

Blue Heaven ℱℱ Finds SEAFOOD/AMERICAN/NATURAL   This hippie-run restaurant has become the place to be in Key West—and with good reason. Be prepared to wait in line. The food here is some of the best in town—especially at breakfast, which features homemade granola, tropical-fruit pancakes, and seafood Benedict. Dinners are just as good and run the gamut from fresh-caught fish and Jamaican jerk chicken to curried soups and vegetarian stews. Some people are put off by the dirt floors and roaming cats and birds, but frankly, it adds to the charm. The building used to be a bordello, where Hemingway was said to hang out watching cockfights. It's still lively here, but not *that* lively!

305 Petronia St. ℂ 305/296-8666. Main courses $10–$30; lunch $6–$14; breakfast $5–$11. DISC, MC, V. Daily 8–11:30am, noon–3pm, and 6–10:30pm; Sun brunch 8am–1pm. Closed mid-Sept to early Oct.

Mangia, Mangia ℱ Value ITALIAN/AMERICAN   Locals appreciate that they can get good, inexpensive food here in a town filled with tourist traps. Off the beaten track, this great Chicago-style pasta place has some of the best Italian food in the Keys. The family-run restaurant serves superb homemade pastas of every description, including one of the tastiest marinara sauces around. The simple grilled chicken breast brushed with olive oil and sprinkled with pepper is another good choice. You wouldn't know it from the front, but there's a fantastic little patio dotted with twinkling pepper lights and lots of plants. While you wait for your table, relax out back with a glass of wine—this place is said to have the largest selection in the Keys—or homemade beer.

900 Southard St. (at Margaret St.). ℂ 305/294-2469. Reservations not accepted. Main courses $9–$15. AE, MC, V. Daily 5:30–10pm.

Pepe's ⍟ *(Finds* AMERICAN   This old dive has been serving good, basic food for nearly a century. Steaks and Apalachicola Bay oysters are the big draws for regulars, who appreciate the rustic barroom setting and historic photos on the walls. Look for original scenes of Key West in 1909, when Pepe's first opened. If the weather is nice, choose a seat on the patio under a stunning mahogany tree. Burgers, fish sandwiches, and standard chili satisfy hearty eaters. Buttery sautéed mushrooms and rich mashed potatoes are the best comfort foods in Key West. There's always a wait, so stop by early for breakfast, when you can get old-fashioned chipped beef on toast and all the usual egg dishes. In the evening, reasonably priced cocktails are served on the deck.

806 Caroline St. (between Margaret and Williams sts.). ⓒ 305/294-7192. Main courses $15–$25; breakfast $2–$10; lunch $5–$10. DISC, MC, V. Daily 6.30am–10.30pm.

Sarabeth's ⍟⍟ *(Finds* AMERICAN   An offshoot of the popular New York City breakfast hot spot, Sarabeth's brings a much-needed shot of cosmopolitan comfort food to Key West in the form of delicious breakfasts with Sarabeth's signature home-made jams and jellies. Choose from buttermilk to lemon ricotta pancakes or almond-crusted cinnamon French toast. For lunch, the traditional Caesar salad, burger, or Key West pinks shrimp roll with avocado are all excellent choices. Dinner is simple, but savory, with top-notch dishes from chicken pot pie and meat loaf to a divine green-chile-pepper macaroni with three cheeses or meaty shrimp-and-crabmeat cakes. The dining room is cozy and intimate, and it feels like you're eating in someone's house; a few tables are on a small outdoor patio.

530 Simonton St. ⓒ 305/293-8181. Main courses $13–$20; breakfast $5.50–$10; lunch $5.75–$14. MC, V. Mon 8am–3pm; Wed–Sun 8am–3pm and 6–10pm.

Turtle Kraals Wildlife Grill ⍟ *(Finds* (Kids SOUTHWESTERN/SEAFOOD   You'll join lots of locals in this out-of-the-way converted warehouse with indoor and dock-side seating, which serves innovative seafood at great prices. Try the twin lobster tails stuffed with mango and crabmeat, stone crabs when in season (Oct–May), or any of the big quesadillas or fajitas. Kids will like the wildlife exhibits, the turtle cannery, and the very cheesy menu. Blues bands play most nights.

213 Margaret St. (at Caroline St.). ⓒ 305/294-2640. Main courses $10–$20. DISC, MC, V. Mon–Thurs 11am–10:30pm; Fri–Sat 11am–11pm; Sun noon–10:30pm. Bar closes at midnight.

INEXPENSIVE

Bahama Mama's Kitchen ⍟ BAHAMIAN   Sit outside under an umbrella and enjoy the authentic Bahamian fare made from recipes that have been handed down for the past 150 years. Try the coconut shrimp: butterflied, soaked in coconut oil, battered with egg, then rolled in fresh shredded coconut and deep-fried. The fresh catch comes blackened, broiled, or fried, and is served with island plantains, shrimp hash cakes, and crab rice. The service is good and the staff is friendly.

In the Bahama Village Market, 324 Petronia St. ⓒ 305/294-3355. Main courses $10–$15; appetizers $4–$10. MC, V. Daily 11am–10pm.

Island Dogs Bar ⍟ AMERICAN   This islandy, Tommy Bahama–esque bar is a cool spot to throw back a few while catching a game or a live band. But more importantly is the fare—not your typical bar fare, but delicious burgers, chicken fingers, chicken wings and, well, you get the picture. Sit at the bar or at one of the few outdoor tables ideally placed for watching the crowds stumble—literally—off Duval Street.

505 Front St. ⓒ 305/295-0501. Main Courses: $5–$10. AE, DISC, MC, V. Daily 11am–2am.

Upper Crust Pizza 🏀🏀 PIZZA   There's nothing better after a day or night of drinking rum runners than chasing them down with a slice or three of this heavenly pizza. The owner hails from Boston and won't tell us his secret to the perfectly crisp, garlicky crust, but as long as he keeps up the good work, we won't bother him for it. All sorts of varieties, from cheese to spinach with goat cheese, are available until the wee hours of the night.

611 Duval St. ℂ 305/293-8890. www.uppercrustkeywest.com. Pizza $3 slice, $13–$16 pie. AE, DISC, MC, V. Daily 11am–2am.

KEY WEST AFTER DARK

Duval Street is the Bourbon Street of Florida. Amid the T-shirt shops and clothing boutiques, you'll find bar after bar serving neon-colored frozen drinks to revelers who bounce from bar to bar from noon 'til dawn. Bands and crowds vary from night to night and season to season. Your best bet is to start at Truman Avenue and head up Duval to check them out for yourself. Cover charges are rare, except in gay clubs (see the "The Gay Scene," below), so stop into a dozen and see which you like. For the most part, Key West is a late-night town, and bars and clubs don't close until around 3 or 4am.

Captain Tony's Saloon   Just around the corner from Duval's beaten path, this smoky old bar is about as authentic as you'll find. It comes complete with old-time regulars who remember the island before cruise ships docked here; they say Hemingway drank, caroused, and even wrote here. The owner, Capt. Tony Tarracino, a former controversial Key West mayor—"immortalized" in Jimmy Buffett's "Last Mango in Paradise"—recently capitalized on the success of this once-quaint tavern by franchising the place. 428 Greene St. ℂ 305/294-1838.

Durty Harry's   This large complex features live rock bands almost every night. You can wander to one of the many outdoor bars or head to Upstairs at Rick's, an indoor/outdoor dance club that gets going late. For racy singles or couples, there is the Red Garter, a pocket-size strip club. The hawker outside reminds couples, in case they've forgotten, that "the family that strips together, sticks together." 208 Duval St. ℂ 305/296-4890.

Sloppy Joe's   You'll have to stop in here just to say you did. Scholars and drunks debate whether this is the same Sloppy Joe's that Hemingway wrote about, but there's no argument that this classic bar's early-20th-century wooden ceiling and cracked-tile floors are Key West originals. There's live music nightly, as well as a cigar room and martini bar. 201 Duval St. ℂ 305/294-5717, ext. 10. www.sloppyjoes.com.

THE GAY SCENE

Key West's bohemian live-and-let-live atmosphere extends to its thriving and quirky gay community. Before and after Tennessee Williams, Key West has provided the perfect backdrop to a gay scene unlike that of many large urban areas. Seamlessly blended with the prevailing culture, there is no "gay ghetto" in Key West, where alternative lifestyles are embraced and even celebrated.

Although restaurants and businesses welcome visitors without discrimination, nightlife *is* inevitably nightlife. In Key West, the best music and dancing can be found at the predominantly gay clubs. While many of the area's other hot spots are geared toward tourists who like to imbibe, the gay clubs are for those who want to rave, gay or not. Covers vary, but are rarely more than $10.

Two popular adjacent late-night spots are the **801 Bourbon Bar/Number One Saloon** (801 Duval St. and 514 Petronia St.; © **305/294-9349** for both), featuring great drag and lots more disco. A mostly male clientele frequents this hot spot from 9pm until 4am. Another Duval Street favorite is **Aqua,** 711 Duval St. (© **305/292-8500**), where you might catch drag queens belting out torch songs or judges voting on the best package in the wet-jockey-shorts contest.

Sunday nights are fun at two local spots. **Tea by the Sea,** on the pier at the Atlantic Shores Motel, 510 South St. (© **800/520-3559**), attracts a faithful following of regulars and visitors alike. The clothing-optional pool is always an attraction. Show up after 7:30pm. Sometime in 2008, the Shores will be demolished to make way for swank condos, to the dismay of many. Better known around town as La Te Da, **La Terraza de Martí,** 1125 Duval St. (© **305/296-6706**), the former Key West home of Cuban exile José Martí, is a great spot to gather poolside for the best martini in town—but don't bother with the food. Just upstairs is the **Crystal Room** (© **305/296-6706**), with a high-caliber cabaret performance featuring the popular Randy Roberts in winter.

4 The Dry Tortugas ★★

70 miles W. of Key West

Few people realize that the Florida Keys don't end at Key West, since about 70 miles west is a chain of seven small islands known as the Dry Tortugas. Since you've come this far, you might wish to visit them, especially if you're into bird-watching, their primary draw.

Ponce de León, who discovered this far-flung cluster of coral keys in 1513, named them Las Tortugas because of the many sea turtles, which still flock to the area during nesting season in the warm summer months. Oceanic charts later carried the preface "dry" to warn mariners that fresh water was unavailable here. Modern intervention has made drinking water available, but little else.

These undeveloped islands make a great day trip for travelers interested in seeing the natural anomalies of the Florida Keys—especially the birds. The Dry Tortugas are nesting grounds and roosting sites for thousands of tropical and subtropical oceanic birds. Visitors will also find a historic fort, good fishing, and terrific snorkeling around shallow reefs.

GETTING THERE

BY BOAT   The **Yankee Fleet,** based in Key West (© **800/634-0939** or 305/294-7009; www.yankeefleet.com/keywest.cfm), offers day trips from Key West for sightseeing, snorkeling, or both. Cruises leave daily at 7:30am for the 3-hour journey from Land's End Marina at Margaret Street to Garden Key. Breakfast is served onboard. Once on the island, you can join a guided tour of Fort Jefferson or explore it on your own. Boats return to Key West by 7pm. Tours cost $139 for adults; $129 for seniors, students, and military personnel; and $94 for children 16 and under. Prices include breakfast, lunch, dinner, and snorkeling equipment. Call for reservations.

Sunny Days Catamarans (© **800/236-7937** or 305/292-6100; www.sunnydays keywest.com) operates the *Fast Cat,* which is faster, quieter, and more high tech than the loud Yankee fleet, as well as a better value. The round-trip fare ($110 for adults, $105 for seniors, $80 for children) includes a continental breakfast; a buffet lunch with cold cuts, fresh veggies, fruits, salads, and unlimited sodas and water; an island tour; and a snorkeling excursion to a shipwreck in 5 to 20 feet of water. The high-speed catamaran leaves Key West for Garden Key at 8am and returns by 6pm.

BY PLANE **Seaplanes of Key West,** based at Key West Airport (© **800/950-2-FLY** or 305/294-0709; www.seaplanesofkeywest.com), offers daily excursions. Weather permitting, flights depart at 8am, 10am, noon, and 2pm. The 40-minute trip at about 500 feet offers a great introduction to the Dry Tortugas. Fares include snorkeling equipment and a cooler for use on the island. A half-day costs $199 for adults, $149 for kids 7 to 12, and $119 for kids 6 and under; a full day costs $345 for adults, $265 for kids 7 to 12, and $210 for kids 6 and under. Bring a bathing suit and snacks to enjoy on these remote and beautiful islands.

EXPLORING THE DRY TORTUGAS

Of the seven islands that make up the Dry Tortugas, Garden Key is the most visited because it is where Fort Jefferson and the visitor center are located. Loggerhead Key, Middle Key, and East Key are open only during the day and are for hiking. Bush Key is for the birds—literally! It's a nesting area for birds only, though it is open from October to January for special excursions. Hospital and Long keys are closed to the public.

Fort Jefferson, a huge six-sided, 19th-century fortress, is set almost at the water's edge of Garden Key, so it appears to float in the middle of the sea. The monumental structure is surrounded by formidable 8-foot-thick walls that rise from the sand to a height of nearly 50 feet. Impressive archways, stonework, and parapets make this 150-year-old monument a grand sight. With the invention of the rifled cannon, the fort's masonry construction became obsolete and the building was never completed. For 10 years, however, from 1863 to 1873, Fort Jefferson served as a prison, a kind of "Alcatraz East." Among its prisoners were four of the "Lincoln Conspirators," including Samuel A. Mudd, the doctor who set the broken leg of fugitive assassin John Wilkes Booth. In 1935, Fort Jefferson became a national monument administered by the National Park Service. Today, however, Fort Jefferson is struggling to resist erosion from the salt and sea, as iron used in the gun openings and the shutters in the fort's walls has accelerated the deterioration, and the structure's openings need to be rebricked. As a result, the National Park Service has designated the fort as the recipient of a $15-million face-lift, a project that may take up to a decade to complete.

For more information on Fort Jefferson and the Dry Tortugas, call the **Everglades National Park Service** (© **305/242-7700**) or visit www.fortjefferson.com. Fort Jefferson is open during daylight hours. A self-guided tour describes the history of the human presence in the Dry Tortugas while leading visitors through the fort.

OUTDOOR ACTIVITIES

BIRD-WATCHING Bring your binoculars and your bird books: Bird-watching is *the* reason to visit this little cluster of tropical islands. The Dry Tortugas, uniquely situated in the middle of the migration flyway between North and South America, serve as an important rest stop for the more than 200 winged varieties that pass through here annually. The season peaks from mid-March to mid-May, when thousands of birds show up, but many species from the West Indies can be found here year-round.

DIVING & SNORKELING The warm, clear, shallow waters of the Dry Tortugas produce optimum conditions for snorkeling and scuba diving. Four endangered species of sea turtles—green, leatherback, Atlantic ridley, and hawksbill—can be found here, along with myriad marine species. The region just outside the seawall of Fort Jefferson is excellent for underwater touring; an abundant variety of fish, coral, and more live in just 3 to 4 feet of water.

FISHING   In July 2001, a federal law closed off all fishing in a 90-square-mile tract of open ocean called the Tortugas North and a 61-square-mile tract of open ocean called the Tortugas South. It basically prohibits all fishing in order to preserve the dwindling population of fish (a result of commercial fishing and environmental factors). Instead, head to Key West.

CAMPING

The rustic beauty of tiny Garden Key (the only island of the Dry Tortugas where campers are allowed to pitch tents) is a camper's dream. Don't worry about sharing your site with noisy RVs or motor homes; they can't get here. The abundance of birds doesn't make it quiet, but the camping—a stone's throw from the water—is as picturesque as it gets. Picnic tables, cooking grills, and toilets are provided, but there are no showers. All supplies must be packed in and out. Sites are $3 per person per night and are available on a first-come, first-served basis. The 10 sites book up fast. For more information, call the **National Park Service** (© **305/242-7700**).

13

The Gold Coast: Hallandale to the Palm Beaches

Named not for the sun-kissed skin of the area's residents, but for the gold salvaged from shipwrecks off its coastline, the Gold Coast embraces more than 60 miles of beautiful Atlantic shoreline—from the pristine sands of Jupiter in northern Palm Beach County to the legendary strip of beaches in Fort Lauderdale.

If you haven't visited the cities along Florida's southeastern coast in the last few years, you'll be amazed at how much has changed. Miles of sprawling grassland and empty lots have been replaced with luxurious resorts and high-rise condominiums. Taking advantage of their proximity to Miami, the cities that make up the Gold Coast have attracted millions of people looking to escape crowded sidewalks, traffic jams, and the everyday routines of life.

Fortunately, amid all the building, much of the natural treasure of the Gold Coast remains. There are 300 miles of Intracoastal Waterway, not to mention Fort Lauderdale's Venetian-inspired canals, and the unspoiled splendor of the Everglades is just a few miles inland.

The most popular areas in the Gold Coast are Fort Lauderdale, Boca Raton, and Palm Beach. While Fort Lauderdale is a favored beachfront destination, Boca Raton and Palm Beach are better known for their country-club lifestyles and excellent shopping. Farther north is the quietly popular Jupiter, best known for spring training at the Roger Dean Stadium and for former resident Burt Reynolds. In

between these better-traveled destinations are a few things worth stopping for, but not much. Driving north along the coastline is one of the best ways to fully appreciate what the Gold Coast is all about—it's a perspective you certainly won't find in a shopping mall.

Tourists come here by the droves, but they aren't the only people coming; thousands of transplants, fleeing the increasing population influx in Miami and the frigid winters up north, have made this area their home. As a result, there has been a construction boom in the existing cities and even westward, into the swampy areas of the Everglades. More than 20 homes per day are being built in Broward County alone. There has also been a great revitalization of several downtown areas, including Hollywood, Fort Lauderdale, and West Palm Beach. These once-desolate urban centers have been spruced up and now attract more young travelers and families than ever.

Unfortunately, like its neighbors to the south, the Gold Coast can be prohibitively hot and buggy in summer. The good news is that bargains are plentiful from May through October, when many locals take advantage of package deals and uncrowded resorts.

For the purposes of this chapter, the Gold Coast will consist of the towns of Hallandale, Hollywood, Pompano Beach, Fort Lauderdale, Dania, Deerfield, Boca Raton, Delray Beach, Boynton Beach, Jupiter, and the Palm Beaches.

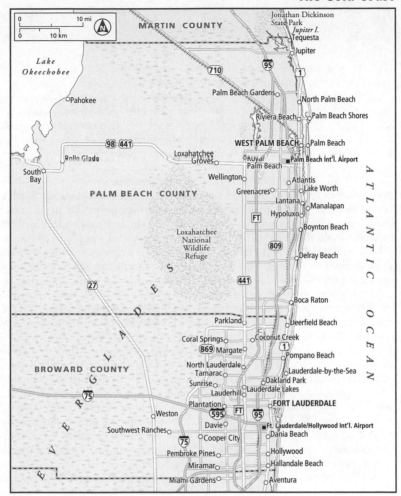

EXPLORING THE GOLD COAST BY CAR

Like most of South Florida, the Gold Coast consists of a mainland and adjacent barrier islands. You'll have to check maps to keep track of the many bridges that allow access to the islands where most tourist activity is centered. Interstate 95, which runs north-south, is the area's main highway. Farther west is the Florida Turnpike, a toll road that can be worth the expense since the speed limit is higher and it's often less congested than I-95. Also on the mainland is U.S. 1, which generally runs parallel to I-95 (to the east) and is a narrower thoroughfare that is mostly crowded with strip malls and seedy hotels.

I recommend taking Florida A1A, a slow oceanside road that connects the long, thin islands of Florida's entire east coast. Although the road is narrow, it is the most scenic and, thus, ushers you into the relaxed atmosphere of these resort towns.

1 Broward County: Hallandale & Hollywood ⧊ to Fort Lauderdale ⧊⧊

23 miles N. of Miami

Less exposed than highly hyped Miami-Dade County, Broward County is a lot calmer and, according to some, a lot friendlier than the Magic City. In fact, a friendly rivalry exists between residents of both counties. Miamians consider themselves more sophisticated and cosmopolitan than their northern neighbors, who, in turn, dismiss the alleged sophistication as snobbery and actually prefer their own county's gentler pace.

With more than 23 miles of beachfront and 300 miles of navigable waterways, Broward County is also a great outdoor destination. Scattered amid the shopping malls, condominiums, and tourist traps is a beautiful landscape lined with hundreds of parks, golf courses, tennis courts, and, of course, beaches.

The City of Hallandale Beach is a small, peaceful oceanfront town just north of Dade County's Aventura. Condos are the predominant landmarks in Hallandale, which is still pretty much a retirement community, although the revamped multimillion-dollar Westin Diplomat Resort (p. 318) is slowly trying to revitalize and liven up the area.

Just north of Hallandale is the more energetic, burgeoning city of Hollywood. Once a sleepy community wedged between Fort Lauderdale and Miami, Hollywood is now a bustling area of 1.5 million people with an array of ethnic and racial identities: from white and African American to Jamaican, Chinese, and Dominican. (*Money* magazine trumpeted the self-described "City of the Future" as having an ethnic makeup that mirrors what the U.S. will look like by the year 2022.) In 2004, the $300-million Seminole Hard Rock Hotel & Casino (p. 321) debuted, with a 500-room hotel, spa, and 130,000-square-foot casino. This was exactly what the city needed to kick its slow renaissance up a notch. A spate of redevelopment has made the pedestrian-friendly center along Hollywood Boulevard and Harrison Street, east of Dixie Highway, a popular destination for travelers and locals alike. Some predict Hollywood will be South Florida's next big destination—South Beach without the attitude and traffic jams. While the prediction is a dubious one, Hollywood is definitely awakening from its long slumber. Prices are a fraction of those at other tourist areas, and a quasi-bohemian vibe is apparent in the galleries, clubs, and restaurants that dot the new "strip." Its gritty undercurrent, however, prevents it from becoming too trendy.

Fort Lauderdale, with its well-known strip of beaches, restaurants, bars, and souvenir shops, has really undergone a major transformation. Once famous (or infamous) for the annual mayhem it hosted during spring break, this area is now attracting a more affluent, better-behaved yachting crowd. The Miami Herald Business section discussed the changes in a 2006 article, *Upscale Inn Crowd,* which agreed that "the city once famous for Spring Break antics undergoes a broad upgrade of its hotel stock." In fact, construction is well underway for Starwood's new W Fort Lauderdale, a 346-room boutique hotel opening here in the fall of 2008, and the swank St. Regis is already open.

In addition to beautiful wide beaches, Fort Lauderdale, known as the Venice of America, has more than 300 miles of navigable waterways and innumerable canals, which permit thousands of residents to anchor boats in their backyards. Boating is not just a hobby here; it's a lifestyle. Visitors can easily get on the water, too, by renting a boat or by hailing a moderately priced water taxi.

Fort Lauderdale

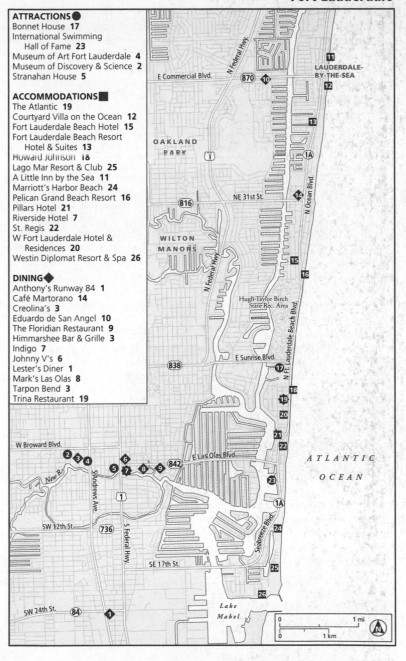

ATTRACTIONS ●
Bonnet House **17**
International Swimming
  Hall of Fame **23**
Museum of Art Fort Lauderdale **4**
Museum of Discovery & Science **2**
Stranahan House **5**

ACCOMMODATIONS ■
The Atlantic **19**
Courtyard Villa on the Ocean **12**
Fort Lauderdale Beach Hotel **15**
Fort Lauderdale Beach Resort
  Hotel & Suites **13**
Howard Johnson **18**
Lago Mar Resort & Club **25**
A Little Inn by the Sea **11**
Marriott's Harbor Beach **24**
Pelican Grand Beach Resort **16**
Pillars Hotel **21**
Riverside Hotel **7**
St. Regis **22**
W Fort Lauderdale Hotel &
  Residences **20**
Westin Diplomat Resort & Spa **26**

DINING ◆
Anthony's Runway 84 **1**
Café Martorano **14**
Creolina's **3**
Eduardo de San Angel **10**
The Floridian Restaurant **9**
Himmarshee Bar & Grille **3**
Indigo **7**
Johnny V's **6**
Lester's Diner **1**
Mark's Las Olas **8**
Tarpon Bend **3**
Trina Restaurant **19**

Huge cruise ships also take advantage of Florida's deepest harbor, Port Everglades. The seaport is on the southeastern coast of the Florida peninsula, near the Fort Lauderdale–Hollywood International Airport on the outskirts of Hollywood and Dania Beach. Port Everglades is the second-busiest cruise-ship base in Florida, after Miami, and one of the top five in the world. For further information on cruises, see p. 179 and consult *Frommer's Caribbean Cruises & Ports of Call* (Wiley Publishing, Inc.).

ESSENTIALS

GETTING THERE   If you're driving from Miami, it's a straight shot north to Hollywood or Fort Lauderdale. Visitors on their way to or from Orlando should take the Florida Turnpike to exits 53, 54, 58, or 62, depending on the location of your accommodations.

The **Fort Lauderdale–Hollywood International Airport** is small, easy to negotiate, and just 15 minutes from both of the downtown areas it services. However, its user-friendliness may not last much longer: Due to its popularity, the airport is still undergoing a $650-million expansion and renovation that often renders it just as maddening as any other major metropolitan airport. The airport has wireless Internet access and a fantastic car-rental center where 10 rental companies are under one roof—very convenient. Levels 1 through 4 are home to Alamo, Avis, Budget, Dollar, Enterprise, E-Z, Hertz, National, Royal, and Thrifty. Levels 5 to 9 provide 5,500 spaces for public parking.

Amtrak (© **800/USA-RAIL**) stations are at 200 SW 21st Terrace (Broward Blvd. and I-95), Fort Lauderdale (© **954/587-6692**), and 3001 Hollywood Blvd. (northwest corner of Hollywood Blvd. and I-95, Hollywood; © **954/921-4517**).

VISITOR INFORMATION   The **Greater Fort Lauderdale Convention & Visitors Bureau,** 1850 Eller Dr., Suite 303 (off I-95 and I-595 E), Fort Lauderdale, FL 33316 (© **954/765-4466;** fax 954/765-4467; www.sunny.org), is an excellent resource for area information in English, Spanish, and French. Call in advance to request a free comprehensive guide covering events, accommodations, and sightseeing in Broward County.

Also available for brochures, information, and vacation packages in Fort Lauderdale are operators at **Greater Than Ever Fort Lauderdale** (© 800/22-SUNNY).

The **Greater Hollywood Chamber of Commerce,** 330 N. Federal Hwy. (at U.S. 1 and Taylor St.), Hollywood, FL 33020 (© **954/923-4000;** fax 954/923-8737; www.hollywoodchamber.org), is open Monday through Friday from 9am to 5pm. Here you'll find the lowdown on all of Hollywood's events, attractions, restaurants, hotels, and tours.

HITTING THE BEACH

The southern part of the Gold Coast, Broward County, has the region's most popular and amenities-laden beaches, which stretch for more than 23 miles. Most do not charge for access and all are well maintained. Here's a selection of some of the county's best, from south to north:

Hollywood Beach, stretching from Sheridan Street to Georgia Street, is a major attraction in the city of Hollywood, a virtual carnival of young hipsters, big families, and sunburned French Canadians who dodge bicyclers and skaters along the rows of tacky souvenir shops, T-shirt shops, game rooms, snack bars, beer stands, hotels, and miniature-golf courses. **Hollywood Beach Broadwalk,** modeled after Atlantic City's legendary boardwalk, is the town's popular beachfront pedestrian thoroughfare, a

Turtle Trail

In June and July, the John U. Lloyd Beach is crawling with nature lovers who come for the spectacular **Sea Turtle Awareness Program**. Park rangers begin the evening with a lecture and slide show while scouts search the beach for nesting loggerhead sea turtles. If a turtle is located—plenty of them usually are—a beach walk allows participants to see the turtles nest and, sometimes, their eggs hatch. The program begins at 9pm on Wednesday and Friday from mid-May to mid-July. Call ℂ **954/923-2833** for reservations. Walks last between 1 and 3 hours. Comfortable walking shoes and insect repellent are necessary. The park entrance fee of $3 to $5 per carload applies.

cement promenade that's 30-feet wide and stretches along the shoreline for 3 miles. A recent makeover added, among other things, a concrete bike path, a crushed-shell jogging path, new trash receptacles, and the relocation of beach showers to each street end (all of are them are handicapped accessible). Popular with runners, skaters, and cruisers, the Broadwalk is also renowned as a hangout for thousands of retirement-age snowbirds who get together for frequent dances and shows at a faded outdoor amphitheater. Despite efforts to clear out a seedy element, the area remains a haven for drunks and scammers, so keep alert.

If you tire of the hectic diversity that defines Hollywood's Broadwalk, enjoy the natural beauty of the beach itself, which is wide and clean. There are lifeguards, showers, restroom facilities, and public areas for picnics and parties.

The **Fort Lauderdale Beach Promenade,** along the beach, underwent a $26-million renovation and looks fantastic. It's especially peaceful in the mornings, when there's just a smattering of joggers and walkers; but even at its most crowded on weekends, the expansive promenade provides room for everyone. Note, however, that the beach is hardly pristine; it is across the street from an uninterrupted stretch of hotels, bars, and retail outlets. Also nearby is a retail-and-dining megacomplex, Beach Place (p. 327)—in the throes of its own renovation that will add newer, hipper stores, bars, and restaurants—on Florida A1A, midway between Las Olas and Sunrise boulevards.

On the sand just across the road, most days you'll find hard-core volleyball players who always welcome anyone with a good spike, and you'll find an inviting ocean for swimmers of any level. The unusually clear waters are under the careful watch of some of Florida's best-looking lifeguards. Freshen up afterward in the clean showers and restrooms conveniently located along the strip. Pets have been banned from most of the beach in order to maintain the impressive cleanliness; a designated area for pets exists away from the main sunbathing areas.

Especially on weekends, parking at the oceanside meters is nearly impossible. Try biking, skating, or hitching a ride on the water taxi instead. The strip is located on Florida A1A, between SE 17th Street and Sunrise Boulevard.

Dania Beach's **John U. Lloyd Beach State Park,** 6503 N. Ocean Dr., Dania (ℂ **954/ 923-2833**), consists of 251 acres of barrier island, situated between the Atlantic Ocean and the Intracoastal Waterway, from Port Everglades on the north to Dania on the south. Its natural setting contrasts sharply with the urban development of Fort Lauderdale. Lloyd Beach, one of Broward County's most important nesting beaches for sea turtles, produces some 10,000 hatchlings a year. The park's broad, flat beach is popular for both swimming and sunning. Self-guided nature trails are great for those too restless to sunbathe. The park and beach received significant damage during 2005's Hurricane Wilma, but you'd never know it. All is restored back to its pristine condition.

OUTDOOR ACTIVITIES & SPECTATOR SPORTS

BOATING   Often called the "yachting capital of the world," Fort Lauderdale provides ample opportunity for visitors to get out on the water, either along the Intracoastal Waterway or on the open ocean. If your hotel doesn't rent boats, try **Aloha Watersports,** Marriott's Harbor Beach Resort, 3030 Holiday Dr., Fort Lauderdale (© 954/462-7245). It can outfit you with a variety of craft, including jet skis, WaveRunners, and catamarans. Rates start at $65 per half-hour for WaveRunners ($15 each additional rider; doubles and triples available), $70 to $125 for sailboats, $60 to $70 for catamarans, $20 per person per hour for ocean kayaks, and $95 per person for a 15-minute parasailing ride. Aloha also offers a Surfing School for $40 (though the waves are hardly rippin' here!) and Coast Guard classes at 9am daily, through which adults can obtain their Florida Boaters License for $3.

FISHING   The **IGFA** (International Game Fish Association) **World Fishing Center,** 300 Gulf Stream Way, Dania Beach (© 954/922-4212; www.igfa.org), is an angler's paradise. One of the highlights of this museum, library, and park is the virtual-reality fishing simulator that allows visitors to actually reel in their own computer-generated catch. Also included in the 3-acre park are displays of antique fishing gear, record catches, famous anglers, various vessels, and a wetlands lab. To get a list of local captains and guides, call **IGFA headquarters** (© 954/927-2628) and ask for the librarian. Admission is $6 for adults, $5 for seniors and children 3 to 16. The museum and library are open daily from 10am to 6pm. On the grounds is also **Bass Pro Shops Outdoor World,** a huge retail complex set on a 3-acre lake.

GOLF   More than 50 golf courses in all price ranges compete for players. Among the best is **Emerald Hills,** 4100 N. Hills Dr., Hollywood (© 954/961-4000; www.theclubatemeraldhills.com), just west of I-95 between Sterling Road and Sheridan Street. This beauty consistently lands on the "best of" lists of golf writers nationwide. The 18th hole, on a two-tier green, is the course's signature; it's surrounded by water and is more than a bit rough. The course is pricey—Friday through Sunday, greens fees start at $150 for tee times after 1pm, and $175 for tee times before noon during high season; Monday through Friday, the fees are $125 before noon and $110 after 1pm. Rates are cheaper during the brutally hot summers.

The **Diplomat Country Club and Spa,** 501 Diplomat Pkwy., Hallandale Beach (© 954/602-6000; www.diplomatcountryclub.com), is across the Intracoastal from the Westin Diplomat Resort. It has fabulous golf facilities, with 8 acres of lakes and rolling fairways, plus a fantastic delivery service that brings lunch and drinks to your cart. You pay for the services, however, with greens fees of about $215 during high season and $95 to $169 off season. Twilight fees at 2pm cost from $50 to $95.

For one of Broward's best municipal challenges, try the 18-holer at the **Orangebrook Golf Course,** 400 Entrada Dr., Hollywood (© 954/967-GOLF). Built in 1937, this is one of the state's oldest courses and one of the area's best bargains. Morning and noon rates are $16.50–$22.50. After 3pm, you can play for about $12.50, including a cart. Men must wear collared shirts to play here, and no spikes are allowed.

SCUBA DIVING   In Broward County, the best dive wreck is the *Mercedes I,* a 197-foot freighter that washed up in the backyard of a Palm Beach socialite in 1984 and was sunk for divers the following year off Pompano Beach. The artificial reef, filled with colorful sponges, spiny lobsters, and barracudas, is 97 feet below the surface, a mile offshore between Oakland Park and Sunrise boulevards. Dozens of reputable dive shops line the beach. Ask at your hotel for a nearby recommendation, or contact **Neil Watson's Undersea Adventures,** 1525 S. Andrews Ave., Fort Lauderdale (℡ 954/462-3400; www.nealwatson.com).

SPECTATOR SPORTS   Baseball fans can get their fix at the **Fort Lauderdale Stadium,** 5301 NW 12th Ave. (℡ **954/828-4980**), where the Baltimore Orioles play spring-training exhibition games starting in early March; call ℡ **954/776-1921** for tickets. General admission is $10, a spot in the grandstand $14, and box seats $20; admission for kids 14 and under is $4. During the season, the Florida Marlins play just south of Hallandale at **Dolphin Stadium,** near the Dade–Broward County line. Tickets go on sale in January for $4 to $100; call **Ticketmaster** (℡ **305/358-5885;** www.ticketmaster.com) to purchase them.

   Pompano Park Racing, 1800 SW 3rd St., Pompano Beach (℡ **954/972-2000**), has parimutuel harness racing from October to early August. Admission is free to both grandstand and clubhouse.

   Wrapped around an artificial lake, **Gulfstream Park Racing and Casino,** at U.S. 1 and Hallandale Beach Boulevard, Hallandale (℡ **954/454-7000;** www.gulfstream park.com), is pretty and popular, especially after its multimillion-dollar renovation, spanking new casino, nightclubs, and restaurants. Large purses and important horse races are commonplace at this recently refurbished suburban course, and the track is often crowded. The most recent renovation has transformed it into a world-class, state-of-the-art facility with four higher-end restaurants, 20 luxury suites, private accommodations for top players, and more. It hosts the Florida Derby each March. Call for schedules. Admission and parking are free. From January 3 to April 25, post times are 1:30pm weekdays and 1pm weekends, and the doors open at 11:30am.

   Jai alai, a sort of Spanish-style indoor lacrosse, was introduced to Florida in 1924 and still draws big crowds that bet on the fast-paced action. Broward's only fronton, **Dania Jai Alai,** 301 E. Dania Beach Blvd., at Florida A1A and U.S. 1 (℡ **954/920-1511**), is a great place to spend an afternoon or evening.

   In the sport of ice hockey, the young **Florida Panthers** (℡ **954/835-7000**) play in Sunrise at the **BankAtlantic Center,** 2555 NW 137th Way (℡ **954/835-8000**). Tickets range from $15 to $100. Call for directions and ticket information.

TENNIS   There are hundreds of courts in Broward County, and plenty are accessible to the public. Many are at resorts and hotels. If yours has none, try the **Jimmy Evert Tennis Center,** 701 NE 12th Ave. (off Sunrise Blvd.), Fort Lauderdale (℡ **954/828-5378**), famous as the spot where Chris Evert got in her early serves. Her coach and father, James Evert, still teaches young players here, though he is very picky about whom he'll accept. There are 18 lit clay courts and 3 hard courts here. Nonresidents of Fort Lauderdale pay $6 per hour before 4pm and $7 after. Reservations are accepted after 2pm for the following day, but cost an extra $3.

SEEING THE SIGHTS

Billie Swamp Safari &   Billie Swamp Safari is an up-close-and-personal view of the Seminole Indians' 2,200-acre Big Cypress Reservation. There are daily tours into reservation wetlands, hardwood hammocks, and areas where wildlife (seemingly strategically placed deer, water buffalo, bison, wild hogs, ornery ostriches, rare birds, and alligators) reside. Tours are provided aboard swamp buggies, customized motorized vehicles specially

One If by Land, Taxi If by Sea

Plan to spend at least an afternoon or evening cruising Fort Lauderdale's 300 miles of waterways the only way you can: by boat. The **Water Bus of Fort Lauderdale** (© 954/467-6677; www.watertaxi.com) is one of the greatest innovations for water lovers since those cool Velcro sandals. A trusty fleet of older port boats serves the dual purpose of transporting and entertaining visitors as they cruise through the "Venice of America." Because of its popularity, the water taxi fleet has welcomed several sleek, 70-passenger "water buses" (featuring indoor and outdoor seating with an atrium-like roof).

Taxis operate on demand and also along a fairly regular route, carrying up to 48 passengers to 20 stops. If you're staying at a hotel on the route, you can be picked up there, usually within 15 minutes of calling, and then be shuttled to any of the dozens of restaurants, bars, and attractions on or near the waterfront. If you aren't sure where you want to go, ask one of the personable captains, who can point out historic and fun spots along the way.

Starting daily at 8am, boats run until midnight 7 days a week, depending on the weather. Check the website for exact times of pickup. The cost is $11 for an all-day pass with unlimited stops on and off. If you want to go to South Beach, it's $19. Tickets are available onboard; no credit cards are accepted.

designed to provide visitors with an elevated view of the frontier while they comfortably ride through the wetlands and cypress heads. The more adventurous may want to take a fast-moving airboat ride or trek a nature trail. Airboat rides run about 20 minutes, while swamp-buggy tours last about an hour. A stop at an alligator farm reeks of Disney, but the kids won't care. You can stay overnight in a native Tiki hut for $35 per night if you're really looking to immerse yourself in the culture.

Big Cypress Seminole Reservation, 1.5 hr. drive west of Fort Lauderdale. © 800/949-6101. www.semtribe.com/safari. Free admission. Swamp-buggy tours $25 adults, $23 seniors 62+, $15 children 4–12; airboat tours $15 for all ages. Daily 8:30am–6pm. Airboats depart every 30 min. from 9:30am to 4:30pm. Swamp-buggy tours leave on the hour between 10am and 5pm. Reptile and Critter Shows daily. Day and overnight packages available.

Bonnet House ♠♠♠   This historic 35-acre plantation home and estate, accessible by guided tour only, will provide you with a fantastic glimpse of Old Florida. Built in 1921, the sprawling two-story waterfront home (surrounded by formal tropical gardens) is really the backdrop of a love story, which the very chatty volunteer guides will share with you if you ask. Some have actually lunched with the former resident of the house, the late Evelyn Bartlett, wife of world-acclaimed artist Frederic Clay Bartlett. The worthwhile 1¼-hour tour introduces you to quirky people, whimsical artwork, lush grounds, and interesting design.

900 N. Birch Rd. (1 block west of the ocean, south of Sunrise Blvd.), Fort Lauderdale. © 954/563-5393. www.bonnet house.org. Admission $20 adults, $18 seniors, $16 students under 18, free for children 6 and under. Call for hours and tour times.

International Swimming Hall of Fame (ISHOF) ♠♠♠   Any aspiring Olympic swimmer or those who appreciate the sport will love this splashy homage to the best backstrokers, frontstrokers, and divers in the world. The museum houses the world's largest collection of aquatic memorabilia and is the single largest source of aquatic books, manuscripts, and literature. Among the highlights are Johnny Weissmuller's Olympic medals; Mark Spitz's starting block used to win six of his seven 1972 Olympic gold medals; and more than 60 Olympic, national, and club uniforms, warm-ups, and swimsuits. For those who don't mind getting their feet wet, the ISHOF Aquatic Complex is the only one of its kind in the world with two 50-meter pools, a diving well, and a swimming flume.

1 Hall of Fame Dr. Fort Lauderdale. (℃) 954/462-6536. www.ishof.org. Admission $8 adults, $6 seniors, $4 children 12 and over. Call for hours and tour times.

Museum of Art Fort Lauderdale *☆* *(Kids* A fantastic modern-art facility, the Museum of Art Fort Lauderdale has permanent collections, including those from William Glackens; the CoBrA Movement in Copenhagen, Brussels, and Amsterdam with more than 200 paintings; 50 sculptures; 1,200 works on paper from 1948 to 1951, including the largest repository of Asger Jorn graphics outside the Silkeborg Kunstmuseum in Denmark; stunning Picasso ceramics; and contemporary works from more than 90 Cuban artists in exile around the world. Traveling exhibits and continuing art classes make the museum a great place to spend a rainy day.

1 E. Las Olas Blvd., Fort Lauderdale. (℃) 954/525-5500. www.moafl.org. Admission $10 adults, $7 seniors and children 6–17; free children 5 and under. Wed and Fri–Mon 11am–7pm; Thurs 11am–9pm.

Museum of Discovery & Science *☆☆* *(Kids* This museum's high-tech, interactive approach to education proves that science can equal fun. Adults won't feel as if they're in a kiddie museum, either. Kids ages 7 and under enjoy navigating their way through the excellent explorations in the Discovery Center. Florida Ecoscapes is particularly interesting, with a living coral reef, bees, bats, frogs, turtles, and alligators. Most weekend nights, you'll find a diverse crowd ranging from hip high-school kids to 30-somethings enjoying a rock film in the IMAX theater, which also shows short, science-related films daily. Out front in the atrium, see the 52-foot-tall *Great Gravity Clock,* the largest kinetic-energy sculpture in the state.

401 SW 2nd St., Fort Lauderdale. (℃) 954/467-6637. www.mods.org. Admission (includes IMAX film) $15 adults, $14 seniors, $12 children 2–12; without IMAX film, $10 adults, $9 seniors, $8 children 2-12. Mon–Sat 10am–5pm; Sun noon–6pm. Movie theater closes later. From I-95, exit on Broward Blvd. E. Continue to SW 5th Ave., turn right; garage is on the right.

Stranahan House *☆☆☆* In a town whose history is under many of its residents, visitors may want to take a minute to see Fort Lauderdale's very oldest standing structure and a prime example of classic "Florida Frontier" architecture. Built in 1901 by the "father of Fort Lauderdale," Frank Stranahan, this house once served as a trading post for Seminole trappers who came here to sell pelts. It's been a post office, town hall, and general store, and now serves as a worthwhile little museum of South Florida pioneer life, containing turn-of-the-19th-century furnishings and historic photos of the area. It is also the site of occasional concerts and social functions; call for details.

335 SE 6th Ave. (Las Olas Blvd. at the New River Tunnel), Fort Lauderdale. (℃) 954/524-4736. www.stranahan house.org. Admission $12 adults, $11 seniors, $7 students and children. Wed–Sat 10am–3pm; Sun 1–3pm. Tours are on the hour; last tour at 3pm. Accessible by water taxi.

SHOPPING & BROWSING

It's all about malls in Broward County and, while most of the best shopping is within Fort Lauderdale proper, other areas are also worth browsing.

Dania is known as the antiques capital of the South because within 1 square mile of Federal Highway, the city has more than 100 dealers selling everything from small collectibles to fine antiques. Parking is best along Federal Highway, on the "row," where Federal Highway meets U.S. 1. For information on "Antique Row," call © 954/924-3627. Also in Dania is the **Design Center of the Americas (DCOTA),** at the intersection of I-95 and Griffin Road (© **954/920-7997;** www.designcenteroftheamericas.com), a 775,000-square-foot interior-design center with furniture showrooms (featuring everything from ultramod to classic), designer studios, and, from time to time, fabulous sample sales. Last time we visited Dania, Matt Damon and his then-fiancée (now wife) were there furnishing their zillion-dollar Miami Beach manse.

For bargain mavens, there's a strip of "fashion" stores on Hallandale Beach Boulevard's "Schmatta Row," east of Dixie Highway and the railroad tracks, where off-brand shoes, bags, and jewelry are sold at deep discounts. Hollywood Boulevard also has some interesting shops, with everything from Indonesian artifacts to used and rare books, leather bustiers, and handmade hats. Dozens of shops line the pedestrian-friendly strip just west of Young Circle. The art galleries are clustered along Harrison Street, just east of Dixie Highway.

The area's only beachfront mall, **The Gallery at Beach Place,** is in Fort Lauderdale on Florida A1A just north of Las Olas Boulevard. This 100,000-square-foot giant sports the usual chains, such as Sunglass Hut, as well as chain bars and restaurants such as Hooter's. While it was once all the rage with the spring-break set, Beach Place is now aiming for a much more upscale clientele, adding many new higher-end stores and restaurants. Still, we think it's just one big tourist trap.

Other more traditional malls include the upscale **Galleria,** at Sunrise Boulevard near the Fort Lauderdale Beach, and **Broward Mall,** west of I-95 on Broward Boulevard, in Plantation.

If you're looking for unusual boutiques, especially art galleries, head to quaint **Las Olas Boulevard** 🐾, located west of A1A and a block east of Federal Highway/U.S. 1, off SE 8th Street, where there are hundreds of shops with alluring window decorations (like kitchen utensils posing as modern-art sculptures) and intriguing merchandise such as mural-size oil paintings. On the edge of the Arts and Science District is **Las Olas Riverfront,** a retail complex with 260,000 square feet of restaurants, clothing stores, arcades, and a multiplex movie theater.

For bargains, there's no better place than **Sawgrass Mills,** 12801 W. Sunrise Blvd. (© **954/846-0179**), featuring over 350 name brand outlets such as Off Fifth and Nordstrom Rack. Nearby is Florida's first ever **Ikea,** 151 NW 36th Ave. (© **954/ 838-9292;** www.ikea.com), purveyor of all things sleek and Swedish—everything from furniture to meatballs.

WHERE TO STAY

The Fort Lauderdale beach has a hotel or motel on nearly every block, ranging from run-down to luxurious. Both the **Howard Johnson,** 700 N. Atlantic Blvd., on Florida A1A south of Sunrise Boulevard (© 800/327-8578 or 954/563-2451); and the **Fort Lauderdale Beach Resort Hotel and Suites,** 4221 N. Ocean Blvd. (© **800/329- 7466** or 954/563-2521), have clean oceanside rooms starting at about $60. For a cushier stay, look into the **St. Regis Resort** (© **954/568-4623**), featuring 183 suites, a gourmet restaurant, and a spa, which opened in May 2007 (see below). Projected to open in the fall of 2008 is the $220-million **W Fort Lauderdale Hotel & Residences**

(© 954/525-8133), a boutique-hotel-slash-condominium with ocean views and a very hip and happening bar.

In Hollywood, where prices are generally cheaper, the **Holiday Inn,** 101 N. Ocean Blvd. (© **954/923-8700**), operates a full-service hotel right on the ocean. With prices starting at around $110 in season and discounts for AAA members, it's a great deal. **Howard Johnson,** 2501 N. Ocean Dr. (I-95 to Sheridan St. E. to Fla. A1A S.; © 800/423-9867 or 954/925-1411), has a good location right on the beach.

Extended Stay America/Crossland Economy Studios (© **800/398-7829**) has four super-clean properties in Fort Lauderdale and offers year-round rates as low as $49 a night and $159 per week. The studios are designed with business travelers in mind: Each includes free local calls, a dataport, a kitchenette, and a well lit desk.

For rentals for a few weeks or months, call **Florida Sunbreak** (© **800/SUN-BREAK**) or check the annual list of small lodgings compiled by the **Greater Fort Lauderdale Convention & Visitors Bureau** (© **954/765-4466**). The latter is especially helpful if you're looking for privately owned, charming, affordable lodgings.

VERY EXPENSIVE

The Atlantic 𝕶𝕶𝕶   The luxe category hit Fort Lauderdale beach with this Starwood Luxury Hotel property. Sitting on 23 miles of white sand, The Atlantic is a study in minimal modernity—soothing colors and comfortable, stylish decor. Besides the usual high-tech amenities found in all rooms of this category—flatscreen TVs, wireless Internet—The Atlantic boasts something other hotels do not: a star chef hailing from New York City's Tribeca Grill and a five-star restaurant. Trina Restaurant and Lounge comes to Fort Lauderdale thanks to celebrated restaurateurs Don Pintabona, former executive chef of Tribeca Grill, and Nick Mautone, former managing partner of Gramercy Tavern. The 6,000-square-foot spa isn't too shabby, either. Service is usually stellar, though we've had some complaints of a bit of attitude, but for some die-hard New Yorkers who stay here, that's a plus!

601 N. Ft. Lauderdale Beach Blvd, Fort Lauderdale, FL 33304. © **866/837-4274** or 954/567-8020. Fax 954/567-8040. www.starwoodhotels.com or www.luxurycollection.com/atlantic. 124 units. Winter $389–$619 double, $969–$999 suite; off season $219–$529 double, $789 suite. AE, DC, DISC, MC, V. Valet parking $28. **Amenities:** 2 restaurants; bar; outdoor heated pool; spa; watersports equipment rental (through concierge); bike rental (through concierge); concierge; business center; salon; 24-hr. room service; laundry service; dry cleaning. *In room:* A/C, TV, dataport, minibar, coffeemaker, microwave, hair dryer, iron, safe.

Hyatt Regency Pier 66 𝕶𝕶   Set on 22 tropical acres on the Intracoastal Waterway, this resort is best known for its world-class marina and a rooftop lounge that spins every 66 minutes. If you experience vertigo after sitting in the revolving lounge, an invigorating treatment at the hotel's exquisite European Spa LXVI will help relocate your sense of balance. Equally invigorating are the recreational amenities, which include a three-pool complex with a 40-person hydrotherapy pool, tennis courts, and an aquatic center with unabridged watersports. Grille 66 and Bar, a classy, upscale steakhouse, is a welcome addition. A $25-million refurbishment has transformed the lobby, lawn, and remaining guest rooms with a retro-modern decor. New lanai guest rooms have cherrywood furnishings and bathrooms with marble floors and granite vanities. All units have flatscreen televisions, wireless Internet access, and balconies with views of the Intracoastal Waterway and the hotel's lushly landscaped gardens.

2301 SE 17th St. Causeway, Fort Lauderdale, FL 33316. © **800/233-1234** or 954/525-6666. Fax 954/728-3541. www.pier66.com. 380 units. Winter $289–$409 double; off season $160–$280 double; year-round from $1,000 suite. Rates are cheaper on the hotel's website. AE, DC, DISC, MC, V. Valet parking $25; self-parking $20 maximum per day.

Amenities: 5 restaurants; 2 bars; 3 pools; 2 lit clay tennis courts; spa; watersports equipment rental; bike rental; concierge; business center; salon; 24-hr. room service; laundry service; dry cleaning; self-service laundry. *In room:* A/C, TV, dataport, minibar, coffeemaker, hair dryer, iron, safe.

Marriott's Harbor Beach ⟨★★ ⟨*Kids* This recently renovated resort is loaded with the same amenities as Pier 66 (above), but has a more secluded setting on 16 ocean-front acres just south of Fort Lauderdale's "strip." Everything in this place is huge—from the guest rooms and suites to the 8,000-square-foot pool and the $8-million, 24,000-square-foot European spa. Accommodations feature marble, crown molding, and bathrooms with granite vanities, marble flooring, and wraparound mirrors. All units open onto private balconies overlooking either the ocean or the Intracoastal Waterway. The hotel's 3030 Ocean is an excellent seafood restaurant and raw bar; the Riva, a Mediterranean-style oceanfront eatery, is also top-notch. Return guests include many convention groups and families who enjoy the space and great location. The hotel's Beachside Buddies kids' program, $45 half-day and $80 full day, including lunch, provides arts and crafts, watersports, and games to keep the young'uns happily occupied. Speaking of watersports, this hotel has the most comprehensive list, from surfing to parasailing.

3030 Holiday Dr., Fort Lauderdale, FL 33316. ⟨ **800/222-6543** or 954/525-4000. Fax 954/766-6193. www.marriott harborbeach.com. 637 units. Winter $439–$679 double; off season $269–$619 double; year-round from $600 suite. AE, DC, DISC, MC, V. Valet parking $27; self-parking $22. From I-95, exit on I-595 E. to U.S. 1 N.; proceed to SE 17th St.; make a right and go over the Intracoastal Bridge past 3 traffic lights to Holiday Dr.; turn right. **Amenities:** 3 restaurants; 2 bars; outdoor heated pool; 4 clay tennis courts; basketball court; health club; European-style spa; extensive watersports equipment; bike rental; children's center and programs; game room; concierge; tour desk; courtesy car; business center; salon; 24-hr. room service; in-room massage; babysitting; laundry service; self-service laundry. *In room:* A/C, TV, PlayStation, dataport, minibar, coffeemaker, hair dryer, iron, safe.

St. Regis ⟨★★★ The first and only five-star hotel on Fort Lauderdale Beach, not to mention the first St. Regis in Florida, this $160 million property has elevated the strip to an entirely new level of luxury. The 183 rooms, including 28 private residences and 34 hotel condominiums, all feature views of the Atlantic or the Intracoastal Waterway, have Wi-Fi Internet access, a state-of-the-art DVD theater entertainment system with a 32" LCD panel TV, a 13" LCD panel TV in each bathroom, Italian linens, designer bath amenities, and a refrigerated minicellar of refreshments. We particularly love the signature butler service as well as Chef Toby Joseph's Cero Restaurant, a stellar seafooder, and the 1,500-bottle wine bar. The oceanfront pool is nice, yet understated, and the spa is sublime. Some people have complained that service is snooty while others say service is discreet and sublime. What's universal is that this is a welcome departure from the norm for the area. Inside tip: all rooms ending in 10 offer floor to ceiling windows and spectacular views!

1 N. Fort Lauderdale Beach Blvd., Fort Lauderdale, FL 33316. ⟨ **800/325-3589** or 954/465-2300. Fax 954/766-6193. www.starwoodhotels.com. 183 units. Winter $439–$679 double; off season $269–$619 double; year-round from $600 suite. AE, DC, DISC, MC, V. Valet parking $27; self-parking $22. From I-95, exit on I-595 E. to U.S. 1 N.; proceed to SE 17th St.; make a right and go over the Intracoastal Bridge past 3 traffic lights to Holiday Dr.; turn right. **Amenities:** 3 restaurants; 2 bars; outdoor heated pool; 4 clay tennis courts; basketball court; health club; European-style spa; extensive watersports equipment; bike rental; children's center and programs; game room; concierge; tour desk; courtesy car; business center; salon; 24-hr. room service; in-room massage; babysitting; laundry service; self-service laundry. *In room:* A/C, TV, dataport, minibar, coffeemaker, hair dryer, iron, safe, PlayStation.

Westin Diplomat Resort & Spa The Diplomat is a 1,060-room, full-service beach resort—the only one of its kind in the somewhat desolate area—loaded with amenities. The main building is a 39-story oceanfront tower surrounded by 8 acres of man-made lakes. A gorgeous bridged, glass-bottomed pool with waterfalls, private cabanas, and a slew of watersports, adds a tropical touch. Rooms are a cross between those in a subtle boutique hotel and in an Art Deco throwback, with dark woods, hand-cut marble and the 10-layer Heavenly Bed, a Westin trademark, with custom-designed pillow-top mattresses and very cushy down blankets. Dining options are aplenty, from the fine-dining steakhouse to several more casual places. Diplomat Landing, the hotel's shopping-and-entertainment complex across the street, features shops and an offshoot of South Beach's Nikki Beach Club. The resort's Country Club and Spa is located across the Intracoastal, featuring 60 luxurious guest rooms, yacht slips, a 155-acre golf course, and a world-class spa and tennis club.

3555 S. Ocean Dr. (Fla. A1A), Hollywood, FL 33019. © 888/627-9057 or 954/602-6000. Fax 954/602-7000. www. diplomatresort.com. 998 units. Winter $305–$515 double, $675–$875 suite; off season $220–$340 double, $475–$675 suite. AE, DC, DISC, MC, V. Valet parking $22. **Amenities:** 8 restaurants; 3 lounges; 2 pools; golf course; 10 clay tennis courts; health club; spa; watersports equipment rental; 24-hr. room service. *In room:* A/C, TV/WebTV, fax, dataport, minibar, coffeemaker, hair dryer.

EXPENSIVE

Lago Mar Resort and Club 𝆑𝆑 *Kids* A charming lobby with a rock fireplace and saltwater aquarium sets the tone of this utterly inviting resort, a casually elegant piece of Old Florida that occupies its own little island between Lake Mayan and the Atlantic. Guests have access to the broadest and best strip of beach in the entire city, not to mention a wonderful bougainvillea-lined, 9,000-square-foot swimming lagoon. Lago Mar is very family oriented, with many facilities and supervised activities for children. Service is spectacular. The plush rooms and suites have Mediterranean or Key West influences. A full-service spa offers a wide array of treatments, while the 1,000-square-foot exercise facility may come in handy after you indulge in the hotel's Northern Italian restaurant, Acquario, which is worth a visit even if you don't stay here. A new $15-million six-story wing of one- and two-bedroom oceanfront suites with individual balconies and larger luxurious bathrooms includes a deck of native tropical landscaping and a 5,000-square-foot saltwater lagoon.

1700 S. Ocean Lane, Fort Lauderdale, FL 33316. © 800/524-6627 or 954/523-6511. Fax 954/524-6627. www.lagomar. com. 212 units. Winter $295 double, from $365 suite; off season $175 double, from $200 suite. AE, DC, MC, V. Free valet parking. From Federal Hwy. (U.S. 1), turn east onto SE 17th St. Causeway; turn right onto Mayan Dr.; turn right again onto S. Ocean Dr.; turn left onto Grace Dr.; then turn left again onto S. Ocean Lane to the hotel. **Amenities:** 4 restaurants; bar; wine room; outdoor pool and lagoon; 2 tennis courts; exercise room; watersports equipment rental; children's programs during holiday periods; game room; concierge; tour desk; business center; 24-hr. room service; laundry service; dry cleaning. *In room:* A/C, TV, dataport, kitchenette, coffeemaker (in some), hair dryer.

Pillars Hotel 𝆑 *Finds* It took me awhile to discover this hotel—and apparently that's exactly the point. One of Fort Lauderdale's best-kept secrets, the Pillars transports you from the neon-hued flash and splash of Fort Lauderdale's strip and takes you to a two-story British Colonial, Caribbean-style retreat tucked away on the bustling Intracoastal Waterway. Since it has just 23 rooms, you'll feel as if you have the grand house all to yourself—albeit a house with white-tablecloth room service, an Edenistic courtyard with a free-form pool, lush landscaping, access to a water taxi, and private chef. Rooms are luxurious and loaded with amenities such as private-label bath products, ultraplush bedding, and, if you're so inclined, a private masseuse to iron out your personal kinks. A library area (with over 500 books and videos) is at your disposal, as is pretty much anything else you request here. Not everyone agrees. One reader complained that her room was small, musty, and far from luxurious.

111 N. Birch Rd., Fort Lauderdale, FL 33304. ⓒ 954/467-9639. Fax 954/763-2845. www.pillarshotel.com. 23 units. Winter $219–$315 double, $339–$515 suite; off season $175–$195 double, $249–$419 suite. AE, DC, DISC, MC, V. Complimentary off-street parking. **Amenities:** Restaurant, waterfront pool; preferred rates at beachfront and downtown health clubs; 24-hr. concierge; business services; 24-hr. room service; same-day laundry service; signing privileges at Max's Beach Place restaurant; water-taxi service. *In room:* A/C, TV/VCR, dataport, minibar, hair dryer, iron, safe.

Riverside Hotel 🎄🎄   A touch of New Orleans hits Fort Lauderdale's popular Las Olas Boulevard in the form of this charming, six-story 1936 hotel. There's no beach here, but the hotel is set on the sleepy and scenic New River, capturing the essence of that ever-elusive Old Florida. Guest rooms, outfitted in Mexican tile and wicker furnishings, are spacious and well maintained. Such details as intricately tiled bathrooms and old-style furniture enhance the charm of the otherwise stark building. The best units face the river, but it's hard to see the water past the parking lot and trees. Twelve rooms offer king-size beds with mirrored canopies and flowing drapes. There are also seven elegantly decorated suites with wet bars and French doors that lead to private balconies. The hotel has two restaurants worth trying: Indigo, a fantastic seafood spot (p. 325), and the Grill Room, for old-world elegance.

620 E. Las Olas Blvd., Fort Lauderdale, FL 33301. ⓒ 800/325-3280 or 954/467-0671. Fax 954/462-2148. www.riverside hotel.com. 217 units. Winter $229–$279 suite; off season $139–$185 suite. Special packages available. Discount for bookings on the hotel's website. AE, DC, MC, V. Valet parking $8–$10. From I-95, exit onto Broward Blvd.; turn right onto Federal Hwy. (U.S. 1); turn left onto Las Olas Blvd. **Amenities:** 2 restaurants; outdoor pool; concierge; secretarial services; limited room service; laundry service; dry cleaning. *In room:* A/C, TV, dataport, minibar, fridge, coffeemaker, hair dryer, iron.

MODERATE

Courtyard Villa on the Ocean 🎄   Nestled between a bunch of larger hotels, this small historic hotel is a romantic getaway right on the beach. Courtyard Villa has spacious oceanfront efficiencies with private balconies, larger suites overlooking the pool, and full two-bedroom apartments. Accommodations are plush, with chenille bedspreads and carved four-poster beds; fully equipped kitchenettes are an added convenience. The tiled bathrooms have strong, hot showers to wash off the beach sand. Room no. 8 is especially nice, with French doors that open to a private balcony overlooking the ocean. Relax in the hotel's unique heated pool/spa or on the second-floor sun deck. You can also swim from the beach to a living reef just 50 feet offshore.

4312 El Mar Dr., Lauderdale-by-the-Sea, FL 33308. ⓒ 800/291-3560 or 954/776-1164. Fax 954/491-0768. www. courtyardvilla.com. 10 units. Winter $249 double; $289–$339 2-bedroom; off season $125–$160 double, $140–$209 2-bedroom. Rates include full breakfast. AE, MC, V. Pets less than 35 lb. accepted with a $200 deposit; must be caged while outside; no pit bulls, Dobermans, or Rottweilers. **Amenities:** Outdoor heated pool; Jacuzzi; free use of bikes; limited room service; scuba instruction; free laptop use with Internet access. *In room:* A/C, TV/VCR, kitchenette, coffeemaker, hair dryer.

Pelican Grand Beach Resort 🎄 *Kids*   The Pelican Beach Resort sits on a 500-foot private beach, with 159 oversized guest rooms (including 117 with balconies) and a sublimely relaxing, wraparound oceanfront veranda and sun deck with rocking chairs. What also rocks about this place are the two heated outdoor pools, complete with a lazy river raft ride. This is a great, low-key luxury resort, especially for families looking for a relaxing vacation with all the amenities of a more harried chain resort overwrought with slews of people. The resort is also completely nonsmoking.

2000 N. Ocean Blvd., Fort Lauderdale, FL 33305. ⓒ 800/525-OCEAN or 954/568-9431. Fax 954/565-2662. www. pelicanbeach.com. 159 units. Winter $299–$349 double, $520 suite; off season $220–$270 double, $420 suite. AE, DC, MC, V. Parking $16 a day. **Amenities:** Restaurant; bar; ice cream parlor; 2 heated outdoor pools; fitness center; sun deck. *In room:* A/C, TV, high-speed Internet, fridge, microwave, coffeemaker, hair dryer.

Anna Nicole & "Room 607"

Anna Nicole Smith died tragically in Room 607 at the **Seminole Hard Rock Hotel** on February 8, 2007. Because the hotel didn't want to create a macabre tourist attraction, they took the room number "out of inventory," meaning the room is still there, but the number has been changed.

Seminole Hard Rock Hotel & Casino 🏨🏨🏨   The Seminole Indians have created a miniature Vegas within Hollywood, Florida, and it's doing a booming business. Although the massive, 130,000-square-foot casino doesn't have typical bet-against-the-house Vegas games (such as blackjack, roulette, or craps), it does have thousands of video slot machines and poker tables, and they're always packed. The main draw here is the casino, but the guest rooms are surprisingly cushy and swank, with flatscreen TVs, Egyptian-cotton linens, and big bathrooms with massive shower heads; the suites are hyperluxurious. Equally impressive is the 4½-acre lagoon-style pool that's very similar to the one at the Hard Rock in Vegas, with waterfalls, hot tubs, wireless Internet access, and, of course, a bar. There are lots of bars here, especially at the attached entertainment complex, with two clubs open 24/7, as well as restaurants and stores. There's also a food court, or you can choose from several on-site, full-service restaurants, including a swank steakhouse. They also offer a massive spa.

1 Seminole Way, Hollywood, FL 33314. ℂ 800/937-0156 or 954/797-5440. Fax 954/797-2376. www.seminole hardrockhollywood.com. 481 units. $189–$259 double, $650–$2,000 suite. AE, DC, DISC, MC, V. Amenities: Casino, 17 restaurants; 11 nightclubs and lounges; pool; spa; Jacuzzi; luxury/exotic car rentals; 22 retail outlets; 24-hr. room service; car wash. *In room:* A/C, TV, Tivoli sound system with CD player, high-speed Internet access, coffeemaker, hair dryer.

INEXPENSIVE

Fort Lauderdale Beach Hostel   For the young, or for backpackers on a budget, this hostel is a great option, with both dorm beds and private rooms at bargain-basement prices. Clean and conveniently located, the hostel is just 654 feet from the ocean. It features free parking, free phones, free self-cook food, free breakfast buffet, and, if you're lucky, free use of the surfboards or in-line skates lying around.

2115 N. Ocean Blvd., Fort Lauderdale, FL 33305. ℂ **954/567-7275.** www.fortlauderdalehostel.com. 12 units. Dorm beds $20 per night, $145 per week; private rooms $45 for 1 person, $55 double. Rates include breakfast buffet. MC, V. **Amenities:** Table tennis; free Internet access; sundeck; garden. *In room:* A/C, TV, iron.

A Little Inn by the Sea 🏨   It's not fancy, but A Little Inn by the Sea sits on a primo piece of oceanfront, and most rooms have private balconies overlooking the ocean. There's also 300 feet of private, palm-tree-lined beach. The accommodations are hardly worthy of a spread in an interior-design magazine, but the views make up for the lackluster decor. A free breakfast buffet, a rooftop terrace, and a heated freshwater pool are lovely perks.

4546 El Mar Dr., Lauderdale-by-the-Sea, FL 33308. ℂ **800/492-0311** or 954/772-2450. Fax 954/938-9354. www. alittleinn.com. 29 units. Winter $159–$169 double, $209–$239 suite, $398 2-bedroom apt; off season $109–$129 double, $129–$169 suite, $179–$298 2-bedroom apt. MC, V. Free parking. **Amenities:** Heated pool; access to nearby tennis court; nearby children's playground; coin laundry. *In room:* A/C, TV.

Sea Downs (and the Bougainvillea) 🏨🏨   This bargain lodging is often booked months in advance by return guests (mostly Europeans) who want to be directly on the beach without paying a fortune. The hosts of this super-clean 1950s motel, Claudia and Karl Herzog, live on the premises and keep things running smoothly. Many

rooms have been redecorated here and at the Herzogs' other, even less expensive property next door, the 11-unit Bougainvillea. Guests at both hotels share the Sea Downs'
pool.

2900 N. Surf Rd., Hollywood, FL 33019. ℂ 954-923-4968. Fax 954/923-8747. www.seadowns.com or www.
bougainvilleahollywood.com. 12 units. Winter $99.–$152 studio, $119–$198 1-bedroom apt; off season $80–$144
studio, $106–$144 1-bedroom apt. No credit cards. From I-95, exit Sheridan St. E. to Fla. A1A and go south; drive
½-mile to Coolidge St.; turn left. **Amenities:** Freshwater outdoor pool; concierge; laundry facilities. *In room:* A/C, TV,
dataport, kitchen, fridge, coffeemaker.

WHERE TO DINE

It took awhile for a more sophisticated, varied epicurean scene to reach these shores,
but Fort Lauderdale—and, to some extent, Hollywood—finally has several fine
restaurants. Increasingly, ethnic options are joining the legions of surf-and-turferies
that have dominated the area for so long. **Las Olas Boulevard** has so many eateries
that the city has put a moratorium on the opening of new restaurants on the 2-mile
street. For celebrated Cantonese food, try **Christine Lee's** (p. 136).

VERY EXPENSIVE

Café Martorano 𝓡𝓡 ITALIAN This small storefront eatery doesn't win any
awards for decor or location, but when it comes to food that's good enough for an
entire Italian family, Café Martorano, which recently opened to rave reviews in Las
Vegas, is one of the best. People wait for a table for upward of 2 hours because the
restaurant accepts no reservations and can get away with it. An almost-offensive sound
system (playing disco tunes and Sinatra) has a tendency to turn off many a diner, but
you don't go to Café Martorano for an intimate dinner. Dining here is like being at a
big, fat, Italian wedding, where eating, drinking, and dancing are paramount. The
menu changes daily, but regulars can request special off-the-menu items. If you don't
ask, you don't get, so open your mouth. Also keep your eyes wide open for such
celebrities as Liza Minnelli, James Gandolfini, and Steven Van Zandt, among others,
who make it a point to stop here for a meal while in town.

3343 E. Oakland Park Blvd., Fort Lauderdale. ℂ 954/561-2554. www.cafemartorano.com. Reservations not
accepted. Main courses $15–$45. MC, V. Daily 5–11pm.

Darrel & Oliver's Cafe Maxx 𝓡𝓡 FLORIDIAN/NEW WORLD Despite its
bleak location in an unassuming storefront, Darrel & Oliver's Cafe Maxx is one of the
best restaurants in Broward County. When it opened in 1984, it was the first restaurant to have an open kitchen, and what a stir that caused! Now, instead of the kitchen,
the marvel is what comes out of it. Consider ancho-rubbed swordfish with corn and
succotash, conch fritters, and avocado salsa; sweet-onion-crusted yellowtail snapper
with Madeira sauce; or blue cheese and pine nut–crusted rack of lamb. Yum. But save
room for dessert—the deep dish Bourbon pecan pie or Bing cherry bread pudding are
just two of many diet- and mind-blowing options.

2601 E. Atlantic Blvd., Pompano Beach. ℂ 954/782-0606. Fax 954/782-0648. www.cafemaxx.com. Reservations
recommended. Main courses $23–$43. AE, DC, DISC, MC, V. Mon–Thurs 5:30–10:30pm; Fri–Sat 5:30–11pm; Sun
5:30–10pm. From I-95, exit at Atlantic Blvd. E. The restaurant is 3 lights east of Federal Hwy.

Mark's Las Olas 𝓡𝓡𝓡 NEW WORLD Star chef Mark Militello opened the eyes
and mouths of discriminating Fort Lauderdale gourmands to his excellent New World
cuisine. Roasted-garlic–stuffed grilled tenderloin of beef with caramelized sweet
onion, Swiss chard, marrow toast, and red-wine short-rib sauce is possibly the best
item on the menu. Everything else served, from the hot-pepper pizza with chorizo to

the crab-crusted black grouper with wild-mushroom/salsify ragout, is delicious. Save room for a chocolate dessert—any one will do.

1032 E. Las Olas Blvd., Fort Lauderdale. ⓒ 954/463-1000. Reservations suggested. Main courses $15–$38. AE, DC, MC, V. Mon–Thurs 11:30am–2:30pm and 6–10:30pm; Fri 11:30am–2:30pm and 6–11pm; Sat 6–11pm; Sun 6–10pm.

EXPENSIVE

Anthony's Runway 84 ✦✦✦ ITALIAN   Meet Anthony, the youthful, gregarious owner of this Fort Lauderdale restaurant with an interior all about jet-setting—albeit in the mid- to late '70s—and a bar crafted out of a plane fuselage. Once you meet him, he will introduce your server, whose name is likely to be Tony. Same goes for the bartender. The quintessential, convivial Italian vibe in here (think Travolta in *Saturday Night Fever*) is conducive to one of the most enjoyable meals you'll ever have. The best way to go is—what else?—family style, in which you'll be able to share lots of dishes such as mussels marinara, fried clams, roasted red peppers in garlic, shrimp parmigiana, an out-of-this-world rigatoni with cauliflower (although it sounds boring, order it no matter what!), and stellar meat and poultry dishes that frequent fliers to Anthony's rave about each time, as if it were their last meal. For the best pizza, try nearby **Anthony's Coal Fired Pizza,** 2203 S. Federal Hwy. (ⓒ 954/462-5555).

330 S.R. 84, Fort Lauderdale. ⓒ 954/467-8484. Reservations not accepted. Main courses $15–$40. AE, DC, DISC, MC, V. Tues–Thurs and Sun noon–10pm; Fri–Sat 5–11pm.

Eduardo De San Angel ✦✦✦ MEXICAN   Gourmet Mexican is *not* an oxymoron, and for those who don't believe that, take one meal at the sublime Eduardo De San Angel and you'll see how true it is. Chef Eduardo Pria has a masterful way with food, as seen in dishes such as *jaibas rellenas* (fresh Florida blue crab, plum tomatoes, onions, jalapeños, and Spanish green olives baked in a shell with melted jack cheese au gratin and mole poblano). Fresh flowers and candlelight, not to mention the fact that the restaurant resembles an intimate hacienda, also drive home the fact that this isn't your mom's Old El Paso taco dinner.

2822 E. Commercial Blvd., Fort Lauderdale. ⓒ 954/772-4731. www.eduardodesanangel.com. Reservations essential. Main courses $26–$38. AE, DC, DISC, MC, V. Mon–Thurs 11:30am–10:30pm; Fri–Sat 5:30–10:30pm.

Himmarshee Bar & Grille ✦ FUSION   Located on a popular street of bars frequented by Fort Lauderdale's young professionals, Himmarshee Bar & Grille is known for its scene and cuisine. A mezzanine bar upstairs is ideal for people-watching; outdoor tables are tight, but strategically situated in front of all the street's action. On weekend nights, in particular, it's difficult to get a table. However, if you can deal with cramming into the bar, it's worth a cocktail or two. The wine list is impressive, and the grilled chili–dusted pork chop with boniato-stuffed poblano chile, Monterey jack cheese, and creamy, spicy corn sauce is to die for. Also try the chorizo taquitos as an appetizer. Check out Side Bar, the restaurant's very ski-lodgey bar next door featuring live music and a bustling crowd of young hipsters.

210 SW 2nd St. (south of Broward Blvd., west of U.S. 1), Fort Lauderdale. ⓒ 954/524-1818. www.himmarshee.com. Reservations recommended. Main courses $19–$39. AE, MC, V. Mon–Thurs 11:30am–2:30pm and 6–10:30pm; Fri 11:30am–2:30pm and 6–11:30pm; Sat 6–11:30pm; Sun 6–10:30pm.

Johnny V's ✦✦✦ SOUTHWESTERN   South Florida's favorite so-called Caribbean Cowboy, Chef Johnny Vinczencz, has moved around quite a bit—from South Beach's Hotel Astor (twice!) to Delray Beach's Sundy House. But this Las Olas hot spot looks to be his final stop and that's good news to all Johnny V's faithful foodies who will travel to the end of the earth to sample some of his Caribbean-influenced new Floridian cuisine. What that means is, smoked pheasant nachos, sage grilled Florida dolphin with lobster pan gravy served atop rock shrimp plantain stuffing with cranberry mango chutney, and a slew of dishes you've likely never seen before. Once you've tasted his fare, you'll understand why a herd of hungry folks are extremely happy to have a place to satisfy their cravings for such gourmet grub. Barbra Streisand dined here while in town for her sold-out concerts in 2006 and couldn't stop singing the praises of Johnny V—onstage during her show! She—and Johnny—were verklempt (falling over themselves with delight)!

625 E. Las Olas Blvd. ⓒ 954/761-7920. www.johnnyvlasolas.com Reservations suggested. $19–$38. AE, DC, MC, V. Mon–Thurs 11:30am–2:30pm and 5:30–11pm; Fri 11:30am–2:30pm and 5:30–midnight; Sat 5:30–midnight; Sun 5:30–11pm.

Sunfish Grill ✿✿✿ SEAFOOD   Unlike its fellow contemporary seafood restaurants, the Sunfish Grill chooses to focus on fish, not fusion. Chef Anthony Sindaco is content to leave the spotlight on his fantastic fish dishes, which are possibly the freshest in town, thanks to the fact that he buys his fish at local markets and often from well-known fishermen who appear at his back door with their catches of the day. The shrimp bisque cappuccino is a deliciously rich soup served in a demitasse cup—because it's that rich. Conch fritters are purely spectacular and not full of filler. Chilean sea bass, expertly cooked with roasted fennel, saffron potatoes, and a caramelized-onion broth, is wonderful. The best dish, in my opinion, is the seared tuna resting on a bed of mushroom and oxtail ragout with garlic mashed potatoes. In fact, almost everything at the Sunfish Grill is better than at most seafood restaurants.

2761 E. Oakland Park Blvd., Pompano Beach. ⓒ 954/788-2434. www.sunfishgrill.com. Reservations recommended. Main courses $25–$32. AE, MC, V. Mon–Thurs 6–9:30pm; Fri–Sat 6–10:30pm.

Trina Restaurant ✿✿✿ MEDITERRANEAN   A bona fide dining hot spot like this is a novelty to the area because restaurants this hot usually open in Miami, not Fort Lauderdale. Thanks to the collaborative efforts of Don Pintabona, former executive chef of Tribeca Grill in New York City and Nick Mautone, formerly of Gramercy Tavern, Miami has some competition. Yes, it's expensive, but the Mediterranean-infused seafood dishes are worth every penny. Try the skewers of diver scallops and braised short ribs with summer truffle reduction and truffled cauliflower. Reservations here are hard to come by, especially in season, but the Trina Lounge is also a great option, offering lighter—and cheaper fare—with high-style ambience. Although we love the buzz of the indoor dining room, request a table outside overlooking the ocean.

601 N. Ft. Lauderdale Beach Blvd., Fort Lauderdale. ⓒ 954/567-8070. www.trinarestaurantandlounge.com. Reservations recommended. Main courses $29–$45. AE, DC, DISC, MC, V. Sun–Thurs 5:30–10pm; Fri–Sat 5:30–10:30pm. Lounge open later.

MODERATE

Cap's Place Island Restaurant ✿ Finds SEAFOOD   Opened in 1928 by a bootlegger who ran in the same circles as gangster Meyer Lansky, this barge-turned-restaurant is one of the area's best-kept secrets. Although it's no longer a rum-running restaurant and casino, its illustrious past (FDR and Winston Churchill dined here together) landed it a spot on the National Register of Historic Places. To get here, you have to take a ferryboat, provided by the restaurant. The short ride across the Intracoastal definitely adds to the Cap's Place experience. The food is good, not great. Traditional seafood dishes such as Florida or Maine lobster, clams casino, and oysters Rockefeller will take you back to the days when a soprano was just an opera singer.

2765 NE 28th Court, Lighthouse Point. (© 954/941-0418. www.capsplace.com. Reservations recommended. Main courses $14–$28. MC, V. Daily 5:30pm–midnight. To get to Cap's Place, motor-launch from I-95, exit at Copan's Rd. and go east to U.S. 1 (Federal Hwy.). At NE 24th St., turn right and follow the double lines and signs to the Lighthouse Point Yacht Basin and Marina (8 miles north of Fort Lauderdale). From here, follow the CAP'S PLACE sign pointing you to the shuttle.

Creolina's *&* CREOLE   You'll find authentic Louisiana Creole cuisine at this small but very popular restaurant situated along the Riverwalk. Try shrimp jambalaya with shrimp, sausage, and vegetables in a rich Cajun sauce served over rice; or perhaps the étouffée with crayfish tail simmered in a mellow Cajun sauce served over rice. The mashed potatoes are homemade, and the delicious lemonade is fresh-squeezed daily. There is also a terrific New Orleans Sunday brunch. Ask to sit in sassy Rosie's section.

209 SW 2nd St., Fort Lauderdale. (© 954/524-2003. Main courses $13–$24. AE, MC, V. Mon 11am–2:30pm and 5–9pm; Tues–Thurs 11am–2:30pm and 5–10pm; Fri 11am–2:30pm and 5–11pm; Sat 5–11pm; Sun 5–9pm.

Indigo *&* SEAFOOD/ECLECTIC   A new seafood-oriented menu makes more sense here than its former incarnation as a funky Asian eatery, especially since it's housed in the New Orleans–style Riverside Hotel. The dining room is nice enough, but sit outside and watch the pedestrian parade that is Las Olas Boulevard. Among the menu highlights: piccata of John Dorie over truffle-scented polenta cakes; tequila-flamed jumbo prawns; and pan-fried, farm-raised catfish coated in corn flakes with andouille sausage and gumbo—the quintessential dish for a Big Easy–style setting.

In the Riverside Hotel, 620 E. Las Olas Blvd., Fort Lauderdale. (© 954/467-0671. Reservations accepted for parties of 6 or more. Main courses $15–$34. AE, DC, DISC, MC, V. Daily 7am–9:45pm.

Rustic Inn Crabhouse *&&* SEAFOOD   A Fort Lauderdale rough-and-tumble landmark for more than 50 years, Rustic Inn isn't the place for a romantic, intimate, quiet dinner. The minute you walk in, you're assaulted by a cacophonous banging—a symphony from a packed house of happy diners cracking their crabs with wooden mallets. Although you don't *have* to crack your own crabs—diva Barbra Streisand didn't when she dined here (she requested them already cracked—heaven forbid she should break a nail!)—it's all part of the experience. Newspaper lines the tables, so prepare to get your hands dirty. Although the restaurant is known for its "world-famous garlic crabs" (and we think they are totally deserving of that lofty tagline), you can also order lobster, pasta, and all sorts of fried fish—even fried alligator (it's chewier than chicken!). The fried clams are especially good, but if you want to gorge yourself, try the Reef Raft, a basket of fried oysters, fried scallops, and fried fish. Dress very casual and prepare to wait awhile for a table, but trust me, it's worth it.

4331 Ravenswood Rd., Fort Lauderdale. (© 954/584-1637. No reservations accepted. Main courses $8–$20; crabs are market price. AE, DC, DISC, MC, V. Mon–Sat 11:30am–10:45pm; Sun 2–9:45 pm.

Sugar Reef *&&* FRENCH CARIBBEAN   I could go on about this restaurant's priceless ocean view, but the menu of Mediterranean, Caribbean, and French dishes is just as outstanding. A pleasant tropical decor is bolstered by fresh air wafting in from the Atlantic. Seafood bouillabaisse in green curry and coconut broth and Sugar Reef pho—a Vietnamese noodle dish with chicken, shrimp, ginger and spices—are among the restaurant's most popular dishes. The kitchen puts a savory spin on duck, roasted and topped with sweet-chile-and-papaya salsa. This is not a place you'd expect to find on a beach boardwalk, which makes it all the more delightful.

600 N. Surf Rd. (on the Broadwalk just north of Hollywood Blvd.), Hollywood. © **954/922-1119.** www.sugarreef grill.com Reservations accepted for parties of 6 or more. Main courses $10–$28. AE, DISC, MC, V. Mon 4–10:30pm; Tues–Thurs 11am–10:30pm; Fri–Sun 11am–11pm (sometimes later in winter).

Sushi Blues Cafe ⚔ SUSHI   Before Hollywood was "hot," Sushi Blues Cafe was singing the blues—in a good way, as the only game in town. Now that the area is bustling, it's singing the blues in an even better way, serving up live music 4 nights a week, along with raw fish that's quite good. Garlic- and ginger-studded tuna steak is also fantastic for those who are bored with sushi. Even better, however, is the fact that, for once, a meal at a sushi restaurant where such restaurants are a dime a dozen actually seems like a unique experience. Attached to the restaurant is the Blue Monk Lounge, where cocktails and live music make for a lively scene.

600 N. Surf Rd. (on the Broadwalk just north of Hollywood Blvd.), Hollywood. © **954/922-1119.** Reservations accepted for parties of 6 or more. Main courses $9–$29; sushi rolls $3–$15. AE, DISC, MC, V. Daily 11:30am–2am.

Tarpon Bend ⚔ SEAFOOD/AMERICAN   This restaurant is one of the few places where the fishermen still bring the fish to the back door. The oysters from the raw bar are shucked to order and are incredible. Try the house specialty, "smoked fish dip"— a kingfish smoked on premises. The steamed clambake, with half a Maine lobster, clams, potatoes, mussels, and corn on the cob, is scrumptious and served in its own pot. For chocolate lovers, the chocolate-brownie sundae is a must. There's live entertainment Wednesday through Saturday and a full bar. A new Tarpon Bend opened in Coral Gables at 65 Miracle Mile (© **305/444-3210**).

200 SW 2nd St., Fort Lauderdale. © **954/523-3233.** Reservations accepted for parties of 6 or more. Main courses $12–$15. AE, MC, V. Mon–Thurs 11:30am–1am; Fri–Sat 11:30am–3am.

INEXPENSIVE

The Floridian Restaurant ⚔ *Value* AMERICAN/DINER   The Floridian has been filling South Florida's diner void for more than 63 years, serving breakfast, lunch, and dinner, 24/7. It's especially busy on weekend mornings when locals and tourists come in for huge omelets, fresh oatmeal, sausage, and biscuits. Just to prove it's up to par with swank Fort Lauderdale, The Floridian offers a $300 Fat Cat meal for two that includes, steak, eggs, and a bottle of Dom Perignon! While some say the place needs a major cleaning, others insist that the grit and grime are part of the greasy spoon's charm.

1410 E. Las Olas Blvd., Fort Lauderdale. © **954/463-4041.** Fax 954/761-3930. Sandwiches $3–$7; breakfast combos $3.50–$8; hot platters $7–$14. No credit cards. Daily 24 hr.

Jaxon's ⚔ *Kids* ICE CREAM   South Florida's best and only authentic old-fashioned ice-cream parlor and country store attracts those with sweet tooths from all over the area. Their cravings are satisfied with an unabridged assortment of homemade ice cream served any which way. Kids love the candy store in the front of the restaurant, and adults love the pre–Ben & Jerry's authenticity. For the calorie-conscious, the sugar-free and fat-free versions are pretty good. Jaxon's most famous everything-but-the-kitchen-sink sundae has countless scoops and endless toppings.

128 S. Federal Hwy., Dania Beach. © **954/923-4445.** Sundaes $2.75–$7.95. AE, DISC, MC, V. Mon–Thurs 11:30am–11pm; Fri–Sat 11:30am–midnight; Sun noon–11pm.

Lester's Diner ⚔ AMERICAN   Since 1968, Lester's Diner has been serving swarms of South Floridians large portions of great greasy-spoon fare until the wee hours. Try the eggs Benedict and the 14-ounce "cup" of classic coffee, or sample one of Lester's many homemade desserts. The place serves breakfast 24 hours a day and is a Fort Lauderdale institution that attracts locals, club crowds, city officials, and a generally motley, friendly crew of hungry people craving no-nonsense food served by seasoned waitresses whose beehive hairdos contribute to the campy atmosphere.

250 S.R. 84, Fort Lauderdale. ✆ 954/525-5641. Main courses $5–$12. AE, MC, V. Daily 24 hr.

Le Tub ★★ *Finds* AMERICAN   Hands down, this is one of the coolest, most unpretentious, quintessential pre-swank South Florida restaurants, if not one of the coolest restaurants, period. Established in 1959 as a Sunoco gas station, Le Tub was purchased in 1974 by a man who personally transformed the place into this waterfront restaurant, made out of flotsam, jetsam, and ocean-bone treasures gathered over 4 years of jogging on Hollywood Beach. But the waterfront location and unique building aren't the only things to marvel at. As you walk in, take note of the hand-painted bathtubs and toilet bowls (it's not at all gross; they're used as planters) lining the walkway. Inside is a divey bar complete with pool table and jukebox; outside seating on the deck is the real gem. Le Tub is famous for its burgers, chili, and seafood, but more appealing than the food is the peaceful, easy feeling exuded by the place.

1100 N. Ocean Dr., Hollywood. ✆ 954/931-9425. Main courses $6–$17. No credit cards. Daily 10:30am–4am.

THE HOLLYWOOD & FORT LAUDERDALE AREA AFTER DARK

Fort Lauderdale no longer mimics the raucous antics of *Animal House* as far as nightlife is concerned. It has become hip to the fact that an active nightlife is vital to the city's desire to distract sophisticated, savvy visitors from the magnetic lure of South Beach. While Lauderdale is no South Beach, it has vastly improved the quality of its nightlife by welcoming places that wouldn't dare host wet T-shirt or beer-chugging contests. It also lacks the South Beach attitude, which is part of the attraction.

Hollywood's nightlife seems to be in the throes of an identity crisis, touting itself as the next South Beach, while at the same time hyping its image as an attitude-free nocturnal playground. Here's the real deal: At press time, Hollywood nightlife was barely awake, with the exception of a few bars and one struggling dance club. If you're looking for a quiet night out, it's probably your best bet. But don't come too late—after midnight, the city is absolutely deserted.

For information on clubs and events, pick up a free copy of Fort Lauderdale's weekly newspaper *City Link,* or the Fort Lauderdale edition of the *New Times.*

The Culture Room   If you consider rock and heavy metal to be culture, visit the Culture Room and bang your head to local bands. Open nightly from 8pm to 3am. 3045 N. Federal Hwy. (at Oakland Park Blvd.), Fort Lauderdale. ✆ 954/564-1074. www.cultureroom.net. Cover varies.

Elbo Room   Formerly spring-break central, the Elbo Room has actually managed to maintain its rowdy and divey reputation by serving up frequent drink specials and live bands. Ironically, it was almost torn down until the Penrod family of chic and sleek Nikki Beach fame bought the place to keep it alive. No matter what, it'll always be a beloved dive, though! Open daily from 10am to 2am. 241 S. Atlantic Blvd. (corner of Las Olas Blvd. and Fla. A1A), Fort Lauderdale. ✆ 954/463-4615. www.elboroom.com.

The Gallery at Beach Place   This outdoor shopping-and-entertainment complex, modeled after Coconut Grove's CocoWalk, landed on the legendary "strip" with several franchised bars and restaurants. It's the beachy version of a mall and is popular with a very young set at night. The view of the ocean makes it worth a stop for a drink. Hours vary by establishment; some places are open until 2 or 3am, while others close around 11pm. 17 S. Fort Lauderdale Beach Blvd., Fort Lauderdale. (C) 954/760-9570.

Harrison's Wine Bar   Dark, cozy, and so comfy that it's hard to get up from the big leather couches, Harrison's attracts a hip crowd that mulls over, sniffs, and sips from more than 100 kinds of vino at reasonable prices. There are also 40 bottled beers. Cheese platters, hummus platters, and panini are available. Open daily from 4pm to 2am. 1916 Harrison St., Hollywood. (C) 954/922-0074. www.harrisonswinebar.com.

Karma Lounge   Almost too hip for Fort Lauderdale, Karma Lounge boasts a British resident DJ, which, if you know anything about DJs or club music, is a big deal. Progressive house music is the soundtrack for this glammy, orange-and-white ultramod spot that's frequented by the dolled-up over-25 set. Open Wednesday through Thursday from 10pm to 3am, Friday and Saturday from 10pm to 4am. 4 W. Las Olas Blvd., Fort Lauderdale. (C) 954/523-7159. Cover varies.

Mai Kai *Moments*   Immerse yourself in this fabulous vestige of Polynesian kitsch: hula dancers, fire eaters, and potent drinks served in coconuts. The food, an ambiguous blend of Chinese, Polynesian, and other Asian cuisine, is tasty but overpriced. No matter; it's bound to get cold as you watch the hilarious show, which includes everything from Tahitian classics to Polynesian versions of American hits. A trip to undeniably fun Mai Kai is a must. *Note:* The cocktails cost almost as much as a meal. Open daily from 5pm until midnight. 3599 N. Federal Hwy. (between Commercial and Oakland Park blvds.), Fort Lauderdale. (C) 954/563-3272. Reservations required. Shows (2 nightly) are $9.95 for adults, free for children 12 and under.

O'Hara's   What used to be a mediocre jazz club has turned into a premier venue for excellent live R&B, pop, and funk music. Two locations: 1905 Hollywood Blvd., Hollywood ((C) 954/925-2555; 24-hr. Jazz & Blues Hot Line: (C) 954/524-2801); and 722 E. Las Olas Blvd., Fort Lauderdale ((C) 954/524-1764).

Pangaea and Gryphon   The two hottest dance clubs and lounges at the Seminole Hard Rock Hotel and Casino opened by a NYC nightlife impresario, Pangaea and Gryphon attract an A-list of club kids spanning the tricounty area. Open 24 hours. 5707 Seminole Way, Hollywood (C) 954/581-5454. Cover Fri–Sat night $20.

The Parrot   Fort Lauderdale's most famous dive bar, The Parrot is a local's and out-of-towner's choice for an evening of beer (16 kinds on tap), bonding, and browsing the bar's gallery of photos of almost everyone who's ever imbibed here since its opening in 1970. Open Sunday through Thursday from 11am to 2am, and Friday and Saturday from 11am to 3am. 911 Sunrise Lane, Fort Lauderdale. (C) 954/563-1493.

The Poor House   There's nothing poor about this microbrew hangout, where excellent live music by local bands starts at midnight and goes on well into the wee hours. A friendly, lively mixed crowd composes a generational cross section where the gap is bridged by a common love of music, cold beer, and good times. Open nightly from 5pm to 2am. 110 SW 3rd Ave., Fort Lauderdale. (C) 954/522-5145.

Revolution   Some of today's hottest indie bands play here, but if you're not into live music, fret not because this cavernous place is a dance club, too. Open Thursday to Sunday until 4am. Opening hours and cover charges vary, depending on what band is playing. 200 W. Broward Blvd., Fort Lauderdale. (C) 954/727-0950.

Riverwalk   You'll find this outdoor shopping-and-entertainment complex in the heart of downtown Fort Lauderdale, on the sleepy yet scenic New River—as a result of its river site, it has more charm than most such complexes. In fact, if you've got a boat, you can sail here. A host of bars, restaurants, and shops, not to mention a high-tech virtual-reality arcade, the Escape, and a multiplex cinema are enough to keep you occupied for at least a few hours. On weekends, this place is packed. 400 SW 2nd St. (along the New River from NE 6th Ave. to SW 6th Ave.), Fort Lauderdale. (C) 954/468-1541.

Shooters   This waterfront bar is quintessential Fort Lauderdale. Inside you'll find nautical types, families, and young professionals mixed with a good dose of sunburned tourists enjoying the live reggae, jazz, or Jimmy Buffett–style tunes, with the gorgeous backdrop of the bay and marinas all around. Open Monday through Friday from 11:30am to 2am, Saturday from 11:30am to 3am, and Sunday from 10am to 2am. 3033 NE 32nd Ave., Fort Lauderdale. (C) 954/566-2855.

2 Boca Raton ★★ & Delray Beach ★

26 miles S of Palm Beach, 40 miles N of Miami, 21 miles N of Fort Lauderdale

Boca Raton is one of South Florida's most expensive, well-maintained cities—home to ladies who lunch and SUV-driving yuppies. The city's name literally translates as "rat's mouth," but you'd be hard-pressed to find rodents in this area's fancy digs.

If you're looking for funky, wacky, and eclectic, look elsewhere. Boca is a luxurious resort community and, for some, the only place worth staying in South Florida. Although Jerry Seinfeld's TV parents retired to the fictional Del Boca Vista, Boca is just too pricey to be a retirement community. With minimal nightlife, entertainment in Boca is restricted to leisure sports, excellent dining, and upscale shopping. The city's residents and vacationers happily comply.

Delray Beach, named after a suburb of Detroit, is a sleepy-yet-starting-to-awaken beachfront community that grew up completely separate from its southern neighbor. Because of their proximity, Boca and Delray can easily be explored together. Budget-conscious travelers would do well to eat and sleep in Delray and dip into Boca for sightseeing and beaching only. The 2-mile stretch of beach here is well maintained and crowded, though not mobbed. Delray's "downtown" area is confined to Atlantic Avenue, which is known for restaurants from casual to chic, quaint shops, and art galleries. During the day, Delray is slumbering, but thanks to the recent addition of trendy restaurants and bars, nighttime is a much more animated hotbed of hipster activity. Still, compared to Boca, Delray is much more laid-back, hardly as chichi, and more cute little beach town than sprawling, swank, suburban Boca.

ESSENTIALS

GETTING THERE   Like the rest of the cities on the Gold Coast, Boca Raton and Delray are easily reached from I-95 or the Florida Turnpike. Both the Fort Lauderdale–Hollywood International Airport and the Palm Beach International Airport are about 20 minutes away. **Amtrak** ((C) **800/USA-RAIL;** www.amtrak.com) trains make stops in Delray Beach at an unattended station at 345 S. Congress Ave.

VISITOR INFORMATION   Contact or stop by the **Palm Beach County Convention and Visitors Bureau,** 1555 Palm Beach Lakes Blvd., Suite 800, West Palm Beach, FL 33401 ((C) **800/554-PALM** or 561/233-3000; fax 561/471-3990; www. palmbeachfl.com). It's open Monday through Friday from 8:30am to 5:30pm and has excellent coupons and discounts. Monday through Friday from 8:30am until at least 4pm, stop by the **Greater Boca Raton Chamber of Commerce,** 1800 N. Dixie Hwy., 4 blocks north of Glades Road, Boca Raton, FL 33432 (© **561/395-4433;** fax 561/392-3780; www.bocaratonchamber.com), for information on attractions, accommodations, and events in the area. You can also try the **Greater Delray Beach Chamber of Commerce,** 64 SE 5th Ave., half a block south of Atlantic Avenue on U.S. 1, Delray Beach, FL 33483 (© **561/278-0424;** fax 561/278-0555; www.delraybeach. com), but I recommend the Palm Beach County Convention and Visitors Bureau since it has information on the entire county.

BEACHES & OUTDOOR ACTIVITIES

BEACHES   Thankfully, Florida had the foresight to set aside some of its most beautiful coastal areas for the public's enjoyment. Many of the area's best beaches are located in state parks and are free to pedestrians and bikers, though most do charge for parking. Among the beaches I recommend are Delray Beach's **Atlantic Dunes Beach,** 1600 S. Ocean Blvd., which charges no admission to access a 7-acre developed beach with lifeguards, restrooms, changing rooms, and a family park area; and Boca Raton's **South Beach Park,** 400 N. Ocean Blvd., with 1,670 feet of beach, 25 acres, lifeguards, picnic areas, restrooms, showers, and 955 feet of developed beach south of the Boca Inlet, accessible for an admission charge of $15 Monday through Friday, and $17 Saturday and Sunday. The two beaches below are also very popular.

Delray Beach, on Ocean Boulevard at the east end of Atlantic Avenue, is one of the area's most popular hangouts. Weekends especially attract a young and good-looking crowd of active locals and tourists. Refreshments, snack shops, bars, and restaurants are just across the street. Families enjoy the protection of lifeguards on the clean, wide strip. Gentle waters make it a good swimming beach, too. Restrooms and showers are available, and there's limited parking at meters along Ocean Boulevard.

Spanish River Park Beach, on North Ocean Boulevard (Fla. A1A), 2 miles north of Palmetto Park Road in Boca Raton, is a huge 95-acre oceanfront park with a half-mile-long beach with lifeguards as well as a large grassy area, making it one of the best choices for picnicking. Facilities include picnic tables, grills, restrooms, showers, and a 40-foot observation tower. You can walk through tunnels under the highway to access nature trails that wind through fertile grasslands. Volleyball nets always have at least one game going on. The park is open from 8am to 8pm. Admission is $16 for vehicles Monday through Friday; $18 on Saturday, Sunday, and major holidays.

Also see the description of **Red Reef Park** under "Scuba Diving & Snorkeling," below.

GOLF   This area has plenty of good courses. The best ones that are not in a gated community are **Boca Raton Resort & Club** (p. 334) and the **Inn at Ocean Breeze Golf and Country Club** (p. 335), formerly known as the Inn at Boca Teeca. Another great place to swing clubs is at the **Deer Creek Golf Club,** 2801 Country Club Blvd., Deerfield Beach (© **954/421-5550**), a 300-plus-yard driving range where a large bucket of balls costs $9 and a small one costs $5. Rates at the Deer Creek Golf Club are seasonal and range from $45 to $130. However, from May to October or November, about a dozen private courses open their greens to visitors staying in Palm Beach County hotels. This "Golf-A-Round" program is free or severely discounted (carts are additional), and reservations can be made through most major hotels. Ask at your

Boca Raton

The Addison **27**
Baja Cafe **25**
Bistro Zenith **16**
Boca Raton Executive
  Country Club **11**
Boca Raton Municipal
  Golf Course **17**
Boca Raton Museum of Art **24**
Boca Raton Resort & Club **28**
Boston's on the Beach **9**
Caldwell Theatre **12**
Crane's BeachHouse **8**
Dada **2**
Daggerwing Nature Center **17**
De La Tierra **7**
Delray Beach Public Beach **9**
Delray Beach Tennis Center **1**
Delux **3**
Elwood's **5**
Falcon House **6**
Gatsby's **29**
Gumbo Limbo
  Environmental Complex **22**
Inn at Ocean Breeze Golf
  and Country Club **14**
Kathy's Gazebo **21**
Mario's of Boca **19**
Max's Grille **24**
Mizner Park **24**
Morikami Museum
  and Japanese Gardens **10**
New York Prime **18**
Old Homestead **28**
Patch Reef Park **15**
Red Reef Park **23**
Sundy House **7**
32 East **4**
The Tin Muffin Cafe **26**
Tom's Place **13**
Town Center Mall **20**
Uncle Tai's **20**

hotel or contact the **Palm Beach County Convention and Visitors Bureau** (℃ 561/ 471-3995) for information on which clubs are available for play.

The **Boca Raton Municipal Golf Course,** 8111 Golf Course Rd. (℃ 561/483- 6100), is the area's best public golf course. There's an 18-hole, par-72 course covering approximately 6,200 yards, as well as a 9-hole, par-30 course. Facilities include a snack bar and a pro shop where clubs can be rented. Greens fees are $16–$32 for 9 holes, and $24 to $56 for 18 holes. Ask about special summer discounts.

SCUBA DIVING & SNORKELING   **Moray Bend,** a 58-foot dive spot about three-quarter miles off Boca Inlet, is the area's most popular. It's home to three moray eels that are used to being fed by scuba divers. The reef is accessible by boat from **Force E Dive Center,** 877 E. Palmetto Park Rd., Boca Raton (℃ 561/368-0555; www.force-e.com). Phone for dive times. Dives cost $60 per person.

Red Reef Park, 1400 N. Ocean Park Blvd. (℃ 561/393-7974), a 67-acre oceanfront park in Boca Raton, has good swimming and year-round lifeguard protection. There's snorkeling around the shallow rocks and reefs that lie just off the beach. The park has restrooms and a picnic area with grills. Located a half-mile north of Palmetto Park Road, it's open daily from 8am to 10pm. The cost is $16 per car Monday through Friday, $18 on Saturday and Sunday; walkers and bikers get in free.

TENNIS   The snazzy **Delray Beach Tennis Center,** 201 W. Atlantic Ave. (℃ 561/ 243-7360; www.delraytennis.com), has 14 lit clay courts and 5 hard courts available by the hour. Phone for rates and reservations.

The 17 public lit hard courts at **Patch Reef Park,** 2000 NW 51st St. (℃ 561/997- 0881; www.ci.boca-raton.fl.us/parks/patchreef.cfm), are available by reservation. The fee for nonresidents is $5.25 per person per 1½ hours. Courts are available Monday through Saturday from 7:30am to 10pm, and Sunday from 7:30am to dusk; call ahead to see whether a court is available. To reach the park from I-95, exit at Yamato Road West and continue past Military Trail to the park.

SEEING THE SIGHTS

Boca Raton Museum of Art ⚐⚐   In addition to a relatively small but well-chosen permanent collection that's strongest in 19th-century European oils (Degas, Klee, Matisse, Picasso, Seurat), the museum stages a wide variety of excellent temporary exhibitions by local and international artists. Lectures and films are offered on a fairly regular basis, so call ahead for details.

Mizner Park, 501 Plaza Real, Boca Raton. ℃ 561/392-2500. www.bocamuseum.org. Admission $8 adults, $6 seniors, $4 students, free for children 11 and under. Additional fees may apply for special exhibits and performances. Free on Wed except during special exhibitions. Tues, Thurs, and Sat 10am–5pm; Wed and Fri 10am–9pm; Sun noon–5pm.

Daggerwing Nature Center ⚐   Seen enough snowbirds? Head over to this 39- acre swampy splendor where birds of another feather reside, including herons, egrets, woodpeckers, and warblers. The trails come complete with a soundtrack provided by songbirds hovering above (watch your head). The park's night hikes will take you on a nocturnal wake-up call for owls at 6pm. Bring a flashlight. A $2 million expansion in 2007 added a new addition, which includes a 3,000-square-foot exhibit hall, a laboratory classroom, and exciting wet forest and conservation exhibits.

South County Regional Park, 11200 Park Access Rd., Boca Raton. ℃ 561/488-9953. Free admission. Tues–Fri 1–4:30pm; Sat 9am–4:30pm. Call for tour and activity schedule.

Gumbo Limbo Environmental Complex ☆☆☆ If manicured lawns and golf courses aren't your idea of communing with nature, head to Gumbo Limbo. Named for an indigenous hardwood tree, the 20-acre complex protects one of the few surviving coastal hammocks, or forest islands, in South Florida. Walk through the hammock on a half-mile-long boardwalk that ends at a 40-foot observation tower, from which you can see the Atlantic Ocean, the Intracoastal Waterway, and much of Boca Raton. From mid-April to September, sea turtles come ashore here to lay eggs.

1801 N. Ocean Blvd. (on Fla. A1A between Spanish River Blvd. and Palmetto Park Rd.), Boca Raton. © 561/338-1473. www.gumbolimbo.org. Free admission ($3 donation suggested). Mon–Sat 9am–4pm; Sun noon–4pm.

Morikami Museum and Japanese Gardens ☆☆☆ Slip off your shoes and enter a scenic Japanese garden that dates from 1905, when an entrepreneurial farmer, Jo Sakai, came to Boca Raton to build a tropical agricultural community. The Yamato Colony, as it was known, was short-lived; by the 1920s, only one tenacious colonist remained: George Sukeji Morikami. But Morikami was quite successful, eventually running one of the largest pineapple plantations in the area. The 200-acre Morikami Museum and Japanese Gardens, which opened to the public in 1977, was Morikami's gift to Palm Beach County and the state of Florida. A stroll through the garden is almost a mile long. An artificial waterfall that cascades into a koi- and carp-filled moat; a small rock garden for meditation; and a large bonsai collection with miniature maple, buttonwood, juniper, and Australian pine trees are all worth contemplation. There's also a cafe with an Asian-inspired menu if you want to stay for lunch.

4000 Morikami Park Rd., Delray Beach. © 561/495-0233. www.morikami.org. Museum $10 adults, $9 seniors, $6 children 6–18. Museum Tues–Sun 10am–5pm; gardens Tues–Sat 10am–5pm. Closed major holidays.

SHOPPING & BROWSING

Even if you don't plan to buy anything, a trip to Boca Raton's **Mizner Park** is essential for capturing the essence of the city. Mizner is the place to see and be seen, where Rolls-Royces and Ferraris are parked curbside, freshly coiffed women sit amid shopping bags at outdoor cafes, and young movers and shakers chat on their constantly buzzing cellphones. Beyond the human scenery, however, Mizner Park is scenic in its own right, with beautiful landscaping. It's really an outdoor mall, with 45 specialty shops, seven good restaurants, and a multiplex. Each shop front faces a grassy island with gazebos, potted plants, and garden benches. Mizner Park is on Federal Highway, between Palmetto Park and Glades roads (© **561/362-0606**).

Boca's **Town Center Mall,** on the south side of Glades Road, just west of I-95, has seven huge department stores, including Nordstrom, Bloomingdale's, Burdines, Lord & Taylor, and Saks Fifth Avenue. Add hundreds of specialty shops, an extensive food court, and a range of other restaurants, and you have the area's most comprehensive shopping center.

On Delray Beach's Atlantic Avenue, especially east of Swinton Avenue, you'll find a few antiques shops, clothing stores, and galleries shaded by palm trees and colorful awnings. Pick up the *Downtown Delray Beach* map and guide at almost any of the stores on this strip, or call © **561/278-0424** for more information.

WHERE TO STAY

A number of national chain hotels worth considering include the moderately priced **Holiday Inn Highland Beach Oceanside,** 2809 S. Ocean Blvd., on Florida A1A, southeast of Linton Boulevard (© **800/234-6835** or 561/278-6241). Although you won't find rows of cheap hotels as in Fort Lauderdale and Hollywood, a handful of mom-and-pop motels have survived along Florida A1A between the towering condominiums of Delray Beach. Look along the beach just south of Atlantic Boulevard. Especially noteworthy is the pleasant little two-story, shingle-roofed **Bermuda Inn,** 64 S. Ocean Blvd. ((C) **561/276-5288**).

Even more economical options can be found in Deerfield Beach, Boca's neighbor, south of the county line. A number of beachfront efficiencies offer great deals, even in the winter months. Try the **Panther Motel and Apartments,** 715 S. A1A ((C) **954/427-0700**), a clean and convenient motel with rates starting as low as $49 (in season, you may have to book for a week at a time; rates then start at $250).

VERY EXPENSIVE

Boca Raton Resort & Club ★★ *Kids*   This landmark resort is a sprawling 350-acre collection of posh, yet oddly matched buildings: the original; the drab pink 27-story Tower; the renovated Beach Club and Pool Oasis, accessible by water shuttle and featuring three redesigned swimming pools, oceanfront bar, beach access, cabana, and sunning terraces; and the brand-new Yacht Club, a Venetian-style wing of 112 luxury rooms and suites. Fans of the old-school resort may be disappointed with the modernization of the hotel; others will be happy things have been spruced up. Everything at this resort, which straddles the Intracoastal, is at your fingertips, but may sometimes require some effort to reach. Amenities include the grand Spa Palazzo, two 18-hole championship golf courses, a $10-million tennis and fitness center, a 25-slip marina, and a private beach with watersports equipment. This resort is foodie heaven, with a choice of 10 places to dine including NYC's Old Homestead steakhouse, Morimoto, and Gordon Ramsay's Cielo.

501 E. Camino Real (P.O. Box 5025), Boca Raton, FL 33432. (C) 888/495-BOCA or 561/447-3000. Fax 561/447-3183. www.bocaresort.com. 1,047 units. Winter $249–$760 double; off season $149–$329 double. Reasonable seasonal packages available. AE, DC, DISC, MC, V. From I-95 N., exit onto Palmetto Park Rd. E. Turn right onto Federal Hwy. (U.S. 1), then left onto Camino Real. **Amenities:** 10 restaurants; 5 bars; 4 pools; 2 18-hole championship golf courses; 30 clay tennis courts; indoor basketball court; 2 fitness centers; Mediterranean spa; watersports equipment rental; extensive children's programs; concierge; business center; 24-hr. room service; laundry service; 32-slip marina. *In room:* A/C, TV, minibar, hair dryer.

Sundy House ★★★   The oldest residence in Delray Beach, Sundy House is a bona fide 1902 Queen Anne that has been restored to its Victorian glory—on the outside, at least. Inside, the four one- and two-bedroom apartments are in a style best described as Caribbean funky, adorned in brilliant colors and outfitted with state-of-the-art electronics, full modern kitchens, and laundry facilities. Six guest rooms known as the Stables are equestrian chic, with rustic appointments in dark woods. While the rooms here are outstanding, it's the surrounding property that garners the most oohs and aahs. Set on an acre of lush gardens, the Sundy House is surrounded by more than 5,000 species of exotic plants, streams, and parrots, making an escape here seem more Hawaii than Florida. You can even swim with fish in the hotel's swimming pond! The on-site restaurant features exquisite New Florida cuisine, oftentimes using fresh fruits and herbs straight from Sundy House's botanical Taru Garden.

106 S. Swinton Ave., Delray Beach, FL 33444. (C) 877/439-9601 or 561/272-5678. Fax 561/272-1115. www.sundy house.com. 11 units. Winter $349–$669 1- or 2-bedroom or cottage; off season $169–$559 1- or 2-bedroom or cottage. AE, DC, DISC, MC, V. **Amenities:** Restaurant; bar; swimming pond; limited room service. *In room:* A/C, TV/DVD, CD player, kitchen, coffeemaker, hair dryer, safe, washer/dryer.

EXPENSIVE

Crane's BeachHouse ⊛⊛   If you can't afford your own South Florida beach house—and why bother with all the maintenance, anyway?—Crane's BeachHouse, meticulously run and maintained by husband and wife Michael and Cheryl Crane, is a haven away from home, located just 1 block from the beach and right in the middle of historic Delray Beach. The main draws here are the whimsical, tropical suites, in which every piece of furniture and bric-a-brac is completely original and oftentimes crafted by local artists. Although each unit has its own theme—Hawaii, Amazon, Anacapri, and Capetown, for instance—the beds are all the same, in that they are downright heavenly. Lush gardens, a Tiki bar, and a swimming pool leave you with little reason to flee the premises, but when you do, you'll want to return as quickly as possible.

82 Gleason St., Delray Beach, FL 33483. ℂ **866/372-7263** or 561/278-1700. Fax 561/278-7826. www.cranesbeach house.com. 27 units. Winter $189–$239 double; $289–$499 suite; off season $139–$169 double; $199–$299 suite. AE, DC, DISC, V. Free parking. **Amenities:** 2 small outdoor pools. *In room:* A/C, TV, VCR, dataport, full kitchen, mini-bar, coffeemaker, hair dryer, iron, safe.

INEXPENSIVE

The Inn at Ocean Breeze Golf and Country Club ⊛   For more than 3 decades, this lodging, formerly known as the Inn at Boca Teeca, has attracted golf fanatics who could care less about the small but comfortable rooms, because they're too busy out on the superb 27-hole golf course, open only to members and guests. For the golf widow(er)s, most of the rooms in this three-story motel style building have balconies or patios from which to watch or signal to their significant others that it's time for dinner.

5800 NW 2nd Ave., Boca Raton, FL 33487. ℂ **561/994-0400.** Fax 561/998-8279. www.theinnatboceanbreeze.com. 46 units. Winter from $119 double; off season from $59 double. AE, DC, MC, V. **Amenities:** Restaurant; small pool; golf course; 6 tennis courts; fitness center. *In room:* A/C, TV, wireless Internet.

WHERE TO DINE

Boca Raton and its surrounding area is the kind of place where you discuss dinner plans at the breakfast table. Nightlife in Boca means going out to a restaurant. But who cares? This is some of the best dining in South Florida.

VERY EXPENSIVE

The Addison ⊛⊛⊛ CONTINENTAL   Located in Addison Mizner's 1925 office building near his famous Boca Raton Resort, The Addison is one of Boca's most popular—and romantic—restaurants, with a stunning courtyard and a setting straight out of a swank Spanish village. The menu ranges from steaks and chops to more nouveau dishes such as corn-crusted soft-shell crab with roasted garlic mash and fennel salad. Service is swift and professional, but people really come here for the ambience.

2 East Camino Real, Boca Raton. ℂ **561/395-9335.** www.theaddison.com. Reservations recommended. Main courses $20–$65. AE, DC, DISC, MC, V. Sun–Thurs 5–10pm; Fri–Sat 5–11pm.

Kathy's Gazebo Cafe ⊛⊛⊛ CONTINENTAL   An elegant, old-school Continental restaurant with chandeliers and white linen tablecloths, Kathy's white-glove restaurant is an ideal spot for special occasions or culinary nostalgia. The food is superb—the Dover sole is flown in from Holland and prepared with nothing fancier than an almandine or meunière sauce; Chateaubriand is also spectacular and, in a city smitten by plain ol' steak and sushi, it's a delicious throwback to simpler, delicious days. Fresh homemade pastries and peach Melba are among the desserts. While jackets aren't commonly required at restaurants in South Florida, you'll want to wear one here just to fit in with the dapper moneyed types who frequent the place.

4199 N. Federal Hwy., Boca Raton. © 561/395-6033. www.kathysgazebo.com. Reservations required. Main courses $12–$39. AE, MC, V. Daily 5:30–10pm.

New York Prime ⊛ STEAKHOUSE   This South Florida outpost of a South Carolina–based chain is the prime spot for carnivores looking to satisfy their cravings for big, succulent steaks. Fish dishes are also available, including lobsters ranging from 3 to 13 pounds. But excess does not come cheap. In fact, the restaurant brazenly states its case on the menu: "We strive to be the Mercedes of steakhouses by offering the very best . . . but you can't drive a Mercedes for the same price as a Buick." Cute motto, but in terms of consistency, New York Prime is a Pinto. On one night the food and service are exquisite, while on another, abysmal. Take your chances, though, because if you do hit it on a good night, you won't be disappointed.

2350 Executive Center Dr., Boca Raton. © 561/998-3881. www.newyorkprime.com. Reservations recommended. Main courses $25–$79. AE, MC, V. Daily 5–11pm.

Old Homestead ⊛⊛⊛ STEAKHOUSE   If you're homesick for New York, this branch of New York's oldest meatery is the place to cure your yearnings, especially if money is no object. The 48-ounce Meatpacking District long bone rib steak for two at $40 per person is pricey, but cheaper than a plane ticket to Gotham—and it's worth it. The meat here is divine. Sides are a la carte and outstanding. The hash-brown potato pie and buttermilk onion rings are my favorites, but all sorts of starches and veggies are available at steep prices from $8 to $12 per dish. Seafood is also aplenty, from fresh shucked oysters to Maine lobsters, and for diners who just can't seem to find the ideal chopped salad, the hand-chopped version of blue cheese, olives, mushrooms, bacon bits, eggs, and hearts of palm is a meal in itself. The restaurant also made news when it decided to charge a whopping $100 for its tri-beef burger, a meaty mixture of Kobe, American, and Argentinean beef, with $10 of its hefty price going to the Make-A-Wish Foundation. After creating a stir regardless of the charity tie in, the burger was reduced to $37.

501 E. Camino Real (in the Boca Raton Resort), Boca Raton. © 561/447-3640. www.bocaresort.com. Reservations required. Main courses $28–$47. AE, MC, V. Sun–Wed 5–10pm; Thurs–Sat 5–11pm.

EXPENSIVE

Max's Grille ⊛ AMERICAN   Max's Grille is a very popular, very good option in Mizner Park, but you'll have to wait to be seated. An exhibition kitchen occupies the back wall of the restaurant, so those diners lucky enough to score a table can watch as their yellowfin tuna steak or filet mignon is seared on a flaming oak grill. There's also a large selection of chicken, meat loaf, pastas, and main-course salads.

404 Plaza Real, in Mizner Park, Boca Raton. © 561/368-0080. Reservations accepted for parties of 6 or more. Main courses $14–$26. AE, DC, DISC, MC, V. Mon–Thurs 11:30am–3pm and 5–10:30pm; Fri–Sat 11:30am–3pm and 5–11pm; Sun 11:30am–10pm.

Sundy House Restaurant ⊛⊛ FLORIBBEAN   This restaurant is a stunning place that combines elegant indoor dining and lush tropical outdoor settings with a gastronomic wizardry of fresh fruits, vegetables, and spices grown on the Sundy House's 5-acre farm. Each dish is prepared with palpable precision. Consider the following: herb-seared Chilean sea bass with truffle oil and chive risotto, or the mojo glazed Caribbean spiced pork tenderloin with Cabernet sauce, chive sour cream and buttered asparagus. Save room for dessert, including a decadent Earl Gray crème brûlée and Mandarin orange chocolate torte. A decadent Sunday brunch buffet makes the day before you return to work infinitely more bearable. On the negative side, the service here can be surly and spotty.

In the Sundy House, 106 S. Swinton Ave., Delray Beach. ℂ **561/272-5678**. www.sundyhouse.com. Reservations essential. Main courses $24–$33. AE, DC, DISC, MC, V. Daily 11:30am–2:30pm and 6–10pm; Sun brunch 10:30am–2:30pm.

32 East ⊛⊛ NEW AMERICAN   The menu changes every day at this popular people-watching outpost of tasty, contemporary American food, which has added a little hipness to the Delray Beach scene. Among the standouts are sauté of Gulf Coast grouper with hedgehog mushrooms, Cipollini onions, and white beans in butternut squash sherry broth; and grilled duck breast and radicchio on parsnip-yam purée and pomegranate-Saba brown butter. The abuzz-with-activity ambience makes 32 East a popular hangout spot for the cocktail set.

32 E. Atlantic Ave., Delray Beach. ℂ **561/276-7868**. www.32east.com. Reservations recommended. Main courses $18–$37. AE, DC, MC, V. Sun–Thurs 5:30–10pm; Fri–Sat 5:30–11pm; bar until 2am.

Uncle Tai's ⊛⊛⊛ CHINESE   Not your average egg-roll-and-lo-mein place, Uncle Tai's, Boca's best upscale Chinese restaurant, offers a savory spin on classics such as garlic chicken and duck with plum sauce. A family-run restaurant, Uncle Tai's is the product of Wen Dah Tai, who studied with master chefs in China, Japan, and the Philippines. Tai wants to make sure you emerge from his restaurant satisfied, and he'll go the extra mile to discourage you from ordering a dish that's less suited to western palates because it was specially created for the restaurant's many Chinese diners.

5250 Town Center Circle (between Glades and Palmetto Park rds.), Boca Raton. ℂ **561/368-8806**. www.uncle-tais. com. Reservations suggested. Main courses $11–$52. AE, DISC, MC, V. Sun–Thurs 11:30am–2:30pm and 5–10pm; Fri–Sat 11:30am–2:30pm and 5–10:30pm.

MODERATE
Bistro Zenith ⊛ NEW AMERICAN   At the height of innovative cuisine, Bistro Zenith's consistently changing menu keeps local foodies coming back for its tasty traditional American dishes graced with Asian, Mediterranean, or Southwestern influences. The pineapple jerk marinated skirt steak with chipotle corn, jicama salsa, fried plantains with yellow rice, and black beans is my favorite. At press time, the restaurant was closed for "renovation" and "vacation" according to a phone recording, so hopefully this Zenith hasn't reached its nadir.

In the Regency Court, 3011 Yamato Rd., Boca Raton. ℂ **561/997-2570**. www.bistrozenith.com. Reservations recommended. Main courses $12–$30. AE, MC, V. Mon–Thurs 11:30am–2:30pm and 5:30–10pm; Fri 11:30am–2:30pm and 5:30–11pm; Sat 5:30–11pm; Sun 5:30–10pm.

Mario's of Boca ⊛ ITALIAN   This extremely popular, bustling Italian bistro keeps Boca's biggest mouths busy with massive portions of great homemade Italian food. The garlic rolls and the pizza are especially worth piping down for. If you're really hungry, an all-you-can-eat buffet is available 7 days a week.

1901 N. Military Trail (at the Holiday Inn, opposite Kings Market), Boca Raton. ℂ **561/392-5595**. www.mariosof boca.com. Reservations not accepted. Main courses $9–$22. AE, MC, V. Mon–Thurs 7–10:30am and 11:30am–10pm; Fri–Sat 7–10:30am and 11:30am–11pm; Sun 7–10:30am and noon–9:30pm.

INEXPENSIVE
Baja Cafe ⊛ MEXICAN   A jeans-and-T-shirt kind of place with wooden tables, Baja Cafe serves fantastic Mexican food at even better prices. Although the salsa borders on somewhat sweet, they do have the hottest sauces; if you like spicy, they will be

happy to slap plenty on your meal if you request it. This place is located right by the Florida East Coast Railway tracks, so don't be surprised if you feel a little rattling. Live music and entertainment make this place a hot spot for an unpretentious crowd.

201 NW 1st Ave., Boca Raton. ✆ **561/394-5449.** Reservations not accepted. Main courses $6–$12. No credit cards. Mon–Thurs 11:30am–10pm; Fri–Sat 11:30am–11pm; Sun 5–10pm.

The Tin Muffin Cafe 🦋 BAKERY/SANDWICH SHOP   Popular with the downtown lunch crowd, this excellent storefront bakery keeps folks lining up for big sandwiches on fresh bread, plus muffins, quiches, and good homemade soups such as split pea or lentil. The curried-chicken sandwich is stuffed with chunks of white meat doused in a creamy curry dressing and fruit. There are a few cafe tables inside and even one outside on a tiny patio. Be warned, however, that service is forgivably slow and parking is a nightmare. Try looking for a spot a few blocks away at a meter.

364 E. Palmetto Park Rd. (between Federal Hwy. and the Intracoastal Bridge), Boca Raton. ✆ **561/392-9446.** Sandwiches and salads $6.50–$11. No credit cards. Mon–Fri 11am–5pm; Sat 11am–4pm.

BOCA RATON & DELRAY BEACH AFTER DARK
THE BAR, CLUB & MUSIC SCENE

Atlantic Avenue in Delray Beach has finally gotten quite hip to nightlife and is now lined with sleek and chic restaurants, lounges, and bars that attract the Palm Beach County "in crowd," along with a few random patrons such as Yanni, who has a house nearby. Although it's hardly South Beach or Fort Lauderdale's Las Olas and Riverfront, Atlantic Avenue holds its own as far as a vibrant nightlife is concerned. In Boca Raton, **Mizner Park** is the nucleus of nightlife, with restaurants masking themselves as nightclubs or, at the very least, sceney bars, such as **Gigi's Tavern,** 346 Plaza Real (✆ **561/368-4488**), and **Mark's Mizner Park,** 334 Plaza Real (✆ **561/395-0770**).

Boston's on the Beach   This is a family restaurant with a somewhat lively bar scene. It's a good choice for post-sunbathing, super-casual happy hours Monday through Friday from 4 to 8pm, or live reggae on Monday. With two decks overlooking the ocean, Boston's is an ideal place to mellow out and take in the scenery. Open daily from 7am to 2am. 40 S. Ocean Blvd., Delray Beach. ✆ **561/278-3364.**

Dada   Dada is a nocturnal outpost of food, drink, music, art, culture, and history. In other words, here you can expect to find neobohemian, arty types lingering in their dark glasses and berets on one of the living room's cozy couches, listening to music, poetry, or dissertations on life. Live music, great food, a bar, an outdoor patio area, and a very eclectic crowd make Dada the coolest hangout in Delray. Open daily from 5:30pm to 2am. 52 N. Swinton Ave., Delray Beach. ✆ **561/330-DADA.**

Delux   Believe it or not, this red-hued dance club on Atlantic Avenue is cooler than some of South Beach's big-shot clubs, thanks to a soundtrack of sexy house music, bedlike seating, and a beautiful crowd in which someone as striking as past patron Gwen Stefani can actually blend in without being noticed. Open Wednesday through Sunday from 7pm to 2am. 16 E. Atlantic Ave., Delray Beach. ✆ **561/279-4792.**

Elwood's   Over the train tracks just steps from the chic bars and restaurants on Atlantic Avenue is this fabulous, blues-themed biker bar housed in a former gas station and garage. No fancy martinis here, just cold beer and good tunes. Open Monday through Friday from 5pm to 2am, Saturday from 11am to 2am, and Sunday from 11am to midnight. 301 E. Atlantic Ave., Delray Beach. ✆ **561/272-7427.**

Falcon House   A cozy wine and tapas bar on a side street off the Atlantic Avenue bustle, Falcon House is reminiscent of a bar you'd find in Napa Valley, with an impressive selection of wine and a hip, well-heeled crowd. It's a haven for those who are over the whole hip-hop scene on Atlantic Avenue. Open Monday through Saturday from 5pm to 2am. 116 NE 6th Ave., Delray Beach. ℂ **561/243-9499.**

Gatsby's   This always-busy bar is singles central, featuring big-screen TVs, microbrews, and martinis. Thursday college nights are especially popular, as are Friday happy hours. Open Monday, Tuesday, and Thursday from 4pm to 2am; Wednesday from 4pm to 3am; Friday from 4pm to 4am; Saturday from 6pm to 4am; and Sunday from 4pm to 3am. 5970 SW 18th St., Boca Raton. ℂ **561/393-3900.**

THE PERFORMING ARTS

For details on upcoming events, check the *Boca News* or the *Sun-Sentinel,* or call the **Palm Beach County Cultural Council** information line at ℂ **800/882-ARTS.** During business hours, a staffer can give details on current performances. After hours, a recorded message describes the week's events.

For live concerts from everyone from Dolly Parton to Kelly Clarkson, the **Mizner Park Amphitheater** (ℂ **866/571-ARTS**) is the place to see them in an open air format, under the stars and, at times, rain. If you're not that big a fan, you'll still hear the concerts from Mizner Park!

The **Florida Symphonic Pops,** a 70-piece professional orchestra, performs jazz, swing, rock, big-band, and classical music throughout Boca Raton. This musical force has entertained audiences for nearly 50 years. Call ℂ **561/393-7677** for a schedule.

Boca's best theater company is the **Caldwell Theatre,** and it's worth checking out. Located in a strip shopping center at 7873 N. Federal Hwy., this equity showcase does well-known dramas, comedies, classics, off-Broadway hits, and new works throughout the year. Ticket prices are reasonable—usually $36 to $42. Full-time students with ID will be especially interested in the little-advertised student rush: When available, tickets are sold for $5 if you arrive at least an hour early. Call ℂ **561/241-7432** for details.

3 Palm Beach ✶✶ & West Palm Beach ✶

65 miles N. of Miami, 193 miles E. of Tampa, 45 miles N. of Fort Lauderdale

Palm Beach County encompasses cities from Boca Raton in the south to Jupiter and Tequesta in the north. But it is Palm Beach, the small island town across the Intracoastal Waterway, that has been the traditional winter home of America's aristocracy— the Kennedys, the Rockefellers, the Pulitzers, the Trumps, titled socialites, and plenty of CEOs. For a perspective on what it means to put on the ritz, there is no better place than Palm Beach, where teenagers cruise around in their parents' Rolls-Royces while socialites seem to jump out of the glossy pages of society magazines and into an even glitzier real life. It's something to be seen, despite the fact that some may consider it all over the top and, frankly, obscene. But this is not only a city of upscale resorts and chic boutiques. In fact, Palm Beach holds some surprises, from a world-class art museum to one of the top bird-watching areas in the state.

Across the water from Palm Beach proper, or the "island" as locals call it, is downtown West Palm Beach, which is where everybody else lives. Clematis Street is the area's nightlife hub, with a great selection of bars, clubs, and restaurants. City Place is West Palm's version of Mizner Park; shops, restaurants, and other entertainment options liven up this once-dead area. In addition to good beaching, boating, and diving, you'll find great golf and tennis throughout the county. *Note:* Palm Beach's population swells from 20,000 in the summer to 40,000 in the winter. Book early if you plan to visit during the winter months.

ESSENTIALS

GETTING THERE   If you're driving up or down the Florida coast, you'll probably reach the Palm Beach area by way of I-95. Exit at Belvedere Road or Okeechobee Boulevard, and head east to reach the most central part of Palm Beach.

Visitors on their way to or from Orlando or Miami should take the Florida Turnpike, a toll road with a speed limit of 65 mph. Tolls are pricey, though; you may pay upward of $9 from Orlando and $4 from Miami. If you're coming from Florida's west coast, you can take either S.R. 70, which runs north of Lake Okeechobee to Fort Pierce, or S.R. 80, which runs south of the lake to Palm Beach.

All major airlines fly to the **Palm Beach International Airport,** at Congress Avenue and Belvedere Road (© 561/471-7400). Amtrak ((© 800/USA-RAIL; www.amtrak.com) has a terminal in West Palm Beach, at 201 S. Tamarind Ave. (© 561/832-6169).

GETTING AROUND   Although a car is almost a necessity in this area, a recently revamped public transportation system is extremely convenient for getting to some attractions in both West Palm and Palm Beach. **Palm Tran** covers 32 routes with more than 140 buses. The fare is $1.50 for adults, 75¢ for children 3 to 18, seniors, and riders with disabilities. Free route maps are available by calling © 561/233-4-BUS. Information operators are available Monday through Saturday from 6am to 7pm.

In downtown West Palm, free shuttles from City Place to Clematis Street operate Monday through Friday from 9am until 4pm, with plans to expand operations to evenings and weekends, too. Allegedly, the shuttles come every 5 minutes, but I'd count on them taking longer. Look for the bubblegum-pink minibuses throughout downtown. Call © 561/833-8873 for details.

For a more nostalgic route, consider the stately wicker chariots that run in the downtown area, especially on weekends and during special events. Rates vary according to the time of day, but average $1 to $2 per block, plus a per-person charge of $1. Call © 561/835-8922 for pickup or information.

VISITOR INFORMATION   The **Palm Beach County Convention and Visitors Bureau,** 1555 Palm Beach Lakes Blvd., Suite 204, West Palm Beach, FL 33401 (© 800/554-PALM or 561/471-3995; www.palmbeachfl.com), distributes an informative brochure and answers questions about visiting the Palm Beaches. Ask for a map as well as a copy of the *Arts and Attractions Calendar,* a day-to-day guide to art, music, stage, and other events in the county.

BEACHES & OUTDOOR ACTIVITIES

BEACHES   Public beaches are a rare commodity here in Palm Beach. Most of the island's best beaches are fronted by private estates and inaccessible to the general public. However, there are a few notable exceptions, including **Midtown Beach,** east of Worth Avenue, on Ocean Boulevard between Royal Palm Way and Gulfstream Road, which boasts more than 100 feet of undeveloped sand. This newly widened coast is now a centerpiece and a natural oasis in a town dominated by commercial glitz. There are no restrooms or concessions here, though a lifeguard is on duty until sundown. A

Palm Beach & West Palm Beach

Amici **18**
Best Western **31**
Bice Restaurant **24**
Brazilian Court **20**
The Breakers **17**
Café Boulud **21**
Cafe l'Europe **19**
Chesterfield Hotel **22**
City Cellar **9**
City Place **10**
The Colony **25**
Comfort Inn **31**
Currie Park **4**
Downtown at the Gardens **1**
Echo **14**
Emerald Dunes Golf Course **8**
Flagler Museum **15**
Four Seasons Resort Palm Beach **34**
Green's Pharmacy **16**
Hibiscus House **3**
Hotel Biba **12**
John G's **35**
Lion Country Safari **26**
Mar-A-Lago **29**
Mark's City Place **8**
Norton Museum of Art **11**
Palm Beach Historic Inn **23**
Palm Beach Hilton **34**
Palm Beach Hotel **13**
Palm Beach Marriott/
  Fairfield Inn and Suites **34**
Palm Beach Outlet Center **7**
Palm Beach Polo & Country Club **31**
Palm Beach Public Golf Course **33**
Palm Beach Zoo at Dreher Park **30**
Parkview Motor Lodge **28**
Phipps Ocean Park **32**
Playmobil Fun Park **1**
Rapids Water Park **2**
Raymond F. Kravis Center
  for the Performing Arts **9**
Rhythm Café **27**
Ritz-Carlton Palm Beach **35**
Rosa Mexicano **1**
The Strip House **1**
Tom's Place **5**

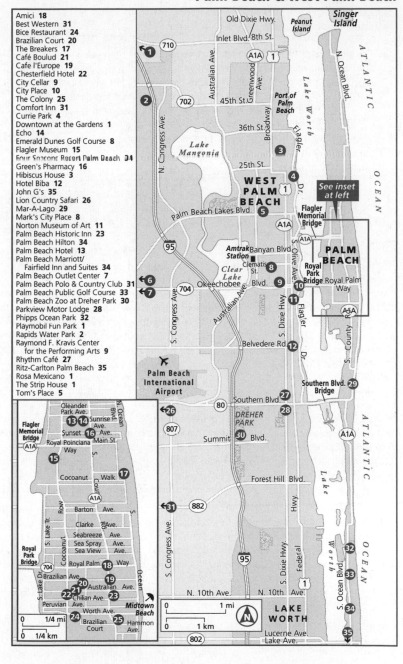

The Sport of Kings

The posh **Palm Beach Polo and Country Club** and the **International Polo Club** are two of the world's premier polo grounds and host some of the sport's top-rated players. Even if you're not a sports fan, you must attend a match at one of these fields, which are on the mainland in a rural area called Wellington. Rest assured, however, that the spectators, and many of the players, are pure Palm Beach. After all, a day at the pony grounds is one of the only good reasons to leave Palm Beach proper. You need not be a Vanderbilt or a Kennedy to attend—matches are open to the public and are surprisingly affordable.

Even if you haven't a clue how the game is played, you can spend your time people-watching. In recent years, stargazers have spotted Prince Charles, Sylvester Stallone, Tommy Lee Jones, Bo Derek, and Ivana Trump, among others. Dozens of lesser-known royalty keep box seats right on the grounds.

Dress is casual; a navy or tweed blazer over jeans or khakis is the standard for men, while neat-looking jeans or a pantsuit is the norm for women. On warmer days, shorts and, of course, polo shirts are fine, too.

General admission is $15 to $45; box seats cost $75 to $100 but are for members only. Matches are held throughout the week. Schedules vary, but the big names usually compete on Sunday at 3:30pm from January to April.

The fields are located at 11809 Polo Club Rd. and 3667 120th Ave. South Wellington, 10 miles west of the Forest Hill Boulevard exit of I-95. Call (C) **561/793-1440** or **561/204-5687** for tickets and a detailed schedule of events.

popular hangout for locals lies about 1½ miles north of here, near Dunbar Street; they prefer it to Midtown Beach because of the relaxed atmosphere. Parking is available at meters along Florida A1A. At the south end of Palm Beach, there's a less-popular but better-equipped beach at **Phipps Ocean Park.** On Ocean Boulevard, between the Southern Boulevard and Lake Avenue causeways, there's a lively public beach encompassing more than 1,300 feet of groomed oceanfront. With picnic and recreation areas and plenty of parking, the area is especially good for families.

BIKING   Rent anything from an English single-speed to a full-tilt mountain bike at the **Palm Beach Bicycle Trail Shop,** 223 Sunrise Ave. ((C) **561/659-4583**). Rates are $10 per hour, $25 per half-day (9am–5pm), and $34 for 24 hours, and include a basket and lock (not that a lock is necessary in this fortress of a town). The most scenic route is called the Lake Trail, running the length of the island along the Intracoastal Waterway. On it, you'll see some of the most magnificent mansions and grounds, and enjoy the views of downtown West Palm Beach as well as some great wildlife.

GOLF   There's good golfing in the Palm Beaches, but many private-club courses are maintained exclusively for members' use. Ask at your hotel or contact the **Palm Beach County Convention and Visitors Bureau** ((C) **561/471-3995**) for information on which clubs are available for play. In the off season, some private courses open to visitors staying in Palm Beach County hotels. This "Golf-A-Round" program offers free greens fees; reservations can be made through most major hotels.

The best hotel for golf in the area is the **PGA National Resort & Spa** (© 800/ 633-9150; p. 358), which features a whopping 90 holes of golf.

The **Palm Beach Public Golf Course,** 2345 S. Ocean Blvd. (© 561/547-0598), a popular public 18-hole course, is a par-54. The course opens at 8am on a first-come, first-served basis. Club rentals are available. Greens fees start at $17 to $47 per person.

SCUBA DIVING   Year-round warm waters, barrier reefs, and plenty of wrecks make South Florida one of the world's most popular places for diving. One of the best-known artificial reefs in this area is a vintage Rolls-Royce Silver Shadow, which was sunk off-shore in 1985. Nature has taken its toll, however, and divers can no longer sit in the car, which has been ravaged by time and saltwater. For gear and excursions, call **Jim Abernaethy's Scuba Adventures,** 2116 Ave. B, Riviera Beach (© 561/691-5808).

TENNIS   There are hundreds of tennis courts in Palm Beach County. Wherever you are staying, you're bound to be within walking distance of one. In addition to the many hotel tennis courts (see "Where to Stay," below), you can play at **Currie Park,** 2400 N. Flagler Dr., West Palm Beach (© 561/835-7025), a public park with three lit hard courts. They're free and available on a first-come, first-served basis.

WATERSPORTS   Call the **Seaside Activities Station** (© 561/835-8922) to arrange sailboat, jet ski, bicycle, kayak, water-ski, and parasail rentals.

SEEING THE SIGHTS

Flagler Museum ★★★   The Gilded Age is preserved in this luxurious mansion commissioned by Standard Oil tycoon Henry Flagler as a wedding present to his third wife. Whitehall, also known as the Taj Mahal of North America, is a classic Edwardian-style mansion containing 55 rooms, including a Louis XIV music room and art gallery, a Louis XV ballroom, and 14 guest suites outfitted with original antique European furnishings. Out back you can climb aboard the *Rambler,* Mr. Flagler's private restored railroad car. Allow at least 1½ hours to tour the stunning grounds and interior. Group tours are available, but for the most part, this is a self-guided museum.

1 Whitehall Way (at Cocoanut Row and Whitehall Way), Palm Beach. © 561/655-2833. www.flaglermuseum.us. Admission $15 adults, $8 ages 13–18, $3 children 6–12. Tues–Sat 10am–5pm; Sun noon–5pm.

Norton Museum of Art ★★★   The Norton is world famous for its prestigious permanent collection and top temporary exhibitions. The museum's major collections are divided geographically. The American galleries contain major works by Hopper, O'Keeffe, and Pollock. The French collection contains Impressionist and post-Impressionist paintings by Cézanne, Degas, Gauguin, Matisse, Monet, Picasso, Pissarro, and Renoir. The Chinese collection contains more than 200 bronzes, jades, and ceramics, as well as monumental Buddhist sculptures. Allow about 2 hours to see this museum, depending on your level of interest.

1451 S. Olive Ave., West Palm Beach. © 561/832-5196. Fax 561/659-4689. www.norton.org. Admission $8 adults, $3 ages 13–21. Mon–Sat 10am–5pm; Sun 1–5pm. Closed Mon May–Oct and all major holidays. Take I-95 to exit 52 (Okeechobee Blvd. E.). Travel east on Okeechobee to Dixie Hwy., and then south ½-mile to the Norton. Access parking through entrances on Dixie Hwy. and S. Olive Ave.

Playmobil Fun Park ★★ *Kids*   For a child, it doesn't get any better than this. The 17,000-square-foot Playmobil Fun Park is housed in a replica castle and loaded with

Unreal Estate

No trip to Palm Beach is complete without at least a glimpse of **Mar-A-Lago**, the stately residence of Donald Trump, the 21st century's answer to Jay Gatsby. In 1985, Trump purchased the estate of cereal heiress Marjorie Merriweather Post for a meager $8 million (for a fully furnished beachfront property of this stature, it was a relative bargain), to the great consternation of locals, who feared that he would turn the place into a casino. Instead, Trump, who sometimes resides in a portion of the palace, opened the house to the public—for a price, of course—as a tony country club (membership fee: $100,000). Rumor has it Trump is selling the place. In the meantime he continues to make his presence loudly known in Palm Beach!

While there are currently no tours open to the public, you can glimpse the gorgeous manse as you cross the bridge from West Palm Beach into Palm Beach. It's located at 1100 S. Ocean Blvd., Palm Beach.

themed areas for imaginative play: a medieval village, a Western town, a fantasy dollhouse, and more. Kids can play with the Playmobil boats on two water-filled tables. Tech-minded youths may get bored, but tots up to age 5 or so will love this place. You *could* spend hours here and not spend a penny, but parents, beware: Everything is available for purchase. There's another Playmobil park in Orlando.

8031 N. Military Trail, Palm Beach Gardens. © **800/351-8697** or 561/691-9880. Fax 561/691-9517. www.playmobil. com. Admission $1. Mon–Sat 10am–6pm; Sun noon–5pm. From I-95, go north to Palm Beach Lakes Blvd., and then west to Military Trail. Turn left; the park is about a mile down on the right.

NATURE PRESERVES & ATTRACTIONS

Lion Country Safari 🎯🎯 *Kids*   More than 1,300 animals on this 500-acre preserve (the nation's first cageless drive-through safari) are divided into their indigenous regions, from the East African preserve of the Serengeti to the American West. Elephants, lions, wildebeest, ostriches, American bison, buffalo, watusi, pink flamingos, and many other unusual species roam the preserve. When I visited, most of the lions were asleep; when awake, they travel freely throughout the cageless grassy landscape (this can be very scary). In fact, you're the one who's confined in your own car without an escort (no convertibles allowed). You're given a detailed pamphlet with photos and descriptions, and are instructed to obey the 15 mph speed limit—unless you see the rhinos charge (a rare occasion), in which case you're encouraged to floor it. Driving the loop takes slightly more than an hour, though you could make a day of just watching the chimpanzees play on their secluded islands. Included in the admission is Safari World, an amusement park with paddle boats, a carousel, miniature golf, and a baby animal nursery. Picnics are encouraged, and camping is available. The best time to go is late afternoon, right before the park closes; it's much cooler then, so the lions are more active. Though some may consider this a tourist trap, I had a great time.

Southern Blvd. W. at S.R. 80, West Palm Beach. © **561/793-1084** or 561/793-9797 for camping reservations. www.lioncountrysafari.com. Admission $22 adults, $20 seniors, $17 children 3–9. Van rental $8 per hour. Daily 9:30am–5:30pm (last vehicle admitted at 4:30pm). From I-95, exit on Southern Blvd. Go west for about 18 miles.

Palm Beach Zoo at Dreher Park *⑂*   If you want animals, go to Lion Country Safari (above). Unlike big-city zoos, this intimate 23-acre attraction is more like a stroll in the park than an all-day excursion. It features about 500 animals representing more than 100 different species. The monkey exhibit and petting zoo are favorites with kids. Stroller and wagon rentals are available. The newest attraction is the Tropics of the Americas, a 3-acre jungle path and complex that immerses guests in the animals, plants, and culture of a New World rainforest. You'll encounter animals such as jaguars, monkeys, giant anteaters, tapirs, bats, birds, snakes, and more. A new Siamang Habitat opened in 2005; it is currently home to a pair of primates known to be the largest species of lesser apes in the world. There are two Malayan tigers at the zoo now—there are only 47 in North America. In May 2007, lemur triplets were born here! Allow at least 2 hours to see all of the sights here.

1301 Summit Blvd. (east of I-95 between Southern and Forest Hill blvds.). *©* 561/547-WILD. Fax 561/585-6085. www.palmbeachzoo.org. Admission $13 adults, $10 seniors, $9 children 3–12. Daily 9am–5pm. Closed Thanksgiving.

Rapids Water Park *⑂* *Kids*   It may not be on the same grand scale as the theme parks in Orlando, but Rapids is a great way to cool off on a hot day. There are 12 acres of water rides, including a children's area and miniature golf course. A few new attractions opened in 2007, including the Black Thunder, involving a huge dark funnel and water; a Raging Rapids ride; and an aquatic obstacle course. Check out the Superbowl, a tubeless water ride that spins and swirls before dumping you into the pool below, and the Big Thunder, a giant funnel that plunges you down 50 feet in a four-person tube. Claustrophobia, anyone?

6566 N. Military Trail, West Palm Beach (1 mile west of I-95 on Military between 45th St./exit 54 and Blue Heron Blvd./exit 55 in West Palm Beach). *©* 561/842-8756. www.rapidswaterpark.com. Admission $32 plus tax; free for children 2 and under. Parking $5. Mid-Mar to Sept Mon–Fri 10am–5pm; Sat–Sun 10am–6pm.

SHOPPING & BROWSING

No matter what your budget, be sure to take a stroll down Worth Avenue, the "Rodeo Drive of the South" and a window-shopper's dream. Between South Ocean Boulevard and Cocoanut Row, there are more than 200 boutiques, posh shops, art galleries, and upscale restaurants. If you want to fit in, dress as if you are going to an elegant luncheon, not the mall down the street.

Despite the presence of the usual suspects (**Gucci, Chanel, Armani, Hermès,** and **Louis Vuitton,** among others), Worth Avenue is not impervious to the mainstream. Several chains such as **Victoria's Secret** and **Limited Express** have snuck in here, but so have a good number of unique boutiques. **History Buff,** 32 Via Mizner (*©* **561/366-8255**), is a virtual museum selling every genre of original historic autographs, some dating back to the 1600s, as well as vintage signed photos, first-edition books, and memorabilia. For privileged feet, **Stubbs & Wooton,** 4 Via Parigi (*©* **561/655-4105**), sells velvet slippers that are a favorite of the loofahed locals. For rare and estate jewelry, **Richter's of Palm Beach,** 224 Worth Ave. (*©* **561/655-0774**), has been specializing in priceless gems since 1893. Just off Worth Avenue is the **Church Mouse,** 374 S. County Rd. (*©* **561/659-2154**), a great consignment/thrift shop with antique furnishings and tableware, as well as lots of good castaway clothing and shoes from socialites who've moved on to the next designers or, worse than that, to the big gala in the sky. This shop usually closes for 2 months during the summer; call to be sure.

City Place, Okeechobee Road (at I-95), West Palm Beach (*©* **561/820-9716**), is a $550-million, Mediterranean-style shopping, dining, and entertainment complex that's responsible for revitalizing what was once a lifeless downtown West Palm Beach. Among the 78 mostly chain stores are **Macy's, FAO Schwarz, Benetton** (which contains an in-line skating track), **Armani Exchange, Pottery Barn,** and **SEE** eyewear. Restaurants include a Ghirardelli ice-cream shop; Legal Seafoods; the legendary Tampa-based Cuban restaurant Columbia; Miami Beach, Fort Lauderdale, and Hollywood's Taverna Opa; City Cellar Wine Bar and Grill; and Cheesecake Factory. Best of all is the Muvico Parisian, a 20-screen movie theater where you can wine and dine while watching a feature.

WHERE TO STAY

The island of Palm Beach is the epitome of *Lifestyles of the Rich and Famous,* oozing with glitz, glamour, and the occasional scandal. Royalty and celebrities come to winter here, and there are plenty of lavishly priced options to accommodate them. Happily, there are also a few special inns that offer reasonably priced rooms in elegant settings. But most of the more modest places to lay your straw hat surround the island.

A few of the larger hotel chains operating in Palm Beach include the **Palm Beach Marriott/Fairfield Inn and Suites,** 2870 S. Ocean Blvd. (© **800/228-2800** or 561/582-2581), across the street from the beach. Also beachside is the pricey **Ocean Club Beach Resort,** formerly known as the Palm Beach Hilton, 2842 S. Ocean Blvd. (© **561/586-6542**). An excellent and affordable alternative right in the middle of Palm Beach's commercial section is a condominium that operates as a hotel, too: the **Palm Beach Hotel and Condominium,** 235 Sunrise Ave., between County Road and Bradley Place, across the street from the Publix supermarket (© **561/655-4586**). With prices starting at about $120 in the off season and $200 during season, this clean and comfortable place for accommodations is a great option for those looking for the rare bargain in Palm Beach.

In West Palm Beach, chain hotels are mostly on the main arteries close to the highways and a short drive from downtown. They include **Best Western,** 1800 Palm Beach Lakes Blvd. (© **800/331-9569** or 561/683-8810), and, just down the road, **Comfort Inn,** 1901 Palm Beach Lakes Blvd. (© **800/221-2222** or 561/689-6100). Farther south is **Parkview Motor Lodge,** 4710 S. Dixie Hwy., just south of Southern Boulevard (© **561/833-4644;** www.parkviewmotorlodge.com). This 28-room motel is the best of many along Dixie Highway (U.S. 1). With rates starting at about $75 for a room with TV, air-conditioning, and phone (don't laugh; some don't have any), you can't ask for more.

For other options, contact **Palm Beach Accommodations** (© 800/543-SWIM).

VERY EXPENSIVE

Brazilian Court ☆☆☆ This elegant, old-world, Mediterranean-style hotel dates from the 1920s and almost looks like a Beverly Hills bungalow. No two rooms are the same as far as decor, but all are elegant and luxurious, with mahogany crown molding, Provence-style wood shutters, imported fabrics, and stunning bathrooms adorned in limestone with Ultra Air Jet tubs and frameless shower enclosures. Service is doting, though a bit aloof—you won't always be received by smiling faces, but you will get whatever you want. There's even room service exclusively for pets (you know the type: held hostage in Mummy's Gucci bag). A large hotel by Palm Beach standards (The Breakers notwithstanding), Brazilian Court sprawls over half a block and features fountains and private courtyards. Celebrity stylist Frederick Fekkai offers the hotel's premier salon and spa. With the addition of renowned Chef Daniel Boulud's hauter-than-thou Café Boulud (which provides stellar 24-hr. room service), Brazilian Court is Palm Beach's number-one place to see and be seen.

301 Australian Ave., Palm Beach, FL 33480. (© **800/552-0335** or 561/655-7740. Fax 561/655-0801. www.the braziliancourt.com. 80 units. From $550 studio, from $950 1-bedroom suite, from $1,145 2-bedroom suite. Special packages available. AE, DC, DISC, MC, V. **Amenities:** Restaurant; private dining room (up to 12); heated outdoor pool; exercise room; spa treatments; concierge; salon; 24-hr. room service; library. *In room:* A/C, TV, Wi-Fi, minibar, coffeemaker, hair dryer, iron.

The Breakers (Kids) This 140-acre beachfront hotel is quintessential Palm Beach, where old money mixes with new money, and the Old World gives way, albeit reluctantly, to a bit of modernity. The seven-story building is a marvel, with a frescoed lobby and long, palatial hallways. Plush rooms feature huge bathrooms and views of the ocean or the magnificently manicured grounds. The oceanfront spa and beach club features four pools, cabanas, and saunas. Spa treatments fill a 16-page book! A revamp of Florida's oldest existing golf course transformed the Ocean Course into a 6,200-yard, championship-level par-70. Kids aren't neglected either at the impressive Family Entertainment Center, a 6,160-square-foot space filled with the latest in high tech toys and games. A $15-million beachfront redevelopment project resulted in stunning landscaping and bungalows available for rent. There's also a free-form pool catering to families, as well as a relaxation pool for peace and quiet. All five restaurants are fantastic, but don't miss the remarkable Sunday brunch.

If you can afford it, the **Flagler Club** is the Breakers' exclusive, hyperluxe hotel within a hotel, featuring private entry, 28 rooms, butlers, concierges, and doting service, as well as tea, cocktails, hors d'oeuvres, and desserts all day and night. The club area is under renovation through October 2008, and prices are typically $100 a night above the Deluxe level suites.

1 S. County Rd., Palm Beach, FL 33480. (© **800/833-3141**, 888/BREAKERS, or 561/655-6611. Fax 561/659-8403. www.thebreakers.com. 560 units. Winter $470–$685 double, $710–$4,500 suite; off season $375–$460 double, $500–$1,980 suite. Special packages available. AE, DC, DISC, MC, V. Valet parking $17. From I-95, exit Okeechobee Blvd. E., head east to S. County Rd., and turn left. **Amenities:** 5 restaurants; 3 bars; 4 outdoor pools; golf course; 14 tennis courts; health club; spa; croquet; shuffleboard; beach volleyball courts; watersports equipment (including scuba and sailing); bike rental; children's programs; game rooms; concierge; business center; shopping arcade; salon; 24-hr. room service; in-room massage; babysitting; laundry service; dry cleaning. *In room:* A/C, TV, CD player, PlayStation, dataport, minibar, hair dryer, iron.

Four Seasons Resort Palm Beach (Kids) Situated on the pristine Palm Beach oceanfront, Four Seasons is a quiet retreat from Worth Avenue—a pricey cab ride from the hotel. Guest rooms are spacious, with private balconies and lavish bathrooms. The full-service spa is excellent and brand new at 9,000 square feet, featuring nine treatment rooms including a "Man Room," a wet room, spa suite, and full-service salon. The main dining room, known simply as The Restaurant, features the Southeastern regional cuisine of Executive Chef Hubert Des Marais. Two other less-formal restaurants, The Ocean Bistro—which is subpar for this kind of hotel—and The Atlantic Bar & Grill, round out the dining options. The resort offers a complimentary kids program, and teens will enjoy the game room with Xbox, a pool table, and a large-screen TV. Meanwhile, parents can entertain themselves in The Living Room, a swank lounge featuring live jazz on weekends.

2800 S. Ocean Blvd., Palm Beach, FL 33480. (© **800/432-2335** or 561/582-2800. Fax 561/547-1557. www.fourseasons. com/palmbeach. 210 units. Winter $429–$745 double, from $2,150 (1-bedroom suite) and $3,850 (2-bedroom suite). Off season (starting June 2008) $299–$599 double, $1,250 (1-bedroom suite) and $3,050 (2-bedroom suite). AE, DC, DISC, MC, V. Valet parking $23. From I-95, take the 6th Ave. exit east and turn left onto Dixie Hwy. Turn east onto Lake

Ave. and north onto A1A (S. Ocean Blvd.); the resort is just ahead on your right. Pets less than 20 lb. accepted. **Amenities:** 3 restaurants; lounge/outdoor patio; outdoor heated pool and whirlpool; 2 tennis courts; spa and fitness center; watersports equipment rentals; complimentary children's programs; multilingual concierge; business center; salon; 24-hr. room service; twice-daily housekeeping service; in-room massage; babysitting; laundry service; dry cleaning; complimentary overnight shoeshine; physician on call. *In room:* A/C, TV/VCR/DVD, LCD TVs, CD/MP3 player, high-speed Internet access, minibar, fridge, hair dryer, iron, safe, robe.

The Ritz-Carlton Palm Beach ⭐⭐⭐ *Kids*   If the Breakers is too mammoth for your taste, consider the Ritz. A lot warmer than the Four Seasons, The Ritz, located on a beautiful beach in a tiny town about 8 miles from Worth Avenue, lacks pretension. A $60-million renovation in March 2007 added flatscreen TVs, bedside electronic control panels, new mahogany furniture, and sleeper sofas in guest rooms and suites. New oceanfront suites have invisible televisions hidden behind mirrors, only visible when turned on. For those who can't stay off their cellphones, the hotel has also enhanced its previously paltry cellular reception. A new pool is hidden in a courtyard area and is ideal for relaxation; the 28,000-square-foot Grand Spa has koi and lily ponds. The specialty restaurant, Angle, is open for dinner only; a casual oceanfront restaurant called Temple Orange features contemporary American fare with fresh seafood. There's also Breeze, a poolside cafe and bar.

100 S. Ocean Blvd., Manalapan, FL 33462. ⓒ **800/241-3333** or 561/533-6000. Fax 561/588-4202. www. ritzcarlton.com. 284 units. Winter $539–$1,039 double, $1,739–$4,500 suite, $6,000 presidential suite; off season $239–$489 double, $599–$3,000 suite, $4,000 presidential suite. AE, DISC, MC, V. Valet parking $25. From I-95, take exit for Lantana Rd., heading east. After 1 mile, turn right onto Federal Hwy. (U.S. 1- Dixie). Continue south to the next light and turn left onto Ocean Ave. Cross the Intracoastal Waterway and turn right onto Fla. A1A. **Amenities:** 4 restaurants; bar; 2 outdoor pools; Boutique Spa and Fitness; Jacuzzi; watersports; equipment rental; bike rental; children's center/programs; teen's center/programs; concierge; business center; salon; 24-hr. room service; in-room massage; laundry service; dry cleaning. *In room:* A/C, flatscreen TV, Wi-Fi, minibar, hair dryer, iron, laptop-friendly safe.

EXPENSIVE

Chesterfield Hotel ⭐⭐⭐   Reminiscent of an English country manor, the Chesterfield in all its flowery, Laura Ashley–inspired glory is a magnificent, charming hotel with exceptional service. Warm and inviting, the Chesterfield is one of the only places in South Florida where the idea of a fireplace (there's one in the hotel's library) doesn't seem ridiculous. Traditional English tea is served every afternoon, including fresh-baked scones, petit fours, and sandwiches. Rooms are decorated with antiques and with bright fabrics and wallpaper. The roomy marble bathrooms are stocked with an array of luxurious toiletries. A small heated pool and courtyard are nice, and the beach is only 3 blocks away, but the real action is inside: The hotel's retro-elegant Leopard Lounge (p. 353) serves decent Continental cuisine, but is better as a late-night hangout for live music, schmoozing, and staring at the local cognoscenti.

363 Cocoanut Row, Palm Beach, FL 33480. ⓒ **800/243-7871** or 561/659-5800. Fax 561/659-6707. www.chester fieldpb.com. 52 units. Winter $395–$465 queen, $495–$570 king, $675–$1,585 suite; off season $175–$249 queen, $259–$319 king, $339–$719 suite. Rollaway bed $15. Packages available. AE, DC, DISC, MC, V. Free valet parking. From I-95, exit onto Okeechobee Blvd. E., cross the Intracoastal Waterway, and turn right onto Cocoanut Row. **Amenities:** Restaurant; lounge; heated pool and hot tub spa; access to nearby health club; concierge; business center; 24-hr. room service; in-room massage; dry cleaning; Wi-Fi access; library. *In room:* Individual A/C/heat, flat-panel TV, high-speed DSL Internet connection, digital alarm w/CD, hair dryer, iron, safe marble bath,. Kings/suites feature refrigerator and entertainment center with DVD/CD.

MODERATE

The Colony ⭐⭐   The sign outside this Palm Beach mainstay should read ROXANNE PULITZER SLEPT HERE. She did, actually, for quite a while after her 7-week marriage went bust. For years, the Colony has been a favorite hangout—hideout, perhaps—for old-timers, socialites, and mysterious luminaries. Beyond that, this Georgian-style hotel is known for its attentive staff, floral-decorated guest rooms, and, unfortunately, really small bathrooms. The 39 suites and apartments, not to mention the seven two-bedroom villas with Jacuzzis, are much more lavish—and lavishly priced.

155 Hammon Ave., Palm Beach, FL 33480. C 800/521-5525 or 561/655-5430. Fax 561/659-8104. www.thecolony palmbeach.com. 92 units. Winter $300–$525 double, $395–$700 suite, $20,000 per month villa; off season $180–$195 double, $225–$295 suite, $5,000–$9,000 per month villa. AE, DC, MC, V. From I-95, exit onto Okeechobee Blvd. E. and cross the Intracoastal Waterway. Turn right on S. County Rd. and then left onto Hammon Ave. **Amenities:** Restaurant; bar; heated Florida-shaped pool; spa; concierge; limited seasonal room service. *In room:* A/C, TV, dataport, hair dryer, iron.

Palm Beach Historic Inn &&   Built in 1923, the Palm Beach Historic Inn is an area landmark within a block's walking distance of the beach (chairs and towels are provided for guests of the hotel), Worth Avenue, and several good restaurants. The small lobby is filled with antiques, books, magazines, and an old-fashioned umbrella stand, all of which add to the homey feel of this intimate B&B. In-room wine, fruit, snacks, tea, and cookies ensure that you won't go hungry—never mind the excellent continental breakfast that is brought to you daily. All bedrooms are uniquely decorated and have hardwood floors, down comforters, Egyptian-cotton linens, fluffy bathrobes, and plenty of good-smelling toiletries. Here you'll find a casual elegance that's comfortable for everyone. In addition, a baby grand piano and guitars for the musically inclined, as well as videotapes to keep the kids entertained, have been added to the hotel's amenities. *Note:* Smoking is not permitted.

365 S. County Rd., Palm Beach, FL 33480. C 561/832-4009. Fax 561/832-6255. www.palmbeachhistoricinn.com. 13 units. Winter $185–$345 double, $345–$395 suite; off season $145–$175 double, $225 suite. Rates include continental breakfast. Children stay free in parent's room. AE, MC, V. Small pets accepted. *In room:* A/C, TV/VCR, fridge, hair dryer, iron.

INEXPENSIVE

Hibiscus House && *Finds*   Inexpensive bed-and-breakfasts are rare in southeast Florida, making the Hibiscus House, one of the area's firsts, a true find. Located a few miles from the coast in a quiet residential neighborhood, this 1920s-era B&B is filled with handsome antiques and tapestries. Every room has a private terrace or balcony. The Red Room has a fabulous bathroom with Jacuzzi. The peaceful backyard retreat has been transformed into a tropical garden, with a heated pool and lounge chairs. There are pretty indoor areas for guests to enjoy; one little sitting room is wrapped in glass and is stocked with playing cards and board games. Huge gourmet breakfast portions are as filling as they are beautiful. Make any special requests in advance; owners Raleigh Hill and Colin Rayer will be happy to oblige.

501 30th St., West Palm Beach, FL 33407. C 800/203-4927 or 561/863-5633. Fax 561/863-5633. www.hibiscus house.com. 8 units. Winter $125–$210 double; off season $100–$150 double. Rates include breakfast. AE, DC, DISC, MC, V. From I-95, exit onto Palm Beach Lakes Blvd. E. and continue 4 miles. Turn left onto Flagler Dr. and continue for about ½-mile; then turn left onto 30th St. Pets accepted. **Amenities:** Heated pool; concierge. *In room:* A/C, TV, hair dryer.

Hotel Biba && *Finds*   Located in the historic El Cid neighborhood, just 1 mile from City Place and Clematis Street, the very cool Biba answers the call for an inexpensive, chic hotel that young hipsters can call their own. Housed in a renovated Colonial-style 1940s motor lodge, Biba has been remarkably updated by de rigueur designer Barbara Hulanicki and features a sleek lobby with the hip hotel bar, gorgeously landscaped outdoor pool area with Asian gardens, and a reflection pond. Guest rooms are shabby chic, with private patios, mosaic-tile floors, custom-made mahogany furniture, Egyptian-cotton linens, down pillows, and high-tech amenities. The bold color schemes mix nicely with the high-fashion crowd that convenes here. *A word of advice:* This place is not exactly soundproof. Rooms may be cloistered by fence and gardens, but they're still extremely close to a major thoroughfare. Ask for a room that's on the quieter Belvedere Road, as opposed to those facing South Olive Avenue.

320 Belvedere Rd., West Palm Beach, FL 33405. ℭ 561/832-0094. Fax 561/833-7848. www.hotelbiba.com. 41 units. $110–$215 double; $200–$300 suite. Rates include complimentary breakfast and are cheaper on the hotel's website. AE, MC, V. **Amenities:** Lounge; outdoor pool; concierge. *In room:* A/C, TV, CD player, free wireless Internet, hair dryer.

WHERE TO DINE

Palm Beach has some of the area's swankiest restaurants. Thanks to the development of downtown West Palm Beach, however, there is also a great selection of trendier, less expensive spots. Dress here is slightly more formal than in most other areas of Florida: Men wear blazers, and women generally put on modest dresses or chic suits when they dine out, even on the oppressively hot days of summer.

VERY EXPENSIVE

Café Boulud 𝕮𝕮𝕮 FRENCH   Snowbird socialites rejoiced over the opening of star chef Daniel Boulud's eponymous restaurant in the Brazilian Court hotel. Nonsocialites said, "Figures, another restaurant where we can't afford even a bread crumb." If you're out to splurge, Boulud is ideal, with an exquisite menu divided into four sections—La Tradition (French and American classics), La Saison (seasonal dishes), Le Potager (dishes inspired by the vegetable market), and Le Voyage (world cuisine). The roasted barramundi with squash, pomegranate, and brown butter is superb. There's also a light menu offering salads, sandwiches, and even a cheeseburger if you prefer—try the chick pea fries with piquillo pepper ketchup. If star chefs, stuffy socialites, and froufrou cuisine aren't your thing, don't even bother.

In the Brazilian Court, 301 Australian Ave., Palm Beach. ℭ 561/655-6060. www.danielnyc.com. Reservations essential. Main courses $16–$46. AE, DC, MC, V. Daily 9am–10pm.

Cafe l'Europe 𝕮𝕮𝕮 CONTINENTAL   One of Palm Beach's finest and most popular spots, this award-winning, romantic, and formal restaurant gives you a good reason to get dressed up. The enticing appetizers served by a superb staff might include Chinese spring rolls, baked-goat-cheese salad with raspberry-walnut dressing, poached salmon, or chilled gazpacho with avocado. Main courses run the gamut from sautéed potato-crusted Florida snapper to roasted rack of lamb. Seafood dishes and steaks in sumptuous but light sauces are always exceptional.

331 S. County Rd. (at Brazilian Ave.), Palm Beach. ℭ 561/655-4020. www.cafeleurope.com. Reservations recommended. Main courses $29–$40. AE, DC, DISC, MC, V. Tues–Sat noon–3pm and 6–10pm; Sun 6–10pm.

Echo 𝕮𝕮𝕮 ASIAN   This hyperstylish, sleek eatery is The Breakers hotel's homage to young and hip. The hotel runs the restaurant even though it's off premises, and it's worth leaving the comfy, upper-crust confines of The Breakers for this resounding Echo. The menu is broken down into categories: Earth, Wind, Fire, Water, and Flavor, which doesn't do the food any real justice. Sushi bar specialties such as the hamachi kama, grilled hamachi, Asian greens and citrus soy, and the outstanding "echo roll" with shrimp tempura, cucumber, avocado, and tobiko in a sesame soy sheet with superspicy sriacha sauce are two of my favorites. But it's not all sushi. There are Chinese dim sum specialties, too. The dim sum sampler at $26 feeds two and is an ideal starter or full-blown meal. Then there's the Thai roast duck, and the open-flame wok specialties. There's too much to choose from, but it's all good. Be sure to check out the restaurant's Dragonfly Lounge after dinner. It's a hopping scene, especially by Palm Beach standards.

230 Sunrise Ave., Palm Beach. (C) 561/802-4222. www.echopalmbeach.com. Reservations essential. Main courses $25–$50. AE, DC, MC, V. Tues–Sun 5:30–9:30pm.

Mark's City Place 🏵🏵🏵 NEW AMERICAN Star chef Mark Militello of Mark's Las Olas and South Beach has landed at West Palm's bustling entertainment-and-dining complex to the delight of foodies in Palm Beach. Wood-burning ovens churn out Militello's specialty pizzas, trendy versions of the thin-crusted classic with toppings such as shrimp, pesto, fontina cheese, and sun-dried tomatoes. The sushi bar here is, frankly, out of place. Focus on entrees that range from risotto with wild mushroom and truffle oil to a seared, black peppercorn–crusted yellowfin tuna. For dessert, try the double-chocolate bread pudding with white-chocolate-chip ice cream.

700 S. Rosemary Ave., West Palm Beach. (C) 561/514-0770. www.chefmark.com. Reservations recommended. Main courses $17–$38. AE, DC, MC, V. Mon–Thurs 5–11pm; Fri–Sat 5pm–midnight; Sun 5–10:30pm.

Rosa Mexicano 🏵🏵🏵 MEXICAN A gourmet Mexican chain hailing from New York, Rosa Mexicano is not your typical trip across the border. A booming salsa-and-tequila-spiked scene can be found here, as young hipsters convene at the trendy bar and foodies marvel over the Mexican fare. The food is as full of flavor as the lively crowd. Guacamole is made tableside and it's quite a show, as enthusiastic servers truly aim to please. Try the grilled skirt steak and jumbo shrimp served in a roasted tomato-chipotle sauce, or just order traditional enchiladas with gourmet sauces such as the mestizas—roasted tomatillos, tomatoes, and chipotles blended to create a rich smoky sauce, just like the scene here.

11708 Lake Victoria Gardens Ave. (Downtown at the Gardens), Palm Beach Gardens. (C) 561/625-3120. www.rosamexicano.com. Reservations recommended. Main courses $7–$24. AE, DC, MC, V. Mon–Wed 11am–10pm; Thurs 11am–4pm; Fri 11am–11:30pm; Sat 4–11:30pm; Sun 4–10pm.

The Strip House 🏵🏵🏵 STEAKHOUSE Yet another New York–based steakhouse has opened in Palm Beach County and, like the others (Old Homestead), this one has opened to rave reviews. The a la carte menu offers impressive porterhouses, but according to some diners, even more impressive are the photos of exotic dancers (hence the restaurant's name), which line the walls. It's a bit of camp with your meat, especially with the bordello-red booths, but that's okay, because once you start slicing into the perfectly prepared steaks here, all memories of scantily clad women as wallpaper may remain just that—scant.

11708 Lake Victoria Gardens Ave. (Downtown at the Gardens), Palm Beach Gardens. (C) 561/296-4900. www.theglaziergroup.com. Reservations recommended. Main courses $15–$46 AE, DC, MC, V. Mon–Wed 11am–10pm; Thurs 11am–4pm; Fri 11am–11:30pm; Sat 4–11:30pm; Sun 4–10pm.

EXPENSIVE

Amici 🏵 *Overrated* ITALIAN This is one of those restaurants whose scene is tastier than its cuisine. An upper-crusty Palm Beach set convenes here and consistently raves about above-average, overpriced Italian food. The best item on the menu is gnocchi with white truffle oil, fontina cheese, and spinach. Everything else is fairly standard: grilled sandwiches, pastas with rustic sauces, pizzas, grilled shrimp, and fish. Despite its less-than-stellar food, Amici is always crowded and very noisy.

288 S. County Rd. (at Royal Palm Way), Palm Beach. ℂ 561/832-0201. www.amicipalmbeach.com. Reservations strongly recommended on weekends. Main courses $26–$44; pizzas $14–$18. AE, DC, MC, V. Mon–Thurs 11:30am–3pm and 5:30–10:30pm; Fri–Sat 11:30am–3pm and 5:30–11pm; Sun 5:30–10:30pm.

Bice Restaurant ☙☙ NORTHERN ITALIAN   Bice's cuisine far surpasses that of Amici's, but as far as atmosphere, the air in here is a bit haughty, bordering on rude. Servers and diners alike have attitudes, but you'll forget all that with one bite of the juicy veal cutlet with tomato salad or the *pasta e fagioli* (pasta with beans).

313½ Worth Ave., Palm Beach. ℂ 561/835-1600. Reservations essential. Main courses $20–$40. AE, DC, MC, V. Daily noon–10pm.

MODERATE

City Cellar ☙☙ AMERICAN   If the Palm Beach–proper dining scene is too stuffy, head over to City Place to find this yuppie brick-and-pressed-tin enclave where people-watching is at a premium. Despite its all-American appearance, City Cellar offers a varied menu, from pizzas and pastas to steak and sea bass. We love the onion and mushroom soup with Pinot Grigio and the twin 7-ounce pork chops with potato puree, sweet and sour shallots, and a sherry mustard butter. The place is mobbed on weekends, so plan for a long wait that's best spent at the action-packed bar.

700 S. Rosemary Ave., West Palm Beach. ℂ 561/659-1853. Reservations suggested. Main courses $11–$32. AE, MC, V. Restaurant Sun–Wed 11:30am–10:30pm; Thurs–Sat 11:30am–11 pm. Bar Sun–Wed 11:30am–1am; Thurs–Sat 11:30am–2am.

Rhythm Café ☙ Finds ECLECTIC AMERICAN   This funky hole-in-the-wall is where those in the know come to eat some of West Palm Beach's most laid-back gourmet food. On the handwritten, photocopied menu (which changes daily), you'll always find a fish specialty accompanied by a hefty dose of greens and garnishes. Reliably outstanding is the pork tenderloin with mango chutney. Salads and soups are a great bargain, since portions are relatively large. The kitschy decor of this tiny cafe comes complete with vinyl tablecloths and a changing display of paintings by local amateurs. Young, handsome waiters are attentive, but not solicitous. The old drugstore where the restaurant recently relocated features an original 1950s lunch counter and stools.

3800 S. Dixie Hwy., West Palm Beach. ℂ 561/833-3406. www.rhythmcafe.cc. Reservations recommended on weekends. Main courses $13–$24. AE, DISC, MC, V. Tues–Sat 6–10pm; Sun (Dec–Mar) 5:30–9pm. Closed in early Sept. From I-95, exit east on Southern Blvd. Go 1 block north of Southern Blvd.; restaurant is on the right.

INEXPENSIVE

Green's Pharmacy ☙ Value AMERICAN   This neighborhood pharmacy offers one of the best meal deals in Palm Beach. Both breakfast and lunch are served coffee-shop style, either at a Formica bar or at tables on a black-and-white checkerboard floor. Breakfast specials include eggs and omelets served with home fries and bacon, sausage, or corned-beef hash. The grill serves burgers and sandwiches, as well as ice-cream sodas and milkshakes, to a loyal crowd of pastel-clad Palm Beachers.

151 N. County Rd., Palm Beach. ℂ 561/832-0304. Fax 561/832-6502. Breakfast $2–$6; burgers and sandwiches $3–$8; soups and salads $2–$8. AE, DISC, MC, V. Mon–Sat 7am–5pm; Sun 7am–3pm.

John G's ☙ AMERICAN   This coffee shop is the most popular in the county. For decades, John G's has been attracting huge breakfast crowds; lines run out the door (on weekends, all the way down the block). Stop in for good, greasy-spoon food served in heaping portions right on the beachfront. This place is known for fresh and tasty fish and chips, and its selection of creative omelets and grill specials.

10 S. Ocean Blvd., Lake Worth. © 561/585-9860. www.johngs.com. Reservations not accepted. Breakfast $3–$10; lunch $4–$15. No credit cards. Daily 7am–3pm. From the Florida Tpk., take the Lake Worth exit and head toward the ocean.

Tom's Place for Ribs *(Finds* BARBECUE   There are two important factors in a successful barbecue: the cooking and the sauce. Tom and Helen Wright's no-nonsense shack wins on both counts, offering flawlessly grilled meats paired with well-spiced sauces. Beef, chicken, pork, and fish are served soul-food style, with corn bread and your choice of sides such as rice with gravy, collard greens, black-eyed peas, coleslaw, or mashed potatoes. There's another very popular branch of Tom's in Boca Raton at 7251 N. Federal Hwy. (© **561/997-0920**).

1725 Palm Beach Lakes Blvd., West Palm Beach. © **561/832 8774.** Reservations not accepted. Main courses $8–$15; sandwiches $5–$6. AE, MC, V. Tues–Thurs 11:30am–10:30pm; Fri 11:30am–10pm; Sat noon–10pm.

THE PALM BEACHES AFTER DARK
THE BAR, CAFE & MUSIC SCENE

A decade-old project to revitalize downtown West Palm Beach has finally become a reality, with **Clematis Street** at its heart. Artists' lofts, sidewalk cafes, bars, restaurants, consignment shops, and galleries dot the street from Flagler Drive to Rosemary Avenue, creating a hot spot for a night out, especially on weekends, when yuppies mingle with stylish Euros and disheveled artists. Every Thursday night is a mob scene of 20- and 30-somethings who come out for "Clematis by Night." Each week features a different rock, blues, or reggae band, plus an art show. Vendors sell food and drinks, and the street's bars and restaurants are packed. Most of the nightspots listed below are open until about 3 or 4am. Check out www.clematisbynight.net for events and club information.

Over the bridge, it's a completely different world. Palm Beach is much quieter and better known for its rather private society balls and estate parties. With the exception of some restaurants that are more of a scene (such as **Amici,** described above, or **Taboo,** reviewed below), Palm Beach nightlife is more likely to entail sipping port at one of the finer hotels such as The Breakers, Colony, Ritz-Carlton, Four Seasons, or Chesterfield.

West Palm Beach
E. R. Bradley's   What used to be a swank saloon on the island of Palm Beach is now a friendly, very casual indoor/outdoor bar in downtown West Palm, attracting a mixed crowd. The later-night bar scene is a real draw. If you're hungry, try the "crab bomb," Maryland lump crabmeat baked in a light cream sauce with steamed vegetables. Open Sunday through Wednesday from 8am to 3am, Thursday through Saturday from 8am to 4am. 104 Clematis St. © 561/833-3520.

Respectable Street Café   This is one of the premier live-music venues in South Florida. In addition to the requisite DJs, the grungy bar features a lineup of alternative-music acts. The plain storefront exterior belies a funky, high-ceilinged interior, decorated with large black booths, psychedelic wall murals, and a checkerboard-tile dance floor. Open Wednesday and Thursday from 9pm to 3am, Friday and Saturday from 9pm to 4am. 518 Clematis St. © 561/832-9999. Cover $5–$20.

Palm Beach
Leopard Lounge *(Finds*   *The Flintstones* meets *Dynasty* at this spotty lounge in the Chesterfield Hotel, in which the carpeting, tablecloths, and waitstaff's waistcoats are

all in leopard print. There's live music every night, ranging from Cole Porter to swing. The crowd's a bit older, but younger couples and a celebrity or two often find their way here, which makes for an amusing scene. Open daily from 6pm to 1:30am. 363 Cocoanut Row. ℂ 561/659-5800.

Ta-boo   Ta-boo is reminiscent of an upscale TGI Friday's (with food that's about on the same level). It caters to a well-heeled crowd, with lots of greenery, a fireplace, and a somewhat cheesy Southwestern decor. But make no mistake, Ta-boo is not about the food: This stellar after-dinner spot is where bejeweled socialites spill out of fancy cars to salsa and show off their best Swarovski jewelry. Find someplace else to eat first. Open Sunday through Thursday from 11:30am to 10pm, and Friday and Saturday from 11:30am to 11pm. 221 Worth Ave., Palm Beach. ℂ 561/835-3500.

THE PERFORMING ARTS
With a number of dedicated patrons and enthusiastic supporters of the arts, this area happily boasts many good venues for those craving culture. Check the *Palm Beach Post* or the *Palm Beach Daily News* for up-to-date listings and reviews.

The **Raymond F. Kravis Center for the Performing Arts,** 701 Okeechobee Blvd., West Palm Beach (ℂ **561/832-7469;** www.kravis.org), is the area's largest and most active performance space. With a huge curved-glass facade and more than 2,500 seats in two lushly decorated indoor spaces, plus a new outdoor amphitheater, the Kravis stages more than 300 performances each year. Phone or check the website for a current schedule of Palm Beach's best music, dance, and theater.

4 Jupiter ⋆ & Northern Palm Beach County ⋆

20 miles N. of Palm Beach, 81 miles N. of Miami, 60 miles N. of Fort Lauderdale

While Burt Reynolds is Jupiter's hometown hero (and Celine Dion just built a sprawling manse here, too), the stars of quaint Jupiter are its beautiful beaches. In the spring, you can also catch the St. Louis Cardinals during their spring-training season. North Palm Beach County's other towns—Tequesta, Juno Beach, North Palm Beach, Palm Beach Gardens, and Singer Island—invite tourists who want to enjoy the outdoor activities that make this area so popular with retirees, seasonal residents, and families.

ESSENTIALS
GETTING THERE   The quickest route from West Palm Beach to Jupiter is on the Florida Turnpike or the sometimes-congested I-95. You can also take a slower but more scenic coastal route, U.S. 1 or Florida A1A. Since Jupiter is so close to Palm Beach, it's easy to fly into **Palm Beach International Airport** (ℂ **561/471-7420**) and rent a car there. The drive should take less than half an hour.

VISITOR INFORMATION   A **visitor center** between I-95 and the Florida Turnpike at 8020 Indiantown Rd., Jupiter (ℂ **561/575-4636;** www.jupiterfloridausa. com), is open Monday through Friday from 8:30am to 5:30pm.

BEACHES, OUTDOOR ACTIVITIES & SPECTATOR SPORTS
BASEBALL   The **Roger Dean Stadium,** 4751 Main St. (ℂ **561/775-1818**), hosts spring training for the St. Louis Cardinals, along with minor-league action from Florida's state league, the Hammerheads. Tickets range in price from $8 to $20. Call for schedules and information.

BEACHES   The farther north you head from populated Palm Beach, the more peaceful and pristine the coast becomes. Just a few miles north of the bustle, castles and condominiums give way to wide-open space and public parkland. There are dozens of recommendable spots. The following are a few of the best.

John D. MacArthur Beach is a spectacular beach that preserves the subtropical coastal habitat that once covered southeast Florida. This state park has a remarkable 4,000-square-foot Nature Center with exhibits, displays, and a video interpreting the barrier island's plant and animal communities. Dominating a large portion of Singer Island, the barrier island just north of Palm Beach, this beach has frontage on both the Atlantic Ocean and Lake Worth Cove. It's great for hiking, swimming, and sunning. Restrooms and showers are available. To reach the park from the mainland, cross the Intracoastal Waterway on Blue Heron Boulevard and turn north on Ocean Boulevard.

Jupiter Inlet meets the ocean at **Dubois Park,** a 29-acre beach that's popular with families. The shallow waters and sandy shore are perfect for kids, while adults can play in the rougher swells of the inlet where there are lifeguards. A footbridge leads to **Ocean Beach,** an area popular with windsurfers and surfers. There's a short fishing pier and plenty of shaded barbecue grills and picnic tables. Explore the Dubois Pioneer Home, situated atop a shell mound built by the Jaega Indians. The home was built of cypress in 1898 by Harry Dubois, a citrus worker, as a wedding gift to his wife, Susan, whose pictures are still in the house. The butter churn, the pump sewing machine in the living room, and the dining room and bedroom are straight out of *Little House on the Prairie.* The park entrance is on Dubois Road, about a mile south of the junction of U.S. 1 and Florida A1A.

BIKING   Bike enthusiasts will enjoy exploring this flat and uncluttered area. North Palm Beach has hundreds of miles of smooth, paved roads. Loggerhead Park in Juno Beach and Florida A1A along the ocean also have great trails for starters. You'll find many more scenic routes over the bridges and west of the highway. Rent a bike at **Jupiter Outdoor Center,** 18095 Coastal A1A, in Jupiter (© **561/747-9666**).

CANOEING   You can rent a boat at several outlets throughout northern Palm Beach County, including **Canoe Outfitters,** 9060 W. Indiantown Rd. (west of I-95), in North Jupiter (© **561/746-7053;** www.canoes-kayaks-florida.com), which provides access to one of the area's most beautiful natural waterways. Canoers start at Riverbend Park along an 8-mile stretch of Intracoastal Waterway, where the lush foliage supports dozens of exotic birds and reptiles. Keep your eyes open for gators, who love to sunbathe on the shallow shores of the river. You'll end up, exhausted, at Jonathan Dickinson Park about 5 or 6 hours later. A pamphlet describing local flora and fauna is available for $1. Trips run Thursday through Monday and cost $50 for two people in a double canoe. Guided trips are also available for $45 per person.

FISHING   Before you leave, order an information-packed fishing kit with details on fish camps, charters, and tournament and tide schedules; it's distributed by the **West Palm Beach Fishing Club** (© **561/832-6780**). The cost is $10 and well worth it. Allow at least 4 weeks for delivery.

In town, several outfitters along U.S. 1 and Florida A1A rent vessels and equipment if your hotel doesn't. One of the most complete facilities is **Sailfish Marina & Resort,** 98 Lake Dr. (off Blue Heron Blvd.), Palm Beach Shores (© **561/844-1724**). Call for equipment, bait, guided trips, or boat rentals.

Discovering a Remarkable Natural World

North Palm Beach is well known for the giant sea turtles that lay their eggs on the county's beaches from May to August. These endangered marine animals return here annually, from as far away as South America, to lay their clutches of about 115 eggs each. Nurtured by the warm sand, but targeted by birds and other predators, only about one or two babies from each nest survives to maturity.

Many environmentalists recommend that visitors take part in an organized turtle-watching program (rather than go on their own), to minimize disturbance to the turtles. **Jupiter Beach Resort** (p. 358) sponsors free guided expeditions to the egg-laying sites from May to August (call to reserve), as does the Marinelife Center of Juno Beach.

Located just south of Jupiter is the **Marinelife Center of Juno Beach,** Loggerhead Park, 14200 U.S. 1, in Juno Beach (℗ **561/627-8280**). Combining a science museum and nature trail, this small center is dedicated to the coastal ecology of northern Palm Beach County. Hands-on exhibits teach visitors about wetlands and beach areas, as well as offshore coral reefs and local sea life. Visitors are encouraged to walk the center's sand-dune nature trails, all of which are marked with interpretive signs. This is one place where you're guaranteed to see live sea turtles year-round. During the peak of breeding season (June–July), the center conducts narrative walks along a nearby beach; reservations are a must. The booking list opens on May 1 and is usually full by midmonth. Admission to the center is free, though donations are accepted. Open Monday through Saturday from 10am to 4pm, and Sunday from noon to 3pm.

GOLF   Even if you're not lucky enough to be staying at the **PGA National Resort & Spa** (p. 358), you may still be able to play on its award-winning courses. If you or someone in your group is a member of another golf or country club, have the head pro write a note on club letterhead to Jackie Rogers at PGA to request a play date. Be sure the pro includes his PGA number and contact information. Allow at least 2 weeks for a response. Also ask about the Golf-A-Round program, in which selected private clubs open their doors to nonmembers for free or discounted rates. Contact the **Palm Beach County Convention and Visitors Bureau** (℗ **561/471-3995**) for details.

Dotting the area are plenty of other great courses, including the **Golf Club of Jupiter,** 1800 Central Blvd., Jupiter (℗ **561/747-6262**), where a well-respected 18-hole, par-70 course is situated on more than 6,200 yards of narrow fairways and fast greens. Fees range from $40–$70; they include a mandatory cart. The course borders I-95, so watch your swing.

HIKING   In an area that's not particularly known for extraordinary natural diversity, **Blowing Rocks Preserve** has a terrific hiking trail along a dramatic limestone outcropping. You won't find hills or scenic vistas, but you will see Florida's unique and varied tropical ecosystem. The well-marked, mile-long trail passes oceanfront dunes, mangrove wetlands, and a coastal hammock. The preserve, owned and managed by the Nature Conservancy, 574 South Beach Rd., Hobe Sound, FL 33455 (© 561/744-6668), also protects an important habitat for West Indian manatees and loggerhead turtles. Located along South Beach Drive (Fla. A1A), north of the Jupiter inlet, Blowing Rocks is about a 10-minute drive northeast of Jupiter. Free guided tours are available Friday at 1pm and Sunday at 11am; no reservations are necessary. From U.S. 1, head east on S.R. 707 and cross the Intracoastal Waterway to the park. Admission is $3 for adults and free for kids 12 and under.

SCUBA DIVING & SNORKELING   Year-round warm, clear waters make northern Palm Beach County great for both diving and snorkeling. The closest coral reef is a quarter-mile from shore and can be reached easily by boat. Three popular wrecks are clustered near one another, less than a mile offshore of the Lake Worth Inlet at about 90 feet. The best wreck, however, is the 16th- or 17th-century Spanish galleon discovered by lifeguard Peter Leo just off Jupiter Beach; any diving outfit off Jupiter Beach will take you there. If your hotel doesn't offer dive trips, call **South Florida Dive Headquarters,** 101 N. Riverside Dr., Pompano Beach (© 800/771-DIVE or 954/783-2299), or **Seafari Dive and Surf,** 75 E. Indiantown Rd., Suite 603, Jupiter (© 561/747-6115).

TENNIS   In addition to the many hotel tennis courts (see "Where to Stay," below), you can swing a racquet at a number of local clubs. The **Jupiter Bay Tennis Club,** 353 U.S. 1, Jupiter (© 561/744-9424; www.jupiterbaytennis.com), has seven clay courts (three lighted) and charges $16 per person per day. Reservations are highly recommended. More economical options are available at relatively well-maintained municipal courts. Call © 561/966-6600 for locations and hours. Many are available free on a first-come, first-served basis.

A HISTORIC LIGHTHOUSE

Jupiter Inlet Lighthouse &   Completed in 1860, this red brick structure is the oldest extant building in Palm Beach County. Still owned and maintained by the U.S. Coast Guard, the lighthouse is now home to a small historical museum, located at its base. The Florida History Museum sponsors tours of the lighthouse, enabling visitors to explore the cramped interior, which is filled with artifacts and photographs illustrating the rich history of the area. A 15-minute video explains the shipwrecks, Indian wars, and other events that helped shape this region. Helpful volunteers are eager to tell colorful stories to highlight the 1-hour tour.

500 S.R. 707, Jupiter. © 561/747-8380. www.lrhs.org Admission $7 adults, $5 children 6–18. Sat–Wed 10am–4pm (last tour departs at 3:15pm). Children must be 4 ft. or taller to climb. No open-backed shoes.

SHOPPING

Northern Palm Beach County may not have the glitzy boutiques of Worth Avenue, but it does have an impressive indoor mall, the **Gardens of the Palm Beaches,** 3101 PGA Blvd. (© 561/775-7750), where you can find department stores such as Bloomingdale's, Burdines, Macy's, and Saks Fifth Avenue, as well as more than 100 specialty shops. A large, diverse food court and fine sit-down restaurants in this 1.3-million-square-foot facility make a shopping excursion an all-day affair.

WHERE TO STAY

The northern part of Palm Beach County is much more laid-back and less touristy than the rest of the Gold Coast. There are relatively few fancy hotels or attractions here.

VERY EXPENSIVE

Jupiter Beach Resort ⚿   The only resort set directly on Jupiter's beach, this unpretentious yet elegant retreat is popular with families and seems a world away from the more luxurious resorts just a few miles to the south. A multimillion-dollar renovation to guest rooms, public areas, and restaurants in 2004–05 transformed the place from shabby-chic to simply chic Caribbean. The guest rooms are furnished in a comfortable island style, and every unit has a private balcony with ocean or sunset views overlooking the beachfront. Speaking of beaches, the resort has a 1,000-foot private beach, as well as a 7,500-square-foot spa. Excursions to top-rated area golf courses are available.

5 N. A1A, Jupiter, FL 33477. Ⓒ 800/228-8810 or 561/746-2511. Fax 561/747-3304. www.jupiterbeachresort.com. 153 units. Winter $350–$450 double, $485–$583 suite, $900–$1,200 penthouse suite; off season $129–$179 double, $189–$219 suite, $600–$850 penthouse suite. AE, DC, DISC, MC, V. Valet parking $5. From I-95, take exit 59A, going east to the end of Indiantown Rd. at A1A. The resort is at this intersection, on the ocean. **Amenities:** 2 restaurants; 2 bars; outdoor heated pool; tennis court; exercise room; extensive watersports equipment rental; bike rental; children's programs; concierge; business center; limited room service; in-room massage; dry cleaning. *In room:* A/C, TV (VCR or DVD player available for $10 additional charge), dataport, kitchenette (in suites), minibar, coffeemaker, iron.

PGA National Resort & Spa ⚿⚿⚿   This rambling resort, the national headquarters of the PGA, is a premier golf-vacation spot—but its top-rated Mediterranean spa could be a destination in itself. With five 18-hole courses on more than 2,300 acres, golfers and other sports-minded travelers will find plenty to keep them occupied—such as croquet, tennis, sailing, a health and fitness center, and that sublime spa. Constant updating has kept the grounds and buildings in like-new condition. The par-72 Champion Course, redesigned in 1990 by Jack Nicklaus, is the resort's most valuable asset. Guest rooms are spacious and comfortable, bordering on residential, with immense bathrooms. Club cottages are especially nice, offering great privacy and serenity. This is not a beach resort, however. Six outdoor therapy pools are surrounded by gorgeous mineral pools. Don Shula's award-winning steakhouse is the hotel's best and most popular restaurant. In 2006, the Honda Classic golf tournament made the resort its official host venue. The tourney is in February.

400 Ave. of the Champions, Palm Beach Gardens, FL 33418. Ⓒ 800/633-9150 or 561/627-2000. Fax 561/225-2595. www.pga-resorts.com. 398 units. Winter $299–$339 double, $369–$829 suite; off season $144–$169 double, $174–$659 suite. Children 16 and under stay free in parent's room. Special packages available. AE, DC, DISC, MC, V. From I-95, take exit 57B (PGA Blvd.) going west and continue for approximately 2 miles to the resort entrance on the left. **Amenities:** 7 restaurants and lounges; 9 pools; 5 18-hole tournament courses plus the PGA National's Academy of Golf; 19 clay tennis courts; aerobics studio; 5 tournament croquet lawns; 5 indoor racquetball courts; Mediterranean spa; watersports equipment rental; concierge; car-rental desk; salon; limited room service; babysitting; laundry. *In room:* A/C, TV, dataport, minibar, hair dryer, safe.

MODERATE/INEXPENSIVE

Baron's Landing Motel & Apartments ⚿ *Value*   This family-run inn is a perfect little beach getaway, a throwback to old Florida. It's not elegant, but it is cozy. The single-story motel fronting the Intracoastal Waterway is often full in winter with snowbirds who dock their boats at the hotel's marina for weeks or months at a time. Nearly all rooms, which are situated around a small pool, have small kitchenettes. Each unit has a funky mix of used furniture; some have pullout sofas. Bathrooms have been remodeled. Considering that you're a few blocks from some of the most expensive real estate in the country, this is a good deal. Dock rentals are available as well.

18125 Ocean Blvd. (Fla. A1A at Clemens St.), Jupiter, FL 33477. ℂ 561/746-8757. 8 units. Winter $90–$125 double, $150–$190 apt; off season $85–$95 double, $140 apt. Monthly rates $1,650–$1,900. MC, V. **Amenities:** Small pool. *In room:* A/C, TV, fax, dataport, kitchen, fridge, coffeemaker, iron.

WHERE TO DINE

In addition to the national fast-food joints that line Indiantown Road and U.S. 1, you'll find a number of touristy fish restaurants serving battered and fried everything. There are only a few really exceptional eateries in North Palm Beach and Jupiter. Try those listed below for guaranteed good food at reasonable prices.

MODERATE

The Bistro ⓡ CONTINENTAL   Locals love this neighborhood country-style restaurant with a menu that runs the gourmet gamut from meaty jumbo lump crab cakes to fish and chips—caught daily by Chef TJ and baked in a tempura batter. Save room for the Grand Marnier or chocolate soufflé and, for oenophiles, The Bistro's wine cellar stores an impressive and diverse selection of reasonably priced vintages that can even be ordered off the restaurant's website.

2133 S. US 1 (in the Driftwood Plaza), Jupiter. ℂ 561/744-5054. www.thebistrojupiter.com. Reservations accepted for parties of 6 or more. Main courses $13–$28. AE, MC, V. Sun–Thurs 5–10pm; Fri–Sat 4–11pm.

Capt. Charlie's Reef Grill ⓡⓡ SEAFOOD/CARIBBEAN   The trick here is to arrive early, ahead of the crowd of local foodies who come for the more than a dozen daily local-catch specials prepared in myriad styles. Imaginative appetizers include Caribbean chili (a rich, chunky stew filled with fresh seafood) and a tuna spring roll big enough for two. The enormous Cuban crab cake is perfectly browned without tasting fried and is served with homemade mango chutney and black beans and rice. Sit at the bar to watch the hectic kitchen turn out perfect dishes on the 14-burner stove. Somehow, the pleasant waitresses keep their cool even when the place is packed. In addition to the terrific seafood, this little dive has an extensive, affordable wine and beer selection—more than 30 of each from around the world.

12846 U.S. 1 (behind O'Brian's and French Connection), Juno Beach. ℂ 561/624-9924. Reservations not accepted. Main courses $10–$28. MC, V. Sun–Fri 11:30am–3pm and 5–9:30pm.

Chef John's ⓡⓡ AMERICAN   One of Jupiter's hottest dinner reservations, this moderately priced American restaurant is heavy on seafood and even heavier on home-made touches, such as the complimentary *amuse-bouche,* from the chef (a variety of delicious small tastes from soup to ceviche), to outstanding dishes made with fish flown in fresh from Hawaii. A husband-and-wife team runs the place and modifies the seasonal menu with the freshest local—and exotic—ingredients.

287 E. Indiantown Rd., Jupiter. ℂ 561/745-8040. Reservations suggested. Main courses $10–$20. AE, MC, V. Sun–Thurs 5–10pm; Fri–Sat 4–11pm.

Nick's Tomato Pie ⓡ ITALIAN   A fun family restaurant, Nick's is a popular attraction that's known to bring folks even from Miami for a piece of this pie. With a huge menu of pastas, pizzas, fish, chicken, and beef, this cheery (and noisy) spot has something for everyone. On Saturday night, you'll see lots of couples on dates and families leaving with doggie bags of leftovers from the impossibly generous portions. The homemade sausage is a delicious treat, served with sautéed onions and peppers. The *pollo Marsala* (chicken in Marsala sauce), too, is good and authentic.

1697 W. Indiantown Rd. (1 mile east of I-95, exit 59A), Jupiter. © 561/744-8935. Reservations accepted for parties of 6 or more. Main courses $12–$20; pastas $10–$15. AE, DC, DISC, MC, V. Mon–Thurs and Sun 5–9:30pm; Fri–Sat 5–10:30pm.

Sinclair's Ocean Grill & Rotisserie 𝒦𝒦 CARIBBEAN   As close to upscale as Jupiter gets, Sinclair's, recently renovated along with the entire hotel, is the Jupiter Beach Resort's excellent restaurant overlooking the pool. It serves fresh, locally caught fish, as well as an excellent filet mignon. Especially popular are the Sunday brunches.

In the Jupiter Beach Resort, 5 N. Fla. A1A. © 561/745-7120. Reservations recommended. Main courses $18–$27. AE, MC, V. Daily 6:30am–2pm and 8–10pm.

14

The Treasure Coast:
Stuart to Sebastian

The area north of Palm Beach is known as the Treasure Coast for the same reason that the area from Fort Lauderdale to Palm Beach is known as the Gold Coast—it was the site of a number of shipwrecks that date back more than 300 years, which led to the discovery of priceless treasures in the water (some historians believe that treasures *still* lie buried deep beneath the ocean floor).

The difference, however, is that while the Gold Coast is a bit, well, tarnished as far as development is concerned, the Treasure Coast remains, for the most part, an unspoiled, quiet natural jewel. Miles of uninterrupted beaches and aquamarine waters attract swimmers, boaters, divers, anglers, and sun worshippers. If you love the great outdoors and prefer a more understated environment than hyperdeveloped Miami and Fort Lauderdale, the Treasure Coast is a real find.

For hundreds of years, Florida's east coast was a popular stopover for European explorers, many of whom arrived from Spain with full coffers of gold and silver. Rough weather and poor navigation often took a toll on their ships, but in 1715, a violent hurricane stunned the northeast coast and sank an entire fleet of Spanish ships laden with gold. Although Spanish salvagers worked for years to collect the lost treasure, much of it remained buried beneath the shifting sand. Workers hired to excavate the area in the 1950s and 1960s discovered centuries-old coins under their tractors.

Today you can still see shipwrecks and incredible barrier reefs in St. Lucie County, which can be reached from the beaches of Fort Pierce and Hutchinson Island. On these same beaches, you'll also find an occasional treasure hunter trolling the sand with a metal detector, alongside swimmers and sunbathers who come to enjoy the stretches of beach that extend into the horizon. The sea, especially around Sebastian Inlet, is a mecca for surfers, who find some of the largest swells in the state.

Along with the pleasures of the talcum-powder sands, the Treasure Coast has good shopping and sports, and numerous other opportunities to take a reprieve from the hubbub of the rat race. Visitors to this part of South Florida should not miss the extensive array of wildlife, which includes the endangered West Indian manatee, loggerhead and leatherback turtles, tropical fish, alligators, deer, and exotic birds. Sports enthusiasts will find boundless opportunities here—from golf and tennis to polo, motorcar racing, the New York Mets during spring training, and the best freshwater fishing around.

The downtown areas of the Treasure Coast have been experiencing a very slow rebirth in the past few years, along with an unprecedented influx of new residents. Fortunately, growth has occurred at a reasonable pace, allowing the neighborhoods to retain their small-town feel. The result is a batch of freshly spruced-up accommodations, shops, and restaurants from Stuart to Sebastian.

Southern Martin County's well-to-do Hobe Sound, in particular, is a Treasure Coast hot spot with its pristine beaches, banyan-tree-canopied streetscapes, one-of-a-kind antiques shops, and art galleries. Hobe Sound rests at the front door of the Gold Coast and the back door of the Treasure Coast, and it has access to both the Atlantic Ocean and the Intracoastal Waterway. Real estate here is at a premium, with multimillion-dollar waterfront mansions lining the shores.

While the Treasure Coast took a major hit during the brutal 2005 hurricane season, all is still golden here.

For the purposes of this chapter, the Treasure Coast runs roughly from Hobe Sound in the south to Sebastian Inlet in the north, encompassing some of Martin, St. Lucie, and Indian River counties, and all of Hutchinson Island.

TREASURE COAST ESSENTIALS
GETTING THERE
Since virtually every town described in this chapter runs along a straight route by the Atlantic Ocean, I've given all directions below.

BY PLANE   The **Palm Beach International Airport** (© 561/471-7420), about 35 miles south of Stuart, is the closest gateway to this region if you're flying. See the "Getting There" section on Palm Beach, on p. 340, for complete information. If you're traveling to the northern part of the Treasure Coast, **Melbourne International Airport,** off U.S. 1 in Melbourne (© 321/723-6227), is less than 25 miles north of Sebastian and about 35 miles north of Vero Beach.

BY CAR   If you're driving up or down the Florida coast, you'll probably reach the Treasure Coast via I-95. If you're heading to Stuart or Jensen Beach, take exits 61 (Rte. 76/Tanner Hwy.) or 62 (Rte. 714); to Port St. Lucie or Fort Pierce, take exits 63 or 64 (Okeechobee Rd.); to Vero Beach, take exit 68 (S.R. 60); to Sebastian, take exit 69 (County Rd.). You can also take the Florida Turnpike; this toll road is the fastest (but not the most scenic) route, especially if you're coming from Orlando. If you're heading to Stuart or Jensen Beach, take exit 133; to Fort Pierce, take exit 152 (Okeechobee Rd.); to Port St. Lucie, take exits 142 or 152; to Vero Beach, take exit 193 (S.R. 60); to Sebastian, take exit 193 to S.R. 60 east and connect to I-95 N.

If you're staying in Hutchinson Island, which runs almost the entire length of the Treasure Coast, you should check with your hotel or see the listings below to find the best route to take.

Finally, if you're coming directly from the west coast, you'll probably take S.R. 70, which runs north of Lake Okeechobee to Fort Pierce, up the road from Stuart.

BY RAIL   Amtrak (© 800/USA-RAIL; www.amtrak.com) stops in West Palm Beach, at 201 S. Tamarind Ave.; and in Okeechobee, at 801 N. Parrot Ave., off U.S. 441 N.

BY BUS   Greyhound (© 800/231-2222; www.greyhound.com) serves the area with bus terminals in Stuart, at 1308 S. Federal Hwy.; in Fort Pierce, at 7005 Okeechobee Rd. (© 772/461-3299); and in Vero Beach, at U.S. 1 and S.R. 60 (© 772/562-6588).

GETTING AROUND
A car is a necessity in this large and rural region. Although heavy traffic is not usually a problem here, on the smaller coastal roads, such as A1A, expect to travel at a slow pace, usually between 25 and 40 mph.

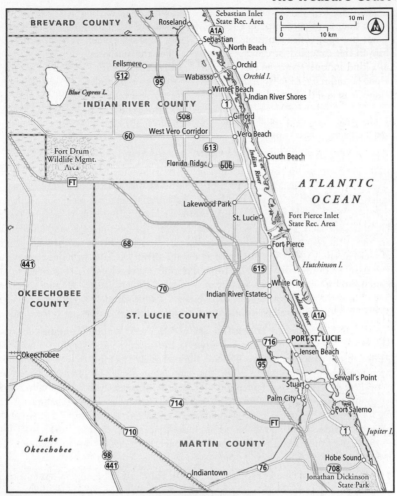

1 Hobe Sound ✶✶✶, Stuart (North Hutchinson Island) ✶✶ & Jensen Beach

Hobe Sound: 45 min. N of Palm Beach; 12 miles S of Stuart

Once just a stretch of pineapple plantations, the towns of Martin County, which include Hobe Sound, Stuart, and Jensen Beach, retain much of their rural character. Between the citrus groves and mangroves are modest homes and an occasional high-rise condominium. Although the area is definitely quiet, the atmosphere is pure small town. Even in historic downtown Stuart, the result of a successful, ongoing restoration, expect the storefronts to be dark and the streets abandoned after 10pm. Martin County did suffer some damage in 2004 and 2005 due to Hurricanes Frances, Jeanne,

Charley, Katrina, and Wilma, and such parks as Jonathan Dickinson State Park were closed for a bit, but everything has since reopened and is fully functional.

ESSENTIALS

The **Stuart/Martin County Chamber of Commerce,** 1650 S. Kanner Hwy., Stuart, FL 34994 (© **800/524-9704** or 772/287-1088; fax 772/220-3437; www.goodnature. org), is the region's main source for information. The **Jensen Beach Chamber of Commerce,** 1901 NE Jensen Beach Blvd., Jensen Beach, FL 34957 (© **772/334-3444;** fax 772/334-0817; www.jensenbeachchamber.biz), also provides visitors with information about its simple beachfront town.

BACK TO NATURE: THE BEACHES & BEYOND

BEACHES   **Hutchinson Island,** one of the most popular beach destinations of the Treasure Coast, is the area just north of Palm Beach on the Atlantic Ocean. Some 70 miles of excellent beaches and laid-back, Old Florida ambience make for an idyllic, frozen-cocktail-on-the-beach resort vacation. The best is **Bathtub Beach,** on North Hutchinson Island. The calm waters here are protected by coral reefs, and visitors can explore the region on dune and river trails. Pick a secluded spot on the wide stretch of sand, or enjoy marked nature trails across the street. Facilities include showers and toilets open during the day. To reach Bathtub Beach from the northern tip of Hutchinson Island, head east on Ocean Boulevard (Stuart Causeway) and turn right onto MacArthur Boulevard. The beach is about a mile ahead on your left, just north of the Hutchinson Island Marriott Beach Resort and Marina. Parking is plentiful.

CANOEING   **Jonathan Dickinson State Park** (see "Wildlife Exploration: From Gators to Manatees to Turtles," below) is the most popular area for canoeing. Although the park experienced a major blow with 2005's Hurricane Wilma, all has been repaired and restored. In 2006, the park debuted the new Jonathan Dickinson State Park Environmental Education and Research Center, which hosts educational programs and activities. The route winds through a variety of botanical habitats. You'll see lots of birds and the occasional manatee. Canoes rent for $14 for 2 hours and $5 for each additional hour, available through the concessions stand (© **561/746-1466**) in the back of the park; it's open Monday through Friday from 9am to 5pm, and Saturday and Sunday from 8am to 5pm.

FISHING   Several charter captains operate on Hutchinson Island and Jensen Beach. One of the largest operators is the **Sailfish Marina,** 3565 SE St. Lucie Blvd., Stuart (© **772/221-9456**), which maintains half a dozen charter boats for fishing excursions year-round. Also on-site is a bait-and-tackle shop and a knowledgeable, helpful staff. Other reputable charter operators include **Hungry Bear Adventures, Inc.,** docked at Indian River Plantation Marriott Resort, 4730-1 SE Teri Place, Stuart (© **772/285-7552;** www.hungrybear.net); and **Bone Shaker Sportfishing,** 3585 SE St. Lucie Blvd., Stuart (© **772/286-5504;** www.boneshakercharters.com).

GOLF   Try the **Champion's Club at Summerfield,** on U.S. 1, south of Cove Road in Stuart (© **772/283-1500;** www.championsclubsummerfield.com), a somewhat challenging championship course designed by Tom Fazio. This rural course, the best in the area, offers great glimpses of wildlife amid the wetlands. Winter greens fees are around $65; carts are mandatory. Reservations are a must and are taken 4 days in advance.

Wildlife Exploration: From Gators to Manatees to Turtles

One of the most scenic areas on this stretch of the coast is **Jonathan Dickinson State Park** 🏕, 2 miles south of Stuart at 16450 S. Federal Hwy. (U.S. 1), Hobe Sound (📞 772/546-2771). The park intentionally receives less maintenance than other, more meticulously maintained parks in order to resemble the rough-around-the-edges, wilderness-like environment of hundreds of years ago, before Europeans started chopping, dredging, and "improving" the area. Dozens of species of Florida's unique wildlife, including alligators and manatees, live on the park's more than 11,300 acres. Bird-watchers will be delighted by glimpses of rare and endangered species such as the bald eagle, the Florida scrub-jay, and the Florida sandhill crane, which still call this park home. You can rent canoes from the concessions stand to explore the Loxahatchee River on your own. Admission is $4 per car of up to eight adults. Day hikers, bikers, and walkers pay $1 each. The park is open from 8am until sundown. See p. 367 for details on camping.

Close to Jonathan Dickinson State Park is **Hobe Sound Wildlife Refuge,** on North Beach Road off S.R. 708, at the north end of Jupiter Island (📞 772/546-6141). This is one of the best places to spot sea turtles that nest on the shore in the summer months, especially in June and July. Because it's home to a large variety of other plant and animal species, the park is worth visiting the rest of the year as well. Admission is $4 per car, and the preserve is open daily from sunrise to sunset. Exact times are posted at each entrance and change seasonally.

For turtle walks on Hutchinson Island, call 📞 877/375-4386. These walks take place from May 22 to July 22 at 9pm on Friday and Saturday. Reservations are necessary and should be made well in advance (they're accepted as of May 1); each walk is limited to only 50 people.

SCUBA DIVING & SNORKELING   Three popular artificial reefs off Hutchinson Island provide excellent scenery for both novice and experienced divers. The **USS Rankin** lies 7 miles east-northeast of the St. Lucie Inlet. The *Rankin* is a 459-foot ship that lies on its port side in 80 feet of water. This ship was used in World War II for troop transportation and was sunk to create the reef in 1988. Deck hatches on the wreck are open and allow exploration. Inside there are thousands of Atlantic Spiny oysters, and a cannon is attached to the bow. The **Donaldson Reef** consists of a cluster of steel tanks and barrels sunk in 58 feet of water to create an artificial reef. It's due east of the Gilbert's House of Refuge Museum (see below). The **Ernst Reef,** made from old tires, is a 60-foot dive located 4½ miles east-southeast of the St. Lucie Inlet. Local dive shops have tips on the best spots, along with rules and regulations for safe diving.

SEEING THE SIGHTS

Balloons Over Florida 🏕🏕🏕 *(Finds*   For a lofty view of Martin County's wildlife, take a hot-air balloon ride above the animals' natural habitat. Two fully licensed and insured balloons and pilots will take a maximum of four people up, up, and away for about an hour first thing in the morning, depending on wind and weather conditions. After you've landed, drink in the sights over a glass of complimentary champagne and a continental breakfast. The entire experience takes about 3½ hours. Book 2 to 3 weeks in advance, especially in season.

Tours begin at approximately 6:30am from a takeoff point to be determined. © 772/334-9393. $195 per person, including continental breakfast and champagne.

Elliott Museum 🎯🎯   A treasure trove of wacky artifacts that really personify Americana, the Elliott Museum is a tribute to inventors, sports heroes, and collectors. The museum was created by the son of turn-of-the-20th-century inventor Sterling Elliott to display the genius of the American spirit. Among the things you'll see here are displays of an apothecary, an ice-cream parlor, a barbershop, and other old-fashioned commercial enterprises, as well as an authentic hand-carved miniature circus. Sports fans will appreciate the baseball memorabilia, including an autographed item from every player in the Baseball Hall of Fame. A gallery of patents and models of machines, invented by the museum's founder and his son, provides an intriguing glimpse into the business of tinkering. The collection of restored antique cars is also impressive. Expect to spend at least an hour seeing the highlights.

825 NE Ocean Blvd. (north of Indian River Plantation Resort), Hutchinson Island, Stuart. © 772/225-1961. www.elliottmuseumfl.org. Admission $6 adults, $2 children 6–13, free for children 5 and under. Mon–Sat 10am–4pm; Sun 1–4pm.

Florida Oceanographic Coastal Center 🎯🎯   This is a nature lover's Disney World. Opened by the South Florida Oceanographic Society in 1994, the 44-acre site (surrounded by coastal hammock and mangroves) is its own little ecosystem and serves as an outdoor classroom, teaching visitors about the region's flora and fauna. The modest main building houses saltwater tanks, and wet and dry "discovery tables" with small indigenous animals. The incredibly eager staff of volunteers encourages visitors to wander the lush, well-marked nature trails. In 2007, the museum began an expansion program to include a fishing center, game fish lagoon, shark pavilion, ray pavilion, children's activity center, and more.

890 NE Ocean Blvd. (across the street from the Elliott Museum), Hutchinson Island, Stuart. © 772/225-0505. www.floridaoceanographic.org. Admission $8 adults, $4 children 3–12. Mon–Sat 10am–5pm; Sun noon–4pm.

Gilbert's House of Refuge Museum 🎯   Gilbert's, the oldest structure in Martin County, dates from 1875, when it functioned as 1 of 10 rescue centers for shipwrecked sailors. After a thorough rehab to its original condition along the rocky shores, the house now displays marine artifacts and turn-of-the-20th-century lifesaving equipment and photographs. It's worth a visit to get a feel for the area's early days.

301 SE MacArthur Blvd. (south of Indian River Plantation Resort), Hutchinson Island, Stuart. © 772/225-1875. Admission $5 adults, $2 children 6–13. Daily 10am–4pm.

A BOAT TOUR

The *Loxahatchee Queen* 🎯🎯🎯 (© 561/746-1466), a 35-foot, 44-passenger pontoon boat in Jonathan Dickinson State Park in Hobe Sound, makes daily tours of the area's otherwise inaccessible backwater, where curious alligators, manatees, eagles, and tortoises often peek out to see who's in their yard. Catch the 2-hour tour, given Wednesday through Sunday as the tide permits, when it includes a stop at Trapper Nelson's home. Known as the "Wildman of Loxahatchee," Nelson lived in primitive conditions on a remote stretch of the water in a log cabin he built himself, now preserved for visitors. Tours leave four times daily—at 9am, 11am, 1pm, and 3pm—and cost $14.50 for adults and $9.50 for children 6 to 12. See "Wildlife Exploration: From Gators to Manatees to Turtles" (p. 365) for more information on the state park.

SHOPPING

Downtown Stuart's historic district, along Flagler Avenue between Confusion Corner and St. Lucie Avenue, offers shoppers diversity and quality in an old small-town setting. Shops sell a range of goods: antique bric-a-brac, old lamps and fixtures, books, gourmet foods, furnishings, and souvenirs. For bargains, check out the **B & A Flea Market** (© 772/288-4915), the Treasure Coast's oldest and largest flea market.

WHERE TO STAY

Although the area boasts some beautiful beaches, the bulk of the hotel scene is downtown, where the nicer (and more reasonably priced) accommodations can be found among the shops and restaurants. There are, however, a few excellent beachfront hotels and inns. There's a pretty nice **Best Western Downtown Stuart,** at 1209 S. Federal Hwy. (© 772/287-6200). This newly remodeled two-story building on a busy main road is kept in very good shape and is convenient to Stuart's historic district. Rates range from $75 to $109. *Note:* A 2% tax is added to accommodations rates in the Stuart–Hutchinson Island area.

VERY EXPENSIVE

Hutchinson Island Marriott Beach Resort and Marina *(★★ (Kids* This sprawling 200-acre compound offers many diversions for active (or not-so-active) vacationers, and families in particular. This is definitely Hutchinson Island's best resort, occupying the lush grounds of a former pineapple plantation. Activities include tennis, golf, boating, sport fishing, scuba diving, and other watersports. Rooms overlook either the Intracoastal and the resort's marina, the ocean, or gardens. All are generously sized and have full kitchens. Be sure to sign up for a summer "turtle watch," so you can observe turtles crawling onto the sand to lay their eggs. Another great activity, offered at an extra cost, is a sightseeing cruise along the St. Lucie and Indian rivers. The Baha Grill seafood restaurant is a great choice on property.

555 NE Ocean Blvd., Hutchinson Island, Stuart, FL 34996. © 800/775-5936 or 772/225-3700. Fax 772/225-0003. www.marriott.com. 298 units. Winter $189–$289 double, $309–$499 suite; off season $159–$199 double, $200–$299 suite. AE, MC, V. From downtown Stuart, take E. Ocean Blvd. over 2 bridges to NE Ocean Blvd.; turn right. Pets accepted with $50 deposit. **Amenities:** Restaurant; coffee shop; lounge; 4 large pools; 18-hole golf course; 13 tennis courts; fitness center and spa; extensive watersports activities; bike rental; childrens programs; game room; concierge; on-property transportation; limited room service; babysitting; laundry services; dry cleaning. *In room:* A/C, TV, high-speed Internet access, kitchenette, minibar, coffeemaker, hair dryer, iron.

CAMPING

There are comfortable campsites (rustic cabins and sites for your tent or camper) in **Jonathan Dickinson State Park,** in Hobe Sound (see "Wildlife Exploration: From Gators to Manatees to Turtles," on p. 365). The River Camp area of the park offers the benefit of the nearby Loxahatchee River, while the Pine Grove site has beautiful shade trees. There are concession areas for daytime snacks and campsites with showers, clean restrooms, water, optional electricity, and open-fire pits for cooking. Overnight rates in winter are $22 with electricity. In summer, rates are about $14 for four people.

For a cushier camping experience, reserve a cabin with furnished kitchen, bathroom with shower, heat and air-conditioning, and outdoor grill. Cabins rent for $85 (one bed and a pullout couch), $95 (two beds and a pullout couch), and up per night. They sleep four people comfortably, or up to six if your group is really into togetherness. Call ℰ 772/546-2771 Monday through Friday between 9am and 5pm, well in advance, to reserve a spot. A $50 key deposit is required. Bring your own linens.

The Treasure Coast RV Resort and Campground of Fort Pierce, 2550 Crossroads Pkwy., Fort Pierce (ℰ 866/468-2099; www.treasurecoastrv.com), has a small lake, oak trees, clubhouse with kitchen, swimming pool, hot tub (!), and shower facilities. There also are full-service hook-ups, free wireless high-speed Internet access, and free cable TV. Rates are $35 to $49.

WHERE TO DINE
EXPENSIVE

Arthur's Dockside Waterfront 𝓴 Finds SEAFOOD   Gorgeous water views and delicious seafood make Arthur's one of the hottest restaurants in town. The expansive dining room provides spectacular views across the St. Lucie River, and the downstairs bar Fiji is so close to the water that, if it's high tide, you may get wet. The food is inconsistent, but a standout is the veal and prawns with garlic and lemon-butter sauce. There's also a sushi bar. Service is spotty at best, but because of the stunning views, everyone seems to always be in a great mood here. That, or it could be the drinks downstairs and Fiji. However, the owner insists he's working on bringing the service up to upscale par. Either way, when you're in town, a visit to Arthur's is a must.

131 SW Flagler Ave., Stuart. ℰ 772/219-3625. Reservations recommended. Main courses $10–$30. AE, DC, MC, V. Sun–Mon 11am–3pm and 4–10pm; Fri–Sat 4–11pm.

The Courtyard Grill 𝓴𝓴 CONTINENTAL   Although this restaurant faces railroad tracks and a station that was never fully built, The Courtyard Grill is the essence of charm, with the warm and inviting vibe of a place where no railroad would ever go. Old-school fare such as clams casino and escargot are juxtaposed with nouveau cuisine such as duck-stuffed ravioli, but old standards such as Dover sole are best. An impressive wine list, a gorgeous garden room, and homemade desserts assure you're on the right track as far as fine food in Hobe Sound is concerned, train or no train.

11970 SE Dixie Hwy., Hobe Sound. ℰ 772/546-2900. Reservations recommended. Main courses $12–$25. MC, V. Tues–Sat 5:30–9:30pm.

11 Maple Street 𝓴𝓴𝓴 AMERICAN   The most highly rated restaurant in Jensen Beach, 11 Maple Street occupies a converted old house. Dining is both indoors and out, in any one of a series of cozy dining rooms or on a covered patio surrounded by gardens. The menu changes daily and features interesting dishes not typically found in these parts of Florida such as wood-grilled North American elk with faro squash, fontina gratin, and a chestnut honey essence; and oak-grilled duck breast with wild huckleberry essence, acorn squash, pine nuts, and warm red cabbage salad. The restaurant uses organic produce from its garden, and poultry and meats that are farm raised and free of additives.

11 Maple St., Jensen Beach. ℰ 772/334-7714. www.11maplestreet.com. Reservations recommended. Main courses $29–$38. MC, V. Wed–Sun 6–10pm. Head east on Jensen Beach Blvd. and turn right after the railroad tracks.

Flagler Grill 𝓴𝓴 AMERICAN/FLORIDA REGIONAL   In the heart of historic downtown, this seemingly out-of-place Manhattan-style bistro serves up classics with

a twist. Dishes are fresh and light enough to quench the appetites of the adventurous—for example, Atlantic salmon filet, honey-lime roasted with green beans, organic
rice blend, confetti corn salad, and a roasted jalapeño aioli. For a main course, the
grilled pork chop with mashed Florida sweet potatoes, Vidalia marmalade, and tomato
confit gives meaning to the term "comfort food." It's hard to go wrong with any of the
many salads, pastas, fish dishes, or delectable beef choices. The desserts, too, are worth
the calories. Ask the bartender to make you the Big Apple martini—apple vodka,
apple schnapps, and a wedge of apple—dessert with a kick! No smoking is allowed in
the restaurant or bar.

47 SW Flagler Ave. (just before the Roosevelt Bridge), downtown Stuart. © 772/221-9517. www.flaglergrill.com.
Reservations strongly suggested in season. Main courses $18–$30. AE, DC, DISC, MC, V. Winter daily 5–10pm; off season Tues–Sat 5:30–9:30pm. Lounge and bar until 11.30pm. Special sunset menu offered 5–6pm.

MODERATE

Black Marlin ⚅ FLORIDA REGIONAL   Although it looks and feels like a dank
English pub, the Black Marlin offers full Floridian flavor. The salmon BLT is typical
of the dishes here—grilled salmon on a toasted bun topped with bacon, lettuce,
tomato, and coleslaw. Pizzas are adorned with shrimp, roasted red peppers, and the
like. Main dishes, served with vegetables and potatoes, range from lobster tail with
honey-mustard sauce to grilled chicken breast on radicchio with caramelized onions.
Ask whether they're serving the fried lobster tail special—it's out of this world!

53 W. Osceola St., downtown Stuart. © 772/286-3126. Reservations not accepted. Salads, pizzas, and sandwiches
$8–$15; main courses $13–$35. AE, MC, V. Mon–Thurs 5–10pm; Fri–Sat 5–11pm (bar open later).

Conchy Joe's Seafood ⚅⚅ (Finds SEAFOOD   Known for fresh seafood and Old
Florida hospitality, Conchy Joe's enjoys an excellent reputation that's far bigger than
the restaurant itself. Shorts and flip-flops are the attire of choice here, and dining is
either indoors or out on a covered patio overlooking the St. Lucie River. The menu
features a variety of freshly shucked shellfish and daily-catch selections that are baked,
broiled, or fried; the conch chowder is sublime. Beer is the drink of choice here,
though other beverages are available. Conchy Joe's has been the most active place in
Jensen Beach since it opened in 1983. The large bar is popular at night and during
weekday happy hours.

3945 NE Indian River Dr. (½-mile from the Jensen Beach Causeway), Jensen Beach. © 772/334-1130. www.
conchyjoes.com. Reservations not accepted. Main courses $12–$20. AE, DISC, MC, V. Daily 11:30am–2:30pm and
5–10pm.

INEXPENSIVE

Harry and the Natives ⚅⚅ AMERICAN   When you dine at this wild and wacky,
kitschy Old Florida institution (to which both Harleys and Bentleys flock), you'll get
decent bar fare (try the venison burger) with a fabulous dish of humor on the side.
They call it Hobe Sounds' only waterfront restaurant—when it rains. It is not at all
on the water, but more of a roadside stop instead. The menu is hysterical, especially
"Acceptable: Visa, MasterCard, our gift certificates, cash, oceanfront homes, table
dancing, honey-dripping, and dishwashing." No offense to our Canadian friends, but
the menu also jokingly has a "Canadian Breakfast—(no tip) $20." The food ranges
from omelets and pancakes to the "President Bush Omelet—$1,000,000,000; Profits
go to the Palm Beach County Election Supervisor to buy more butterfly ballots, voting machines, and incompetent help." I won't spoil it all, so be sure to read the entire

menu. There's live music Wednesday through Saturday; request the Harry and the Natives theme song.

11910 S. Federal Hwy., Hobe Sound. ℭ 772/546-3061. www.harryandthenatives.com. Main courses $5–$10. MC, V. Daily 6:30am–2:30am.

Nature's Way Cafe ℱ HEALTH FOOD   This lovely dining room has dozens of little tables, a few bar stools, and some sidewalk seating, too. A sort of health-food deli, Nature's Way excels in serving quick and nutritious meals such as huge salads, vegetarian sandwiches, and frozen yogurts. Try some of the homemade baked goods. Sit outside on quaint Osceola Street or get your lunch packed up to take to the beach.

25 SW Osceola St., in the Post Office Arcade, Stuart. ℭ 772/220-7306. Sandwiches and salads $4–$9; juices and shakes $1–$5. No credit cards. Mon–Fri 10am–4pm; Sat 11am–3pm.

STUART & JENSEN BEACH AFTER DARK

Nightlife on the Treasure Coast may as well be called night*dead* because there really isn't any! This is not the place if you're looking for active nightlife. That said, Stuart and Jensen Beach are the closest to nightlife in the region; local restaurants serve as the centers of after-dark happenings. "Night" ends pretty early here, even on weekends.

Fiji at **Arthur's Dockside Waterfront** (see "Where to Dine," above), is a happening, splashy spot, especially around happy hour, which seems to start earlier than most. The bar at the **Black Marlin** (see "Where to Dine," above) is popular with locals and out-of-towners alike. No list of Jensen nightlife would be complete without mention of **Conchy Joe's Seafood** (see "Where to Dine," above), one of the region's most active spots. Inside, locals chug beer and watch a large-screen TV, while outside on the waterfront patio, live bands perform a few nights a week for a raucous crowd of dancers. Happy hours, Monday through Friday from 3 to 6pm, draw large crowds.

The centerpiece of Stuart's slowly expanding cultural offerings is the newly restored **Lyric Theater,** 59 SW Flagler Ave. (ℭ 772/286-7827). This beautiful 1920s-era theater hosts a variety of shows, readings, concerts, and films throughout the year.

2 Port St. Lucie & Fort Pierce

Port St. Lucie: 120 miles N of Miami; 120 miles S of Orlando

Port St. Lucie and Fort Pierce are two true Old Florida towns—reminiscent of the pre-neon, pre-condo-maniacal Florida, a sleepy world apart from the Gold Coast and Miami. Both towns thrive on sport fishing, and a seemingly endless row of piers juts out along the Intracoastal Waterway and the Fort Pierce Inlet for both river and ocean runs. Visitors can dive, snorkel, beachcomb, and sunbathe in an area left untouched by the overdevelopment that has altered its neighbors to the south and north.

Most sightseeing takes place along the main beach road (the strip across from the Ocean/A1A). Driving along Florida A1A on Hutchinson Island, you'll discover several secluded beach clubs interspersed with 1950s-style homes, a few small inns, grungy raw bars, and a few high-rise condominiums. Much of this island is government owned and kept undeveloped for the public's enjoyment.

ESSENTIALS

The **St. Lucie County Chamber of Commerce,** 2200 Virginia Ave., Fort Pierce, FL 34982 (ℭ 772/595-9999; www.stluciechamber.org), is the region's main source of information. There's another branch at 1626 SE Port St. Lucie Blvd., in Port St. Lucie. Both spots are open Monday through Friday from 9am to 5pm.

BEACHES & NATURE PRESERVES

North Hutchinson Island's beaches are the most pristine in this area. You won't find restaurants, hotels, or shopping; instead, you'll spend your time swimming, surfing, fishing, and diving. Most of the beaches along this stretch of the Atlantic Ocean are private, but thankfully the state has set aside some of the best areas for the public.

Fort Pierce Inlet State Recreation Area (© 772/468-3985) is a stunning 340-acre park with almost 4,000 feet of sandy shores that were once the training ground for the original navy frogmen. A short nature trail leads through a canopy of live oaks, cabbage palms, sea grapes, and strangler figs. The western side of the area has swamps of red mangroves that are home to fiddler crabs, osprey, and a multitude of wading birds. Jack Island State Preserve, in the state recreation area, is popular with bird watchers and has hiking trails. Jutting into the Indian River, the mangrove-covered peninsula contains several marked trails, varying in distance from .5 mile to more than 4 miles. The trails through mangrove forests lead to a short observation tower.

The best beach in the state recreation area, **Jetty Park**, lies in the northern part. Families will enjoy the picnic areas and barbecue grills here. There are also restrooms and outdoor showers, and lifeguards look after swimmers. The park is at 905 Shorewinds Dr., north of Fort Pierce Inlet. To get here from I-95, take exit 66 E. (Rte. 68) and turn left onto U.S. 1 North; in about 2 miles, you will see signs to Florida A1A and the North Bridge Causeway. Turn right on A1A and cross over to North Hutchinson Island. Admission is $4 per vehicle; the park is open daily from 8am to sunset.

SPECTATOR SPORTS & OUTDOOR PURSUITS

BASEBALL   The **New York Mets** hold spring training in Port St. Lucie from late February to the end of March at **Tradition Field**, 525 NW Peacock Blvd. (© 772/871-2115). Tickets for games and practices cost $6 to $25. From April to August, their farm team, the Vero Beach Dodgers, plays home games in the stadium.

FISHING   The **Fort Pierce City Marina**, 1 Ave. A, Fort Pierce (© 772/464-1245), has more than a dozen charter captains who keep their motors running for anglers anxious to catch a few. Brochures available at the marina list all of the privately owned charter operators, who organize trips on an as-desired basis. The price usually starts at $150 per person for half-day tours, depending on the season.

GOLF   The most notable courses in Port St. Lucie are at the **PGA Golf Club**, 1916 Perfect Dr. (© 772/467-1300). The club's first of three 18-hole public golf courses opened in 1996 and was designed by Tom Fazio; another course was designed by Pete Dye. The South Course, a classic Old Florida–style course, is set on wetlands, affords views of native wildlife, and is the most popular. The center also provides lessons for amateurs. The club is open daily from 7am to 6pm. Greens fees are usually $55–$65, but after 2pm they go down to $29. Reserve at least 9 days in advance.

SEEING THE SIGHTS

Harbor Branch Oceanographic Institution ✸✸   Harbor Branch is a working nonprofit scientific institute that studies oceanic resources and welcomes visitors on scheduled tours. Stops include the J. Seward Johnson Marine Education Center, which houses submersibles used to conduct research at depths of up to 3,000 feet. A video details current projects, and several large aquariums simulate the environments of the Indian River Lagoon and a saltwater reef. Visitors see the Aqua-Culture Farming Center, a research facility that contains tanks growing seaweed and other oceanic plants. The 90-minute Lagoon Wildlife Tour examines the Indian River Lagoon from a pontoon boat. The boat tours are offered Monday through Saturday at 10am and 1 and 3pm; the cost is $17 for adults, $12 for children 6 to 12. The bus tour of the 600-acre campus costs $10 and leaves Monday through Saturday at 10am, noon, and 2pm.

5600 U.S. 1 N., Fort Pierce. ℂ 772/465-2400. www.hboi.edu. Admission $10 adults, $6 children 6–12. Mon–Fri 8am–5pm; visitor center gift shop Mon–Sat 9am–5pm. Arrive at least 20 min. before tour.

Savannahs Recreation Area 𝓕𝓕𝓕 *Finds*   A 550-acre former reservoir, Savannahs is one of the most interesting places in these parts—it's a veritable wilderness, with botanical gardens, nature trails, campsites, a petting zoo, and scenery reminiscent of the Florida Everglades, but in a much more contained environment.

1400 E. Midway Rd., Fort Pierce. ℂ 772/464-7855. Admission $1 per car. Daily 8am–6pm.

UDT-SEAL Museum (Underwater Demolition Team Museum)   Florida is full of unique museums, but none more curious than the UDT-SEAL Museum, an interesting tribute to the secret forces of the U.S. Navy frogmen and their successors, the SEAL teams. Chronological displays trace the history of these clandestine divers and detail their most important achievements. The best exhibits are those on the intricately detailed equipment used by the navy's most elite members. Expect to spend about an hour here, depending on your interests.

3300 N. S.R. A1A, Fort Pierce. ℂ 772/595-5845. www.navysealmuseum.com. Admission $6 adults, $3 children 6–12. Mon–Sat 10am–4pm; Sun noon–4pm. Closed Mon in off season.

WHERE TO STAY

The Port St. Lucie mainland is pretty run-down, but there are a number of inexpensive hotel options on scenic Hutchinson Island that are charming and well priced. Probably the best choice is the **Hampton Inn,** 2831 Reynolds Dr. (ℂ 800/426-7866 or 772/828-4100), which is beautifully maintained. If you want to be closer to the water, try the **Mariner's Bay Inn and Suites,** 1920 Seaway Dr. (ℂ 800/325-2525 or 772/461-8737), a simple, very well-kept motel that sits along the Intracoastal Inlet.

EXPENSIVE

Club Med Sandpiper 𝓕𝓕 *Kids*   This 400-acre, all-inclusive resort isn't your typical bacchanalian Club Med, but rather a fabulous getaway for families with kids. The hotel markets itself to Europeans looking for a Florida getaway. They come in droves (Americans, too) with all the kids and nannies for an active vacation with lavish meals, from buffets to sit-downs, for a package price. Thanks to tailored programs for kids—there's Baby Club Med, Petit Club Med, Mini Club Med, and Junior's Club Med—the resort is all about families with kids. Rooms are so-so and retro, but not in a cool way. However, there's so much to do that you really won't be spending much time inside anyway. The drawback is that guests are 20 minutes from the nearest beach. The buildings could use an overhaul, but there are plenty of diversions on-site, such as golf, tennis, bocce ball, volleyball, water-skiing, sailing, and boating on the Indian River, and even a circus school!

4500 SE Pine Valley, Port St. Lucie, FL 34952. ℂ 800/CLUB-MED or 772/398-5100. Fax 772/398-5101. www.clubmed.com. 337 units. Winter $800–$2,320 per week per adult; off season $700–$2,180 per week per adult (reduced rates are offered for children). Rates include all meals; unlimited wine, beer, and soft drinks with lunch and dinner; sports equipment and instruction; and nightly entertainment. Transportation from your city of departure to the village, as well as transfers to and from the village, is available. AE, MC, V. Closed Nov–Mar. From U.S. 1 S., turn left onto Westmoreland Blvd. Make another left onto Pine Valley Rd.; the resort entrance is straight ahead. **Amenities:** 2 restaurants; bar; 4 pools; 3 golf courses; 19 tennis courts (9 lit); fitness center; watersports equipment; game rooms; coin-op washers and dryers. *In room:* A/C, TV, hair dryer.

MODERATE

Dockside Inn and Resort 👁️   Fronting the Intracoastal Waterway, the Dockside Inn is an ideal choice for boating and fishing enthusiasts, with 15 boat slips and two private fishing piers. The hotel itself carries on the nautical theme with pierlike wooden stairs and rope railings. While not exactly captain's quarters, the rooms (straight out of Rooms to Go, albeit with a bit of a nautical flair) are attractive enough. Higher-priced units have either waterfront balconies or small kitchenettes.

1160 Seaway Dr., S. Hutchinson Island, FL 34949. © **800/286-1745** or 772/468-3555. Fax 772/489-9848. www. docksideinn.com. 64 units. Winter $79 standard room, $95–$130 efficiency; $130–$155 suite; off season $70–$105 standard room or efficiency; $119–$145 suite. **Amenities:** 2 outdoor heated pools; self-service laundry; 5 lit fishing docks; boat dockage; grilling areas. *In room:* A/C, TV, dataport, kitchenette (in higher-priced rooms), minibar, coffeemaker.

WHERE TO DINE

Fort Pierce and St. Lucie aren't exactly gourmet destinations, but there are a few good restaurants. It's also easy to drive to Stuart for more diverse dining options. See p. 368 for recommendations in Stuart.

MODERATE

Alumni's International Grill AMERICAN   Formerly the Governor's Grill, Alumni's is the kind of place that serves beer and wings—and hosts short-skirt contests. It's far from fancy, but with a full bar, a major selection of beer, and live music on select nights, it's certainly a lively one.

122 N. 2nd St., Fort Pierce. © **772/466-6944**. Main courses $6–$18. AE, DISC, MC, V. Daily 11am–2am.

Mangrove Mattie's 👁️👁️ SEAFOOD   A rustic restaurant on the Fort Pierce Inlet, Mangrove Mattie's is the best place for outdoor dining, thanks to both its priceless location—right on the inlet, affording panoramic views of the Atlantic—and its excellent fresh seafood. Happy hours, Monday through Friday from 4 to 7pm, are especially popular and feature a free buffet.

1640 Seaway Dr., Fort Pierce. © **772/466-1044**. Main courses $11–$20. AE, DISC, MC, V. Daily 11:30am–10pm.

PORT ST. LUCIE & FORT PIERCE AFTER DARK

Wednesday Walkabout, an event to showcase the galleries, restaurants, and shops of Fort Pierce, is held the second Wednesday of every month from 5 to 8pm and costs $5 per person. It begins in front of the Sunrise Theater (© **772/466-3880**). All galleries are usually open for this event, and they supply free beverages and cheese. The free **Friday Fest Street Festival** (www.mainstreetfortpierce.org), on the first Friday of every month at the Historic Downtown Riverfront, has live music and refreshments for sale. **Whiskey Jay's,** 338 Port St. Lucie Blvd. (© **772/873-1111**), has jazz, blues, and rock music Tuesday through Sunday nights; reservations are recommended.

3 Vero Beach 👁️ & Sebastian 👁️👁️

Vero Beach: 87 miles S of Orlando; 95 miles N of Fort Lauderdale

Old Florida is thriving in these remote and tranquil villages. Vero Beach, known for its exclusive and affluent winter population, and Sebastian, known as one of the last remaining fishing villages, are set at the northern tip of the Treasure Coast region in Indian River County. These two beach towns are populated with folks who appreciate the area's small-town feel, and that's exactly the appeal for visitors: a laid-back atmosphere, friendly people, and friendlier prices.

A crowd of well-tanned surfers from all over the state descends on the region, especially the Sebastian Inlet, to catch some of the state's biggest waves. Other watersports enthusiasts enjoy the area's fine diving and windsurfing. Anglers are also in heaven here. In spring, baseball buffs can catch some action from the L.A. Dodgers as they train in exhibition games.

ESSENTIALS

The **Indian River County Tourist Council,** 1216 21st St., Vero Beach, FL 32961 (© 772/567-3491; fax 772/778-3181; www.vero-beach.fl.us/chamber), will send visitors a detailed information packet on the county (which includes Vero Beach and Sebastian), with a full-color map, a list of upcoming events, a hotel guide, and more.

BEACHES & OUTDOOR ACTIVITIES

BEACHES   You'll find plenty of free and open beachfront along the coast—most areas are uncrowded and are open from 7am until 10pm.

South Beach Park, on South Ocean Drive, at the end of Marigold Lane, is a busy, developed, lifeguarded beach with picnic tables, restrooms, and showers. It's known as one of the best swimming beaches in Vero Beach and attracts a young crowd that plays volleyball in a tranquil setting. A nature walk takes you onto beautiful secluded trails.

At the very north tip of the island, **Sebastian Inlet State Park** 🖈, 9700 S. Fla. A1A, Melbourne (© 321/984-4852), has flat, sandy beaches with lots of facilities, including kayak, paddleboat, and canoe rentals; a well-stocked surf shop; picnic tables; and a snack shop. The winds seem to stir up the surf with no jetty to stop the swells, to the delight of surfers and boarders who come here to catch the big waves. Campers enjoy fully equipped sites in a woody area. At press time, the park was readying itself for the arrival of cozy, 1,150- to 1,600-square-foot cabins with high-tech amenities, such as Internet access, as well as woodsy amenities, such as rocking chairs, porches, and fireplaces. According to one park official, however, it's not happening anytime soon, but rather, "in the distant future." Stay tuned. Entry fees to the park are $5 per car and $1 for those who walk or bike in.

FISHING   Capt. Terry Lamielle has been fishing the area for more than 40 years and will teach you all about fly-fishing for red fish, snook, and tarpon. His **Indian River Adventures** (© 321/725-7255; www.indianriveradventures.com) takes anglers on his *Sterling Flats* fishing boat for private river excursions. Half-day jaunts on the Indian River cost $300 for one or two people (the minimum required for a charter), tackle, rigs, and everything included; it's $50 extra for a third person.

Many other charters, guides, party boats, and tackle shops operate in this area. Consult your hotel for suggestions, or call the **Vero Beach Chamber of Commerce** (© 772/567-3491). You can also contact **Captain Hiram's** (© 772/589-4345; www.hirams.com), a restaurant/bar/hotel/marina that houses many charter boats.

GOLF   Hard-core golfers insist that of the dozens of courses in the area, only a handful are worth their plots of grass. Set on rolling hills with uncluttered views of sand dunes and sky, the **Sandridge Golf Club,** 5300 73rd St., Vero Beach (© 772/770-5000; www.sandridgegc.com), offers two par-72 18-holers. The Dunes is a long course with rolling fairways, while the newer Lakes course has lots of water. Both charge $27 to $47, including cart. Reservations are recommended and are taken 2 days in advance.

Although less challenging, the **Sebastian Municipal Golf Course,** 1010 E. Airport Dr. (© 772/589-6801; www.sebastiangolfcourse.org), is a good 18-hole par-72 course. It's scenic, well maintained, and a relative bargain. Greens fees are $18 to $44 per player, with cart.

Golfers who are also baseball fans will be pleased to know there are two golf courses at **Dodgertown** (p. 376).

TENNIS   Many of the tennis courts around Vero Beach and Sebastian are at hotels and resorts, and are thus closed to nonguests. Try **Riverside Racquet Complex,** 350 Dahlia Lane, at Royal Palm Boulevard at the east end of Barber Bridge, Vero Beach (© 772/231-4787). This popular park has 10 hard courts (6 lit) that can be rented for $4 per person per hour if you're a county resident, and $5 if not. Reservations are accepted up to 24 hours in advance.

SEEING THE SIGHTS

Environmental Learning Center 🎯🎯 🎯ids
The Indian River is not really a river at all, but a large, brackish lagoon that's home to a greater variety of species than any other estuary in North America—it has thousands of species of plants, animals, fish, and birds, including 36 species on the endangered list. The privately funded Environmental Learning Center was created to educate visitors about the Indian River area's environment. Situated on 51 island acres, the center features a 600-foot boardwalk through the mangroves and dozens of hands-on exhibits that are geared to both children and adults. There are touch tanks, exhibits, and microscopes for viewing the smallest sea life up close. The best thing to do is join one of the center's field excursion programs, from guided nature walks and stargazing to river cruise adventures. Best of all, prices range from free to $14 for adults and $6 for children.

255 Live Oak Dr. (just off the 510 Causeway), Wabasso Island (a 51-acre island in the Indian River Lagoon). © 772/ 589-5050. www.elcweb.org. Free admission. Tues–Fri 10am–4pm; Sat 9am–noon; Sun 1–4pm.

Indian River Citrus Museum
The tiny Indian River Citrus Museum exhibits artifacts relating to the history of the citrus industry, from its initial boom in the late 1800s to the present; a small grove displays several varieties. The gift shop sells citrus-themed items along with, of course, ready-to-ship fruit.

2140 14th Ave., Vero Beach. © 772/770-2263. Admission $1 donation. Tues–Fri 10am–4pm.

McKee Botanical Garden 🎯🎯
This impressive 18-acre attraction was originally opened in 1932 and featured a virtual jungle of orchids, exotic and native trees, monkeys, and birds. After years of neglect, it was placed on the National Register of Historic Places in 1998 and renovated; you can now again experience the full charms of this little Eden.

350 U.S. 1, Vero Beach. © 772/794-0601. Fax 772/794-0602. www.mckeegarden.org. Admission $6 adults, $5 seniors, $3.50 children 5–12. Tues–Sat 10am–5pm; Sun noon–5pm.

McLarty Treasure Museum 🎯
If you're unsure of why this area is called the Treasure Coast, this is a must-see. Built on the site of a salvage camp from a 1715 shipwreck, this little museum is full of interesting history. It may not have the treasures of the nearby Mel Fisher museum, but it shows an engaging 45-minute video describing the many aspects of treasure hunting. You'll also see household items salvaged from the Spanish fleet and dioramas of life in the 18th century.

13180 N. Fla. A1A, Sebastian Inlet State Recreation Area, Vero Beach. (✆ 772/589-2147. Admission $1, free for children 5 and under. Daily 10am–4:30pm.

DODGERTOWN

Vero is the winter home of the **Los Angeles Dodgers** (at least for the time being, as there's been talk of a move to Arizona in 2009; in order to move, the Dodgers will either have to pay off a bond issue or buy the stadium to get out of the local agreement, and it could cost the Dodgers about $16 million to break the lease, which expires in 2021). The 450-acre compound, **Dodgertown**, at 3901 26th St. ((✆ 772/569-4900; www.dodgertownverobeach.com), encompasses spring-training camp, two golf courses, a conference center, a country club, a movie theater, a recreation room, citrus groves, and a residential community. It is a city unto its own for baseball fanatics, though critics say it's not exactly state-of-the-art and, well, a bit long in the tooth. You can watch afternoon exhibition games between mid-February and the end of March in the comfortable 6,500-seat outdoor stadium. Even if the game sells out, you can sprawl on the lawn for just $8 (the stadium has never turned away an eager fan). When spring training is over, you can still catch a game: The Dodgers' farm team, the Vero Beach Devil Rays, has a full season of minor-league baseball in summer. Admission to the complex is free; tickets to games are about $15 for a reserved seat. The complex is open daily from 9am to 5pm, with game time usually at 1pm. From I-95, take the exit for S.R. 60 East to 43rd Avenue and turn left; continue to 26th Street and turn right.

SHOPPING

Ocean Boulevard and Cardinal Drive are Vero's two main shopping streets. Both are near the beach and lined with boutiques, including antiques and home-decor shops.

If you want to send fruit back home, the local source is **Hale Indian River Groves,** 615 Beachland Blvd. ((✆ **800/562-4502**; www.halegroves.com), a shipper of local citrus and jams since 1947, with four locations in Vero Beach. The grove is closed 2 to 3 months a year, usually from summer to early fall, depending on the crops; the season generally runs from November to Easter.

The **Horizon Outlet Center,** at S.R. 60 and I-95, Vero Beach ((✆ **877/GO-OUTLET** or 772/770-6171), contains more than 80 discount stores selling name-brand shoes, kitchenware, clothing, and more. The center is open Monday through Saturday from 9am to 8pm, and Sunday from 11am to 6pm.

Indian River Mall, 6200 20th St. (S.R. 60), about 5 miles east of I-95 ((✆ **772/770-6255**), is a monster mall with the big chains and several department stores. It's open Monday through Saturday from 10am to 9pm, and Sunday from noon to 6pm.

WHERE TO STAY

You can choose to stay on the mainland or on the beach. As you might expect, the beachfront accommodations are a bit more expensive—but, I think, worth it. A great spot to know, especially if you're planning to fish, is the **Key West Inn at Captain Hiram's,** 1580 U.S. Hwy. 1, Sebastian ((✆ **772/388-8588**; www.hirams.com), where 70 rooms are available adjacent to the restaurant and overlooking the water. (Also see "Fishing," above, and "Vero Beach & Sebastian After Dark," below.)

Comfortable and inexpensive chain options near the Horizon Outlet Center, off S.R. 60, include **Holiday Inn Express** ((✆ **800/465-4329** or 772/567-2500) and **Hampton Inn** ((✆ **800/426-7866** or 772/770-4299). Rates for both run between $99 and $120, and include breakfast and local calls.

EXPENSIVE

Vero Beach Hotel & Club It was only a matter of time before a luxurious condo/hotel rose on Vero Beach's scenic Ocean Drive. If it's luxury you want, this is the place, with 83 one-, two-, and three-bedroom, fully furnished suites, each with views of the ocean or pool and featuring West Indies–style decor with dark woods, Jerusalem stone flooring, granite countertops, and plasma and flatscreen TVs. Among the hotel's many amenities: a 5,000-square-foot spa and salon a high-end restaurant, the Indigo Room; and, best of all, a private beach club catering to your every whim.

3500 Ocean Dr., Vero Beach, FL 32963. © 866/602-VERO or 772/231-5666. Fax 772/234-4866. www.verobeach hotelandclub.com. 83 units. $179–$2,100. AE, MC, V. **Amenities:** Private beach club; oceanfront restaurant; pool bar & grill; heated oceanfront pool; private cabanas; golf privileges at local clubs; fitness center; spa concierge and valet parking services; room service. *In room:* A/C, TV/DVD, MP3 player, refrigerator, microwave, minibar.

MODERATE

The Caribbean Court *Finds* Although this looks like your typically charming Florida rental community, The Caribbean Court is a 17-room island-style inn with a heated pool, private beach, and the excellent on-site French restaurant, Maison Martinique (see "Where to Dine," below). Rooms are nicely furnished with four-poster beds, antique furniture, original Caribbean artwork, French country–style bathrooms with ceramic washbasins, kitchenettes, and balconies overlooking the pool. More for couples looking for romance than the area's other beachy keen hotels, The Caribbean Court has a beautiful honeymoon suite, too.

1601 Ocean Dr., Vero Beach, FL 32963. © 772/231-7211. www.thecaribbeancourt.com. 17 units. Winter $145–$195 double; off season $110–$125 double. Efficiencies cost $10 extra. AE, MC, V. **Amenities:** Restaurant; lounge; heated pool; private beach. *In room:* A/C, TV/DVD, fridge.

Driftwood Resort *Finds* Originally planned in the 1930s as a private estate by eccentric entrepreneur Waldo Sexton, the Driftwood was opened to the public in the late '30s. Since it was the largest property in Vero Beach, people assumed it was an attraction or, at least, a hotel. All of the guest rooms were renovated in 2000, and each is unique. Some have terra-cotta floors and lighter furniture, while others have a more rustic feel with hardwoods and antiques. Some of the rooms contain Jacuzzis, and all are equipped with full kitchens. Two of the best units are the Captain's Quarters, which overlooks the ocean with a private staircase to the pool, and the town house in the breezeway building, featuring a spiral staircase as well as living-room and bedroom views of the ocean. The resort is listed on the National Register of Historic Places and, to say the least, has lots of quirky charm.

3150 Ocean Dr., Vero Beach, FL 32963. © 772/231-0550. Fax 772/234-1981. www.thedriftwood.com. 100 units. Winter $140–$190 double, $200–$400 apt.; off season $100–$130 double, $140–$270 apt. AE, DISC, MC, V. **Amenities:** Oceanfront, Waldo's Restaurant, 2 outdoor heated pools; dry-cleaning. *In room:* A/C, TV, full or partial kitchen in all units, all units sleep at least 4, Jacuzzi (in some).

Islander Inn This is one of the most comfortable and welcoming inns in the area. Well located in downtown Vero Beach, the small, quaint Key West–meets–Old Florida–style motel is just a short walk to the beach, restaurants, and shops. Every breezy guest room has a small refrigerator, either a king-size bed or two double beds, paddle fans, wicker furniture, and vaulted ceilings. Rooms open onto a pretty courtyard and sparkling pool. Efficiencies have full kitchens.

3101 Ocean Dr., Vero Beach, FL 32963. © 800/952-5886 or 772/231-4431. 16 units. Winter $155–$185 double; off season $89–$109 double. Efficiencies cost $10 extra. AE, MC, V. **Amenities:** Cafe; pool. *In room:* A/C, TV, fridge.

Sea Turtle Inn & Apartments ⟨★⟩   This two-part, smoke-free property offers the best value on the beach (just 2 blocks from the ocean). The 1950s motel and an adjacent apartment building have been fully renovated and outfitted with understated yet efficient furnishings. You won't find any fancy amenities, but the price and location make up for what the place lacks in frills. The properties share a small pool and sun deck. Book early, especially in season, since they fill up quickly with long-term visitors.

835 Azalea Lane, Vero Beach, FL 32963. ⟨✆⟩ 877/998-8785 or 772/234-0788. www.seaturtleinn.net. 20 units. $99–$145 double; $135–$215 apt. Weekly and monthly rates available. MC, V. From I-95, go east on S.R. 60; it's about 10 miles to Cardinal Dr. Turn right onto Azalea Lane. **Amenities:** Small pool; bike rental; laundry facilities. *In room:* A/C, TV, minifridge, coffeemaker.

CAMPING

The Vero Beach and Sebastian areas of the Treasure Coast are popular with campers, who choose from nearly a dozen camping locations. If you aren't camping at the scenic and popular **Sebastian Inlet State Park** (p. 374), try the **Vero Beach RV Park,** 8850 U.S. 1, Wabasso (⟨✆⟩ **772/589-5665**). This 120-site campground is 2 miles from the ocean and the Intracoastal Waterway, and a quarter-mile from the Indian River, a big draw for fishing fanatics. There's access to running water and electricity, as well as showers, a shop, and hookups for RVs. Rates are $46 per site and $29 for tents. To get here, take I-95 to exit 69 East; at U.S. 1, turn left.

WHERE TO DINE
EXPENSIVE
Maison Martinique ★★★   FRENCH/CONTINENTAL   Exquisite country French cooking, a comprehensive wine list, and white-glove service complement the fine linens and imported china at this romantic standout owned and operated by Yannick Martin. Formerly known as Café du Soir, Maison Martinique is in the charming waterfront Caribbean Court Hotel. Excellent starters include Louisiana sausage with sautéed apples, foie gras with caramelized raisins, and exceptional escargot. Main courses include sautéed Dover sole and filet mignon stuffed with Roquefort cheese. Desserts might include raspberry and strawberry Napoleons and country apple tarts.

1605 Ocean Dr., Vero Beach. ⟨✆⟩ **772/231-7299.** www.thecaribbeancourt.com. Reservations recommended. Main courses $15–$40. AE, MC, V. Mon–Sat from 6pm; closing time varies based on last reservation.

MODERATE
Ocean Grill ★★ *(Finds)* STEAKS/SEAFOOD   The Ocean Grill attracts faithful devotees with its simple but rich cooking and its stunning locale, right on the ocean's edge; ask for a table along the wall of windows that open onto the sea. Built more than 60 years ago by Vero Beach eccentric Waldo Sexton, the restaurant was once an officers' club for residents of the nearby naval airbase during World War II. All fish can be prepared Cajun style, wood grilled, or deep-fried. Indian River crab cakes make for a memorable meal, deep-fried with fresh backfin and claw meat rolled in cracker meal. Try stone crab claws when they're in season, or the house shrimp scampi baked in butter and herbs and served with a tangy mustard sauce, or any of the big servings of meats. I especially recommend the Cajun rib-eye, featuring a béarnaise sauce that's delightfully jolting to the taste buds. Dinners are uniformly good here; the only tacky element of this place is the gift shop.

1050 Sexton Plaza (by the ocean at the end of S.R. 60), Vero Beach. ⟨✆⟩ **772/231-5409.** www.ocean-grill.com. Reservations accepted only for parties of 5 or more. Main courses $20–$35. AE, DC, DISC, MC, V. Mon–Fri 11:30am–2:30pm and 5:30–10pm; Sat–Sun 5:30–10pm. Closed Thanksgiving, Super Bowl Sun, and July 4.

INEXPENSIVE

Nino's Cafe 𝒦 ITALIAN   This little beachside cafe looks like a stereotypical pizza joint, complete with fake brick walls, murals of the Italian countryside, and red-and-white checked tablecloths. The atmosphere is pure cheese and so is much of the food—pizza and parmigiana dishes are smothered in the stuff. Still, the thin crust and fresh toppings make pizzas here a cut above the rest—just ask the New York transplants who live for the place. Entrees and pastas are also tasty.

1006 Easter Lily Lane (off Ocean Dr., next to Humiston Park), Vero Beach. ℭ **772/231-9311.** Main courses $9–$15. No credit cards. Mon–Thurs 11am–9pm; Fri–Sat 11am–10pm; Sun 4–9pm.

VERO BEACH & SEBASTIAN AFTER DARK

More than half of the residents in this area are retirees, so it shouldn't be a surprise that, even on weekends, this town retires early. Hotel lounges often have live music and a good bar scene, however, especially in high season, and sometimes stay open as late as 1am, if you're lucky. For beachside drinks, go to the **Driftwood Resort** (p. 377).

A mostly 30-something and younger crowd goes to **Bombay Louie's,** 398 21st St., Vero Beach (ℭ **772/978-0209**), where a DJ spins dance music after 9pm Wednesday through Saturday.

Vero Beach is also known as an artsy enclave, hosting galleries such as the **Admiralty Gallery,** 3315 Ocean Dr., Vero Beach (ℭ **772/231-3178**). The **Civic Arts Center,** at Riverside Park, is a hub of culture; it includes the **Riverside Theatre** (ℭ **772/231-6990**), the **Agnes Wahlstrom Youth Playhouse** (ℭ **772/234-8052**), and the **Center for the Arts** (ℭ **772/231-0707**), known for films and an excellent lecture series.

In Sebastian, you'll find live music every weekend (and daily in season) at **Captain Hiram's,** 1606 N. Indian River Dr. (ℭ **772/589-4345**), a salty outdoor restaurant and bar on the Intracoastal Waterway that locals and tourists love at all hours of the day and night (well, until it closes at 11pm, that is). The feel is tacky Key West, complete with a sand floor and thatched-roof bar.

North of the inlet, head for the tried-and-true **Sebastian Beach Inn** (SBI to locals), 7035 S. Fla. A1A (ℭ **321/728-4311**), for live music on weekends. Jazz, blues, or sometimes rock 'n' roll starts at 9pm on Friday and Saturday. On Sunday, it's old-style reggae after 2pm. The inn is open daily for drinks from 11am until anytime between midnight and 2am.

4 A Side Trip Inland: Fishing at Lake Okeechobee 𝒦𝒦𝒦

60 miles SW of West Palm Beach

Many visitors to the Treasure Coast come to fish, and they certainly get their fill off the miles of Atlantic shore and on the inland rivers. But if you want to fish freshwater and nothing else, head for "The Lake"—**Lake Okeechobee,** that is. The state's largest, it's chock-full of good eating fish. Only about a 1½-hour drive from the coast, it makes a great day or weekend excursion.

ESSENTIALS

GETTING THERE   From Palm Beach, take I-95 S. to Southern Boulevard (U.S. 98 W.) in West Palm Beach, which merges with S.R. 80 and S.R. 441. Follow signs for S.R. 80 West through Belle Glade to South Bay. In South Bay, turn right onto U.S. 27 North, which leads directly to Clewiston.

VISITOR INFORMATION   Contact the **Clewiston Chamber of Commerce,** 544 W. Sugarland Hwy., Clewiston, FL 33440 (℃ **863/983-7979;** www.clewiston.org), for maps, business directories, and the names of numerous fishing guides throughout the area. In addition, you might contact the **Pahokee Chamber of Commerce,** 115 E. Main St., Pahokee, FL 33476 (℃ **772/924-5579;** fax 772/924-8116; www.pahokee. com), which will send a complete package of magazines, guides, and accommodations listings.

OUTDOOR ACTIVITIES

FISHING   See "Going After the Big One," below.

SKY DIVING   Besides fishing, the biggest sport in Clewiston is jumping out of planes, due to the area's limited air traffic and vast areas of flat, undeveloped land. **Air Adventures** (℃ **800/533-6151** or 863/983-6151; www.skydivefl.com) operates a year-round program from the Airglades Airport. If you've never jumped before, you can go on a tandem dive, where you'll be attached to a "jumpmaster." For the first 60 seconds, the two of you free-fall from about 12,500 feet. Then a quick pull of the chute turns your rapid descent into a gentle, balletlike cruise to the ground, with time to see the whole majestic lake from a privileged perspective. Dive packages start at $185; group rates start at $175. (**Note:** You must be 18 or older and weigh less than 240 lb.)

WHERE TO STAY

If you aren't camping, book a room at the **Clewiston Inn** *(★★,* 108 Royal Palm Ave., Clewiston (℃ **800/749-4466** or 863/983-8151; www.clewistoninn.com). Built in 1938, this allegedly haunted, Southern plantation–inspired hotel is the oldest in the Lake Okeechobee region. Rumor has it that a very friendly, pretty female ghost roams the halls at night. Its 52 rooms are simply decorated and nondescript. The lounge area sports a 1945 mural depicting the animals of the region. Double rooms start at $99 a night; suites begin at $129. All have air-conditioning and TVs.

Another choice, especially if you're here to fish, is **Roland Martin,** 920 E. Del Monte (℃ **800/473-6766** or 863/983-3151; www.rolandmartinmarina.com), the "Disney of fishing." This RV park (no tent sites) has modest motel rooms, efficiencies, condominiums, apartments, RV hookups and trailers, with two heated pools, gift and marina shops, and a restaurant. The modern complex, dotted with prefab buildings, is clean and well manicured. Rooms rent from $68 to $95; efficiencies cost from $88 to $105. Condominiums are about $150 to $185 a night, with a 3-night minimum. One- or two-bedroom trailers with full kitchen and living room are $65 to $105. Full hook-up RV Sites are $30 a night and include power, water, sewage, and cable TV.

CAMPING

During the winter, campers own the Clewiston area. Campsites are jammed with regulars who come year after year for the simple pleasures of the lake and, of course, the warm weather. Every manner of RV, from simple pop-top Volkswagens to Winnebagos to fully decked-out mobile homes, finds its way to a lakeside campsite.

Okeechobee Landings, U.S. 27 E. (℃ **863/983-4144;** www.okeechobeelandingsrv. com), is one of the best; it has every conceivable amenity included in the price of a site. More than 250 sites are situated around a lake, clubhouse, snack bar, pool, Jacuzzi, horseshoe pit, shuffleboard court, and tennis court. Full hookup includes a sewage connection, which is not the case throughout the county. RV spots are sold to regulars, but there are usually some spots available for rental to one-time visitors. Rates start at $38.50 a day or $192.50 a week, plus tax, including hookup.

Going After the Big One

Fishing on Lake Okeechobee is a year-round affair, though the fish tend to bite a little better in the winter, perhaps for the benefit of the many snowbirds who flock here (especially Feb–Mar). RV camps are mobbed almost year-round with fish-frenzied anglers who come down for weeks at a time for a decent catch.

You'll need a fishing license to go out with a rod and reel. It's a simple matter to apply. The chamber of commerce and most fishing shops can sign you up on the spot. The cost for non-Florida residents is $17 for 7 days or $47 for the year.

You can rent, charter, or bring your own boat to Clewiston; just be sure to schedule your trip in advance. You don't want to show up during one of the frequent fishing tournaments only to find you can't get a room, campsite, or fishing boat. All tournaments are held at Roland Martin's marina (see below). For more information on tournaments, check out www.roland martinmarina.com.

There are several marinas where you can rent or charter boats. If it's your first time on the lake, I suggest chartering a boat with a guide who can show you the most fertile spots and help you handle your tackle. **Roland Martin, 920 E. Del Monte** (© **863/983-3151**; www.rolandmartinmarina.com), is the one-stop spot where you can find a guide, tackle, rods, bait, coolers, picnic supplies, and a choice of boats. Rates for a guided fishing tour are $250 for a half-day and $350 for a full day, for one or two people. You need a fishing license, which is available here for $17. There are also boat rentals: A 16-foot johnboat goes for $40 half-day and $60 full day, with a $40 deposit. Rentals for a 14-footer start at $60 for a half-day, for a maximum of four people. A full day costs $80. If you want a guide, rates start at $250 (for two people) for a half-day, though in the summer (June–Oct), when it's slow, you can get a cheaper deal.

Also see **Roland Martin,** described above.

WHERE TO DINE

If you aren't frying up your own catch for dinner, you may want to reconsider it, as dining options here are few and far between. Thank goodness for the **Clewiston Inn** (see "Where to Stay," above), where you can get catfish, beef stroganoff, ham hocks, fried chicken, and liver and onions in a setting as Southern as the food. The dining room is open daily from 6am to 2pm and 5 to 9pm; entrees cost $10 to $18. Sunday brunch is served from 11:30am to 3pm and a new lunch buffet served Monday through Friday features traditional southern foods, a salad bar, dessert assortment, and beverage for $8.95. **Lightsey's,** 1040 Rte. 78 (© **863/763-4276**), housed in a lodge, started as a fish company and has expanded to a full-service restaurant. Any catch of the day can be broiled, fried, grilled, or steamed. Try the frogs' legs, gator, and catfish. Entrees are less than $10. Open daily from 11am to 9pm.

Appendix:
Fast Facts, Toll-Free
Numbers & Websites

1 Fast Facts: South Florida

AMERICAN EXPRESS You'll find American Express offices in downtown Miami at 330 Biscayne Blvd. (© **305/ 358-7350**); 9700 Collins Ave., Bal Harbour (© **305/865-5959**); and 32 Miracle Mile, Coral Gables (© **305/446-3381**). Offices are open weekdays from 9am to 5pm and Saturday from 10am to 4pm. The Bal Harbour office is also open on Sunday from noon to 6pm. To report lost or stolen traveler's checks, call © **800/ 221-7282**. Other South Florida American Express offices include 2451 E. Atlantic Blvd., Pompano Beach (© **954/ 952-2300**), and 3312 NE 32nd St., Fort Lauderdale (© **954/565-9481**).

AREA CODES The original area code for Miami and all of Dade County was 305. That is still the code for older phone numbers, but all phone numbers assigned since July 1998 have the area code 786 (SUN). For all local calls, even if you're calling across the street, you must dial the area code (305 or 786) first. Even though the Keys still share the Dade County area code of 305, calls to there from Miami are considered long distance and must be preceded by 1-305. (Within the Keys, simply dial the seven-digit number.) The area code for Fort Lauderdale is 954; for Palm Beach, Boca Raton, Vero Beach, and Port St. Lucie, it's 561.

ATM NETWORKS ATMs are as ubiquitous in South Florida as the palm trees. Machines are found on nearly every street corner, in main shopping areas, and, in most cases, in supermarkets and even convenience stores.

AUTOMOBILE ORGANIZATIONS Auto clubs will supply maps, suggested routes, guidebooks, accident and bail-bond insurance, and emergency road service. The **American Automobile Association (AAA)** is the major auto club in the United States. If you belong to an auto club in your home country, inquire about AAA reciprocity before you leave. You may be able to join AAA even if you're not a member of a reciprocal club; to inquire, call AAA (© **800/222-4357**). AAA is actually an organization of regional auto clubs, so look under "AAA Automobile Club" in the White Pages of the telephone directory. AAA has a nationwide emergency road service telephone number (© **800/AAA-HELP**).

BUSINESS HOURS Banking hours vary, but most banks are open weekdays from 9am to 3pm. Several stay open until 5pm or so at least 1 day during the week, and many banks feature ATMs for 24-hour banking. Most stores are open daily from 10am to 6pm; however, there are many exceptions. In Miami, shops in the Bayside Marketplace are usually open until 9 or 10pm, as are the boutiques in Coconut Grove. Boutiques on South Beach operate in their own time zone and hours range from 11am to midnight, sometimes earlier, sometimes later. Stores in Bal Harbour and other malls are usually open an extra hour 1 night during the week (usually Thurs). As far as business offices are concerned, Miami is generally a 9-to-5 town. In the Keys, hours are much more leisurely, and often left at the discretion of the proprietors. Call ahead before you go. In Key West, however, hours are similar to those in South Beach. Things are open rather late there. In Fort Lauderdale, hours are typically 9am to 5pm for businesses, but on the "Strip" (Las Olas Blvd. and downtown Fort Lauderdale), shops, restaurants, and clubs tend to stay open into the wee hours, or at least after midnight. Boca Raton, Palm Beach, and the Treasure Coast are entirely different and tend to keep earlier hours, with stores closing between 5 and 6pm and restaurants closing around 11pm, with the exception of those stores and restaurants on Clematis Street.

CAR RENTALS See "Getting Around," p. 39.

CLIMATE See "When to Go," p. 30.

CURRENCY The most common bills are the $1 (a "buck"), $5, $10, and $20 denominations. There are also $2 bills (seldom encountered), $50 bills, and $100 bills (the last two are usually not welcome as payment for small purchases).

Coins come in seven denominations: 1¢ (1 cent, or a penny); 5¢ (5 cents, or a nickel); 10¢ (10 cents, or a dime); 25¢ (25 cents, or a quarter); 50¢ (50 cents, or a half dollar); the gold-colored Sacagawea coin, worth $1; and the rare silver dollar.

For additional information see "Money," p. 29.

DRINKING LAWS The legal age for purchase and consumption of alcoholic beverages is 21; proof of age is required and often requested at bars, nightclubs, and restaurants, so it's always a good idea to bring ID when you go out.

Do not carry open containers of alcohol in your car or any public area that isn't zoned for alcohol consumption. The police can fine you on the spot. And nothing will ruin your trip faster than getting a citation for DUI ("driving under the influence"), so don't even think about driving while intoxicated. Beer and wine are sold in most supermarkets and convenience stores. Most liquor stores throughout South Florida are closed on Sundays, but liquor stores in the city of Miami Beach are open all week.

ELECTRICITY Like Canada, the United States uses 110 to 120 volts AC (60 cycles), compared to 220 to 240 volts AC (50 cycles) in most of Europe, Australia, and New Zealand. Downward converters that change 220 to 240 volts to 110 to 120 volts are difficult to find in the United States, so bring one with you.

EMBASSIES & CONSULATES All embassies are located in the nation's capital, Washington, D.C. Some consulates are located in major U.S. cities, and most nations have a mission to the United Nations in New York City. If your country isn't listed below, call for directory information in Washington, D.C. (© 202/ 555-1212) or log on to www.embassy. org/embassies.

The embassy of **Australia** is at 1601 Massachusetts Ave. NW, Washington, DC 20036 (© 202/797-3000; www. austemb.org). There are consulates in New York, Honolulu, Houston, Los Angeles, and San Francisco.

The embassy of **Canada** is at 501 Pennsylvania Ave. NW, Washington, DC 20001 (© 202/682-1740; www.canadian embassy.org). Other Canadian consulates are in Buffalo (New York), Detroit, Los Angeles, New York, and Seattle.

The embassy of **Ireland** is at 2234 Massachusetts Ave. NW, Washington, DC 20008 (© 202/462-3939; www. irelandemb.org). Irish consulates are in Boston, Chicago, New York, San Francisco, and other cities. See website for complete listing.

The embassy of **New Zealand** is at 37 Observatory Circle NW, Washington, DC 20008 (② **202/328-4800;** www.nzemb.org). New Zealand consulates are in Los Angeles, Salt Lake City, San Francisco, and Seattle.

The embassy of the **United Kingdom** is at 3100 Massachusetts Ave. NW, Washington, DC 20008 (② **202/588-7800;** www.britainusa.com). Other British consulates are in Atlanta, Boston, Chicago, Cleveland, Houston, Los Angeles, New York, San Francisco, and Seattle.

EMERGENCIES To reach the police, ambulance, or fire department, dial ② **911** from any phone. No coins are needed. Emergency hot lines include **Crisis Intervention** (② **305/358-HELP** or 305/358-4357) and the **Poison Information Center** (② **800/282-3171**). For crisis emergencies in Broward County, call **First Call for Help** (② **954/467-6333**), and in Palm Beach, call **Crisis Line** (② **561/930-1234**).

GASOLINE (PETROL) At press time, in the U.S., the cost of gasoline (also known as gas, but never petrol), is abnormally high. Taxes are already included in the printed price. One U.S. gallon equals 3.8 liters or .85 imperial gallons. Fill-up locations are known as gas or service stations.

HOLIDAYS Banks, government offices, post offices, and many stores, restaurants, and museums are closed on the following legal national holidays: January 1 (New Year's Day), the third Monday in January (Martin Luther King, Jr., Day), the third Monday in February (Presidents' Day), the last Monday in May (Memorial Day), July 4th (Independence Day), the first Monday in September (Labor Day), the second Monday in October (Columbus Day), November 11 (Veterans' Day/Armistice Day), the fourth Thursday in November (Thanksgiving Day), and December 25 (Christmas). The Tuesday after the first Monday in November is Election Day, a federal government holiday in presidential-election years (2008, 2012, and so on).

For more information on holidays see "South Florida Calendar of Events" (p. 31).

LEGAL AID If you are "pulled over" for a minor infraction (such as speeding), never attempt to pay the fine directly to a police officer; this could be construed as attempted bribery, a much more serious crime. Pay fines by mail, or directly into the hands of the clerk of the court. If accused of a more serious offense, say and do nothing before consulting a lawyer. Here the burden is on the state to prove a person's guilt beyond a reasonable doubt, and everyone has the right to remain silent, whether he or she is suspected of a crime or actually arrested. Once arrested, a person can make one telephone call to a party of his or her choice. International visitors should call their embassy or consulate.

LOST & FOUND Be sure to tell all of your credit card companies the minute you discover your wallet has been lost or stolen and file a report at the nearest police precinct. Your credit card company or insurer may require a police report number or record of the loss. Most credit card companies have an emergency toll-free number to call if your card is lost or stolen; they may be able to wire you a cash advance immediately or deliver an emergency credit card in a day or two. Visa's U.S. emergency number is ② **800/847-2911** or 410/581-9994. American Express cardholders and traveler's check holders should call ② **800/221-7282.** MasterCard holders should call ② **800/307-7309** or 636/722-7111. For other credit cards, call the toll-free number directory at ② **800/555-1212.**

If you need emergency cash over the weekend when all banks and American Express offices are closed, you can have money wired to you via **Western Union**

(☎ 800/325-6000; www.westernunion. com).

MAIL At press time, domestic postage rates were 24¢ for a postcard and 39¢ for a letter. For international mail, a first-class letter of up to 1 ounce costs 84¢ (63¢ to Canada and Mexico); a first-class postcard costs 75¢ (55¢ to Canada and Mexico); and a preprinted postal aerogramme costs 75¢. For more information go to www.usps.com and click on "Calculate Postage."

If you aren't sure what your address will be in the United States, mail can be sent to you, in your name, c/o General Delivery, at the main post office of the city or region where you expect to be. (Call ☎ 800/275-8777 for information on the nearest post office.) The addressee must pick up mail in person and must produce proof of identity (driver's license, passport, or other). Most post offices will hold your mail for up to 1 month, and are open Monday to Friday from 8am to 6pm, and Saturday from 9am to 3pm.

Always include zip codes when mailing items in the U.S. If you don't know your zip code, visit www.usps.com/zip4.

NEWSPAPERS & MAGAZINES The *Miami Herald* is Miami's only English-language daily. It is especially known for its extensive Latin American coverage and has a decent Friday "Weekend" entertainment guide. It also publishes a Broward County edition for the Fort Lauderdale area. Fort Lauderdale's major daily is the *Sun-Sentinel*, while Palm Beach has the *Post*. The most respected alternative weekly in South Florida is the give-away tabloid called *New Times*, which contains up-to-date listings and reviews of food, films, theater, music, and whatever else is happening in town. There are Miami as well as Broward/Palm Beach editions. Also free is *Ocean Drive*, an oversized glossy magazine that's limited on text and heavy on ads and society photos; it's available at a number of chic boutiques, hotels, restaurants, and newsstands.

PASSPORTS For Residents of Australia: You can pick up an application from your local post office or any branch of Passports Australia, but you must schedule an interview at the passport office to present your application materials. Call the **Australian Passport Information Service** at ☎ 131-232, or visit the government website at www.passports.gov.au.

For Residents of Canada: Passport applications are available at travel agencies throughout Canada or from the central **Passport Office,** Department of Foreign Affairs and International Trade, Ottawa, ON K1A 0G3 (☎ 800/567-6868; www.ppt.gc.ca). *Note:* Canadian children who travel must have their own passport. However, if you hold a valid Canadian passport issued before December 11, 2001, that bears the name of your child, the passport remains valid for you and your child until it expires.

For Residents of Ireland: You can apply for a 10-year passport at the **Passport Office,** Setanta Centre, Molesworth Street, Dublin 2 (☎ 01/671-1633; www.irlgov.ie/iveagh). Those under age 18 and over 65 must apply for a €12 3-year passport. You can also apply at 1A South Mall, Cork (☎ 021/272-525) or at most main post offices.

For Residents of New Zealand: You can pick up a passport application at any New Zealand Passports Office or download it from their website. Contact the **Passports Office** at ☎ 0800/225-050 in New Zealand or 04/474-8100, or log on to www.passports.govt.nz.

For Residents of the United Kingdom: To pick up an application for a standard 10-year passport (5-year passport for children 15 and under), visit your nearest passport office, major post office, or travel agency or contact the **United Kingdom Passport Service** at ☎ 0870/521-0410 or search its website at www.ukpa.gov.uk.

POLICE   For emergencies, dial ✆ **911** from any phone. No coins are needed. For other matters, call ✆ **305/595-6263.** The Broward County Sheriff's Office number is (✆ **954/831-8900**); the Palm Beach County Sheriff's Office number is (✆ **561/470-5257**).

SAFETY   See "Health & Safety" (p. 41).

SMOKING   Smoking is no longer allowed in restaurants. A law passed prohibiting smoking in any establishment that makes the bulk of its money in food sales. Outdoor areas are immune to these laws, and some restaurants have ignored the law and still permit smoking indoors.

TAXES   A 6% state sales tax (plus 0.5% local tax, for a total of 6.5% in Miami) is added on at the register for all goods and services purchased in Florida. In addition, most municipalities levy special taxes on restaurants and hotels. In Surfside, hotel taxes total 10.5%; in Bal Harbour, 9.5%; in Miami Beach (including South Beach), 11.5%; and in the rest of Dade County, a whopping 12.5%. In Miami Beach, Surfside, and Bal Harbour, the resort (hotel) tax also applies to hotel restaurants and restaurants with liquor licenses. Broward and Palm Beach County sales tax is 6.5%. Resort taxes in Palm Beach are 4%, while Broward County charges a 5% tax only for conventions, not for tourists.

TELEPHONE & FAX   Generally, hotel surcharges on long-distance and local calls are astronomical, so you're better off using your **cellphone** or a **public pay telephone.** Many convenience groceries and packaging services sell **prepaid calling cards** in denominations up to $50; for international visitors these can be the least expensive way to call home. Many public phones at airports now accept American Express, MasterCard, and Visa credit cards. **Local calls** made from public pay phones in most locales cost either 25¢ or 35¢. Pay phones do not accept pennies, and few will take anything larger than a quarter.

Most long-distance and international calls can be dialed directly from any phone. **For calls within the United States and to Canada,** dial 1 followed by the area code and the seven-digit number. **For other international calls,** dial 011 followed by the country code, city code, and the number you are calling.

Calls to area codes **800, 888, 877,** and **866** are toll-free. However, calls to area codes **700** and **900** (chat lines, bulletin boards, "dating" services, and so on) can be very expensive—usually a charge of 95¢ to $3 or more per minute, and they sometimes have minimum charges that can run as high as $15 or more.

For **reversed-charge or collect calls,** and for **person-to-person calls,** dial the number 0 and then the area code and number; an operator will come on the line, and you should specify whether you are calling collect, person-to-person, or both. If your operator-assisted call is international, ask for the overseas operator.

For **local directory assistance** ("information"), dial 411; for long-distance information, dial 1, and then the appropriate area code and 555-1212.

Most hotels have **fax machines** available for guest use (be sure to ask about the charge to use it). Many hotel rooms are even wired for guests' fax machines. A less expensive way to send and receive faxes may be at stores such as **The UPS Store** (formerly Mail Boxes Etc.).

TIME   Florida, like New York, is in the **Eastern Standard Time (EST)** zone. The continental United States is divided into **four time zones:** Eastern Standard Time (EST), Central Standard Time (CST), Mountain Standard Time (MST), and Pacific Standard Time (PST). Alaska and Hawaii have their own zones. For example, when it's 9am in Los Angeles (PST), it's 7am in Honolulu (HST),10am in Denver (MST), 11am in Chicago (CST), noon in New York City (EST), 5pm in London (GMT), and 2am the next day in Sydney.

Daylight saving time takes effect at 2am the second Sunday in March until 2am the last Sunday in October, except in Arizona, Hawaii, the U.S. Virgin Islands, and Puerto Rico. Daylight savings moves the clock 1 hour ahead of standard time.

TIPPING Tips are a very important part of certain workers' income, and gratuities are the standard way of showing appreciation for services provided. (Tipping is certainly not compulsory if the service is poor!) In hotels, tip **bellhops** at least $1 per bag ($2–$3 if you have a lot of luggage) and tip the **chamber staff** $1 to $2 per day (more if you've left a disaster area for him or her to clean up). Tip the **doorman** or **concierge** only if he or she has provided you with some specific service (for example, calling a cab for you or obtaining difficult-to-get theater tickets). Tip the **valet-parking attendant** $1 every time you get your car.

In restaurants, bars, and nightclubs, tip **service staff** 15% to 20% of the check, tip **bartenders** 10% to 15%, tip **checkroom attendants** $1 per garment, and tip **valet-parking attendants** $1 per vehicle.

As for other service personnel, tip **cab drivers** 15% of the fare; tip **skycaps** at airports at least $1 per bag ($2–$3 if you have a lot of luggage); and tip **hairdressers** and **barbers** 15% to 20%.

TOILETS You won't find public toilets or "restrooms" on the streets in most U.S. cities but they can be found in hotel lobbies, bars, restaurants, museums, department stores, railway and bus stations, and service stations. Large hotels and fast-food restaurants are often the best bet for clean facilities. If possible, avoid the toilets at parks and beaches, which tend to be dirty; some may be unsafe. Restaurants

and bars in resorts or heavily visited areas may reserve their restrooms for patrons.

USEFUL PHONE NUMBERS U.S. Department of State Travel Advisory: ℭ **202/647-5225** (manned 24 hr.).

U.S. Passport Agency: ℭ **202/647-0518.**

U.S. Centers for Disease Control International Traveler's Hot Line: ℭ **404/332-4559.**

VISAS For information about U.S. visas go to **http://travel.state.gov** and click on "Visas." Or go to one of the following websites.

Australian citizens can obtain up-to-date visa information from the **U.S. Embassy Canberra,** Moonah Place, Yarralumla, ACT 2600 (ℭ **02/6214-5600**) or by checking the U.S. Diplomatic Mission's website at http://us embassy-australia.state.gov/consular.

British subjects can obtain up-to-date visa information by calling the **U.S. Embassy Visa Information Line** (ℭ **0891/200-290**) or by visiting the "Visas to the U.S." section of the American Embassy London's website at www. usembassy.org.uk.

Irish citizens can obtain up-to-date visa information through the **Embassy of the USA Dublin,** 42 Elgin Rd., Dublin 4, Ireland (ℭ **353/1-668-8777**), or by checking the "Consular Services" section of the website at http://dublin. usembassy.gov.

Citizens of **New Zealand** can obtain up-to-date visa information by contacting the **U.S. Embassy New Zealand,** 29 Fitzherbert Terrace, Thorndon, Wellington (ℭ **644/472-2068**), or get the information directly from the "For New Zealanders" section of the website at http://usembassy.org.nz.

WEATHER Hurricane season runs from August through November. For an up-to-date recording of current weather conditions and forecast reports, call ℭ **305/229-4522.**

2 Toll-Free Numbers & Websites

MAJOR U.S. AIRLINES

(*flies internationally as well)

Alaska Airlines/Horizon Air
© 800/252/7522
www.alaskaair.com

American Airlines*
© 800/433-7300 (in U.S. or Canada)
© 020/7365-0777 (in U.K.)
www.aa.com

ATA Airlines
© 800/435-9282
www.ata.com

Cape Air
© 800/352-0714
www.flycapeair.com

Continental Airlines*
© 800/523-3273 (in U.S. or Canada)
© 084/5607-6760 (in U.K.)
www.continental.com

Delta Air Lines*
© 800/221-1212 (in U.S. or Canada)
© 084/5600-0950 (in U.K.)
www.delta.com

Frontier Airlines
© 800/432-1359
www.frontierairlines.com

Hawaiian Airlines*
© 800/367-5320 (in U.S. or Canada)
www.hawaiianair.com

JetBlue Airways
© 800/538-2583 (in U.S.)
© 080/1365-2525 (in U.K. or Canada)
www.jetblue.com

Midwest Airlines
© 800/452-2022
www.midwestairlines.com

Nantucket Airlines
© 800/635-8787
www.nantucketairlines.com

North American Airlines*
© 800/371-6297
www.flynaa.com

Northwest Airlines
© 800/225-2525 (in U.S.)
© 870/0507-4074 (in U.K.)
www.flynaa.com

Pan Am Clipper Connection
© 800/359-7262
www.flypanam.com

PenAir (The Spirit of Alaska)
© 800/448-4226 (in U.S.)
www.penair.com

Skybus
© no phone
www.skybus.com

United Airlines*
© 800/864-8331 (in U.S. or Canada)
© 084/5844-4777 (in U.K.)
www.united.com

US Airways*
© 800/428-4322 (in U.S. or Canada)
© 084/5600-3300 (in U.K.)
www.usairways.com

Virgin America*
© 877/359-8474
www.virginamerica.com

MAJOR INTERNATIONAL AIRLINES

Aeroméxico
© 800/237-6639 (in U.S.)
© 020/7801-6234 (in U.K.,
    information only)
www.aeromexico.com

Air France
© 800/237-2747 (in U.S.)
© 800/375-8723 (in U.S. or Canada)
© 087/0142-4343 (in U.K.)
www.airfrance.com

Air India
- 212/407-1371 (in U.S.)
- 91 22 2279 6666 (in India)
- 020/8745-1000 (in U.K.)
- www.airindia.com

Air Jamaica
- 800/523-5585 (in U.S. or Canada)
- 208/570-7999 (in Jamaica)
- www.airjamaica.com

Air New Zealand
- 800/262-1234 (in U.S.)
- 800/663-5494 (in Canada)
- 0800/028-4149 (in U.K.)
- www.airnewzealand.com

Air Tahiti Nui
- 877/824-4846 (in U.S. or Canada)
- www.airtahitinui-usa.com

Alitalia
- 800/223-5730 (in U.S.)
- 800/361-8336 (in Canada)
- 087/0608-6003 (in U.K.)
- www.alitalia.com

American Airlines
- 800/433-7300 (in U.S. or Canada)
- 020/7365-0777 (in U.K.)
- www.aa.com

Aviacsa (Mexico and southern U.S.)
- www.aviacsa.com.mx

Bahamasair
- 800/222-4262 (in U.S.)
- 242/300-8359 (in Family Islands)
- 242/377-5505 (in Nassau)
- www.bahamasair.com

British Airways
- 800/247-9297 (in U.S. or Canada)
- 087/0850-9850 (in U.K.)
- www.british-airways.com

Caribbean Airlines (formerly BWIA)
- 800/920-4225 (in U.S. or Canada)
- 084/5362 4225 (in U.K.)
- www.caribbean-airlines.com

China Airlines
- 800/227-5118 (in U.S.)
- 022/715-1212 (in Taiwan)
- www.china-airlines.com

Continental Airlines
- 800/523-3273 (in U.S. or Canada)
- 084/5607-6760 (in U.K.)
- www.continental.com

Cubana
- 888/667-1222 (in Canada)
- 020/7538-5933 (in U.K.)
- www.cubana.cu

Delta Air Lines
- 800/221-1212 (in U.S. or Canada)
- 084/5600-0950 (in U.K.)
- www.delta.com

EgyptAir
- 212/581-5600 (in U.S.)
- 020/7734-2343 (in U.K.)
- 09/007-0000 (in Egypt)
- www.egyptair.com

El Al Airlines
- 972/3977-1111 (outside Israel)
- *2250 (from any phone in Israel)
- www.el.co.il

Emirates Airlines
- 800/777-3999 (in U.S.)
- 087/0243-2222 (in U.K.)
- www.emirates.com

Finnair
- 800/950-5000 (in U.S. or Canada)
- 087/0241-4411 (in U.K.)
- www.finnair.com

Hawaiian Airlines
- 800/367-5320 (in U.S. or Canada)
- www.hawaiianair.com

Iberia Airlines
- 800/722-4642 (in U.S. or Canada)
- 087/0609-0500 (in U.K.)
- www.iberia.com

Icelandair
- 800/223-5500 ext 2 prompt 1 (in U.S. or Canada)
- 084/5758-1111 (in U.K.)
- www.icelandair.com
- www.icelandair.co.uk (in U.K.)

Israir Airlines
- 877/477-2471 (in U.S. or Canada)
- 700/505-777 (in Israel)
- www.israirairlines.com

Japan Airlines
℃ 012/025-5931 (international)
www.jal.co.jp

Korean Air
℃ 800/438-5000 (in U.S. or Canada)
℃ 0800/413-000 (in U.K.)
www.koreanair.com

Lan Airlines
℃ 866/435-9526 (in U.S.)
℃ 305/670-9999 (in other countries)
www.lanchile.com

Lufthansa
℃ 800/399-5838 (in U.S.)
℃ 800/563-5954 (in Canada)
℃ 087/0837-7747 (in U.K.)
www.lufthansa.com

North American Airlines
℃ 800/359-6222
www.flynaa.com

Olympic Airlines
℃ 800/223-1226 (in U.S.)
℃ 514/878-9691 (in Canada)
℃ 087/0606-0460 (in U.K.)
www.olympicairlines.com

Philippine Airlines
℃ 800/I-Fly-Pal (800/435-9725) (in U.S. or Canada)
℃ 632/855-8888 (in Philippines)
www.philippineairlines.com

Qantas Airways
℃ 800/227-4500 (in U.S.)
℃ 084/5774-7767 (in U.K. or Canada)
℃ 13 13 13 (in Australia)
www.qantas.com

BUDGET AIRLINES

Aegean Airlines
℃ 210/626-1000 (in U.S., Canada, or U.K.)
www.aegeanair.com

Aer Lingus
℃ 800/474-7424 (in U.S. or Canada)
℃ 087/0876-5000 (in U.K.)
www.aerlingus.com

South African Airways
℃ 271/1978-5313 (international)
℃ 0861 FLYSAA (086/135-9122) (in South Africa)
www.flysaa.com

Swiss Air
℃ 877/359-7947 (in U.S. or Canada)
℃ 084/5601-0956 (in U.K.)
www.swiss.com

TACA
℃ 800/535-8780 (in U.S.)
℃ 800/722-TACA (8222) (in Canada)
℃ 087/0241-0340 (in U.K.)
℃ 503/2267-8222 (in El Salvador)
www.taca.com

Thai Airways International
℃ 212/949-8424 (in U.S.)
℃ 020/7491-7953 (in U.K.)
www.thaiair.com

Turkish Airlines
℃ 90 212 444 0 849
www.thy.com

United Airlines*
℃ 800/864-8331 (in U.S. or Canada)
℃ 084/5844-4777 (in U.K.)
www.united.com

US Airways*
℃ 800/428-4322 (in U.S. or Canada)
℃ 084/5600-3300 (in U.K.)
www.usairways.com

Virgin Atlantic Airways
℃ 800/821-5438 (in U.S. or Canada)
℃ 087/0574-7747 (in U.K.)
www.virgin-atlantic.com

Aero California
℃ 800/237-6225 (in U.S. or Mexico)
www.aerocalifornia.com.mx

Air Berlin
℃ 087/1500-0737 (in U.K.)
℃ 018/0573-7800 (in Germany)
℃ 180/573-7800 (all others)
www.airberlin.com

AirTran Airways
© 800/247-8726
www.airtran.com

Avolar
© 888/3-AVOLAR (800/326-8527)
  (in U.S.)
© 800/21-AVOLAR (800/326-8527)
  (in Mexico)
© 086/6370-4065 (in U.K.)
www.avolar.com.mx

BMI Baby
© 087/1224-0224 (in U.K.)
© 870/126-6726 (in U.S.)
www.bmibaby.com

Cape Air
© 800/352-0714
www.flycapeair.com

Click Mexicana
© 800/11-click (800/112-5425)
  (international)
© 800/112-5425 (in Mexico)
www.clickmx.com

easyJet
© 870/600-0000 (in U.S.)
© 090/5560-7777 (in U.K.)
www.easyjet.com

Frontier Airlines
© 800/432-1359
www.frontierairlines.com

go!
© 888/435-9462
www.iflygo.com
(Hawaii based)

CAR-RENTAL AGENCIES

Advantage
© 800/777-5500 (in U.S.)
© 021/0344-4712 (outside of U.S.)
www.advantagerentacar.com

Alamo
© 800/GO-ALAMO (800/462-5266)
www.alamo.com

Auto Europe
© 888/223-5555 (in U.S. or Canada)
© 0800/2235-5555 (in U.K.)
www.autoeurope.com

Interjet
© 800/101-2345
www.interjet.com.mx

JetBlue Airways
© 800/538-2583 (in U.S.)
© 801/365-2525 (in U.K. or Canada)
www.jetblue.com

Jetstar (Australia)
© 866/397-8170
www.jetstar.com

RyanAir
© 353/1249-7700 (in U.S.)
© 081/830-3030 (in Ireland)
© 087/1246-0000 (in U.K.)
www.ryanair.com

Southwest Airlines
© 800/435-9792 (in U.S., U.K., or
  Canada)
www.southwest.com

Spirit Airlines
© 800/772-7117
www.spiritair.com

Ted (part of United Airlines)
© 800/225-5561
www.flyted.com

Volaris
© 866/988-3527
© 800/7-VOLARIS (800/786-5274)
  (in Mexico)
www.volaris.com.mx

WestJet
© 800/538-5696 (in U.S. or Canada)
www.westjet.com

Avis
© 800/331-1212 (in U.S. or Canada)
© 084/4581-8181 (in U.K.)
www.avis.com

Budget
© 800/527-0700 (in U.S.)
© 087/0156-5656 (in U.K.)
© 800/268-8900 (in Canada)
www.budget.com

Dollar
© 800/800-4000 (in U.S.)
© 800/848-8268 (in Canada)
© 080/8234-7524 (in U.K.)
www.dollar.com

Enterprise
© 800/261-7331 (in U.S.)
© 514/355-4028 (in Canada)
© 012/9360-9090 (in U.K.)
www.enterprise.com

Hertz
© 800/645-3131
© 800/654-3001 (for international reservations)
www.hertz.com

MAJOR HOTEL & MOTEL CHAINS

Best Western International
© 800/780-7234 (in U.S. or Canada)
© 0800/393-130 (in U.K.)
www.bestwestern.com

Clarion Hotels
© 800/CLARION or 877/424-6423 (in U.S. or Canada)
© 0800/444-444 (in U.K.)
www.choicehotels.com

Comfort Inns
© 800/228-5150
© 0800/444-444 (in U.K.)
www.ComfortInnChoiceHotels.com

Courtyard by Marriott
© 888/236-2427 (in U.S.)
© 0800/221-222 (in U.K.)
www.marriott.com/courtyard

Crowne Plaza Hotels
© 888/303-1746
www.ichotelsgroup.com/crowneplaza

Days Inn
© 800/329-7466 (in U.S.)
© 0800/280-400 (in U.K.)
www.daysinn.com

Doubletree Hotels
© 800/222-TREE (800/222-8733) (in U.S. or Canada)

Kemwel (KHA)
© 877/820-0668
www.kemwel.com

National
© 800/CAR-RENT (800/227-7368)
www.nationalcar.com

Payless
© 800/PAYLESS (800/729-5377)
www.paylesscarrental.com

Rent-A-Wreck
© 800/535-1391
www.rentawreck.com

Thrifty
© 800/367-2277
© 918/669-2168 (international)
www.thrifty.com

© 087/0590-9090 (in U.K.)
www.doubletree.com

Econo Lodges
© 800/55-ECONO (800/552-3666)
www.choicehotels.com

Embassy Suites
© 800/EMBASSY (800/362-2779)
www.embassysuites.hilton.com

Farfield Inn by Marriott
© 800/228-2800 (in U.S. or Canada)
© 0800/221-222 (in U.K.)
www.marriott.com/farfieldinn

Four Seasons
© 800/819-5053 (in U.S. or Canada)
© 0800/6488-6488 (in U.K.)
www.fourseasons.com

Hampton Inn
© 800/HAMPTON (800/426-4766)
www.hamptoninn.hilton.com

Hilton Hotels
© 800/HILTONS (800/445-8667) (in U.S. or Canada)
© 087/0590-9090 (in U.K.)
www.hilton.com

Holiday Inn
© 800/315-2621 (in U.S. or Canada)
© 0800/405-060 (in U.K.)
www.holidayinn.com

Howard Johnson
© 800/446-4656 (in U.S. or Canada)
www.hojo.com

Hyatt
© 888/591-1234 (in U.S. or Canada)
© 084/5888-1234 (in U.K.)
www.hyatt.com

InterContinental Hotels & Resorts
© 800/424-6835 (in U.S. or Canada)
© 0800/1800-1800 (in U.K.)
www.ichotelsgroup.com

La Quinta Inns and Suites
© 800/642-4271 (in U.S. or Canada)
www.lq.com

Loews Hotels
© 800/23LOEWS (800/235-6397)
www.loewshotels.com

Marriott
© 877/236-2427 (in U.S. or Canada)
© 0800/221-222 (in U.K.)
www.marriott.com

Motel 6
© 800/4MOTEL6 (800/466-8356)
www.motel6.com

Omni Hotels
© 888/444-OMNI (888/444-6664)
www.omnihotels.com

Quality
© 877/424-6423 (in U.S. or Canada)
© 0800/444-444 (in U.K.)
www.QualityInn.ChoiceHotels.com

Radisson Hotels & Resorts
© 888/201-1718 (in U.S. or Canada)
© 0800/374-411 (in U.K.)
www.radisson.com

Ramada Worldwide
© 888/2-RAMADA (888/272-6232)
   (in U.S. or Canada)
© 080/8100-0783 (in U.K.)
www.ramada.com

Red Carpet Inns
© 800/251-1962
www.bookroomsnow.com

Red Lion Hotels
© 800/RED-LION (800/733-5466)
www.redlion.rdln.com

Red Roof Inns
© 866/686-4335 (in U.S. or Canada)
© 614/601-4075 (international)
www.redroof.com

Renaissance
© 888/236-2427
www.renaissance.com

Residence Inn by Marriott
© 800/331-3131
© 800/221-222 (in U.K.)
www.marriott.com/residenceinn

Rodeway Inns
© 877/424-6423
www.RodewayInn.ChoiceHotels.com

Sheraton Hotels & Resorts
© 800/325-3535 (in U.S.)
© 800/543-4300 (in Canada)
© 0800/3253-5353 (in U.K.)
www.starwoodhotels.com/sheraton

Super 8 Motels
© 800/800-8000
www.super8.com

Travelodge
© 800/578-7878
www.travelodge.com

Vagabond Inns
© 800/522-1555
www.vagabondinn.com

Virgin America
© 877/359-847446
www.virginamerica.com

Westin Hotels & Resorts
© 800/937-8461 (in U.S. or Canada)
© 0800/3259-5959 (in U.K.)
www.starwoodhotels.com/westin

Wyndham Hotels & Resorts
© 877/999-3223 (in U.S. or Canada)
© 050/6638-4899 (in U.K.)
www.wyndham.com

Index

AAA (American Automobile Association), 38, 382
AARP, 43
The Abbey (Miami), 211
Access America, 40
Accommodations. *See also specific destinations*
best, 11–13
surfing for hotels, 46
Actors' Playhouse (Miami), 225
African American Association of Innkeepers International, 45
African-American travelers, 44–45
Agua Spa at the Delano (Miami), 88
AIDSinfo, 29
Air Adventures (Clewiston), 380
Airboat tours, Everglades National Park, 239
Airfares, 45
Air travel, 37, 40
toll free numbers and websites of airlines, 388–391
Alabama Jack's (Card Sound), 250
Alf's Golf Shop (Miami), 208
Alhambra Antiques (Miami), 200
Aloha Watersports (Fort Lauderdale), 312
Amelia Earhart Park (Miami), 177
American Airlines Arena (Miami), 192
American Airlines Vacations, 48
American Automobile Association (AAA), 38, 382
American Express, 30, 68, 382
American Watersports (Miami), 184
Amtrak, 39
Anhinga Trail (Everglades National Park), 236–237
Animal parks and attractions. *See also* Aquariums and marine-life attractions; Zoos
Billie Swamp Safari (Big Cypress Seminole Reservation), 313–314

Jonathan Dickinson State Park, 365
Lion Country Safari (West Palm Beach), 344
Miami, 193–196
Upper and Middle Keys, 255
Anne's Beach, 253
Antique Show (Miami), 199
Aqua (Key West), 303
Aquariums and marine-life attractions
Florida Oceanographic Coastal Center (Stuart), 366
Harbor Branch Oceanographic Institution (Fort Pierce), 371–372
Key West, 280
Marinelife Center of Juno Beach (near Jupiter), 356
Miami, 195
Upper and Middle Keys, 255–257
Aquasino (Miami), 188
Aquatic Rental Center (Miami), 184
Arabian Nights Festival (Hialeah), 34
Architectural Antiques (Miami), 200
Area codes, 382
Arroyo, Angel, 224
The Arsht Center for the Performing Arts (Miami), 226, 227
Art Basel Miami Beach, 36
ArtCenter/South Florida (Miami), 167–168
Art Deco Weekend (South Beach), 31
Art Deco Welcome Center (Miami), 164, 166
Art galleries, Miami, 170–171
Arturo Sandoval Jazz Club (Miami), 221–222
Atlantic Avenue (Delray Beach), 338
Atlantic Dunes Beach (Delray Beach), 330
ATMs (automated-teller machines), 30
Atrium (Miami), 202
Audubon House & Tropical Gardens (Key West), 279

Automatic Slim's (Miami), 211
Auto Train, 39
Aventura (Miami), 63, 198
Aventura Mall (Miami), 206

Bahia Honda State Park (Big Pine Key), 270, 272–273
Bal Harbour (Miami), 63
restaurants, 132–134
Bal Harbour Beach (Miami), 163
Bal Harbour Shops (Miami), 206
Ballet Flamenco La Rosa (Miami), 224, 226
Balloons Over Florida, 365–366
Bally's Total Fitness (Miami), 190
B & A Flea Market (Stuart), 367
BankAtlantic Center (Sunrise), 313
Barbara Gillman Gallery (Miami), 170
Barnacle State Historic Site (Miami), 174
Barnes & Noble (Miami), 200
Barneys Co-Op (Miami), 202
Baseball
Fort Lauderdale, 313
Jupiter, 354
Miami, 191–192
Port St. Lucie, 371
Vero Beach, 376
Base USA (Miami), 202
Basketball, Miami, 192
Bass Museum of Art (Miami), 168
Bass Pro Shops Outdoor World (Dania Beach), 312
Bass Pro Shops Outdoor World (Miami), 208
Bathtub Beach (North Hutchinson Island), 364
Bayside Marketplace (Miami), 206
Beaches. *See also specific beaches*
best, 10–11
Broward County, 310–312
Delray Beach and Boca Raton, 330

Fort Pierce area, 371
Jupiter area, 355
Key West, 285–286
Miami, 160–163
Palm Beach, 340, 342
Vero Beach area, 374
Beethoven by the Beach (Fort Lauderdale), 35
Belinda's Designs (Miami), 203
Bicycle Center (Key West), 278
Big Cypress National Preserve (Everglades National Park), 231
Bike Shop (Key West), 278
Biking
Everglades National Park, 237
Jupiter area, 355
Key West, 278, 286
the Lower Keys, 271
Miami, 68, 185–186
Palm Beach, 342
Bill Baggs Cape Florida State Park, 162, 177
Bill Cosford Cinema (Miami), 228
Billie Swamp Safari (Big Cypress Seminole Reservation), 313–314
Biltmore Hotel (Miami), golf course at, 189
Biltmore Hotel Tour (Miami), 182
Birds and bird-watching
Daggerwing Nature Center (Boca Raton), 332
the Dry Tortugas, 304
Everglades National Park, 237
Florida Keys Wild Bird Center (Tavernier), 255–256
Jonathan Dickinson State Park, 365
the Lower Keys, 271
Biscayne Corridor (Miami), 64, 198
Biscayne National Park, 244–247
Biscayne National Underwater Park, 246
Black Travel Online, 44
Blowing Rocks Preserve, 356–357
Blue (Miami), 211
Blue Hole, 271
Blue Moon Outdoor Center (Miami), 184
Blue Planet Kayak Tours, 259
Blues Festival at Riverwalk (Fort Lauderdale), 36

Boating and sailing (rentals and charters). See also Canoeing; Kayaking; Motorboating
Broward County, 312
the Lower Keys, 271
Miami, 183, 184
Upper and Middle Keys, 258
Boat Rental Plus (Miami), 183
Boat tours and cruises
Biscayne National Park, 246–247
Jonathan Dickinson State Park, 366–367
Key West, 285
Boca Chita Key, 244, 246
Boca Raton, 329–339
accommodations, 333–335
beaches and outdoor activities, 330, 332
nightlife, 338–339
restaurants, 335–338
shopping, 333
sights and attractions, 332–333
traveling to, 329
visitor information, 329
Boca Raton Municipal Golf Course, 332
Boca Raton Museum of Art, 332
Boingo, 47
Bone Shaker Sportfishing (Stuart), 364
Bongo's Cuban Café (Miami), 218, 224
Bonnet House (Fort Lauderdale), 314
Books, recommended, 25
Books & Books (Miami), 201, 228
Bookstores, Miami, 200–201
Borders (Miami), 200
Boston's on the Beach (Delray Beach), 338
Britto Central (Miami), 170–171
Broward County, 308–329
accommodations, 316–322
beaches, 310–312
nightlife, 327–329
outdoor activities and spectator sports, 312–313
restaurants, 322–327
shopping, 315–316
sights and attractions, 313–315
traveling to, 310
visitor information, 310

Brownes & Co. Apothecary (Miami), 201–202
Browne's Beauty Lounge (Miami), 72
Bud n' Mary's Fishing Marina (Islamorada), 260
Burr's Berry Farms (Goulds), 186
Business hours, 382–383

Cajun Zydeco Crawfish Festival (Fort Lauderdale), 34
Caldwell Theatre (Boca Raton), 339
Calendar of events, 31–37
Calle Ocho (Miami), shopping, 198
Calle Ocho Festival (Miami), 33
Cameo (Miami), 218
Camping
Clewiston area, 380
the Dry Tortugas, 305
Everglades National Park, 240–241
Fort Pierce, 368
Jonathan Dickinson State Park, 367–368
the Lower Keys, 273
Upper and Middle Keys, 265
Vero Beach, 378
Canoeing
Biscayne National Park, 245
Everglades National Park, 237–240
Jonathan Dickinson State Park, 364
Jupiter area, 355
the Lower Keys, 271
Upper and Middle Keys, 257, 258–259
Cape Air, 40
Captain Doug's (Everglades City), 239
Captain Pip's (Marathon), 258
Captain Tony's Saloon (Key West), 286, 302
Caribbean Carnival (Miami), 35
Car Rental Referral Service, 67
Car rentals, 38–40
surfing for, 46
Car travel, 37
planning your trip, 39
Casa Casaurina (Miami), 167
Casa Panza (Miami), 223
Casino Records Inc. (Miami), 208
Casinos, Miami area, 188
Celebration Cruising (Miami), 179–180

Celebrity sightings, Miami, 214
Cellphones, 48, 386
Centers for Disease Control and Prevention, 42
Central Reservation Service (Miami), 75
Charter Boat Row (Key West), 287
The Children's Exchange (Miami), 209
Churchill's Hideaway (Miami), 222
Church Mouse (Palm Beach), 345
Cigar Alley (Key West), 288
Cigars, Miami, 201
City Limousine (Miami), 61
City Place (West Palm Beach), 345–346
Clarke's (Miami), 211
Clematis Street (West Palm Beach), 353
Clevelander (Miami), 212
Clewiston, 380
Climate, 30–31
Clinton Street Market (Key West), 288
Club Nautico (Miami), 183
Club Space (Miami), 218–219
C. Madeleines's (Miami), 209
Coconut Grove (Miami), 65–66, 174
    accommodations, 106–108
    restaurants, 150–152
    shopping, 198
Coconut Grove Arts Festival, 32
Coconut Grove Convention Center (Miami), 199
Coconut Grove Goombay Festival, 34
Coconut Grove Playhouse (Miami), 225
CocoWalk (Miami), 206
Collins Aviation, 40
Collins Park Cultural Center (Miami), 166–167
Colony Theater (Miami), 227
Columbus Day Regatta (Miami), 35, 184
Concert Association of Florida (CAF; Miami), 225
Conch Republic Cigar Factory (Key West), 288
Conch Tour Train (Key West), 283
Consulates, 383–384
Continental Airlines Vacations, 48
Convoy Point Visitor Center (Biscayne National Park), 245

Coopertown Airboat Tours (Everglades National Park), 239
Coral Castle (Miami), 175
Coral Gables (Miami), 65
    accommodations, 104–106
    restaurants, 152–156
Coral Reef Park Co. (Key Largo), 259
Country Club of Miami, golf courses at, 189
Crandon Park Beach (Miami), 162
Crandon Park Golf Course (Miami), 189
Crandon Tennis Center (Miami), 190
Crane Point Hammock (Marathon), 254
Credit cards, 30
Crisis Intervention, 384
Crunch (Miami), 191
Crystal Room (Key West), 303
Cuba, Cuba! (Key West), 289
Cuban coffee, in Miami, 146
The Culture Room (Fort Lauderdale), 327
Currency, 383
Currie Park (West Palm Beach), 343
Customs regulations, 29
CWS Tours & Transportation, 48

Dada (Delray Beach), 338
Dade Human Rights Foundation, 43
Dadeland Mall (Miami), 207
Daggerwing Nature Center (Boca Raton), 332
Dania/Dania Beach, 311–312.
    See also Broward County
Dania Jai Alai, 313
Dante Fascell Visitor Center (Biscayne National Park), 245
Daylight saving time, 387
Debit cards, 30
Delray Beach, 329, 330, 332–339
Delray Beach Tennis Center, 332
Delta Vacations, 48
Delux (Delray Beach), 338
Design Center of the Americas (DCOTA; Dania), 316
Diana Lowenstein Fine Arts (Miami), 171
Diaspora Vibe Art Gallery (Miami), 168

Diesel Jeans (Miami), 202
Diplomat Country Club and Spa (Hallandale Beach), 312
Disabilities, travelers with, 43
Dive Key West, 286
Diver's Paradise (Miami), 185
Dodgertown (Vero Beach), 376
Dolphin Mall (Miami), 207
Dolphin Research Center (Marathon), 255
Dolphins, swimming with, 42
    Marathon, 255
Dolphin Stadium (Miami), 192
Donaldson Reef, 365
Don's Bait & Tackle (Homestead), 235
Doral Golf Resort and Spa (Miami), golf courses at, 189
Doral Park Golf and Country Club, golf courses at, 189
Doral Ryder Golf Open (West Miami), 32
Douglas Gardens Jewish Home and Hospital Thrift Shop (Miami), 209
Drinking laws, 383
The Dry Tortugas, 303–305
Dubois Park (Jupiter), 355
Durty Harry's (Key West), 302

Eastern Standard Time (EST), 386
East Martello Museum and Gallery (Key West), 279
Eco-Adventure Tours (Miami), 182
Ecotourism, 42
Edwin Watts Golf Shops (Miami), 208
801 Bourbon Bar/Number One Saloon (Key West), 303
85th Street Beach (Miami), 162
Elbo Room (Fort Lauderdale), 327
El Credito Cigars (Miami), 201
Electricity, 383
Elite Fine Art (Miami), 171
Elliott Key, 244, 246
Elliott Museum (Stuart), 366
Elwood's (Delray Beach), 338
Embassies and consulates, 383–384
Emergencies, 384
En Avance (Miami), 202
Entry requirements, 28–29
Environmental Learning Center (Wabasso Island), 375
Epicure (Miami), 204–205

Equinox Fitness (Miami), 191
E. R. Bradley's (West Palm
    Beach), 353
Ernest F. Coe Visitor Center
    (Everglades National Park),
    234
Ernest Hemingway Home and
    Museum (Key West), 280
Ernst Reef, 365
Escorted general-interest tours,
    49
ESPA at Acqualina (Miami), 89
Evelyn S. Poole Ltd. (Miami), 171
Everglades Adventures, 238,
    240
Everglades Alligator Farm
    (Everglades National Park),
    239
Everglades City accommoda-
    tions, 241–242
Everglades National Park, 22,
    230–243
    accommodations, 240–243
    entrance fees, permits and
        regulations, 234–235
    getting there and access
        points, 231, 234
    highlights, 236–237
    organized tours, 239–240
    ranger programs, 235–236
    restaurants, 243
    safety, 236
    seasons, 235
    sports and outdoor activities,
        237–239
    visitor information, 234
Everglades National Park Boat
    Tours, 238
Everglades National Park Head-
    quarters (Homestead), 234
Everglades Seafood Festival
    (Florida City), 32
Eyre Tour and Travel, 48

Fairchild Tropical Garden
    (Miami), 177–178
Fairmont Turnberry Isle Resort
    & Club (Miami)
    golf courses at, 189
    spa at, 88
Falcon House (Delray Beach),
    339
The Falls (Miami), 207
Families with children, 43–44
    suggested itinerary, 55–58
Fantasy Fest (Key West), 35–36
Fashions (clothing), Miami,
    202–204

Fast Buck Freddie's (Key West),
    289
Fax machines, 386
FedEx Orange Bowl Classic
    (Miami), 31
Festival Miami, 35
Festivals and special events,
    31–37
Fillmore Miami Beach, 227
First Call for Help, 384
Fishing
    Biscayne National Park,
        245–246
    Broward County, 312
    the Dry Tortugas, 305
    Everglades National Park, 238
    Fort Pierce, 371
    Hutchinson Island and Jensen
        Beach, 364
    Jupiter, 355
    Key West, 287
    Lake Okeechobee, 379, 381
    the Lower Keys, 271–272
    Miami, 187–188
    Upper and Middle Keys,
        259–260
    Vero Beach, 374
Flagler Museum (Palm Beach),
    343
Flamingo Park (Miami), tennis
    facilities at, 190
Flamingo Visitor Center (Ever-
    glades National Park), 234,
    241
Florida Bay Outfitters (Key
    Largo), 259
Florida City, 234
    accommodations, 242–243
Florida Grand Opera (Miami),
    226
Florida Keys Boat Rental, 271
Florida Keys Dive Center (Tav-
    ernier), 259
Florida Keys Eco-Discovery
    Center (Key West), 279
Florida Keys Kayak and Sail
    (Islamorada), 259
Florida Keys Wild Bird Center
    (Tavernier), 255–256
Florida Marlins (Miami),
    191–192
Florida Oceanographic Coastal
    Center (Stuart), 366
Florida Panthers, 192, 313
Florida Philharmonic Orchestra
    (Miami), 226
The Florida Room (Miami), 212
Florida Symphonic Pops (Boca
    Raton), 339

Food stores and markets,
    Miami, 204–205
Football, Miami, 192
Force E Dive Center (Boca
    Raton), 332
Forge (Miami), 212
Fort Jefferson, 304
Fort Lauderdale, 308, 310. See
    also Broward County
    accommodations, 316–321
    history of, 22–23
    nightlife, 327–329
    restaurants, 322–327
Fort Lauderdale Beach Prome-
    nade, 311
Fort Lauderdale-Hollywood
    International Airport, 310
Fort Lauderdale International
    Boat Show, 35
Fort Lauderdale Stadium, 313
Fort Pierce, 370–373
Fort Pierce City Marina, 371
Fort Pierce Inlet State Recre-
    ation Area, 371
Fort Zachary Beach, 286
Fox's Sherron Inn (Miami), 212
Freedom Tower (Miami), 175
Friday Fest Street Festival (Fort
    Pierce), 373
Fritz's Skate Shop (Miami),
    190
Frommers.com, 45
Frost, Robert, 284
    Cottage (Key West), 281

Gables Stage (Miami), 225
The Gallery at Beach Place
    (Fort Lauderdale), 316,
    327–328
Gambling, Miami, 188
GameWorks (Miami), 196,
    228–229
Gardens of the Palm Beaches
    (North Palm Beach County),
    357
Gardner's Market (Miami), 205
Garrison Bight Marina (Key
    West), 287
Gasoline, 384
Gator Park, 239
Gatsby's (Boca Raton), 339
Gay, Lesbian & Bisexual Com-
    munity Services of Central
    Florida, 43
Gay and Lesbian Community
    Center of Fort Lauderdale, 43
Gay Key West, 285
Gay Men's Health Crisis, 29

Gays and lesbians, 43
  Key West, 278, 285, 302–303
  Miami, 163, 222–223
Genius Jones (Miami), 204
George, Dr. Paul, 181–182
Gigi's Tavern (Boca Raton), 338
Gilbert's House of Refuge
  Museum (Stuart), 366
Giorgio's European Clothing
  (Miami), 204
GoCar (Miami), 166
The Gold Coast, 3–4, 306–360
Golden Access Passport, 43
Golf
  Boca Raton area, 330, 332
  Broward County, 312
  Jupiter, 356
  Key West, 288
  Miami, 189
  Palm Beach, 342–343
  Port St. Lucie, 371
  Stuart, 364
  Vero Beach area, 374–375
Grand Prix of Miami (Home-
  stead), 33
Greater Fort Lauderdale Con-
  vention & Visitor's Bureau, 27
Greater Miami and Beaches
  Hotel Association, 27
Greater Miami Convention and
  Visitor's Bureau, 27, 61
Gryphon (Hollywood), 328
Gulf Coast Visitor Center (Ever-
  glades National Park), 241
Gulfstream III (Key West), 287
Gulfstream Park Casino and
  Racing (Hallandale), 192, 313
Gumbo Limbo Environmental
  Complex (Boca Raton), 333
Gumbo Limbo Trail (Everglades
  National Park), 236
Gusman Center for the Per-
  forming Arts (Miami), 227
Gusman Concert Hall (Miami),
  227

Haitian Art Co. (Key West),
  289
Hale Indian River Groves (Vero
  Beach), 376
Half Buck Freddie's (Key West),
  289
Hallandale, 308
Hall's Dive Center & Career
  Institute (Marathon), 259
Harbor Branch Oceanographic
  Institution (Fort Pierce),
  371–372

Harrison's Wine Bar (Holly-
  wood), 328
Harry S. Truman Little White
  House (Key West), 280
Hatsume Fair (Delray Beach),
  32–33
Haulover Beach Park (Miami),
  163, 187, 189
Health concerns, 41–42
Health insurance, 41
Heavy Hitters Charters (Key
  West), 287
Hell's Bay Canoe Trail (Ever-
  glades National Park), 238
Hemingway, Ernest, 284
  Home and Museum (Key
  West), 280
Hemingway Days Festival (Key
  West), 35
Henderson Travel & Tours, 45
Herencia Hispana Tour (Miami),
  182
Heritage Miami II Topsail
  Schooner, 180
Higgs Beach, 286
HiHo Batik (Miami), 203
Hiking
  Biscayne National Park, 246
  Jupiter area, 356–357
  Long Key State Recreation
  Area, 257
  the Lower Keys, 272
History Buff (Palm Beach), 345
History of Florida, 19–25
HIV-positive visitors, 29
Hobe Sound, 363–370
Hobe Sound Wildlife Refuge,
  365
Hobie Beach (Miami), 163
Hog Heaven (Islamorada), 269
Holidays, 384
Hollywood Beach Broadwalk,
  310–311
Hollywood/Hollywood Beach,
  308, 310. See also Broward
  County
  accommodations, 321–322
  nightlife, 327–329
  restaurants, 326, 327
Holocaust Memorial (Miami),
  168, 170
Homestead, 234
  accommodations, 242
Homestead Rodeo, 32
Horizon Outlet Center (Vero
  Beach), 376
Horse racing, 192, 313
Hot lines, 384
Hoy Como Ayer (Miami), 223

Hungry Bear Adventures (Stuart), 364
Hutchinson Island, 364

IAMAT (International Associa-
  tion for Medical Assistance
  to Travelers), 41–42
Ice hockey, Miami, 192
Immigration and customs
  clearance, 37
Independence Day (Miami), 34
Indian Key, 253
Indian River Adventures (Vero
  Beach), 374
Indian River Citrus Museum
  (Vero Beach), 375
Indian River County Tourist
  Council (Vero Beach), 374
Indian River Mall (near Vero
  Beach), 376
Industrian (Miami), 200
In-line skating, Miami, 189–190
Insurance, 40–41
Intermix (Miami), 203
International Association for
  Medical Assistance to Travel-
  ers (IAMAT), 41–42
The International Jewelry
  Exchange (Miami), 205
International Polo Club (Palm
  Beach), 342
International Society of Travel
  Medicine, 42
International Swimming Hall of
  Fame (ISHOF; Fort Laud-
  erdale), 314–315
Internet access, 47
InTouch USA, 48
IPass network, 47
Islamorada, 251
Island Airplane Tours (Key
  West), 284
Island Water Sports (Miami),
  208
Italian Renaissance Festival
  (Miami), 33
Itineraries, suggested, 50–59
I2roam, 47

Jackie Gleason Theater
  (Miami), 227
Jai alai, 193, 313
Jazid (Miami), 222
Jensen Beach, 363, 364,
  368–370
Jerry Herman Ring Theatre
  (Miami), 225

Jet skis/WaveRunners (Miami), 183–184
Jetty Park (Fort Pierce), 371
Jiffy Lube Miami 300 Weekend of NASCAR (Homestead), 36
Jimmy Evert Tennis Center (Fort Lauderdale), 313
Joe's Takeaway (Miami), 205
John D. MacArthur Beach (Jupiter), 355
John Pennekamp Coral Reef State Park, 251, 256–257, 265
John U. Lloyd Beach State Park, 311–312
Jonathan Dickinson State Park, 364, 365
Jose Cuervo Underwater Bar (Miami), 185
Journeywoman, 44
J Sisters (Miami), 72
Jungle Island (Miami), 193–194
Jupiter, 354–360
Jupiter Bay Tennis Club, 357
Jupiter Inlet Lighthouse, 357

Kafka's Cyberkafe (Miami), 69, 201
Kampong (Miami), 178
Karma Lounge (Fort Lauderdale), 328
Kayaking
  Biscayne National Park, 245
  Key West, 288
  the Lower Keys, 271
  Miami, 184
  Upper and Middle Keys, 258–259
Kelley Fishing Fleet (Miami), 187
Key Biscayne (Miami), 63
  accommodations, 100–101
  beaches, 162
  restaurants, 148–150
Key Cycling (Miami), 186
Key deer, 270–271
Key Largo, 251
Key Lime Pie Co. (Key West), 289
The Keys, 3, 248–303. See also Key West; The Lower Keys; Upper and Middle Keys
  exploring by car, 250–251
  history of, 21–22
  10 "Keymandments," 258
Keys Fisheries (Marathon), 260
Keys Shipwreck Heritage Trail (Key West), 287

Key West, 249, 275–303
  accommodations, 289–296
  getting around, 278
  literary sights, 284
  nightlife, 302–303
  organized tours, 283–285
  orientation, 278–279
  outdoor activities, 285–288
  parking, 278
  restaurants, 297–302
  shopping, 288–289
  sights and attractions, 279–285
  sunset viewing, 282
  traveling to, 275, 278
  visitor information, 278
Key West Aloe, 289
Key West Aquarium, 280
Key West Butterfly & Nature Conservatory, 280–281
Key West Cemetery, 281
Key West Express, 278
Key West Golf Club, 288
Key West Heritage House Museum, 281
Key West Island Bookstore, 289
Key West Lighthouse Museum, 281
Key West Literary Seminar, 32
Key West Marine Park, 286–287
Key West Pub Crawl, 285
Key West's Shipwreck Historeum, 281
Key West Tropical Forest Botanical Gardens, 283
Key West Visitor Center, 278
Kidding Around (Miami), 204
Knaus Berry Farm (the Redlands), 186
Knight Concert Hall (Miami), 227
Kokomo's (Islamorada), 269
KW Light Gallery (Key West), 289

La Brioche Doree (Miami), 205
La Casa de las Guayaberas (Miami), 204
La Covacha (Miami), 223
La Perla (Miami), 203
Lapidus, Morris, 167
Las Olas Boulevard (Fort Lauderdale), 316
Las Olas Riverfront (Fort Lauderdale), 316
La Terraza de Martí (Key West), 303

Lauderdale-by-the-Sea, accommodations, 320, 321
Laundry Bar (Miami), 212, 223
Laurenzo's Italian Supermarket and Farmer's Market (Miami), 205
Legal aid, 384
Leopard Lounge (Palm Beach), 353–354
Le Spa Miami, 72
Lignumvitae Key, 253
Lincoln Road (Miami), 166, 167
Lion Country Safari (West Palm Beach), 344
Literary tour, 59
Little Acorns International Kite Festival (South Beach), 34
Little Havana (Miami), 65
  restaurants, 145–148
Little Havana Walking Tour (Miami), 182
Long Key State Park, 265
Long Key State Recreation Area, 257
Looe Key Dive Center, 272
Looe Key National Marine Sanctuary, 272
Los Angeles Dodgers (Vero Beach), 376
Lost and found, 384–385
Lost-luggage insurance, 41
Lost Reef Adventures (Key West), 287
The Lower Keys, 249, 270–275
Lower Keys Underwater Music Fest (Looe Key), 34–35
Loxahatchee Queen (Jonathan Dickinson State Park), 366
Lucky Strike Lanes (Miami), 221
Lummus Park Beach (Miami), 162
Lyric Theater (Stuart), 370

Macarena (Miami), 214
McDonald's Air & Sea Show (Fort Lauderdale), 34
McKee Botanical Garden (Vero Beach), 375
McLarty Treasure Museum (Vero Beach), 375–376
Mac's Club Deuce (Miami), 214
Mai Kai (Fort Lauderdale), 328
Mail, 385
Main Park Road (Everglades National Park), 237
Mango's Tropical Café (Miami), 223–224

Mansion (Miami), 219
Mar-A-Lago (Palm Beach), 344
Marathon, 252
Marinelife Center of Juno Beach (near Jupiter), 356
Marjory Stoneman Douglas Biscayne Nature Center (Miami), 178
Mark's Mizner Park (Boca Raton), 338
Martin Luther King, Jr., Day Parade, 31–32
Matheson Hammock Park Beach (Miami), 163
Me & Ro Jewelery (Miami), 204
Medical insurance, 41
Medical requirements for entry, 28–29
Melbourne International Airport, 362
Mel Fisher Maritime Heritage Museum (Key West), 281–282
Mermaid Sculpture (Miami), 167
Metro-Dade Transit Agency, 66
Metrorail (Miami), 66
Miami, 60–229. See also specific neighborhoods
    accommodations, 1–2, 74–112
        bars in hotels, 78, 216
        Coconut Grove, 106–108
        Coral Gables, 104–106
        downtown, 101–104
        Key Biscayne, 100–101
        long-term stays, 75
        Miami Beach, 96–100
        North Dade County, 110–112
        price categories, 75
        reservation services, 75–76
        restaurants inside hotels, 85
        seasons and rates, 75
        South Beach, 76–96
        spas, 88–89
        West Miami/Airport Area, 108–110
    American Express, 68
    animal parks and attractions, 193–196
    area code, 68
    arriving in, 60–61
    art galleries, 170–171
    beaches, 160–163
    business hours, 69
    curfew, 69
    dentists, 69
    doctors, 69

downtown, 64
    accommodations, 101–104
    restaurants, 137–145
    shopping, 198–199
emergencies, 69
finding an address in, 62
getting around, 66–68
history of, 21
Internet access, 69
laundry and dry cleaning, 69
layout of, 62
liquor laws, 70
lost property, 70
luggage storage and lockers, 70
neighborhoods in brief, 62–66
newspapers and magazines, 70
nightlife, 210–229
    bars and lounges, 211–217
    cinemas, 228
    dance clubs, 217–221
    gay and lesbian scene, 222–223
    ground rules, 218
    Latin clubs, 223–224
    literary scene, 228
    live music, 221–222
    performing arts, 224–228
    what's new, 3
outdoor activities, 185–191
parking, 67–68
pharmacies, 70
photographic needs, 70
police, 70
post office, 71
radio, 71
religious services, 71
restaurants, 2–3, 113–159
    Coconut Grove, 150–152
    Coral Gables, 152–156
    downtown Miami, 137–145
    Key Biscayne, 148–150
    late-night bites, 229
    Latin (Cuban) cuisine, 147
    Little Havana, 145–148
    Miami Beach, North Beach, Surfside, Bal Harbour, Sunny Isles & North Miami, 132–134
    North Miami Beach, 134–137
    South Beach, 114–132
    South Miami and West Miami, 156–159
    tipping, 114

restrooms, 71
safety, 71
shopping, 197–209
    areas, 198–199
    malls, 206–208
    sights and attractions, 160–183
        Art Deco District (South Beach), 163–166
        cruises and organized tours, 179–183
        historic homes and sites, 174–177
        museum and art scene, 166–174
        nature preserves, parks and gardens, 177–179
    spas and massage, 71–72
    spectator sports, 191–193
    street maps, 62
    taxes, 72
    taxis, 60–61, 68
    television, 72–73
    time zone, 73
    transit information, 73
    video arcades and entertainment centers, 196
    visitor information, 61
    watersports, 183–185
    weather forecasts, 73
    what's new in, 1–3
Miami Art Museum at the Miami-Dade Cultural Center, 171–172
Miami Beach, 62–63. See also Miami
    accommodations, 96–100
    beaches, 161
    restaurants, 132–134
Miami Beach Architecture Cruise, 180
Miami Beach Bicycle Center, 185
Miami Beach Botanical Garden, 178
Miami Beach Cinematheque, 228
Miami Beach Golf Club, 189
Miami Beach Polo Cup, 192
Miami Book Fair International, 36
Miami Chamber Symphony, 226
Miami Children's Museum, 172
Miami City Ballet, 226
Miami City Web, 48
Miami Dade and South Beach Business Guild, 43
Miami-Dade County Auditorium (Miami), 227
Miami Design Preservation League, 164, 182

Miami Dolphins, 192
Miami Duck Tours, 180–181
Miami Film Festival, 32
Miami Gay & Lesbian Film Festival, 33
Miami Heat, 192
Miami International Airport (MIA), 60
Miami International Boat Show, 32
Miami Jai Alai Fronton, 193
Miami Metrozoo, 194–195
Miami Nice Excursion Travel and Service, 181
Miami River Circle, 176
Miami Science Museum, 172
Miami Seaquarium, 195
Miami SkyLift Balloon, 182–183
Miami Twice, 200
Miccosukee Everglades Festival (West Miami), 35
Miccosukee Indian Gaming (West Miami), 188
Miccosukee Indian Village, 239
Miccosukee Resort, 240
Midtown Beach (Palm Beach), 340
Mike's Cigars Distributor's Inc. (Miami), 201
Miracle Mile (Coral Gables; Miami), 199
Mizner Park (Boca Raton), 333, 338
Mizner Park Amphitheater (Boca Raton), 339
Mobil Station (Miami), 69
Modernism Gallery (Miami), 200
Mokai (Miami), 214
Money matters, 29–30
Monkey Jungle (Miami), 195
Moped Hospital (Key West), 278
Moray Bend (Boca Raton), 332
Morgan Miller (Miami), 203
Morikami Museum and Japanese Gardens (Delray Beach), 333
Morning Call Bakery (Miami), 205
Mosquito Coast Outfitters (Key West), 287, 288
Motorboating
   Everglades National Park, 238–240
   Upper and Middle Keys, 253
Movies filmed in Florida, 26
   Miami, 191
Museum of Art Fort Lauderdale, 315

Museum of Contemporary Art (MOCA; Miami), 172–173
Museum of Discovery & Science (Fort Lauderdale), 315
Music, 26
Mynt (Miami), 214
Mystery, Mayhem and Vice Crime Bus Tour (Miami), 183

NASDAQ 100 Open (Key Biscayne), 33
National Hurricane Center (Miami), 168
National Key Deer Refuge (Big Pine Key), 270, 272
Native Americans, 19–20
   Miami River Circle, 176
Neil Watson's Undersea Adventures (Fort Lauderdale), 313
Newspapers and magazines, 385
New Theater (Miami), 225
New World Symphony (Miami), 226
New York Mets (Port St. Lucie), 371
Nikki Beach (Miami), 219
Nine-mile Pond (Everglades National Park), 238
Noble Hammock Canoe Trail (Everglades National Park), 238
North Beach (Miami), 63
   restaurants, 132–134
North Dade County, accommodations, 110–112
North Miami, restaurants, 132–134
North Miami Beach, restaurants, 134–137
North Palm Beach County, 354–360
Norton Museum of Art (West Palm Beach), 343

Ocean Beach (Jupiter), 355
Ocean Drive (Miami), 166
Ocean Key Resort (Key West), bar at, 282
Oceanside Marina (Key West), 287–288
O'Hara's (Fort Lauderdale), 328
Okeechobee, Lake, 379–381
Okeechobee Landings (Clewiston), 380
Oldest House/Wrecker's Museum (Key West), 282

Old Town Trolley (Key West), 283
Oleta River State Recreation Area (Miami), 178–179
Opium Garden (Miami), 219
Orangebrook Golf Course (Hollywood), 312
Original Penguin Store (Miami), 204

Package tours, 48–49
Palm Beach, 339–354
   accommodations, 346–350
   beaches and outdoor activities, 340, 342–343
   getting around, 340
   history of, 23
   nightlife, 353–354
   restaurants, 350–353
   shopping, 345
   sights and attractions, 343–345
   traveling to, 340
   visitor information, 340
Palm Beach Bicycle Trail Shop, 342
Palm Beach County Convention and Visitors Bureau (West Palm Beach), 27, 329, 340
Palm Beach County Cultural Council, 339
Palm Beach International Airport, 340, 354, 362
Palm Beach International Art and Antiques Fair, 32
Palm Beach Polo and Country Club, 342
Palm Beach Public Golf Course, 343
Palm Beach Zoo at Dreher Park, 345
Palm Tran, 340
Pangaea (Hollywood), 328
Paradise Waterfont (Lower Keys), 274
Parkwest Nightclub (Miami), 220
The Parrot (Fort Lauderdale), 328
Passports, 385
Patch Reef Park (Boca Raton), 332
Pawn Shop Lounge (Miami), 220–221
Peacock Education Center (Miami), 227
Peppers of Key West, 289
Petrol, 384
PGA Golf Club (Port St. Lucie), 371

PGA Seniors Golf Championship (Palm Beach Gardens), 34
Phipps Ocean Park (Palm Beach), 342
Pigeon Key, 254
Pinecrest Gardens (Miami), 194
Pinto, Luz, 224
Pirate Soul (Key West), 282–283
Place Vendome (Miami), 203
Planning your trip, 27–49
  cellphones, 48
  customs regulations, 29
  entry requirements, 28–29
  escorted general-interest tours, 49
  getting around, 39–40
  health and safety, 41–42
  insurance, 40–41
  Internet access, 47
  money matters, 29–30
  online resources, 45–46
  package tours, 48–49
  specialized travel resources, 43–45
  traveling to South Florida, 37–39
  visitor information, 27–28
  websites, 46–47
  when to go, 30–37
Playmobil Fun Park (Palm Beach Gardens), 343–344
Playwright Irish Pub (Miami), 214
Plaza for the Arts (Miami), 227
Poison Information Center, 384
Police, 386
Polo Season (Palm Beach), 31
Pompano Park Racing, 313
The Poor House (Fort Lauderdale), 328
Port St. Lucie, 370–373
Prescription medications, 42
Preston B. Bird and Mary Heinlein Fruit and Spice Park (Homestead), 179
The Purdy Lounge (Miami), 214–215

Rags to Riches (Miami), 209
Rapids Water Park (West Palm Beach), 345
Raymond F. Kravis Center for the Performing Arts (West Palm Beach), 354

Rebel (Miami), 203
Redland Tropical Trail Tours (Miami), 183
Red Reef Park (Boca Raton), 332
Red White & Blue Thrift Store (Miami), 209
Reflections Kayak Nature Tours (Big Pine Key), 271
Reflections Nature Tours, 259
Respectable Street Café (West Palm Beach), 353
Restaurants, best, 13–16
Revolution (Fort Lauderdale), 328
Richter's of Palm Beach, 345
Rickenbacker Causeway (Miami), 186
The Ritz-Carlton Key Biscayne Spa (Miami), 72, 88
Riverside Racquet Complex (Vero Beach), 375
Riverwalk (Fort Lauderdale), 329
RoadPost, 48
Robbie's Partyboats & Charters (Islamorada), 259
Robbie's Pier (Islamorada), 256
Robbie's Rent-A-Boat (Islamorada), 253–254, 258
Robert Frost Cottage (Key West), 281
Rodgers Travel, 44–45
Roger Dean Stadium (Jupiter), 354
Rok Bar (Miami), 215
The Room (Miami), 215
Rose Bar at the Delano (Miami), 215
Royal Palm Visitor Center (Everglades National Park), 234
Rubell Family Art Collection (Miami), 173
Russian Turkish Baths (Miami), 71–72

Safety concerns, 42
Sailboards Miami (Miami), 185
Sailfish Marina (Stuart), 364
Sailfish Marina & Resort (Palm Beach Shores), 355
San-Ai-An Japanese Garden (Miami), 194
Sandridge Golf Club (Vero Beach), 374

Sanford and Dolores Ziff Ballet Opera House (Miami), 227
Sanford L. Ziff Jewish Museum of Florida (Miami), 173
Santa's Enchanted Forest (Miami), 36
Savannahs Recreation Area (Fort Pierce), 372
Sawgrass Mills (Sunrise), 207, 316
Scoop (Miami), 203
Score (Miami), 223
The Scott Rakow Youth Center (Miami), 196
Scratch DJ Academy (Miami), 217, 220
Scuba diving
  Biscayne National Park, 246
  Boca Raton, 332
  Broward County, 312–313
  the Dry Tortugas, 304–305
  Hutchinson Island, 365
  Key West, 286–287
  the Lower Keys, 272
  Miami, 184–185
  North Palm Beach County, 357
  Palm Beach, 343
  Upper and Middle Keys, 259
Sea Grass Adventures (Miami), 195–196
Seaplanes of Key West, 304
Seasons, 30–31
Sea Turtle Awareness Program, 311
Sea turtles, 257, 303, 305, 311, 333, 356, 365
Sebastian, 373–379
Sebastian Inlet State Park, 378
Sebastian Inlet State Park (Melbourne), 374
Sebastian Municipal Golf Course, 375
SEE (Miami), 204
Segafredo Espresso (Miami), 215
Seminole Hard Rock Winterfest Boat Parade (Fort Lauderdale), 36–37
Senior travel, 43
Senzatempo (Miami), 200
Sephora (Miami), 202
SET (Miami), 221
Seven-mile Bridge, 254–255
Seybold Buchwald's Jewelers (Miami), 205
Shark Valley (Everglades National Park), 186, 231, 236, 237

Shark Valley Tram Tours (Everglades National Park), 237, 240
Shark Valley Visitor Center (Everglades National Park), 234
Shooters (Fort Lauderdale), 329
Shops at Sunset Place (Miami), 207
Simons and Green (Miami), 204
Skybar at The Shore Club (Miami), 215
Sky diving, Clewiston, 380
Sloppy Joe's (Key West), 302
Smathers Beach, 286
Smoking, 386
Snatch (Miami), 215–216
Snorkeling
    Bahia Honda State Park (Big Pine Key), 270
    Biscayne National Park, 246
    Boca Raton, 332
    the Dry Tortugas, 304–305
    Hutchinson Island, 365
    Long Key State Recreation Area, 257
    the Lower Keys, 272
    Miami, 184–185
    North Palm Beach County, 357
    Upper and Middle Keys, 259
SoHo Lounge (Miami), 221
Sombrero Beach, 253
Soul of America, 44
South Beach Dive and Surf Shop (Miami), 209
South Beach Divers (Miami), 185
South Beach Internet Cafe (Miami), 69
South Beach Park
    Boca Raton, 330
    Vero Beach, 374
South Beach—The Art Deco District (Miami), 62
    accommodations, 76–96
    restaurants, 114–132
    shopping, 199
    sights and attractions, 163–166
South Beach Wine & Food Festival (Miami), 33
Southern Glades Trail, 237
Southern Miami-Dade County, 66
South Florida International Auto Show (Miami Beach), 36

South Miami restaurants, 156–159
South Pointe Park (Miami), 187
The Spa at Mandarin Oriental (Miami), 72, 89
Spa Internazionale at Fisher Island (Miami), 88–89
Spanish Monastery Cloisters (Miami), 175
Spanish River Park Beach (Boca Raton), 330
Spa V at the Hotel Victor (Miami), 89
Special events and festivals, 31–37
Sports Club/LA at the Four Seasons (Miami), 89, 190
The Standard (Miami Beach), spa at, 88
Standard Hotel (Miami), 72
Stone Age Antiques (Miami), 200
Stranahan House (Fort Lauderdale), 315
Streets of Mayfair (Miami), 207–208
Strike Zone Charters (Big Pine Key), 272
Stuart (North Hutchinson Island), 363
Stubbs & Wooton (Palm Beach), 345
Studio A (Miami), 222
Studio Theater (Miami), 227
Sun exposure, 42
Sunfest (West Palm Beach), 34
Sunny Isles (Miami), 63
    restaurants, 132–134
Sunset Culinaire Tours (Key West), 285
Sunset Deck (Key West), 282
Sunset Limited, 39
SuperShuttle (Miami), 61
Surfside (Miami), 63
    restaurants, 132–134
Swimming, Biscayne National Park, 246

Ta-boo (Palm Beach), 354
Taste of the Grove Food and Music Festival (Coconut Grove), 37
Taverna Opa (Miami), 216
Taxes, 386
Tea by the Sea (Key West), 303
Telephones, 386

Tennis, 332
    Broward County, 313
    Jupiter, 357
    Miami, 190
    Palm Beach, 343
    Vero Beach, 375
Texaco Key West Classic (Key West), 34
Theater
    Boca Raton, 339
    Miami, 225
Theater of the Sea (Islamorada), 256
Three Kings Parade (Miami), 31
Tiki Bar at the Holiday Isle Resort (Islamorada), 269
Time zones, 386–387
Tipping, 387
T-Mobile Hotspot, 47
Tobacco Road (Miami), 222
Toilets, 387
Tourist information, 27–28
Tower Theater (Miami), 171
Town Center Mall (Boca Raton), 333
Tradition Field (Port St. Lucie), 371
Trails of Margaritaville (Key West), 286
Train travel, 39
Transit Lounge (Miami), 216
Traveler's checks, 30
Travelex Insurance Services, 40–41
Travel Guard International, 40
Traveling to South Florida, 37–39
Travel insurance, 40–41
Travel Insured International, 40
The Treasure Coast, 23, 361–381
    getting around, 362
    traveling to, 362
Triangle (newsletter), 43
Trip-cancellation insurance, 40–41
Tropical Bicycles & Scooter Rentals (Key West), 278
Tropical Boat Tours (Miami), 181
Tropical Everglades Visitor's Center (Florida City), 28
Tropical Park (Miami), 179
Truman, Harry S., Little White House (Key West), 280
Turtles, sea, 257, 303, 305, 311, 333, 356, 365
12th Street Beach (Miami), 163
Twist (Miami), 223

UDT-SEAL Museum (Underwater Demolition Team
Museum; Fort Pierce), 372
United Vacations, 48
Upper and Middle Keys, 249,
251–269
accommodations, 260–265
animal parks and attractions,
255–256
nightlife, 269
outdoor sights and activities,
253–255
restaurants, 265–269
state parks, 256–257
traveling to, 252
watersports, 258–260
Upstairs at the Van Dyke Cafe
(Miami), 222
Urban Outfitters (Miami), 203
USA Rail Pass, 39

Venetian Causeway (Miami),
180
Venetian Pool (Miami), 176
Vero Beach, 373–379
Versace Mansion (Miami), 167
Village of Merrick Park
(Miami), 199, 208
Vino Miami, 216–217
Virginia Key (Miami), 163
Visas, 28, 387
Visitor information, 27–28
Visit USA, 40
Vizcaya Museum and Gardens
(Miami), 176–177

Wabasso Island, 375
Wallflower Gallery (Miami),
171
Water Bus of Fort Lauderdale,
314
Watersports, 258–260, 343. *See
also specific sports*
Watson Hammock Trail, 271
Wayport, 47
Weather, 30–31, 387
Websites, 46–47
traveler's toolbox, 44
Wednesday Walkabout (Fort
Pierce), 373
Wells, Sharon, 285
Western Union, 384–385
Western Union (schooner),
285
West Miami
accommodations, 108–110
restaurants, 156–159
West Palm Beach, 339. *See also*
Palm Beach
accommodations, 346,
349–350
nightlife, 353, 354
restaurants, 351–353
West Palm Beach Fishing Club,
355
Wet Willie's (Miami), 217
Wheelchair accessibility, 43
Whiskey Jay's (Port St. Lucie),
373
White Party Week (Miami and
Fort Lauderdale), 36
The White Room (Miami), 221

Wi-Fi access, 47
Windsurfing, Miami, 185
Wine and All That Jazz (Boca
Raton), 35
Winter Equestrian Festival
(West Palm Beach), 32
Winter Music Conference
(South Beach/Miami), 33
Winter Party (Miami Beach),
33
Wolfsonian-Florida Interna-
tional University (Miami),
173–174
Women travelers, 44
Woody's Saloon and Restaurant
(Islamorada), 269
World Chess Hall of Fame and
Sidney Samole Chess
Museum (Miami), 172
World Cup Polo Tournament
(Palm Beach), 33–34
The World Erotic Art Museum
(Miami), 174
World Fishing Center (Dania
Beach), 312

Yesterday and Today Records
(Miami), 208
Y-3 (Miami), 203

Zane Grey's (Islamorada),
269
Zoos
Miami, 194–195
Palm Beach , 345

FROMMER'S® COMPLETE TRAVEL GUIDES

Alaska
Amalfi Coast
American Southwest
Amsterdam
Argentina
Arizona
Atlanta
Australia
Austria
Bahamas
Barcelona
Beijing
Belgium, Holland & Luxembourg
Belize
Bermuda
Boston
Brazil
British Columbia & the Canadian
  Rockies
Brussels & Bruges
Budapest & the Best of Hungary
Buenos Aires
Calgary
California
Canada
Cancún, Cozumel & the Yucatán
Cape Cod, Nantucket & Martha's
  Vineyard
Caribbean
Caribbean Ports of Call
Carolinas & Georgia
Chicago
Chile & Easter Island
China
Colorado
Costa Rica
Croatia
Cuba
Denmark
Denver, Boulder & Colorado Springs
Eastern Europe
Ecuador & the Galapagos Islands
Edinburgh & Glasgow
England
Europe
Europe by Rail

Florence, Tuscany & Umbria
Florida
France
Germany
Greece
Greek Islands
Guatemala
Hawaii
Hong Kong
Honolulu, Waikiki & Oahu
India
Ireland
Israel
Italy
Jamaica
Japan
Kauai
Las Vegas
London
Los Angeles
Los Cabos & Baja
Madrid
Maine Coast
Maryland & Delaware
Maui
Mexico
Montana & Wyoming
Montréal & Québec City
Morocco
Moscow & St. Petersburg
Munich & the Bavarian Alps
Nashville & Memphis
New England
Newfoundland & Labrador
New Mexico
New Orleans
New York City
New York State
New Zealand
Northern Italy
Norway
Nova Scotia, New Brunswick &
  Prince Edward Island
Oregon
Paris
Peru

Philadelphia & the Amish Country
Portugal
Prague & the Best of the Czech
  Republic
Provence & the Riviera
Puerto Rico
Rome
San Antonio & Austin
San Diego
San Francisco
Santa Fe, Taos & Albuquerque
Scandinavia
Scotland
Seattle
Seville, Granada & the Best of
  Andalusia
Shanghai
Sicily
Singapore & Malaysia
South Africa
South America
South Florida
South Korea
South Pacific
Southeast Asia
Spain
Sweden
Switzerland
Tahiti & French Polynesia
Texas
Thailand
Tokyo
Toronto
Turkey
USA
Utah
Vancouver & Victoria
Vermont, New Hampshire & Maine
Vienna & the Danube Valley
Vietnam
Virgin Islands
Virginia
Walt Disney World® & Orlando
Washington, D.C.
Washington State

FROMMER'S® DAY BY DAY GUIDES

Amsterdam
Barcelona
Beijing
Boston
Cancun & the Yucatan
Chicago
Florence & Tuscany

Hong Kong
Honolulu & Oahu
London
Maui
Montréal
Napa & Sonoma
New York City

Paris
Provence & the Riviera
Rome
San Francisco
Venice
Washington D.C.

PAULINE FROMMER'S GUIDES: SEE MORE. SPEND LESS.

Alaska
Hawaii
Italy

Las Vegas
London
New York City

Paris
Walt Disney World®
Washington D.C.

FROMMER'S® PORTABLE GUIDES

Acapulco, Ixtapa & Zihuatanejo
Amsterdam
Aruba, Bonaire & Curacao
Australia's Great Barrier Reef
Bahamas
Big Island of Hawaii
Boston
California Wine Country
Cancún
Cayman Islands
Charleston
Chicago
Dominican Republic

Florence
Las Vegas
Las Vegas for Non-Gamblers
London
Maui
Nantucket & Martha's Vineyard
New Orleans
New York City
Paris
Portland
Puerto Rico
Puerto Vallarta, Manzanillo &
    Guadalajara

Rio de Janeiro
San Diego
San Francisco
Savannah
St. Martin, Sint Maarten, Anguila &
    St. Bart's
Turks & Caicos
Vancouver
Venice
Virgin Islands
Washington, D.C.
Whistler

FROMMER'S® CRUISE GUIDES

Alaska Cruises & Ports of Call

Cruises & Ports of Call

European Cruises & Ports of Call

FROMMER'S® NATIONAL PARK GUIDES

Algonquin Provincial Park
Banff & Jasper
Grand Canyon

National Parks of the American West
Rocky Mountain
Yellowstone & Grand Teton

Yosemite and Sequoia & Kings
    Canyon
Zion & Bryce Canyon

FROMMER'S® WITH KIDS GUIDES

Chicago
Hawaii
Las Vegas
London

National Parks
New York City
San Francisco

Toronto
Walt Disney World® & Orlando
Washington, D.C.

FROMMER'S® PHRASEFINDER DICTIONARY GUIDES

Chinese
French

German
Italian

Japanese
Spanish

SUZY GERSHMAN'S BORN TO SHOP GUIDES

France
Hong Kong, Shanghai & Beijing
Italy

London
New York
Paris

San Francisco
Where to Buy the Best of Everything.

FROMMER'S® BEST-LOVED DRIVING TOURS

Britain
California
France
Germany

Ireland
Italy
New England
Northern Italy

Scotland
Spain
Tuscany & Umbria

THE UNOFFICIAL GUIDES®

Adventure Travel in Alaska
Beyond Disney
California with Kids
Central Italy
Chicago
Cruises
Disneyland®
England
Hawaii

Ireland
Las Vegas
London
Maui
Mexico's Best Beach Resorts
Mini Mickey
New Orleans
New York City
Paris

San Francisco
South Florida including Miami &
    the Keys
Walt Disney World®
Walt Disney World® for
    Grown-ups
Walt Disney World® with Kids
Washington, D.C.

SPECIAL-INTEREST TITLES

Athens Past & Present
Best Places to Raise Your Family
Cities Ranked & Rated
500 Places to Take Your Kids Before They Grow Up
Frommer's Best Day Trips from London
Frommer's Best RV & Tent Campgrounds in the U.S.A.

Frommer's Exploring America by RV
Frommer's NYC Free & Dirt Cheap
Frommer's Road Atlas Europe
Frommer's Road Atlas Ireland
Retirement Places Rated